Get more out of your textbook with the FREE Book Companion Site.

bedfordstmartins.com/roarkcompact

Created to help you master key themes and concepts and build skills, the activities in this free resource help you test and broaden your knowledge.

Online Study Guide. Get immediate feedback on your progress with Self-Tests and Defining Terms activities designed to check your understanding of chapter concepts and key terms. Other resources, such as map and visual activities, note-taking outlines, and more, help reinforce concepts and ideas presented in the textbook.

Make History. Access our online database with thousands of images, maps, Web links, and documents. Browse by topic, date, or resource type.

Online Research and Reference Aids. Research guides, models for documenting sources, plagiarism tutorials, and other resources provide you with the support you need to refine your research skills, effectively evaluate sources, and organize your findings.

Study on the move with Audio Reviews.

bedfordstmartins.com/audioreviews

These 25- to 30-minute chapter summaries highlight the major themes of the book. Download them to your portable audio device and use them to fit solid study time into your hectic schedule. And at just $.99 per chapter (or $9.99 per volume), they fit your budget too.

THE CONTEMPORARY WORLD

ARCTIC OCEAN

NORWAY
SWEDEN
FINLAND
ESTONIA
LATVIA
LITHUANIA
DEN.
RMANY POLAND BELARUS
UX.
CZ.
SLK. UKRAINE
AUS. HUNG. MOLDOVA
SLN.
CR. SE. ROMANIA
Z. ITALY B.H. BULGARIA
MO. KO. MAG. GEORGIA
ALB. GREECE ARMENIA
TUNISIA MALTA TURKEY
CYPRUS SYRIA
ISRAEL LEBANON
Gaza Strip IRAQ
West Bank JORDAN
LIBYA EGYPT KUWAIT
SAUDI ARABIA
QATAR
UNITED ARAB
EMIRATES OMAN

RUSSIAN FEDERATION

KAZAKHSTAN
MONGOLIA

UZBEKISTAN
KYRGYZSTAN
TURKMENISTAN TAJIKISTAN
AZERBAIJAN
AFGHANISTAN
IRAN
PAKISTAN
BAHRAIN

CHINA
N. KOREA
S. KOREA JAPAN

PACIFIC OCEAN

BHUTAN
NEPAL
BANGLADESH
INDIA MYANMAR
(BURMA)
VIETNAM
LAOS
Taiwan

NIGER CHAD SUDAN ERITREA
YEMEN
DJIBOUTI

THAILAND
CAMBODIA

Mariana Is.
(U.S.)

Guam
(U.S.)

MARSHALL
IS.

GERIA
NIN
GO CENTRAL
AFRICAN REP. ETHIOPIA
CAMEROON
GABON CONGO
RWANDA
DEM. REP. OF
THE CONGO
BURUNDI TANZANIA
COMOROS
SEYCHELLES

UGANDA
KENYA

SOMALIA

MALDIVES SRI
LANKA

BRUNEI

MALAYSIA

PALAU

FEDERATED STATES
OF MICRONESIA

SINGAPORE

INDONESIA

NAURU
KIRIBATI

TUVALU

PAPUA
NEW
GUINEA

SOLOMON
IS.

ANGOLA ZAMBIA MALAWI
ZIMBABWE MADAGASCAR
NAMIBIA BOTSWANA
MAURITIUS

INDIAN OCEAN

TIMOR
LESTE

VANUATU FIJI

New Caledonia
(Fr.)

AUSTRALIA

MOZAMBIQUE
SOUTH SWAZILAND
AFRICA LESOTHO

ABBREVIATIONS

ALB. ALBANIA
AUS. AUSTRIA
BEL. BELGIUM
B.H. BOSNIA AND HERZEGOVINA
CR. CROATIA
CZ. CZECH REPUBLIC
DEN. DENMARK
HUNG. HUNGARY
KO. KOSOVO
LUX. LUXEMBOURG
MAC. MACEDONIA
MO. MONTENEGRO
NETH. NETHERLANDS
SE. SERBIA
SLK. SLOVAKIA
SLN. SLOVENIA
SWITZ. SWITZERLAND

NEW
ZEALAND

Tasmania
(AUST.)

ANTARCTICA

20°E   40°E   60°E   80°E   100°E   120°E   140°E   160°E

The American Promise

A COMPACT HISTORY

Laura James, *Family Portrait*, 1998.

The American Promise

A COMPACT HISTORY FOURTH EDITION

Volume II: From 1865

JAMES L. ROARK *Emory University*

MICHAEL P. JOHNSON *Johns Hopkins University*

PATRICIA CLINE COHEN *University of California, Santa Barbara*

SARAH STAGE *Arizona State University*

ALAN LAWSON *Boston College*

SUSAN M. HARTMANN *The Ohio State University*

BEDFORD/ST. MARTIN'S

Boston • New York

FOR BEDFORD/ST. MARTIN'S

Publisher for History: Mary Dougherty
Director of Development for History: Jane Knetzger
Senior Developmental Editor: Laura Arcari
Senior Production Editor: Christina M. Horn
Assistant Production Manager: Joe Ford
Executive Marketing Manager: Jenna Bookin Barry
Associate Editor: Lynn Sternberger
Editorial Assistant: Robin Soule
Production Assistants: David Ayers, Alexis Biasell, and Alexandra Leach
Senior Art Director: Anna Palchik
Text Design: Brian Salisbury
Copyeditor: Sybil Sosin
Map Editor: Charlotte Miller
Indexer: Leoni Z. McVey
Photo Research: Pembroke Herbert/Sandi Rygiel, Picture Research Consultants & Archives, Inc.
Cover Design: Billy Boardman
Cover and Title Page Art: Family Portrait, 1998, by Laura James (contemporary artist). Private Collection/
    The Bridgeman Art Library.
Cartography: Mapping Specialists, Ltd.
Composition: Macmillan Publishing Solutions
Printing and Binding: RR Donnelley and Sons

President: Joan E. Feinberg
Editorial Director: Denise B. Wydra
Director of Marketing: Karen R. Soeltz
Director of Editing, Design, and Production: Marcia Cohen
Assistant Director of Editing, Design, and Production: Elise S. Kaiser
Managing Editor: Elizabeth M. Schaaf

Library of Congress Control Number: 2009924719

Copyright © 2010, 2007, 2003, 2000 by Bedford/St. Martin's

Manufactured in the United States of America.
4   3   2   1   0
f   e   d   c

For information, write: Bedford/St. Martin's, 75 Arlington Street, Boston, MA 02116 (617-399-4000)

ISBN-10: 0-312-53406-X ISBN-13: 978-0-312-53406-6 (combined edition)
ISBN-10: 0-312-53407-8 ISBN-13: 978-0-312-53407-3 (Vol. I)
ISBN-10: 0-312-53408-6 ISBN-13: 978-0-312-53408-0 (Vol. II)

Credits and copyrights appear at the back of the book on page CR-1, which constitutes an extension of this copyright page.

★ CONTENTS

Reconstruction 16
1863–1877   385

The Contested West

1870–1900 411

Business and Politics in the Gilded Age

1870–1895 435

The City and Its Workers

19

1870–1900   461

Dissent, Depression, and War

20

1890–1900   487

Progressivism from the Grass Roots to the White House

1890–1916   513

World War I: The Progressive Crusade at Home and Abroad

1914–1920   541

From New Era to Great Depression

23

1920–1932   569

The New Deal Experiment

24

1932–1939   595

The United States and the Second World War

Cold War Politics in the Truman Years

The Politics and Culture of Abundance
1952–1960   673

Reform, Rebellion, and Reaction
1960–1974   697

Vietnam and the Limits of Power

1961–1975 723

America Moves to the Right

1969–1989 747

The End of the Cold War and the Challenges of Globalization

Since 1989　773

★ MAPS, FIGURES, AND TABLES

Seeking the American Promise

GETTING STUDENTS TO OPEN THE BOOK IS ONE of the biggest hurdles instructors face. *The American Promise: A Compact History* grew from the concerns most frequently voiced by instructors: that students often find history boring, unfocused, and difficult and their textbooks lifeless and overwhelming. We asked ourselves how our text could address these concerns and engage students in ways that would help them understand and remember the main developments in American history. To make the political, social, economic, and cultural changes vivid and memorable and to portray fully the diversity of the American experience, we stitched into our narrative the voices of hundreds of contemporaries — from presidents to pipe fitters and sharecroppers to suffragists — whose ideas and actions shaped their times and whose efforts still affect our lives. More maps and illustrations than in any other brief book — including hundreds of artifacts that highlight material culture — engage, inform, and make the past tangible to students. By incorporating a rich selection of authentic American voices and contemporaneous illustrations, we seek to capture history as it happened and to create a compelling narrative that captures students' interests and sparks their historical imagination.

From the beginning, *The American Promise* has been shaped by our firsthand knowledge that the survey course is the most difficult to teach and the most difficult to take. Collectively, we have logged considerably more than a century in introductory American history classrooms in institutions that range from small community colleges to large research universities. Our experience as teachers informs every aspect of our text, beginning with its framework. In our classrooms, we have found that students need **both** the structure a political narrative provides and the insights gained from examining social and cultural experience. To write a comprehensive, balanced account of American history, we focused on the public arena — the place where politics intersects social and cultural developments — to show how Americans confronted the major issues of their day and created far-reaching historical change.

Our title, *The American Promise*, reflects our emphasis on human agency and our conviction that American history is an unfinished story. For millions, the nation has held out the promise of a better life, unfettered worship, representative government, democratic politics, and other freedoms seldom found elsewhere. But none of these promises has come with guarantees. As we see it, much of American history is a continuing struggle over the definition and realization of the nation's promise. Abraham Lincoln, in the midst of what he termed the "fiery trial" of the Civil War, pronounced the nation "the last best hope of Earth." That hope has been marred by compromises, disappointments, and denials, but it lives still. Barack Obama declared that it is the "promise that has always set this country apart," adding that "when that promise was in jeopardy, ordinary men and women — students and soldiers, farmers and teachers, nurses and janitors — found the courage to keep it alive."

In developing the fourth edition, we sought to provide an alternative for colleagues searching for an affordable text with all the features of a full-length text. Many of our competitors continue to chase after the goals we achieved with this book: to offer a readable, accessible, briefer text that really works for students and teachers. With so many choices, we've been deeply gratified by the continued success of the compact edition. The fourth edition rests solidly on our original goals and premises. We continue to pair all the color, pedagogy, and features of a full-length text with a briefer narrative at a lower price. As authors, we continue to do our own abridgment to make a narrative that is both brief and rich with memorable details. To engage students more fully in the American story, we've given the book a new look, redesigned all of the book's maps, added a new biographical feature, and found new ways to position American history in the global world in which students live. Finally, in our quest to make this book even easier to study from, we've strengthened the pedagogical aids to provide students with greater guidance in reading, understanding, and remembering American history. Like America itself over the centuries, the fourth edition of *The American Promise: A Compact History* is both recognizable and new.

Features

From the beginning, readers have proclaimed this textbook a visual feast, richly illustrated in ways that extend and reinforce the narrative. The fourth edition offers almost **500** contemporaneous **illustrations**. In our effort to make history tangible, we include over **200 artifacts**—from boots and political buttons to guns and sewing machines—that emphasize the importance of material culture in the study of the past and enrich the historical account. **Comprehensive captions** for the illustrations in the book entice students to delve deeper into the text itself.

Our highly regarded **map program**, with **170** maps in all, rests on the old truth that "History is not intelligible without geography." Each chapter offers, on average, three **full-size maps** showing major developments in the narrative and two or three **spot maps** embedded in the narrative that emphasize detail from the discussion. To help students think critically about the role of geography in American history, we include **one critical-thinking map exercise** per chapter. New maps in the fourth edition highlight such topics as the Treaty of Fort Stanwix, Zululand and Cape Colony in 1878, major sources of oil in 1980, the recent conflict in Iraq, and the election of 2008.

To draw students in, each chapter begins with a colorful **opening vignette** featuring lively accounts of individuals or groups who embody the central themes of the chapter. New vignettes in this edition include, among others, Queen Isabella supporting Columbus's expedition to the New World, the Robin Johns's experiences in the Atlantic slave trade, Deborah Sampson masquerading as a man to join the Continental army, Alexander Hamilton as a polarizing figure, James T. Rapier emerging in the early 1870s as Alabama's most prominent black leader, Frances Willard participating in the creation of the Populist Party in 1892, and congresswoman Helen Gahagan Douglas during the Cold War.

As part of our ongoing efforts to make this the most teachable and readable survey text available, we paid renewed attention to the fourth edition's pedagogy. Chapters are constructed to preview, reinforce, and review the narrative in the most memorable and engaging ways possible. Designed to help students get the most out of their reading, each chapter includes **chapter outlines**, **review questions** that check the comprehension of main ideas, and boldfaced **key terms**. **Reviewing the Chapter** sections at the end of each chapter help students prepare for exams, with key terms, review questions repeated from within the narrative, **Making Connections** questions that ask students to think about broad developments, and **Suggested Readings**. These comprehensive reading and study tools offer students all the support of a full-sized text.

An enriched array of special features reinforces the narrative and offers teachers more points of departure for assignments and discussion. We've developed two new special features for this edition. To increase the book's emphasis on human agency, we've added **new Seeking the American Promise essays**. Biographical in nature, each essay explores a different promise of America—from the promise of freedom to the promise of home ownership, for example—while recognizing that the promises fulfilled for some have meant promises denied to others. Students connect to the broader themes through the stories of Americans such as Elizabeth Freeman, a slave who sued for her freedom in 1781, and paraplegic Beverly Jones, who sued for access under the Americans with Disabilities Act in her home state of Tennessee.

To support our increased emphasis on the global context of U.S. history, this edition also debuts fourteen **new Global Comparison figures** that showcase data visually with an emphasis on global connections. Features are focused on a wide range of topics, from comparing "Nineteenth-Century School Enrollment and Literacy Rates" worldwide to "Energy Consumption per Capita" in 1980.

Fresh topics in our three enduring special features further enrich this edition. Each **Documenting the American Promise** feature juxtaposes three or four primary documents to dramatize the human dimension of major events and show varying perspectives on a topic or issue. Feature introductions and document headnotes contextualize the sources, and Questions for Analysis and Debate promote critical thinking about primary sources. New topics in this edition include "Virginia Laws Governing Servants and Slaves," "Defending Slavery," and "The Final Push for Woman Suffrage." **Historical Question** essays pose and interpret specific questions of continuing interest so as to demonstrate the depth and variety of possible answers, thereby countering the belief of many beginning students that historians simply gather facts and string them together in a chronological narrative. Students recognize that history is an interpretive enterprise by joining in the questioning of, arguing about, and wrestling with the past. New questions in this edition include "Who Were the

First Americans?"; "Progressives and Conservation: Should Hetch Hetchy Be Dammed or Saved?"; and "Why Did the Allies Win World War II?" In addition, 50 percent of the **Beyond America's Borders** features are new. These essays seek to widen students' perspectives and help students see that this country did not develop in isolation. New essays as varied as "Prisoners of War in the Eighteenth Century" and "Imperialism, Colonialism, and the Treatment of the Sioux and the Zulu" consider the reciprocal connections between the United States and the wider world and challenge students to think about the effects of transnational connections over time.

Textual Changes

Because students live in an increasingly global world and benefit from making connections with the world outside the United States, we have substantially increased our attention to the global context of American history in the fourth edition. In addition to the two global features — Beyond America's Borders and the Global Comparison figures — the transnational context of American history has been integrated throughout the narrative as appropriate, including a new section on international diplomacy during the Civil War and a comparison of the welfare state in the United States and Europe during the Cold War. By contributing to a broader notion of American history, these additions help students understand more fully the complex development of their nation's history and help prepare them to live in the twenty-first century.

In our ongoing effort to offer a comprehensive text that braids all Americans into the national narrative, we have increased our attention to women's history. In addition to enhancing our coverage of women in the narrative—including a new section on women's education in the early Republic and more on woman suffrage—we've added eleven new vignettes and features focused around women. These additions continue to position women firmly in the national narrative while introducing students in more depth to women such as Queen Liliuokalani, Frances Willard, and Helen Gahagan Douglas, among others who have contributed to this nation's story.

To strengthen coverage and increase clarity and accessibility, we reorganized certain chapters. In particular, reorganization in Chapter 11, "The Expanding Republic, 1815–1840," and Chapter 12, "The New West and Free North, 1840–1860,"

provides clearer themes with smoother transitions. Chapter 17 — newly titled "The Contested West" — has also been reorganized to incorporate the latest scholarship on the colonization of the West and to accommodate an expanded treatment of the struggles of Native Americans.

Staying abreast of current scholarship is a primary concern of ours, and this edition reflects that keen interest. We incorporated a wealth of new scholarship in myriad ways to benefit students. Readers will note that we made good use of the latest works on a number of topics, such as the French and Indian borderlands, the education of women in the early Republic, the Barbary wars, Denmark Vesey, black soldiers in the Civil War, the colonization of the West and the struggles of Native Americans in response to it, and American imperialism in Hawaii, as well as providing up-to-date coverage of the George W. Bush administration, the Middle East, Hurricane Katrina, the Iraq War, the 2008 election of Barack Obama, and the recent economic downturn.

Flexible Format

To accommodate the different ways that the American history survey is taught, *The American Promise: A Compact History*, Fourth Edition, is published in several versions:

- Combined edition (Chapters 1–31): paperback or e-Book
- Volume I, To 1877 (Chapters 1–16): paperback or e-Book
- Volume II, From 1865 (Chapters 16–31): paperback or e-book

For more information on the e-Book, see below.

Supplements

Developed with our guidance and thoroughly revised to reflect the changes in the fourth edition, the comprehensive collection of free and premium resources accompanying the textbook provide a host of practical learning and teaching aids. We learned much from the book's community of adopters, and we broadened the scope of the supplements to create a learning package that responds to the real needs of instructors and students. Many of the new media options not only will save you and your students time and money but also will add sound to the voices, movement to the images, and interactivity to the documents that help bring history to life. Cross-references in the textbook to the Online Study Guide and to the primary source reader signal the tight integration of the core text with the supplements.

For Students

Print Resources

Reading the American Past: Selected Historical Documents, **Fourth Edition.** Edited by Michael P. Johnson (Johns Hopkins University), one of the authors of *The American Promise,* and designed to complement the textbook, *Reading the American Past* provides a broad selection of more than 150 primary source documents, as well as editorial apparatus to help students understand the sources. Emphasizing the important social, political, and economic themes of U.S. history courses, 32 new documents (at least one per chapter) were added to provide a multiplicity of perspectives on environmental, western, ethnic, and gender history and to bring a global dimension to the anthology. Available free when packaged with the text and now available as an e-book (see below).

NEW *Rand McNally Atlas of American History.* This collection of more than 80 full-color maps illustrates key events and eras from early exploration, settlement, expansion, and immigration to U.S. involvement in wars abroad and on U.S. soil. Introductory pages for each section include brief overviews, timelines, graphs, and photos to quickly establish a historical context. Available for $3 when packaged with the text.

Maps in Context: A Workbook for American History. Written by historical cartography expert Gerald A. Danzer (University of Illinois at Chicago), this skill-building workbook helps students comprehend essential connections between geographic literacy and historical understanding. Organized to correspond to the typical U.S. history survey course, *Maps in Context* presents a wealth of map-centered projects and convenient pop quizzes that give students hands-on experience working with maps. Available free when packaged with the text.

The Bedford Glossary for U.S. History. This handy supplement for the survey course gives students clear, concise definitions of the political, economic, social, and cultural terms used by historians and contemporary media alike. The terms are historically contextualized to aid comprehension. Available free when packaged with the text.

U.S. History Matters: A Student Guide to U.S. History Online, **Second Edition.** This resource, written by Alan Gevinson, Kelly Schrum, and Roy Rosenzweig (all of George Mason University), provides an illustrated and annotated guide to 250 of the most useful Web sites for student research in U.S. history as well as advice on evaluating and using Internet sources. This essential guide is based on the acclaimed "History Matters" Web site developed by the American History Social Project and the Center for History and New Media. Available free when packaged with the text.

Bedford Series in History and Culture. More than 100 titles in this highly praised series combine first-rate scholarship, historical narrative, and important primary documents for undergraduate courses. Each book is brief, inexpensive, and focused on a specific topic or period. Package discounts are available.

Historians at Work Series. Brief enough for a single assignment yet meaty enough to provoke thoughtful discussion, each volume in this series examines a single historical question by combining unabridged selections by distinguished historians, each with a different perspective on the issue, with helpful learning aids. Package discounts are available.

Trade Books. Titles published by sister companies Farrar, Straus and Giroux; Henry Holt and Company; Hill and Wang; Picador; St. Martin's Press; and Palgrave Macmillan are available at a 50 percent discount when packaged with Bedford/St. Martin's textbooks. For more information, visit **bedfordstmartins .com/tradeup**.

Student Course Guides for *Shaping America: U.S. History to 1877* **and** *Transforming America: U.S. History since 1877.* These guides by Kenneth G. Alfers (Dallas County Community College District) are designed for students using *The American Promise* in conjunction with the Dallas TeleLearning telecourses *Shaping America* and *Transforming America.* Lesson overviews, assignments, objectives, and focus points provide structure for distance learners, while enrichment ideas, suggested readings, and brief primary sources extend the unit lessons. Practice tests help students evaluate their mastery of the material.

New Media Resources

NEW *The American Promise: A Compact History e-Book.* This electronic version of the fourth edition offers students unmatched value—the complete text of the print book with easy-to-use highlighting, searching, and note-taking tools, at a significantly reduced price.

NEW *Reading the American Past e-Book.* An online version of the fourth edition of *Reading the American Past* offers more than 150 primary source documents and editorial apparatus to aid students' understanding of the sources. This e-Book allows you to add an electronic dimension to your class or to integrate sources with your existing online course.

FREE Online Study Guide at bedfordstmartins .com/roarkcompact. The popular Online Study Guide for *The American Promise: A Compact History* is a free learning tool to help students master themes and information presented in the textbook and improve their historical skills. Assessment quizzes let students evaluate their comprehension, and a wide range of quizzing, map, and primary document analysis activities provides them with the opportunity for further study. Instructors can monitor students' progress through the online Quiz Gradebook or receive e-mail updates.

Audio Reviews. These 25- to 30-minute chapter summaries of each chapter in *The American Promise: A Compact History*, Fourth Edition, highlight the major themes of the text and help reinforce student learning. They fit easily into students' lifestyles and provide a practical way for them to study.

Online Bibliography at bedfordstmartins.com/ roark compact. Organized by book chapter and topic, the online bibliography provides an authoritative and comprehensive list of references to jump-start student research.

Jules R. Benjamin's *A Student's Online Guide to History Reference Sources* at bedfordstmartins .com/roarkcompact. This Web site provides links to history-related databases, indexes, and journals, plus contact information for state, provincial, local, and professional history organizations.

Bedford Bibliographer at bedfordstmartins .com/roarkcompact. This simple but powerful Web-based tool assists students with the process of collecting sources and generates bibliographies in four commonly used documentation styles.

Diana Hacker's *Research and Documentation Online* at bedfordstmartins.com/roarkcompact. This Web site provides clear advice on how to integrate primary and secondary sources into research papers, how to cite sources correctly, and how to format in MLA, APA, *Chicago*, or CBE style.

The St. Martin's Tutorial on Avoiding Plagiarism at bedfordstmartins.com/roark compact. This online tutorial reviews the consequences of plagiarism and explains what sources to acknowledge, how to keep good notes, how to organize research, and how to integrate sources appropriately. The tutorial includes exercises to help students practice integrating sources and recognize acceptable summaries.

Critical Thinking Modules at bedfordstmartins .com/roarkcompact. This Web site offers more than two dozen online modules for interpreting maps and audio, visual, and textual sources centered on events covered in the U.S. history survey.

For Instructors

Print Resources

Transparencies. This set of full-color acetate transparencies includes all full-size maps and many other images from *The American Promise* to help instructors present lectures and teach students important map-reading skills. A correlation guide showing how the transparencies align with the compact edition appears in the Instructor's Resource Manual and at bedfordstmartins.com/roarkcompact.

New Media Resources

Instructor's Resource Manual at bedfordstmartins .com/roarkcompact/catalog. This popular manual by Sarah E. Gardner (Mercer University) and Catherine A. Jones (Johns Hopkins University) offers both experienced and first-time instructors tools for presenting textbook material in exciting and engaging ways—learning objectives, annotated chapter outlines, lecture strategies, tips for helping students with common misconceptions and difficult topics, and suggestions for in-class activities, including using film and video, ways to start discussions, topics for debate, and analyzing primary sources. The new edition includes model answers for the questions in the book as well as a chapter-by-chapter guide to all of the supplements available with *The American Promise: A Compact History*. An extensive guide for first-time teaching assistants and sample syllabi are also included.

Instructor's Resource CD-ROM. This disc provides instructors with ready-made and customizable PowerPoint multimedia presentations built around chapter outlines, maps, figures, and selected images from the textbook plus jpeg versions of all maps and figures and of selected images. Also included are chapter questions formatted in PowerPoint and MS Word for use with i<clicker, a classroom response system, and blank outline maps in PDF format.

Computerized Test Bank. The test bank offers over 80 exercises per chapter, including multiple-choice, matching, map, and short and long essay questions. The answer key includes textbook page numbers, correct answers, and model essay responses. Instructors can customize quizzes, add or edit both questions and answers, and export questions to a variety of formats, including WebCT and Blackboard. The disc includes separate test banks for the associated telecourses *Shaping America* and *Transforming America*.

Book Companion Site at bedfordstmartins .com/roark compact. This companion Web site gathers all the electronic resources for the text, including the Online Study Guide and related Quiz Gradebook, at a single Web address providing convenient links to lecture, assignment, and research materials such as PowerPoint chapter outlines and the digital libraries at Make History.

Make History at bedfordstmartins.com/ roarkcompact. Comprising the content of our five acclaimed online libraries—Map Central, the Bedford History Image Library, DocLinks, HistoryLinks, and PlaceLinks, Make History provides one-stop access to relevant digital content including maps, images, documents, and Web links. Students and instructors alike can browse this free, easy-to-use database by course, topic, date, or resource type and can download the content they find. Instructors can also create entire collections of content and store them online for later use or post their collections to the Web to share with students.

Content for Course Management Systems. A variety of student and instructor resources developed for this textbook are ready for use in course management systems such as WebCT, Blackboard, and other platforms. This e-content includes nearly all of the offerings from the book's Online Study Guide as well as the book's test bank and the test banks from the associated telecourses *Shaping America* and *Transforming America*.

Reel Teaching. A valuable tool for enhancing media-rich lectures, short segments in VHS and DVD format are available to qualified adopters from the award-winning telecourses *Shaping America* and *Transforming America* by Dallas Tele-Learning at the LeCroy Center for Educational Telecommunications.

***The American Promise* via Telecourse.** *The American Promise* has been selected as the textbook for the award-winning U.S. history telecourses *Shaping America: U.S. History to 1877* and *Transforming America: U.S. History since 1877* by Dallas TeleLearning at the LeCroy Center for Educational Telecommunications, Dallas County Community College District. Guides for students and instructors fully integrate the narrative of *The American Promise* into each telecourse. For more information on these distance-learning opportunities, visit the Dallas Tele-Learning Web site at http://telelearning.dcccd.edu, e-mail tlearn@dcccd.edu, or call 972-669-6650.

Videos and Multimedia. A wide assortment of videos and multimedia CD-ROMs on various topics in American history is available to qualified adopters.

Acknowledgments

We gratefully acknowledge all of the helpful suggestions from those who have read and taught from the previous editions of *The American Promise: A Compact History*, and we hope that our many classroom collaborators will be pleased to see their influence in the fourth edition. In particular, we wish to thank the talented scholars and teachers who gave generously of their time and knowledge to review this book; their critiques and suggestions contributed greatly to the published work: Virginia Bellows, *Tulsa Community College;* Deborah Blackwell, *Texas A&M;* Harry Carpenter, *Western Piedmont Community College;* John Duke, *Alvin Community College;* Ronald B. Frankum, *Millersville University;* Barry Gidcomb, *Columbia State Community College;* Cecilia Gowdy-Wygant, *Front Range Community College–Westminster;* Eric

Hall, *Purdue University;* Arnette Hawkins, *University of Toledo;* Laurie Hochstetler, *Western Washington University;* David Howard-Pitney, *De Anza College;* Patricia Kaiser, *Erie Community College;* Carol Keller, *San Antonio College;* Ross Kennedy, *Illinois State University;* Peggy Lambert, *Kingwood College (a North Harris Montgomery Community College District school);* John Leiby, *Paradise Valley Community College;* Susan Oliver, *Cerritos College;* Anne Paulet, *Humboldt State University;* Dr. Patrick Reagan, *Tennessee Technological University;* Dan Rezny, *St. Charles County Community College;* Walter Sargent, *University of Maine–Farmington;* Jeff Smith, *Lindenwood University;* Norton Wheeler, *Washburn University;* and James Whitt, *Ozarks Technical Community College.*

A project as complex as this requires the talents of many individuals. First, we would like to acknowledge our families for their support, forbearance, and toleration of our textbook responsibilities. Pembroke Herbert and Sandi Rygiel of Picture Research Consultants, Inc., contributed their unparalleled knowledge, soaring imagination, and diligent research to make possible the extraordinary illustration program.

We would also like to thank the many people at Bedford/St. Martin's who have been crucial to this project. No one contributed more than developmental editor Laura Arcari, who managed the entire revision and oversaw the development of each chapter. The results of her dedication to excellence and commitment to creating the best textbook imaginable are evident on every page. We greatly appreciate the acute intelligence and indomitable good humor that Laura brought to this revision. Thanks also go to associate editor Lynn Sternberger, for her assistance managing the reviews, and editorial assistant Robin Soule, who provided unflagging assistance and who coordinated the turnover of manuscript. We are also grateful to Jane Knetzger, director of development for history; William Lombardo, executive editor; and Mary Dougherty, publisher, for their support and guidance. For their imaginative and tireless efforts to promote the book, we want to thank Jenna Bookin Barry, executive marketing manager; John Hunger, senior history specialist; and Amanda Byrnes, senior marketing associate. With great skill and professionalism, Christina Horn, senior production editor, pulled together the many pieces related to copyediting, design, and typesetting, with the able assistance of David Ayers and the guidance of managing editor Elizabeth Schaaf and assistant managing editor John Amburg. Senior production supervisor Joe Ford oversaw the manufacturing of the book. Designer Brian Salisbury, copyeditor Sybil Sosin, and proofreaders Andrea Martin and Angela Hoover Morrison attended to the myriad details that help make the book shine. Leoni McVey provided an outstanding index. The book's gorgeous covers were designed by Billy Boardman. New media associate editor Marissa Zanetti, associate editor Jack Cashman, and new media production associate Rebecca Merrill made sure that *The American Promise: A Compact History* remains at the forefront of technological support for students and instructors. Editorial director Denise Wydra provided helpful advice throughout the course of the project. Finally, Charles H. Christensen, former president, took a personal interest in *The American Promise* from the start, and Joan E. Feinberg, president, guided all editions through every stage of development.

James L. Roark

Born in Eunice, Louisiana, and raised in the West, James L. Roark received his B.A. from the University of California, Davis, and his Ph.D. from Stanford University. His dissertation won the Allan Nevins Prize. He has taught at the University of Nigeria, Nsukka; the University of Nairobi, Kenya; the University of Missouri, St. Louis; and, since 1983, Emory University, where he is Samuel Candler Dobbs Professor of American History. In 1993, he received the Emory Williams Distinguished Teaching Award, and in 2001–2002 he was Pitt Professor of American Institutions at Cambridge University. He has written *Masters without Slaves: Southern Planters in the Civil War and Reconstruction* (1977). With Michael P. Johnson, he is author of *Black Masters: A Free Family of Color in the Old South* (1984) and editor of *No Chariot Let Down: Charleston's Free People of Color on the Eve of the Civil War* (1984). He has received research assistance from the American Philosophical Society, the National Endowment for the Humanities, and the Gilder Lehrman Institute of American History. Active in the Organization of American Historians and the Southern Historical Association, he is also a fellow of the Society of American Historians.

Michael P. Johnson

Born and raised in Ponca City, Oklahoma, Michael P. Johnson studied at Knox College in Galesburg, Illinois, where he received a B.A., and at Stanford University in Palo Alto, California, where he earned his Ph.D. He is currently professor of history at Johns Hopkins University in Baltimore, having previously taught at the University of California, Irvine; San Jose State University; and LeMoyne (now LeMoyne-Owen) College in Memphis. His publications include *Toward a Patriarchal Republic: The Secession of Georgia* (1977); with James L. Roark, *Black Masters: A Free Family of Color in the Old South* (1984) and *No Chariot Let Down: Charleston's Free People of Color on the Eve of the Civil War* (1984); *Abraham Lincoln, Slavery, and the Civil War: Selected Speeches and Writings* (2001); *Reading the American Past: Selected Historical Documents*, the documents reader for *The American Promise*; and articles that have appeared in the *William and Mary Quarterly,* the *Journal of Southern History, Labor History,* the *New York Review of Books,* the *New Republic,* the *Nation,* and other journals. Johnson has been awarded research fellowships by the American Council of Learned Societies, the National Endowment for the Humanities, and the Center for Advanced Study in the Behavioral Sciences and Stanford University, and the Times Mirror Foundation Distinguished Research Fellowship at the Huntington Library. He has directed a National Endowment for the Humanities Summer Seminar for College Teachers and has been honored with the University of California, Irvine, Academic Senate Distinguished Teaching Award and the University of California, Irvine, Alumni Association Outstanding Teaching Award. He won the *William and Mary Quarterly* award for best article and the Organization of American Historians ABC-CLIO *America: History and Life* Award for best American history article. He is an active member of the Society of American Historians, the American Historical Association, the Organization of American Historians, and the Southern Historical Association.

Patricia Cline Cohen

Born in Ann Arbor, Michigan, and raised in Palo Alto, California, Patricia Cline Cohen earned a B.A. at the University of Chicago and a Ph.D. at the University of California, Berkeley. In 1976, she joined the history faculty at the University of California, Santa Barbara. In 2005–2006 she received the university's Distinguished Teaching Award. Cohen has written *A Calculating People: The Spread of Numeracy in Early America* (1982; reissued 1999) and *The Murder of Helen Jewett: The Life and Death of a Prostitute in Nineteenth-Century New York* (1998). She has also published articles on quantitative literacy, mathematics education, prostitution, and murder in journals including the *Journal of Women's History, Radical History Review,* the *William and Mary Quarterly,* and the *NWSA Journal.* Her scholarly work has received support from the National Endowment for the Humanities, the National Humanities Center, the University of California President's Fellowship in the Humanities, the Mellon Foundation, the American Antiquarian Society, the Schlesinger Library, and the Newberry Library. She is an active associate of the Omohundro Institute of Early American History and Culture, sits on the advisory council of the Society for the History of the Early American Republic, and is past president of the Western Association of Women Historians. She has served as chair of the history department, as chair of the Women's Studies Program, and as acting dean of the humanities and fine arts at the University of California at Santa Barbara. In 2001–2002 she was the Distinguished Senior Mellon Fellow at the American Antiquarian Society. Currently she is working on a book about women's health advocate Mary Gove Nichols.

Sarah Stage

Sarah Stage was born in Davenport, Iowa, and received a B.A. from the University of Iowa and a Ph.D. in American studies from Yale University. She has taught U.S. history for more than twenty-five years at Williams College and the University of California, Riverside. Currently she is professor of Women's Studies at Arizona State University at the West campus in Phoenix. Her books include *Female Complaints: Lydia*

Pinkham and the Business of Women's Medicine (1979) and *Rethinking Home Economics: Women and the History of a Profession* (1997), which has been translated for a Japanese edition. Among the fellowships she has received are the Rockefeller Foundation Humanities Fellowship, the American Association of University Women dissertation fellowship, a fellowship from the Charles Warren Center for the Study of History at Harvard University, and the University of California President's Fellowship in the Humanities. She recently returned from China where she was a visiting scholar at Beijing University and Sichuan University.

Alan Lawson

Born in Providence, Rhode Island, Alan Lawson received his B.A. from Brown University and his M.A. from the University of Wisconsin. After army service and experience as a high school teacher, he earned his Ph.D. from the University of Michigan. Since winning the Allan Nevins Prize for his dissertation, Lawson has served on the faculties of the University of California, Irvine; Smith College; and, currently, Boston College. He has written *The Failure of Independent Liberalism* (1971) and coedited *From Revolution to Republic* (1976). While completing the forthcoming *Ideas in Crisis: The New Deal and the Mobilization of Progressive Experience,* he has published book chapters and essays on political economy, the cultural legacy of the New Deal, multiculturalism, and the arts in public life. He has served as editor of the *Review of Education* and the *Intellectual History Newsletter* and contributed articles to those journals as well as to the *History of Education Quarterly.* He has been active in the field of American studies as director of the Boston College American studies program and as a contributor to the *American Quarterly.* Under the auspices of the United States Information Agency, Lawson has been coordinator and lecturer for programs to instruct faculty from foreign nations in the state of American historical scholarship and teaching.

Susan M. Hartmann

Professor of history at Ohio State University, Susan M. Hartmann received her B.A. from Washington University and her Ph.D. from the University of Missouri. After specializing in the political economy of the post–World War II period and publishing *Truman and the 80th Congress* (1971), she expanded her interests to the field of women's history, publishing many articles and three books: *The Home Front and Beyond: American Women in the 1940s* (1982); *From Margin to Mainstream: American Women and Politics since 1960* (1989); and *The Other Feminists: Activists in the Liberal Establishment* (1998). Her work has been supported by the Truman Library Institute, the Rockefeller Foundation, the National Endowment for the Humanities, the American Council of Learned Societies, and the Woodrow Wilson International Center for Scholars. At Ohio State she has served as director of women's studies, and in 1995 she won the Exemplary Faculty Award in the College of Humanities. Hartmann has taught at the University of Missouri, St. Louis, and Boston University, and she has lectured on American history in Australia, Austria, France, Germany, Greece, Japan, Nepal, and New Zealand. She is a fellow of the Society of American Historians and has served on award committees of the American Historical Association, the Organization of American Historians, the American Studies Association, and the National Women's Studies Association. She has also served on the Board of Directors at the Truman Library Institute. Her current research is on gender and the transformation of politics since 1945.

★ SUGGESTED READINGS

Ira Berlin et al., eds., *Freedom: A Documentary History of Emancipation, 1861–1867*, 5 vols. (1982–2008). A monumental collection of contemporary documents that recount the black experience in the war.

Richard J. Carwardine, *Lincoln* (2003). A fresh biography of Lincoln as war leader.

Drew Gilpin Faust, *This Republic of Suffering: Death and the American Civil War* (2008). A moving examination of how Americans coped with the unprecedented scale of death.

William B. Gould IV, ed., *Diary of a Contraband: The Civil War Passage of a Black Sailor* (2002). A remarkable account of an ex-slave's service in the Union navy.

Anne Sarah Rubin, *A Shattered Nation: The Rise and Fall of the Confederacy, 1861–1868* (2005). An investigation of how home front and battlefield contributed to the construction of Confederate identity.

Nina Silber, *Daughters of the Union: Northern Women Fight the Civil War* (2006). A reconsideration of the role of ordinary northern women in the Union war effort.

FOR MORE BOOKS ABOUT TOPICS IN THIS CHAPTER, see the Online Bibliography at **bedfordstmartins.com/roarkcompact**.

FOR ADDITIONAL FIRSTHAND ACCOUNTS OF THIS PERIOD, see Chapter 15 in Michael Johnson, ed., *Reading the American Past,* Fourth Edition.

FOR WEB SITES, IMAGES, AND DOCUMENTS RELATED TO TOPICS AND PLACES IN THIS CHAPTER, visit Make History at **bedfordstmartins.com/roarkcompact**.

★ TIMELINE

1861
- **April.** Attack on Fort Sumter.
- **April–May.** Four Upper South states join Confederacy.
- **July.** Union forces routed in first battle of Bull Run (Manassas).
- **August.** First Confiscation Act.

1862
- **February.** Grant captures Fort Henry and Fort Donelson.
- **March.** Confederates defeated at battle of Glorieta Pass. Union victory at battle of Pea Ridge.
- **April.** Battle of Shiloh in Tennessee ends Confederate bid to control Mississippi valley.
- **April.** Confederate Congress authorizes draft.
- **May.** Homestead Act.
- **May–July.** Union forces defeated during Virginia peninsula campaign.
- **July.** Second Confiscation Act. Militia Act.
- **September.** Battle of Antietam stops Lee's advance into Maryland.

1863
- **January.** Emancipation Proclamation becomes law.
- **February.** National Banking Act.
- **March.** Congress authorizes draft.
- **July.** Fall of Vicksburg to Union forces.
- **July.** Lee defeated at battle of Gettysburg.
- **July.** New York City draft riots.

1864
- **March.** Grant appointed Union general in chief.
- **May–June.** Wilderness campaign.
- **September.** Fall of Atlanta to Sherman.
- **November.** Lincoln reelected.
- **December.** Fall of Savannah to Sherman.

1865
- **April 2–3.** Fall of Petersburg and Richmond.
- **April 9.** Lee surrenders to Grant.
- **April 15.** Lincoln dies from bullet wound; Vice President Andrew Johnson becomes president.

CARPETBAG

A carpetbag was a nineteenth-century suitcase made from carpet, often brightly colored. Applied first to wildcat bankers on the western frontier, "carpetbagger" was a derogatory name for rootless and penniless adventurers who could carry everything they owned in a single bag. Critics of Republican administrations in the South hurled the name "carpetbaggers" at white Northerners who moved South during Reconstruction and became active in politics. According to white Southerners, carpetbaggers exploited gullible ex-slaves to gain power and wealth. In fact, many Northerners who came to the South joined with blacks and some southern whites to form Republican state and local governments that were among the most progressive anywhere in the nineteenth century. Private Collection/Picture Research Consultants & Archives.

Reconstruction

1863–1877

IN 1856, JOHN RAPIER, a free black barber in Florence, Alabama, urged his four freeborn sons to flee the increasingly repressive and dangerous South. Searching for a color-blind society, the brothers scattered around the world. **James T. Rapier** chose Canada, where he went to live with his uncle in a largely black community and studied Greek and Latin in a log schoolhouse. After his conversion at a Methodist revival, James wrote to his father: "I have not thrown a card in 3 years[,] touched a woman in 2 years[,] smoked nor drunk any Liquor in going on 2 years." He vowed, "I will endeavor to do my part in solving the problems [of African Americans] in my native land."

The Union victory in the Civil War gave James Rapier the opportunity to redeem his pledge. In 1865, after more than eight years of exile, the twenty-seven-year-old Rapier returned to Alabama, where he presided over the first political gathering of former slaves in the state. Alabama freedmen produced a petition that called on the federal government to thoroughly reconstruct the South, to guarantee suffrage, free speech, free schools, and equal rights for all men, regardless of color.

Rapier soon discovered that Alabama's whites found it agonizingly difficult to accept defeat and black freedom. They responded to the revolutionary changes under the banner "White Man — Right or Wrong — Still the White Man!" In 1868, when Rapier and other Alabama blacks vigorously supported the Republican presidential candidate, former Union general Ulysses S. Grant, the recently organized Ku Klux Klan went on a bloody rampage of whipping, burning, and shooting. A mob of 150 outraged whites scoured Rapier's neighborhood seeking four black politicians they claimed were trying to "Africanize Alabama." They caught and hanged three, but the "nigger carpetbagger from Canada" escaped. Badly shaken, Rapier considered fleeing the state, but he decided to stay and fight.

Rapier emerged in the early 1870s as Alabama's most prominent black leader. He demanded that the federal government end the violence against ex-slaves, guarantee their civil rights, and give them land. In 1872, he won election to the House of Representatives and joined six other black congressmen in Washington, D.C. Even those who sought to destroy him and so-called Negro rule admitted that Rapier was "the best intellect under a

James T. Rapier Only two years after emancipation, ex-slaves in the United States gained full political rights and wielded far more political power than former bondsmen anywhere else in the New World. Black suffrage sent fourteen African American congressmen to Washington, D.C., during Reconstruction, among them James T. Rapier of Alabama. Temporarily at least, he and his black colleagues helped shape post-emancipation society. In 1874, when Rapier spoke on behalf of a civil rights bill, he described the humiliation of being denied service at inns all along his route from Montgomery to Washington. Elsewhere in the world, he said, class and religion were invoked to defend discrimination. In Europe, "they have princes, dukes, lords"; in India, "brahmans or priests, who rank above the sudras or laborers." But in America, "our distinction is color." Alabama Department of Archives and History.

colored skin in Alabama." Defeated for reelection in 1874 in a fraudulent campaign, Rapier turned to cotton farming, generously giving thousands of dollars of his profits to black schools and churches.

Embittered by persistent black poverty and demoralized by continuing racial violence, Rapier again chose exile. Rapier purchased land in Kansas and urged Alabama's blacks to escape with him. Buoyant and confident when he returned to Alabama in 1865, he had over the years grown to believe that blacks could never achieve equality and prosperity in the South. But in 1883, before he could leave Alabama, Rapier died of tuberculosis at the age of forty-five.

In 1865, Union general Carl Schurz had foreseen many of the troubles Rapier would encounter in the postwar South. Schurz concluded that the Civil War was "a revolution but half accomplished." Northern victory had freed the slaves, he observed, but it had not changed former slaveholders' minds about blacks' unfitness for freedom. Left to themselves, whites would "introduce some new system of forced labor, not perhaps exactly slavery in its old form but something similar to it." To defend their freedom, Schurz concluded, blacks would need federal protection, land of their own, and voting rights. Until whites "cut loose from the past, it will be a dangerous experiment to put Southern society upon its own legs."

As Schurz discovered, the end of the war did not mean peace. The United States was one of only two societies in the New World in which slavery ended in a bloody war. (The other was Haiti.) Not surprisingly, racial turmoil continued in the South after the armies quit fighting in 1865. The nation entered one of its most chaotic and conflicted eras — Reconstruction, a violent period that would define the defeated South's status within the Union and the meaning of freedom for ex-slaves.

The place of the South within the nation and the extent of black freedom were determined not only in Washington, D.C., where the federal government played an active role, but also in the state legislatures and county seats of the South, where blacks participated in the process. Moreover, on farms and plantations from Virginia to Texas, ex-slaves struggled to become free workers while ex-slaveholders clung to the Old South. A small band of white women joined in the struggle for racial equality, and soon their crusade broadened to include gender equality. Their attempts to secure voting rights for women as well as blacks were thwarted, however. Reconstruction witnessed a gigantic struggle to determine the consequences of Confederate defeat and emancipation. In the end, white Southerners prevailed. Their New South was a different South from the one to which most whites wished to return but also vastly unlike the one of which James Rapier dreamed.   ★

Wartime Reconstruction

Reconstruction did not wait for the end of war. As the odds of a northern victory increased, thinking about reunification quickened. Immediately, a question arose: Who had authority to devise a plan for reconstructing the Union?

President Abraham Lincoln believed firmly that reconstruction was a matter of executive responsibility. Congress just as firmly asserted its jurisdiction. Fueling the argument about who had the authority to set the terms of reconstruction were significant differences about the terms themselves.

In their eagerness to formulate a plan for political reunification, neither Lincoln nor Congress gave much attention to the South's land and labor problems. But as the war rapidly eroded slavery and traditional plantation agriculture, Yankee military commanders in the Union-occupied areas of the Confederacy had no choice but to oversee the emergence of a new labor system.

"To Bind Up the Nation's Wounds" As early as 1863, Lincoln contemplated how "to bind up the nation's wounds" and achieve "a just, and a lasting peace." While deep compassion for the enemy guided his thinking, his plan for reconstruction aimed primarily at shortening the war and ending slavery.

Lincoln's Proclamation of Amnesty and Reconstruction in December 1863 set out his terms. He offered a full pardon, restoring property (except slaves) and political rights, to rebels willing to renounce secession and to accept emancipation. His offer excluded only high-ranking Confederate military and political officers and a few other groups. When 10 percent of a state's voting population had taken an oath of allegiance, the state could organize a new government. Lincoln's plan did not require ex-rebels to extend social or political rights to ex-slaves, nor did it anticipate a program of long-term federal assistance to freedmen. Clearly, the president looked forward to the speedy, forgiving restoration of the broken Union.

Lincoln's easy terms enraged abolitionists such as Wendell Phillips of Boston, who charged that the president "makes the negro's freedom a mere sham." He "is willing that the negro should be free but seeks nothing else for him." Phillips and other northern radicals called instead for a thorough overhaul of southern society. Their ideas proved to be too drastic for most Republicans during the war years, but Congress agreed that Lincoln's plan was inadequate. Congress feared that the president's program amounted to restoring the old southern ruling class to power. It wanted greater assurances of white loyalty and greater guarantees of black rights.

In July 1864 Congressman Henry Winter Davis of Maryland and Senator Benjamin Wade of Ohio jointly sponsored a bill that demanded that at least half of the voters in a conquered rebel state take the oath of allegiance before reconstruction could begin. The **Wade-Davis bill** also banned all ex-Confederates from participating in the drafting of new state constitutions. Finally, the bill guaranteed the equality of freedmen before the law. When Lincoln refused to sign the bill and let it die, Wade and Davis charged the president with usurpation of power. They warned Lincoln to confine himself to "his executive duties—to obey and execute, not make the laws—to suppress by arms armed rebellion, and leave political organization to Congress."

Undeterred, Lincoln continued to nurture the formation of loyal state governments under his own plan. Four states—Louisiana, Arkansas, Tennessee, and Virginia—fulfilled the president's requirements, but Congress refused to seat representatives from the "Lincoln states." In his last public address in April 1865, Lincoln defended his plan but for the first time expressed publicly his endorsement of suffrage for southern blacks, at least "the very intelligent, and . . . those who serve our cause as soldiers." The announcement demonstrated that Lincoln's thinking about reconstruction was still evolving. Four days later, he was dead.

Land and Labor Of all the problems raised by the North's victory in the war, none proved more critical than the South's transition from slavery to free labor. As federal armies invaded and occupied the Confederacy, hundreds of thousands of slaves became free workers. In addition, Union armies controlled vast territories in the South where legal title to land had become unclear. The Confiscation Acts punished "traitors" by taking away their property. The question of what to do with federally occupied land and how to organize labor on it engaged former slaves, former slaveholders, Union military commanders, and federal government officials long before the war ended.

In the Mississippi valley, occupying federal troops announced a new labor code. It required slaveholders to sign contracts with ex-slaves and to pay wages. It obligated employers to provide food, housing, and medical care. It outlawed whipping, but it reserved to the army the right to discipline blacks who refused to work. The code required black laborers to enter into contracts, work diligently, and remain subordinate and obedient. Military leaders clearly had no intention of promoting a social or economic revolution. Instead, they sought to restore plantation agriculture with wage labor. The effort resulted in a hybrid system that one contemporary called "compulsory free labor," something that satisfied no one.

Planters complained because the new system fell short of slavery. Blacks could not be "transformed by proclamation," a Louisiana sugar planter declared. Yet under the new system, blacks "are expected to perform their new obligations without coercion, & without the fear of punishment which is essential to stimulate the idle and correct the vicious." Without the right to whip, he argued, the new labor system did not have a chance.

African Americans found the new regime too reminiscent of slavery to be called free labor. Its

Military Auction of Condemned Property, Beaufort, South Carolina, 1865 During the war, thousands of acres of land in the South came into federal hands as abandoned property or as a result of seizures due to nonpayment of taxes. The government authorized the sale of some of this land at public auction. This rare photograph shows expectant blacks (and a few whites) gathered in Beaufort, South Carolina, for a sale. Very few former slaves could raise enough money to purchase land, and even when they pooled their resources, they usually lost out to northern army officers, government officials, or speculators with deeper pockets. Several of the individuals here are wearing Union army caps, strong affirmation of their political loyalties. The Huntington Library, San Marino, California.

chief deficiency, they believed, was the failure to provide them with land of their own. Freedmen believed they had a moral right to land because they and their ancestors had worked it without compensation for more than two centuries. "What's the use of being free if you don't own land enough to be buried in?" one man asked. Several wartime developments led freedmen to believe that the federal government planned to undergird black freedom with landownership.

In January 1865, General William Tecumseh Sherman set aside part of the coast south of Charleston for black settlement. By June 1865, some 40,000 freedmen sat on 400,000 acres of "Sherman land." In March 1865, Congress passed a bill establishing the Bureau of Refugees, Freedmen, and Abandoned Lands. The **Freedmen's Bureau**, as it was called, distributed food and clothing to destitute Southerners and eased the transition of blacks from slaves to free persons. Congress also authorized the agency to divide abandoned and confiscated land into 40-acre plots, to rent them to freedmen, and eventually to sell them "with such title as the United States can convey." By June 1865, the bureau had situated nearly 10,000 black families on a half million acres abandoned by fleeing planters. Other ex-slaves eagerly anticipated farms of their own.

Despite the flurry of activity, wartime reconstruction failed to produce agreement about whether the president or Congress had the authority to devise policy or what proper policy should be.

The African American Quest for Autonomy

Ex-slaves never had any doubt about what they wanted from freedom. They had only to contemplate what they had been denied as slaves. (See "Documenting the American Promise," page 390.) Slaves had to remain on their plantations; freedom allowed blacks to see what was on the other side of the hill. Slaves had to be at work in the fields by dawn; freedom permitted blacks to sleep through a sunrise. Freedmen also tested the etiquette of racial subordination. "Lizzie's maid passed me today when I was coming from church *without speaking to me*," huffed one plantation mistress.

To whites, emancipation looked like pure anarchy. Blacks, they said, had reverted to their natural condition: lazy, irresponsible, and wild. Without the discipline of slavery, whites predicted, blacks would go the way of "the Indian and the

> "The way we can best take care of ourselves is to have land," one former slave declared in 1865, "and turn it and till it by our own labor."

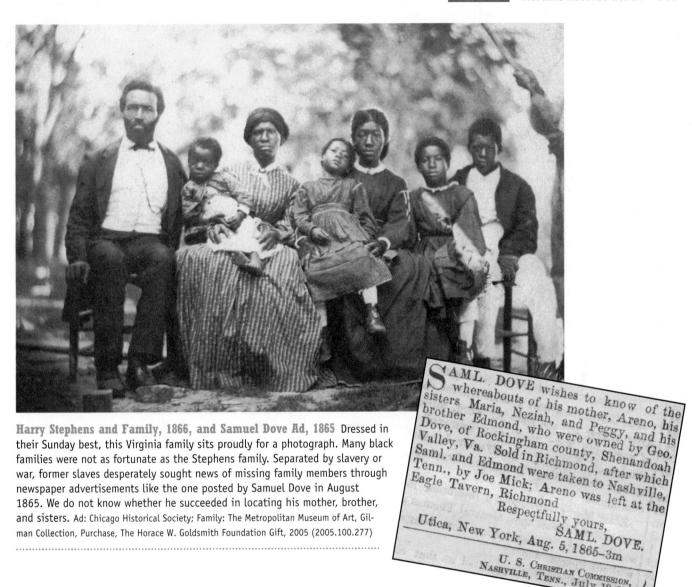

Harry Stephens and Family, 1866, and Samuel Dove Ad, 1865 Dressed in their Sunday best, this Virginia family sits proudly for a photograph. Many black families were not as fortunate as the Stephens family. Separated by slavery or war, former slaves desperately sought news of missing family members through newspaper advertisements like the one posted by Samuel Dove in August 1865. We do not know whether he succeeded in locating his mother, brother, and sisters. Ad: Chicago Historical Society; Family: The Metropolitan Museum of Art, Gilman Collection, Purchase, The Horace W. Goldsmith Foundation Gift, 2005 (2005.100.277)

SAML. DOVE wishes to know of the whereabouts of his mother, Areno, his sisters Maria, Neziah, and Peggy, and his brother Edmond, who were owned by Geo. Dove, of Rockingham county, Shenandoah Valley, Va. Sold in Richmond, after which Saml. and Edmond were taken to Nashville, Tenn., by Joe Mick; Areno was left at the Eagle Tavern, Richmond

Respectfully yours,
SAML. DOVE.

Utica, New York, Aug. 5, 1865—3m

U. S. Christian Commission, Nashville, Tenn., July 19, 1865.

buffalo." Actually, former slaves were experimenting with freedom, but they could not long afford to roam the countryside, neglect work, and casually provoke whites. Soon, most were back at work in whites' kitchens and fields.

But other items on ex-slaves' agenda of freedom endured. They continued to dream of land and economic independence. "The way we can best take care of ourselves is to have land," one former slave declared in 1865, "and turn it and till it by our own labor." Freedmen also wanted to learn to read and write. Many black soldiers had become literate in the Union army, and they understood the value of the pen and book. "I wishes the Childern all in School," one black veteran asserted. "It is beter for them then to be their Surveing a mistes [mistress]."

The restoration of broken families was another persistent black aspiration. Thousands of freedmen took to the roads in 1865 to look for kin who had been sold away or to free those who were being held illegally as slaves. A black soldier from Missouri wrote his daughters that he was coming for them. "I will have you if it cost me my life," he declared. "Your Miss Kitty said that I tried to steal you," he told them. "But I'll let her know that god never intended for a man to steal his own flesh and blood." And he swore that "if she meets me with ten thousand soldiers, she [will] meet her enemy."

Independent worship was another continuing aspiration. African Americans greeted freedom with a mass exodus from white churches, where they had been required to worship when slaves. Some joined the newly established southern branches of all-black northern churches, such as the African Methodist Episcopal Church. Others formed black versions of the major southern denominations, Baptists

The Meaning of Freedom

On New Year's Day 1863, President Abraham Lincoln issued the Emancipation Proclamation. It states that "all persons held as slaves" within the states still in rebellion "are, and henceforward shall be, free." Although the Proclamation in and of itself did not free any slaves, it transformed the character of the war. Despite often intolerable conditions, black people focused on the possibilities of freedom.

DOCUMENT 1
Letter from John Q. A. Dennis to Edwin M. Stanton, July 26, 1864

John Q. A. Dennis, formerly a slave in Maryland, wrote to ask Secretary of War Edwin M. Stanton for help in reuniting his family.

Boston

Dear Sir I am Glad that I have the Honour to Write you afew line I have been in troble for about four yars my Dear wife was taken from me Nov 19th 1859 and left me with three Children and I being a Slave At the time Could Not do Anny thing for the poor little Children for my master it was took me Carry me some forty mile from them So I Could Not do for them and the man that they live with half feed them and half Cloth them & beat them like dogs & when I was admitted to go to see them it use to brake my heart & Now I say again I am Glad to have the honour to write to you to see if you Can Do Anny thing for me or for my poor little Children I was keap in Slavy untell last Novr 1863. then the Good lord sent the Cornel borne [federal Colonel William Birney?] Down their in Marland in worsester Co So as I have been recently freed I have but letle to live on but I am Strieving Dear Sir but what I went too know of you Sir is it possible for me to go & take my Children from those men that keep them in Savery if it is possible will you pleas give me a permit from your hand then I think they would let them go. . . .

    Hon sir will you please excuse my Miserable writeing & answer me as soon as you can I want get the little Children out of Slavery, I being Criple would like to know of you also if I Cant be permited to rase a Shool Down there & on what turm I Could be admited to Do so No more At present Dear Hon Sir

SOURCE: *Freedom: A Documentary History of Emancipation, 1861–1867*, ser. 1, vol. 1, *The Destruction of Slavery*, 386, by Ira Berlin, Joseph P. Reidy, and Leslie S. Rowland, eds. Copyright © 1985. Reprinted with the permission of Cambridge University Press.

DOCUMENT 2
Report from Reverend A. B. Randall, February 28, 1865

Freedom prompted ex-slaves to seek legal marriages, which under slavery had been impossible. Writing from Little Rock, Arkansas, to the adjutant general of the Union army, A. B. Randall, the white chaplain of a black regiment, affirmed the importance of marriage to freed slaves and emphasized their conviction that emancipation was only the first step toward full freedom.

Weddings, just now, are very popular, and abundant among the Colored People. They have just learned, of the Special Order No. 15. of Gen Thomas [Adjutant General Lorenzo Thomas] by which, they may not only be lawfully married, but have their Marriage Certificates, Recorded; in a book furnished by the Government. This is most desirable. . . . Those who were captured . . . at Ivy's Ford, on the 17th of January, by Col Brooks, had their Marriage Certificates, taken from them; and destroyed; and then were roundly cursed, for having such papers in their posession. I have married, during the month, at this Post; Twenty five couples; mostly, those, who have families; & have been living together for years. I try to dissuade single men, who are soldiers, from marrying, till their time of enlistment is out: as that course seems to me, to be most judicious. The Colord People here, generally consider, this war not only; their exodus, from bondage; but the road, to Responsibility; Competency; and an honorable Citizenship — God grant that their hopes and expectations may be fully realized.

SOURCE: *Freedom: A Documentary History of Emancipation, 1861–1867*, ser. 2, vol. 1, *The Black Military Experience*, 712, by Ira Berlin, Joseph P. Reidy, and Leslie S. Rowland, eds. Copyright © 1982. Reprinted with the permission of Cambridge University Press.

DOCUMENT 3
Petition "to the Union Convention of Tennessee Assembled in the Capitol at Nashville," January 9, 1865

Early efforts at political reconstruction prompted petitions from former slaves and free blacks demanding civil and political rights. In January 1865, black Tennesseans petitioned a convention of white Unionists debating the reorganization of state government.

We the undersigned petitioners, American citizens of African descent, natives and residents of Tennessee, and devoted friends of the great National cause, do most respectfully ask a patient hearing of your honorable body in regard to matters deeply affecting the future condition of our unfortunate and long suffering race.

First of all, however, we would say that words are too weak to tell how profoundly grateful we are to the Federal Government for the good work of freedom which it is gradually carrying forward; and for the Emancipation Proclamation which has set free all the slaves in some of the rebellious States, as well as many of the slaves in Tennessee. . . .

We claim freedom, as our natural right, and ask that in harmony and co-operation with the nation at large, you should cut up by the roots the system of slavery, which is not only a wrong to us, but the source of all the evil which at present afflicts the State. For slavery, corrupt itself, corrupted nearly all, also, around it, so that it has influenced nearly all the slave States to rebel against the Federal Government, in order to set up a government of pirates under which slavery might be perpetrated.

In the contest between the nation and slavery, our unfortunate people have sided, by instinct, with the former. We have little fortune to devote to the national cause, for a hard fate has hitherto forced us to live in poverty, but we do devote to its success, our hopes, our toils, our whole heart, our sacred honor, and our lives. We will work, pray, live, and, if need be, die for the Union, as cheerfully as ever a white patriot died for his country. The color of our skin does not lessen in the least degree, our love either for God or for the land of our birth. . . .

We know the burdens of citizenship, and are ready to bear them. We know the duties of the good citizen, and are ready to perform them cheerfully, and would ask to be put in a position in which we can discharge them more effectually. . . .

This is a democracy—a government of the people. It should aim to make every man, without regard to the color of his skin, the amount of his wealth, or the character of his religious faith, feel personally interested in its welfare. Every man who lives under the Government should feel that it is his property, his treasure, the bulwark and defence of himself and his family, his pearl of great price, which he must preserve, protect, and defend faithfully at all times, on all occasions, in every possible manner.

This is not a Democratic Government if a numerous, law-abiding, industrious, and useful class of citizens, born and bred on the soil, are to be treated as aliens and enemies, as an inferior degraded class, who must have no voice in the Government which they support, protect and defend, with all their heart, soul, mind, and body, both in peace and war. . . .

The possibility that the negro suffrage proposition may shock popular prejudice at first sight, is not a conclusive argument against its wisdom and policy. No proposition ever met with more furious or general opposition than the one to enlist colored soldiers in the United States army. The opponents of the measure exclaimed on all hands that the negro was a coward; that he would not fight; that one white man, with a whip in his hand could put to flight a regiment of them; that the experiment would end in the utter rout and ruin of the Federal army. Yet the colored man has fought so well, on almost every occasion, that the rebel government is prevented, only by its fears and distrust of being able to force him to fight for slavery as well as he fights against it, from putting half a million of negroes into its ranks.

The Government has asked the colored man to fight for its preservation and gladly has he done it. It can afford to trust him with a vote as safely as it trusted him with a bayonet.

SOURCE: *Freedom: A Documentary History of Emancipation, 1861–1867*, ser. 2, vol. 1, *The Black Military Experience*, 811–16, by Ira Berlin, Joseph P. Reidy, and Leslie S. Rowland, eds. Copyright © 1982. Reprinted with the permission of Cambridge University Press.

Questions for Analysis and Debate

1. How does John Q. A. Dennis interpret his responsibility as a father?

2. Why do you think ex-slaves wanted their marriages legalized?

3. Why, according to petitioners to the Union Convention of Tennessee, did blacks deserve voting rights?

and Methodists. Freedmen interpreted the events of the Civil War and reconstruction as Christian people. One black woman thanked Lincoln for the Emancipation Proclamation, declaring, "When you are dead and in Heaven, in a thousand years that action of yours will make the Angels sing your praises I know it."

Q: Why did Congress object to Lincoln's wartime plan for reconstruction?

Presidential Reconstruction

Abraham Lincoln died on April 15, 1865, just hours after John Wilkes Booth shot him at a Washington, D.C., theater. Chief Justice Salmon P. Chase immediately administered the oath of office to Vice President **Andrew Johnson** of Tennessee. Congress had adjourned in March and would not reconvene until December. Throughout the summer and fall, the "accidental president" made critical decisions about the future of the South without congressional advice. With dizzying speed, he drew up and executed a plan of reconstruction.

Congress returned to the capital in December to find that, as far as the president and former Confederates were concerned, reconstruction was completed. Most Republicans, however, thought Johnson's puny demands of ex-rebels made a mockery of the sacrifice of Union soldiers. Instead of honoring the dead by insisting on "a new birth of freedom," as Lincoln had promised in his 1863 speech at Gettysburg, Johnson had acted as midwife to the rebirth of the Old South and the stillbirth of black liberty. They proceeded to dismantle Johnson's program and substitute a program of their own.

Johnson's Program of Reconciliation Born in 1808 in Raleigh, North Carolina, Andrew Johnson was the son of illiterate parents. Self-educated and ambitious, Johnson moved to Tennessee, where he worked as a tailor, accumulated a fortune in land, acquired five slaves, and built a career in politics championing the South's common white people and assailing its "illegitimate, swaggering, bastard, scrub aristocracy." The only senator from a Confederate state to remain loyal to the Union, Johnson held the planter class responsible for secession. Less than two weeks before he became president, he announced what he would do to planters if he ever had the chance: "I would arrest them—I would try them—I would convict them and I would hang them."

Despite such statements, Johnson was no friend of the Republicans. A Democrat all his life,

Johnson occupied the White House only because the Republican Party in 1864 had needed a vice presidential candidate who would appeal to loyal, Union-supporting Democrats. Johnson vigorously defended states' rights (but not secession) and opposed Republican efforts to expand the power of the federal government. A steadfast supporter of slavery, Johnson had owned slaves until 1862, when Tennessee rebels, angry at his Unionism, confiscated them. When he grudgingly accepted emancipation, it was more because he hated planters than sympathized with slaves. "Damn the negroes," he said. "I am fighting those traitorous aristocrats, their masters." At a time when the nation confronted the future of black Americans, the new president harbored unshakable racist convictions. Africans, Johnson said, were "inferior to the white man in point of intellect—better calculated in physical structure to undergo drudgery and hardship."

Like Lincoln, Johnson stressed the rapid restoration of civil government in the South. Like Lincoln, he promised to pardon most, but not all, ex-rebels. Johnson recognized the state governments created by Lincoln but set out his own requirements for restoring the other rebel states to the Union. All that the citizens of a state had to do was to renounce the right of secession, deny that the debts of the Confederacy were legal and binding, and ratify the Thirteenth Amendment abolishing slavery, which became part of the Constitution in December 1865.

Johnson's eagerness to restore relations with southern states and his lack of sympathy for blacks also led him to return to pardoned ex-Confederates all confiscated and abandoned land, even if it was in the hands of freedmen. Reformers were shocked. They had expected the president's hatred of planters to mean the permanent confiscation of the South's plantations and the distribution of the land to loyal freedmen. Instead, his instructions canceled the promising beginnings made by General Sherman and the Freedmen's Bureau to settle blacks on land of their own. As one freedman observed, "Things was hurt by Mr. Lincoln getting killed."

White Southern Resistance and Black Codes In the summer of 1865, delegates across the South gathered to draw up the new state constitutions required by Johnson's plan of reconstruction. Rather than take their medicine, delegates choked on even the president's mild requirements. Refusing to renounce secession, the South Carolina and Georgia conventions merely "repudiated" their secession ordinances, preserving in principle their right to secede. South Carolina and Mississippi refused to disown their Confederate

The Black Codes Titled "Selling a Freeman to Pay His Fine at Monticello, Florida," this 1867 drawing from a northern magazine equates black codes with the reinstitution of slavery. The laws stopped short of reenslavement but sharply restricted blacks' freedom. In Florida, as in other southern states, certain acts, such as breaking a labor contract, were made criminal offenses, the penalty for which could be involuntary plantation labor for a year. Granger Collection.

war debts. Mississippi rejected the Thirteenth Amendment outright, and Alabama rejected it in part. Despite these defiant acts, Johnson did nothing. White Southerners began to think that by standing up for themselves they—not victorious Northerners—would shape reconstruction.

State governments across the South adopted a series of laws known as **black codes**, which made a travesty of black freedom. The codes sought to keep ex-slaves subordinate to whites by subjecting them to every sort of discrimination. Several states made it illegal for blacks to own a gun. Mississippi made insulting gestures and language by blacks a criminal offense. The codes barred blacks from jury duty. Not a single southern state granted any black the right to vote.

At the core of the black codes, however, lay the matter of labor. Faced with the death of slavery, legislators sought to hustle freedmen back to the plantations. South Carolina attempted to limit blacks to either farmwork or domestic service by requiring them to pay annual taxes of $10 to $100 to work in any other occupation. Mississippi declared that blacks who did not possess written evidence of employment could be declared vagrants and be subject to involuntary plantation labor. Under so-called apprenticeship laws, courts bound thousands of black children—orphans and others whose parents they deemed unable to support them—to work for planter "guardians."

Johnson refused to intervene. A staunch defender of states' rights, he believed that the citizens of every state should be free to write their own constitutions and laws. Moreover, Johnson was as eager as other white Southerners to restore white supremacy and black subordination.

But Johnson also followed the path that he believed offered him the greatest political return. A conservative Tennessee Democrat at the head of a northern Republican Party, he began to look southward for political allies. By pardoning powerful whites, by accepting governments even when they failed to satisfy his minimal demands, and by acquiescing in the black codes, he won useful southern friends.

In the fall elections of 1865, white Southerners dramatically expressed their mood. To represent them in Congress, they chose former Confederates. Of the eighty senators and representatives they sent to Washington, fifteen had served in the Confederate army, ten of them as generals. Another sixteen had served in civil and judicial posts in the Confederacy. Nine others had served in the Confederate Congress. One—Alexander Stephens—had been vice president of the Confederacy. As one Georgian remarked, "It looked as though Richmond had moved to Washington."

Expansion of Federal Authority and Black Rights

Southerners had blundered monumentally. They had assumed that what Andrew Johnson was willing to accept, Republicans would accept as well. But southern intransigence compelled even moderates to conclude that ex-rebels were a "generation of vipers," still untrustworthy and dangerous. So angry were Republicans with the rebels that the federal government refused to supply artificial limbs to disabled Southerners, as they did for Union veterans.

The black codes became a symbol of southern intentions to "restore all of slavery but its name." Northerners were hardly saints when it came to racial justice, but black freedom had become a hallowed war aim. "We tell the white men of Mississippi," the *Chicago Tribune* roared, "that the men of the North will convert the State of Mississippi into a frog pond before they will allow such laws to disgrace one foot of the soil in which the bones of our soldiers sleep and over which the flag of freedom waves."

The moderate majority of the Republican Party wanted only assurance that slavery and treason were dead. They did not champion black equality, the confiscation of plantations, or black voting, as did the radicals. But southern obstinacy had succeeded in forging unity (at least temporarily) among Republican factions. In December 1865, exercising Congress's right to determine the qualifications of its members, Republicans refused to seat the southern representatives elected in the fall elections. Rather than accept Johnson's claim that

THE PROMISE OF TECHNOLOGY

Artificial Limbs Approximately 45,000 of the 60,000 Civil War amputees survived. After the war, the great demand for artificial limbs prompted businesses to apply industrial manufacturing processes to limbs. The search for a functional, lightweight artificial limb drew on a number of advancing fields, including photography, physiology, physics, material science, mathematics, and psychology. Artificial limbs advanced quickly from crude peg legs to hollow willow legs with movable ankles that simulated the natural motions of the foot. Newly invented vulcanized rubber (called India rubber) increased strength and flexibility and allowed disabled veterans to dispense with metal bolts and springs in their new limbs. These "before and after" images of a veteran with and without his artificial legs from an A. A. Marks business card in about 1878 sent a clear message: Marks legs make maimed men whole again. Marks promised that, thus restored, the wounded man would be the "equal of his fellowmen in every employment of life." Warshaw Collection, National Museum of American History, Smithsonian Institution.

the "work of restoration" was done, Congress challenged his executive power.

Republican senator Lyman Trumbull declared that the president's policy meant that an ex-slave would "be tyrannized over, abused, and virtually reenslaved without some legislation by the nation for his protection." Early in 1866, the moderates produced two bills that strengthened the federal shield. The first, the Freedmen's Bureau bill, prolonged the life of the agency established by the previous Congress. It had distributed food, supervised labor contracts, and sponsored schools for freedmen. Arguing that the Constitution never contemplated a "system for the support of indigent persons," President Andrew Johnson vetoed the bill. Congress failed by a narrow margin to override the president's veto.

The moderates designed their second measure, the **Civil Rights Act**, to nullify the black codes by affirming African Americans' rights to "full and equal benefit of all laws and proceedings for the security of person and property as is enjoyed by white citizens." The act boldly required the end of racial discrimination in state laws and represented an extraordinary expansion of black rights and federal authority. The president argued that the civil rights bill amounted to "unconstitutional invasion of states' rights" and vetoed it. In essence, he denied that the federal government possessed the authority to protect the civil rights of blacks.

In April 1866, an incensed Republican Party again pushed the civil rights bill through Congress and overrode the presidential veto. In July, it passed another Freedmen's Bureau bill and overrode Johnson's veto. For the first time in American history, Congress had overridden presidential vetoes of major legislation. As a worried South Carolinian observed, Johnson had succeeded in uniting the Republicans and probably touched off "a fight this fall such as has never been seen."

Q: How did the North respond to the passage of black codes in the southern states?

Congressional Reconstruction

By the summer of 1866, President Andrew Johnson and Congress had dropped their gloves and stood toe-to-toe in a bare-knuckle contest unprecedented in American history. Johnson made it clear that he would not budge on either constitutional issues or policy. Moderate Republicans responded by amending the Constitution. But the obstinacy of Johnson and white Southerners pushed Republican moderates ever closer to the radicals and to

acceptance of additional federal intervention in the South. Congress also voted to impeach the president. In time, Congress debated whether to make voting rights color-blind, while women sought to make voting sex-blind as well.

The Fourteenth Amendment and Escalating Violence In June 1866, Congress passed the **Fourteenth Amendment** to the Constitution, and two years later it gained the necessary ratification of three-fourths of the states. The most important provisions of this complex amendment made all native-born or naturalized persons American citizens and prohibited states from abridging the "privileges and immunities" of citizens, depriving them of "life, liberty, or property without due process of law," and denying them "equal protection of the laws." By making blacks national citizens, the amendment provided a national guarantee of equality before the law. In essence, it protected blacks against violation by southern state governments.

The Fourteenth Amendment also dealt with voting rights. It gave Congress the right to reduce the congressional representation of states that withheld suffrage from some of its adult male population. In other words, white Southerners could either allow black men to vote or see their representation in Washington slashed. Whatever happened, Republicans stood to benefit from the Fourteenth Amendment. If southern whites granted voting rights to freedmen, Republicans would gain valuable black votes. If whites refused, representation of southern Democrats would plunge.

The Fourteenth Amendment's suffrage provisions ignored the small band of politicized women who had emerged from the war demanding "the ballot for the two disenfranchised classes, negroes and women." Founding the **American Equal Rights Association** in 1866, **Susan B. Anthony** and **Elizabeth Cady Stanton** lobbied for "a government by the people, and the whole people; for the people and the whole people." They felt betrayed when their old antislavery allies refused to work for their goals. "It was the Negro's hour," Frederick Douglass explained. Senator Charles Sumner suggested that woman suffrage could be "the great question of the future."

The Fourteenth Amendment provided for punishment of any state that excluded voters on the basis of race but not on the basis of sex. The amendment also introduced the word *male* into the Constitution when it referred to a citizen's right to vote. Stanton predicted that "if that word 'male' be inserted, it will take us a century at least to get it out."

Tennessee approved the Fourteenth Amendment in July, and Congress promptly welcomed

Susan B. Anthony Like many outspoken suffragists, Anthony, depicted here in 1852, began her public career working on behalf of temperance and abolition. But she grew tired of laboring under the direction of male clergymen — "white orthodox little saints," she called them — who controlled the reform movements and routinely dismissed the opinions of women. Anthony's continued passion for other causes — improving working conditions for labor, for example — led some conservatives to oppose women's political rights because they equated the suffragist cause with radicalism in general. Women could not easily overcome such views, and the long struggle for the vote eventually drew millions of women into public life. Susan B. Anthony House, Inc.

the state's representatives and senators back. Had President Johnson counseled other southern states to ratify this relatively mild amendment and warned them that they faced the fury of an outraged Republican Party if they refused, they might have listened. Instead, Johnson advised Southerners to reject the Fourteenth Amendment and to rely on him to trounce the Republicans in the fall congressional elections.

Johnson had decided to make the Fourteenth Amendment the overriding issue of the 1866 elections and to gather its white opponents into a new conservative party, the National Union Party. The president's strategy suffered a setback when whites in several southern cities went on rampages against blacks. When a mob in New Orleans assaulted delegates to a black suffrage convention, thirty-four blacks died. In Memphis, white mobs killed at least forty-six people. The slaughter shocked Northerners and renewed skepticism about Johnson's claim that southern whites could be trusted. "Who doubts that the Freedmen's Bureau ought to be abolished forthwith," a New Yorker observed sarcastically, "and the blacks remitted to the

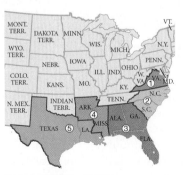

Reconstruction Military Districts, 1867

paternal care of their old masters, who 'understand the nigger, you know, a great deal better than the Yankees can.'"

The 1866 elections resulted in an overwhelming Republican victory. Johnson had bet that Northerners would not support federal protection of black rights and that a racist backlash would blast the Republican Party. But the war was still fresh in northern minds, and as one Republican explained, southern whites "with all their intelligence were traitors, the blacks with all their ignorance were loyal."

Radical Reconstruction and Military Rule

When Johnson continued to urge Southerners to reject the Fourteenth Amendment, every southern state except Tennessee voted it down. "The last one of the sinful ten," thundered Representative James A. Garfield of Ohio, "has flung back into our teeth the magnanimous offer of a generous nation." After the South rejected the moderates' program, the radicals seized the initiative.

Each act of defiance by southern whites had boosted the standing of the radicals within the Republican Party. Except for freedmen themselves, no one did more to make freedom the "mighty moral question of the age." Radicals such as Massachusetts senator Charles Sumner and Pennsylvania representative Thaddeus Stevens did not speak with a single voice, but they united in demanding civil and political equality. Southern states were "like clay in the hands of the potter," Stevens declared in January 1867, and he called on Congress to begin reconstruction all over again.

In March 1867, Congress overturned the Johnson state governments and initiated military rule of the South. The **Military Reconstruction Act** (and three subsequent acts) divided the ten unreconstructed Confederate states into five military districts. Congress placed a Union general in charge of each district and instructed him to "suppress insurrection, disorder, and violence" and to begin political reform. After the military had completed voter registration, which would include black men, voters in each state would elect delegates to conventions that would draw up new state constitutions. Each constitution would guarantee black suffrage. When the voters of each state had approved the constitution and the state legislature had ratified the Fourteenth Amendment, the state could submit its work to Congress. If Congress approved, the state's senators and representatives could be seated, and political reunification would be accomplished.

Radicals proclaimed the provision for black suffrage "a prodigious triumph," for it extended far beyond the limited suffrage provisions of the Fourteenth Amendment. Republicans now believed that only the voting power of ex-slaves could bring about a permanent revolution in the South. When combined with the disfranchisement of thousands of ex-rebels, it promised to cripple any neo-Confederate resurgence and guarantee Republican state governments in the South.

Despite its bold suffrage provision, the Military Reconstruction Act of 1867 disappointed those who also advocated the confiscation and redistribution of southern plantations to ex-slaves. Thaddeus Stevens agreed with the freedman who said, "Give us our own land and we take care of ourselves, but without land, the old masters can hire us or starve us, as they please." But most Republicans believed they had provided blacks with what they needed: equal legal rights and the ballot. If blacks were to get land, they would have to gain it themselves.

Declaring that he would rather sever his right arm than sign such a formula for "anarchy and chaos," Andrew Johnson vetoed the Military Reconstruction Act. Congress overrode his veto,

dramatizing the shift in power from the executive to the legislative branch of government. With the passage of the Reconstruction Acts of 1867, congressional reconstruction was virtually completed. Congress left whites owning most of the South's land but, in a departure that justified the term "radical reconstruction," had given black men the ballot. In 1867, the nation began an unprecedented experiment in interracial democracy — at least in the South, for Congress's plan did not touch the North. But before the spotlight swung away from Washington to the South, the president and Congress had one more scene to play.

Impeaching a President Despite his defeats, Andrew Johnson had no intention of yielding control of reconstruction. In a dozen ways, he sabotaged Congress's will and encouraged southern whites to resist. He issued a flood of pardons, waged war against the Freedmen's Bureau, and replaced Union generals eager to enforce Congress's Reconstruction Acts with conservative men eager to defeat them. Johnson claimed that he was merely defending the "violated Constitution." At bottom, however, the president subverted congressional reconstruction to protect southern whites from what he considered the horrors of "Negro domination."

THIS LITTLE BOY WOULD PERSIST IN HANDLING BOOKS ABOVE HIS CAPACITY.

AND THIS WAS THE DISASTROUS RESULT.

Andrew Johnson Cartoon Appearing in 1868 during President Andrew Johnson's impeachment trial, this cartoon includes captions that read: "This little boy would persist in handling books above his capacity" and "And this was the disastrous result." The cartoonist's portrait of Johnson being crushed by the Constitution refers to the president's flouting of the Tenure of Office Act, which caused Republicans to vote for his impeachment. The cartoon's celebration of Johnson's destruction proved premature, however. Granger Collection.

According to the Constitution, the House of Representatives can impeach and the Senate can try any federal official for "treason, bribery, or other high crimes and misdemeanors." Radicals argued that Johnson's abuse of constitutional powers and his failure to fulfill constitutional obligations to enforce the law were impeachable offenses. But moderates interpreted the constitutional provision to mean violation of criminal statutes. As long as Johnson refrained from breaking the law, **impeachment** (the process of formal charges of wrongdoing against the president or other federal official) remained stalled.

Then in August 1867, Johnson suspended secretary of war Edwin M. Stanton from office. As required by the Tenure of Office Act, which demanded the approval of the Senate for the removal of any government official who had been appointed with Senate approval, the president requested the Senate to consent to the dismissal. When the Senate balked, Johnson removed Stanton anyway. "Is the President crazy, or only drunk?" asked a dumbfounded Republican moderate. "I'm afraid his doings will make us all favor impeachment."

News of Johnson's open defiance of the law convinced every Republican in the House to vote for a resolution impeaching the president. Supreme Court chief justice Salmon Chase presided over the Senate trial, which lasted from March until May 1868. Chase refused to allow Johnson's opponents to raise broad issues of misuse of power and forced them to argue their case exclusively on the narrow legal grounds of Johnson's removal of Stanton. Johnson's lawyers argued that the president had not committed a criminal offense, that the Tenure of Office Act was unconstitutional, and that in any case it did not apply to Stanton, who had been appointed by Lincoln. When the critical vote came, thirty-five senators voted guilty and nineteen not guilty. The impeachment forces fell one vote short of the two-thirds needed to convict.

After his trial, Johnson called a truce, and for the remaining ten months of his term, congressional reconstruction proceeded unhindered by presidential interference. Without interference from Johnson, Congress revisited the suffrage issue.

The Fifteenth Amendment and Women's Demands In February 1869, Republicans passed the **Fifteenth Amendment** to the Constitution, which prohibited states from depriving any citizen of the right to vote because of "race, color, or previous condition of servitude." The Reconstruction Acts of 1867 already required black suffrage in the South; the Fifteenth Amendment extended black voting nationwide.

Some Republicans, however, found the final wording of the Fifteenth Amendment "lame and halting." Rather than absolutely guaranteeing the right to vote, the amendment merely prohibited exclusion on grounds of race. The distinction would prove to be significant. In time, white Southerners would devise tests of literacy and property and other apparently nonracial measures that would effectively disfranchise blacks yet not violate the Fifteenth Amendment. But an amendment that fully guaranteed the right to vote courted defeat outside the South. Rising antiforeign sentiment—against the Chinese in California and European immigrants in the Northeast—caused states to resist giving up total control of suffrage requirements. In March 1870, after three-fourths of the states had ratified it, the Fifteenth Amendment became part of the Constitution. Republicans generally breathed a sigh of relief, confident that black suffrage was "the last great point that remained to be settled of the issues of the war."

Woman suffrage advocates, however, were sorely disappointed with the Fifteenth Amendment's failure to extend voting rights to women. The amendment denied states the right to forbid suffrage only on the basis of race. Elizabeth Cady Stanton and Susan B. Anthony condemned the Republicans' "negro first" strategy and pointed out that women remained "the only class of citizens wholly unrepresented in the government." Stanton wondered aloud why ignorant black men should legislate for educated and cultured white women. Increasingly, activist women concluded that woman "must not put her trust in man." The Fifteenth Amendment severed the early feminist movement from its abolitionist roots. Over the next several decades, feminists established an independent suffrage crusade that drew millions of women into political life.

Republicans took enough satisfaction in the Fifteenth Amendment to promptly scratch the "Negro question" from the agenda of national politics. Even that steadfast crusader for equality Wendell Phillips concluded that the black man now held "sufficient shield in his own hands. . . . Whatever he suffers will be largely now, and in future, his own fault." Northerners had no idea of the violent struggles that lay ahead.

Q: **Why did Johnson urge the southern states to reject the Fourteenth Amendment?**

The Struggle in the South

Northerners believed they had discharged their responsibilities with the Reconstruction Acts and the amendments to the Constitution, but

Southerners knew that the battle had just begun. Black suffrage established the foundation for the rise of the Republican Party in the South. Gathering together outsiders and outcasts, southern Republicans won elections, wrote new state constitutions, and formed new state governments.

Challenging the established class for political control was dangerous business. Equally dangerous were the confrontations that took place on southern farms and plantations, where blacks sought to give economic meaning to their newly won legal and political equality. Ex-masters had their own ideas about the labor system that should replace slavery. Freedom remained contested territory, and Southerners fought pitched battles with one another to determine the contours of their new world.

Freedmen, Yankees, and Yeomen African Americans made up the majority of southern Republicans. After gaining voting rights in 1867, nearly all eligible black men registered to vote as Republicans, grateful to the party that had freed them and granted them the franchise. Southern blacks did not have identical political priorities, but they united in their desire for education and equal treatment before the law.

Northern whites who made the South their home after the war were a second element of the South's Republican Party. Conservative white Southerners called them **carpetbaggers**, men so poor that they could stuff all their earthly belongings in a single carpet-sided suitcase and swoop southward like buzzards to "fatten on our misfortunes." But most Northerners who moved south were young men who looked upon the South as they did the West — as a promising place to make a living. Northerners in the southern Republican Party consistently supported programs that encouraged vigorous economic development along the lines of the northern free-labor model.

Southern whites made up the third element of the South's Republican Party. Approximately one out of four white Southerners voted Republican. The other three condemned the one who did as a traitor to his region and his race and called him a **scalawag**, a term for runty horses and low-down, good-for-nothing rascals. Yeoman farmers accounted for the majority of southern white Republicans. Some were Unionists who emerged from the war with bitter memories of Confederate persecution. Others were small farmers who wanted to end state governments' favoritism toward plantation owners. Yeomen supported initiatives for public schools and for expanding economic opportunity in the South.

The South's Republican Party, then, was made up of freedmen, Yankees, and yeomen — an improbable coalition. The mix of races, regions, and classes inevitably meant friction as each group maneuvered to define the party. But Reconstruction represents an extraordinary moment in American politics: Blacks and whites joined together in the Republican Party to pursue political change. Formally, of course, only men participated in politics — casting ballots and holding offices — but white and black women also played a part in the political struggle by joining in parades and rallies, attending stump speeches, and even campaigning.

Reconstruction politics was not for cowards. Most whites in the South condemned southern Republicans as illegitimate and felt justified in doing whatever they could to stamp them out. Violence against blacks — the "white terror" — took brutal institutional form in 1866 with the formation in Tennessee of the **Ku Klux Klan**, a social club of Confederate veterans that quickly developed into a paramilitary organization supporting Democrats. The Klan went on a rampage of whipping, hanging, shooting, burning, and throat-cutting to defeat Republicans and restore white supremacy. Rapid demobilization of the Union army after the war left only twenty thousand troops to patrol the entire South. Without effective military protection, southern Republicans had to take care of themselves.

Republican Rule In the fall of 1867, southern states held elections for delegates to state constitutional conventions, as required by the Reconstruction Acts. About 40 percent of the white electorate stayed home because they had been disfranchised or because they had decided to boycott politics. Republicans won three-fourths of the seats. About 15 percent of the Republican delegates to the conventions were Northerners who had moved south, 25 percent were African Americans, and 60 percent were white Southerners. As a British visitor observed, the delegate elections reflected "the mighty revolution that had taken place in America."

The reconstruction constitutions introduced two broad categories of changes in the South: those that reduced aristocratic privilege and increased democratic equality and those that expanded the state's responsibility for the general welfare. In the first category, the constitutions adopted universal male suffrage, abolished property qualifications for holding office, and made more offices elective and fewer appointed. In the second category, they

> Conservative white Southerners called them "carpetbaggers," men so poor that they could stuff all their earthly belongings in a single carpet-sided suitcase and swoop southward like buzzards to "fatten on our misfortunes."

enacted prison reform; made the state responsible for caring for orphans, the insane, and the deaf and mute; and exempted debtors' homes from seizure.

To Democrats, however, these forward-looking state constitutions looked like wild revolution. They were blind to the fact that no constitution confiscated and redistributed land, as virtually every former slave wished, or disfranchised ex-rebels wholesale, as most southern Unionists advocated. And Democrats were convinced that the new constitutions initiated "Negro domination" in politics. In fact, although four out of five Republican voters were black men, more than four out of five Republican officeholders were white. Southerners sent fourteen black congressmen and two black senators to Washington, but only 6 percent of Southerners in Congress during Reconstruction were black (Figure 16.1). And no state legislature experienced "Negro rule," despite black majorities in the populations of some states.

Southern voters ratified the new constitutions and swept Republicans into power. When the former Confederate states ratified the Fourteenth Amendment, Congress readmitted them. Southern Republicans then turned to a staggering array of problems. Wartime destruction—burned cities, shattered bridges, broken levees—littered the landscape. Manufacturing limped along, and agricultural production remained anemic. The region's railroads lay devastated. Making matters worse, racial harassment and reactionary violence dogged Southerners

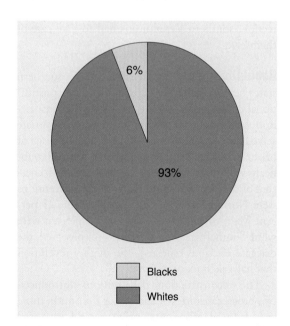

FIGURE 16.1 Southern Congressional Delegations, 1865–1877
The statistics contradict the myth of black domination of congressional representation during Reconstruction.

who sought reform. In this desperate context, Republicans struggled to breathe life into the region.

Activity focused on three areas—education, civil rights, and economic development. Every state inaugurated a system of public education. Before the Civil War, whites had deliberately kept slaves illiterate, and planter-dominated governments rarely spent tax money to educate the children of yeomen. By 1875, half of Mississippi's and South Carolina's eligible children (the majority of whom were black) were attending school. Although schools were underfunded, literacy rates rose sharply. Public schools were racially segregated, but education remained for many blacks a tangible, deeply satisfying benefit of freedom and Republican rule.

State legislatures also attacked racial discrimination and defended civil rights. Republicans especially resisted efforts to segregate blacks from whites in public transportation. Mississippi levied fines of up to $1,000 and three years in jail for railroads and steamboats that pushed blacks into "smoking cars" or to lower decks. A Mississippian complained: "Money cannot buy for a colored man or woman decent treatment and the comforts that white people claim and can obtain." But passing color-blind laws was one thing; enforcing them was another. Despite the laws, segregation—later called Jim Crow—developed at white insistence and became a feature of southern life long before the end of the Reconstruction era.

Republican governments also launched ambitious programs of economic development. They envisioned a South of diversified agriculture, roaring factories, and booming towns. State legislatures chartered scores of banks and industrial companies, appropriated funds to fix ruined levees and drain swamps, and went on a railroad-building binge. These efforts fell far short of solving the South's economic troubles, however. Republican spending to stimulate economic growth also meant rising taxes and enormous debt that drained funds from schools and other programs.

The southern Republicans' record, then, was mixed. To their credit, the biracial party took up an ambitious agenda to change the South. Money was scarce, the Democrats continued their harassment, and factionalism threatened the Republican Party from within. However, corruption infected Republican governments in the South. Public morality reached new lows everywhere in the nation after the Civil War, and the chaos of the postwar South proved fertile soil for bribery, fraud, and influence peddling. Despite shortcomings, however, the Republican Party made headway in its efforts to purge the South of aristocratic privilege and racist oppression. Republican governments had less success in overthrowing the long-established white oppression of black farm laborers in the rural South.

White Landlords, Black Sharecroppers

Ex-slaves who wished to escape slave labor and ex-masters who wanted to reinstitute old ways clashed repeatedly. Except for having to pay subsistence wages, planters had not been required to offer many concessions to emancipation. They continued to believe that African Americans would not work without coercion. Whites moved quickly to restore the antebellum world of work gangs, white overseers, field labor for black women and children, clustered cabins, minimal personal freedom, and even whipping whenever they could get away with it.

Ex-slaves resisted every effort to turn back the clock. They argued that if any class could be described as "lazy," it was the planters, who, as one ex-slave noted, "lived in idleness all their lives on stolen labor." Land of their own would anchor their economic independence, they believed, and end planters' interference in their personal lives. They could then, for example, make their own decisions about whether women and children would labor in the fields. Indeed, within months after the war, perhaps one-third of black women abandoned field labor to work on chores in their own cabins just as poor white women did. Hundreds of thousands of black children enrolled in school. But without their own land, ex-slaves had little choice but to work on plantations.

Although forced to return to the planters' fields, freedmen resisted efforts to restore slavelike conditions. Instead of working for wages, a South Carolinian observed, "the negroes all seem disposed to rent land," which increased their independence from whites. Out of this tug-of-war between white landlords and black laborers emerged a new system of southern agriculture.

Sharecropping was a compromise that offered both ex-masters and ex-slaves something but satisfied neither. Under the new system, planters divided their cotton plantations into small farms that freedmen rented, paying with a share of each year's crop, usually half. Sharecropping gave blacks more freedom than the system of wages and labor gangs and released them from the day-to-day supervision of whites. Black families abandoned the old slave quarters and scattered over plantations, building separate cabins for themselves on the patches of land they rented (Map 16.1). Black families now decided who would work, for how long, and how hard. Still, most blacks remained dependent on white landlords, who had the power to expel them at the end of each growing season. For planters, sharecropping offered a way to resume agricultural production, but it did not allow them to restore the old slave plantation.

Sharecropping introduced a new figure—the country merchant—into the agricultural equation. Landlords supplied sharecroppers with land, mules,

Black Woman in Cotton Fields, Thomasville, Georgia Few images of everyday black women during the Reconstruction era survive. This photograph was taken in 1895, but it nevertheless goes to the heart of the labor struggle after the Civil War. Before emancipation, black women worked in the fields; after emancipation, white landlords wanted them to continue working there. Freedom allowed some women to escape field labor, but not this Georgian, who probably worked to survive. The photograph reveals a strong person with a clear sense of who she is. Though worn to protect her head and body from the fierce heat, her intricately wrapped headdress dramatically expresses her individuality. Her bare feet also reveal something about her life. Courtesy, Georgia Department of Archives and History, Atlanta, Georgia.

seeds, and tools, but blacks also needed credit to obtain essential food and clothing before they harvested their crops. Thousands of small crossroads stores sprang up to offer credit. Under an arrangement called a crop lien, a merchant would advance goods to a sharecropper in exchange for a lien, or legal claim, on the farmer's future crop. Some merchants charged exorbitant rates of interest, as much as 60 percent, on the goods they sold. At the end

MAP 16.1 A Southern Plantation in 1860 and 1881

These maps of the Barrow plantation in Georgia illustrate some of the ways in which ex-slaves expressed their freedom. Freedmen and freedwomen deserted the clustered living quarters behind the master's house, scattered over the plantation, built family cabins, and farmed rented land. The former Barrow slaves also worked together to build a school and a church.

READING THE MAP: Compare the number and size of the slave quarters in 1860 with the homes of the former slaves in 1881. How do they differ? Which buildings were prominently located along the road in 1860, and which could be found along the road in 1881?

CONNECTIONS: How might the former master feel about the new configuration of buildings on the plantation in 1881? In what ways did the new system of sharecropping replicate the old system of plantation agriculture? In what ways was it different?

FOR MORE HELP ANALYZING THIS MAP, see the map activity for this chapter in the Online Study Guide at bedfordstmartins.com/roarkcompact.

of the growing season, after the landlord had taken half of the farmer's crop for rent, the merchant took most of the rest. Sometimes, the farmer's debt to the merchant exceeded the income he received from his remaining half of the crop, and the farmer would have no choice but to borrow more from the merchant and begin the cycle all over again.

An experiment at first, sharecropping spread quickly and soon dominated the cotton South. Lien merchants forced tenants to plant cotton, which was easy to sell, instead of food crops. The result was excessive production of cotton and falling cotton prices, developments that cost thousands of small white farmers their

land and pushed them into the great army of sharecroppers. The new sharecropping system of agriculture took shape just as the political power of Republicans in the South began to buckle under Democratic pressure.

Q: **Why was the Republican Party in the South a coalition party?**

Reconstruction Collapses

By 1870, after a decade of war and reconstruction, Northerners wanted to put "the southern problem" behind them. Increasingly, practical, business-minded men came to the forefront of the Republican Party, replacing the band of reformers and idealists who had been prominent in the 1860s. While northern commitment to defend black freedom eroded, southern commitment to white supremacy intensified. Without northern protection, southern Republicans were no match for the Democrats' economic coercion, political corruption, and bloody violence. One by one, Republican state governments fell in the South. The election of 1876 both confirmed and completed the collapse of reconstruction.

Grant's Troubled Presidency In 1868, the Republican Party's presidential nomination went to Ulysses S. Grant, the North's favorite general. Hero of the Civil War and a supporter of congressional reconstruction, Grant was the obvious choice. His Democratic opponent, Horatio Seymour of New York, ran on a platform that blasted congressional reconstruction as "a flagrant usurpation of power . . . unconstitutional, revolutionary, and void." The Republicans answered by **waving the bloody shirt**—that is, they reminded voters that the Democrats were "the party of rebellion." During the campaign, the Ku Klux Klan erupted in a reign of terror across the South, murdering hundreds of Republicans. Violence cost Grant votes, but he gained a narrow 309,000-vote margin in the popular vote and a substantial victory (214 votes to 80) in the electoral college (Map 16.2).

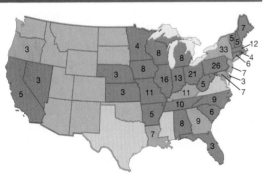

Grant was not as good a president as he was a general. The talents he had demonstrated on the battlefield—decisiveness, clarity, and resolution—were less obvious in the White House. He surrounded himself with fumbling kinfolk

Grant and Scandal This anti-Grant cartoon by Thomas Nast, the nation's most celebrated political cartoonist, shows the president falling headfirst into the barrel of fraud and corruption that tainted his administration. During Grant's eight years in the White House, many members of his administration failed him. Sometimes duped, sometimes merely loyal, Grant stubbornly defended wrongdoers, even to the point of perjuring himself to keep an aide out of jail. Library of Congress.

FOR MORE HELP ANALYZING THIS IMAGE, see the visual activity for this chapter in the Online Study Guide at bedfordstmartins.com/roarkcompact.

and old friends from his army days. He also made a string of dubious appointments that led to a series of damaging scandals. Charges of corruption tainted his vice president, Schuyler Colfax, and brought down two of his cabinet officers. Though never personally implicated in any scandal, Grant was aggravatingly naive and blind to the rot that filled his administration. Congressman James A. Garfield declared: "His imperturbability is amazing. I am in doubt whether to call it greatness or stupidity."

In 1872, anti-Grant Republicans bolted and launched the Liberal Party. To clean up the graft and corruption, Liberals proposed ending the spoils system, by which victorious parties rewarded loyal workers with public office, and replacing it with a nonpartisan civil service commission that would oversee competitive examinations for appointment to office. Liberals also demanded that the federal government remove its troops from the South and restore "home rule" (southern white control). Democrats liked the Liberals' southern policy and endorsed the Liberal

Candidate	Electoral Vote	Popular Vote	Percent of Popular Vote
Ulysses S. Grant (Republican)	214	3,012,833	52.7
Horatio Seymour (Democrat)	80	2,703,249	47.3
Nonvoting states (Reconstruction)			

MAP 16.2 The Election of 1868

presidential candidate, Horace Greeley, the longtime editor of the *New York Tribune*. The nation, however, still felt enormous affection for the man who had saved the Union and reelected Grant with 56 percent of the popular vote.

Grant's ambitions for his administration extended beyond reconstruction, but not even foreign affairs could escape the problems of the South. Grant coveted Santo Domingo in the Caribbean and argued that the acquisition of this tropical land would permit the United States to expand its trade and also provide a new home for the South's blacks, who were so desperately harassed by the Klan. Aggressive foreign policy had not originated with the Grant administration. Lincoln's and Johnson's secretary of state, William H. Seward, had thwarted French efforts to set up a puppet empire under Maximilian in Mexico, and his purchase of Alaska ("Seward's Ice Box") from Russia in 1867 for only $7 million fired Grant's imperialist ambition. But in the end, Grant could not convince Congress to approve the treaty annexing Santo Domingo. The South preoccupied Congress and undermined Grant's initiatives.

Grant's Proposed Annexation of the Dominican Republic

Northern Resolve Withers Although Grant genuinely wanted to see blacks' civil and political rights protected, he understood that most Northerners had grown weary of reconstruction and were increasingly willing to let southern whites manage their own affairs. Citizens wanted to shift their attention to other issues, especially after the nation slipped into a devastating economic depression in 1873. More than eighteen thousand businesses collapsed, leaving more than a million workers on the streets. Northern businessmen wanted to invest in the South but believed that recurrent federal intrusion was itself a major cause of instability in the region. Republican leaders began to question the wisdom of their party's alliance with the South's lower classes—its small farmers and sharecroppers. One member of Grant's administration proposed allying with the "thinking and influential native southerners . . . the intelligent, well-to-do, and controlling class."

Congress, too, wanted to leave reconstruction behind, but southern Republicans made that difficult. When the South's Republicans begged for federal protection from Klan violence, Congress enacted three laws in 1870 and 1871 that were intended to break the back of white terrorism. The severest of the three, the Ku Klux Klan Act (1871), made interference with voting rights a felony. Federal marshals arrested thousands of Klansmen and came close to destroying the Klan, but they did not end all terrorism against blacks. Congress also passed the Civil Rights Act of 1875, which boldly outlawed racial discrimination in transportation, public accommodations, and juries. But federal authorities never enforced the law aggressively, and segregated facilities remained the rule throughout the South.

By the early 1870s, the Republican Party had lost its leading champions of African American rights to death or defeat at the polls. Other Republicans concluded that the quest for black equality was mistaken or hopelessly naive. In May 1872, Congress restored the right of officeholding to all but three hundred ex-rebels. Many Republicans had come to believe that traditional white leaders offered the best hope for honesty, order, and prosperity in the South.

Underlying the North's abandonment of reconstruction was unyielding racial prejudice. Northerners had learned to accept black freedom during the war, but deep-seated prejudice prevented many from accepting black equality. Even the actions they took on behalf of blacks often served partisan political advantage. Northerners generally supported Indiana senator Thomas A. Hendricks's harsh declaration that "this is a white man's Government, made by the white man for the white man."

The U.S. Supreme Court also did its part to undermine reconstruction. The Court issued a series of decisions that significantly weakened the federal government's ability to protect black Southerners. In the *Slaughterhouse* cases (1873), the Court distinguished between national and state citizenship and ruled that the Fourteenth Amendment protected only those rights that stemmed from the federal government, such as voting in federal elections and interstate travel. Since the Court decided that most rights derived from the states, it sharply curtailed the federal government's authority to defend black citizens. Even more devastating, the *United States v. Cruikshank* ruling (1876) said that the reconstruction amendments gave Congress the power to legislate against discrimination only by states, not by individuals. The "suppression of ordinary crime," such as assault, remained a state responsibility. The Supreme Court did not declare reconstruction unconstitutional but eroded its legal foundation.

The mood of the North found political expression in the election of 1874, when for the first time in eighteen years the Democrats gained control of the House of Representatives. As one Republican observed, the people had grown tired of the "negro question, with all its complications, and the reconstruction of Southern States, with all its interminable embroilments." Reconstruction had come apart. The people were tired of it. Grant grew increasingly unwilling to enforce it. Congress gradually abandoned it. And the Supreme Court denied the constitutionality of significant parts of it.

Rather than defend reconstruction from its southern enemies, Northerners steadily backed away from the challenge. By the early 1870s, southern Republicans faced the forces of reaction largely on their own.

White Supremacy Triumphs

Republican governments in the South attracted more hatred than any other political regimes in American history. To most whites, Republican rule meant intolerable insults: Black militiamen patrolled town streets, black laborers negotiated contracts with former masters, black maids stood up to former mistresses, black voters cast ballots, and black legislators such as James T. Rapier enacted laws. The northern retreat from reconstruction permitted southern Democrats to harness this white rage to politics.

Taking the name **Redeemers**, they promised to replace "bayonet rule" (a few federal troops continued to be stationed in the South) with "home rule." They branded Republican governments a carnival of extravagance, waste, and fraud and promised that honest, thrifty Democrats would supplant the irresponsible tax-and-spend Republicans. Above all, Redeemers swore to save southern civilization from a descent into "African barbarism." As one man put it, "We must render this either a white man's government, or convert the land into a Negro man's cemetery."

Southern Democrats adopted a multi-pronged strategy to overthrow Republican governments. First, they sought to polarize the parties around color. They went about gathering all the South's white voters into the Democratic Party, leaving the Republicans to depend on blacks, who made up a minority of population in almost every southern state. To dislodge whites from the Republican Party, Democrats fanned the flames of racial prejudice. A South Carolina Democrat crowed that his party appealed to the "proud Caucasian race, whose sovereignty on earth God has proclaimed." Local newspapers published the names of whites who kept company with blacks, and neighbors ostracized offenders.

Democrats also exploited the severe economic plight of small white farmers by blaming it on Republican financial policy. Government spending soared during reconstruction, and small farmers saw their tax burden skyrocket. "This is tax time," a South Carolinian reported. "We are nearly all on our head

"Of Course He Wants to Vote the Democratic Ticket" This Republican cartoon from the October 21, 1876, issue of *Harper's Weekly* comments sarcastically on the possibility of honest elections in the South. The caption reads, "You're free as air, ain't you? Say you are or I'll blow yer black head off." The cartoon demonstrates not only some Northerners' concern that violence would deliver the election to the Democrats but also the perception that white Southerners were crude, drunken, ignorant brutes. Granger Collection.

FOR MORE HELP ANALYZING THIS IMAGE, see the visual activity for this chapter in the Online Study Guide at bedfordstmartins.com/roarkcompact.

"White Man's Country" White supremacy emerged as a central tenet of the Democratic Party before the Civil War, and Democrats kept up a vicious racist attack on Republicans throughout Reconstruction. This silk ribbon from the 1868 presidential campaign between Republican Ulysses S. Grant and his Democratic opponent, New York governor Horatio Seymour, openly declares the Democrats' racial goal. During the campaign, Democratic vice presidential nominee Francis P. Blair Jr. promised that a Seymour victory would restore "white people" to power by declaring the reconstruction governments in the South "null and void." The Democrats' promotion of white supremacy reached new levels of shrillness in the 1870s, when northern support for reconstruction began to waver. Collection of Janice L. and David J. Frent.

about them. They are so high & so little money to pay with" that farmers were "selling every egg and chicken they can get." In 1871, Mississippi reported that one-seventh of the state's land—3.3 million acres—had been forfeited for nonpayment of taxes. The small farmers' economic distress had a racial dimension. Because few freedmen succeeded in acquiring land, they rarely paid taxes. In Georgia in 1874, blacks made up 45 percent of the population but paid only 2 percent of the taxes. From the perspective of a small white farmer, Republican rule meant that he was paying more taxes and paying them to aid blacks.

If racial pride, social isolation, and financial hardship proved insufficient to drive yeomen from the Republican Party, Democrats turned to terrorism. "Night riders" targeted white Republicans as well as blacks for murder and assassination. Whether white or black, a "dead Radical is very harmless," South Carolina Democratic leader Martin Gary told his followers.

But the primary victims of white violence were black Republicans. The object was to "kill out the leading men of the republican party," a black Republican from Florida declared. But violence targeted all black voters, not just leaders. And it escalated to unprecedented levels. In 1873, a clash between black militiamen and gun-toting whites in Louisiana killed two white men and an estimated seventy black men. The whites slaughtered half of the black men after they surrendered. Although the federal government indicted more than one hundred of the white men, local juries failed to convict even one.

Even before adopting the all-out white supremacist tactics of the 1870s, Democrats had taken control of the governments of Virginia, Tennessee, and North Carolina. The new campaign brought fresh gains. The Redeemers retook Georgia in 1871, Texas in 1873, and Arkansas and Alabama in 1874. Mississippi became a scene of open, unrelenting, and often savage intimidation of black voters and their few remaining white allies. As the state election approached in 1876, Governor Adelbert Ames appealed to Washington for federal troops to control the violence, only to hear from the attorney general that the "whole public are tired of these annual autumnal outbreaks in the South." Abandoned, Mississippi Republicans succumbed to the Democratic onslaught in the fall elections. By 1876, only three Republican state governments survived in the South (Map 16.3).

An Election and a Compromise

The centennial year of 1876 witnessed one of the most tumultuous elections in American history. Its chaos and confusion provided a fitting conclusion to the experiment known as reconstruction. The election took place in November, but not until March 2 of the following year did the nation know who would be inaugurated president on March 4. The Democrats nominated New York's governor, **Samuel J. Tilden**, who immediately targeted the corruption of the Grant administration and the "despotism" of Republican reconstruction. The Republicans put forward **Rutherford B. Hayes**, governor of Ohio. Privately, Hayes considered "bayonet rule" a mistake but concluded that waving the bloody shirt — reminding voters that the Democrats were the "party of rebellion" — remained the Republicans' best political strategy.

On election day, Tilden tallied 4,288,590 votes to Hayes's 4,036,000. But in the all-important electoral college, Tilden fell one vote short of the majority required for victory. The electoral votes of three states — South Carolina, Louisiana, and Florida, the only remaining Republican governments in the South — remained in doubt because both Republicans and Democrats in those states claimed victory. To win, Tilden needed only one of the nineteen contested votes. Hayes had to have all of them.

Congress had to decide who had actually won the elections in the three southern states and thus who would be president. The Constitution provided no guidance for this situation. Moreover, Democrats controlled the House, and Republicans controlled the Senate. Congress created a special electoral commission to arbitrate the disputed returns. All of the commissioners voted their party affiliation, giving every state to the Republican Hayes and putting him over the top in electoral votes (Map 16.4).

Some outraged Democrats vowed to resist Hayes's victory. Rumors flew of an impending

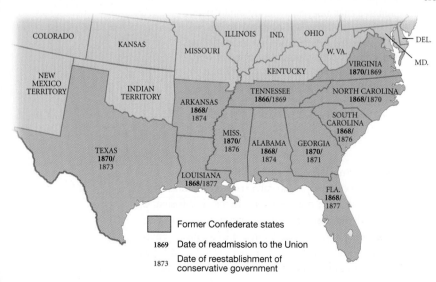

MAP 16.3 The Reconstruction of the South
Myth has it that Republican rule of the former Confederacy was not only harsh but long. In most states, however, conservative southern whites stormed back into power in months or just a few years. By the election of 1876, Republican governments could be found in only three states, and they soon fell.

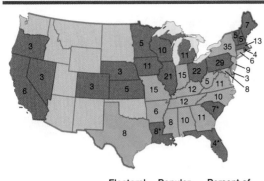

Candidate	Electoral Vote	Popular Vote	Percent of Popular Vote
Rutherford B. Hayes (Republican)	185*	4,036,298	47.9**
Samuel J. Tilden (Democrat)	184	4,288,590	51.0

*19 electoral votes were disputed.

**Percentages do not total 100 because some popular votes went to other parties.

MAP 16.4 The Election of 1876

coup and renewed civil war. But the impasse was broken when negotiations behind the scenes resulted in an informal understanding known as the **Compromise of 1877**. In exchange for a Democratic promise not to block Hayes's inauguration and to deal fairly with the freedmen, Hayes vowed to refrain from using the army to uphold the remaining Republican regimes in the South and to provide the South with substantial federal subsidies for internal improvements. Two days later, the nation celebrated Hayes's peaceful inauguration.

Stubborn Tilden supporters bemoaned the "stolen election" and damned "His Fraudulency," Rutherford B. Hayes. Old-guard radicals such as William Lloyd Garrison denounced Hayes's bargain as a "policy of compromise, of credulity, of weakness, of subserviency, of surrender." But the nation as a whole celebrated, for the country had weathered a grave crisis. The last three Republican state governments in the South fell quickly once Hayes abandoned them and withdrew the U.S. army. Reconstruction came to an end.

Q: How did the Supreme Court undermine the Fourteenth and Fifteenth Amendments?

Conclusion: "A Revolution But Half Accomplished"

In 1865, when General Carl Schurz visited the South, he discovered "a revolution but half accomplished." White Southerners resisted the passage from slavery to free labor, from white racial despotism to equal justice, and from white political monopoly to biracial democracy. The old elite wanted to get "things back as near to slavery as possible," Schurz reported, while African Americans such as James T. Rapier and some whites were eager to exploit the revolutionary implications of defeat and emancipation.

The northern-dominated Republican Congress pushed the revolution along. Although it refused to provide for blacks' economic welfare, Congress employed constitutional amendments to require ex-Confederates to accept legal equality and share political power with black men. Congress was not willing to extend such power to women, however. Conservative southern whites fought ferociously to recover their power and privilege. When Democrats regained control of politics, whites used both state power and private violence to wipe out many of the gains of Reconstruction, leading one observer to conclude that the North had won the war but the South had won the peace.

The Redeemer counterrevolution, however, did not mean a return to slavery. Northern victory in the Civil War ensured that ex-slaves no longer faced the auction block and could send their children to school, worship in their own churches, and work independently on their own rented farms. Sharecropping, with all its hardships, provided more autonomy and economic welfare than bondage had. It was limited freedom, to be sure, but it was not slavery.

The Civil War and emancipation set in motion the most profound upheaval in the nation's history, and nothing reactionary whites did entirely erased its revolutionary impact. War destroyed the largest slave society in the New World. The world of masters and slaves succumbed to that of landlords and sharecroppers, a world in which white racial dominance continued, though with greater freedom for blacks. War also gave birth to a modern nation-state, and Washington increased its role in national affairs. When the South returned to the Union, it did so as a junior partner. The victorious North set the nation's compass toward the expansion of industrial capitalism and the final conquest of the West.

Despite massive changes, however, the Civil War remained only a "half accomplished" revolution. By not fulfilling the promises the nation seemed to hold out to black Americans at war's end, Reconstruction represents a tragedy of enormous proportions. The failure to protect blacks and guarantee their rights had enduring consequences. Almost a century after Reconstruction, the nation would embark on what one observer called a "second reconstruction." The solid achievements of the Thirteenth, Fourteenth, and Fifteenth Amendments to the Constitution would provide a legal foundation for the renewed commitment. It is worth remembering, though, that it was only the failure of the first reconstruction that made the modern civil rights movement necessary.

Reviewing the Chapter

★ KEY TERMS

Explain each term's significance

WHO
James T. Rapier (p. 385)
Andrew Johnson (p. 392)
Susan B. Anthony (p. 395)
Elizabeth Cady Stanton (p. 395)
Samuel J. Tilden (p. 406)
Rutherford B. Hayes (p. 406)

WHAT
Wade-Davis bill (p. 387)
Freedmen's Bureau (p. 388)
black codes (p. 393)
Civil Rights Act of 1866 (p. 395)
Fourteenth Amendment (p. 395)
American Equal Rights Association (p. 395)
Military Reconstruction Act (p. 396)
impeachment (p. 398)
Fifteenth Amendment (p. 398)
carpetbagger (p. 399)
scalawag (p. 399)
Ku Klux Klan (p. 399)
sharecropping (p. 401)
waving the bloody shirt (p. 403)
Redeemers (p. 405)
Compromise of 1877 (p. 407)

FOR PRACTICE QUIZZES AND OTHER STUDY TOOLS, see the Online Study Guide at **bedfordstmartins.com/roarkcompact**.

★ REVIEW QUESTIONS Q:

Use key terms and dates to support your answer

1. Why did Congress object to Lincoln's wartime plan for reconstruction? (pp. 386–92)

2. How did the North respond to the passage of black codes in the southern states? (pp. 392–95)

3. Why did Johnson urge the southern states to reject the Fourteenth Amendment? (pp. 395–98)

4. Why was the Republican Party in the South a coalition party? (pp. 398–402)

5. How did the Supreme Court undermine the Fourteenth and Fifteenth Amendments? (pp. 402–07)

★ MAKING CONNECTIONS

Draw on key terms, timeline, and review questions

1. Reconstruction succeeded in advancing black civil rights but failed to secure them over the long term. Why and how did the federal government retreat from defending African Americans' civil rights in the 1870s? In your answer, cite specific actions by Congress and the Supreme Court.

2. Why was distributing plantation land to former slaves such a controversial policy? In your answer, discuss why landownership was important to freedmen and why Congress rejected redistribution as a general policy.

3. At the end of the Civil War, it remained to be seen exactly how emancipation would transform the South. How did emancipation change political and labor organization in the region? In your answer, discuss how ex-slaves exercised their new freedoms and how white Southerners attempted to limit them.

4. The Republican Party shaped Reconstruction through its control of Congress and state legislatures in the South. How did the identification of the Republican Party with Reconstruction policy affect the party's political fortunes in the 1870s? In your answer, be sure to address developments on the federal and state levels.

★ SUGGESTED READINGS

Jane Turner Censer, *The Reconstruction of White Southern Womanhood, 1865–1895* (2003). A lively investigation of the consequences of the Civil War for white southern women.

Eric Foner, *Reconstruction: America's Unfinished Revolution* (1988). A masterful synthesis that makes African Americans central actors in the Reconstruction era.

John Hope Franklin and Loren Schweninger, *In Search of the Promised Land: A Slave Family in the Old South* (2006). A careful retelling of the history of the Rapier family.

Stephen Kantrowitz, *Ben Tillman and the Reconstruction of White Supremacy* (2000). An eloquent biography of a leading white supremacist in South Carolina.

Hyman Rubin III, *South Carolina Scalawags* (2006). A probing analysis of white South Carolinians who became Republicans.

Brooks D. Simpson, *The Reconstruction Presidents* (1998). A thoughtful interpretation that emphasizes the differences between the policies and styles of Lincoln, Johnson, Grant, and Hayes.

FOR MORE BOOKS ABOUT TOPICS IN THIS CHAPTER, see the Online Bibliography at **bedfordstmartins.com/roarkcompact**.

FOR ADDITIONAL FIRSTHAND ACCOUNTS OF THIS PERIOD, see Chapter 16 in Michael Johnson, ed., *Reading the American Past*, Fourth Edition.

FOR WEB SITES, IMAGES, AND DOCUMENTS RELATED TO TOPICS AND PLACES IN THIS CHAPTER, visit Make History at **bedfordstmartins.com/roarkcompact**.

★ TIMELINE

1863
- Proclamation of Amnesty and Reconstruction.

1864
- Wade-Davis bill.

1865
- Freedmen's Bureau established.
- President Abraham Lincoln shot; dies on April 15; succeeded by Andrew Johnson.
- Black codes enacted.
- Thirteenth Amendment becomes part of Constitution.

1866
- Congress approves Fourteenth Amendment.
- Civil Rights Act.
- American Equal Rights Association founded.
- Ku Klux Klan founded.

1867
- Military Reconstruction Act.
- Tenure of Office Act.

1868
- Impeachment trial of President Johnson.
- Republican Ulysses S. Grant elected president.

1869
- Congress approves Fifteenth Amendment.

1871
- Ku Klux Klan Act.

1872
- Liberal Party formed; calls for end of government corruption.
- President Grant reelected.

1873
- Economic depression sets in for remainder of decade.
- *Slaughterhouse* cases.

1874
- Democrats win majority in House of Representatives.

1875
- Civil Rights Act.

1876
- *United States v. Cruikshank.*

1877
- Republican Rutherford B. Hayes assumes presidency; Reconstruction era ends.

LAKOTA VEST This Lakota vest belonged to Thomas American Horse, a member of the Oglala band of Lakota Sioux who lived on the Pine Ridge Reservation in South Dakota at the end of the nineteenth century. His initials are worked in beads across the shoulders. Made of tanned hide, with glass beads and tanned leather binding and lining, the vest shows how Native Americans adopted Euro-American articles of clothing and decorative motifs while employing materials that perpetuated native traditions. On the vest, two mounted Indians in feathered headdresses face each other under American flags. The American flag appeared frequently as a decorative motif in Indian bead art and testifies to some of the great changes taking place in the American West. Private Collection, Photograph: American Hurrah Archive, NYC.

17

The Contested West

1870–1900

TO CELEBRATE INDIAN CITIZENSHIP DAY in 1892, students at Hampton Institute's Indian boarding school in Virginia staged a pageant honoring the four hundredth anniversary of the "discovery" of the New World. Students appeared dressed as the nation's heroes — among them Christopher Columbus, Miles Standish, and George Washington. Halfway through the program, the pageant finally honored some Native American heroes, but the Indians selected — Samoset, Pocahontas — all came from the distant past in lands east of the Appalachians. There was no mention of Crazy Horse, Sitting Bull, or Geronimo — Indians who resisted white encroachment and appropriation of their land in the West.

Only two years earlier, the massacre of more than two hundred Miniconjou Sioux at Wounded Knee, South Dakota, marked the end of three decades of war against the Indians in the trans-Mississippi West. The Indian wars left the Native American population in the continental United States at 250,000 according to the census of 1900 (admittedly an undercount), down from estimates as high as 15 million at the time of first contact with Europeans. Not only had the population been decimated by war and disease, but Indian lands had shrunk so much that by 1890 Euro-Americans controlled 97.5 percent of the territory formerly occupied by Native Americans.

The Hampton pageant could not entirely ignore a catastrophe of this magnitude. Yet it managed to end on a note of reconciliation with a student proclaiming:

> You have taken our rivers and fountains
>   And the plains where we loved to roam, —
> Banish us not to the mountains
>   And the lonely wastes for home!
> Our clans that were strongest and bravest,
>   Are Broken and powerless through you:
> Let us join the great tribe of the white men,
>   As brothers to dare and to do!

How the students felt about the lines they spoke we cannot know. But the pageant clearly reflected the values and beliefs that Indian boarding

Hampton Pageant, 1892 The Indian students in this picture are dressed for Columbia's Roll Call, a pageant at Hampton Institute honoring the nation's heroes on Indian Citizenship Day, 1892. Among those portrayed are Christopher Columbus, Pocahontas, George Washington, and, in the center, a student dressed as Columbia, symbol of the Republic, draped in the American flag. Courtesy of Hampton University Archives.

schools hoped to inculcate in their pupils at the end of the nineteenth century.

Indian schools constituted the cultural battleground of the Indian wars in the West, their avowed purpose "to destroy the Indian in him and save the man." In 1877, Congress appropriated funds for Indian education, reasoning "it was less expensive to educate Indians than to kill them." Hampton Institute, created in 1868 to school newly freed slaves, accepted its first Indian students in 1878. Although many Indian schools operated on the reservations, authorities much preferred boarding facilities that isolated students from the "contamination" of tribal values.

Many Native American parents resisted sending their children away. When all else failed, the military kidnapped the children and sent them off to school. An agent at the Mescalero Apache Agency in Arizona Territory reported in 1886 how "it became necessary to visit the camps unexpectedly with a detachment of police, and seize such children as were proper and take them away to school, willing or unwilling." The parents put up a struggle. "Some hurried their children off to the mountains or hid them away in camp, and the police had to chase and capture them like so many wild rabbits," the agent observed. "This unusual proceeding created quite an outcry. The men were sullen and muttering, the women loud in their lamentations, and the children almost out of their wits with fright."

Once at school, the children were stripped and scrubbed, their clothing and belongings confiscated, their hair hacked off and doused with kerosene to kill lice. Issued stiff new uniforms, shoes, and what one boy recalled as the "torture" of woolen long underwear, the children often lost not only their possessions but also their names: Hehakaavita (Yellow Elk) became Thomas Goodwood; Polingaysi Qoyawayma became Elizabeth White.

The curriculum featured agricultural and manual arts for boys and domestic skills for girls, training designed to make Indians "willing workers" who would no longer be a burden to the government. The **Carlisle Indian School** in Pennsylvania, founded in 1879, became the model for later institutions. To encourage assimilation, Carlisle pioneered the "outing system"—sending students to live with white families during summer vacations. The policy reflected the school's slogan, "To civilize the Indian, get him into civilization. To keep him civilized, let him stay."

Merrill Gates, a member of the Board of Indian Commissioners, summed up the goal of Indian education: "To get the Indian out of the blanket and into trousers,—and trousers with a pocket in them, *and with a pocket that aches to be filled with dollars!*" Gates's faith in the "civilizing" power of the dollar reflected the unabashed materialism of his age. In 1871, author Mark Twain published *Roughing It*, a chronicle of his days spent in mining towns in California and Nevada. There he found the same corrupt politics, vulgar display, and mania for speculation that he later skewered in *The Gilded Age* (1873), his biting satire of greed and corruption in the nation's capital. Far from being an antidote to the meretricious values of the East—an innocent idyll out of place and time—the American West, with its get-rich-quick ethos and its addiction to gambling and speculation, played an integral part in the politics and economics of the Gilded Age. With its rich natural resources and land, the West became fiercely contested terrain, not only for the Indians who struggled to preserve their sovereignty and their cultural identity but also among competing groups of Anglos, Hispanics, and a host of others following the promise of land and riches. ★

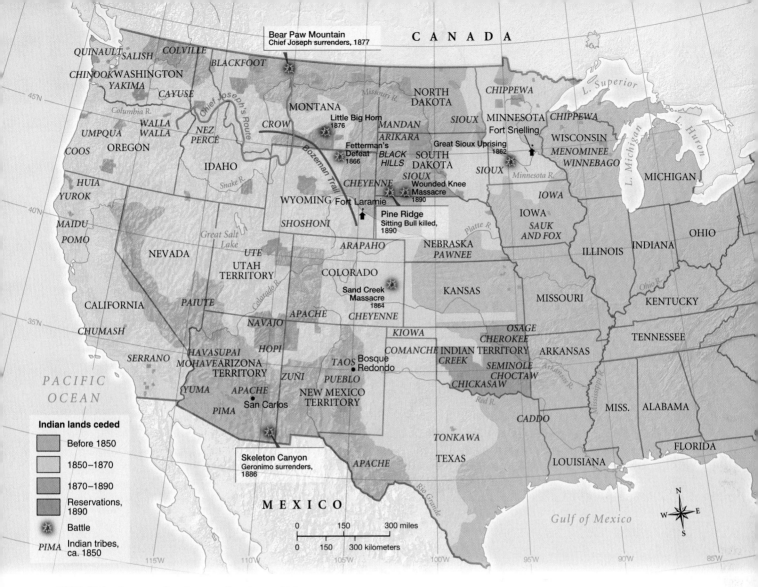

MAP 17.1 The Loss of Indian Lands, 1850–1890

By 1890, western Indians were isolated on small, scattered reservations. Native Americans had struggled to retain their land in major battles, from the Santee Uprising in Minnesota in 1862 to the massacre at Wounded Knee, South Dakota, in 1890.

READING THE MAP: Where was the largest reservation located in 1890? Which states on this map show no reservations in 1890? Compare this map to Map 17.3, Federal Land Grants to Railroads and the Development of the West.

CONNECTIONS: Why did the federal government force Native Americans onto reservations? What developments prompted these changes?

FOR MORE HELP ANALYZING THIS MAP, see the map activity for this chapter in the Online Study Guide at bedfordstmartins.com/roarkcompact.

Conquest and Empire in the West

While the European powers expanded their authority and wealth through imperialism and colonialism, establishing far-flung empires abroad, the United States focused its attention on the West. American exceptionalism has stressed how the history of the United States differs from that of western European nations, and America's preoccupation with its western frontier has often been cited as a case in point. Yet recent historians have argued that

the process by which the United States expanded its borders in the nineteenth century can best be understood in the global context of imperialism and colonialism—language applied to European powers in this period that makes explicit how expansion in the American West involved the conquest, displacement, and rule over native peoples. (See "Beyond America's Borders," page 414.) The federal government, through chicanery and conquest, pushed the Indians off their land (Map 17.1). Removed to Indian Territory or confined on reservations, Indians

Imperialism, Colonialism, and the Treatment of the Sioux and the Zulu

Viewed through the lens of colonialism, the British war with the Zulu in South Africa offers a compelling contrast to the United States' war against the Lakota Sioux. Comparing the subjugation of the Zulu and the Sioux highlights the escalation of conflict between white imperialist powers and indigenous peoples of color over land, labor, and resources in the context of the global economic expansion of the nineteenth century.

The Zulu, like the Sioux, came to power as a result of devastating intertribal warfare. In the area that is today the KwaZulu-Natal province of the Republic of South Africa, Shaka, the Zulu king, united his empire by 1826 with an army of more than twenty thousand. And like the Sioux, the Zulu earned a formidable reputation as brave warriors who fought to protect their land from white encroachment.

The British and the Boers made up the two dominant European groups in South Africa. Dutch-speaking white settlers came to the Cape of Good Hope, at the southernmost tip of Africa, in the seventeenth century, when the place was little more than a way station for the Dutch East India Company on the long sea route to the East Indies. They stayed and become farmers, mingling with French and German settlers to create a tough new breed known as Afrikaners, or Boers. By the nineteenth century, the Cape Colony consisted of a community of more than ten thousand settlers stretching six hundred miles inland from Cape Town.

The British seized the Cape in 1806 to protect their sea route to India, and land-hungry British settlers poured into the colony in the wake of the agricultural depression that followed the long Napoleonic Wars in Europe. The British settlers and the Boers soon clashed over land and labor. The Boers relied on slave labor to work their vast farmlands. When the British passed the Act of Emancipation in 1834, the Boers

Zululand and Cape Colony, 1878

rebelled. Clashes between Britons and Boers resulted in the Great Trek, the migration of nearly twelve thousand Boers to the northeast beginning in 1835. There they claimed land and established the South African Republic (the Transvaal) in 1853 and the Orange Free State in 1854, both independent of British rule. But the Great Trek brought the Boers into Zululand, where they met with bold and bloody resistance.

The Zulu lived in a highly complex society, with all the young men organized into *amabutho*, regiments of warriors arranged by age and bound to local chiefs under the supreme command of the Zulu king, who demanded obedience and bravery. During Shaka's harsh reign, he inspected his regiments after each battle, picking out cowards and putting them to death on the spot. Young men could not start their own households without the local chief's permission, thus ensuring an ample stock of warriors and making the Zulu army, in the words of one English observer, "a celibate, man-slaying machine." The Boer settlers repeatedly faced the wrath of the Zulu, who slaughtered the first trekkers to arrive in Zululand after promising them permission to settle and luring them to a feast. But it was the Zulu's dependence on cattle that put them in permanent conflict with the Boers. To pay for a wife, a Zulu man had to acquire an *ilobolo*, a dowry payment of cattle. The more cattle a man owned, the more wives he could buy. The Zulu regarded the Boer herds as theirs for the taking and repeatedly raided settlements to steal cattle.

To restore order, the British entered the fray in 1879, sparking the Anglo-Zulu War, which a recent historian has condemned "as unnecessary as it was unjust." Britain issued an ultimatum to the Zulu king Cetshwayo, a former British ally who ruled with Queen Victoria's blessing. Sir Theophilus Shepstone, British secretary for native affairs, hinted at a motive for

became wards of the federal government, their culture assaulted by policies designed to force assimilation. Through the lens of colonialism, we can see how the United States' commitment to an imperialist, expansionist ideology resulted in the displacement of Native Americans and the establishment of new territories and eventually states. The colonizing of the West was a dynamic process in which Native Americans actively resisted, contested, and adapted to colonial rule.

the invasion when he wrote in 1878, "Had Cetshwayo's 30,000 warriors been in time changed to labourers working for wages, Zululand would have been a prosperous peaceful country instead of what it is now, a source of perpetual danger to itself and its neighbors." Clearly, the incentive for invasion came not only from a desire to placate the Boers but also from the desire to secure a source of labor for British economic expansion, made paramount by the discovery of diamonds in the region.

Crack British troops under Lord Chelmsford, armed with the latest rifles and artillery, expected to subdue the Zulu easily. With a confidence reminiscent of that of George Armstrong Custer, the British commander wrote, "I am inclined to think that the first experience of the power of the Martini-Henrys [rifles] will be such a surprise to the Zulus, that they will not be formidable after the first effort." But in January 1879, at the battle of Isandhlwana, the Zulu army of more than 25,000 surprised a British encampment. The battle lasted less than two hours, but when it was over, more than 4,000 Zulu and British bodies lay indiscriminately piled on top of one another across the British position. Only a handful of British soldiers managed to escape. Chelmsford lost 1,300 officers and men — the biggest single defeat of British troops since the Crimean War.

★ **Zulu Warriors** Chief Ngoza (center) poses with Zulu men in full war dress. Their distinctive cowhide shields date to the reign of King Shaka. Each warrior also carried two or three throwing spears and an *ikwa*, or flat-bladed stabbing spear used in close combat. Zulu warriors marched at the double and could cover up to fifty miles a day. Campbell Collections of the University of KwaZulu-Natal.

When news of Isandhlwana reached London, commentators compared the massacre to Custer's defeat at the Little Big Horn three years earlier, and noted that native forces armed with spears had defeated a modern army. The military disaster shocked and outraged the nation, damaging the British military's reputation of invincibility.

Vowing that the Zulu would "pay dearly for their triumph of a day," the British immediately launched unconditional war against the Zulu. In the ensuing battles, neither side took prisoners. The Zulu beat the British twice more, but the tide turned at Rorke's Drift, and after seven months of battle, the British defeated the Zulu. After routing the Zulu army, the British marched away, imprisoning Cetshwayo on Robben Island and abandoning Zululand to its fate — partition, starvation, and civil war.

Historians would later compare the British victory at Rorke's Drift to the U.S. army's defeat of the Sioux at Wounded Knee. But the Zulu and the Sioux met different economic fates. As Shepstone hinted in 1878, the British goal had been to subdue the Zulu and turn them into a reservoir of plentiful, cheap labor. In 1887, the British formally annexed Zululand, and in 1902 they defeated their white rivals in the Anglo-Boer War and gained dominance in the region. The Zulu ended up laboring on the estates and in the mines of the white colonialists in a condition little better than slavery. Compared to the naked economic exploitation of the Zulu, the U.S. policy toward the Sioux, with its forced assimilation on reservations and its misguided attempts to turn the nomadic tribes into sedentary, God-fearing farmers, may seem less exploitative if no less ruthless in its cultural imperialism.

Both the Little Big Horn and Isandhlwana became legends that spawned a romantic image of the "noble savage": fierce in battle, honored in defeat. Describing this myth, historian James Gump, who has chronicled the subjugation of the Sioux and the Zulu, observed, "Each western culture simultaneously dehumanized and glamorized the Sioux and Zulu," and noted that the noble savage mythology marked "a product of the racist ideologies of the late nineteenth century as well as the guilt and compassion associated with the bloody costs of empire building." Imperial powers, both Britain and the United States defeated indigenous rivals and came to dominate their lands (and, in the case of the Zulu, their labor) in the global expansion that marked the nineteenth century.

Indian Removal and the Reservation System

Beginning in the early days of the Republic, Americans advocated a policy of **Indian removal**. With plenty of land open in the West, the government removed eastern tribes — often against their will — to territory west of the Mississippi. In the 1830s, President Andrew Jackson pushed the Five Civilized Tribes — the Cherokee, Choctaw, Chickasaw, Creek, and Seminole peoples — off their land in the southern United States. Jackson's

Indian removal forced thousands of men, women, and children to leave their homes in Georgia and Tennessee and walk hundreds of miles west. So many died of hunger, exhaustion, and disease along the way that the Cherokees called their path "the trail on which we cried." At the end of this trail of tears stood land set aside as Indian Territory (present-day Oklahoma). Here, the government promised, the Indians could remain "as long as grass shall grow" (see chapter 11). But hunger for western land soon negated that promise.

Manifest destiny—the belief that the United States had a "God-given" right to aggressively spread the values of white civilization and expand the nation from ocean to ocean—dictated U.S. policy. In the name of manifest destiny, Americans forced the removal of the Five Civilized Tribes to Oklahoma; colonized Texas and won its independence from Mexico in 1836; conquered California, Arizona, New Mexico, and parts of Utah and Colorado in the Mexican-American War of 1846–1848; and invaded Oregon in the 1840s (see chapter 12).

By midcentury, settlers in unprecedented numbers crossed the Great Plains on their way to the goldfields of California or the rich farmland of Washington and Oregon. In their path stood a solid wall of Indian land, stretching from Minnesota to Texas, much of it granted through the policy of Indian removal. As the *United States Magazine* observed, "Now the removed tribes are precisely in the center of this path." The "Indian problem" needed to be solved—through treaties if possible or coercion if necessary. In 1851, some ten thousand Plains Indians came together at Fort Laramie in Wyoming to negotiate a treaty that ceded a wide swath of their land to allow passage of the wagon trains. In return, the government promised that the rest of the Indian land would remain inviolate.

The Indians who "touched the pen" to the 1851 **Treaty of Fort Laramie** hoped to preserve their culture in the face of the white onslaught, which already had decimated their population and despoiled their environment. White invaders cut down trees, miners polluted streams, and hunters killed off bison and small game. Whites brought alcohol, guns, and something even more deadly—disease. Smallpox was the biggest killer of Native Americans in the West. Epidemics spread from Mexico up to Canada. Between 1780 and 1870, the population of the Plains tribes declined by half. Cholera, diphtheria, measles, scarlet fever, and other contagious diseases also took their toll. "If I could see this thing, if I knew where it came from, I would go there and fight it," a Cheyenne warrior anguished. Disease shifted the balance of power on the plains from Woodland agrarian tribes like the Mandan and Hidatsa (who died at the rate of 79 percent) to the Lakota (Western) Sioux, who fled the contagion of villages to take up life as equestrian (horse-riding) nomads on the western plains. As the Sioux pushed west, they displaced weaker tribes.

The Indian wars in the West marked the last resistance of a Native American population devastated by disease and demoralized by the removal policy pursued by the federal government. More accurately called "settlers' wars" (since they began with "peaceful settlers," often miners, overrunning Native American land), the wars flared up again only a few years after the signing of the Fort Laramie treaty. The Dakota Sioux in Minnesota went to war in 1862. For years, under the leadership of Chief Little Crow, the Dakota, also known as the Santee, had pursued a policy of accommodation, ceding land in return for the promise of annuities. But with his people on the verge of starvation (the local Indian agent told the hungry Dakota, "Go and eat grass"), Little Crow reluctantly led his angry warriors in a desperate campaign against the intruders, killing more than 1,000 settlers. American troops quelled what was called the Great Sioux Uprising (also called the Santee Uprising) and marched 1,700 Sioux to Fort Snelling, where 400 Indians were put on trial for murder and 38 died in the largest mass execution in American history.

On the southern plains, the conflict reached its nadir in November 1864 at the Sand Creek Massacre in Colorado Territory. There Colonel John M. Chivington and his Colorado militia descended on a village of Cheyenne, mostly women and children. Their leader, Black Kettle, raised a white flag and an American flag to signal surrender, but the charging cavalry ignored his signal and butchered 270 Indians. Chivington watched as his men scalped and mutilated their victims and later justified the killing of Indian children with the terse remark, "Nits make lice." The city of Denver treated Chivington and his men as heroes, but a congressional inquiry castigated the soldiers for their "fiendish malignity" and condemned the "savage cruelty" of the massacre.

To Americans like Chivington, fed theories of racial superiority, the Indians constituted, in the words of one Colorado militia major, "an obstacle to civilization . . . [and] should be exterminated." After the Civil War, President Ulysses S. Grant faced the prospect of protracted Indian war on the Great Plains. Reluctant to spend more money and sacrifice more lives in battle, Grant adopted a "peace policy" designed to segregate and control the Indians while

> General William Tecumseh Sherman summed up the new Indian policy succinctly: "Remove all to a safe place and then reduce them to a helpless condition."

opening up land to white settlers. The government sought control of Indian lands and promised in return to pay annuities and put the Indians on lands reserved for their use—reservations. This policy won the support of both friends of the Indians, who feared for their survival, and Indian haters, who coveted their land and wished to confine them to the least desirable areas in the West. General William Tecumseh Sherman summed up the new Indian policy succinctly: "Remove all to a safe place and then reduce them to a helpless condition." The army herded the Indians onto reservations (see Map 17.1), where the U.S. Bureau of Indian Affairs supposedly ministered to their needs.

Poverty and starvation stalked the reservations. Confined by armed force, the Indians eked out an existence on stingy government rations. These once proud peoples found themselves dependent on government handouts and the assistance of Indian agents who, in the words of Paiute Sarah Winnemucca, did "nothing but fill their pockets." Winnemucca launched a lecture campaign in the United States and Europe denouncing the government's reservation policy.

Indian reservations soon became cultural battlegrounds. Styled as stepping-stones on the road to "civilization," they closely resembled colonial societies where native populations, ruled by outside bureaucrats, saw their culture assaulted, their religious practices outlawed, their children sent away to school, and their way of life attacked in the name of progress and civilization. Self-styled "friends of the Indians," many of them easterners with little experience in the West, maintained that reservations would provide a classroom of civilization where Indians could be taught to speak English, to worship a Christian god, to give up hunting for farming, and to reject tribal ways. In the face of this assault, Indians found ways to resist and hold on to their cultural identity.

The Decimation of the Great Bison Herds and the Fight for the Black Hills

By the nineteenth century, more than two hundred years of contact with whites had utterly transformed Native American societies. Indians had been pushed off their lands east of the Mississippi and moved west. Through trade with the Spanish and French, Indians had acquired horses and guns. The Sioux, hunting on horseback, staked their survival on the buffalo (American bison). But the great herds, once numbering as many as thirty million, fell into decline. A host of environmental and human factors contributed to the destruction of the bison. The dynamic ecology of the Great Plains, with its drought, fires, and blizzards, combined with the ecological imperialism of humans (Indian buffalo robe traders as well

as whites and their cattle), put increasing pressure on the bison. By the 1850s, a combination of drought and commerce had driven the great herds onto the far western plains.

"Slaughtered for the Hide" *Harper's Weekly* in 1874 featured this cover with its illustration of a buffalo hide hunter skinning a carcass on the southwestern plains. By 1872, the Santa Fe railroad reached Kansas, making Dodge City the center for the shipment of buffalo hides to the East, where they were made into leather belting used to run the nation's machinery. In a matter of months, hunters decimated the great southern bison herds. City father Colonel Richard Dodge wrote of the carnage, "The air was foul with sickening stench, and the vast plain which only a short twelve months before teemed with animal life, was a dead, solitary putrid desert." Dodge estimated that hunters slaughtered more than three million bison between 1872 and 1874. The grim reality of the trade makes the magazine's subtitle, "A Journal of Civilization," highly ironic. Library of Congress.

FOR MORE HELP ANALYZING THIS IMAGE, see the visual activity for this chapter in the Online Study Guide at bedfordstmartins.com/roarkcompact.

After the Civil War, the accelerating pace of industrial expansion brought about the near extinction of the bison. Industrial demand for heavy leather belting used in machinery and the development of larger, more accurate rifles combined to hasten the slaughter of the bison. At the same time, the nation's growing transcontinental rail system cut the range in two and divided the herds. For the nomadic tribes of the plains, the buffalo constituted a way of life—a source of food, fuel, and shelter and a central part of their religion and rituals. To the railroads, the bison were a nuisance, at best a cheap source of meat for their workers and a target for sport. "It will not be long before all the buffaloes are extinct near and between the railroads," Ohio senator John Sherman predicted in 1868. The army took credit for the conquest of the Plains Indians, but victory came about largely as a result of the decimation of the great bison herds. General Philip Sheridan acknowledged as much when he applauded white hide hunters for "destroying the Indians' commissary." With their food supply gone, Indians had to choose between starvation and the reservation. "A cold wind blew across the prairie when the last buffalo fell," the great Sioux leader **Sitting Bull** lamented, "a death wind for my people."

On the southern plains in 1867, more than five thousand warring Comanches, Kiowas, and Southern Arapahos gathered at Medicine Lodge Creek in Kansas to negotiate a treaty. Satak, or Sitting Bear, a prominent Kiowa chief and medicine man, explained why the Indians sought peace: "In the far-distant past . . . the world seemed large enough for both the red man and the white man." But, he observed, "its broad plains seem now to contract, and the white man grows jealous of his red brother." To preserve their land from white encroachment, the Indians signed the Treaty of Medicine Lodge, agreeing to move to a reservation. But after 1870, hide hunters poured into the region, and within a decade, they had nearly exterminated the southern bison herds. Luther Standing Bear recounted the sight and stench: "I saw the bodies of hundreds of dead buffalo lying about, just wasting, and the odor was terrible. . . . They were letting our food lie on the plains to rot."

On the northern plains, the fever for gold fueled the conflict between Indians and Euro-Americans. In 1866, the Cheyenne united with the Sioux in Wyoming to protect their hunting grounds in the Powder River valley, which were threatened by the construction of the Bozeman Trail connecting Fort Laramie with the goldfields in Montana. Captain William Fetterman, who had boasted that with eighty men he could ride through the Sioux nation, was killed along with all of his troops in an Indian attack. The Sioux's impressive victories led to the second **Treaty of Fort Laramie** in 1868, in which the United States agreed to abandon the Bozeman Trail and guaranteed the Indians control of the **Black Hills**, land sacred to the Lakota Sioux. The treaty was full of contradictions—in one breath promising to preserve Indian land and in the next forcing the tribes to relinquish all territory outside their reservations. A controversial provision of the treaty guaranteed the Indians access to their traditional hunting grounds "so long as the buffalo may range thereon in such numbers as to justify the chase." With the bison facing extermination, the provision was ominous. Yet the government's fork-tongued promises induced some of the tribes to accept the treaty. The great Sioux chief Red Cloud led many of his people onto the reservation. Red Cloud soon regretted his decision. "Think of it!" he told a visitor to the Pine Ridge Reservation. "I, who used to own . . . country so extensive that I could not ride through it in a week . . . must tell Washington when I am hungry. I must beg for that which I own." Several Sioux chiefs, among them **Crazy Horse** of the Oglala band and Sitting Bull of the Hunkpapa, refused to sign the treaty. Crazy Horse said that he wanted no part of the "piecemeal penning" of his people.

In 1874, the discovery of gold in the Black Hills of the Dakotas led the government to break its promise to Red Cloud. Miners began pouring into the region, and the Northern Pacific Railroad made plans to lay track. Lieutenant Colonel George Armstrong Custer, whose troopers found gold in the area, trumpeted news of the strike. At first, the government offered to purchase the Black Hills. But to the Lakota Sioux the Black Hills were sacred—"the heart of everything that is." They refused to sell. The army responded by issuing an ultimatum ordering all Lakota Sioux and Northern Cheyenne bands onto the Pine Ridge Reservation and threatening to hunt down those who refused.

In the summer of 1876, the army launched a three-pronged attack led by Custer, General **George Crook**, and Colonel John Gibbon. Crazy Horse stopped Crook at the Battle of the Rosebud. Custer, leading the second prong of the army's offensive, divided his troops and ordered an attack. On June 25, he spotted signs of the Indians' camp and crying "Hurrah Boys, we've got them," led 265 men of the Seventh Cavalry into the largest Indian camp ever assembled on the Great Plains. Nomadic bands of Sioux, Cheyenne, and Arapaho had come together for a summer buffalo hunt and camped along the banks of the Greasy Grass River (whites called it the Little Big Horn). Indian warriors led by Sitting Bull and Crazy Horse set upon Custer and his men and quickly annihilated them. "It took us about as long as a hungry man to eat his dinner," the Cheyenne chief Two Moons recalled.

Gibbon arrived two days later to discover the carnage. "Custer's Last Stand," as the **Battle of the Little Big Horn** was styled in myth, turned out to be the last stand for the Sioux. The Indians' nomadic way of life meant they could not remain a combined force for long. The bands that had massed at the Little Big Horn scattered, and the army hunted them down. "Wherever we went," wrote the Oglala holy man Black Elk, "the soldiers came to kill us." In 1877, Crazy Horse was captured and killed. Four years later, in 1881, Sitting Bull surrendered. The government took the Black Hills and confined the Lakota to the Great Sioux Reservation. The Sioux never accepted the loss of the Black Hills. In 1923, they filed suit, demanding the return of the land taken illegally from them. After a protracted court battle lasting nearly sixty years, the U.S. Supreme Court ruled in 1980 that the government had illegally abrogated the Treaty of Fort Laramie and upheld an award of $122.5 million in compensation to the tribes. The Sioux refused the settlement and continue to press for the return of the Black Hills.

The Dawes Act and Indian Land Allotment In the 1880s, the practice of rounding up Indians and herding them onto reservations lost momentum in favor of allotment — a new policy designed to encourage assimilation through farming and the ownership of private property. Americans vowing to avenge Custer urged the government to get tough with the Indians. Reservations, they argued, took up too much good land that white settlers could put to better use. At the same time, those sympathetic to the Indians were appalled at the desperate poverty on the reservations and feared for the Indians' survival. Helen Hunt Jackson, in her classic work *A Century of Dishonor* (1881), convinced many readers that the Indians had been treated unfairly. "Our Indian policy," the *New York Times* concluded, "is usually spoliation behind the mask of benevolence."

The Indian Rights Association, a group of mainly white easterners formed in 1882, campaigned for the dismantling of the reservations, now viewed as obstacles to progress. To "cease to treat the Indian as a red man and treat him as a man" meant putting an end to tribal communalism and fostering individualism. "Selfishness," declared Senator Henry Dawes of Massachusetts, "is at the bottom of civilization." Dawes called for "allotment in severalty" — the institution of private property.

In 1887, Congress passed the **Dawes Allotment Act**, dividing up reservations and allotting parcels of land to individual Indians as private property. Each Indian household was eligible to receive 160 acres of land from reservation property. Indians who took allotments earned U.S. citizenship. Since Indian land far surpassed the acreage needed for allotments, the government reserved the right to sell the "surplus" to white settlers. The Dawes Act effectively reduced Indian land from 138 million acres to a scant 48 million. The legislation, in the words of one critic, worked "to despoil the Indians of their lands and to make them vagabonds on the face of the earth." The Dawes Act completed the dispossession of the western Indian peoples and dealt a crippling blow to traditional tribal culture. It remained in effect until 1934, when the United States restored the right of Native Americans to own land communally (see chapter 24).

Indian Resistance and Survival Faced with the extinction of their entire way of life, different groups of Indians responded in different ways in the waning decades of the nineteenth century. Some tribes, including the Crow, Arikara, Pawnee, and Shoshoni, fought alongside the U.S. army against their old enemies, the Sioux. The Crow chief Plenty Coups explained why he allied with the United States: "Not because we loved the white man . . . or because we hated the Sioux . . . but because we plainly saw that this course was the only one which might save our beautiful country for us." The Crow and Shoshoni got to stay in their homelands and avoided the fate of other tribes shipped to reservations far away.

Indians who refused to stay on reservations risked being hunted down — a clear indication that reservations were intended to keep Indians in, not to keep whites out, as the friends of the Indians had intended. The Nez Percé war of 1877 is perhaps the most harrowing example of the army's policy. In 1863, the government dictated a treaty drastically reducing Nez Percé land. Most of the chiefs refused to sign the treaty and did not move to the reservation. In 1877, the army issued an ultimatum — come in to the reservation or be hunted down. Some eight hundred Nez Percé people, many of them women and children, fled across the mountains of Idaho, Wyoming, and Montana, heading for the safety of Canada. At the end of their 1,300-mile trek, 50 miles from freedom, they stopped to rest in the snow. The army's Indian scouts spotted their tepees, and the soldiers attacked. Yellow Wolf recalled their plight: "Children crying with cold. No fire. There could be no light. Everywhere the crying, the death wail." After a five-day siege, the Nez Percé leader, **Chief Joseph**, surrendered. His speech, reported by a white soldier, would become famous. "I am tired of fighting," he said as he surrendered his rifle. "Our chiefs are killed. It is cold and we have no blankets. The little children are freezing to death. . . . I am tired. My heart is sick and sad. From where the sun now stands, I will fight no more forever."

In the Southwest, the Apaches resorted to armed resistance. They roamed the Sonoran Desert of southern Arizona and northern Mexico, perfecting a hit-and-run guerrilla warfare that terrorized white settlers and bedeviled the army in the 1870s and 1880s. General George Crook combined a policy of dogged pursuit with judicious diplomacy. Crook relied on Indian scouts to track the raiding parties, recruiting nearly two hundred, including Apaches along with Navajos and Paiutes. By 1882, Crook had succeeded in persuading most of the Apaches to settle on the San Carlos Reservation in Arizona Territory. A desolate piece of desert inhabited by scorpions and rattlesnakes, San Carlos, in the words of one Apache, was "the worst place in all the great territory stolen from the Apaches."

Geronimo, a respected shaman (medicine man) of the Chiricahua Apache, refused to stay at San Carlos and repeatedly led raiding parties in the early 1880s. His warriors attacked ranches to obtain ammunition and horses. Among Geronimo's band was **Lozen**, a woman who rode with the warriors, armed with a rifle and a cartridge belt. The sister of a great chief who described her as being as "strong as a man, braver than most, and cunning in strategy," Lozen never married and remained a warrior in Geronimo's band even after her brother's death. In the spring of 1885, Geronimo and his followers, including Lozen, went on a ten-month offensive, moving from the Apache sanctuary in the Sierra Madre to raid and burn ranches and towns on both sides of the Mexican border. General Crook caught up with Geronimo in the fall and persuaded him to return to San Carlos, only to have him slip away on the way back to the reservation. Chagrined, Crook resigned his post. General **Nelson Miles**, Crook's replacement, adopted a policy of hunt and destroy.

Geronimo's band of thirty-three Apaches, including women and children, managed to elude Miles's troops for more than five months. In the end, this small band fought two thousand soldiers to a stalemate. After months of pursuit, Lieutenant Leonard Wood, a member of Miles's spit-and-polish cavalry, discarded his horse and most of his clothes until he was reduced to wearing nothing "but a pair of canton flannel drawers, and an old blue blouse, a pair of moccasins and a hat without a crown."

Eventually, Miles's scouts cornered Geronimo in 1886 at Skeleton Canyon. Caught between Mexican regulars and the U.S. army, Geronimo agreed to march north with the soldiers and negotiate a settlement. "We have not slept for six months," he admitted, "and we are worn out." Although fewer than three dozen Apaches had been considered "hostile," when General Miles induced them to surrender, the government rounded up nearly five hundred Apaches, including the scouts who had helped track Geronimo, and sent them as prisoners to Florida. By 1889, more than a quarter of them had died, some due to illnesses contracted in the damp lowland climate and some by suicide. Their plight roused public opinion, and in 1892 they were moved to Fort Sill in Oklahoma and later to New Mexico.

Geronimo lived to become something of a celebrity. He appeared at the St. Louis Exposition in 1904, and he rode in President Theodore Roosevelt's inaugural parade in 1905. In a newspaper interview, he confessed, "I want to go to my old home before I die. . . . Want to go back to the mountains again. I asked the Great White Father to allow me to go back, but he said no." None of the Apaches were permitted to return to Arizona; when Geronimo died in 1909, he was buried in Oklahoma.

On the plains, many tribes turned to a nonviolent form of resistance—a compelling new religion called the **Ghost Dance**. The Paiute shaman Wovoka, drawing on a cult that had developed in the 1870s, combined elements of Christianity and traditional Indian religion to found the Ghost Dance religion in 1889. Wovoka claimed that he had received a vision in which the Great Spirit spoke through him to all Indians, prophesying that if they would unite in the Ghost Dance ritual, whites would be destroyed in an apocalypse. The shaman promised that Indian warriors slain in battle would return to life and that buffalo once again would roam the land unimpeded. This religion, born of despair and with a message of hope, spread like wildfire over the plains. The Ghost Dance was performed in Idaho, Montana, Utah, Wyoming, Colorado, Nebraska, Kansas, the Dakotas, and Indian Territory by tribes as diverse as the Sioux, Arapaho, Cheyenne, Pawnee, and Shoshoni. Dancers often went into hypnotic trances, dancing until they dropped from exhaustion.

The Ghost Dance was nonviolent, but it frightened whites, especially when the Sioux taught that wearing a white ghost shirt made Indians immune to soldiers' bullets. Soon whites began to fear an uprising. "Indians are dancing in the snow and are wild and crazy," wrote the Bureau of Indian Affairs agent at the Pine Ridge Reservation in South Dakota. Frantic, he pleaded for reinforcements. "We are at the mercy of these dancers. We need protection, and we need it now." President Benjamin Harrison dispatched several thousand federal troops to Sioux country to handle any outbreak.

In December 1890, when Sitting Bull joined the Ghost Dance, he was killed by Indian police as they tried to arrest him at his cabin on the Standing Rock Reservation. His people, fleeing the scene, joined with a larger group of Miniconjou Sioux, who were apprehended by the Seventh Cavalry, Custer's old regiment, near Wounded Knee Creek, South Dakota. As the Indians laid down their arms, a shot rang out, and the soldiers opened fire. In the ensuing melee, Indian men, women, and children

Ghost Dancers Arapaho women at the Darlington Agency in Indian Territory (Oklahoma) participate in the Ghost Dance. Different tribes performed variations of the dance, but generally dancers formed a circle and danced until they reached the trancelike state shown here. The ceremonial drum (right) features a drawing of a thunderbird. Whites feared the dancers and demanded that the army dispatch troops to subdue them. The result was the killing of Sitting Bull and the massacre at Wounded Knee. Ghost Dance: National Anthropological Archives, Smithsonian Institution, Washington, D.C. (#81-9626); Drum: Copyright the Dorothea Lange Collection, Oakland Museum of California, City of Oakland. Gift of Paul S. Taylor.

were mowed down in minutes by the army's brutally efficient Hotchkiss rapid-fire guns. More than two hundred Sioux lay dead or dying in the snow. Settler Jules Sandoz surveyed the scene the day after the massacre at **Wounded Knee**. "Here in ten minutes an entire community was as the buffalo that bleached on the plains," he wrote. "There was something loose in the world that hated joy and happiness as it hated brightness and color, reducing everything to drab agony and gray." It had taken Euro-Americans 250 years to wrest control of the eastern half of the United States from the Indians. It took them less than 40 years to take the western half. The subjugation of the American Indians marked the first chapter in a national mission of empire that would later lead to overseas imperialistic adventures in Asia, Latin America, the Caribbean, and the Pacific Islands.

Q: **How did the slaughter of the bison contribute to the Plains Indians' removal to reservations?**

Gold Fever and the Mining West

Mining stood at the center of the United States' quest for empire in the West. The California gold rush of 1849 touched off the frenzy. The four decades following witnessed equally frenetic rushes for gold and other metals, most notably on the **Comstock Lode** in Nevada and later in New Mexico, Colorado, the Dakotas, Montana, Idaho, Arizona, and Utah. Each rush built on the last, producing new mining technologies and innovations in financing as hordes of miners, eager to strike it rich, moved from one boomtown to the next. Mining in the West, however, was a story not only of boom and bust but also of community building and the development of territories into states (Map 17.2). At first glance, the mining West may seem much different from the East, but by the 1870s, the term *urban industrialism* described Virginia City, Nevada, as accurately

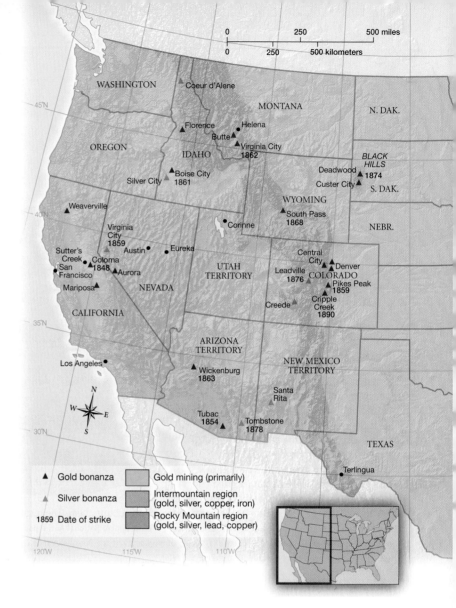

MAP 17.2 Western Mining, 1848–1890
Rich deposits of gold, silver, copper, lead, and iron larded the mountains of the West, from the Sierra Nevada of California to the Rockies of Colorado and the Black Hills of South Dakota. Beginning with the gold strike on Sutter's Creek in California in 1848 and continuing through the rush for gold in Cripple Creek, Colorado, in 1890, miners from all over the world flocked to the West. Few struck it rich, but many stayed on as paid workers in the increasingly mechanized corporate mines. Source: After Francaviglia.

as it did Pittsburgh or Cleveland. And the diverse peoples drawn to the West by the promise of mining riches made the region the most cosmopolitan in the nation. A close look at mining on the Comstock Lode indicates some of the patterns and paradoxes of western mining. And a look at territorial government uncovers striking parallels with corruption and cupidity in politics east of the Mississippi.

Mining on the Comstock Lode By 1859, refugees from California's played-out goldfields flocked to the Washoe basin in Nevada. There prospectors found the gold they sought mired in blackish sand they called "that blasted blue stuff." Eventually, an enterprising miner had the stuff assayed, and it turned out the Washoe miners had stumbled on the richest vein of silver ore on the continent—the legendary Comstock Lode, named for prospector Henry Comstock.

To exploit even potentially valuable silver claims required capital and expensive technology well beyond the means of the prospector. An active San Francisco

stock market sprang up to finance operations on the Comstock. Shrewd businessmen soon recognized that the easiest way to get rich was not to mine at all but to sell their claims or to form mining companies and sell shares of stock. The most unscrupulous mined the wallets of gullible investors by selling shares in bogus mines. Speculation, misrepresentation, and outright thievery ran rampant. In twenty years, more than $300 million poured from the earth in Nevada alone. A little stayed in Virginia City, but a great deal more went to speculators in California, some of whom got rich without ever leaving San Francisco.

The promise of gold and silver drew thousands to the mines of the West, the honest as well as the unprincipled. As Mark Twain observed, the Comstock attracted an international array of immigrants. "All the peoples of the earth had representative adventures in the Silverland," he wrote. Irish, Chinese, Germans, English, Scots, Welsh, Canadians, Mexicans, Italians, Scandinavians, French, Swiss, Chileans, and other South and Central

Americans came to share in the bonanza. With them came a sprinkling of Russians, Poles, Greeks, Japanese, Spaniards, Hungarians, Portuguese, Turks, Pacific Islanders, and Moroccans, as well as other North Americans, African Americans, and American Indians. This polyglot population, typical of mining boomtowns, made Virginia City in the 1870s more cosmopolitan than New York or Boston. In the part of Utah Territory that eventually became Nevada, as many as 30 percent of the people came from outside the United States, compared to 25 percent in New York and 21 percent in Massachusetts.

Irish immigrants formed the largest ethnic group in the mining district. In Virginia City, fully one-third of the population claimed at least one parent from Ireland. Irish and Irish American women constituted the largest group of women on the Comstock. As servants, boardinghouse owners, and washerwomen, they made up a significant part of the workforce. In contrast, the Chinese community, numbering 642 in 1870, remained overwhelmingly male. Virulent anti-Chinese sentiment barred the men from work in the mines, but despite the violent anti-Asian rhetoric, the mining community came to depend on Chinese labor. Many boardinghouses and affluent homes employed a Chinese cook or servant along with an Irish parlor maid.

As was so often the case in the West, where Euro-American ambitions clashed with Native American ways, the discovery of precious metals on the Comstock spelled disaster for the Indians. No sooner had the miners struck pay dirt than they demanded army troops to "hunt Indians" and establish forts to protect transportation to and from the diggings. This sudden and dramatic intrusion left Nevada's native tribes — the Northern Paiute and Bannock Shoshoni — exiles in their own land. At first they resisted, but over time they made peace with the invaders and proved resourceful in finding ways to adapt and preserve their culture and identity despite the havoc wrought by western mining and settlement.

In 1873, Comstock miners uncovered a new vein of ore, a veritable cavern of gold and silver. This "Big Bonanza" speeded the transition from small-scale industry to corporate oligopoly, creating a radically new social and economic environment. The Comstock became a laboratory for new mining technology. Huge stamping mills pulverized rock with pistonlike hammers driven by steam engines. Enormous Cornish pumps sucked water from the mine shafts, and huge ventilators circulated air in the underground chambers. No backwoods mining camp, Virginia City was an industrial center with more than 1,200 stamping mills working on average a ton of ore every day. Almost 400 men worked in milling, nearly 300 labored in manufacturing industries, and roughly 3,000 toiled in the mines. The Gould and Curry mine covered sixty acres. Most of the miners who came to the Comstock ended up as laborers for the big companies.

New technology eliminated some of the dangers of mining but often created new ones. In the hard-rock mines of the West, accidents in the 1870s disabled 1 out of every 30 miners and killed 1 in 80. Ross Moudy, who worked as a miner in Cripple Creek, Colorado, recalled how a stockholder visiting the mine nearly fell to his death. The terrified visitor told the miner next to him that "instead of being paid $3 a day, they ought to have all the gold they could take out." Moudy's biggest worry was carbon dioxide, which often filled the tunnels because of poor ventilation. "Many times," he confessed, "I have been carried out unconscious." Those who avoided accidents still breathed air so dangerous that respiratory diseases eventually disabled them. After a year on the job, Moudy joined a labor union "because I saw it would help me to keep in work and for protection in case of accident or sickness." The union provided good sick benefits and hired nurses, "so if one is alone and sick he is sure to be taken care of." On the Comstock Lode, because of the difficulty of obtaining skilled labor, the richness of the ore, and the need for a stable workforce, labor unions formed early and held considerable bargaining power. Comstock miners commanded $4 a day, the highest wage in the mining West.

The mining towns of the "Wild West" are often portrayed as lawless outposts, filled with saloons and rough gambling dens and populated almost exclusively by men, except for the occasional dance-hall floozy. The truth is more complex, as Virginia City's development attests. An established urban community built to serve an industrial giant, Virginia City in its first decade boasted churches, schools, theaters, an opera house, and hundreds of families. By 1870, women composed 30 percent of the population, and 75 percent of the women listed their occupation in the census as housekeeper. Mary McNair Mathews, a widow from Buffalo, New York, who lived on the Comstock in the 1870s, worked as a teacher, nurse, seamstress, laundress, and lodging-house operator. She later published a book on her adventures. By 1875, Virginia City boasted a population of 25,000 people, making it one of the largest cities between St. Louis and San Francisco. A must-see stop on the way west, the Queen of the Comstock hosted American presidents as well as legions of lesser dignitaries. No rough outpost of the Wild West, Virginia City represented, in the words of a recent chronicler, "the distilled essence of America's newly established course — urban, industrial, acquisitive, and materialistic, on the move, 'a living polyglot' of cultures that collided and converged."

Chinese Workers Chinese section hands, wearing their distinctive conical hats, are shown here in 1898 shoveling dirt for the North Pacific Coast Railroad in Corte Madera, California. Charles Crocker was the first railroad executive to hire Chinese laborers to work on the Central Pacific railroad in the 1860s, reasoning that "the race that built the Great Wall" could build tracks through the Sierra Nevada. California Historical Society, FN-25345.

Territorial Government The federal government practiced a policy of benign neglect when it came to territorial government in the West. The president appointed a governor, a secretary, and two to four judges, along with an attorney and a marshal. In Nevada Territory, that meant that a handful of officials governed an area the size of New England. Originally a part of the larger Utah Territory and propelled by mining interests, Nevada moved on the fast track to statehood, entering the Union in 1864, long before its population or its development merited statehood.

More typical were the territories extant in 1870 — New Mexico, Utah, Washington, Colorado, Dakota, Arizona, Idaho, Montana, and Wyoming. These areas remained territories for inordinately long periods ranging from twenty-three to sixty-two years. While awaiting statehood, they were subject to territorial governors who were underpaid, often unqualified, and largely ignored in Washington.

In theory, territorial governors received adequate salaries, as high as $3,500 in an era when the average workingman earned less than $500 a year. In practice, the funds rarely arrived in a timely fashion, and more than one governor found that he had to pay government expenses out of his own pocket. As one cynic observed, "Only the rich or those having 'no visible means of support,' can afford to accept office."

Nearly all territorial appointees tried to make ends meet by maintaining business connections with the East or by taking advantage of investment opportunities in the West. Distance and the lack of funds made it difficult to summon officers from Washington to investigate charges of corruption. Officials who ventured west to look into such charges often felt intimidated by gun-packing westerners. One judge sent to New Mexico Territory in 1871 reported that he "stayed three days, made up his mind that it would be dangerous to do any investigating, . . . and returned to his home without any action." Underfunded and overlooked, victims of political cronyism and prey to local interests, territorial governments were rife with conflicts of interest and corruption, mirroring the self-serving political and economic values of the country as a whole in the rush for riches that followed the Civil War.

The Diverse Peoples of the West The West of the late nineteenth century was a polyglot place, as much so as the big cities of the East. The sheer number of peoples who mingled in the West produced a complex blend of racism and prejudice. One historian has noted, not entirely facetiously, that there were at least eight oppressed "races" in the West — Indians, Latinos, Chinese, Japanese, blacks, Mormons, strikers, and radicals.

African Americans who ventured out to the territories faced hostile settlers determined to keep the West "for whites only." In response, they formed all-black communities such as Nicodemas, Kansas. That settlement, founded by thirty black Kentuckians in 1877, grew to a community of seven hundred by 1880. Isolated and often separated by great distances, small black settlements grew up throughout the West, in Nevada, Utah, and the Pacific Northwest as well as in Kansas. Black soldiers who served in the West during the Indian wars often stayed on as settlers. Called **buffalo soldiers** because Native Americans thought their hair resembled that of the buffalo, these black troops numbered up to 25,000. In the face of discrimination, poor treatment, and harsh conditions, the buffalo soldiers served with distinction and boasted the lowest desertion rate in the army.

Hispanic peoples had lived in Texas and the Southwest since Juan de Oñate led pioneer settlers up the Rio Grande in 1598. Hispanics had occupied the Pacific coast since San Diego was founded in 1769. Overnight, they were reduced to a "minority" after the United States annexed Texas in 1845 and took land stretching to California after the Mexican-American War ended in 1848. At first, the Hispanic owners of large *ranchos* in California, New Mexico, and Texas greeted conquest as an economic opportunity—new markets for their livestock and buyers for their lands. But racial prejudice soon ended their optimism. Californios (Mexican residents of California), who had been granted American citizenship by the Treaty of Guadalupe Hidalgo (1848), faced discrimination by Anglos who sought to keep them out of California's mines and commerce. Whites illegally squatted on *rancho* land while protracted litigation over Spanish and Mexican land grants forced the Californios into court. Although the U.S. Supreme Court eventually validated most of their claims, it took so long—seventeen years on average—that many Californios sold their property to pay taxes and legal bills. The city of Oakland, California, sits on what was once a 19,000-acre ranch owned by the Peralta family, who lost the land to Anglos.

Swindles, chicanery, and intimidation dispossessed scores of Californios. Many ended up segregated in urban barrios (neighborhoods) in their own homeland. Their percentage of California's population declined from 82 percent in 1850 to 19 percent in 1880 as Anglos migrated to the state. In New Mexico and Texas, Mexicans remained a majority of the population but became increasingly impoverished as Anglos dominated business and took the best jobs. Skirmishes between Hispanics and whites in northern New Mexico over the fencing of the open range lasted for decades. Groups of Hispanics with names such as *Las Manos Negras* (the Black Hands) cut fences and burned barns. In Texas, violence along the Rio Grande pitted Tejanos (Mexican residents of Texas) against the Texas Rangers, who saw their role as "keeping Mexicans in their place."

Like the Mexicans, the Mormons faced prejudice and hostility. The followers of Joseph Smith, the founder and prophet of the Church of Jesus Christ of Latter-Day Saints, fled west to avoid religious persecution. They believed that they had a divine right to the land, and their messianic militancy contributed to making them outcasts. The Mormon practice of polygamy (a man taking more than one wife) became a convenient point of attack for those who hated and feared the group. After Smith was killed by an Illinois mob in 1844, **Brigham Young** led the flock, which numbered more than 20,000, over the Rockies to the valley of the Great Salt Lake in Utah Territory. The Mormons quickly set to work irrigating the desert. They relied on cooperation and communalism, a strategy that excluded competition from those outside the faith. By 1882,

the Mormons had built Salt Lake City, a thriving metropolis of more than 150,000 residents.

The Mormon practice of polygamy (Brigham Young had twenty-seven wives) had come under attack as early as 1857, when U.S. troops occupied Salt Lake City (see chapter 12). To counter criticism of polygamy, the Utah territorial legislature gave women the right to vote in 1870, the first universal woman suffrage act in the nation. (Wyoming had granted suffrage to white women in 1869.) Although woman's rights advocates argued that the newly enfranchised women would "do away with the horrible institution of polygamy," it remained in force. Not until 1890 did the church hierarchy give in to pressure to renounce polygamy. The fierce controversy over polygamy postponed statehood for Utah until 1896.

The Chinese suffered brutal treatment at the hands of employers and other laborers. Drawn by the promise of gold, more than 20,000 Chinese had joined the rush to California by 1852. Miners determined to keep "California for Americans" succeeded in passing prohibitive foreign license laws to keep the Chinese out of the mines. But Chinese immigration continued. In the 1860s, when white workers moved on to find riches in the bonanza mines of Nevada, Chinese laborers took jobs abandoned by the whites. Railroad magnate Charles Crocker hired Chinese gangs to work on the Central Pacific, reasoning that "the race that built the Great Wall" could lay tracks across the treacherous Sierra Nevada. Some 12,000 Chinese, representing 90 percent of Crocker's workforce, completed America's first transcontinental railroad in 1869.

By 1870, more than 63,000 Chinese immigrants lived in America, 77 percent of them in California. A 1790 federal statute that limited naturalization to "white persons" was modified after the Civil War to extend naturalization to blacks ("persons of African descent"). But the Chinese and other Asians continued to be denied access to citizenship. As perpetual aliens, they constituted a reserve army of transnational laborers that many saw as a threat to American labor. For the most part, the Chinese did not displace white workers but instead found work as railroad laborers, cooks, servants, and farmhands while white workers sought out more lucrative fields. In the 1870s, when California and the rest of the nation weathered a major economic depression, the Chinese became easy scapegoats. California workingmen rioted and fought to keep Chinese workers out of the state, claiming they were "coolie labor"—involuntary contract laborers recruited by business interests determined to keep wages at rock bottom.

In 1876, the Workingmen's Party formed to fight for Chinese exclusion. Racial and cultural animosities stood at the heart of anti-Chinese agitation. Denis Kearney, the fiery San Francisco leader of the movement, made clear this racist bent when he

Railroad Locomotive In the years following the Civil War, the locomotive replaced the covered wagon, enabling settlers to travel from Chicago or St. Louis to the West Coast in two days. By the 1890s, more than 72,000 miles of track stretched west of the Mississippi River. The first transcontinental railroad, completed in 1869, soon led to the creation of competing systems, so that by the 1880s, travelers going west could choose from four railroad lines. In this photograph, men and women perched on a locomotive celebrate the completion of a section of track. Library of Congress.

urged legislation to "expel every one of the moon-eyed lepers." Nor was California alone in its anti-immigrant nativism. As the country confronted growing ethnic and racial diversity with the rising tide of global immigration in the decades following the Civil War, many questioned the principle of racial equality at the same time they argued against the assimilation of "nonwhite" groups. In this climate, Congress passed the **Chinese Exclusion Act** in 1882, effectively barring Chinese immigration and setting a precedent for further immigration restrictions. The Chinese Exclusion Act led to a sharp drop in the Chinese population—from 105,465 in 1880 to 89,863 in 1900—because Chinese immigrants, overwhelmingly male, did not have families to sustain their population. Eventually, Japanese immigrants, including women as well as men, replaced the Chinese,

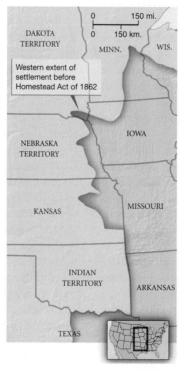

Midwestern Settlement before 1862

particularly in agriculture. As "nonwhite" immigrants, they could not become naturalized citizens, but their children born in the United States claimed the rights of citizenship. Japanese parents, seeking to own land, purchased it in their children's names. Although anti-Asian prejudice remained strong in California and elsewhere in the West, Asian immigrants formed an important part of the economic fabric of the western United States.

The American West in the nineteenth century witnessed more than its share of conflict and bloodshed. Violent prejudice against the Chinese and other Asian immigrants remained common. But violence also broke out between cattle ranchers and sheep ranchers, between ranchers and farmers, between striking miners and their bosses, among rival Indian groups, and between whites and Indians. At issue was who would control the vast resources of the emerging region.

Q: How did industrial technology change mining in Nevada?

Land Fever

In the three decades following 1870, more land was settled than in all the previous history of the country. Americans by the hundreds of thousands packed up and moved west, goaded if not by the hope of striking gold, then by the promise of owning land. The agrarian West shared with the mining West a persistent restlessness, an equally pervasive addiction to speculation, and a penchant for exploiting natural resources and labor.

Two factors stimulated the land rush in the trans-Mississippi West. The **Homestead Act of 1862** promised 160 acres free to any citizen or prospective citizen, male or female, who settled on the land for five years. Even more important, transcontinental railroads opened up new areas and actively recruited settlers. After the completion of the first transcontinental railroad in 1869, homesteaders abandoned the covered wagon, and by the 1880s they could choose from four competing rail lines and make the trip west in a matter of days.

Although the country was rich in land and resources, not all who wanted to own land achieved their goal. During the transition from the family farm to large commercial farming, small farms gave way to vast spreads worked by migrant labor or paid farmworkers. Just as industry corporatized and consolidated in the East, the period from 1870 to 1900 witnessed corporate consolidation in mining, ranching, and agriculture.

Moving West: Homesteaders and Speculators

A Missouri homesteader remembered packing as her family pulled up stakes and headed west to Oklahoma in 1890. "We were going to God's Country," she wrote. "You had to work hard on that rocky country in Missouri. I was glad to be leaving it. . . . We were going to a new land and get rich."

People who ventured west searching for "God's Country" faced hardship, loneliness, and deprivation. To carve a farm from the raw prairie of Iowa, the plains of Nebraska, or the forests of the Pacific Northwest took more than fortitude and backbreaking toil. It took luck. Blizzards, tornadoes, grasshoppers, hailstorms, drought, prairie fires, accidental death, and disease were only a few of the catastrophes that could befall even the best farmer. Homesteaders on free land still needed as much as $1,000 for a house, a team of farm animals, a well, fencing, and seed. Poor farmers called "sodbusters" did without even these basics, living in dugouts carved into hillsides and using muscle instead of machinery.

"Father made a dugout and covered it with willows and grass," one Kansas girl recounted. When it rained, the dugout flooded, and "we carried the water out in buckets, then waded around in the mud until it dried." Rain wasn't the only problem. "Sometimes the bull snakes would get in the roof and now and then one would lose his hold and fall down on the bed. . . . Mother would grab the hoe . . . and after the fight was over Mr. Bull Snake was dragged outside." The sod house, a step up from the dugout, had walls cut from blocks of sod and a roof of sod, lumber, or tin.

For women on the frontier, obtaining simple daily necessities such as water and fuel meant backbreaking labor. Out on the plains, where water was scarce, women often had to trudge to the nearest creek or spring. "A yoke was made to place across [Mother's] shoulders, so as to carry at each end a bucket of water," one daughter recollected, "and then water was brought a half mile from spring to house." Gathering fuel was another heavy chore. Without ready sources of coal or firewood, settlers on the plains turned to what substitutes they could scavenge—twigs, tufts of grass, corncobs, sunflower stalks. But by far the most prevalent fuel was "chips"—chunks of dried cattle and buffalo dung, found in abundance on the plains.

Despite the hardships, some homesteaders succeeded in building comfortable lives. The sod hut made way for a more substantial house; the log cabin yielded to a white clapboard home with a porch and a rocking chair. For others, the promise of the West failed to materialize. Already by the 1870s, much of the best land had been taken. Too often, homesteaders found that only the least desirable tracts were left—poor land, far from markets, transportation, and society. "There is plenty of land for sale in California," one migrant complained in 1870, but "the majority of the available lands are held by speculators, at prices far beyond the reach of a poor man." The railroads, flush from land grants provided by the state and federal governments, owned huge swaths of land in the West and actively recruited settlers. Altogether, the land grants totaled approximately 180 million acres—an area almost one-tenth the size of the United States (Map 17.3). Of the 2.5 million farms established between 1860 and 1900, homesteading accounted for only one in five; the vast majority of farmland sold for a profit.

As land grew scarce on the prairie in the 1870s, farmers began to push farther west, moving into western Kansas, Nebraska, and eastern Colorado—the region called the **Great American Desert** by settlers who had passed over it on their way to California and Oregon. Many agricultural experts warned that the semiarid land (where less than twenty inches of rain fell annually) would not support a farm on the 160 acres allotted to homesteaders. But their words of caution were drowned out by the extravagant claims of western promoters, many employed by the railroads to sell off their land grants. "Rain follows the plow" became the slogan of western boosters, who insisted that cultivation would alter the climate of the region and bring more rainfall. Instead, drought followed the plow. Droughts were a cyclical fact of life on the Great Plains. Plowed up, the dry topsoil blew away in the wind. A period of relatively good rainfall in the early 1880s encouraged farming; then a protracted drought in the late 1880s and early 1890s sent starving farmers reeling back from the plains. Thousands left, some in wagons carrying the slogan "In God we trusted, in Kansas we busted."

Fever for fertile land set off a series of spectacular land runs in Oklahoma. When two million acres of land in former Indian Territory opened for settlement in 1889, thousands of homesteaders massed on the border. At the opening pistol shot, "with a shout and a yell the swift riders shot out, then followed the light buggies or wagons," a reporter wrote. "Above all, a great cloud of dust hover[ed] like smoke over a battlefield." By nightfall, Oklahoma boasted two tent cities with more than ten

MAP 17.3 **Federal Land Grants to Railroads and the Development of the West, 1850–1900**
Generous federal land grants meant that railroads could sell the desirable land next to the track at a profit or hold it for speculation. Railroads received more than 180 million acres, an area as large as Texas. Notice how the railroads connect with major cattle trailheads in Dodge City, Abilene, and Kansas City and to mining towns in Montana, Nevada, Colorado, and New Mexico.

Cattle Trails, 1860–1890

thousand residents. In the last frenzied land rush on Oklahoma's Cherokee strip in 1893, several settlers were killed in the stampede, and nervous men guarded their claims with rifles. As public land grew scarce, the hunger for land grew fiercer for both farmers and ranchers.

Ranchers and Cowboys Cattle ranchers followed the railroads onto the plains, establishing a cattle kingdom from Texas to Wyoming between 1865 and 1885. Cowboys drove huge herds, as many as three thousand head of cattle that grazed on public lands as they followed cattle tracks like the Chisholm Trail from Texas to railheads in Kansas. More than a million and a half Texas longhorns went to market before the range began to close in the 1880s.

Barbed wire revolutionized the cattle business and sounded the death knell for the open range. In 1874, Joseph F. Glidden, an Illinois sheriff, invented and patented barbed wire. Gambler and promoter John "Bet a Million" Gates made his fortune by corralling a herd of Texas longhorns in downtown San Antonio, proving the merit of the flimsy-looking wire he went on to market profitably.

As the largest ranches in Texas began to fence, nasty fights broke out between big ranchers and "fence cutters," who resented the end of the free range. One old-timer observed, "Those persons, Mexicans and Americans, without land but who had cattle were put out of business by fencing." Fencing forced small-time ranchers who owned land but could not afford to buy barbed wire or sink wells to sell out for the best price they could get. The displaced ranchers, many of them Mexicans, ended up as wageworkers on the huge spreads owned by Anglos or by European syndicates.

Barbed Wire The original working model of Joseph Glidden's barbing machine, patented in 1874, consisted of an old-fashioned coffee mill with its casing cut away and its grinder altered to cut and coil small lengths of wire. The barbs were strung by hand between strands of plain wire. Despite its flimsiness, barbed wire could contain cattle, as master promoter John "Bet a Million" Gates demonstrated by corralling a herd of Texas longhorns in downtown San Antonio in 1879. Ellwood House Museum, De Kalb, Illinois.

THE PROMISE OF TECHNOLOGY

On the range, the cowboy gave way to the cattle king and, like the miner, became a wage laborer. Many cowboys were African Americans (as many as five thousand in Texas alone). Writers of western literature chose to ignore the presence of black cowboys like Deadwood Dick (Nat Love), who was portrayed as a white man in the dime novels of the era.

By 1886, cattle overcrowded the range. Severe blizzards during the winters of 1886–87 and 1887–88 decimated the herds. "A whole generation of cowmen," wrote one chronicler, "went dead broke." Fencing worsened the situation. During blizzards, cattle stayed alive by keeping on the move. But when they ran up against barbed wire fences, they froze to death. In the aftermath of the "Great Die Up," new labor-intensive forms of cattle ranching replaced the open-range model.

Tenants, Sharecroppers, and Migrants In the post–Civil War period, as agriculture became a big business tied to national and global markets, an increasing number of laborers worked land that they would never own. In the southern United States, farmers labored under particularly heavy burdens (see chapter 16). The Civil War wiped out much of the region's capital, which had been invested in slaves, and crippled the plantation economy. Newly freed slaves rarely obtained land of their own and often ended up as farm laborers. "The colored folks stayed with the old boss man and farmed and worked on the plantations," a black Alabama sharecropper observed bitterly. "They were still slaves, but they were free slaves." Some freedpeople did manage to pull together enough resources to go west. In 1879, more than fifteen thousand black **Exodusters** moved from Mississippi and Louisiana to take up land in Kansas.

California's Mexican cowboys, or *vaqueros*, commanded decent wages throughout the Southwest. Skilled horsemen, the vaqueros boasted that five of them could do the work of thirty Anglo cowboys. The vocabulary of ranching with words such as *rodeo, lasso,* and *lariat* testified to the centrality of the vaqueros' place in the cattle industry. But by 1880, as the coming of the railroads ended the long cattle drives and large feedlots began to replace the open range, the value of their skills declined. Many vaqueros ended up as migrant laborers, often on land their families had once owned. Similarly, in Texas, Tejanos found themselves displaced. After the heyday of cattle ranching ended in the late 1880s, cotton production rose in the southeastern regions of the state. Ranchers turned their pastures into sharecroppers' plots and hired displaced cowboys, most of them Mexicans, as seasonal laborers for as little as seventy-five cents a day, thereby creating a growing army of agricultural wageworkers.

Land monopoly and large-scale farming fostered tenancy and migratory labor on the West Coast. By the 1870s, less than 1 percent of California's population owned half the state's available agricultural land. The rigid economics of large-scale commercial agriculture and the seasonal nature of the crops spawned a ragged army of migratory agricultural laborers.

> Severe blizzards during the winters of 1886–87 and 1887–88 decimated the herds. "A whole generation of cowmen," wrote one chronicler, "went dead broke."

Derisively labeled "blanket men" or "bindle stiffs," these transients worked the fields in the growing season and wintered in the flophouses of San Francisco. Most farm laborers were Chinese immigrants. After passage of the Chinese Exclusion Act of 1882, Mexicans, Filipinos, and Japanese immigrants filled the demand for migratory workers.

Commercial Farming and Industrial Cowboys

In the late nineteenth century, America's population remained overwhelmingly rural. The 1870 census showed that nearly 80 percent of the nation's people lived on farms and in villages of fewer than 8,000 inhabitants. By 1900, the figure had dropped to 66 percent. At the same time, the number of farms rose. Rapid growth in the West increased the number of the nation's farms from 2 million in 1860 to more than 5.7 million in 1900.

Despite the hardships individual farmers experienced, new technology and farming techniques revolutionized American farm life. Mechanized plows and reapers halved the time and labor cost of production and made it possible to cultivate vast tracts of land. Urbanization provided farmers with expanding markets for their produce, and railroads carried crops to markets thousands of miles away. Even before the start of the twentieth century, American agriculture had entered the era of what would come to be called agribusiness—farming as a big business—with the advent of huge commercial farms.

As farming moved onto the prairies and plains, mechanization took command. Steel plows, reapers, mowers, harrows, seed drills, combines, and threshers replaced human muscle. Horse-drawn implements gave way to steam-powered machinery. By 1880, a single combine could do the work of twenty men, vastly increasing the acreage a farmer could cultivate. Mechanization spurred the growth of bonanza wheat farms, some more than 100,000 acres, in California and the Red River Valley of North Dakota and Minnesota. This agricultural revolution meant that Americans raised more than four times the corn, five times the hay, and seven times the wheat and oats they had before the Civil War.

Like cotton farmers in the South, western grain and livestock farmers increasingly depended on foreign markets for their livelihood. A fall in global market prices meant that a farmer's entire harvest went to pay

Buffalo Bill Poster Buffalo Bill Cody used colorful posters to publicize his Wild West show during the 1880s and 1890s. This poster advertises the reenactment of Custer's Last Stand. Buffalo Bill performed for Queen Victoria in London and at the World's Columbian Exposition in Chicago. Sitting Bull, who fought at the Battle of the Little Big Horn, toured with the company in 1885 and traveled to England with the show. Cody's romantic depictions of western history helped create the myth of the Old West. Buffalo Bill Historical Center, Cody, Wyoming.

FOR MORE HELP ANALYZING THIS IMAGE, see the visual activity for this chapter in the Online Study Guide at bedfordstmartins.com/roarkcompact.

off debts. In the depression that followed the panic of 1893, many heavily mortgaged farmers lost their land to creditors. As a Texas cotton farmer complained, "By the time the World Gets their Liveing out of the Farmer as we have to Feed the World, we the Farmer has nothing Left but a Bear Hard Liveing." Commercial farming, along with mining, represented another way in which the West developed its own brand of industrialism. The far West's industrial economy sprang initially from California gold and the vast territory that came under American control following the Mexican-American War. In the ensuing rush on land and resources, environmental factors interacted with economic and social forces to produce enterprises as vast in scale and scope as anything found in the East.

Two Alsatian immigrants, Henry Miller and Charles Lux, pioneered the West's mix of agriculture and industrialism. Beginning as meat wholesalers, Miller and Lux quickly expanded their business to encompass cattle, land, and land reclamation projects such as dams and irrigation systems. With a labor force of migrant workers, a highly coordinated corporate system, and large sums of investment capital, the firm of **Miller & Lux** became one of America's industrial behemoths. Eventually, these "industrial cowboys" grazed a herd of 100,000 cattle on 1.25 million acres of company land in California, Oregon, and Nevada and employed more than 1,200 migrant laborers on their corporate ranches. Miller & Lux dealt with the labor problem by offering free meals to migratory workers, thus keeping wages low while winning goodwill among an army of unemployed who competed for the work. When the company's Chinese cooks rebelled at washing the dishes resulting from the free meals, the migrant laborers were forced to eat after the ranch hands and use their dirty plates. By the 1890s, more than eight hundred migrants a year followed what came to be known as the "Dirty Plate Route" on Miller & Lux ranches throughout California.

Since the days of Thomas Jefferson, agrarian life had been linked with the highest ideals of a democratic society. Now agrarianism itself had been transformed. The farmer was no longer a self-sufficient yeoman but often a businessman or a wage laborer tied to a global market. And even as farm production soared, industrialization outstripped it. More and more farmers left the fields for urban factories or found work in the "factories in the fields" of the new industrialized agribusiness. Now that the future seemed to lie not with the small farmer but with industrial enterprises, was democracy itself at risk? This question would ignite a farmers' revolt in the 1880s and dominate political debate in the 1890s.

Q: **Why did many homesteaders find it difficult to acquire good land in the West?**

Conclusion: The Mythic West

Even as the Old West was changing, the mythic West was being born. The prince of the dime novel, Buffalo Bill, became its icon. Born William F. Cody, the real-life Buffalo Bill panned for gold, rode for the Pony Express, scouted for the army, and earned his nickname hunting buffalo for the railroad. The masterful showman formed a touring Wild West company in 1883. Part circus, part theater, the Wild West extravaganza featured exhibitions of riding, shooting, and roping and presented dramatic reenactments of great moments in western lore. Highly dubious as history, as spectacle the Wild West show was unbeatable. At the World's Columbian Exposition in 1893, crowds numbering tens of thousands packed the bleachers to cheer. By the turn of the twentieth century, the high drama of the struggle for the West had become little more than a thrilling but harmless entertainment.

While Buffalo Bill's show entertained the crowds on the Midway, across the fairgrounds historian Frederick Jackson Turner addressed the American Historical Association on "The Significance of the Frontier in American History." Turner noted that by 1890, the census could no longer discern a clear frontier line. His tone was elegiac: "The existence of an area of free land, its continuous recession, and the advance of settlement westward," he observed, "explained American development" and was inextricably linked to what was best and unique in America. Of course, land in the West had never been empty or free. And the pastoral agrarianism Turner celebrated belied the urban, industrial West found on the Comstock and in the commercial farms of California. Nevertheless, Turner's **frontier thesis** became one of the most enduring myths of the American West.

The real West was no less dramatic than the mythic West. In the decades following the Civil War, as the United States pursued empire in the American West, new problems replaced the old issues of slavery and sectionalism. The growing power of big business, the exploitation of labor and natural resources, corruption in politics, and ethnic and racial tensions exacerbated by colonial expansion and unparalleled immigration dominated the debates of the day in both East and West. As the nineteenth century ended, Americans had more questions than answers. Could the American promise survive in the new world of corporations, wage labor, and mushrooming cities? Neither out of place nor out of time, the West contributed its share to both the promise and the problems of the era Mark Twain would brand the Gilded Age.

Reviewing the Chapter

★ KEY TERMS

Explain each term's significance

WHO

Sitting Bull (p. 418)

Crazy Horse (p. 418)

George Crook (p. 418)

Chief Joseph (p. 419)

Geronimo (p. 420)

Lozen (p. 420)

Nelson Miles (p. 420)

Brigham Young (p. 425)

WHAT

Carlisle Indian School (p. 412)

Indian removal (p. 415)

Treaties of Fort Laramie (1851 and 1868) (pp. 416, 418)

Black Hills (p. 418)

Battle of the Little Big Horn (p. 418)

Dawes Allotment Act (p. 419)

Ghost Dance (p. 420)

Wounded Knee massacre (p. 421)

Comstock Lode (p. 421)

buffalo soldiers (p. 424)

Chinese Exclusion Act (p. 426)

Homestead Act of 1862 (p. 426)

Great American Desert (p. 427)

barbed wire (p. 428)

Exodusters (p. 429)

Miller & Lux (p. 431)

frontier thesis (p. 431)

★ REVIEW QUESTIONS Q:

Use key terms and dates to support your answer

1. How did the slaughter of the bison contribute to the Plains Indians' removal to reservations? (pp. 413–21)

2. How did industrial technology change mining in Nevada? (pp. 421–26)

3. Why did many homesteaders find it difficult to acquire good land in the West? (pp. 426–31)

★ MAKING CONNECTIONS

Draw on key terms, timeline, and review questions

1. Westward migration brought settlers into conflict with Native Americans. What was the U.S. government's policy toward Indians in the West, and how did it evolve over time? How did the Indians resist and survive white encroachment? In your answer, discuss the cultural and military features of the conflict.

2. The economic and industrial developments characteristic of the East after the Civil War also made their mark on the West. How did innovations in business and technology transform mining and agriculture in the West? In your answer, be sure to consider effects on production and the consequences for the lives of miners and agricultural laborers.

3. Settlers from all over the world came to the American West seeking their fortunes but found that opportunity was not equally available to all. In competition for work and land, why did Anglo-American settlers usually have the upper hand? How did legal developments contribute to this circumstance?

FOR PRACTICE QUIZZES AND OTHER STUDY TOOLS, see the Online Study Guide at **bedfordstmartins.com/roarkcompact**.

★ SUGGESTED READINGS

David Wallace Adams, *Education for Extinction: American Indians and the Boarding School Experience, 1875–1928* (1995). A vivid and often heartbreaking study of the experiences of Indian youth sent to boarding schools.

James O. Gump, *The Dust Rose Like Smoke: The Subjugation of the Zulu and the Sioux* (1994). A fascinating comparison of U.S. Indian policy and colonial practices in South Africa.

David Igler, *Industrial Cowboys: Miller & Lux and the Transformation of the Far West, 1850–1920* (2001). A case study of how two neighborhood butchers became the West's leading industrialists.

Andrew C. Isenberg, *The Destruction of the Bison: An Environmental History, 1730–1920* (2000). How the environment of the plains and the acts of Indians and settlers led to the decimation of the great bison herds.

Ronald M. James, *The Roar and the Silence: The History of Virginia City and the Comstock Lode* (1998). A lively account of life on the Comstock.

Jeffrey Ostler, *The Plains Sioux and U.S. Colonialism from Lewis and Clark to Wounded Knee* (2004). A pioneering work comparing colonialism abroad with U.S. policies in the West.

FOR MORE BOOKS ABOUT TOPICS IN THIS CHAPTER, see the Online Bibliography at **bedfordstmartins.com/roarkcompact**.

FOR ADDITIONAL FIRSTHAND ACCOUNTS OF THIS PERIOD, see Chapter 17 in Michael Johnson, ed., *Reading the American Past*, Fourth Edition.

FOR WEB SITES, IMAGES, AND DOCUMENTS RELATED TO TOPICS AND PLACES IN THIS CHAPTER, visit Make History at **bedfordstmartins.com/roarkcompact**.

★ TIMELINE

1851	• First Treaty of Fort Laramie.
1862	• Homestead Act. • Great Sioux Uprising (Santee Uprising).
1864	• Sand Creek Massacre.
1867	• Treaty of Medicine Lodge.
1868	• Second Treaty of Fort Laramie.
1869	• First transcontinental railroad completed.
1870	• Hunters begin to decimate bison herds.
1873	• "Big Bonanza" on Comstock Lode.
1874	• Discovery of gold in Black Hills.
1876	• Battle of the Little Big Horn.
1877	• Chief Joseph surrenders. • Crazy Horse surrenders and is later arrested and killed.
1878	• Indian students enroll at Hampton Institute in Virginia.
1879	• Carlisle Indian School opens in Pennsylvania. • More than fifteen thousand Exodusters move to Kansas.
1881	• Sitting Bull surrenders.
1882	• Chinese Exclusion Act. • Indian Rights Association formed.
1883	• Buffalo Bill Cody begins touring.
1886	• Geronimo surrenders.
1886–1888	• Severe blizzards decimate cattle herds.
1887	• Dawes Allotment Act.
1889	• Rise of Ghost Dance. • Two million acres in Oklahoma opened for settlement.
1890	• Sitting Bull killed. • Massacre at Wounded Knee, South Dakota.
1893	• Last land rush takes place in Oklahoma Territory.
1900	• Census finds 66 percent of population lives in rural areas, compared to 80 percent in 1870.

CAMPAIGN PINS, 1884 These gilt campaign pins from the election of 1884 show Republican candidate James G. Blaine, on the right, thumbing his nose at Democratic candidate Grover Cleveland. Styled by a contemporary journalist as "the vilest campaign ever waged," the 1884 race pitted Cleveland, who had made his political reputation on his honest dealings, against Blaine, who was tainted with charges of corruption. However, when the *Buffalo Telegraph* revealed that the bachelor Cleveland had fathered an illegitimate child, the tables turned, and Cleveland and his followers lost the high moral ground. Perhaps this is why Blaine is portrayed in this mechanical pin as thumbing his nose at Cleveland. His gesture proved premature; Cleveland squeaked past Blaine in a close race. The gilt pins are a good symbol for Gilded Age politics — an era characterized by corruption and party strife. Collection of Janice L. and David J. Frent.

Business and Politics in the Gilded Age

1870–1895

ONE NIGHT OVER DINNER, humorist and author Mark Twain and his friend Charles Dudley Warner teased their wives about the popular novels they read. When the two women challenged them to write something better, they set to work. Warner supplied the sentimental melodrama, while Twain "hurled in the facts." The result was a runaway best seller, a savage satire of the "get-rich-quick" era that forever after would be known by the book's title, **_The Gilded Age_** (1873).

Twain left no one unscathed in the novel — political hacks, Washington lobbyists, Wall Street financiers, small-town boosters, wildcat miners, and the "great putty-hearted public" that tolerated the plunder. Underneath the glitter of the Gilded Age, as Twain's title implied, lurked baser stuff. Twain had witnessed up close the corrupt partnership of business and politics in the administration of Ulysses S. Grant. Drawing on this experience, he described how a lobbyist could get an appropriation bill through Congress:

> Why the matter is simple enough. A Congressional appropriation costs money. Just reflect, for instance. A majority of the House Committee, say $10,000 apiece — $40,000; a majority of the Senate Committee, the same each — say $40,000; a little extra to one or two chairmen of one or two such committees, say $10,000 each — $20,000; and there's $100,000 of the money gone, to begin with. Then, seven male lobbyists, at $3,000 each — $21,000; one female lobbyist, $3,000; a high moral Congressman or Senator here and there — the high moral ones cost more, because they give tone to a measure — say ten of these at $3,000 each, is $30,000; then a lot of small fry country members who won't vote for anything whatever without pay — say twenty at $500 apiece, is $10,000 altogether; lot of jimcracks for Congressmen's wives and children — those go a long way — you can't spend too much money in that line — well, those things cost in a lump, say $10,000 — along there somewhere; — and then comes your printed documents. . . . Oh, my dear sir, printing bills are destruction itself. Ours, so far amount to — let me see — . . . well, never mind the details, the total in clean numbers foots up $118,254.42 thus far!

Mark Twain and *The Gilded Age*
Popular author Mark Twain (Samuel Langhorne Clemens) wrote acerbically about the excesses of the Gilded Age in his novel of that name written with Charles Dudley Warner and published in 1873. No one knew the meretricious lure of the era better than Twain, who succumbed to a get-rich-quick scheme that led him to the brink of bankruptcy. Book: Beinecke Rare Book and Manuscript Library, Yale University; Photo: Newberry Library.

In Twain's satire, Congress is for sale to the highest bidder. The unseemly intimacy between government and business meant that more often than not, senators, representatives, and even members of the executive branch were on the payroll of business interests, if not in their pockets. The corrupt interplay of business and politics raised serious questions about the health of American democracy.

The Gilded Age seemed to tarnish all who touched it. No one would learn that lesson better than Twain, who, even as he attacked it as an "era of incredible rottenness," fell prey to its enticements. Born Samuel Langhorne Clemens, he grew up in a rough Mississippi River town, where he first became a journeyman printer and then a riverboat pilot. Taking the pen name Mark Twain, he moved west and gained fame chronicling mining booms in California and Nevada. In 1866, he came east to launch a career as an author, public speaker, and itinerant humorist. Twain played to packed houses, but his work about common people using common language was judged too vulgar for the genteel tastes of the time. His masterpiece, *The Adventures of Huckleberry Finn*, was banned in Boston when it appeared in 1884.

Huck Finn's creator eventually stormed the citadels of polite society, hobnobbing with the wealthy and living in increasingly elegant and lavish style. Succumbing to the money fever of his age, Twain plunged into one scheme after another in the hope of making millions. The Paige typesetting machine proved his downfall. Twain invested heavily in this invention that promised to mechanize typesetting. The idea was a good one; a competing invention, the Linotype, eventually replaced hand type. The Paige machine, however, proved too complicated and temperamental to be practical. By the 1890s, Twain faced bankruptcy. Only the help of his friend Standard Oil millionaire Henry H. Rogers enabled him to begin his dogged climb out of debt.

Twain's tale was common in an age when the promise of wealth led as many to ruin as to riches. In the Gilded Age, fortunes were made and lost with dizzying frequency. Wall Street panics, like those in 1873 and 1893, periodically interrupted the boom times and plunged the country into economic depression. But with railroads and cities to be built and industry expanding on every level, the mood of the country remained buoyant.

The rise of industrialism in the United States and the interplay of business and politics strike the key themes in the Gilded Age. In the decades from 1870 to 1890, the transition from a rural, agricultural economy to urban industrialism, global in its reach, transformed American society. The growth of old industries and the creation of new ones, along with the rise of big business, signaled the coming of age of industrial capitalism. With new times came new economic and political issues. Old divisions engendered by sectionalism and slavery still influenced politics. But increasingly, economic issues such as the tariff and monetary policy shaped party politics. And as concern grew over the power of big business and the growing chasm between the rich and the poor, many Americans looked to the government for solutions.

Perhaps nowhere were the hopes and fears that industrialism inspired more evident than in the public's attitude toward the great business moguls of the day, men like Jay Gould, Andrew Carnegie, John D. Rockefeller, and J. P. Morgan. These larger-than-life figures dominated business and sparked the popular imagination as the heroes and villains in the high drama of industrialization. At no other period in U.S. history would the industrial giants and the businesses they built (and sometimes wrecked) loom so large in American life. ★

Old Industries Transformed, New Industries Born

In the years following the Civil War, the scale and scope of American industry expanded dramatically. Old industries like iron transformed into modern industries typified by the behemoth U.S. Steel. Discovery and invention stimulated new industries from oil refining to electric light and power. The expansion of the nation's rail system in the decades after the Civil War played the key role in the transformation of the American economy. New rail lines created a national market that enabled businesses to expand from a regional to a nationwide scale. The railroads became America's first big business.

Jay Gould, Andrew Carnegie, John D. Rockefeller, and other business leaders pioneered new strategies to seize markets and consolidate power in the rising railroad, steel, and oil industries. Always with an eye to the main chance, these business tycoons set the tone in the get-rich-quick era of freewheeling capitalism that came to be called the Gilded Age.

Railroads: America's First Big Business In the decades following the Civil War, the United States built the greatest railroad network in the world. The first transcontinental railroad was completed in 1869 when the tracks of the Union Pacific and Central Pacific railroads came together at Promontory Point, Utah, linking new markets in the West to the nation's economy (Map 18.1).

MAP 18.1 Railroad Expansion, 1870–1890

Railroad mileage nearly quadrupled between 1870 and 1890, with the greatest growth occurring in the trans-Mississippi West. New transcontinental lines — the Great Northern, Northern Pacific, Southern Pacific, and Atlantic and Pacific — were completed in the 1880s. Small feeder lines such as the Oregon Short Line and the Atchison, Topeka, and Santa Fe fed into the great transcontinental systems, knitting the nation together.

READING THE MAP: Where were most of the railroad lines located in 1870? What cities were the major railroad centers? What was the end point of the only western route?

CONNECTIONS: Why were so many rails laid between 1870 and 1890? How did the railroads affect the nation's economy?

FOR MORE HELP ANALYZING THIS MAP, see the map activity for this chapter in the Online Study Guide at bedfordstmartins.com/roarkcompact.

Railroad Track Mileage, 1890

	Completed Track in Miles
India	16,918
Great Britain	17,291
Russia	19,012
France	20,679
Germany	26,638
United States	208,152

By 1850, the railway network in Great Britain was already well established, and most of the main lines in Germany had been built. France was slower to invest in railroads, but during the period 1850 to 1860, the government invested heavily in laying track, and the French soon caught up with, and then bypassed, their European neighbors. Russia's railway development experienced its greatest growth in the late nineteenth century. This growth was driven by the country's need to access its newly developing industrial regions and the vast natural resources of its far-flung territories in Asia. Like Russia, most of India's railroad growth occurred late in the century. This development was financed by the British, who were eager to tap the economic potential of their profitable overseas colony. By 1890, the United States had laid more railroad track than Britain, Germany, France, Russia, and India combined. Most of this growth occurred in the period 1870 to 1890, when railroad mileage in the United States nearly quadrupled. The vast area of the United States and its western territories accounted for some of the disparity between railroad mileage here and in Europe. England, France, and Germany combined contained less land than the states east of the Mississippi River.

Between 1870 and 1880, the amount of track in the country doubled, and it nearly doubled again in the following decade. By 1900, the nation boasted more than 193,000 miles of railroad track—more than in all of Europe and Russia combined (see Global Comparison). To understand how the railroads developed and came to dominate American life, there is no better place to start than with the career of **Jay Gould**, who pioneered the expansion of America's railway system and became the era's most notorious speculator. Jason "Jay" Gould bought his first railroad before he turned twenty-five. It was only sixty-two miles long, in bad repair, and on the brink of failure, but within two years, he sold it at a profit of $130,000.

Gould, by his own admission, knew little about railroads and cared less about their operation. The secretive Gould operated in the stock market like a shark, looking for vulnerable railroads, buying enough stock to take control, and threatening to undercut his competitors until they bought him out at a high profit. The railroads that fell into his hands fared badly and often went bankrupt. Gould's genius lay in cleverly buying and selling railroad stock, not in providing transportation. In the 1880s, he moved to put together a second transcontinental railroad. To defend their interests, his competitors had little choice but to adopt his strategy of expansion and consolidation, which in turn encouraged railroad building and stimulated a national market.

The dramatic growth of the railroads created the country's first big business. Before the Civil War, even the largest textile mill in New England employed no more than 800 workers. In contrast, the Pennsylvania Railroad by the 1870s boasted a payroll of more than 55,000 workers. Capitalized at more than $400 million, the Pennsylvania Railroad constituted the largest private enterprise in the world.

The Republican Party, firmly entrenched in Washington, worked closely with business interests, subsidizing the transcontinental railroad system with land grants of a staggering 100 million acres of public land and $64 million in tax incentives and direct aid. States and local communities joined the railroad boom, knowing that only those towns and villages along the tracks would grow and flourish. The combined federal and state giveaway amounted to more than 180 million acres, an area larger than Texas.

A revolution in communication accompanied and supported the growth of the railroads. The telegraph, developed by Samuel F. B. Morse, marched across the continent alongside the railroad. By transmitting coded messages along electrical wire, the telegraph formed the "nervous system" of the new industrial order. Telegraph service quickly replaced Pony Express mail carriers in the West and transformed business by providing instantaneous communication. Again Jay Gould took the lead. In 1879, through stock manipulation, he seized control of Western Union, the company that monopolized the telegraph industry.

The railroads soon fell on hard times. Already by the 1870s, lack of planning led to overbuilding. On the eastern seaboard, railroads competed fiercely for business. A manufacturer in an area served by competing railroads could get substantially reduced shipping rates in return for promises of steady business. Because railroad owners lost money through this kind of competition, they tried to set up agreements, or "pools," to end cutthroat competition by dividing up territory and setting rates. But these informal gentlemen's agreements invariably failed because men like Jay Gould, intent on undercutting all competitors, refused to play by the rules.

The public's alarm at the control wielded by the new railroad magnates provided a barometer of attitudes toward big business itself. When Gould died in 1892, the press described him as "the world's richest man," estimating his fortune at more than $100 million. His competitor "Commodore" Cornelius Vanderbilt, who built the New York Central Railroad, judged Gould "the smartest man in America." But to the public, he was, as he himself admitted shortly before his death, "the most hated man in America."

Andrew Carnegie, Steel, and Vertical Integration

If Jay Gould was the man Americans loved to hate, **Andrew Carnegie** became one of America's heroes. Unlike Gould, for whom speculation was the game and wealth the goal, Carnegie turned his back on speculation and worked to build something enduring — Carnegie Steel, the biggest steel business in the world during the Gilded Age.

The growth of the steel industry proceeded directly from railroad building. The first railroads ran on iron rails, which cracked and broke with alarming frequency. Steel, both stronger and more flexible than iron, remained too expensive for use

in rails until Englishman Henry Bessemer developed a way to make steel more cheaply from pig iron. Andrew Carnegie, among the first to champion the new "King Steel," came to dominate the emerging industry.

Carnegie, a Scottish immigrant, landed in New York in 1848 at the age of twelve. He rose from a job cleaning bobbins in a textile factory to become one of the richest men in America. Before he died, he gave away more than $300 million, most notably to public libraries. His generosity, combined with his own rise from poverty, burnished his public image. But Carnegie had a darker side: He was a harsh taskmaster who made nearly inhuman demands on his employees.

> When Gould died in 1892, the press described him as "the world's richest man," estimating his fortune at more than $100 million.

When Carnegie was a teenager, his skill as a telegraph operator caught the attention of Tom Scott, superintendent of the Pennsylvania Railroad. Scott hired Carnegie, soon promoted him, and lent him the money for his first foray into Wall Street investment. A millionaire before his thirtieth birthday, Carnegie turned away from speculation and struck out on his own to reshape the iron and steel industry. "My preference was always manufacturing," he wrote. "I wished to make something tangible." By applying the lessons of cost accounting and efficiency that he had learned from twelve years with the Pennsylvania Railroad, Carnegie turned steel into the nation's first manufacturing big business.

In 1872, Andrew Carnegie acquired one hundred acres in Braddock, Pennsylvania, on the outskirts of Pittsburgh, convenient to two railroad lines and fronted by the Monongahela River, a natural highway to Pittsburgh and the Ohio River and to the coal and iron mines farther north. There Carnegie built the largest, most up-to-date Bessemer steel plant in the world. At that time, steelmakers produced about 70 tons a week. Within two decades, Carnegie's blast furnaces poured out an incredible 10,000 tons a week. He soon cut the cost of making rails by more than half, from $58 to $25 a ton. His formula for success was simple: "Cut the prices, scoop the market, run the mills full; watch the costs and profits will take care of themselves."

To guarantee the lowest costs and the maximum output, Carnegie pioneered a system of business organization called **vertical integration**. All aspects of the business were under Carnegie's control — from the mining of iron ore, to its transport on the Great Lakes, to the production of steel. Vertical integration, in the words of one observer, meant that "from the moment these crude stuffs

"What a Funny Little Government" The power wielded by John D. Rockefeller and the Standard Oil Company is captured in this political cartoon by Horace Taylor, which appeared in the January 22, 1900, issue of the *Verdict*. Rockefeller is pictured holding the White House and the Treasury Department in the palm of his hand, while in the background the U.S. Capitol has been converted into an oil refinery. Rockefeller and the company he ran held so much power that many feared democracy itself was threatened in the Gilded Age. Collection of The New-York Historical Society.

FOR MORE HELP ANALYZING THIS IMAGE, see the visual activity for this chapter in the Online Study Guide at bedfordstmartins.com/roarkcompact.

were dug out of the earth until they flowed in a stream of liquid steel in the ladles, there was never a price, profit, or royalty paid to any outsider."

Always Carnegie kept his eyes on the account books, looking for ways to cut costs. The great productivity Carnegie encouraged came at a high price. He deliberately pitted his managers against one another, firing the losers and rewarding the winners with a share in the company. Workers achieved the output Carnegie demanded by enduring low wages, dangerous working conditions, and twelve-hour days six days a week. One worker, commenting on the contradiction between Carnegie's generous philanthropy in endowing public libraries and his tightfisted labor policy, observed, "After working twelve hours, how can a man go to a library?"

By 1900, Andrew Carnegie had become the best-known manufacturer in the nation, and the age of iron had yielded to an age of steel. Steel from Carnegie's mills supported the elevated trains in New York and Chicago, formed the skeleton of the Washington Monument, supported the first steel bridge to span the Mississippi, and girded America's first skyscrapers. Carnegie steel armored the naval fleet that helped make the United States a world power. As a captain of industry, Carnegie's only rival was the titan of the oil industry, John D. Rockefeller.

John D. Rockefeller, Standard Oil, and the Trust Edwin Drake's discovery of oil in Pennsylvania in 1859 sent thousands rushing to the oil fields in search of "black gold." In the days before the automobile and gasoline, crude oil was refined into lubricating oil for machinery and kerosene for lamps, the major source of lighting in nineteenth-century houses before the invention of gas lamps and electric lighting. The amount of capital needed to buy or build an oil refinery in the 1860s and 1870s remained relatively low—less than $25,000, or roughly what it cost to lay one mile of railroad track. With start-up costs so low, the new petroleum industry experienced riotous competition among many small refineries. Ultimately, **John D. Rockefeller** and his Standard Oil Company succeeded in controlling nine-tenths of the oil-refining business.

Rockefeller grew up the son of a shrewd Yankee who peddled quack cures for cancer. Under his father's rough tutelage, he learned how to drive a hard bargain. "I trade with the boys and skin 'em and just beat 'em every time I can," "Big Bill" Rockefeller boasted. "I want to make 'em sharp." John D. learned his lessons well. In 1865, at the age of twenty-five, he controlled the largest oil refinery in Cleveland. Like a growing number of business owners, Rockefeller abandoned partnership or single proprietorship to embrace the corporation as the business structure best suited to maximize profit and minimize personal liability. In 1870, he incorporated his oil business, founding the Standard Oil Company, a behemoth so huge it served as the precursor not only of today's Exxon-Mobil but also of Amoco, Chevron, Sunoco, and ConocoPhillips.

As the largest refiner in Cleveland, Rockefeller demanded secret rebates from the railroads in exchange for his steady business. Rebates enabled Rockefeller to drive out his competitors through predatory pricing. The railroads, facing the pressures of cutthroat competition, needed Rockefeller's business so badly that they gave him a share of the rates that his competitors paid. A Pennsylvania Railroad official later confessed that Rockefeller extracted such huge rebates that the railroad, which could not risk losing his business, sometimes ended up paying him to transport Standard's oil. Secret deals, predatory pricing, and rebates enabled Rockefeller to undercut his competitors and pressure competing refiners to sell out or face ruin.

To gain legal standing for Standard Oil's secret deals, Rockefeller in 1882 pioneered a new form of corporate structure—the **trust**. The trust differed markedly from Carnegie's vertical approach in steel. Instead of attempting to control all aspects of the oil business, from the well to the consumer, Rockefeller used horizontal integration to control the refining process. Several trustees held stock in various refinery companies "in trust" for Standard's stockholders. This elaborate stock swap allowed the trustees to coordinate policy among the refineries, giving Rockefeller a virtual monopoly on the oil-refining business. The Standard Oil trust, valued at more than $70 million, paved the way for trusts in sugar, whiskey, matches, and many other products.

When the federal government responded to public pressure to outlaw the trust as a violation of free trade, Standard Oil changed tactics and reorganized as a holding company. Instead of stockholders in competing companies acting through trustees to set prices and determine territories, the holding company simply brought competing companies under one central administration. No longer technically separate businesses, they could act in concert without violating antitrust laws that forbade companies from forming "combinations in restraint of trade." As Standard Oil's empire grew, Rockefeller ended the independence of the refinery operators and closed inefficient plants. Next he moved to control sources of crude oil and took charge of the transportation and marketing of petroleum products. By the 1890s, Standard Oil ruled more than 90 percent of the oil business, employed 100,000 people, and was the biggest, richest, most feared, and most admired business organization in the world.

John D. Rockefeller enjoyed enormous success in business, but he was not well liked by the public. Before he died in 1937 at the age of ninety-eight, Rockefeller had become the country's first billionaire. But despite his modest habits, his pious Baptist faith, and his many charitable gifts, he never shared in the public affection that Carnegie enjoyed. Editor and journalist Ida M. Tarbell's "History of the Standard Oil Company," which ran for three years (1902–1905) in serial form in *McClure's Magazine*, largely shaped the public's harsh view of Rockefeller.

Ida M. Tarbell had grown up in the Pennsylvania oil region, and her father had owned one of the small refineries gobbled up by Standard Oil. Her devastatingly thorough history chronicled the methods Rockefeller had used to take over the oil industry. Publicly, Rockefeller refused to respond to her allegations, although in private he dubbed her "Miss Tarball." "If I step on that worm I will call attention to it," he explained. "If I ignore it, it will disappear." Yet by the time Tarbell finished publishing her story, Rockefeller slept with a loaded revolver by his bed in fear of would-be assassins. Standard Oil and the man who created it had become the symbol of heartless monopoly. (See "Documenting the American Promise," page 442.)

New Inventions: The Telephone and Electricity The second half of the nineteenth century was an age of invention. Men like Thomas Alva Edison and Alexander Graham Bell became folk heroes. But no matter how dramatic the inventors or the inventions, the new electric and telephone industries pioneered by Edison and Bell soon eclipsed their inventors and fell under the control of bankers and industrialists.

Alexander Graham Bell came to America from Scotland at the age of twenty-four with a passion to find a way to teach the deaf to speak (his wife and mother were deaf). Instead, he developed a way to transmit voice over wire—the telephone. Bell's invention astounded the world when he

Rockefeller and His Critics

No one inspired the nation's fear of industrial consolidation more than John D. Rockefeller, creator of the Standard Oil trust. To many Americans, Rockefeller and "the sovereign state of Standard Oil" came to represent a danger to democracy itself because of the secretive methods and enormous political influence of the corporation and its founder.

DOCUMENT 1
"The Smokeless Rebate," from Henry Demarest Lloyd's *Wealth against Commonwealth*, 1894

As early as 1881, Henry Demarest Lloyd introduced Rockefeller to a national audience by attacking Standard Oil and its founder in "The Story of a Great Monopoly," published in the February issue of Atlantic Monthly. *The public snapped up the exposé—the issue went through six printings. In 1894, Lloyd published* Wealth against Commonwealth, *a full-scale exposé of the company. To avoid charges of libel, Lloyd used no names, but readers knew he referred to Rockefeller and Standard Oil. Here Lloyd describes how Rockefeller used illegal railroad rebates to best his competitors.*

That entirely modern social arrangement—the private ownership of [railroads]—has introduced a new weapon into business warfare which means universal dominion to him who will use it with an iron hand.

This weapon is the rebate, smokeless, noiseless, invisible, of extraordinary range, and the deadliest gun known to commercial warfare. It is not a lawful weapon.

. . . It has to be used secretly. All the rates [Rockefeller] . . . got were a secret between himself and the railroads. "It has never been otherwise," testified one of the oil combination.

The smokeless rebate makes the secret of success in business to be not manufacture, but manufacture—breaking down with a strong hand the true makers of things. To those who can get the rebate it makes no difference who does the digging, building, mining, making, producing the million forms of wealth they covet for themselves. They need only get control of the roads. . . . Builders, not of manufactories, but of privileges; inventors only of schemes . . . , contrivers, not of competition, but of ways to tax the property of their competitors into their pockets. They need not make money; they can take it from those who have made it.

SOURCE: Henry Demarest Lloyd, *Wealth against Commonwealth* (New York: Harper & Brothers, 1894), 474–75, 488.

DOCUMENT 2
Ida M. Tarbell, "The Oil War of 1872"

Editor and journalist Ida Minerva Tarbell, whose "History of the Standard Oil Company" ran for three years (1902–1905) in serial form in McClure's Magazine, *proved Rockefeller's most damaging critic. Tarbell grew up in the Pennsylvania oil region; her father had owned a small refinery gobbled up by Standard Oil. In a devastatingly thorough history, she chronicled the underhanded methods Rockefeller used*

demonstrated it at the Philadelphia Centennial Exposition in 1876. Dumbfounded by the display, the emperor of Brazil cried out, "My God, it talks!"

In 1880, Bell's company, American Bell, pioneered "long lines" (long-distance telephone service), creating American Telephone and Telegraph (AT&T) as a subsidiary. In 1900, AT&T became the parent company of the system as a whole, controlling Western Electric, which manufactured and installed the equipment, and coordinating the Bell regional divisions. This complicated organizational structure meant that Americans could communicate not only

locally but also across the country. And unlike a telegraph message, which had to be written out and taken to a telegraph station, sent over the wire, and then delivered by hand to the recipient, the telephone connected both parties immediately and privately. Bell's invention proved a boon to business, contributing to speed and efficiency. The number of telephones soared, reaching 310,000 in 1895 and more than 1.5 million in 1900.

Even more than Alexander Graham Bell, inventor **Thomas Alva Edison** embodied the old-fashioned virtues of Yankee ingenuity and rugged individualism that Americans most admired. A self-educated dynamo, he worked twenty hours *to gain control of the oil-refining industry. Here she portrays a critical chapter in the history of Standard Oil: In 1879, Rockefeller's first attempt to consolidate the oil industry through the use of illegal rebates had failed.*

If Mr. Rockefeller had been an ordinary man the outburst of popular contempt and suspicion which suddenly poured on his head would have thwarted and crushed him. But he was no ordinary man. He had the powerful imagination to see what might be done with the oil business if it could be centered in his hands—the intelligence to analyze the problem into its elements and to find the key to control. He had the essential element to all great achievement, a steadfastness to a purpose once conceived which nothing can crush. The Oil Regions might rage, call him a conspirator and those who sold to him traitors; the railroads might withdraw their contracts and the legislature annul his charter; undisturbed and unresting he kept at this great purpose. . . .

He got a rebate. . . . How much less a rate than $1.25 Mr. Rockefeller had before the end of April the writer does not know. Of course the rate was secret and he probably understood now, as he had not two months before, how essential it was that he keep it secret. His task was more difficult now, for he had an enemy active, clamorous, contemptuous, whose suspicions had reached that acute point where they could believe nothing but evil of him—the producers and independents of the Oil Regions. . . .

They believed in independent effort—every man for himself and fair play for all. They wanted competition, loved open fight. They considered that all business should be done openly—that railways were bound as public carriers to give equal rates—that any combination which favored one firm or one locality at the expense of another was unjust and illegal. . . .

Those theories which the body of oil men held as vital and fundamental Mr. Rockefeller and his associates either did not comprehend or were deaf to. This lack of comprehension by many men of what seems to other men to be the most obvious principles of justice is not rare. Many men who are widely known as good, share it. Mr. Rockefeller was "good." There was no more faithful Baptist in Cleveland than he. Every enterprise of that church he had supported liberally from youth. He gave to its poor. He visited its sick. He wept with its suffering. Moreover, he gave unostentatiously to many outside charities of whose worthiness he was satisfied. He was simple and frugal in his habits. He never went to the theater, never drank wine. He was a devoted husband, and he gave much time to the training of his children. . . . Yet he was willing to strain every nerve to obtain for himself special and illegal privileges from the railroads.

SOURCE: From pages 77–79 in *Muckraking: Three Landmark Articles* by Ellen F. Fitzpatrick, ed. Copyright © 1994. Reprinted with permission of St. Martin's Press. Originally published in *McClure's Magazine,* January 1903.

Questions for Analysis and Debate

1. Henry Demarest Lloyd and Ida Tarbell agree that Rockefeller gained control of the oil industry through illegal methods. What was his primary weapon, and how did it operate?

2. Compare Lloyd's style to that of Tarbell. Which is more effective and why? Was either one of these journalists an impartial observer?

3. Rockefeller never responded to his critics. Do you think Rockefeller's silence was a good strategy? Why or why not?

a day in his laboratory in Menlo Park, New Jersey, vowing to turn out "a minor invention every ten days and a big thing every six months or so." He almost made good on his promise. At the height of his career, he averaged a patent every eleven days and invented such "big things" as the phonograph, the motion picture camera, and the filament for the incandescent lightbulb.

Edison, in competition with George W. Westinghouse, pioneered the use of electricity as an energy source. By the late nineteenth century, electricity had become a part of American urban life. It powered trolley cars and lighted factories, homes, and office buildings. Indeed, electricity

became so prevalent in urban life that it symbolized the city, whose bright lights contrasted with rural America, left largely in the dark because private enterprise judged it not profitable enough to run electric lines to outlying farms and ranches.

While Americans thrilled to the new electric cities and the changes wrought by inventors, the day of the inventor quietly yielded to the heyday of the corporation. In 1892, the electric industry consolidated. Reflecting a nationwide trend in business, Edison General Electric dropped the name of its inventor, becoming simply General Electric (GE). For years, an embittered Edison refused to set foot

THE PROMISE OF TECHNOLOGY

AN UNRESTRAINED DEMON.

Electrifying America This 1889 cartoon was part of a campaign Thomas Edison waged against George Westinghouse in what came to be known as the "war of the currents." With the system of how best to provide electric current to the nation at stake, Edison launched a massive public relations campaign to discredit the high-voltage alternating current (AC) favored by Westinghouse. In the cartoon, innocent pedestrians are electrocuted by the wires as a policeman runs for help. The skull in the wires attached to the electric lightbulb warns that this new technology can be deadly. Although the direct current (DC) Edison championed was less dangerous to handle, it could reach only a one-mile radius from a power station. Despite his campaign to discredit Westinghouse, Edison lost the war of the currents. Cities that wanted electric lighting found Westinghouse's alternating current (AC), despite the dangers of high voltage, less expensive and better suited to their needs. Granger Collection.

inside a GE building. General Electric could afford to overlook the slight. A prime example of the trend toward business consolidation taking place in the 1890s, GE soon dominated the market.

> **Q:** How did John D. Rockefeller gain control of 90 percent of the oil-refining business by 1890?

From Competition to Consolidation

Even as Rockefeller and Carnegie built their empires, the era of the "robber barons," as they were dubbed by their detractors, was drawing to a close. Increasingly, businesses replaced partnerships and sole proprietorships with the anonymous corporate structure that would come to dominate the twentieth century. At the same time, mergers led to the creation of huge new corporations.

Banks and financiers played a key role in this consolidation, so much so that the decades at the turn of the twentieth century can be characterized as a period of **finance capitalism**—investment sponsored by banks and bankers. When the depression that followed the panic of 1893 bankrupted many businesses, bankers stepped in to bring order and to reorganize major industries. During these years, a new social philosophy based on the theories of naturalist Charles Darwin helped to justify consolidation and to inhibit state or federal regulation of business. A conservative Supreme Court further frustrated attempts to control business by consistently declaring unconstitutional legislation designed to regulate railroads or to outlaw trusts and monopolies.

J. P. Morgan and Finance Capitalism John Pierpont Morgan, the preeminent finance capitalist of the late nineteenth century, loathed competition and sought whenever possible to eliminate it by substituting consolidation and central control. Morgan's passion for order made him the architect of business mergers. The son of a prominent banker, **J. P. Morgan** inherited along with his wealth the stern business code of the old-fashioned merchant bankers, men who valued character and

J. P. Morgan, Photograph by Edward Steichen Few photographs of J. P. Morgan exist. Morgan, who suffered from a skin condition that left him with a misshapen strawberry of a nose, rarely allowed his picture to be taken. But it was his eyes that people remembered — eyes so piercing that Edward Steichen, who took this photograph, observed that "meeting his gaze was a little like confronting the headlights of an express train." George Eastman House. Reprinted with permission of Joanna T. Steichen.

reputation. Aloof and silent, Morgan looked down on the climbers and the speculators with a haughtiness that led his rivals to call him "Jupiter," after the ruler of the Roman gods. At the turn of the twentieth century, he dominated American banking, exerting an influence so powerful that his critics charged he controlled a vast "money trust."

Morgan acted as a power broker in the reorganization of the railroads and the creation of industrial giants such as General Electric and U.S. Steel. When the railroads fell on hard times in the 1890s, he used his access to capital to rescue embattled, wrecked, and ruined companies. Morgan quickly took over the struggling railroads and moved to eliminate competition by creating what he called "a community of interest" among the managers he handpicked. By the time he finished reorganizing the railroads, Morgan had concentrated the nation's rail lines in the hands of a few directors who controlled two-thirds of the nation's track.

Banker control of the railroads rationalized, or coordinated, the industry. But stability came at a high price. To keep investors happy and to guarantee huge profits from the sale of stock, Morgan heavily "watered" the stock of the railroads, issuing more shares than the assets of the company warranted. J. P. Morgan & Co. made millions of dollars from commissions and from blocks of stock acquired through reorganization. The flagrant overcapitalization created by the watered stock hurt the railroads in the long run, saddling them with enormous debt. Equally harmful was the management style of the Morgan directors. Bankers, not railroad men, they aimed at short-term profit and discouraged the continued technological and organizational innovation needed to run the railroads effectively.

In 1898, Morgan moved into the steel industry, directly challenging Andrew Carnegie. Morgan supervised the mergers of several smaller steel companies, which soon expanded from the manufacture of finished goods to compete head-to-head with Carnegie in steel production. The pugnacious Carnegie cabled his partners in the summer of 1900: "Action essential: crisis has arrived . . . have no fear as to the result; victory certain." The press trumpeted news of the impending fight between the feisty Scot and the haughty Wall Street banker, but what the papers called the "battle of the giants" in the end proved little more than the wily maneuvering of two businessmen so adept that even today it is difficult to say who won. For all his belligerence, the sixty-six-year-old Carnegie yearned to retire to Skibo Castle, his home in Scotland. He may well have welcomed Morgan's bid for power. Morgan, who disdained haggling, agreed to pay Carnegie's asking price, $480 million (the equivalent of about $10 billion in today's currency). According to legend, when Carnegie later teased Morgan, saying that he should have asked $100 million more, Morgan replied, "You would have got it if you had."

Morgan's acquisition of Carnegie Steel signaled the passing of the old entrepreneurial order personified by Andrew Carnegie and the arrival of a new, anonymous corporate world. The banker quickly moved to pull together Carnegie's chief competitors to form a huge new corporation, United States Steel, known today as USX. Created in 1901 and capitalized at $1.4 billion, U.S. Steel was the largest corporation in the world. Yet for all its size, it did not hold a monopoly in the steel industry. Significant small competitors, such as Bethlehem Steel, remained independent, creating a competitive system called an oligopoly, in which several companies control production. The smaller manufacturers simply followed the lead of U.S. Steel in setting prices and dividing the market so that each company held a comfortable share. Although oligopoly did not entirely eliminate competition, it did effectively blunt it.

Homestead Steelworks The Homestead steelworks, outside Pittsburgh, is pictured shortly after J. P. Morgan bought out Andrew Carnegie and created U.S. Steel, the precursor of today's USX. Try to count the smokestacks in the picture. Air pollution on this scale posed a threat to the health of citizens and made for a dismal landscape. Workers complained that trees would not grow in Homestead. Hagley Museum & Library.

When J. P. Morgan died in 1913, his estate totaled $68 million, not counting an estimated $50 million in art treasures. Andrew Carnegie, who gave away more than $300 million before his death six years later, is said to have quipped, "And to think he was not a rich man!" But Carnegie's gibe missed the mark. The quest for power, not wealth, had motivated J. P. Morgan, and his power could best be measured not in the millions he owned but in the billions he controlled. Even more than Carnegie or Rockefeller, Morgan left his stamp on the twentieth century and formed the model for corporate consolidation that economists and social scientists soon justified with a new social theory known as social Darwinism.

Social Darwinism, Laissez Faire, and the Supreme Court John D. Rockefeller Jr., the son of the founder of Standard Oil, once remarked to his Baptist Bible class that the Standard Oil Company, like the American Beauty rose, resulted from "pruning the early buds that grew up around it." The elimination of smaller, inefficient units, he said, was "merely the working out of a law of nature and a law of God." The comparison of the business world to the natural world gave rise to a theory of society based on the law of evolution formulated by British naturalist Charles Darwin.

In his monumental work *On the Origin of Species* (1859), Darwin theorized that in the struggle for survival, adaptation to the environment triggered among species a natural selection process that led to evolution. Herbert Spencer in Britain and William Graham Sumner in the United States developed the theory of **social Darwinism**. The social Darwinists concluded that progress came about as a result of relentless competition in which the strong survived and the weak died out.

In social terms, the idea of the "survival of the fittest" had profound significance, as Sumner, a professor of political economy at Yale University, made clear in his 1883 book *What Social Classes Owe to Each Other*. "The drunkard in the gutter is just where he ought to be, according to the fitness and tendency of things," Sumner insisted. Conversely, "millionaires are the product of natural selection," and although "they get high wages and live in luxury," Sumner claimed, "the bargain is a good one for society."

Social Darwinists equated wealth and power with "fitness" and believed that the unfit should be allowed to die off to advance the progress of humanity. Any efforts by the rich to aid the poor would only tamper with the rigid laws of nature and slow down evolution. Social Darwinism acted to curb social reform while at the same time glorifying great wealth. In an age when Rockefeller and Carnegie amassed hundreds of millions of dollars (billions in today's currency) and the average worker earned $500 a year, social Darwinism justified economic inequality.

Andrew Carnegie softened some of the harshness of social Darwinism in his essay "The Gospel of Wealth," published in 1889. The millionaire, Carnegie wrote, acted as a "mere trustee and agent for his poorer brethren, bringing to their service his superior wisdom, experience, and ability to administer, doing for them better than they could or would do for themselves." Carnegie preached philanthropy and urged the rich to "live unostentatious lives" and "administer surplus wealth for the good of the people." His **gospel of wealth** earned much praise but won few converts. Most millionaires followed the lead of J. P. Morgan, who contributed to charity but amassed private treasures in his marble library.

Social Darwinism nicely suited an age in which the gross inequalities accompanying industrialization seemed to cry out for action. Assuaging the nation's conscience, social Darwinism justified neglect of the poor in the name of "race progress." With so many of the poor coming from different races and ethnicities, social Darwinism fueled racism. A new "scientific racism" purported to prove "Anglo-Saxons" superior to all other groups. Social Darwinism buttressed the status quo and reassured comfortable, white Americans that all was as it should be. Even the gospel of wealth, which mitigated the harshest dictates of social Darwinism, insisted that Americans lived in the best of all possible worlds and that the rich were the natural rulers.

Social Darwinism, with its emphasis on the free play of competition and the survival of the fittest, encouraged the economic theory of **laissez-faire** (French for "let it alone"). Business argued that government should not meddle in economic affairs, conveniently ignoring the huge land grants and protective tariffs that benefited industry. During the 1880s and 1890s, a conservative Supreme Court in a series of landmark decisions used the Fourteenth Amendment—originally intended to protect freed slaves from state laws violating their rights—to protect corporations from taxation, regulation, labor organization, and antitrust legislation. Only in the arena of politics did Americans attempt to tackle the power of corporate capitalism.

> **Q:** Why did the ideas of social Darwinism appeal to many Americans in the late nineteenth century?

Politics and Culture

For many Americans, politics provided a source of identity, a means of livelihood, and a ready form of entertainment. A variety of factors contributed to the complicated interplay of politics and culture. Patronage provided an economic incentive for voter participation, but ethnicity, religion, sectional loyalty, race, and gender all influenced the political life of the period.

Political Participation and Party Loyalty

Patronage proved a strong motivation for party loyalty among many voters. Political parties in power doled out federal, state, and local government jobs to their loyal supporters. With hundreds of thousands of jobs to be filled, the choice of party affiliation could mean the difference between a paycheck and an empty pocket. Money greased the wheels of this system of patronage, dubbed the **spoils system** from the adage "to the victor go the spoils." With their livelihoods tied to their party identity, government employees in particular had an incentive to vote in great numbers.

Political affiliation provided a powerful sense of group identity for many voters proud of their loyalty to the Democrats or the Republicans. Democrats, who traced the party's roots back to Thomas Jefferson, called theirs "the party of the fathers." The Republican Party, founded in the 1850s, still claimed strong loyalties as a result of its alignment with the Union during the Civil War. Noting the power of old sectional loyalties, one of the party faithful observed, "Iowa will go Democratic when Hell goes Methodist." Republicans proved particularly adept at evoking Civil War loyalty, using a tactic called "waving the bloody shirt"—reminding voters which side they had fought for in the Civil War.

Religion and ethnicity also played a significant role in politics. In the North, Protestants from the old-line denominations, particularly Presbyterians and Methodists, flocked to the Republican Party, which championed a series of moral reforms, including local laws requiring businesses to close in observance of the Sabbath. In the burgeoning cities, the Democratic Party courted immigrants and working-class Catholic and Jewish voters charging, rightly, that Republican moral crusades often masked attacks on immigrant culture.

Sectionalism and the New South

After the end of Reconstruction, most white voters in the former Confederate states remained loyal Democrats, voting for Democratic candidates in every presidential election for the next seventy years. Labeling the Republican Party the agent of "Negro rule," Democrats urged white southerners to "vote the way you shot." Yet the so-called solid South proved far from solid on the state and local levels. The economic plight of the South led to shifting political alliances and to third-party movements that challenged Democratic attempts to define politics along race lines and maintain the Democratic Party as the white man's party.

The South's economy, devastated by the war, foundered at the same time the North experienced an unprecedented industrial boom. Soon an influential group of southerners called for a **New South** modeled on the industrial North. Henry Grady, the ebullient young editor of the *Atlanta Constitution*, used his paper's influence (it boasted the largest circulation of any weekly in the country) to extol the virtues of a new industrial South. Part bully, part booster, Grady exhorted the South to use its natural advantages—cheap labor and abundant natural resources—to go head-to-head in competition with northern industry.

Grady's message fell on receptive ears. Many southerners, men and women, black and white, joined the national migration from farm to city, leaving the old plantations to molder and decay. With the end of military rule in 1877, southern Democrats took back state governments, calling themselves "Redeemers." Yet rather than restore the economy of the old planter class, they embraced northern promoters who promised prosperity and profits.

The railroads came first, opening up the region for industrial development. Southern railroad mileage grew fourfold from 1865 to 1890. The number of cotton spindles also soared as textile mill owners abandoned New England in search of the cheap labor and proximity to raw materials promised in the South. By 1900, the South had become the nation's leading producer of cloth, and more than 100,000 southerners, many of them women and children, worked in the region's textile mills.

The New South prided itself most on its iron and steel industry, which grew up in the area surrounding Birmingham, Alabama. During this period, the smokestack replaced the white-pillared plantation as the symbol of the New South. Andrew Carnegie toured the region in 1889 and observed, "The South is Pennsylvania's most formidable industrial enemy." But southern industry remained controlled by northern investors, who had no intention of letting the South beat the North at its own game. Elaborate mechanisms rigged the price of southern steel, inflating it, as one northern insider confessed, "for the purpose of protecting the Pittsburgh mills and in turn the Pittsburgh steel users." Similarly, in the lumber and mining industries, investors in the North and abroad, not southerners, reaped the lion's share of the profits.

In only one industry did the South truly dominate—tobacco. Capitalizing on the invention of a machine for rolling cigarettes, the American Tobacco Company, founded by the Duke family of North Carolina, eventually dominated the industry. As cigarettes replaced chewing tobacco in popularity at the turn of the twentieth century, a booming market developed for Duke's "ready mades." Soon the company sold 400,000 cigarettes a day.

In practical terms, the industrialized New South proved an illusion. Much of the South remained agricultural, caught in the grip of the insidious crop lien system (see chapter 16). White southern farmers, desperate to get out of debt, sometimes joined with African Americans to pursue their goals politically. Between 1865 and 1900, voters in every state south of the Mason-Dixon line experimented with political alliances that crossed the color line. In Virginia, the "Readjusters," a coalition of blacks and whites determined to "readjust" (lower) the state debt and spend more money on public education, captured state offices from 1879 to 1883. In southern politics, the interplay of race and gender made coalitions like the Readjusters a potent threat to the status quo.

Gender, Race, and Politics Gender—society's notion of what constitutes acceptable masculine or feminine behavior—influenced politics throughout the nineteenth century. From the early days of the Republic, citizenship had been defined in male terms. Citizenship and its prerogatives (voting and officeholding) served as a badge of manliness and rested on its corollary, patriarchy—the power and authority men exerted over their wives and families. With the advent of universal (white) male suffrage in the early nineteenth century, gender eclipsed class as the defining feature of citizenship; men's dominance over women provided the common thread that knit all white men together politically. The concept of separate spheres dictated political participation for men only. Once the public sphere of political participation became equated with manhood, women found themselves increasingly restricted to the private sphere of home and hearth.

Gender permeated politics in other ways, especially in the New South. Cross-racial alliances like the Readjusters rested on the belief that universal political rights (voting, officeholding, patronage) could be extended to black males in the public sphere without eliminating racial barriers in the private sphere. Democrats, for their part, fought back by trying to convince voters that black voting would inevitably lead to miscegenation (racial mixing). Black male political power and sexual power, they warned, went hand in hand. Ultimately, their arguments prevailed, and many whites returned to the Democratic fold to protect "white womanhood" and with it white supremacy.

The notion that black men threatened white southern womanhood reached its most vicious form in the practice of lynching—the killing and mutilation of black men by white mobs. By 1892, the practice had become so prevalent that a courageous black woman, **Ida B. Wells**, launched an antilynching movement. That year, a white mob lynched a friend of Wells's whose grocery store competed too successfully with a white-owned store. Wells shrewdly concluded that lynching served "as an excuse to get rid of Negroes who were acquiring wealth and property and thus keep the race terrorized." She began to collect data on lynching and discovered that in the decade between 1882 and 1892, lynching rose in the South by an overwhelming 200 percent, with more than 241 people killed. The vast increase in lynching testified to the retreat of the federal government following Reconstruction and to white southerners' determination to maintain supremacy through terrorism and intimidation.

Wells struck back. As the first salvo in her attack, she put to rest the "old threadbare lie that Negro men assault white women." As she pointed out, violations of black women by white men, which were much more frequent than black attacks on white women, went unnoticed and unpunished. Wells articulated lynching as a problem of race and gender. She insisted that the myth of black attacks on white southern women masked the reality that mob violence had more to do with economics and the shifting social structure of the South than with rape. She demonstrated in a sophisticated way how the southern patriarchal system, having lost its control over blacks with the end of slavery, used its control over women to circumscribe the liberty of black men.

Wells's strong stance immediately resulted in reprisal. While she was traveling in the North, vandals ransacked her office in Tennessee and destroyed her printing equipment. Yet the warning that she would be killed on sight if she ever returned to Memphis only stiffened her resolve. As she wrote in her autobiography, *Crusade for Justice* (1928), "Having lost my paper, had a price put on my life and been made an exile . . . , I felt that I owed it to myself and to my race to tell the whole truth now that I was where I could do so freely." As a reporter, first for the *New York Age* and later for the *Chicago Inter-Ocean*, she used every opportunity to hammer home her message. Beginning in 1894 and continuing for decades, antilynching bills were introduced in Congress, only to be defeated by southern opposition.

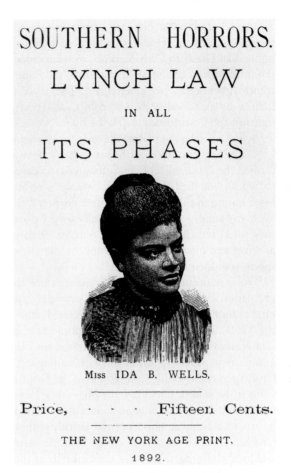

Ida B. Wells Ida B. Wells began her antilynching campaign in 1892 after a friend's murder led her to examine the problem of lynching in the South. She spread her message in lectures and pamphlets like this one, distributed for fifteen cents. Wells brought the horror of lynching to a national and international audience and mobilized other African American women to undertake social action under the auspices of the National Association of Colored Women. She later became a founding member of the National Association for the Advancement of Colored People (NAACP). Manuscript, Archives and Rare Books Division, Schomburg Center for Research in Black Culture, The New York Public Library, Astor, Lenox, and Tilden Foundations.

Lynching did not end during Ida B. Wells's lifetime, but Wells's forceful voice brought the issue to national and international prominence. At her funeral in 1931, black leader W. E. B. Du Bois eulogized Wells as the woman who "began the awakening of the conscience of the nation." Wells's determined campaign against lynching provided just one example of women's political activism during the Gilded Age. The suffrage and temperance movements, along with the growing popularity of women's clubs, dramatized how women refused to be relegated to a separate sphere that kept them out of politics.

Women's Activism No one better recognized the potency of the gendered notion of political rights than Elizabeth Cady Stanton, who lamented the introduction of the word *male* into the Fourteenth Amendment (see chapter 16). The explicit linking of manhood with citizenship and voting rights in the Constitution marked a major setback for reformers who supported the vote for women. In 1869, Stanton along with Susan B. Anthony formed the National Woman Suffrage Association (NWSA), the first independent woman's rights organization in the United States (see chapter 20). Women found ways to act politically long before they voted and cleverly used their moral authority as wives and mothers to move from the domestic sphere into the realm of politics.

The extraordinary activity of women's clubs in the period following the Civil War provides just one example. Women's clubs proliferated from the 1860s to the 1890s, often in response to the exclusionary policies of men's organizations. In 1868, newspaper reporter Jane Cunningham Croly (pen name Jennie June) founded the Sorosis Club in New York City after the New York Press Club denied entry to women journalists wishing to attend a banquet honoring the British author Charles Dickens. In 1890, Croly brought state and local clubs together under the umbrella of the **General Federation of Women's Clubs** (GFWC). Not wanting to alienate southern women, the GFWC barred black women's clubs from joining, despite their vehement objections. Women's clubs soon turned from literary pursuits to politics and reform, endorsing an end to child labor, supporting the eight-hour workday, and helping pass pure food and drug legislation.

The temperance movement (the movement to end drunkenness) attracted by far the largest number of organized women in the late nineteenth century. By the late 1860s and 1870s, the liquor business flourished, with about one saloon for every fifty males over the age of fifteen. During the winter of 1873–74, temperance women adopted a radical new tactic. Armed with Bibles and singing hymns, they marched on taverns and saloons and refused to leave until the proprietors signed a pledge to quit selling liquor. Known as the Woman's Crusade, the movement spread like a prairie fire through small towns in Ohio, Indiana, Michigan, and Illinois and soon moved east into New York, New England, and Pennsylvania. Before it was over, more than 100,000 women had marched in more than 450 cities and towns.

The women's tactics may have been new, but the temperance movement dated back to the 1820s. Originally, the movement was led by Protestant men who organized clubs to pledge voluntary abstinence from liquor. By the 1850s, temperance advocates won significant victories when states, starting with Maine, passed laws to prohibit the sale of liquor (known as "Maine laws"). The Woman's Crusade dramatically brought the issue of temperance back into the national spotlight and led to the formation of a new organization, the **Woman's Christian Temperance Union** (WCTU) in 1874. Composed entirely of women, the WCTU advocated total abstinence from alcohol.

Temperance provided women with a respectable outlet for their increasing resentment of women's inferior status and their growing recognition of women's capabilities. In its first five years, the WCTU relied on education and moral suasion, but when Frances Willard became president in 1879, she politicized the organization (see chapter 20). When the women of the WCTU joined with the Prohibition Party (formed in 1869 by a group of evangelical clergymen), one wag observed, "Politics is a man's game, an' women, childhern, and prohyibitionists do well to keep out iv it." By sharing power with women, the Prohibitionist men violated the old political rules and risked attacks on their honor and manhood.

Even though they could not yet vote, women found ways to affect the political process. Like men, they displayed strong party loyalties and rallied around traditional Republican and Democratic candidates. Third parties courted women, recognizing that their volunteer labor and support could be key assets in party building. Nevertheless, despite growing political awareness among women, politics, particularly presidential politics, remained an exclusively male prerogative.

 How did race and gender influence politics?

Presidential Politics

The presidents of the Gilded Age, from Rutherford B. Hayes (1877–1881) to William McKinley (1897–1901), are largely forgotten men, primarily because so little was expected of them. Until the 1890s, few Americans thought the president or the national government had any role to play in addressing the problems accompanying the nation's industrial transformation. The dominant creed of laissez-faire, coupled with the dictates of social Darwinism, warned government to leave business alone. Still, presidents in the Gilded Age grappled with corruption and party strife and struggled toward the creation of new political ethics designed to replace patronage with a civil service system that promised to award jobs on the basis of merit, not party loyalty.

Corruption and Party Strife

The political corruption and party factionalism that characterized the administration of Ulysses S. Grant (1869–1877) continued to trouble the nation in the 1880s. The spoils system—awarding jobs for political purposes—remained the driving force in party politics at all levels of government in the Gilded Age. Pro-business Republicans generally held a firm grip on the White House, while Democrats had better luck in Congress. Both parties relied on patronage to cement party loyalty. Reformers eager to replace the spoils system with civil service faced an uphill battle.

A small but determined group of reformers championed a new ethics that would preclude politicians from getting rich from public office. The selection of U.S. senators particularly concerned them. Under the Constitution, senators were selected by state legislatures, not directly elected by the voters. Powerful business interests often contrived to control state legislatures and through them U.S. senators. As journalist Henry Demarest Lloyd quipped, Standard Oil "had done everything to the Pennsylvania legislature except to refine it." Nothing prevented a senator from collecting a paycheck from any of the great corporations. So many did so that political cartoonists often portrayed senators as huge money bags labeled with the names of the corporations they served. In this climate, a constitutional amendment calling for the direct election of senators faced stiff opposition from entrenched interests.

Republican president **Rutherford B. Hayes**, whose disputed election in 1876 signaled the end of Reconstruction in the South, tried to steer a middle course between spoilsmen and reformers. Although the Democratic press ridiculed him as "Rutherfraud" because he had not been popularly elected (see chapter 16), Hayes proved a hard-working, well-informed executive who wanted peace, prosperity, and an end to party strife. Yet the Republican Party remained divided into factions led by strong party bosses who boasted that they could make or break any president.

Foremost among the Republican bosses in the Senate stood **Roscoe Conkling** of New York, a master spoilsman who ridiculed civil service as "snivel service." He and his followers, called the "Stalwarts," represented the Grant faction of the party. Conkling's archrival, Senator **James G. Blaine** of Maine, led the "Half Breeds." Not as openly corrupt as the Grant wing of the party, the Half Breeds and their champion were

nevertheless tainted with charges of corruption. A third group, called the "Mugwumps," consisted primarily of reform-minded Republicans from Massachusetts and New York who deplored the spoils system and advocated **civil service reform**. The name "Mugwump" came from the Algonquian word for chief, but critics used the term derisively, punning that the Mugwumps straddled the fence on issues of party loyalty, "with their mug on one side and wump on the other."

President Hayes's middle course pleased no one, and he soon managed to alienate all factions of his party. No one was surprised when he announced that he would not seek reelection in 1880. To avoid choosing among its factions, the Republican Party in 1880 nominated a dark-horse candidate, Representative **James A. Garfield** from Ohio. To appease Conkling, they picked Stalwart Chester A. Arthur as the vice presidential candidate. The Democrats made an attempt to overcome sectionalism and establish a national party by selecting as their presidential standard-bearer an old Union general, Winfield Scott Hancock. But as one observer noted, "It is a peculiarly constituted party that sends rebel brigadiers to Congress because of their rebellion, and then nominates a Union General as its candidate for president because of his loyalty." Hancock garnered only lukewarm support, receiving just 155 electoral votes to Garfield's 214, although the popular vote was less lopsided.

> As journalist Henry Demarest Lloyd quipped, Standard Oil "had done everything to the Pennsylvania legislature except to refine it."

Hayes Campaign Lantern, 1876 Republicans carried this lantern in the presidential campaign of 1876. Designed for nighttime rallies, the lantern featured paper transparencies that allowed light to shine through the stars and illuminate the portrait of the candidate, Rutherford B. Hayes. Marching men with lighted lanterns held aloft must have been a dramatic sight in small towns across the country, where politics constituted a major form of entertainment in the nineteenth century. Collection of Janice L. and David J. Frent.

Garfield's Assassination and Civil Service Reform

"My God," Garfield swore after only a few months in office, "what is there in this place that a man should ever want to get into it?" Garfield, like Hayes, faced the difficult task of remaining independent while pacifying the party bosses and placating the reformers. As the federal bureaucracy grew to nearly 150,000 jobs, thousands of office seekers swarmed to the nation's capital, each clamoring for a position. In the days before Secret Service protection, the White House door stood open to all comers. Garfield took a fatalistic view. "Assassination," he told a friend, "can no more be guarded against than death by lightning, and it is best not to worry about either."

On July 2, 1881, less than four months after taking office, Garfield was shot. His assailant, Charles Guiteau, though clearly insane, turned out to be a disappointed office seeker who claimed to be motivated by political partisanship. He told the police officer who arrested him, "I did it; I will go to jail for it; Arthur is president, and I am a Stalwart." Throughout the hot summer, the country kept a deathwatch as Garfield lingered. When he died in September, Chester A. Arthur became president. The press almost universally condemned Republican factionalism for creating the political climate that produced Guiteau and led to the second political assassination in a generation.

Stalwart Roscoe Conkling saw his hopes for the White House dashed. Attacks on the spoils system increased, and the public joined the chorus calling for reform. Both parties claimed credit for passage of the Pendleton Civil Service Act of 1883, which established a permanent Civil Service Commission consisting of three members appointed by the president. Some fourteen thousand jobs came under a merit system that required examinations for office and made it impossible to remove jobholders for political reasons. The new law also prohibited federal jobholders from contributing to political campaigns, thus drying up the major source of the party bosses' revenue. Soon, business interests stepped in to replace officeholders as the nation's chief political contributors. Ironically, civil service reform thus gave business an even greater influence in political life.

Reform and Scandal: The Campaign of 1884

With Conkling's downfall, James G. Blaine assumed leadership of the Republican Party and at long last captured the presidential nomination in 1884. A magnetic Irish American, Blaine inspired such devotion that his supporters called themselves Blainiacs. But Mugwumps like editor Carl Schurz insisted that Blaine "wallowed in spoils like a rhinoceros in an African pool." They bolted the party and embraced the Democrats' presidential nominee, the stolid **Grover Cleveland**, reform governor of New York. The burly, beer-drinking Cleveland distinguished himself from an entire generation of politicians by the simple motto "A public office is a public trust." First as mayor of Buffalo and later as governor of New York, he built a reputation for honesty, economy, and administrative efficiency. The Democrats, who had not won the presidency since 1856, had high hopes for his candidacy, especially after the Mugwumps threw their support to Cleveland, insisting that "the paramount issue this year is moral rather than political."

The Mugwumps soon regretted their words. The 1884 contest degenerated so far into scandal and nasty mudslinging that one disgusted journalist styled it "the vilest campaign ever waged." In July, Cleveland's hometown paper, the *Buffalo Telegraph*, dropped the bombshell that the candidate had fathered an illegitimate child in an affair with a local widow. Cleveland, a bachelor, stoically accepted responsibility for the child. Crushed by the scandal, the Mugwumps lost much of their enthusiasm. At public rallies, Blaine's partisans taunted Cleveland, chanting, "Ma, Ma, where's my Pa?" Silent but fuming, Cleveland waged his campaign in the traditional fashion by staying home.

Blaine set a new campaign style by launching a whirlwind national tour. On a last-minute stop in New York City, the exhausted candidate committed a misstep that may have cost him the election. He overlooked a remark by a supporter, a local clergyman who cast a slur on Catholic voters by styling

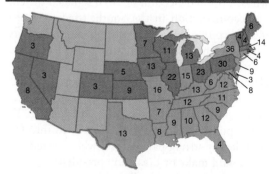

Candidate	Electoral Vote	Popular Vote	Percent of Popular Vote
Grover Cleveland (Democrat)	219	4,874,986	48.5*
James G. Blaine (Republican)	182	4,851,981	48.3

*Percentages do not total 100 because some popular votes went to other parties.

MAP 18.2 The Election of 1884

the Democrats as the party of "Rum, Romanism, and Rebellion." Linking drinking (rum) and Catholicism (Romanism) offended Irish Catholic voters, whom Blaine had counted on to desert the Democratic Party and support him because of his Irish background.

With less than a week to go until the election, Blaine had no chance to recover from the negative publicity. He lost New York State by fewer than 1,200 votes and with it the election. In the final tally, Cleveland defeated Blaine by a scant 23,005 votes nationwide but won with 219 electoral votes to Blaine's 182 (Map 18.2), ending twenty-five years of Republican control of the presidency. Cleveland's followers had the last word. To the chorus of "Ma, Ma, where's my Pa?" they retorted, "Going to the White House, ha, ha, ha."

Q: How did the question of civil service reform contribute to divisions within the Republican Party?

Economic Issues and Party Realignment

Four years later, in the election of 1888, fickle voters turned Cleveland out, electing Republican Benjamin Harrison, the grandson of President William Henry Harrison. Then, in the only instance in America's history when a president once defeated at the polls returned to office, the voters brought Cleveland back in the election of 1892. What factors account for such a surprising turnaround? The 1880s witnessed a remarkable political realignment as a set of economic concerns replaced appeals to Civil War sectional loyalties. The tariff, federal regulation of the railroads and trusts, and the campaign for free silver restructured American politics.

The Tariff and the Politics of Protection

The tariff became a potent political issue in the 1880s. The concept of a protective tariff to raise the price of imported goods and stimulate American industry dated back to Alexander Hamilton in the founding days of the Republic. The Republicans turned the tariff to political ends in 1861 by enacting a measure that both raised revenues for the Civil War and rewarded their industrial supporters, who wanted protection from foreign competition. After the war, the pro-business Republicans continued to revise and enlarge the tariff. Manufactured goods such as steel and textiles, and some agricultural products, including sugar and wool, benefited from

protection. Most farm products, notably wheat and cotton, did not. By the 1880s, the tariff produced more than $2.1 billion in revenue. The high tariff not only paid off the nation's Civil War debt and funded pensions for Union soldiers, but it also created a huge surplus that sat idly in the Treasury's vaults while the government argued about how (or even whether) to spend it.

To many Americans, particularly southern and midwestern farmers who sold their crops in a world market but had to buy goods priced artificially high because of the protective tariff, the answer was simple: Reduce the tariff. Advocates of free trade and moderates agitated for tariff reform. But those who benefited from the tariff—industrialists insisting that America's "infant industries" needed protection and some westerners producing protected raw materials such as wool, hides, and lumber—firmly opposed lowering the tariff. Many argued that workers, too, benefited from high tariffs that protected American wages by giving American products an edge over imported goods.

The Republican Party seized on the tariff question to forge a new national coalition. "Fold up the bloody shirt and lay it away," Blaine advised a colleague in 1880. "It's of no use to us. You want to shift the main issue to protection." By encouraging an alliance among industrialists, labor, and western producers of raw materials—groups seen to benefit from the tariff—Blaine hoped to solidify the North, Midwest, and West against the solidly Democratic South. Although the tactic failed for Blaine in the presidential election of 1884, it worked for the Republicans four years later.

Cleveland, who had straddled the tariff issue in the election of 1884, startled the nation in 1887 by calling for tariff reform. Cleveland attacked the tariff as a tax levied on American consumers by powerful industries. And he pointed out that high tariffs impeded the expansion of American markets abroad at a time when American industries needed to expand if they were to keep growing. The Republicans countered by arguing that "tariff tinkering" would only unsettle prosperous industries, drive down wages, and shrink the farmers' home market. Republican Benjamin Harrison, who supported the high tariff, ousted Cleveland from the White House in 1888, carrying all the western and northern states except Connecticut and New Jersey.

Back in power, the Republicans brazenly passed the highest tariff in the nation's history in 1890. The new tariff, sponsored by Republican representative William McKinley of Ohio and signed into law by Harrison, stirred up a hornet's nest of protest across the United States. The American people had elected Harrison to preserve protection but not to enact a higher tariff. Democrats condemned the **McKinley tariff** and labeled the Republican Congress that passed it the "Billion Dollar Congress" for its carnival of spending, which depleted the nation's surplus by enacting a series of pork barrel programs shamelessly designed to bring federal money to congressmen's own constituents. In the congressional election of 1890, angry voters swept the hapless Republicans, including tariff sponsor McKinley, out of office. Two years later, Harrison himself was defeated. Grover Cleveland, whose call for tariff revision had cost him the election in 1888, triumphantly returned to the White House vowing to lower the tariff. Such were the changes in the political winds whipped up by the tariff issue.

Controversy over the tariff masked deeper divisions in American society. Conflict between workers and farmers on the one side and bankers and corporate giants on the other erupted throughout the 1880s and came to a head in the 1890s. Both sides in the tariff debate spoke to concern over class conflict when they insisted that their respective plans, whether McKinley's high tariff or Cleveland's tariff reform, would bring prosperity and harmony. For their part, many working people shared the sentiment voiced by one labor leader that the tariff was "only a scheme devised by the old parties to throw dust in the eyes of laboring men."

Railroads, Trusts, and the Federal Government

American voters may have divided on the tariff, but increasingly they agreed on the need for federal regulation of the railroads and federal legislation to curb the power of the "trusts" (a term loosely applied to all large business combinations). As early as the 1870s, angry farmers in the Midwest who suffered from the unfair shipping practices of the railroads organized to fight for railroad regulation. The Patrons of Husbandry, or the Grange, founded in 1867 as a social and educational organization for farmers, soon became an independent political movement. By electing Grangers to state office, farmers made it possible for several midwestern states to pass laws in the 1870s and 1880s regulating the railroads. At first, the Supreme Court ruled in favor of state regulation (*Munn v. Illinois*, 1877). But in 1886, the Court reversed itself, ruling that because railroads crossed state boundaries, they fell outside state jurisdiction (*Wabash v. Illinois*). With more than three-fourths of railroads crossing state lines, the Supreme Court's decision effectively quashed the states' attempts at railroad regulation.

Anger at the *Wabash* decision finally led to the first federal law regulating the railroads, the **Interstate Commerce Act**, passed in 1887 during Cleveland's first administration. The act established the nation's first federal regulatory agency, the Interstate Commerce Commission (ICC), to oversee the railroad industry. In its early years, the ICC was never strong enough to pose a serious threat to the railroads. It could not, for example, end rebates to big shippers. In its early decades, the ICC proved more important as a precedent than effective as a watchdog.

Concern over the growing power of the trusts led Congress to pass the **Sherman Antitrust Act** in 1890. The act outlawed pools and trusts, ruling that businesses could no longer enter into agreements to restrict competition. It did nothing to restrict huge holding companies such as Standard Oil, however, and proved to be a weak sword against the trusts. In the following decade, the government successfully struck down only six trusts but used the law four times against labor by outlawing unions as a "conspiracy in restraint of trade." In 1895, the conservative Supreme Court dealt the antitrust law a crippling blow in *United States v. E. C. Knight Company*. In its decision, the Court ruled that "manufacture" did not constitute "trade." This semantic quibble drastically narrowed the law, in this case allowing the American Sugar Refining Company, which had bought out a number of other sugar companies (including E. C. Knight) and controlled 98 percent of the production of sugar, to continue its virtual monopoly.

Both the ICC and the Sherman Antitrust Act testified to the nation's concern about corporate abuses of power and to a growing willingness to use federal measures to intervene on behalf of the public interest. As corporate capitalism became more and more powerful, public pressure toward government intervention grew. Yet not until the twentieth century would more active presidents sharpen and use these tools effectively against the large corporations.

The Fight for Free Silver

While the tariff and regulation of the trusts gained many backers, the silver issue stirred passions like no other issue of the day. On one side stood those who believed that gold constituted the only honest money. Although other forms of currency circulated, notably paper money such as banknotes and greenbacks, the government's support of the gold

U.S. Currency Gold remained the nation's standard currency, but silver supporters, including farmers and western mining interests, demanded the minting of silver dollars and the issuance of silver certificates. On the left is a dollar gold piece and above it a silver dollar. The American Numismatic Assn.; Picture Research Consultants & Archives.

standard meant that anyone could redeem paper money for gold. Many who supported the gold standard were eastern creditors who did not wish to be paid in devalued dollars. On the opposite side stood a coalition of western silver barons and poor farmers from the West and South who called for **free silver**. The mining interests, who had seen the silver bonanza in the West drive down the price of the precious metal, wanted the government to buy silver and mint silver dollars. Farmers from the West and South who had suffered from deflation during the 1870s and 1880s hoped that increasing the money supply with silver dollars, thus causing inflation, would give them some debt relief by enabling them to pay off their creditors with cheaper dollars.

During the depression following the panic of 1873, critics of hard money organized the Greenback Labor Party, an alliance of farmers and urban wage laborers. The Greenbackers favored issuing paper currency not tied to the gold supply, citing the precedent of the greenbacks issued during the Civil War. The government had the right to define what constituted legal tender, the Greenbackers reasoned: "Paper is equally money, when . . . issued according to law." They proposed that the nation's currency be based on its wealth — land, labor, and capital — and not simply on its reserves of gold. The Greenback Labor Party captured more than a million votes and

elected fourteen members to Congress in 1878. Although conservatives considered the Greenbackers dangerous cranks, their views eventually prevailed in the 1930s, when the country abandoned the gold standard.

After the Greenback Labor Party collapsed, proponents of free silver came to dominate the monetary debate in the 1890s. Advocates of free silver pointed out that until 1873, the country had enjoyed a system of bimetallism — the minting of both silver and gold into coins. In that year, at the behest of those who favored gold, the Republican Congress had voted to stop buying and minting silver, an act silver supporters denounced as the "crime of '73." By sharply contracting the money supply at a time when the nation's economy was burgeoning, the Republicans had enriched bankers and investors at the expense of cotton and wheat farmers and industrial wageworkers. In 1878 and again in 1890, with the Sherman Silver Purchase Act, Congress took steps to ease the tight money policy and appease advocates of silver by passing legislation requiring the government to buy silver and issue silver certificates. Though good for the mining interests, the laws did little to promote the inflation desired by farmers. Soon monetary reformers began to call for "the free and unlimited coinage of silver," a plan whereby nearly all the silver mined in the West would be minted into coins circulated at the rate of sixteen ounces of silver to one ounce of gold.

By the 1890s, the silver issue crossed party lines. The Democrats hoped to use it to achieve a union between western and southern voters. Unfortunately for them, Democratic president Grover Cleveland remained a staunch conservative in money matters and supported the gold standard as vehemently as any Republican. After a panic on Wall Street in the spring of 1893, Cleveland called a special session of Congress and bullied the legislature into repealing the Silver Purchase Act because he believed it threatened economic confidence. Repeal proved disastrous for Cleveland, not only economically but also politically. It did nothing to bring prosperity and dangerously divided the country. Angry farmers, furious at the president's harsh monetary policy, warned Cleveland not to travel west of the Mississippi River if he valued his life.

Panic and Depression President Cleveland had scarcely begun his second term in office in 1893 when the country faced the worst depression it had yet seen. In the face of economic disaster, Cleveland clung to the economic orthodoxy of the gold standard. In the winter of 1894–95, the president walked the floor of the White House, sleepless over the prospect that the United States might go bankrupt. Individuals and investors, rushing to trade in their banknotes for gold, strained the country's monetary system. The Treasury's gold reserves dipped so low that unless they could be buttressed, the unthinkable might happen: The U.S. Treasury might not be able to meet its obligations.

At this juncture, J. P. Morgan stepped in and suggested a plan. A group of bankers would purchase gold abroad and supply it to the Treasury. Cleveland knew that such a scheme would unleash a thunder of protest, yet to save the gold standard, the president had no choice but to turn to Morgan for help. A storm of controversy erupted over the deal. The press claimed that Cleveland had lined his own pockets and rumored that Morgan had made $8.9 million. Neither allegation was true. Cleveland had not profited a penny, and Morgan made far less than the millions his critics claimed.

But if President Cleveland's action managed to salvage the gold standard, it did not save the country from hardship. The winter of 1894–95 was one of the worst times in American history. People faced unemployment, cold, and hunger.

A firm believer in limited government, Cleveland insisted that nothing could be done to help. "I do not believe that the power and duty of the General Government ought to be extended to the relief of individual suffering which is in no manner properly related to the public service or benefit." Nor did it occur to Cleveland that his great faith in the gold standard prolonged the depression, favored creditors over debtors, and caused immense hardship for millions of Americans.

Q: Why were Americans split on the question of the tariff and currency?

Conclusion: Business Dominates an Era

The gold deal between J. P. Morgan and Grover Cleveland underscored a dangerous reality: The federal government was so weak that its solvency depended on a private banker. This lopsided power relationship signaled the dominance of business in the era Mark Twain satirically but accurately characterized as the Gilded Age. Perhaps no other era in American history spawned greed, corruption, and vulgarity on so grand a scale—an era when speculators like Jay Gould not only built but wrecked businesses to turn paper profits; an era when business boasted openly of buying politicians, who in turn lined their pockets at the public's expense.

Nevertheless, the Gilded Age was not without its share of solid achievements. In these years, America made the leap into the industrial age. Factories and refineries poured out American steel and oil at unprecedented rates. Businessmen like Carnegie, Rockefeller, and Morgan developed new strategies to consolidate American industry. New inventions, including the telephone and electric light and power, changed Americans' everyday lives. By the end of the nineteenth century, the country had achieved industrial maturity. It boasted the largest, most innovative, most productive economy in the world. No other era in the nation's history witnessed such a transformation.

Yet the changes that came with these developments worried many Americans and gave rise to the era's political turmoil. Race and gender profoundly influenced American politics, leading to new political alliances. Fearless activist Ida B. Wells fought racism in its most brutal form — lynching. Women's organizations championed causes, notably suffrage and temperance, and challenged prevailing views of woman's proper sphere. Reformers fought corruption by instituting civil service. And new issues — the tariff, the regulation of the trusts, and currency reform — restructured the nation's politics.

The Gilded Age witnessed a nation transformed. Where dusty roads and cattle trails once sprawled across the continent, steel rails now bound the country together. Cities grew exponentially, not only with new inhabitants from around the globe but also with new bridges, subways, and skyscrapers. The nation's workers and the great cities they labored to build are the focus of Chapter 19.

Reviewing the Chapter

★ KEY TERMS

Explain each term's significance

WHO

Jay Gould (p. 438)

Andrew Carnegie (p. 439)

John D. Rockefeller (p. 440)

Ida M. Tarbell (p. 441)

Thomas Alva Edison (p. 442)

J. P. Morgan (p. 444)

Ida B. Wells (p. 449)

Rutherford B. Hayes (p. 451)

Roscoe Conkling (p. 451)

James G. Blaine (p. 451)

James A. Garfield (p. 451)

Grover Cleveland (p. 452)

WHAT

The Gilded Age (p. 435)

vertical integration (p. 439)

trust (p. 441)

finance capitalism (p. 444)

social Darwinism (p. 446)

gospel of wealth (p. 447)

laissez-faire (p. 447)

spoils system (p. 447)

New South (p. 448)

General Federation of Women's Clubs (p. 450)

Woman's Christian Temperance Union (p. 450)

civil service reform (p. 451)

McKinley tariff (p. 454)

Interstate Commerce Act (p. 454)

Sherman Antitrust Act (p. 454)

free silver (p. 455)

FOR PRACTICE QUIZZES AND OTHER STUDY TOOLS, see the Online Study Guide at **bedfordstmartins.com/roarkcompact**.

★ REVIEW QUESTIONS Q:

Use key terms and dates to support your answer

1. How did John D. Rockefeller gain control of 90 percent of the oil-refining business by 1890? (pp. 436–44)

2. Why did the ideas of social Darwinism appeal to many Americans in the late nineteenth century? (pp. 444–47)

3. How did race and gender influence politics? (pp. 447–50)

4. How did the question of civil service reform contribute to divisions within the Republican Party? (pp. 450–53)

5. Why were Americans split on the question of the tariff and currency? (pp. 453–56)

★ MAKING CONNECTIONS

Draw on key terms, timeline, and review questions

1. Late-nineteenth-century industrialization depended on developments in technology and business strategy. What were some of the key innovations in both arenas? How did they facilitate the maturation of American industry? How did the railroads contribute to the growth of American industry? In your answer, discuss the drawbacks and benefits of these developments.

2. By the 1870s, several new concerns had displaced slavery as the defining question of American politics. What were these new issues, and how did they shape new regional, economic, and racial alliances and rivalries? In your answer, consider the part political parties played in this process.

3. Energetic political activity characterized Gilded Age America, both within and beyond formal party politics. How did the activism of women denied the vote contribute to the era's electoral politics? In your answer, be sure to cite specific examples of political action.

4. The U.S. Congress and the Supreme Court facilitated the concentration of power in the hands of private business concerns during the Gilded Age. Citing specific policies and court decisions, discuss how government helped augment the power of big business in the late nineteenth century.

★ SUGGESTED READINGS

Rebecca Edwards, *New Spirits: Americans in the Gilded Age, 1865–1905* (2006). A lively new survey of a diverse and conflicted nation.

Patricia J. Giddings, *Ida, a Sword among Lions: Ida B. Wells and the Campaign against Lynching* (2008). A biography of the complicated woman who made the fight against lynching her life's work.

David Nasaw, *Andrew Carnegie* (2006). A recent biography of the multifaceted and contradictory industrialist-philanthropist.

Jean Strouse, *Morgan: American Financier* (1999). This prize-winning biography of J. P. Morgan tells the engrossing story of the larger-than-life banker and the era he dominated.

LeeAnn Whites, *Gender Matters: Civil War, Reconstruction, and the Making of the New South* (2005). A collection of essays that includes analysis of the centrality of gender and class in the creation of the New South.

FOR MORE BOOKS ABOUT TOPICS IN THIS CHAPTER, see the Online Bibliography at **bedfordstmartins.com/roarkcompact**.

FOR ADDITIONAL FIRSTHAND ACCOUNTS OF THIS PERIOD, see Chapter 18 in Michael Johnson, ed., *Reading the American Past*, Fourth Edition.

FOR WEB SITES, IMAGES, AND DOCUMENTS RELATED TO TOPICS AND PLACES IN THIS CHAPTER, visit Make History at **bedfordstmartins.com/roarkcompact**.

★ TIMELINE

1869	• First transcontinental railroad completed. • National Woman Suffrage Association (NWSA) founded.
1870	• John D. Rockefeller incorporates Standard Oil Company.
1872	• Andrew Carnegie builds the largest, most up-to-date Bessemer steel plant in the world.
1873	• U.S. government stops minting silver. • Wall Street panic leads to major economic depression. • Woman's Crusade begins.
1874	• Woman's Christian Temperance Union (WCTU) founded.
1876	• Alexander Graham Bell demonstrates telephone.
1877	• Republican Rutherford B. Hayes sworn in as president. • "Redeemers" come to power in South. • *Munn v. Illinois*.
1880	• Republican James A. Garfield elected president.
1881	• Garfield assassinated; Vice President Chester A. Arthur becomes president.
1882	• John D. Rockefeller develops the trust.
1883	• Pendleton Civil Service Act.
1884	• Democrat Grover Cleveland elected president.
1886	• *Wabash v. Illinois*.
1887	• Interstate Commerce Act.
1888	• Republican Benjamin Harrison elected president.
1890	• McKinley tariff. • General Federation of Women's Clubs (GFWC) founded. • Sherman Antitrust Act.
1892	• Ida B. Wells launches antilynching campaign.
1893	• Wall Street panic touches off national depression.
1895	• J. P. Morgan bails out U.S. Treasury.
1901	• U.S. Steel incorporated for $1.4 billion.

BROOKLYN BRIDGE FAN This commemorative fan celebrates the opening of the Great East River Bridge on May 24, 1883. A testament in stone and steel to the growing importance of urban America, the Brooklyn Bridge stood as a symbol not only of New York but of the era as well. Conceived amid the corruption of Boss Tweed's regime and inaugurated at a ceremony that pointedly excluded the workers who had risked their lives to build it, the bridge evoked all the contradictions of the Gilded Age. In an age of enterprise and hucksterism, the bridge became a popular motif in advertising. The lithograph on the fan depicts a view of the bridge over the East River with ships in the foreground and the Manhattan skyline, as well as commerce along the quays illustrated in detail in the background. On the back is an advertisement for the Cowperthwaits Furniture Company. The firm's sign is visible among the buildings in the lithograph, and an image of the company's building, along with its address and telephone number, is printed on the back. Museum of the City of New York.

The City and Its Workers

1870–1900

19

"A TOWN THAT CRAWLED NOW STANDS ERECT**, and we whose backs were bent above the hearths know how it got its spine," boasted a steelworker surveying New York City. Where once wooden buildings stood rooted in the mire of unpaved streets, cities of stone and steel sprang up in the last decades of the nineteenth century. The labor of millions of workers, many of them immigrants, laid the foundations for urban America.

No symbol better represented the new urban landscape than the Brooklyn Bridge, opened in May 1883 and quickly hailed as "one of the wonders of the world." The great bridge soared over the East River in a single mile-long span. Begun in 1869, the bridge was the dream of builder John Roebling, who died in a freak accident almost as soon as construction began.

The building of the Brooklyn Bridge took fourteen years and cost the lives of thirty men. Nearly three hundred workers labored around the clock in three shifts, six days a week, most for $2 a day. To sink the foundation deep into the riverbed, common laborers tunneled down through mud and debris, working in reinforced wooden boxes called caissons, which were open at the bottom and pressurized to keep the water from flooding in. Before long, the workers experienced a mysterious malady they called "bends" because it left them doubled over in pain after they came to the surface. (Scientists later discovered that nitrogen bubbles trapped in the bloodstream caused the condition and that it could be prevented if the men came up slowly to allow for decompression.)

The first death occurred when the caisson reached a depth of seventy-one feet. On April 22, 1872, a heavyset German immigrant named John Meyers complained that he did not feel well and headed home to his boardinghouse. Before he could reach his bed, he collapsed and died. Eight days later, another man dropped dead, and the entire workforce in the caissons went out on strike. Conditions had become so hazardous, so terrifying that the workers demanded a higher wage for fewer hours of work.

One worker, Frank Harris, remembered the men's fear of working in the caissons. As a scrawny sixteen-year-old from Ireland, Harris started to work a few days after landing in America. He described how the men went into a coffin-like "air-lock" to acclimate to the pressure of the compressed air in the caissons:

Construction of the Brooklyn Bridge This photograph shows the giant cables of the Brooklyn Bridge being put in place. The sloping wooden footpath that leads to the Gothic tower provided access for the workers. The massive bridge took fourteen years to build and cost the lives of thirty men. © Bettmann/Corbis.

When the air was fully compressed, the door of the air-lock opened at a touch and we all went down to work with pick and shovel on the gravelly bottom. My headaches soon became acute. The six of us were working naked to the waist in the small iron chamber with the temperature of about 80 degrees Fahrenheit: In five minutes the sweat was pouring from us, and all the while we were standing in icy water that was only kept from rising by the terrific pressure. No wonder the headaches were blinding.

Harris recalled the big Swede who headed the work gang telling him that "I could stay as long as I liked, but he advised me to leave at the end of a month: It was too unhealthy." By the fifth day, Harris experienced terrible shooting pains in his ears, and fearing he might go deaf, he quit. Like Harris, many immigrant workers walked off the job, often as many as a hundred a week. But a ready supply of immigrants meant that the work never slowed or stopped; new workers eagerly entered the caissons, where they could earn in a day more than they made in a week in Ireland or Italy.

Washington Roebling, who took over as chief engineer after his father's death, routinely worked twelve to fourteen hours six days a week. Soon he, too, fell victim to the bends and ended up an invalid, directing the completion of the bridge through a telescope from his window in Brooklyn Heights. His wife, Emily Warren Roebling, acted as site superintendent and general engineer of the project. At the dedication of the bridge, Roebling turned to his wife and said, "I want the world to know that you, too, are one of the Builders of the Bridge." Arching 130 feet above the East River, the bridge carried a roadway for vehicles and above it a pedestrian walkway. Together, they pierced massive granite towers at each end through two huge Gothic arches. Roebling intended the bridge to stand as "a great work of art" as well as "a successful specimen of advanced Bridge engineering." Generations of artists and poets have testified to his success.

At the end of the nineteenth century, the Brooklyn Bridge stood as a symbol of many things: the industrial might of the United States; the labor of the nation's immigrants; the ingenuity and genius of its engineers and inventors; the rise of iron and steel; and, most of all, the ascendancy of urban America. Poised on the brink of the twentieth century, the nation was shifting inexorably from a rural, agricultural society to an urban, industrial nation. In the burgeoning cities, tensions would erupt into conflict as workers squared off to fight for their rights to organize into labor unions and demand safer working conditions, shorter hours, and better pay. And the explosive growth of the cities would foster political corruption as unscrupulous bosses and entrepreneurs cashed in on the building boom. Immigrants, political bosses, middle-class managers, poor laborers, and the very rich populated the nation's cities, crowding the streets, laboring in the stores and factories, and taking their leisure at the new ballparks, amusement parks, dance halls, and municipal parks that dotted the urban landscape. As the new century dawned, the city and its workers moved to center stage in American life. ★

The Rise of the City

"We cannot all live in cities, yet nearly all seem determined to do so," New York editor Horace Greeley complained. The last three decades of the nineteenth century witnessed an urban explosion. Cities and towns grew more than twice as rapidly as the total population. Among the fastest-growing cities, Chicago expanded at a meteoric rate, from 100,000 in 1860 to over a million by 1890, doubling its population each decade. By 1900, the number of cities with more than 100,000 inhabitants had jumped from eighteen in 1870 to thirty-eight. Most of the nation's largest cities were east of the Mississippi, although St. Louis and San Francisco both ranked among the top ten urban areas in 1900. In the far West, Los Angeles mushroomed from a sleepy village of 5,000 in 1870 to a metropolis of more than 100,000 a scant thirty years later. By 1900, the United States boasted three cities with more than a million inhabitants—New York, Chicago, and Philadelphia.

Patterns of **global migration** contributed to the rise of the city. In the port cities of the East Coast, more than fourteen million people arrived, many from southern and eastern Europe, and huddled together in dense urban ghettos. The word *slum* entered the American vocabulary and with it growing concern over the rising tide of newcomers. In the city, the widening gap between rich and poor became more visible, exacerbated by changes in the city landscape brought about by advances in transportation and technology.

The Urban Explosion, a Global Migration

The United States grew up in the country and moved to the city, or so it seemed by the end of the nineteenth century. Between 1870 and 1900, eleven million people moved into cities.

Burgeoning industrial centers such as Pittsburgh, Chicago, New York, and Cleveland acted as giant magnets, attracting workers from the countryside. But migrants to the cities were by no means only rural Americans. Worldwide in scope, the movement from rural areas to urban industrial centers attracted millions of immigrants to American shores in the waning decades of the nineteenth century.

By the 1870s, the world could be conceptualized as three interconnected geographic regions (Map 19.1). At the center stood an industrial core bounded by Chicago and St. Louis in the west; Toronto, Glasgow, and Berlin in the north; Warsaw in the east; and Milan, Barcelona, Richmond, and Louisville in the south. Surrounding this industrial core lay a vast agricultural domain encompassing Canada, much of Scandinavia, Russia and Poland, Hungary, Greece, Italy and Sicily, southern Spain, the South and the western plains of America, central and northern Mexico, the hinterlands of northern China, and the southern islands of Japan. Capitalist development in the late nineteenth century shattered traditional patterns of economic activity in this rural periphery. As old patterns

MAP 19.1 Economic Regions of the World, 1890s

The global nature of the world economy at the turn of the twentieth century is indicated by three interconnected geographic regions. At the center stands the industrial core—western Europe and the northeastern United States. The second region—the agricultural periphery—supplied immigrant laborers to the industries in the core. Beyond these two regions lay a vast area tied economically to the industrial core by colonialism.

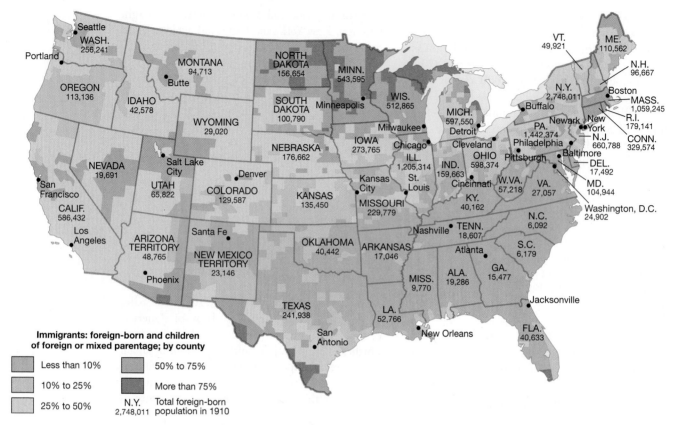

Immigrants: foreign-born and children of foreign or mixed parentage; by county

Less than 10%

10% to 25%

25% to 50%

50% to 75%

More than 75%

N.Y. 2,748,011   Total foreign-born population in 1910

MAP 19.2 The Impact of Immigration, to 1910

Immigration flowed in all directions—south from Canada, north from Mexico and Latin America, east from Asia to Seattle and San Francisco, and west from Europe to East Coast port cities including Boston and New York.

READING THE MAP: Which states had high percentages of immigrants? Which cities attracted the most immigrants? Which cities the fewest?

CONNECTIONS: Why did most immigrants gravitate toward the cities? Why do you think the South drew such a low percentage of immigrants?

FOR MORE HELP ANALYZING THIS MAP, see the map activity for this chapter in the Online Study Guide at bedfordstmartins.com/roarkcompact.

broke down, these rural areas exported, along with other raw materials, new recruits for the industrial labor force.

Beyond this second circle lay an even larger third world including the Caribbean, Central and South America, the Middle East, Africa, India, and most of Asia. Ties between this part of the world and the industrial core strengthened in the late nineteenth century, but most of the people living there stayed put. They worked on plantations and railroads, in mines and ports, as part of a huge export network managed by foreign powers that staked out spheres of influence and colonies in this vast region.

In the 1870s, railroad expansion and low steamship fares gave the world's peoples a new-found mobility that enabled industrialists to draw on a global population for cheap labor. When Andrew Carnegie opened his first steel mill in

1872, his superintendent hired workers he called "buckwheats"—young American boys just off the farm. By the 1890s, however, Carnegie's work-force was liberally sprinkled with other rural boys, Hungarians and Slavs who had migrated to the United States, willing to work for low wages.

Altogether, more than 25 million immigrants came to the United States between 1850 and 1920. They came from all directions: east from Asia, south from Canada, north from Latin America, and west from Europe (Map 19.2). Part of a worldwide migration, immigrants traveled to South America and Australia as well as to the United States. Yet more than 70 percent of all European immigrants chose North America as their destination. (See "Global Comparison.")

The largest number of immigrants to the United States came from the British Isles and

European Emigration, 1870–1890

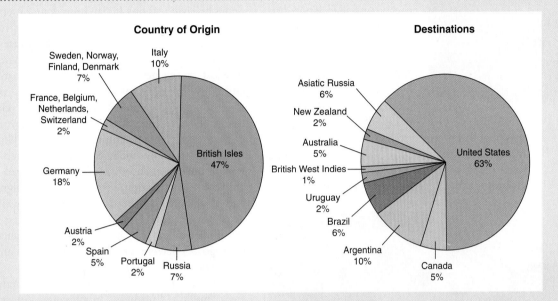

Country of Origin

- Italy 10%
- Sweden, Norway, Finland, Denmark 7%
- France, Belgium, Netherlands, Switzerland 2%
- Germany 18%
- Austria 2%
- Spain 5%
- Portugal 2%
- Russia 7%
- British Isles 47%

Destinations

- Asiatic Russia 6%
- New Zealand 2%
- Australia 5%
- British West Indies 1%
- Uruguay 2%
- Brazil 6%
- Argentina 10%
- Canada 5%
- United States 63%

A comparison of European emigrants and their destinations between 1870 and 1890 shows that emigrants from Germany and the British Isles (including England, Ireland, Scotland, and Wales) formed the largest group of out-migrants. The United States, which took in 63 percent of these emigrants, was by far the most popular destination, with Argentina, Brazil, Australia, Canada, and Asiatic Russia also attracting a share of the European immigrants. After 1890, the origin of European emigrants would tilt south and east, with Italians and eastern Europeans growing in number. Argentina proved a particularly popular destination for Italian emigrants, who found the climate and geography to their liking. In the United States, the number of German and British immigrants declined. What factors might account for why Europeans immigrated to the port cities of the eastern United States rather than to South America or Australia?

from German-speaking lands. The vast majority of immigrants were white; Asians accounted for fewer than one million immigrants, and other people of color numbered even fewer. Yet ingrained racial prejudices increasingly influenced the country's perception of immigration patterns. One of the classic formulations of the history of European immigration divided immigrants into two distinct waves that have been called the "old" and the "new" immigration. According to this theory, before 1880 the majority of immigrants came from northern and western Europe, with Germans, Irish, English, and Scandinavians making up approximately 85 percent of the newcomers. After 1880, the pattern shifted, with more and more ships carrying passengers from southern and eastern Europe. Italians, Hungarians, eastern European Jews, Turks, Armenians, Poles, Russians, and other

Slavic peoples accounted for more than 80 percent of all immigrants by 1896. Implicit in the distinction was an invidious comparison between "old" pioneer settlers and "new" unskilled proletarians. Yet this sweeping generalization spoke more to perception than to reality. In fact, many of the earlier immigrants from Ireland, Germany, and Scandinavia came not as settlers or farmers, but as wage laborers, much like the Italians and Slavs who followed them.

The "new" immigration resulted from a number of factors. Improved economic conditions in western Europe coupled with increased immigration to Australia and Canada slowed the flow of immigrants coming into the United States from northern and western Europe. At the same time, economic depression in southern Italy, the persecution of Jews in eastern Europe, and a general desire

> People left for the United States believing, as one Italian immigrant observed, "that if they were ever fortunate enough to reach America, they would fall into a pile of manure and get up brushing the diamonds out of their hair."

to avoid conscription into the Russian army led many people from southern and eastern Europe to move to the United States. The need of America's industries for cheap, unskilled labor during prosperous years also stimulated immigration.

Steamship companies courted immigrants — a highly profitable, self-loading cargo. By the 1880s, the price of a ticket from Liverpool had dropped to less than $25. Would-be immigrants eager for information about the United States relied on letters from friends and relatives, advertisements, and word of mouth — sources

Russian Immigrant Family A Russian immigrant family is shown leaving Ellis Island in 1900. Notice the white slips of paper pinned to their coats indicating that they have been processed. The couple is well dressed, she in a dark dress and scarf and he in a suit and tie. But the paucity of their possessions testifies to the struggles they would face in their new country. She carries her belongings in a white cloth sack, and he has a suitcase in one hand and bedding draped over his arm. An immigration official in uniform stands on the left. Ellis Island opened the year this photograph was taken, replacing the old immigration station at Castle Garden in lower Manhattan. Keystone-Mast Collection, UCR/California Museum of Photography, University of California, Riverside.

that were not always dependable or truthful. Even photographs proved deceptive: Workers dressed in their Sunday best looked more prosperous than they actually were to relatives in the old country, where only the very wealthy wore white collars or silk dresses. No wonder people left for the United States believing, as one Italian immigrant observed, "that if they were ever fortunate enough to reach America, they would fall into a pile of manure and get up brushing the diamonds out of their hair."

Most of the newcomers stayed in the nation's cities. By 1900, almost two-thirds of the country's immigrant population resided in cities, many of the immigrants too poor to move on. (The average laborer immigrating to the United States carried only about $21.50.) Although the foreign-born population rarely outnumbered the native-born population, taken together immigrants and their American-born children did constitute a majority, particularly in the nation's largest cities: Philadelphia, 55 percent; Boston, 66 percent; Chicago, 75 percent; and New York City, an amazing 80 percent in 1900.

Not all the newcomers came to stay. Perhaps eight million European immigrants — most of them young men — worked for a year or a season and then returned to their homelands. Immigration officers called these immigrants, many of them Italians, "birds of passage" because they followed a regular pattern of migration to and from the United States. By 1900, almost 75 percent of the new immigrants were young, single men.

Women generally had less access to funds for travel and faced tighter family control. For these reasons, women most often came to the United States as wives, mothers, or daughters, not as single wage laborers. Only among the Irish did women immigrants outnumber men by a small margin from 1871 to 1891.

Jews from eastern Europe most often came with their families and came to stay. Beginning in the 1880s, a wave of violent **pogroms**, or persecutions, in Russia and Poland prompted the departure of more than a million Jews in the next two decades. Most of the Jewish immigrants settled in the port cities of the East, creating distinct ethnic enclaves. Hester Street in the heart of New York City's Lower East Side rang with the calls of pushcart peddlers and vendors hawking their wares, from pickles to feather beds.

Racism and the Cry for Immigration Restriction

Ethnic diversity and racism played a role in dividing skilled workers (those with a craft or specialized ability) from the globe-hopping proletariat of unskilled workers (those who supplied muscle or tended machines). As industrialists mechanized to replace skilled workers with lower-paid unskilled labor, they drew on immigrants, particularly those from southern and eastern Europe, who had come to the United States in the hope of bettering their lives. Skilled workers, frequently members of older immigrant groups, criticized the newcomers. One Irish worker complained, "There should be a law . . . to keep all the Italians from comin' in and takin' the bread out of the mouths of honest people."

The Irish worker's resentment brings into focus the impact of racism on America's immigrant laborers. Throughout the nineteenth century and into the twentieth, members of the educated elite as well as the uneducated viewed ethnic and even religious differences as racial characteristics, referring to the Polish or the Jewish "race." Americans judged "new" immigrants of southern and eastern European "races" as inferior to those of Anglo-Teutonic "stock." Each wave of newcomers was deemed somehow inferior to the established residents.

The Irish who criticized the Italians so harshly had themselves been stigmatized as a lesser "race" a generation earlier. Immigrants not only brought their own religious and racial prejudices to the United States but also absorbed the popular prejudices of American culture. Social Darwinism, with its strongly racist overtones, decreed that whites stood at the top of the evolutionary ladder. But who was "white"? Skin color supposedly served as a marker for the "new" immigrants—"swarthy" Italians; dark-haired, olive-skinned Jews. But even blond, blue-eyed Poles were not considered white. The social construction of "race" is nowhere more apparent than in the testimony of an Irish dockworker who boasted that he hired only "white men," a category that he insisted excluded "Poles and Italians." For the new immigrants, Americanization and assimilation would prove inextricably part of becoming "white."

For African Americans, the cities of the North promised not just economic opportunity but also an end to institutionalized segregation and persecution. Jim Crow laws—restrictions that segregated blacks—became common throughout the South in the decades following Reconstruction. Intimidation and lynching terrorized blacks throughout the South (see chapter 18). "To die from the bite of frost is far more glorious than at the hands of a mob," proclaimed the *Defender*, Chicago's largest African American newspaper. In the 1890s, many blacks moved north, settling for the most part in the growing cities. Racism relegated them to poor jobs and substandard living conditions, but by 1900 New York, Philadelphia, and Chicago had the largest black communities in the nation. Although the most significant African American migration out of the South would occur during and after World War I, the great exodus was already under way.

On the West Coast, Asian immigrants became scapegoats of the changing economy. After California's gold rush, many Chinese who had come to work "on the gold mountain" found jobs on the country's transcontinental railroads. When the railroad work ended, they took work other groups shunned, including domestic service. But hard times in the 1870s made them a target for disgruntled workers. Prohibited from owning land, the Chinese migrated to the cities. In 1870, San Francisco housed a Chinese population estimated at 12,022, and it continued to grow until passage of the Chinese Exclusion Act in 1882 (see chapter 17). For the first time in the nation's history, U.S. law excluded an immigrant group on the basis of race. Some Chinese managed to come to America using a loophole that allowed relatives to join their families. In contrast, the nation's small Japanese community of about 3,000 expanded rapidly after 1890, until pressures to keep out all Asians led in 1910 to the creation of an immigration station at Angel Island in San Francisco Bay. Asian immigrants were detained there, sometimes for months, and many were deported as "undesirables."

On the East Coast, the volume of immigration from Europe in the last two decades of the century proved unprecedented. In 1888 alone, more than half a million Europeans landed in America, 75 percent of them in New York City. The Statue of Liberty, a gift from the people of France erected in 1886, stood sentinel in the harbor. The nation's response to the new immigrants was best summed up in the verse inscribed at Liberty's base, penned by a young Jewish girl named Emma Lazarus:

Give me your tired, your poor,
Your huddled masses yearning to breathe free,
The wretched refuse of your teeming shore,
Send these, the homeless, tempest-tost to me,
I lift my lamp beside the golden door!

The tide of immigrants to New York City soon swamped the immigration office at Castle Garden in lower Manhattan. An imposing new brick facility opened on **Ellis Island** in New York harbor in 1900. Its overcrowded halls became the gateway to the United States for millions.

To many Americans, the "new" immigrants seemed uneducated, backward, and uncouth—impossible to assimilate. "These people are not Americans," editorialized the popular journal *Public Opinion*, "they are the very scum and offal of Europe." Terence V. Powderly, head of the broadly inclusive Knights of Labor, complained that the newcomers "herded together like animals and lived like beasts." Blue-blooded Yankees led by Senator Henry Cab

Lodge of Massachusetts formed an unlikely alliance with organized labor to press for immigration restrictions. Lodge and his followers championed a literacy test, knowing that the vast majority of Italian and Slavic peasants were unable to read. In 1896, Congress approved a literacy test for immigrants, but President Grover Cleveland promptly vetoed it. "It is said," the president reminded Congress, "that the quality of recent immigration is undesirable. The time is quite within recent memory when the same thing was said of immigrants, who, with their descendants, are now numbered among our best citizens." Cleveland's veto forestalled immigration restriction but did not stop anti-immigrant forces from seeking to close the gates. They would continue to press for restrictions until they achieved their goal in the 1920s (see chapter 23).

The Social Geography of the City During the Gilded Age, cities experienced demographic and technological changes that greatly altered the social geography of the city. Cleveland, Ohio, provides a good example. In the 1870s, Cleveland was a small city in both population and area. Oil magnate John D. Rockefeller could, and often did, walk from his large brick house on Euclid Avenue to his office downtown. On his way, he passed the small homes of his clerks and other middle-class families. Behind these homes ran miles of alleys crowded with the dwellings of Cleveland's working class. Farther out, on the shores of Lake Erie, close to the factories and foundries, clustered the shanties of the city's poorest laborers.

Within two decades, the Cleveland that Rockefeller knew no longer existed. The coming of mass transit transformed the walking city. In its place emerged a central business district surrounded by concentric rings of residences organized by ethnicity and income. First the horsecar in the 1870s and then the electric streetcar in the 1880s made it possible for those who could afford the five-cent fare to work downtown and flee after work to the "cool green rim" of the city, with its single-family homes, lawns, gardens, and trees. Social segregation—the separation of rich and poor, and of ethnic and old-stock Americans—was one of the major social changes engendered by the rise of the industrial metropolis, evident not only in Cleveland but in cities across the nation.

Race and ethnicity affected the way cities evolved. Newcomers to the nation's cities faced hostility and not surprisingly sought out their kin and country folk as they struggled to survive. Distinct ethnic neighborhoods often formed around a synagogue or church. Blacks typically experienced the greatest residential segregation, but every large city had its ethnic enclaves—Little Italy, Chinatown,

Bohemia Flats, Germantown—where English was rarely spoken.

Poverty, crowding, dirt, and disease constituted the daily reality of New York City's immigrant poor—a plight documented by photo-journalist **Jacob Riis** in his best-selling book *How the Other Half Lives* (1890). By taking his camera into the hovels of the poor, Riis opened the nation's eyes to conditions in the city's slums. While Riis's audience shivered at his revelations about the "other half," many middle-class Americans worried equally about the excesses of the wealthy. They feared the class antagonism fueled by the growing chasm between rich and poor so visible in the nation's cities and shared Riis's view that "the real danger to society comes not only from the tenements, but from the ill-spent wealth which reared them."

The excesses of the Gilded Age's newly minted millionaires were nowhere more visible than in the lifestyle of the Vanderbilts. With a fortune amassed in the railroads, the Vanderbilts spent their money conspicuously on Fifth Avenue mansions and "cottages" in Newport, Rhode Island, that sought to rival the palaces of Europe. In 1883, Alva (Mrs. William) Vanderbilt launched herself into New York society by throwing a costume party so lavish that not even old New York society, which turned up its nose at the nouveau riche, could resist an invitation. Dressed as a Venetian princess, the hostess greeted her twelve hundred guests. But her sister-in-law Alice Vanderbilt stole the show by appearing as that miraculous new invention, the electric light, resplendent in a white satin evening dress studded with diamonds (see photo, page 469). The *New York World* speculated that Alva Vanderbilt's party cost more than a quarter of a million dollars (more than $4 million today).

Such ostentatious displays of wealth became especially alarming when they were coupled with disdain for the well-being of ordinary people. When a reporter in 1882 asked William Vanderbilt whether he considered the public good when running his railroads, he shot back, "The public be damned." The fear that America had become a plutocracy—a society ruled by the rich—gained credence from the fact that the wealthiest 1 percent of the population owned more than half the real and personal property in the country. As the new century dawned, reformers would form a progressive movement to address the problems of urban industrialism and the substandard living and working conditions it produced.

Q: **Why did American cities experience explosive growth in the late nineteenth century?**

How Both Halves Lived The gap between the rich and poor documented in Jacob Riis's best seller *How the Other Half Lives* is underscored here by juxtaposing the photographs of two women. Riis took the photograph of a "scrub" or washerwoman (left) in one of the notorious Police Station lodging houses, the shelters of last resort for the city's poor. Notice how large and misshapen her hands are from her heavy work. On the right is Alice Vanderbilt costumed as the "Spirit of Electricity" for her sister-in-law Alva Vanderbilt's costume ball in 1883. Her silk and satin gown, trimmed with velvet, gilt metallic bullion, and real diamonds, epitomized what political economist Thorstein Veblen would brand "conspicuous consumption." Washerwoman: Museum of the City of New York; Vanderbilt: Collection of the New York Historical Society.

FOR MORE HELP ANALYZING THIS IMAGE, see the visual activity for this chapter in the Online Study Guide at bedfordstmartins.com/roarkcompact.

At Work in Industrial America

The number of industrial wageworkers in the United States exploded in the second half of the nineteenth century, more than tripling from 5.3 million in 1860 to 17.4 million in 1900. These workers toiled in a variety of settings. Many skilled workers and artisans still earned a living in small workshops. But with the rise of corporate capitalism, large factories, mills, and mines increasingly dotted the landscape. Sweatshops and outwork, the contracting of piecework to be performed in the home, provided work experiences different from those of factory operatives and industrial workers. Pick-and-shovel labor, whether on the railroads or in the building trades, constituted yet another kind of work. Managers, as well as women "typewriters" and salesclerks, formed a new white-collar segment of America's workforce. The best way to get a sense of the diversity of workers and workplaces is to look at the industrial nation at work.

America's Diverse Workers Common laborers formed the backbone of the American labor force. They built the railroads and subways, tunneled under New York's East River to anchor the Brooklyn Bridge, and helped lay the foundation of industrial America. These "human machines" stood at the bottom of the country's economic ladder and generally came from the most recent immigrant groups. Initially, the Irish wielded the picks and shovels that built American cities, but by the turn of the century, as the Irish bettered their lot, Slavs and Italians took up their tools.

At the opposite end of labor's hierarchy stood skilled craftsmen like iron puddler James J. Davis, a Welsh immigrant who worked in the Pennsylvania mills. Using brains along with brawn, puddlers took the melted pig iron in the heat of the furnace and, with long poles, formed the cooling metal into 200-pound balls, relying on eye and intuition to make each ball uniform. Possessing such a skill meant earning good wages. Davis made up to $7 a day, when there was work. But most industry and manufacturing work in the nineteenth century remained seasonal; few workers could count on year-round pay. In addition, two major depressions only twenty years apart, beginning in 1873 and 1893, spelled unemployment and hardship. In an era before unemployment insurance, workers' compensation, or old-age pensions, even the best worker could not guarantee security for his family. "The fear of ending in the poor-house is one of the terrors that dog a man through life," Davis confessed.

Skilled workers like Davis wielded power on the shop floor. Employers attempted to limit workers' control by replacing people with machines, breaking down skilled work into ever smaller tasks that could be performed by unskilled factory operatives. New England's textile mills provide a classic example of the effects of mechanized factory labor in the nineteenth century. Mary, a weaver at the mills in Fall River, Massachusetts, went to work in the 1880s at the age of twelve. By then, mechanization of the looms had reduced the job of the weaver to watching for breaks in the thread. "At first the noise is fierce, and you have to breathe the cotton all the time, but you get used to it," Mary told a reporter from *Independent*. "When the bobbin flies out and a girl gets hurt, you can't hear her shout—not if she just screams, you can't. She's got to wait, 'till you see her. . . . Lots of us is deaf."

During the 1880s, the number of foreign-born mill workers almost doubled. At Fall River, Mary and her Scots-Irish family resented the new immigrants. "The Polaks learn weavin' quick," she remarked, using a common derogatory term to identify a rival group. "They just as soon live on nothin' and work like that. But it won't do 'em much good for all they'll make out of it." Employers encouraged racial and ethnic antagonism because it inhibited labor organization.

The majority of factory operatives in the textile mills were young, unmarried women like Mary. They worked from six in the morning to six at night six days a week, and they took home about $1 a day. The seasonal nature of the work also drove wages down. "Like as not your mill will 'shut down' three months," and "some weeks you only get two or three days' work," Mary recounted.

After twenty years of working in the mill, Mary's family had not been able to scrape together enough money to buy a house: "We saved some, but something always comes."

Mechanization transformed the garment industry as well. With the introduction of the foot-pedaled sewing machine in the 1850s and the use of mechanical cloth-cutting knives in the 1870s, independent tailors were replaced with workers hired by contractors to sew pieces of cloth into suits and dresses. Working in sweatshops, small rooms hired for the season or even in the contractor's own tenement, women and children formed an important segment of garment workers. Discriminated against in the marketplace, where they earned less than men, women generally worked for wages only eight to ten years, until they married.

Sadie Frowne, a sixteen-year-old Polish Jew, went to work in a Brooklyn sweatshop in the 1890s. Frowne sewed for eleven hours a day in a room twenty feet long and fourteen feet wide containing fourteen machines. "The machines go like mad all day, because the faster you work the more money you get," she recalled. Paid by the piece, she earned about $4.50 a week and, by rigid economy, tried to save $2. Young and single, Frowne typified the woman wage earner in the late nineteenth century. In 1890, the average workingwoman was twenty-two and had been working since the age of fifteen, laboring twelve hours a day six days a week and earning less than $6 a week.

The Family Economy: Women and Children

In 1890, the typical male worker earned $500 a year, about $9,000 in today's dollars. Many working-class families, whether native-born or immigrant, lived in or near poverty, their economic survival dependent on the contributions of all family members, regardless of sex or age. One statistician estimated that in 1900, as many as 64 percent of working-class families relied on income other than the husband's wages to make ends meet. The paid and unpaid work of women and children proved essential for family survival and economic advancement.

In the cities, boys as young as six years old plied their trades as bootblacks and newsboys. Often working under an adult contractor, these children earned as little as fifty cents a day. Many of them were homeless—orphaned or cast off by their families. "We wuz six, and we ain't got no father," a child of twelve told reporter Jacob Riis. "Some of us had to go."

Child labor increased decade by decade after 1870. The percentage of children under fifteen engaged in paid labor did not drop until after World War I. The 1900 census estimated that 1,750,178 children ages ten to fifteen were employed, an increase of more than a million over thirty years. Children in this age range constituted more than 18 percent of the industrial labor force. Many younger children not counted by the census worked in mills, in factories, and on the streets.

In the late nineteenth century, the number of women workers also rose sharply, with their most common occupations changing slowly from domestic service to factory work and then to office work. In 1870, the census listed 1.5 million women working for wages in nonagricultural occupations. By 1890, the number had more than doubled, with 3.7 million women working for pay (Figure 19.1). Women's working patterns varied considerably according to race and ethnicity. White married women, even among the working class, rarely worked for wages outside the home. In 1890, only 3 percent were employed. Black women, married and unmarried, worked for wages in much greater numbers. The 1890 census showed that 25 percent of married African

American women were employed, often as domestics in the houses of white families.

White-Collar Workers: Managers, "Typewriters," and Salesclerks

In the late nineteenth century, business expansion and consolidation led to a managerial revolution, creating a new class of white-collar workers who worked in offices and stores. As skilled workers saw their crafts replaced by mechanization, some moved into management positions. "The middle class is becoming a salaried class," a writer for the *Independent* magazine observed, "and is rapidly losing the economic and moral independence of former days." As large business organizations consolidated, corporate development separated management from ownership, and the job of directing the firm became the province of salaried executives and managers, the majority of whom were white men drawn from the 8 percent of Americans who held high school diplomas. These managers earned on average more than thirty times what the average worker earned — compared to today's top CEOs who receive compensation 400 times greater than the rank and file worker.

Until late in the century, when engineering schools began to supply recruits, many skilled workers moved from the shop floor to positions of considerable responsibility. William "Billy" Jones, the son of a Welsh immigrant, was one such worker. Beginning as an apprentice at the age of ten, Jones rose through the ranks to become plant superintendent at Andrew Carnegie's Pittsburgh steelworks in 1872. By all accounts, Jones was the best steel man in the industry, and Carnegie rewarded him with a "hell of a big salary," $25,000 — the same salary as the president of the United States.

The new white-collar workforce also included women "typewriters" and salesclerks. In the decades after the Civil War, as businesses became larger and more far-flung, the need for more elaborate and exact records, as well as the greater volume of correspondence, led to the hiring of more office workers. Mechanization transformed business as it had industry and manufacturing. The adding machine, the cash register, and the typewriter came into general use in the 1880s. Employers seeking literate workers soon turned to nimble-fingered women. Educated men had many other career choices, but for middle-class white women, secretarial work constituted one of very few areas where they could put their literacy to use for wages.

Sylvie Thygeson was typical of the young women who went to work as secretaries. Thygeson grew up in an Illinois prairie town. When her father died in 1884, she went to work as a country schoolteacher at the age of sixteen, after graduating high school.

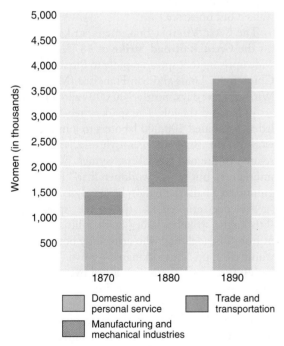

FIGURE 19.1 Women and Work, 1870–1890
In 1870, close to 1.5 million women worked in nonagricultural occupations. By 1890, that number had more than doubled to 3.7 million. More and more women sought work in manufacturing and mechanical industries, although domestic service still constituted the largest employment arena for women.

Realizing that teaching school did not pay a living wage, she mastered typing and stenography and found work as a secretary to help support her family. According to her account, she made "a fabulous sum of money." Nevertheless, she gave up her job after a few years when she met and married her husband.

Called "typewriters," women workers like Thygeson were seen as indistinguishable from the machines they operated. Far from viewing their jobs as dehumanizing, women typewriters took pride in their work and relished the economic independence it afforded them. By the 1890s, secretarial work was the overwhelming choice of native-born white women, who constituted more than 90 percent of the female clerical force. Not only considered more genteel than factory work or domestic labor, office work also meant more money for shorter hours. Boston's clerical workers made more than $6 a week in 1883, compared with less than $5 for women working in manufacturing.

As a new consumer culture came to dominate American urban life in the late nineteenth century, department stores offered another employment opportunity for women in the cities. Boasting ornate facades, large plate-glass display windows, and marble and brass fixtures, stores such as Macy's in New York, Wanamaker's in Philadelphia, and Marshall Field in Chicago stood as monuments to the material promise of the era. Within these palaces of consumption, cash girls, stock clerks, and wrappers earned as little as $3 a week, while at the top of the scale, buyers like Belle Cushman of the fancy goods department at Macy's earned $25 a week, an unusually high salary for a woman in the 1870s. Salesclerks counted themselves a cut above factory workers. Their work was neither dirty nor dangerous, and even when they earned less than factory workers, they felt a sense of superiority.

> **Q:** How did business expansion and consolidation change workers' occupations in the late nineteenth century?

Workers Organize

By the late nineteenth century, industrial workers were losing ground in the workplace. In the fierce competition to reduce prices and cut costs, industrialists like Andrew Carnegie invested heavily in new machinery that enabled them to replace skilled workers with unskilled labor. The erosion of skills and the redefinition of labor as mere "machine tending" left the worker with a growing sense of

individual helplessness that served as a spur to collective action. In the 1870s and 1880s, labor organizations grew, and the Knights of Labor and the American Federation of Labor attracted workers. Convinced of the inequity of the wage-labor system, labor organizers spoke eloquently of abolishing class privileges and monopoly. The rhetoric frightened many middle-class Americans and led them to equate the labor movement with the specter of violence and anarchism. Strikes particularly underscored the tensions produced by rapid industrialization. In 1877, in the midst of a depression that left many workers destitute, labor flexed its muscle in the Great Railroad Strike and showed the power of collective action.

The Great Railroad Strike of 1877 Economic depression following the panic of 1873 threw as many as three million people out of work. Those who were lucky enough to keep their jobs watched as pay cuts eroded their wages until they could no longer feed their families. In the summer of 1877, the Baltimore and Ohio (B&O) Railroad announced a 10 percent wage cut at the same time it declared a 10 percent dividend to its stockholders. Angry brakemen in West Virginia, whose wages had already fallen from $70 to $30 a month, walked out on strike.

The West Virginia brakemen's strike touched off the **Great Railroad Strike** of 1877, a nationwide uprising that spread rapidly to Pittsburgh and Chicago, St. Louis and San Francisco (Map 19.3). Within a few days, nearly 100,000 railroad workers walked off the job. The spark of rebellion soon led an estimated 500,000 laborers to join the train workers. In Reading, Pennsylvania, militiamen refused to fire on the strikers, saying, "We may be militiamen, but we are workmen first." Rail traffic ground to a halt; the nation lay paralyzed.

Violence erupted as the strike spread. In Pittsburgh, strikers clashed with militia brought in from Philadelphia, who arrogantly boasted they would clean up "the workingmen's town." Opening fire on the crowd, the militia killed twenty people. Angry workers retaliated by reducing an area two miles long beside the tracks to smoldering rubble. Before the day ended, twenty more workers had been shot, and the railroad had sustained property damage totaling $2 million.

Within eight days, the governors of nine states, acting at the prompting of the railroad owners and managers, defined the strike as an "insurrection" and called for federal troops. President Rutherford B. Hayes, after hesitating briefly, called out the army. By the time the troops arrived, the violence had run its course. Federal troops did not shoot

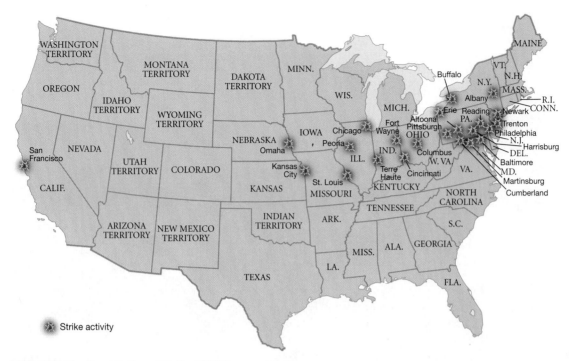

MAP 19.3 The Great Railroad Strike of 1877
Starting in West Virginia and Pennsylvania, the strike spread as far north as Albany, New York, and as far west as San Francisco, bringing rail traffic to a standstill. Called the Great Uprising, the strike heralded the beginning of a new era of working-class protest and trade union organization.

a single striker in 1877. But they struck a blow against labor by acting as strikebreakers—opening rail traffic, protecting nonstriking "scab" train crews, and maintaining peace along the line. In three weeks, the strike was over.

Although many middle-class Americans initially sympathized with the conditions that led to the strike, they condemned the strikers for the violence and property damage that occurred. The *New York Times* editorialized about the "dangerous classes," and the *Independent* magazine offered the following advice on how to deal with "rioters": "If the club of a policeman, knocking out the brains of the rioter, will answer then well and good; but if it does not promptly meet the exigency, then bullets and bayonets . . . constitutes [*sic*] the one remedy and one duty of the hour."

"The strikes have been put down by force," President Hayes noted in his diary on August 5. "But now for the real remedy. Can't something be done by education of the strikers, by judicious control of the capitalists, by wise general policy to end or diminish the evil? The railroad strikers, as a rule, are good men, sober, intelligent, and industrious." While Hayes acknowledged the workers' grievances, most businessmen and industrialists did

not and fought the idea of labor unions, arguing that workers and employers entered into contracts as individuals and denying the right of unions to bargain collectively for their workers. For their part, workers quickly recognized that they held little power individually and flocked to join unions. As labor leader Samuel Gompers noted, the strike served as an alarm bell to labor "that sounded a ringing message of hope to us all."

The Knights of Labor and the American Federation of Labor The **Knights of Labor**, the first mass organization of America's working class, proved the chief beneficiary of labor's new-found consciousness. The Noble and Holy Order of the Knights of Labor had been founded in 1869 by Uriah Stephens, a Philadelphia garment cutter. A secret society of workers, the Knights envisioned a "universal brotherhood" of all workers, from common laborers to master craftsmen. The organization's secrecy and ritual served to bind Knights together at the same time that it discouraged company spies and protected members from reprisals.

Although the Knights played no active role in the 1877 railroad strike, membership swelled as a

Destruction from the Great Railroad Strike of 1877 Pictures of the devastation caused in Pittsburgh during the strike shocked many Americans. When militiamen fired on striking workers, killing more than twenty strikers, the mob retaliated by destroying a two-mile area along the track, reducing it to a smoldering rubble. Property damage totaled $2 million. Curious pedestrians came out to view the destruction. Carnegie Library of Pittsburgh.

result of the growing interest in labor organizing that followed the strike. In 1878, the Knights abandoned secrecy and launched an ambitious campaign to organize workers regardless of skill, sex, race, or nationality. The Knights of Labor attempted to bridge the boundaries of ethnicity, gender, ideology, race, and occupation in a badly fragmented society. **Leonora Barry** served as general investigator for women's work from 1886 to 1890, helping the Knights recruit teachers, waitresses, housewives, and domestics along with factory and sweatshop workers. Women composed perhaps 20 percent of the membership. The Knights also made good on its vow to include African Americans, organizing more than 95,000 black workers. That the Knights of Labor often fell short of its goals to unify the working class proved less surprising than the scope of its efforts.

Under the direction of Grand Master Workman **Terence V. Powderly**, the Knights became the dominant force in labor during the 1880s. The organization advocated a kind of workers' democracy that embraced reforms including public ownership of the railroads, an income tax, equal pay for women workers, and the abolition of child labor. A loose mix of ideology, unionism, culture, fraternalism, and mysticism, the Knights called for one big union to create a cooperative commonwealth that would supplant the wage system and remove class distinctions. Only the "parasitic" members of society—gamblers, stockbrokers, lawyers, bankers, and liquor dealers—were denied membership.

In theory, the Knights of Labor opposed strikes. Powderly championed arbitration and preferred to use boycotts. But in practice, much of the organization's appeal came from a successful strike the Knights mounted in 1885 against railroads controlled by Jay Gould. In the Great Southwest strike, the Knights won a sweeping victory. Despite the reservations of its leadership, the Knights became a militant labor organization that won passionate support from working people with the slogan "An injury to one is the concern of all."

The Knights of Labor was not without rivals. Many skilled workers belonged to craft unions organized by trade. Among the largest and richest of these unions stood the Amalgamated Association of Iron and Steel Workers, founded in 1876 and counting twenty thousand skilled workers as members. Trade unionists spurned the broad reform goals of the Knights and focused on workplace issues. **Samuel Gompers**, a cigar maker born in London of Dutch Jewish ancestry, promoted what he called "pure and simple" unionism. Gompers founded the Organized Trades and Labor Unions in 1881 and reorganized it in 1886 into the **American Federation of Labor** (AFL), which coordinated the activities of craft unions throughout the United States. His plan was simple: organize skilled workers such as machinists and locomotive engineers — those with the most bargaining power — and use strikes to gain immediate objectives such as higher pay and better working conditions. Gompers at first drew few converts. The AFL had only 138,000 members in 1886, compared with 730,000 for the Knights of Labor. But events soon brought down the Knights, and Gompers's brand of unionism came to prevail.

Haymarket and the Specter of Labor Radicalism

While the AFL and the Knights of Labor competed for members, more radical labor groups, including socialists and anarchists, believed that reform was futile and called instead for social revolution. Both groups, sensitive to criticism that they preferred revolution in theory to improvements here and now, rallied around the popular issue of the eight-hour day.

Since the 1840s, labor had sought to end the twelve-hour workday, which was standard in industry and manufacturing. By the mid-1880s, it seemed clear to many workers that labor shared too little in the new prosperity of the decade, and pressure mounted for the eight-hour day. Labor rallied to the popular issue and launched major rallies in cities across the nation. Supporters of the movement set May 1, 1886, as the date for a nationwide general strike in support of the eight-hour workday.

All factions of the nascent labor movement came together in Chicago on May Day for what was billed as the largest demonstration to date. A group of labor radicals led by anarchist Albert Parsons, a *Mayflower* descendant, and August Spies, a German socialist, spearheaded the eight-hour movement in Chicago. Chicago's Knights of Labor rallied to the cause even though Terence Powderly and the union's national leadership, worried about the increasing activism of the rank and file, refused to endorse the movement for shorter hours. Samuel Gompers was on hand, too, to lead the city's trade unionists, although he privately urged the AFL assemblies not to participate in the general strike.

Gompers's skilled workers were labor's elite. Many still worked in small shops where negotiations between workers and employers took place in an environment tempered by personal relationships. Well dressed in their frock coats and starched shirts, the AFL's skilled workers stood in sharp contrast to the dispossessed workers out on strike across town at Chicago's huge McCormick reaper works. There strikers watched helplessly as the company brought in strikebreakers to take their jobs and marched the "scabs" to work under the protection of the Chicago police and security guards supplied by the Pinkerton Detective Agency. Cyrus McCormick Jr., son of the inventor of the mechanical reaper, viewed labor organization as a threat to his power as well as to his profits; he was determined to smash the union.

During the May Day rally, 45,000 workers paraded peacefully down Michigan Avenue in support of the eight-hour day, many singing the song that had become the movement's anthem:

> We mean to make things over;
>   we're tired of toil for naught
> But bare enough to live on: never
>   an hour for thought.
> We want to feel the sunshine; we
>   want to smell the flowers;
> We're sure that God has willed it,
>   and we mean to have eight hours.
> Eight hours for work, eight hours for rest,
>   eight hours for what we will!

Trouble came two days later, when strikers attacked scabs outside the McCormick works and police opened fire, killing or wounding six men. Angry radicals rushed out a circular urging workers to "arm yourselves and appear in full force" at a rally in Haymarket Square.

On the evening of May 4, the turnout at Haymarket was disappointing. No more than two or three thousand gathered in the drizzle to hear Spies, Parsons, and the other speakers. Mayor Carter Harrison, known as a friend of labor, mingled conspicuously in the crowd, pronounced the meeting peaceable, and went home to bed. A short

> On the gallows, August Spies spoke for the Haymarket martyrs: "The time will come when our silence will be more powerful than the voices you throttle today."

time later, police captain John "Blackjack" Bonfield, who had made his reputation cracking skulls, marched his men into the crowd, by now fewer than three hundred people, and demanded that it disperse. Suddenly, someone threw a bomb into the police ranks. After a moment of stunned silence, the police drew their revolvers. "Fire and kill all you can," shouted a police lieutenant. When the melee ended, seven policemen and an unknown number of other people lay dead. An additional sixty policemen and thirty or forty civilians suffered injuries.

"The Chicago Riot" Inflammatory pamphlets like this one published in the wake of the Haymarket bombing presented a one-sided view of the incident and stirred public passion. In this charged atmosphere, the anarchist speakers at the rally were tried and convicted for the bombing even though witnesses testified that none of them had thrown the bomb. The identity of the bomb thrower remains uncertain. Chicago Historical Society.

FOR MORE HELP ANALYZING THIS IMAGE, see the visual activity for this chapter in the Online Study Guide at bedfordstmartins.com/roarkcompact.

News of the "Haymarket riot" provoked a nationwide convulsion of fear, followed by blind rage directed at anarchists, labor unions, strikers, immigrants, and the working class in general. Eight men, including Parsons and Spies, went on trial in Chicago, although witnesses testified that none of them had thrown the bomb. "Convict these men," thundered the state's attorney, Julius S. Grinnell, "make examples of them, hang them, and you save our institutions." Although the state could not link any of the defendants to the **Haymarket bombing**, the jury nevertheless found them all guilty. Four were executed, one committed suicide, and three received prison sentences. On the gallows, Spies spoke for the Haymarket martyrs: "The time will come when our silence will be more powerful than the voices you throttle today."

The bomb blast at Haymarket had lasting repercussions. To commemorate the death of the Haymarket martyrs, labor made May 1 an annual international celebration of the worker. But the Haymarket bomb, in the eyes of one observer, proved "a godsend to all enemies of the labor movement." It effectively scotched the eight-hour day movement and dealt a blow to the Knights of Labor, already wracked by internal divisions. With the labor movement everywhere under attack, many skilled workers turned to the American Federation of Labor. Gompers's narrow economic strategy made sense at the time and enabled one segment of the workforce — the skilled — to organize effectively and achieve tangible gains. But the nation's unskilled workers remained untouched by the AFL's brand of trade unionism. The vast majority of America's workers would have to wait another forty years before a mainstream labor union, the Congress of Industrial Organizations (CIO), moved to organize the unskilled (see chapter 24).

Q: Why did the fortunes of the Knights of Labor rise in the late 1870s and decline in the 1890s?

At Home and at Play

The growth of urban industrialism not only dramatically altered the workplace but also transformed home and family life and gave rise to new forms of commercialized leisure. Industrialization redefined the very concepts of work and home. Increasingly, men went out to work for wages, while most white married women stayed home, either working in the home without pay — cleaning, cooking, and rearing children—or supervising paid domestic servants who did the housework.

Domesticity and "Domestics" The separation of the workplace and the home that marked the shift to industrial society redefined the home as a "haven in the heartless world," presided over by a wife and mother who made the household her separate sphere. The growing separation of workplace and home led to a new ideology, one that sentimentalized the home and women's role in it. The cultural ideology that dictated woman's place in the home has been called the cult of domesticity, a phrase used to prescribe an ideal of middle-class, white womanhood that dominated the period from 1820 to the end of the nineteenth century (see chapter 11).

The cult of domesticity and the elaboration of the middle-class home led to a major change in patterns of hiring household help. The live-in servant, or domestic, became a fixture in the North, replacing the hired girl of the previous century. (The South continued to rely on black female labor, first slave and later free.) In American cities by 1870, 15 to 30 percent of all households included live-in domestic servants, more than 90 percent of them women. By the mid-nineteenth century, native-born women increasingly took up other work and left domestic service to immigrants. In the East, the maid was so often Irish that "Bridget" became a generic term for female domestics.

Servants by all accounts resented the long hours and lack of privacy. "She is liable to be rung up at all hours," one study reported. "Her very meals are not secure from interruption, and even her sleep is not sacred." No wonder tension between domestic servants and their female employers proved endemic. Domestic service became the occupation of last resort, a "hard and lonely life" in the words of one servant girl.

For women of the white middle class, domestics were a boon, freeing them from household drudgery and giving them more time to spend with their children or to pursue club work or reform. Thus, while domestic service supported the cult of domesticity, it created for those women who could afford it opportunities that expanded their horizons outside the home in areas such as women's clubs and the temperance and suffrage movements.

Cheap Amusements Growing class divisions manifested themselves in patterns of leisure as well as in work and home life. The poor and working class took their leisure, when they had any, not in the crowded tenements that housed their families, but increasingly in the cities' new dance halls, music houses, ballparks, and amusement arcades, which by the 1890s formed a familiar part of the urban landscape.

The growing anonymity of urban industrial society posed a challenge to traditional rituals of courtship. Adolescent working girls no longer met prospective husbands only through their families. Fleeing crowded tenements, the young sought each other's company in dance halls and other commercial retreats. Scorning proper introductions, working-class youths "picked up" partners at dance halls, where drinking was part of the evening's entertainment. Young workingwomen, who rarely could afford more than trolley fare when they went out, counted on being "treated" by men, a transaction that often implied sexual payback. Young women's need to negotiate sexual encounters if they wished to participate in commercial amusements blurred the line between respectability and promiscuity and made the dance halls a favorite target of reformers who feared they lured girls into prostitution.

For men, baseball became a national pastime in the 1870s—then, as now, one force in urban life capable of uniting a city across class lines. Cincinnati mounted the first entirely paid team, the Red Stockings, in 1869. Soon professional teams proliferated in cities across the nation, and Mark Twain hailed baseball as "the very symbol, the outward and visible expression, of the drive and push and rush and struggle of the raging, tearing, booming nineteenth century."

The increasing commercialization of entertainment in the late nineteenth century can best be seen at **Coney Island**. A two-mile stretch of sand nine miles from Manhattan by trolley or steamship, Coney Island in the 1870s and 1880s attracted visitors to its beaches, dance pavilions, and penny arcades, where they consumed treats ranging from oysters to saltwater taffy. In the 1890s, Coney Island was transformed into the site of some of the largest and most elaborate amusement parks in the country. Promoter George Tilyou built Steeplechase Park in 1897, advertising "10 hours of fun for 10 cents." With its mechanical thrills and fun-house laughs, the amusement park encouraged behavior that one schoolteacher aptly described as "everyone with the brakes off." By 1900, as many as a million New Yorkers flocked to Coney Island on any given weekend, making the amusement park the unofficial capital of a new mass culture.

Q: **How did urban industrialism shape the world of leisure?**

Beach Scene at Coney Island Opened in the 1870s, Coney Island came into its own at the turn of the twentieth century with the development of elaborate amusement parks. It became a symbol of commercialized leisure and mechanical excitement. This fanciful rendering captures the frenetic goings-on. Men and women, along with costumed clowns, frolic in the waves. Notice the women's bathing outfits, with their leggings, modest skirts and blouses, and bathing hats. Men box and play ball, while a uniformed policeman wades into the fray, brandishing his billy club. On the shore are the rides — with the Ferris wheel dominating the skyline — and the famous hotel in the shape of an elephant. Sunday crowds on the island reportedly reached 100,000. Beach scene: Library of Congress; Sand pail: Private Collection.

City Growth and City Government

Private enterprise, not planners, built the cities of the United States. Boosters, builders, businessmen, and politicians all had a hand in creating the modern metropolis. With a few notable exceptions, such as Washington, D.C., and Savannah, Georgia, there was no such thing as a comprehensive city plan. Cities simply mushroomed, formed by the dictates of private enterprise and the exigencies of local politics. With the rise of the city came the need for public facilities, transportation, and services that would tax the imaginations of America's architects and engineers and set the scene for the rough-and-tumble of big-city government, politics, and politicians.

Building Cities of Stone and Steel Skyscrapers and mighty bridges dominated the imagination and the urban landscape. Less imposing but no less significant were the paved streets, the parks and public libraries, and the subways and sewers. In the late nineteenth century, Americans rushed to embrace new technology of all kinds, making their cities the most modern in the world.

Structural steel made enormous advances in building possible. A decade after the completion of the Brooklyn Bridge, engineers used the new technology to construct the Williamsburg Bridge two miles to the north. More prosaic and utilitarian than its neighbor, the new bridge was never as acclaimed, but it was longer by four feet and completed in half the time. It became the model for future building as the age of steel supplanted the age of stone and iron.

Chicago, not New York, gave birth to the modern skyscraper. Rising from the ashes of the Great Fire of 1871, which destroyed three square miles and left eighteen thousand people homeless, Chicago offered a generation of skilled architects and engineers the chance to experiment. Commercial architecture became an art form at the hands of a skilled group of architects who together constituted the "Chicago school." Men of genius such as Louis Sullivan and John Wellborn Root gave Chicago some of the world's finest commercial buildings. Employing the dictum "Form follows function," they built startlingly modern structures. A fitting symbol of modern America, the skyscraper expressed the domination of corporate power.

Across the United States, municipal governments undertook public works on a scale never before seen. They paved streets, built sewers and water mains, replaced gas lamps with electric lights, ran trolley tracks on the old horsecar lines, and dug underground to build subways, tearing down the unsightly elevated tracks that had clogged city streets. In San Francisco, Andrew Smith Hallidie mastered the city's hills, building a system of cable cars in 1873. Boston completed the nation's first subway system in 1897, and New York and Philadelphia soon followed.

Cities became more beautiful with the creation of urban public parks to complement the new buildings that quickly filled city lots. Much of the credit for America's greatest parks goes to one man—landscape architect **Frederick Law Olmsted**. The indefatigable Olmsted designed parks in Atlanta, Boston, Brooklyn, Hartford, Detroit, Chicago, and Louisville, as well as the grounds for the U.S. Capitol. But he is best remembered for the creation of New York City's Central Park. Completed in 1873, it became the first landscaped public park in the United States. Olmsted and his partner, Calvert Vaux, directed the planting of more than five million trees, shrubs, and vines to transform the eight hundred acres between 59th and 110th streets into an oasis for urban dwellers. We want a place, he wrote, where people "may stroll for an hour, seeing, hearing, and feeling nothing of the bustle and jar of the streets."

American cities did not overlook the mind in their efforts at improvement. They created a comprehensive free public school system that educated everyone from the children of the middle class to the sons and daughters of immigrant workers. The exploding urban population strained the system and led to crowded and inadequate facilities. In 1899, more than 544,000 pupils attended school in New York's five boroughs. The United States provided the only opportunity in the world for free secondary school education.

In addition to schools, the cities built libraries to educate their citizens. In the late nineteenth century, American cities created the most extensive free public library system in the world. In 1895, the Boston Public Library opened its bronze doors under the inscription "Free to All." Designed in the style of a Renaissance palazzo, with more than 700,000 books on the shelves ready to be checked out, the library earned the description "a palace of the people."

Despite the Boston Public Library's legend "Free to All," the poor did not share equally in the advantages of city life. The parks, the libraries, and even the subways and sewers benefited some city dwellers more than others. Few library cards were held by Boston's laborers, who worked six days a week and found the library closed on Sunday. And in the 1890s, there was nothing central about New York's Central Park. It was a four-mile walk from the tenements of Hester Street to the park's entrance at 59th Street and Fifth Avenue. Then, as now, the comfortable majority, not the indigent minority, reaped a disproportionate share of the benefits in the nation's big cities.

Any story of the American city, it seems, must be a tale of two cities—or, given the cities' great diversity, a tale of many cities within each metropolis. At the turn of the twentieth century, a central paradox emerged: The enduring monuments of America's cities—the bridges, skyscrapers, parks, and libraries—stood as the undeniable achievements of the same system of municipal government that reformers dismissed as boss-ridden, criminal, and corrupt.

City Government and the "Bosses" The physical growth of the cities required the expansion of public services and the creation of entirely new facilities: streets, subways, elevated trains, bridges, docks, sewers, and public utilities. There was work to be done and money to be made. The professional politician—the colorful **big-city boss**—became a phenomenon of urban growth. Though corrupt and often criminal, the boss saw to the building of the city and provided needed social services for the new residents. Yet not even the big-city boss could be said to rule the unruly city. The governing of America's cities resembled more a tug-of-war than boss rule.

The most notorious of all the city bosses was **William Marcy "Boss" Tweed** of New York. At mid-century, Boss Tweed's Democratic Party "machine" held sway. A machine was really no more than a political party organized at the grassroots level. Its purpose was to win elections and reward its followers, often with jobs on the city's payroll. New York's citywide Democratic machine, **Tammany Hall**, commanded an army of party functionaries. At the bottom were district captains. In return for votes, they provided services for their constituents, everything from a scuttle of coal in the winter to housing for an evicted family. At the top were powerful ward bosses who distributed lucrative franchises for subways and streetcars. They formed a shadow government more powerful than the city's elected officials.

The only elected office Tweed ever held was alderman. But as chairman of the Tammany general committee, he wielded more power than the mayor. Through the use of bribery and graft, he kept the Democratic Party together and ran the city. "As long as I count the votes," he shamelessly boasted, "what are you going to do about it?"

The excesses of the Tweed ring soon led to a clamor for reform and cries of "Throw the rascals out." Cartoonist Thomas Nast pilloried Tweed in the pages of *Harper's Weekly*. His cartoons, easily understood even by those who could not read, did the boss more harm than hundreds of outraged editorials. Tweed's rule ended in 1871. Eventually, he was tried and convicted and later died in jail.

Tammany Bank This cast-iron bank, a campaign novelty, bears the name of the New York City Democratic machine. It conveys its political reform message graphically: When you put a penny in the politician's hand, he puts it in his pocket. Tammany Hall dominated city politics for more than a century, dispensing contracts and franchises worth millions of dollars. Some of those dollars invariably found their way into the pockets of Tammany politicians. Collection of Janice L. and David J. Frent.

New York was not the only city to experience bossism and corruption. The British visitor James Bryce concluded in 1888, "There is no denying that the government of cities is the one conspicuous failure of the United States." More than 80 percent of the nation's thirty largest cities experienced some form of boss rule in the decades around the turn of the twentieth century. However, infighting among powerful ward bosses often meant that no single boss enjoyed exclusive power in the big cities.

Urban reformers and proponents of good government (derisively called "goo goos" by their rivals) challenged machine rule and sometimes succeeded in electing reform mayors. But the reformers rarely managed to stay in office for long. Their detractors called them "mornin' glories," observing that they "looked lovely in the mornin' and withered up in a short time." The bosses enjoyed continued success largely because the urban political machines helped the cities' immigrants and poor, who remained its staunchest allies. "What tells in holding your district," a Tammany ward boss observed, "is to go right down among the poor and help them in the different ways they need help. It's philanthropy, but it's politics, too—mighty good politics."

A few reform mayors managed to achieve success and longevity by following the bosses' model. **Hazen S. Pingree** of Detroit exemplified the successful reform mayor. A businessman who went into politics in the 1890s, Pingree, like most good-government candidates, promised to root out dishonesty and inefficiency. But when the depression of 1893 struck, Pingree emerged as a champion of the working class and the poor. He hired the unemployed to build schools, parks, and public baths. By providing jobs and needed services, he built a powerful political organization based on working-class support. Detroit's voters kept him in the mayor's office for four terms and then helped elect him governor twice.

The big-city boss, through the skillful orchestration of rewards, exerted powerful leverage and lined up support for his party from a broad range of constituents, from the urban poor to wealthy industrialists. In 1902, when journalist **Lincoln Steffens** began "The Shame of the Cities," a series of articles exposing city corruption, he found that business leaders who fastidiously refused to mingle socially with the bosses nevertheless struck deals with them. "He is a self-righteous fraud, this big businessman," Steffens concluded. "I found him buying boodlers [bribers] in St. Louis, defending grafters in Minneapolis, originating corruption in Pittsburgh, sharing with bosses in Philadelphia, deploring reform in Chicago, and beating good government with corruption funds in New York."

The complexity of big-city government, apparent in the many levels of corruption that Steffens uncovered, pointed to one conclusion: For all the color and flamboyance of the big-city boss, he was simply one of many actors in the drama of municipal government. Old-stock aristocrats, new professionals, saloonkeepers, pushcart peddlers, and politicians all fought for their interests in the hurly-burly of city government. They didn't much like each other, and they sometimes fought savagely. But they learned to live with one another. Compromise and accommodation—not boss rule—best characterized big-city government by the turn of the twentieth century, although the cities' reputation for corruption left an indelible mark on the consciousness of the American public.

White City or City of Sin? Americans have always been of two minds about the city. They like to boast of its skyscrapers and bridges, its culture and sophistication, and they pride themselves on its bigness and bustle. At the same time, they fear it as the city of sin, the home of immigrant slums, the center of vice and crime. Nowhere did the divided view of the American city take form more graphically than in Chicago in 1893.

In that year, Chicago hosted the **World's Columbian Exposition**, the grandest world's fair in the nation's history. The fairground, called the White

City and built on the shores of Lake Michigan, offered a lesson in what Americans on the eve of the twentieth century imagined a city might be. Only five miles down the shore from downtown Chicago, the White City seemed light-years away. Its very name celebrated a harmony and pristine beauty unknown in Chicago, with its stockyards, slums, and bustling terminals. Frederick Law Olmsted and architect Daniel Burnham supervised the transformation of a swampy wasteland into a paradise of lagoons, fountains, wooded islands, gardens, and imposing buildings.

"Sell the cookstove and come," novelist Hamlin Garland wrote to his parents on the farm. And come they did, in spite of the panic and depression that broke out only weeks after the fair opened in May 1893. In six months, fairgoers purchased more than 27 million tickets, turning a profit of nearly a half million dollars for promoters. Visitors from home and abroad strolled the elaborate grounds, visited the exhibits—everything from a model of the Brooklyn Bridge carved in soap to the latest goods and inventions. (See "Beyond America's Borders," page 482.) Half carnival, half culture, the great fair offered something for everyone. On the Midway Plaisance, crowds thrilled to the massive wheel built by Mr. Ferris and watched agog as Little Egypt danced the hootchy-kootchy.

In October, the fair closed its doors in the midst of the worst depression the country had yet seen. During the winter of 1894, Chicago's unemployed and homeless took over the grounds, vandalized the buildings, and frightened the city's comfortable citizens out of their wits. When reporters asked Daniel Burnham what should be done with the moldering remains of the White City, he responded, "It should be torched." And it was. In July 1894, in a clash between federal troops and striking railway workers, incendiaries set fires that leveled the fairgrounds.

In the end, the White City remained what it had always been, a dreamscape. Buildings that looked like marble were actually constructed of staff, a plaster of paris substance that began to crumble even before fire destroyed the fairgrounds. Perhaps it was not so strange, after all, that the legacy of the White City could be found on Coney Island, where two new amusement parks, Luna and Dreamland, sought to combine, albeit in a more tawdry form, the beauty of the White City and the thrill of the Midway Plaisance. More enduring than the White City itself was what it represented: the emergent industrial might of the United States, at home and abroad, with its inventions, manufactured goods, and growing consumer culture.

Q: How did municipal governments respond to the challenges of urban expansion?

Conclusion: Who Built the Cities?

As much as the great industrialists and financiers, as much as eminent engineers like John and Washington Roebling, common workers, most of them immigrants, built the nation's cities. The unprecedented growth of urban, industrial America resulted from the labor of millions of men, women, and children who toiled in workshops and factories, in sweatshops and mines, on railroads and construction sites across America.

America's cities in the late nineteenth century teemed with life. Immigrants and blue bloods, poor laborers and millionaires, middle-class managers and corporate moguls, secretaries, salesgirls, sweatshop laborers, and society matrons lived in the cities and contributed to their growth. Town houses and tenements jostled for space with skyscrapers and great department stores, while parks, ball fields, amusement arcades, and public libraries provided the city masses with recreation and entertainment.

Municipal governments, straining to build the new cities, experienced the rough-and-tumble of machine politics as bosses and their constituents looked to profit from city growth. Reformers deplored the graft and corruption that accompanied the rise of the cities. But they were rarely able to oust the party bosses for long because they failed to understand the services the political machines provided for their largely immigrant and poor constituents, as well as the ties between the politicians and wealthy businessmen who sought to benefit from franchises and contracts.

For America's workers, urban industrialism along with the rise of big business and corporate consolidation drastically changed the workplace. Industrialists replaced skilled workers with new machines that could be operated by cheaper unskilled labor. And during hard times, employers did not hesitate to cut workers' already meager wages. As the Great Railroad Strike of 1877 demonstrated, when labor united, it could bring the nation to attention. Organization held out the best hope for the workers; first the Knights of Labor and later the American Federation of Labor won converts among the nation's working class.

The rise of urban industrialism challenged the American promise, which for decades had been dominated by Jeffersonian agrarian ideals. Could such a promise exist in the changing world of cities, tenements, immigrants, and huge corporations? In the great depression that came in the 1890s, mounting anger and frustration would lead workers and farmers to join forces and create a grassroots movement to fight for change under the banner of a new People's Party.

The World's Columbian Exposition and Nineteenth-Century World's Fairs

Dedicated more to commerce than to culture, the 1893 World's Columbian Exposition in Chicago and the other great world's fairs of the nineteenth century represented a unique phenomenon of industrial capitalism and a testament to the expanding global market economy. The Chicago fair, named to celebrate the four hundredth anniversary of Columbus's arrival in the New World, offered a cornucopia of international exhibits testifying to growing international influences ranging from cultural to technological exchange. Such a celebration of global commerce and influence seemed an appropriate way to honor Columbus, whose voyage in 1492, after all, initiated one of the world's most significant international exchanges.

Beginning with London's Great Exhibition in 1851, with its famous Crystal Palace, and continuing through the age of commercial and cultural expansion in the late nineteenth century, international exhibitions proliferated and flourished. By the time Chicago secured the right to host its celebration, world's fairs had evolved into monumental extravaganzas that showcased the products of the host country and city along with impressive international displays. Great cities vied to host world's fairs, as much to promote commercial growth as to demonstrate their cultural refinement. Each successive fair sought to outdo its predecessor. Chicago's fair followed on the great success of the 1889 Universal Exposition in Paris, commissioned to celebrate the one hundredth anniversary of the French Revolution. The Paris Exposition featured as its crowning glory the 900-foot steel tower constructed by Alexander Gustav Eiffel. What could Chicago, a prairie upstart, do to top that?

The answer was the creation of the White City, with its monumental architecture, landscaped grounds, and first Ferris wheel. Itself a tribute to the international style of architecture, the White City celebrated the classicism of the French Beaux Arts school, which borrowed heavily from the massive geometric styling and elaborate detailing of Greek and Renaissance architecture. With the exception of Louis Sullivan's Transportation Building, nothing hinted of the clean and simple lines of indigenous American design soon to be celebrated with the advent of Frank Lloyd Wright.

Beneath its Renaissance facade, the White City acted as an enormous emporium dedicated to the unabashed materialism of the Gilded Age. Participants from more than one hundred states, territories, countries, and colonies, as well as thousands of concessionaires — from small businesses to the largest corporations — mounted exhibits to demonstrate their wares and compete for international attention. Fairgoers could view virtually every kind of manufactured product in the world inside the imposing Manufactures and Liberal Arts Building, including Swiss glassware and clocks, Japanese lacquerware and bamboo, British woolen products, and French perfumes and linens. The German pavilion displayed fine wooden furniture as well as tapestries, porcelain, and jewelry belonging to the ruling family.

As suited an industrial age, manufactured products and heavy machinery received privileged status and drew the largest crowds. Displays introduced visitors to the latest mechanical and technological innovations, many the result of international influences. For five cents, fairgoers could put two hard rubber tubes into their ears and listen for the first time to a Gramophone playing the popular tune "The Cat Came Back." The Gramophone, which signaled the beginning of the recorded music industry, was itself the work of a German immigrant, Emile Berliner (Thomas Edison later claimed credit for a similar invention, calling it the phonograph).

Such international influences were evident throughout the Columbian Exposition. At the Tiffany pavilion, one of the most popular venues at the fair, visitors oohed and aahed over the display of lamps, ornamental metalwork, and fine jewelry that Louis Comfort Tiffany credited to the influence of Japanese art forms. Juxtaposed with Tiffany's finery stood a display of firearms in the Colt gallery. Colt had been an international company since 1851, when it opened a factory in England. The company's revolvers enjoyed an international reputation — the best-known firearms not only in America but also in Canada, Mexico, and many European countries. Colt's new automatic weapon, the machine gun, would soon play a major role on the world stage in both the Boxer uprising in China and the Spanish-American War.

★ **"All Nations Are Welcome"** Uncle Sam, flanked by the city of Chicago, welcomes representatives carrying the flags of many nations to the World's Columbian Exposition in 1893. In the background are the fairgrounds on the shores of Lake Michigan. More than one hundred nations participated in the fair by sending exhibits and mounting pavilions to showcase their cultures and products. Chicago Historical Society.

All manner of foodstuffs—teas from India, Irish whiskey, and pastries and other confectionery from Germany and France—tempted fairgoers. American food products such as Shredded Wheat, Aunt Jemima syrup, and Juicy Fruit gum debuted at the fair, where they competed for ribbons. Winners such as Pabst "Blue Ribbon" Beer used the award in advertisements. And the fair introduced two new foods—carbonated soda and the hamburger—destined to become America's best-known contributions to international cuisine.

The Columbian Exposition also served as a testimony to American technological achievement and progress. By displaying technology in action, the White City tamed it and made it accessible to American and world consumers. The fair helped promote new technologies, particularly electric light and power. With 90,000 electric lights, 5,100 arc lamps, electric fountains, an electric elevated railroad, and electric launches plying the lagoons, the White City provided a glowing advertisement for electricity. Indeed, an entire building was devoted to it. In the Electricity Building, fairgoers visited the Bell Telephone Company exhibit, marveled at General Electric's huge dynamo (electric generator), and gazed into the future at the all-electric home and model demonstration kitchen.

Consumer culture received its first major expression and celebration at the Columbian Exposition. Not only did this world's fair anticipate the mass marketing, packaging, and advertising of the twentieth century, but the vast array of products on display also cultivated the urge to consume. Thousands of concessionaires with products for sale sent a message that tied enjoyment inextricably to spending money and purchasing goods, both domestic and foreign. The Columbian Exposition set a pattern for the twentieth-century world's fairs that followed, making a powerful statement about the possibilities of urban life in an industrial age and encouraging the rise of a new middle-class consumer culture. As G. Brown Goode, head of the Smithsonian Institution in 1893, observed, the Columbian Exposition was in many ways "an illustrated encyclopedia of civilization."

Reviewing the Chapter

★ KEY TERMS

Explain each term's significance

WHO

Washington Roebling (p. 462)

Jacob Riis (p. 468)

Leonora Barry (p. 474)

Terence V. Powderly (p. 474)

Samuel Gompers (p. 475)

Frederick Law Olmsted (p. 479)

William Marcy "Boss" Tweed (p. 479)

Hazen S. Pingree (p. 480)

Lincoln Steffens (p. 480)

WHAT

global migration (p. 463)

pogroms (p. 466)

Ellis Island (p. 467)

Great Railroad Strike (p. 472)

Knights of Labor (p. 473)

American Federation of Labor (p. 475)

Haymarket bombing (p. 476)

Coney Island (p. 477)

big-city boss (p. 479)

Tammany Hall (p. 479)

World's Columbian Exposition (p. 480)

FOR PRACTICE QUIZZES AND OTHER STUDY TOOLS, see the Online Study Guide at **bedfordstmartins.com/roarkcompact.**

★ REVIEW QUESTIONS Q:

Use key terms and dates to support your answer

1. Why did American cities experience explosive growth in the late nineteenth century? (pp. 462–68)

2. How did business expansion and consolidation change workers' occupations in the late nineteenth century? (pp. 469–72)

3. Why did the fortunes of the Knights of Labor rise in the late 1870s and decline in the 1890s? (pp. 472–76)

4. How did urban industrialism shape the world of leisure? (pp. 476–77)

5. How did municipal governments respond to the challenges of urban expansion? (pp. 478–81)

★ MAKING CONNECTIONS

Draw on key terms, timeline, and review questions

1. Americans expressed both wonder and concern at the nation's mushrooming cities. Why did cities provoke such divergent responses? In your answer, discuss the dramatic demographic, environmental, and political developments associated with urbanization.

2. Why did patterns of immigration to the United States in the late nineteenth century change? How did Americans respond to the immigrants who arrived late in the century? In your answer, consider how industrial capitalism, nationally and globally, contributed to these developments.

3. How did urban industrialization affect Americans' lives outside of work? Describe the impact of late-nineteenth-century economic developments on home life and leisure. In your answer, consider how class, race, gender, and ethnicity contributed to diverse urban experiences.

4. When workers began to embrace organization in the late 1870s, what did they hope to accomplish? Were they successful? Why or why not? In your answer, discuss both general conditions and specific events that shaped these developments.

★ SUGGESTED READINGS

Gary S. Cross and John K. Walton, *The Playful Crowd: Pleasure Places in the Twentieth Century* (2005). A lively comparative history of popular leisure in the United States and Britain.

Roger Daniels, *Guarding the Golden Door: American Immigration Policy and Immigrants since 1882* (2004). A comprehensive history of immigration restriction from the Chinese Exclusion Act to Homeland Security.

Ileen A. DeVault, *United Apart: Gender and the Rise of Craft Unionism* (2004). How gender shaped labor protest and gender bias became a central tenet of trade unionism.

Dirk Hoerder, *Cultures in Contact: World Migrations in the Second Millennium* (2002). An impressive overview of who moved where and why.

David R. Roediger, *Working toward Whiteness: How America's Immigrants Became White* (2005). How immigrants had to overcome prejudice to be considered "white."

Robert E. Weir, *Knights Unhorsed: Internal Conflict in a Gilded Age Social Movement* (2000). A sympathetic study of the rise and fall of the Knights of Labor.

FOR MORE BOOKS ABOUT TOPICS IN THIS CHAPTER, see the Online Bibliography at **bedfordstmartins.com/roarkcompact**.

FOR ADDITIONAL FIRSTHAND ACCOUNTS OF THIS PERIOD, see Chapter 19 in Michael Johnson, ed., *Reading the American Past*, Fourth Edition.

FOR WEB SITES, IMAGES, AND DOCUMENTS RELATED TO TOPICS AND PLACES IN THIS CHAPTER, visit Make History at **bedfordstmartins.com/roarkcompact**.

★ TIMELINE

1869	• Knights of Labor founded. • Cincinnati mounts first paid baseball team, the Red Stockings.
1871	• Boss Tweed's rule in New York ends. • Chicago's Great Fire.
1873	• Panic on Wall Street touches off depression. • San Francisco's cable car system opens.
1877	• Great Railroad Strike.
1878	• Knights of Labor organizes workers.
1880s	• Immigration from southern and eastern Europe rises.
1882	• Chinese Exclusion Act.
1883	• Brooklyn Bridge opens.
1886	• American Federation of Labor (AFL) founded. • Haymarket bombing.
1890s	• African American migration from the South begins.
1890	• Jacob Riis publishes *How the Other Half Lives*.
1893	• World's Columbian Exposition. • Panic on Wall Street touches off major economic depression.
1895	• Boston Public Library opens.
1896	• President Grover Cleveland vetoes immigrant literacy test.
1897	• Steeplechase Park opens on Coney Island. • Nation's first subway system opens in Boston.
1900	• Ellis Island opens.

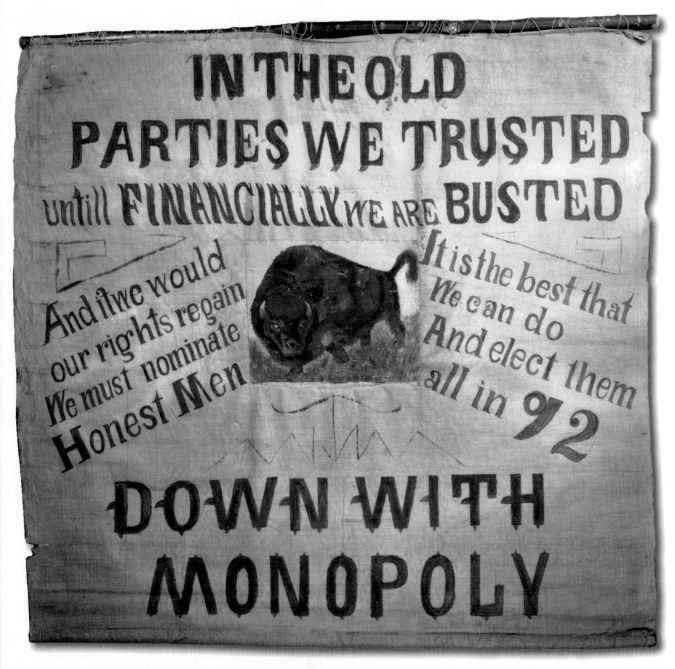

BUFFALO BANNER FROM THE 1892 POPULIST CONVENTION This flag graphically declares the frustration with the Democratic and Republican parties that led angry Americans, particularly farmers, to gather in St. Louis in 1892 to create a new People's Party. Featuring the buffalo (American bison) as a symbol, the flag urged the election of "honest men" and proclaimed as its motto "Down with Monopoly." The buffalo was perhaps a poor choice as a mascot, for just as the great herds on the western plains had been decimated during the 1880s, the People's (or Populist) Party would not survive the '90s. Nebraska State Historical Society.

Dissent, Depression, and War

1890–1900

FRANCES WILLARD TRAVELED to St. Louis in February 1892 with high hopes. She was not alone. Farmers, laborers, and reformers of all stripes flocked to Missouri to attend a meeting, in the words of one reporter, "different from any other political meeting ever witnessed in St. Louis." The cigar-chomping politicians who generally worked the convention circuit were nowhere to be seen. In their place, "mostly gray-haired, sunburned and roughly clothed men" assembled under a banner that proclaimed, "We do not ask for sympathy or pity. We ask for justice."

Political change was in the air, and Willard was there to help fashion a new reform party, one that she hoped would embrace her two passions — temperance and woman suffrage. As head of the Woman's Christian Temperance Union, an organization with members in every state and territory in the nation, Willard wielded considerable clout. At her invitation, twenty-eight of the country's leading reformers had already met in Chicago to draft a set of principles to bring to St. Louis. Always expedient, **Frances Willard** had settled for a statement condemning the saloon rather than an endorsement for a stronger measure to prohibit the sale of alcohol. But at the convention she hoped to press the case for woman suffrage and prohibition. Willard knew it would not be easy, but in the heady atmosphere of 1892, she determined to try. No American woman before her had played such a central role in a political movement. At the height of her political power, Willard took her place among the leaders on the podium in St. Louis.

Exposition Music Hall presented a colorful spectacle. "The banners of the different states rose above the delegates throughout the hall, fluttering like the flags over an army encamped," wrote one reporter. The fiery orator Ignatius Donnelly attacked the money kings of Wall Street. Mary Elizabeth Lease, a veteran campaigner from Kansas known for exhorting farmers to "raise less corn and more hell," added her powerful voice to the cause. Terence V. Powderly, head of the Knights of Labor, called on workers to join hands with farmers against the "nonproducing classes." Frances Willard urged the crowd to outlaw the liquor traffic and give the vote to women. Between speeches, the crowd sang labor songs like "Hurrah for the Toiler" and "All Hail the Power of Laboring Men."

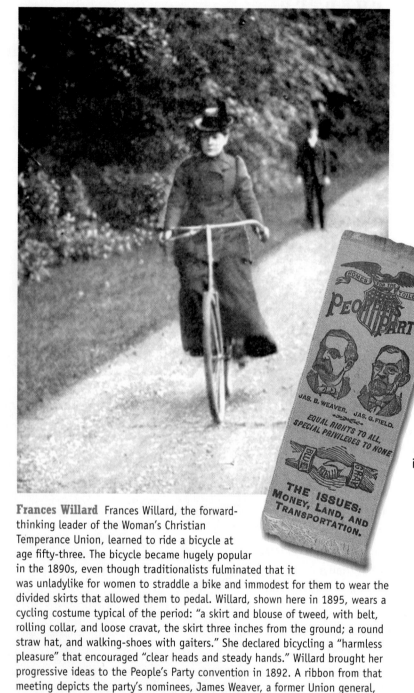

Frances Willard Frances Willard, the forward-thinking leader of the Woman's Christian Temperance Union, learned to ride a bicycle at age fifty-three. The bicycle became hugely popular in the 1890s, even though traditionalists fulminated that it was unladylike for women to straddle a bike and immodest for them to wear the divided skirts that allowed them to pedal. Willard, shown here in 1895, wears a cycling costume typical of the period: "a skirt and blouse of tweed, with belt, rolling collar, and loose cravat, the skirt three inches from the ground; a round straw hat, and walking-shoes with gaiters." She declared bicycling a "harmless pleasure" that encouraged "clear heads and steady hands." Willard brought her progressive ideas to the People's Party convention in 1892. A ribbon from that meeting depicts the party's nominees, James Weaver, a former Union general, and ex-Confederate James Field. The Populists hoped that the issues proclaimed on the ribbon — "money, land, and transportation" — would trump sectional loyalties, and symbolized their wish by portraying the Blue (Union) and Gray (Confederate) hands shaking. Photo: Courtesy of the Frances E. Willard Memorial Library and Archives (WCTU); Ribbon: Collection of Janice L. and David J. Frent.

In the course of the next few days, delegates hammered out a series of demands, breathtaking in their scope. They tackled the tough questions of the day — the regulation of business, the need for banking and currency reform, the right of labor to organize and bargain collectively, and the role of the federal government in regulating business, curbing monopoly, and guaranteeing democracy. But the new party determined to stick to economic issues and resisted endorsing either temperance or woman suffrage. As a member of the platform committee, Willard fought for both and complained of the "crooked methods . . . employed to scuttle these planks." Outmaneuvered in committee, she brought the issues to the floor of the convention, only to go down to defeat by a vote of 352 to 238.

Despite Willard's disappointment, the convention ended its work amid a chorus of cheers. According to one eyewitness, "Hats, paper, handkerchiefs, etc., were thrown into the air; . . . cheer after cheer thundered and reverberated through the vast hall reaching the outside of the building where thousands who had been waiting the outcome joined in the applause till for blocks in every direction the exultation made the din indescribable."

What was all the shouting about? The cheering crowd was celebrating the birth of a new political party, officially named the People's Party. Fed up with the Democrats and Republicans, a broad coalition of groups came together in St. Louis to fight for change. They resolved to reconvene in Omaha in July to nominate candidates for the upcoming presidential election. Defeated but not willing to abandon the new party, Willard resolved to work for the nomination of a presidential candidate committed to temperance and suffrage.

The St. Louis gathering marked a milestone in one of the most turbulent decades in U.S. history. Unrest, agitation, agrarian revolt, labor strikes, a severe financial panic and depression, and a war of expansion shook the 1890s. While the two major political parties continued to do business as usual, Americans flocked to organizations including the Farmers' Alliance, the American Federation of Labor, and the Woman's Christian Temperance Union, and they worked together to create the political alliance that gave birth to the People's (or Populist) Party. In a decade of unrest and uncertainty, the People's Party countered laissez-faire economics by insisting that the federal government play a more active role to ensure greater economic equity in industrial America. This challenge to the status quo culminated in 1896 in one of the most hotly contested presidential elections in the nation's history. At the close of the tumultuous decade, the Spanish-American War helped to bring the country together as Americans rallied to support the troops. But disagreement over American imperialism and overseas expansion raised questions about the nation's role on the world stage as the United States stood poised to enter the twentieth century. ★

The Farmers' Revolt

Hard times in the 1880s and 1890s created a ground-swell of agrarian revolt. A bitter farmer wrote from Minnesota, "I settled on this Land in good Faith Built House and Barn. Broken up Part of the Land. Spent years of hard Labor in grubbing fencing and Improving." About to lose his farm to foreclosure, he lamented, "Are they going to drive us out like trespassers . . . and give us away to the Corporations?"

Farm prices fell decade after decade, even as American farmers' share of the world market grew. Wheat that sold for a dollar a bushel in 1870 dropped to sixty cents in the 1890s. Cotton plummeted from fifteen cents to five cents a pound. Corn started at forty-five cents and fell to thirty cents a bushel. In parts of Kansas, it sold for as little as ten cents, and angry farmers burned their corn for fuel rather than market it at that price. At the same time, consumer prices soared. In Kansas alone, almost half the farms had fallen into the hands of the banks by 1894 because poor farmers could no longer afford to pay their mortgages.

At the heart of the problem stood a banking system dominated by eastern commercial banks committed to the gold standard, a railroad rate system that was capricious and unfair, and rampant speculation that drove up the price of land. In the West, farmers rankled under a system that allowed railroads to charge them exorbitant freight rates while granting rebates to large shippers (see chapter 18). The railroads' policy of charging higher rates for short hauls meant that large grain elevator companies could ship their wheat from Chicago to New York for less money than it cost a Dakota farmer to send his crop to nearby Minneapolis. In the South, lack of currency and credit drove farmers to the stop-gap credit system of the crop lien, turning the entire region into "a vast pawn shop." To pay for seed and supplies, farmers had to pledge their crops to local creditors, called "furnishing merchants," whose exorbitant prices meant chronic debt and destitution for southern farmers. Determined to do something, farmers banded together to fight for change.

The Farmers' Alliance Farm protest was not new. In the 1870s, farmers had supported the Grange and the Greenback Labor Party. As the farmers' situation grew more desperate, they organized, forming regional alliances. The first **Farmers' Alliance** came together in Lampasas County, Texas, to fight "landsharks and horse thieves." During the 1880s, the movement spread rapidly. In frontier farmhouses in Texas, in log cabins in the

Nebraska Farm Family A Nebraska farm family posed in front of their sod hut in Custer County, Nebraska, in 1889. The house is formed of blocks of sod cut from the prairie. The wife stands in the doorway, wearing a hat, while the husband stands with a team of horses and the family dog keeps a vigilant eye on the photographer. The photo testifies to the hard, lonely life of farmers on the Great Plains. Drought and falling crop prices devastated farmers in the 1880s, and many lost their land to bank foreclosures when they could not make their mortgage payments. Growing discontent among farmers in the Midwest and South led to the growth of the Farmers' Alliance in the 1880s and the creation of the People's Party in the 1890s. Nebraska State Historical Society.

backwoods of Arkansas, and in the rural parishes of Louisiana, separate groups of farmers formed similar alliances for self-help.

As the movement grew, farmers' groups consolidated into two regional alliances. The Northwestern Farmers' Alliance was active in Kansas, Nebraska, and other midwestern Granger states. The more radical Southern Farmers' Alliance got its start in Texas and spread rapidly. In the 1880s, traveling lecturers preached the Alliance message. Worn-out men and careworn women did not need to be convinced that something was wrong. Overnight, scores of local alliances sprang up, each with its own lecturer, who in turn carried the word to every crossroads in the South. By 1887, the Southern Farmers' Alliance had grown to more than 200,000 members, and by 1890 it counted more than 3 million members.

Radical in its inclusiveness, the Southern Alliance reached out to African Americans, women, and industrial workers. Through cooperation with the **Colored Farmers' Alliance**, an African American group founded in Texas in the 1880s, blacks and whites attempted to make common cause. As Georgia's Tom Watson, a Southern Alliance stalwart, pointed out, "The colored tenant is in the same boat as the white tenant, . . . and . . . the accident of color can make no difference in the interests of farmers, croppers, and laborers." The political culture of the Alliance encouraged the inclusion of women and children and used the family as its defining symbol. Women rallied to the Alliance banner along with their menfolk, drawn to meetings that combined picnic, parade, revival, country fair, and political convention. "I am going to work for prohibition, the Alliance, and for Jesus as long as I live," swore one woman. And during the Great Southwestern Strike in 1886, the Alliance rushed food and supplies to the striking workers and issued a proclamation in support of the Knights of Labor.

At the heart of the Alliance movement stood a series of farmers' cooperatives. By "bulking" their cotton—that is, selling it together—farmers could negotiate a better price. And by setting up trade stores and exchanges, they sought to escape the grasp of the merchant/creditor. Through the cooperatives, the Farmers' Alliance promised to change the way farmers lived. "We are going to get out of debt and be free and independent people once more," exulted one Georgia farmer.

Cooperatives sprang up throughout the South and West. But the Alliance faced insurmountable difficulties in running successful cooperatives. Opposition by merchants, bankers, wholesalers, and manufacturers made it impossible for the cooperatives to get credit. As the cooperative

movement died, the Farmers' Alliance moved toward direct political action. Confounded by the failure of the Democrats and Republicans to break with commercial interests and support the farmers, Alliance leaders moved, often reluctantly, toward the formation of a third party.

The Populist Movement In the earliest days of the Alliance movement, a leader of the Southern Farmers' Alliance insisted, "The Alliance is a strictly white man's nonpolitical, secret business association." But by 1892, it was none of those things. Advocates of a third party carried the day at the convention of laborers, farmers, and common folk in St. Louis in 1892. There, the Farmers' Alliance gave birth to the **People's Party** and launched the Populist movement. "There is something at the back of all this turmoil more than the failure of crops or the scarcity of ready cash," a journalist observed in 1892.

The same spirit of religious revival that animated the Farmers' Alliance infused the People's

Mary Elizabeth Lease This photograph of Lease, taken in 1895 at the height of her political activities in Kansas, shows a well-dressed, mild-eyed woman—belying her reputation as a hell-raiser who supposedly exhorted Kansas farmers to "raise less corn and more hell." Lease brought her considerable oratorical skills to the causes of temperance, suffrage, and the Populist Party. Her admirers styled her "The People's Joan of Arc." But in the eyes of her detractors, who attacked not only her speeches but the propriety of a woman who dared to pursue a career as a public speaker, she was "a lantern-jawed, google-eyed nightmare" and "a petticoated smut-mill." Kansas State Historical Society.

Party. The Populists built on the work of the Farmers' Alliance to mount a critique of industrial society and a call for action. Convinced that the money and banking systems worked to the advantage of the wealthy few, they demanded economic democracy. To help farmers get the credit they needed at reasonable rates, southern farmers hit on the ingenious idea of a **subtreasury**—a plan that would allow farmers to store their nonperishable crops and receive commodity credit from the federal government. The subtreasury promised to get rid of the crop lien system once and for all. Although the idea would be enacted piecemeal in progressive and New Deal legislation in the twentieth century, conservatives in the 1890s dismissed it as farfetched "corn tassel communism."

To the western farmer, the Populists promised land reform, championing a plan that would claim excessive land granted to railroads or sold to foreign investors. The Populists' boldest proposal called for government ownership of the railroads and the telegraph system to put an end to discriminatory rates. Citing examples of how the powerful railroads had corrupted the political system, the Populists did not shrink from advocating what their opponents branded state socialism.

The Populists also demanded currency reform. Farmers in all sections rallied to the cry for cheaper currency, calling for free silver and greenbacks—attempts to increase the nation's tight money supply and thus make credit easier to obtain. And to empower the common people, the Populist platform called for the direct election of senators and for other electoral reforms, including the secret ballot and the right to initiate legislation, to recall elected officials, and to submit issues to the people by means of a referendum. Because the Populists shared common cause with labor against corporate interests, they also supported the eight-hour workday and an end to contract labor.

The sweeping array of Populist reforms enacted in the Populist platform changed the agenda of politics for decades to come. More than just a response to hard times, Populism presented an alternative vision of American economic democracy.

Q: Why did American farmers organize alliances in the late nineteenth century?

The Labor Wars

While farmers united to fight for change, industrial laborers fought their own battles in a series of bloody strikes so fiercely waged on both sides that historians have called them the "labor wars."

Industrial workers felt increasingly threatened as businesses combined into huge corporations, and in the 1890s labor took a stand. At issue was the right of workers to organize and to speak through unions to bargain collectively and fight for better working conditions, higher wages, shorter hours, and greater worker control in the face of increased mechanization.

Three major conflicts of the period—the lockout of steelworkers in Homestead, Pennsylvania, in 1892; the miners' strike in Cripple Creek, Colorado, in 1894; and the Pullman strike in Illinois that same year—raised fundamental questions about the rights of labor and the sanctity of private property.

The Homestead Lockout In 1892, steelworkers in Pennsylvania squared off against Andrew Carnegie in a decisive struggle over the right to organize in the Homestead steel mills. Carnegie was unusual among industrialists as a self-styled friend of labor. In 1886, he had written, "The right of the workingmen to combine and to form trade unions is no less sacred than the right of the manufacturer to enter into associations and conferences with his fellows."

Yet as much as he cherished his liberal beliefs, Carnegie cherished his profits more. In 1892, Carnegie resolved to crush the Amalgamated Iron and Steel Workers, one of the largest and richest craft unions in the American Federation of Labor. When the Amalgamated attempted to renew its contract at Carnegie's Homestead mill, its leaders were told that since "the vast majority of our employees are Non union, the Firm has decided that the minority must give place to the majority." While it was true that only 800 skilled workers belonged to the elite Amalgamated, the union had long enjoyed the support of the plant's 3,000 nonunion workers. Slavs, who did much of the unskilled work, made common cause with the Welsh, Scots, and Irish skilled workers who belonged to the union. Never before had the Amalgamated been denied a contract.

Carnegie preferred not to be directly involved in the union busting that lay on the horizon, so that spring he sailed to Scotland and left **Henry Clay Frick**, the toughest antilabor man in the industry, in charge of the Homestead plant. By summer, a strike looked inevitable. Frick prepared by erecting a fifteen-foot fence around the plant and topping it with barbed wire. Workers aptly dubbed it "Fort Frick." To defend his fort and protect strikebreakers, Frick hired 316 mercenaries from the Pinkerton National Detective Agency at the rate of $5 per day, more than double the wage of the average Homestead worker.

Homestead Workers Attack the Pinkertons The nation's attention was riveted on labor strife at the Homestead steel mill in the summer of 1892. Frank Leslie's *Illustrated Weekly* ran a cover story on the violence that Pinkerton agents faced from a crowd of men, women, and children armed with clubs, guns, and ax handles. The workers, who had been locked out by Henry Clay Frick, were enraged that Frick had hired the Pinkertons to bring in strikebreakers. In a standoff with the workers, the Pinkertons fired into the crowd, killing three men and wounding scores. A truce was negotiated, but the crowd could not contain its rage and viciously attacked the hated "Pinks." The illustration shows a boy with a gun in the foreground. Although the mob was armed, not one of the Pinkertons was shot as they ran the gantlet. All, however, were beaten. The New-York Society Library.

FOR MORE HELP ANALYZING THIS IMAGE, see the visual activity for this chapter in the Online Study Guide at **bedfordstmartins.com/roarkcompact**.

The Pinkerton Agency, founded before the Civil War, came into its own in the 1880s as a private security force for hire. Pinkerton agents were a motley crew, recruited from all levels of society, from urban thugs to college boys. The "Pinks" earned the hatred of workers by protecting strikebreakers and acting as company spies.

On June 28, the **Homestead lockout** began when Frick locked the workers out of the mills and prepared to bring in scab workers. Hugh O'Donnell, the young Irishman who led the union, vowed to prevent strikebreakers from entering the plant. On July 6 at four in the morning, a lookout spotted two barges moving up the Monongahela River in the fog. Frick was attempting to smuggle Pinkertons into Homestead.

Workers sounded the alarm, and within minutes a crowd of more than a thousand, hastily armed with rifles, hoes, and fence posts, rushed to the riverbank to meet the enemy. When the Pinkertons attempted to come ashore, gunfire broke out, and more than a dozen Pinkertons and some thirty strikers fell, killed or wounded. The Pinkertons retreated to the barges. For twelve hours, the workers, joined by their family members, threw everything they had at the barges, from fireworks to dynamite. Finally, the Pinkertons hoisted a white flag and arranged with O'Donnell to surrender. With three workers dead and scores wounded, the crowd, numbering perhaps ten thousand, was in no mood for conciliation. As the hated "Pinks" came up the hill, they were forced to run a gantlet of screaming, cursing men, women, and children. When a young guard dropped to his knees, weeping for mercy, a woman used her umbrella to poke out his eye. One Pinkerton had been killed in the siege on the barges. In the grim rout that followed their surrender, not one avoided injury.

The "battle of Fort Frick" ended in a dubious victory for the workers. They took control of the plant and elected a council to run the community. At first, public opinion favored their cause. Newspapers urged Frick to negotiate or submit to arbitration. A congressman castigated Carnegie for "skulking in his castle in Scotland." Populists, meeting in St. Louis, condemned the use of "hireling armies."

The action of the Homestead workers struck at the heart of the capitalist system, pitting the workers' right to their jobs against the rights of private property. The workers' insistence that "we are not destroying the property of the company—merely protecting our rights" did not prove as compelling to the courts and the state as the property rights of the mill owners. Four days after the confrontation, Pennsylvania's governor, who sympathized with the workers, nonetheless yielded to pressure from Frick and ordered eight thousand National Guard troops into Homestead to protect Carnegie's property. The strikers, thinking they had nothing to fear from the militia, welcomed the troops with a brass band. But they soon understood the reality. The troops' ninety-five-day occupation not only protected Carnegie's property but also enabled Frick to reopen the mills and bring in strikebreakers. "We have been deceived," one worker complained bitterly. "We have stood idly by and let the town be occupied by soldiers who come here, not as our protectors, but as the protectors of non-union men. . . . If we undertake to resist the seizure of our jobs, we will be shot down like dogs."

Then, in a misguided effort to ignite a general uprising, **Alexander Berkman**, a Russian immigrant and anarchist, attempted to assassinate Frick. Berkman bungled his attempt. Shot twice and stabbed with a dagger, Frick survived and showed considerable courage, allowing a doctor to remove the bullets but refusing to leave his desk until the day's work was completed. "I do not think that I shall die," Frick remarked coolly, "but whether I do or not, the Company will pursue the same policy and it will win."

After the assassination attempt, public opinion turned against the workers. Berkman was quickly tried and sentenced to prison. Although the Amalgamated and the AFL denounced his action, the incident linked anarchism and unionism, already associated in the public mind as a result of the Haymarket bombing in 1886 (see chapter 19). Hugh O'Donnell later wrote, "The bullet from Berkman's pistol, failing in its foul intent, went straight through the heart of the Homestead strike."

In the end, the workers capitulated. The Homestead mill reopened in November, and the men returned to work, except for the union leaders, now blacklisted in every steel mill in the country. With the owners firmly in charge, the company slashed wages, reinstated the twelve-hour day, and eliminated five hundred jobs.

In the drama of events at Homestead, the significance of what occurred often remained obscured: The workers at Homestead had been taught a lesson. They would never again, in the words of the National Guard commander, "believe the works are their's [*sic*] quite as much as Carnegie's." Another forty-five years would pass before steelworkers, unskilled as well as skilled, successfully unionized. In the meantime, Carnegie's production tripled, even in the midst of a depression. "Ashamed to tell you profits these days," Carnegie wrote a friend in 1899. And no wonder: Carnegie's profits had grown from $4 million in 1892 to $40 million in 1900.

The Cripple Creek Miners' Strike of 1894
Less than a year after the Homestead lockout, a panic on Wall Street in the spring of 1893 touched off a bitter economic depression. In the West, silver mines fell on hard times, touching off the **Cripple Creek miners' strike of 1894**. When mine owners moved to lengthen the workday from eight to ten

hours, the newly formed Western Federation of Miners (WFM) vowed to hold the line in Cripple Creek, Colorado. In February 1894, the WFM threatened to strike all mines working more than eight-hour shifts. The mine owners divided: Some quickly settled with the WFM; others continued to demand ten hours, provoking a strike.

The striking miners received help from many quarters. Working miners paid $15 a month to a strike fund, and miners in neighboring districts sent substantial contributions. The miners enjoyed the support and assistance of local businesses and grocers, who provided credit to the strikers. With these advantages, the Cripple Creek strikers could afford to hold out for their demands.

Even more significant, Governor Davis H. Waite, a Populist elected in 1892, had strong ties to the miners and refused to use the power of the state against the strikers. Governor Waite asked the strikers to lay down their arms and demanded that the mine owners disperse their hired deputies. The miners agreed to arbitration and selected Waite as their sole arbitrator. By May, the recalcitrant mine owners capitulated, and the union won an eight-hour day.

Governor Waite's intervention demonstrated the pivotal power of the state in the nation's labor wars. Having a Populist in power made a difference. A decade later, in 1904, with Waite out of office, mine owners relied on state troops to take back control of the mines, defeating the WFM and blacklisting all of its members. In retrospect, the Cripple Creek miners' strike of 1894 proved the exception to the rule of state intervention on the side of private property. More typical was the outcome of another strike in 1894 in Pullman, Illinois.

Eugene V. Debs and the Pullman Strike
The economic depression that began in 1893 swelled the ranks of the unemployed to three million, almost half of the working population. "A fearful crisis is upon us," wrote a labor publication. Nowhere were workers more demoralized than in the model town of Pullman, on the outskirts of Chicago.

In the wake of the Great Railroad Strike of 1877, **George M. Pullman**, the builder of Pullman railroad cars, had moved his plant and workers away from the "snares of the great city." In 1880, he purchased 4,300 acres nine miles south of Chicago and built a model town. The town of Pullman boasted parks, fountains, playgrounds, an auditorium, a

> One Homestead worker complained bitterly, "We have stood idly by and let the town be occupied by soldiers. . . . If we undertake to resist the seizure of our jobs, we will be shot down like dogs."

A Pullman Craftsworker Pullman Palace cars were known for their luxurious details. Here, a painter working in the 1890s applies elaborate decoration to the exterior of a Pullman car. In the foreground is an intricately carved door, an example of fine hand-detailing. The Pullman workers' strike in 1894 stemmed in part from the company's efforts to undermine the status of craftsworkers by reducing them to low-paid piecework. Control of the workplace, as much as issues related to wages and hours, fueled the labor wars of the 1890s. Chicago Historical Society.

library, a hotel, shops, and markets, along with 1,800 units of housing. Noticeably absent was a saloon.

The housing in Pullman was clearly superior to that in neighboring areas, but workers paid a high price to live in the model town. George M. Pullman expected a 6 percent return on his investment. As a result, Pullman's rents ran 10 to 20 percent higher than housing costs in nearby communities.

And a family in Pullman could never own its own home. George Pullman refused to "sell an acre under any circumstances." As long as he controlled the town absolutely, he held the powerful whip of eviction over his employees and could quickly get rid of "troublemakers." Although observers at first praised the beauty and orderliness of the town, critics by the 1890s compared Pullman's model town to a "gilded cage" for workers.

The depression brought hard times to Pullman. Workers saw their wages slashed five times between May and December 1893, with cuts totaling at least 28 percent. At the same time, Pullman refused to lower the rents in his model town, insisting that "the renting of the dwellings and the employment of work men at Pullman are in no way tied together." When workers went to the bank to cash their paychecks, they found the rent had been taken out. One worker discovered only forty-seven cents in his pay envelope for two weeks' work. When the bank teller asked him whether he wanted to apply it to his back rent, he retorted, "If Mr. Pullman needs that forty-seven cents worse than I do, let him have it." At the same time, Pullman continued to pay his stockholders an 8 percent dividend, and the company accumulated a $25 million surplus.

At the heart of the labor problems at Pullman lay not only economic inequity but also the company's attempt to control the work process, substituting piecework for day wages and undermining skilled craftsworkers. The Pullman workers rebelled. During the spring of 1894, Pullman's desperate workers, seeking help, flocked to the ranks of the **American Railway Union (ARU)**, led by the charismatic **Eugene V. Debs**. The ARU, unlike the skilled craft unions of the AFL, pledged to organize all railway workers—from engineers to engine wipers.

George Pullman responded to union organization at his plant by firing three of the union's leaders the day after they led a delegation to protest wage cuts. Angry men and women walked off the job in disgust. What began as a spontaneous protest in May 1894 quickly blossomed into a strike that involved more than 90 percent of Pullman's 3,300 workers. "We do not know what the outcome will be, and in fact we do not much care," one worker confessed. "We do know that we are working for less wages than will maintain ourselves and families in the necessaries of life, and on that proposition we refuse to work any longer." Pullman countered by shutting down the plant.

In June, the Pullman strikers appealed to the ARU to come to their aid. Debs hesitated to commit his fledgling union to a major strike in the midst of a depression. He pleaded with the workers to find another solution. When George Pullman adamantly refused arbitration, the ARU membership voted to boycott all Pullman cars. Beginning on June 29, switchmen across the United States refused to handle any train that carried Pullman cars.

The conflict escalated quickly. The General Managers Association (GMA), an organization of managers from twenty-four different railroads, acted in concert to quash the **Pullman boycott**. Determined to kill the ARU, they recruited strikebreakers and fired all the protesting switchmen. Their tactics set off a chain reaction. Entire train crews walked off the job in a show of solidarity with the Pullman workers. In a matter of days, the boycott/strike spread to more than fifteen railroads and affected twenty-seven states and territories. By July 2, rail lines from New York to California lay paralyzed. Even the GMA was forced to concede that the railroads had been "fought to a standstill."

The boycott remained surprisingly peaceful. In contrast to the Great Railroad Strike of 1877, no major riots broke out, and no serious property damage occurred. Debs, in a whirlwind of activity, fired off telegrams to all parts of the country advising his followers to avoid violence and respect law and order. But the nation's newspapers, fed press releases by the GMA, distorted the issues and misrepresented the strike. Across the country, papers ran headlines like "Wild Riot in Chicago" and "Mob Is in Control."

In Washington, Attorney General Richard B. Olney, a lawyer with strong ties to the railroads, determined to put down the strike. In his way stood the governor of Illinois, John Peter Altgeld, who, observing that the boycott remained peaceful, refused to call out troops. To get around Altgeld, Olney convinced President Grover Cleveland that federal troops had to intervene to protect the mails. To further cripple the boycott, two conservative Chicago judges issued an injunction so sweeping that it prohibited Debs from speaking in public. By issuing the injunction, the court made the boycott a crime punishable by a jail sentence for contempt of court, a civil process that did not require a jury trial. Even the conservative *Chicago Tribune* judged the injunction "a menace to liberty . . . a weapon ever ready for the capitalist." Furious, Debs risked jail by refusing to honor it.

Olney's strategy worked. With the strikers violating a federal injunction and with the mails in jeopardy (the GMA made sure that Pullman cars were put on every mail train), Cleveland called out the army. On July 5, nearly 8,000 troops marched into Chicago. Violence immediately erupted. In one day, troops killed 25 workers and wounded more than 60. In the face of bullets and bayonets, the strikers held firm. "Troops cannot move trains," Debs reminded his followers, a fact that was borne out as the railroads remained paralyzed despite the military intervention. But if the army could not put down the boycott, the injunction could and did. Debs was arrested and imprisoned for contempt of court. With its leader in jail, its headquarters raided and ransacked, and its members demoralized, the ARU was defeated along with the boycott. Pullman reopened his factory, hiring new workers to replace many of the strikers and leaving 1,600 workers without jobs.

In the aftermath of the strike, a special commission investigated the events at Pullman, taking testimony from 107 witnesses, from the lowliest workers to George M. Pullman himself. Stubborn and self-righteous, Pullman spoke for the business orthodoxy of his era, steadfastly affirming the right of business to safeguard its interests through confederacies such as the GMA and at the same time denying labor's right to organize. "If we were to receive these men as representatives of the union," he stated, "they could probably force us to pay any wages which they saw fit."

From his jail cell, Eugene Debs reviewed the events of the Pullman strike. With the courts and the government ready to side with industrialists in the interest of defending private property, Debs realized that labor had little recourse. Strikes seemed futile, and unions remained helpless; workers would have to take control of the state itself. Debs went into jail a trade unionist and came out six months later a socialist. At first, he turned to the Populist Party, but after its demise, he formed the Socialist Party in 1900 and ran for president on its ticket five times. Debs's dissatisfaction with the status quo was shared by another group even more alienated from the political process — women.

Q: **Why did the strikes of the 1890s fail to produce permanent gains for workers?**

Women's Politics

"Do everything," Frances Willard urged her followers in 1881. The new president of the Woman's Christian Temperance Union (WCTU) meant what she said. The WCTU followed a trajectory that was common for women in the late nineteenth century. As women organized to deal with issues that touched their homes and families, they moved into politics, lending new urgency to the cause of woman suffrage. Urban industrialism dislocated women's lives no less than men's. Like men, women sought political change and organized to promote issues central to their lives, campaigning for temperance and woman suffrage.

Frances Willard and the Woman's Christian Temperance Union

Frances Willard, the visionary leader of the WCTU, spoke for a group left almost entirely out of the U.S. electoral process—women. In 1890, only one state, Wyoming, allowed women to vote in national elections. But lack of the franchise did not mean that women were apolitical. The WCTU demonstrated the breadth of women's political activity in the late nineteenth century.

When Frances Willard became president in 1879, she radically changed the direction of the organization. Social action replaced prayer as women's answer to the threat of drunkenness. Viewing alcoholism as a disease rather than a sin and poverty as a cause rather than a result of drink, the WCTU became involved in labor issues, joining with the Knights of Labor to press for better working conditions for women workers. Describing workers in a textile mill, a WCTU member wrote in the *Union Signal*, "It is dreadful to see these girls, stripped almost to the skin . . . and running like racehorses from the beginning to the end of the day." She concluded, "The hard slavish work is drawing the girls into the saloon."

Willard capitalized on the cult of domesticity as a shrewd political tactic to move women into public life and gain power to ameliorate social problems. Using "home protection" as her watchword, she argued as early as 1884 that women needed the vote to protect home and family. By the 1890s, the WCTU's grassroots network of local unions had spread to all but the most isolated rural areas of the country. Strong and rich, with more than 200,000 dues-paying members, the WCTU was a formidable group.

Willard worked to create a broad reform coalition in the 1890s, embracing the Knights of Labor, the People's Party, and the Prohibition Party. Until her death in 1898, she led, if not a woman's rights movement, then the first organized mass movement of women united around a women's issue. By 1900, thanks largely to the WCTU, women could claim a generation of experience in political action—speaking, lobbying, organizing, drafting legislation, and running private charitable institutions. As Willard observed, "All this work has tended more toward the liberation of women than it has toward the extinction of the saloon."

Elizabeth Cady Stanton, Susan B. Anthony, and the Movement for Woman Suffrage

Unlike the WCTU, the organized movement for woman suffrage remained small and relatively weak in the late nineteenth century. The woman's rights movement, begun by **Elizabeth Cady Stanton** at Seneca Falls in 1848 (see chapter 12), split in 1867 over whether the Fourteenth and Fifteenth Amendments, which granted voting rights to African American men, should have extended the vote to women as well. Stanton and her ally, **Susan B. Anthony**, launched the National Woman Suffrage Association (NWSA) in 1869, demanding the vote for women (see chapter 18). A more conservative group, the American Woman Suffrage Association (AWSA), formed the same year. Composed of men as well as women, the AWSA believed that women should vote in local but not national elections.

By 1890, the split had healed, and the newly united National American Woman Suffrage Association (NAWSA) launched campaigns on the state level to gain the vote for women. Twenty years had made a great change. Woman suffrage, though not yet generally supported, was no longer considered a crackpot idea. Thanks to the WCTU's support of the "home protection" ballot, suffrage had become accepted as a means to an end even when it was not embraced as a woman's natural right. The NAWSA honored Elizabeth Cady Stanton by electing her its first president, but Susan B. Anthony, who took the helm in 1892, emerged as the leading figure in the new united organization.

Stanton and Anthony, both in their seventies, were coming to the end of their public careers. Since the days of the Seneca Falls woman's rights convention, they had worked for reforms for their sex, including property rights, custody rights, and the right to education and gainful employment. But the prize of woman suffrage still eluded them. Suffragists won victories in Colorado in 1893 and Idaho in 1896. One more state joined the suffrage column in 1896 when Utah entered the Union. But women suffered a bitter defeat in a California referendum on woman suffrage that same year. Never losing faith, Susan B. Anthony remarked in her last public appearance, in 1906, "Failure is impossible." Although it would take until 1920 for all women to gain the vote with the ratification of the Nineteenth Amendment, the unification of the two woman suffrage groups in 1890

> Never losing faith, Susan B. Anthony remarked in her last public appearance, in 1906, "Failure is impossible."

Campaigning for Woman Suffrage In 1896, women voted in only four states — Wyoming, Colorado, Idaho, and Utah. The West led the way in the campaign for woman suffrage, with Wyoming Territory granting women the vote as early as 1869. Sparse population meant that only sixteen votes were needed in the state's territorial legislature to obtain passage of woman suffrage. The poster calls on Nebraska to join the suffrage column, while the flag illustrates the number of states in which women could vote. Poster: Nebraska State Historical Society; Flag: Smithsonian Institution, Washington, D.C.

signaled a new era in women's fight for the vote just as Frances Willard's place on the platform in 1892 at the founding of the People's Party in St. Louis symbolized women's growing role in politics and reform.

Q: How did women's temperance activism contribute to the cause of woman suffrage?

Depression Politics

The depression that began in the spring of 1893 and lasted for more than four years put nearly half of the labor force out of work, a higher percentage than during the Great Depression of the 1930s. The human cost of the depression was staggering. "I Take my pen in hand to let you know that we are Starving to death," a Kansas farm woman wrote to the governor in 1894. "Last cent gone," wrote a young widow in her diary. "Children went to work without their breakfasts." The burden of feeding and sheltering the unemployed and their families fell to private charity, city government, and some of the stronger trade unions. Following the harsh dictates of social Darwinism and laissez-faire, the majority of America's elected officials believed

that it was inappropriate for the government to intervene. But the scope of the depression made it impossible for local agencies to supply sufficient relief, and increasingly Americans called on the federal government to take action. Armies of the unemployed marched on Washington to demand relief, and the Populist Party experienced a surge of support as the election of 1896 approached.

Coxey's Army Masses of unemployed Americans marched to Washington, D.C., in the spring of 1894 to call attention to their plight and to urge Congress to enact a public works program to end unemployment. Jacob S. Coxey of Massilon, Ohio, led the most publicized contingent. Convinced that men could be put to work building badly needed roads for the nation, Coxey proposed a scheme to finance public works through non-interest-bearing bonds. "What I am after," he maintained, "is to try to put this country in a condition so that no man who wants work shall be obliged to remain idle." His plan won support from the AFL and the Populists.

Starting out from Ohio with one hundred men, **Coxey's army**, as it was dubbed, swelled as it marched east through the spring snows of the Alleghenies. In Pennsylvania, Coxey recruited several hundred from the ranks of those left unemployed by the

Coxey's Army A contingent of Coxey's army stops to rest on its way to Washington, D.C. A "petition in boots," Coxey's followers were well dressed, as evidenced by the men in this photo wearing white shirts, vests, neckties, and bowler hats. Music was an important component of the march, including the anthem "Marching with Coxey," sung to the tune of "Marching through Georgia." Band members are pictured on the right with their instruments. Despite their peaceful pose, the marchers stirred the fears of many conservative Americans, who predicted an uprising of the unemployed. Only a few Populist members of Congress—notably Senator William V. Allen of Nebraska—supported them and urged Congress to hear their grievances. Instead, Coxey and a contingent of his marchers were arrested and jailed for "walking on the grass" when they reached the nation's capital. Ohio Historical Society.

Homestead lockout. Called by Coxey the Commonweal of Christ, the army advanced to the tune of "Marching through Georgia":

> We are not tramps nor vagabonds,
>   that's shirking honest toil,
> But miners, clerks, skilled artisans,
>   and tillers of the soil
> Now forced to beg our brother worms
>   to give us leave to toil,
> While we are marching with Coxey.
> Hurrah! hurrah! for the unemployed's appeal
> Hurrah! hurrah! for the marching commonweal!

On May 1, Coxey's army arrived in Washington. When Coxey defiantly marched his men onto the Capitol grounds, police set upon the demonstrators with nightsticks, cracking skulls and arresting Coxey and his lieutenants. Coxey went to jail for twenty days and was fined $5 for "walking on the grass."

Those who had trembled for the safety of the Republic heaved a sigh of relief after Coxey's arrest, hoping that it would halt the march on Washington. But other armies of the unemployed, totaling possibly as many as five thousand people, were still on their way. Too poor to pay for railway tickets,

they rode the rails as "freeloaders." The more daring contingents commandeered entire trains, stirring fears of revolution. Journalists who covered the march did little to quiet the nation's fears. They delighted in military terminology, describing themselves as "war correspondents." To boost newspaper sales, they gave to the episode a tone of urgency and heightened the sense of a nation imperiled.

By August, the leaderless, tattered armies dissolved. Although the "On to Washington" movement proved ineffective in forcing federal relief legislation, Coxey's army dramatized the plight of the unemployed and acted, in the words of one participant, as a "living, moving object lesson." Like the Populists, Coxey's army called into question the underlying values of the new industrial order and demonstrated how ordinary citizens turned to means outside the regular party system to influence politics in the 1890s.

The People's Party and the Election of 1896
Even before the depression of 1893 gave added impetus to their cause, the Populists had railed against the status quo. "We meet in the midst of a nation brought to the verge of moral, political, and material ruin," Ignatius Donnelly had declared

in his keynote address at the creation of the People's Party in St. Louis in 1892. "The fruits of the toil of millions are boldly stolen to build up colossal fortunes for a few. . . . From the same prolific womb of governmental injustice we breed the two great classes—tramps and millionaires."

The fiery rhetoric frightened many who saw in the People's Party a call not to reform but to revolution. Throughout the country, the press denounced the Populists as "cranks, lunatics, and idiots." When one self-righteous editor dismissed them as "calamity howlers," Populist governor Lorenzo Lewelling of Kansas shot back, "If that is so I want to continue to howl until those conditions are improved."

The People's Party captured more than a million votes in the presidential election of 1892, a respectable showing for a new party (Map 20.1). But increasingly, sectional and racial animosities threatened its unity. In the South, the Populists' willingness to form common cause with black farmers made them anathema. Realizing that race prejudice obscured the common economic interests of black and white farmers, Tom Watson of Georgia openly courted African Americans, appearing on platforms with black speakers and promising "to wipe out the color line." When angry Georgia whites threatened to lynch a black Populist preacher, Watson rallied two thousand gun-toting Populists to the man's defense. Although many Populists remained racist in their attitudes toward African Americans, the spectacle of white Georgians riding through the night to protect a black man from lynching was symbolic of the enormous changes the Populist Party promised in the South.

As the presidential election of 1896 approached, the depression intensified cries for reform not only from the Populists but also throughout the electorate. Depression worsened the tight money problem caused by the deflationary pressures of the gold standard. Once again, proponents of free silver (the unlimited coinage of silver in addition to gold) stirred rebellion in the ranks of both the Democratic and the Republican parties. When the Republicans nominated Ohio governor **William McKinley** on a platform pledging the preservation of the gold standard, western advocates of free silver representing miners and farmers walked out of the convention. Open rebellion also split the Democratic Party as vast segments in the West and South repudiated President Grover Cleveland because of his support for gold. In South Carolina, Benjamin Tillman won his race for Congress by promising, "Send me to Washington and I'll stick my pitchfork into [Cleveland's] old ribs!"

The spirit of revolt animated the Democratic National Convention in Chicago in the summer

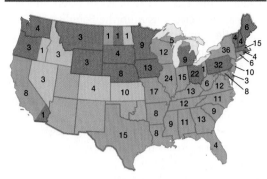

Candidate	Electoral Vote	Popular Vote	Percent of Popular Vote
Grover Cleveland (Democrat)	277	5,555,426	46.1
Benjamin Harrison (Republican)	145	5,182,690	43.0
James B. Weaver (People's)	22	1,029,846	8.5

MAP 20.1 The Election of 1892

of 1896. **William Jennings Bryan** of Nebraska, the thirty-six-year-old "boy orator from the Platte," whipped the convention into a frenzy with his passionate call for free silver. In his keynote address, Bryan masterfully cataloged the grievances of farmers and laborers, closing his dramatic speech with a ringing exhortation: "Do not crucify mankind upon a cross of gold." Pandemonium broke loose as delegates stampeded to nominate Bryan, the youngest candidate ever to run for the presidency.

The juggernaut of free silver rolled out of Chicago and on to St. Louis, where the People's Party met a week after the Democrats adjourned. Smelling victory, many western Populists urged the party to ally with the Democrats and endorse Bryan. A major obstacle in the path of fusion, however, was Bryan's running mate, Arthur M. Sewall. A Maine railway director and bank president, Sewall, who had been placed on the ticket to appease conservative Democrats, embodied everything the Populists detested.

Populism's regional constituencies remained as divided over tactics as they were uniform in their call for change. Western Populists, including a strong coalition of farmers and miners in states such as Idaho and Colorado, championed free silver. In these largely Republican states, Populists had joined forces with Democrats in previous elections and saw no problem with becoming "Popocrats" once Bryan led the Democratic ticket on a free-silver platform. Similarly in the Midwest, a Republican stronghold, Populists who had used fusion with the Democrats as a tactic to win elections had little trouble backing Bryan. But in the South, where Democrats had resorted to fraud and violence to steal elections from the Populists in 1892 and 1894, support for a Democratic ticket proved especially hard to swallow. Die-hard southern Populists wanted no part of fusion.

All of these tactical differences emerged as the Populists met in St. Louis in 1896 to nominate a candidate for president. To show that they remained true to their principles, delegates first voted to support all the planks of the 1892 platform, added to it a call for public works projects for the unemployed, and only narrowly defeated a plank for woman suffrage. To deal with the problem of fusion, the convention selected the vice presidential candidate first. The nomination of **Tom Watson** undercut opposition to Bryan's candidacy. And although Bryan quickly sent a telegram to protest that he would not drop Sewall as his running mate, mysteriously his message never reached the convention floor. Fusion triumphed. Watson's vice presidential nomination paved the way for the selection of Bryan by a lopsided vote. The Populists did not know it, but their cheers for Bryan signaled not a chorus of victory, but the death knell of the People's Party.

Few contests in the nation's history have been as fiercely fought and as full of emotion as the presidential election of 1896. On one side stood Republican William McKinley, backed by the wealthy industrialist and party boss Mark Hanna. Hanna played on the business community's fears of Populism to raise a Republican war chest more than double the amount of any previous campaign. On the other side, William Jennings Bryan, with few assets beyond his silver tongue, struggled to

make up in energy and eloquence what his party lacked in campaign funds, crisscrossing the country in a whirlwind tour, traveling more than eighteen thousand miles and delivering more than six hundred speeches in three months. According to his own reckoning, he visited twenty-seven states and spoke to more than five million Americans.

As election day approached, the silver states of the Rocky Mountains lined up solidly for Bryan. The Northeast stood solidly for McKinley. Much of the South, with the exception of the border states, abandoned the Populists and returned to the Democratic fold, leaving Tom Watson to lament that "[Populists] play Jonah while [Democrats] play the whale." The Midwest hung in the balance. Bryan intensified his campaign in Illinois, Michigan, Ohio, and Indiana. But midwestern farmers proved less receptive than western voters to the blandishments of free silver.

In the cities, Democrats charged the Republicans with mass intimidation. "Men, vote as you please," the head of New York's Steinway Piano Company reportedly announced to his workers on the eve of the election, "but if Bryan is elected tomorrow the whistle will not blow Wednesday morning." Intimidation alone did not explain the failure of urban labor to rally to Bryan. Republicans repeatedly warned workers that if the Democrats won, the inflated silver dollar would be worth only fifty cents. However much farmers and laborers might insist that they were united as producers against the nonproducing bosses, it was equally true that inflation did not offer the boon to urban laborers that it did to western farmers.

On election day, four out of five voters went to the polls in an unprecedented turnout. In the critical midwestern states, as many as 95 percent of the eligible voters cast their ballots. In the end, the election hinged on between 100 and 1,000 votes in several key states, including Wisconsin, Iowa, and Minnesota. Although McKinley won twenty-three states to Bryan's twenty-two, the electoral vote showed a lopsided 271 to 176 in McKinley's favor (Map 20.2).

The biggest losers in 1896 turned out to be the Populists. On the national level, they polled fewer than 300,000 votes, a million less than in 1894. In the clamor to support Bryan, Populists in the South had drifted back to the Democratic Party. The People's Party was crushed, and with it the agrarian revolt.

But if Populism proved unsuccessful at the polls, it nevertheless set the domestic political agenda for the United States in the next decades, highlighting issues such as banking and currency reform, electoral reforms, and an enlarged role for the federal government in the economy. Meanwhile, as

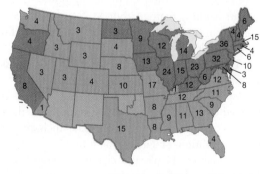

Candidate	Electoral Vote	Popular Vote	Percent of Popular Vote
William McKinley (Republican)	271	7,104,779	51.1
William J. Bryan (Democrat-People's)	176	6,502,925	47.7

MAP 20.2 The Election of 1896

the decade ended, the bugle call to arms turned America's attention to foreign affairs and effectively drowned out the trumpet of reform. The struggle for social justice gave way to a war for empire as the United States asserted its power on the world stage.

Q: Why was the People's Party unable to translate national support into victory in the 1896 election?

The United States and the World

Throughout much of the second half of the nineteenth century, U.S. interest in foreign policy took a backseat to territorial expansion in the American West. The United States stood aloof while Great Britain, France, Germany, Spain, Belgium, and the increasingly powerful Japan competed for empires in Asia, Africa, Latin America, and the Pacific. Between 1870 and 1900, European nations colonized more than 20 percent of the world's landmass and 10 percent of the world's population.

At the turn of the twentieth century, American foreign policy consisted of two currents—isolationism and expansionism. Although the determination to remain aloof from European politics had been a hallmark of U.S. foreign policy since the nation's founding, Americans simultaneously believed in manifest destiny—the "obvious" right to expand the nation from ocean to ocean. The United States' determination to protect its sphere of influence in the Western Hemisphere at the same time it expanded its trading in Asia moved the nation away from isolationism and toward a more active role on the world stage. The push for commercial expansion joined with a sense of Christian mission to refocus the nation's attention abroad and led both to the strengthening of the Monroe Doctrine in the Western Hemisphere and to a new Open Door policy in Asia.

Markets and Missionaries The depression of the 1890s provided a powerful impetus to American commercial expansion. As markets weakened at home, American businesses looked abroad for profits. As early as 1890, Captain Alfred Thayer Mahan, leader of a growing group of American expansionists, prophesied, "Whether they will or not, Americans must now begin to look outward. The growing production of the country requires it." As the depression deepened, one diplomat warned that Americans "must turn [their] eyes abroad, or they will soon look inward upon discontent."

Exports constituted a small but significant percentage of the profits of American business in the 1890s (Figure 20.1). And where American interests led, businessmen expected the government's power and influence to follow to protect their investments. Companies like Standard Oil actively sought to use the U.S. government as their agent, often putting foreign service employees on the payroll. "Our ambassadors and ministers and consuls," wrote John D. Rockefeller appreciatively, "have aided to push our way into new markets and to the utmost corners of the world." Whether "our" referred to the United States or to Standard Oil remained ambiguous; in

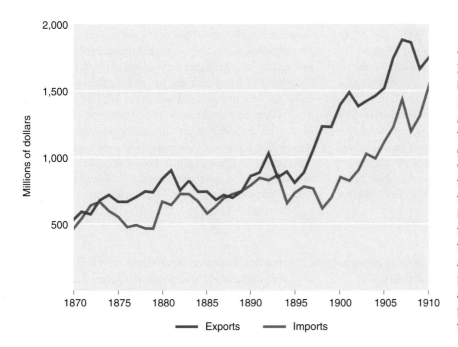

FIGURE 20.1 Expansion in U.S. Trade, 1870–1910 Between 1870 and 1910, American exports more than tripled. Imports generally rose, but they were held in check by the high protective tariffs championed by Republican presidents from Ulysses S. Grant to William Howard Taft. A decline in imports is particularly noticeable after the passage of the prohibitive McKinley tariff in 1890.

Regime Change in Hawaii

Queen Liliuokalani came to the throne in Hawaii in 1891 determined to take back power for her monarchy and her people. As a member of Hawaii's native royalty, or *alii*, she had received a first-rate education in missionary school. A convert to Christianity, she had taken the English name Lydia and married the *haole* (white) governor of Maui. Yet she maintained a reverence for traditional Hawaiian ways and resented the treatment of her people by the white minority.

Her brother, King Kalakaua, had proved to be a weak and compliant leader. In 1876, he signed a treaty that turned Hawaii essentially into an American protectorate. And in 1887, while Liliuokalani was traveling in Europe, the white elite coerced Kalakaua to sign the "Bayonet Constitution," which leased Pearl Harbor to the United States and put the government squarely in the hands of the white minority. When Liliuokalani learned of the power grab, she bluntly styled it "a revolutionary movement inaugurated by those of foreign blood, or American blood." After the death of her brother, Liliuokalani assumed the throne resolved to institute a new constitution that would restore power to the Hawaiian people by making only native Hawaiians eligible to vote.

Her task would not be easy. She had already been warned by a member of the haole elite, "You will live longer and happier and be more popular by not trying to do too much." Yet determined to rule, not simply to reign, Liliuokalani moved ahead with plans to wrest power from the minority she referred to as Hawaii's "guests."

For Hawaiians, contact with outsiders had followed a course very similar to that of Native Americans on the mainland—death, disease, and dispossession. Not long after Captain James Cook sailed into the islands in 1778, things turned deadly. Cook killed one of the chiefs, and the Hawaiians retaliated by hacking Cook to pieces. But more deadly than armed conflict were the diseases carried by the sailors who soon made Hawaii a Pacific port of call. Lacking immunity, the native Hawaiian population shrank over the next century from more than 300,000 to barely 50,000.

American missionaries first came to Hawaii in 1820 and soon intermarried with their Christian converts, creating a group of *hapa haole* (half whites), as well as a growing number of children born in Hawaii to white parents. The temptations of wealth led many missionaries, like Amos Starr Cooke, to acquire land and try their hand at sugar planting. In 1851, he founded Castle & Cooke, which became one of the world's largest sugar producers. By the end of the century, missionaries and planters had blended into one ruling class and gained control of extensive tracts of land. Thanks to the Bayonet Constitution, they controlled the islands, even though native Hawaiians and the Japanese and Chinese "coolie" laborers imported to work on the sugar plantations outnumbered the whites ten to one.

Sugar became a booming business in Hawaii as a result of favorable reciprocity treaties with the United States. Exports grew from 21 million pounds in 1876 to 225 million pounds by 1890. But hard times came to the islands with the passage of the McKinley tariff in 1890. The tariff wiped out the advantage Hawaiian sugar had enjoyed in the American market, with devastating results. Within two years, the value of Hawaiian sugar exports plummeted from $13 million to $8 million.

One way to avoid the tariff was by incorporating Hawaii into the United States through annexation. Foremost among those who championed this scheme was Lorrin Thurston, the thirty-five-year-old grandson of American missionaries. Thurston, born in Hawaii and educated in the United States, was zealous in his belief that Hawaii should be ruled by "the intelligent part of the community"—white Americans and their children. In 1892, he founded the secret Annexation Club and traveled to Washington, D.C., where he won the support of Republican secretary of state James G. Blaine, an enthusiastic supporter of American expansion. Blaine went so far as to suggest that Thurston bribe Queen Liliuokalani, offering her $250,000 to abdicate and assign the sovereignty of Hawaii to the United States. Unfortunately, Thurston replied, there was

practice, the distinction was of little importance in late-nineteenth-century foreign policy.

America's foreign policy often appeared little more than a sidelight to business development. In Hawaii (first called the Sandwich Islands), American sugar interests fomented a rebellion in 1893, toppling the increasingly independent Queen Liliuokalani. (See "Beyond America's Borders.") They pushed Congress to annex the islands, which would allow planters to avoid the high McKinley tariff on sugar.

"no probability" that the independent-minded queen would accept such an offer. But he returned to Hawaii armed with the knowledge that annexation had influential friends in Washington.

Queen Liliuokalani picked Saturday, January 14, 1893, as the day to promulgate her new constitution. She dressed with care in a lavender silk gown and a diamond coronet and called her cabinet to meet at the Iolani Palace. Learning of her intentions, Thurston quickly sprang into action. He persuaded four of the cabinet ministers to oppose the constitution, stalling for time while he plotted to overthrow the monarchy. Thurston's daring plan could work only with the cooperation of the United States. So late that night, he knocked on the door of John L. Stevens, the American minister to Hawaii. Laying out his plan, he urged Stevens, a staunch annexationist, to support the overthrow of the queen and to pledge U.S. support for his actions. Without hesitating, Stevens promised to land Marines from the USS *Boston* "to protect American lives and property."

Two days later, 162 American Marines and sailors marched into Honolulu armed with carbines and dragging howitzers (small cannons) and Gatling guns. The next day, Thurston and 17 of his confederates seized control of a government building across the street from the palace and proclaimed themselves a "provisional government." Minister Stevens promptly recognized the revolutionaries as the legitimate government of Hawaii.

To avoid bloodshed, Queen Liliuokalani bowed to the inevitable and agreed to step aside. But in a masterstroke, she sat down and composed a letter addressed not to her enemies in the provisional government, but to the U.S. government. Protesting her overthrow, she yielded her authority "until such time as the Government of the United States, shall, upon the facts being presented to it, undo the action of its representatives and reinstate me in the authority which I claim as the constitutional sovereign of the Hawaiian Islands." The action now shifted to Washington, where Grover Cleveland, a Democrat skeptical of America's adventures abroad, came to the presidency in March 1893. Cleveland quickly squelched plans for

★ **Queen Liliuokalani (1838–1917)** An accomplished woman who straddled two cultures, Lydia Kamakaeha Dominis, or Queen Liliuokalani, spoke English as easily as her native Hawaiian and was fluent in French and German as well. She traveled widely in Europe and the United States. Despite President Cleveland's belief that the monarchy should be restored, Liliuokalani never regained her throne. In 1898, she published *Hawaii's Story by Hawaii's Queen*, outlining her version of the events that had led to her downfall. In 1993, on the one hundredth anniversary of the revolution that deposed her, Congress passed and President Bill Clinton signed a resolution offering an apology to native Hawaiians for the overthrow of their queen. Courtesy of the Liliuokalani Trust.

annexation and called for an inquiry. When his investigation concluded that the Hawaiian people did not support the takeover, Cleveland admonished Stevens for his role in the overthrow and called for the restoration of the monarchy. The provisional government, however, enjoyed the support of Republicans in Congress and refused to step down. In a bid to gain American sympathy, Hawaii's provisional government declared itself a republic on July 4, 1894, and then bided its time, waiting for the Republicans to take back the White House.

In 1898, as the taste for empire swept the United States in the wake of the Spanish-American War, President William McKinley quietly signed a treaty annexing Hawaii. His action pleased not only Hawaii's sugar growers but also American expansionists, who judged Hawaii strategically important in expanding U.S. trade with China.

"Hawaii is ours," Grover Cleveland wrote sadly. "As I look back upon the first steps in this miserable business, and as I contemplate the means used to complete the outrage, I am ashamed of the whole affair."

When President Cleveland learned that Hawaiians opposed annexation, he withdrew the proposal from Congress. But expansionists still coveted the islands and continued to look for an excuse to push through annexation.

However compelling the economic arguments about overseas markets proved, business interests alone did not account for the new expansionism that seized the nation during the 1890s. As Mahan confessed, "Even when material interests are the original exciting cause, it is the sentiment to which they give rise, the moral tone which emotion takes that constitutes the greater force." Much of that moral tone was set by American missionaries intent on spreading the gospel of Christianity to the "heathen." No area on the globe constituted a greater challenge than China.

The 1858 Tientsin treaty admitted foreign missionaries to China. Although Christians converted only 100,000 in a population of 400 million, the Chinese nevertheless resented the interference of missionaries in village life. Opposition to foreign missionaries took the form of antiforeign secret societies, most notably the Boxers, whose Chinese name translated to "Righteous Harmonious Fist."

No simple boxing club, in 1899 the Boxers began to hunt down and kill Chinese Christians and missionaries in northwestern Shandong Province. With the tacit support of China's Dowager Empress, the Boxers became bolder. Under the slogan "Uphold the Ch'ing Dynasty, Exterminate the Foreigners," they marched on the cities. Their rampage eventually led to the massacre of some 30,000 Chinese converts and 250 foreign nuns, priests, and missionaries along with their families. In August 1900, 2,500 U.S. troops joined an international force sent to rescue the foreigners besieged in Beijing. The European powers imposed the humiliating Boxer Protocol in 1901, giving them the right to maintain military forces in the Chinese capital and requiring the Chinese government to pay an exorbitant indemnity of $333 million for the loss of life and property resulting from the **Boxer uprising**.

In the aftermath of the uprising, missionaries voiced no concern at the paradox of bringing Christianity to China at gunpoint. "It is worth any cost in money, worth any cost in bloodshed," argued one bishop, "if we can make millions of Chinese true and intelligent Christians." Merchants and missionaries alike shared such moralistic reasoning. Indeed, they worked hand in hand; trade and Christianity marched into Asia together. "Missionaries," admitted the American clergyman Charles Denby, "are the pioneers of trade and commerce. . . . The missionary, inspired by holy zeal, goes everywhere and by degrees foreign commerce and trade follow."

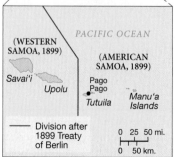

The Samoan Islands, 1889

The Monroe Doctrine and the Open Door Policy The emergence of the United States as a world power pitted the nation against other colonial powers, particularly Germany and Japan, which posed a threat to the twin pillars of America's expansionist foreign policy—one dating back to President James Monroe in the 1820s, the other formalized in 1900 under President William McKinley. The first, the **Monroe Doctrine**, came to be interpreted as establishing the Western Hemisphere as an American "sphere of influence" and warned European powers to stay away or risk war. The second, the Open Door, dealt with maintaining market access to China.

American diplomacy actively worked to buttress the Monroe Doctrine, with its assertion of American hegemony (domination) in the Western Hemisphere. In the 1880s, Republican secretary of state James G. Blaine promoted hemispheric peace and trade through Pan-American cooperation but at the same time used American troops to intervene in Latin American border disputes. In 1895, Americans risked war with Great Britain to enforce the Monroe Doctrine when a conflict developed between Venezuela and British Guiana. After American saber rattling, the British backed down and accepted U.S. mediation in the area despite their territorial claims in Guiana.

In Central America, American business triumphed in a bloodless takeover that saw French and British interests routed by behemoths such as the United Fruit Company of Boston. United Fruit virtually dominated the Central American nations of Costa Rica and Guatemala, while an importer from New Orleans turned Honduras into a "banana republic" (a country run by U.S. business interests). Thus, by 1895, the United States, through business as well as diplomacy, had successfully achieved hegemony in Latin America and the Caribbean, forcing even the British to concur with the secretary of state that "the infinite resources [of the United States] combined with its isolated position render it master of the situation and practically invulnerable as against any or all other powers."

At the same time that American foreign policy warned European powers to stay out of the Western Hemisphere, the United States competed for trade in the Eastern Hemisphere. As American interests in China grew, the United States became more aggressive in

The Open Door The trade advantage gained by the United States through the Open Door policy, enunciated by Secretary of State John Hay in 1900, is portrayed graphically in this political cartoon. Uncle Sam stands prominently in the "open door," while representatives of the other great powers seek admittance to the "Flowery Kingdom" of China. Uncle Sam holds the golden key of "American diplomacy," while the Chinese man on the other side of the door beams with pleasure. In fact, the Open Door policy promised equal access for all powers to the China trade, not U.S. preeminence as the cartoon implies. Culver Pictures.

FOR MORE HELP ANALYZING THIS IMAGE, see the visual activity for this chapter in the Online Study Guide at bedfordstmartins.com/roarkcompact.

defending its presence in Asia and the Pacific. The United States risked war with Germany in 1889 to guarantee the U.S. navy access to Pago Pago in the Samoan Islands, a port for refueling on the way to Asia. Germany, seeking dominance over the islands, challenged the United States by sending warships to the region. But before fighting broke out, a great typhoon destroyed the German and American ships. Acceding to the will of nature, the potential combatants later divided the islands amicably in the 1899 Treaty of Berlin.

The biggest prize in Asia remained the China market. In the 1890s, China, weakened by years of internal warfare, was beginning to be partitioned into spheres of influence by Britain, Japan, Germany, France, and Russia. Concerned about the integrity of China and no less about American trade, Secretary of State John Hay in 1899–1900 wrote a series of notes calling for an "open door" policy

that would ensure trade access to all and maintain Chinese sovereignty. The notes—sent to Britain, Germany, and Russia and later to France, Japan, and Italy—were greeted by the major powers with polite evasion. Nevertheless, Hay skillfully managed to maneuver the major powers into doing his bidding, and in 1900 he boldly announced the Open Door as international policy. The United States, by insisting on the **Open Door policy**, managed to secure access to Chinese markets, expanding its economic power while avoiding the problems of maintaining a far-flung colonial empire on the Asian mainland. But as the Spanish-American War soon demonstrated, Americans found it hard to resist the temptations of overseas empire.

Q: **Why did the United States largely abandon its isolationist foreign policy in the 1890s?**

War and Empire

The **Spanish-American War** began as a humanitarian effort to free Cuba from Spain's colonial grasp and ended with the United States itself acquiring territory overseas and fighting a dirty guerrilla war with Filipino nationalists, who, like the Cubans, sought independence. Behind the contradiction stood the twin pillars of American foreign policy: The Monroe Doctrine made Spain's presence in Cuba unacceptable, and U.S. determination to keep open the door to Asia made the Philippines attractive as a stepping-stone to China. Precedent for its imperial adventures also came from the recent Indian Wars in the American West, which provided a template for the subjugation of native peoples in the name of civilization.

"A Splendid Little War" Looking back on the Spanish-American War of 1898, Secretary of State John Hay judged it "a splendid little war; begun with the highest motives, carried on with magnificent intelligence and spirit, favored by that fortune which loves the brave." At the close of a decade marred by bitter depression, social unrest, and political upheaval, the war offered Americans a chance to wave the flag and march in unison. Few argued the merits of the conflict until it was over and the time came to divide the spoils.

The war began with moral outrage over the treatment of Cuban revolutionaries, who had launched a fight for independence against the Spanish colonial regime in 1895. In an attempt to isolate the guerrillas, the Spanish general Valeriano Weyler herded Cubans into crowded and unsanitary concentration camps, where thousands died of hunger, disease, and exposure. Starvation soon spread to the cities. Tens of thousands of Cubans died, and countless others were left without food, clothing, or shelter. By 1898, fully a quarter of the island's population had perished in the Cuban revolution.

As the Cuban rebellion dragged on, pressure for American intervention mounted. American newspapers fueled public outrage at Spain. A fierce circulation war raged in New York City between William Randolph Hearst's *Journal* and Joseph Pulitzer's *World*. Their competition provoked what came to be called **yellow journalism**, named for the colored ink used in a popular comic strip. Practitioners of yellow journalism pandered to the public's appetite for sensationalism. The Cuban war provided a wealth of dramatic copy. Newspapers fed the American people a daily diet of "Butcher" Weyler and Spanish atrocities. Hearst sent artist Frederic Remington to document the horror, and when Remington wired home, "There is no trouble here. There will be no war," Hearst shot back, "You furnish the pictures and I'll furnish the war."

American interests in Cuba were, in the words of the U.S. minister to Spain, more than "merely theoretical or sentimental." American business had more than $50 million invested in Cuban sugar, and American trade with Cuba, a brisk $100 million a year before the rebellion, had dropped to near zero. Nevertheless, the business community balked, wary of a war with Spain. When industrialist Mark Hanna, the Republican kingmaker and senator from Ohio, urged restraint, hotheaded **Theodore Roosevelt** exploded, "We will have this war for the freedom of Cuba, Senator Hanna, in spite of the timidity of commercial interests."

To expansionists like Roosevelt, more than Cuban independence was at stake. War with Spain opened up the prospect of expansion into Asia as well, since Spain controlled not only Cuba and Puerto Rico but also Guam and the Philippine Islands. Appointed assistant secretary of the navy in April 1897, Roosevelt took the helm in the absence of his boss and audaciously ordered the U.S. fleet to Manila in the Philippines. In the event of conflict with Spain, Roosevelt put the navy in a position to capture the islands and gain an entry point to China.

President McKinley slowly moved toward intervention. In a show of American force, he dispatched the battleship *Maine* to Cuba. On the night of February 15, 1898, a mysterious explosion destroyed the *Maine*, killing 267 crew members. The source of the explosion remained unclear, but inflammatory stories in the press enraged Americans, who immediately blamed the Spanish government. Rallying to the cry "Remember the *Maine*," Congress declared war on Spain in April. In a surge of patriotism, more than 235,000 men enlisted. War brought with it a unity of purpose and national harmony that ended a decade of political dissent and strife. "In April, everywhere over this good fair land, flags were flying," wrote Kansas editor William Allen White. "At the stations, crowds gathered to hurrah for the soldiers, and to throw hats into the air, and to unfurl flags."

Soon they had something to cheer about. Five days after McKinley signed the war resolution, a U.S. navy squadron commanded by Admiral George Dewey destroyed the Spanish fleet in Manila Bay (Map 20.3). Dewey's stunning victory caught the United States by surprise. Although naval strategists including Theodore Roosevelt had been orchestrating the move for some time, few Americans had ever heard of the Philippines. Even McKinley confessed that he could not immediately locate the archipelago on the map. He nevertheless recognized the strategic importance of the Philippines and dispatched U.S. troops to secure the islands.

The war in Cuba ended almost as quickly as it began. The first troops landed on June 22, and

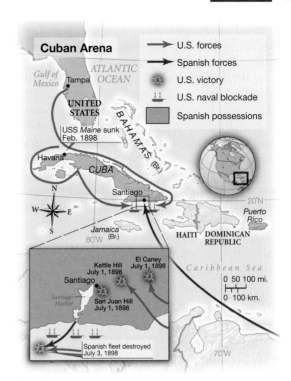

MAP 20.3 The Spanish-American War, 1898

The Spanish-American War was fought in two theaters, the Philippine Islands and Cuba. Five days after President William McKinley called for a declaration of war, Admiral George Dewey captured Manila without the loss of a single American sailor. The war lasted only eight months. Troops landed in Cuba in mid-June and by mid-July had taken Santiago and Havana and destroyed the Spanish fleet.

READING THE MAP: Which countries held imperial control over countries and territories immediately surrounding the Philippine Islands and Cuba?

CONNECTIONS: What role did American newspapers play in the start of the war? How did the results of the war serve American aims in both Asia and the Western Hemisphere?

FOR MORE HELP ANALYZING THIS MAP, see the map activity for this chapter in the Online Study Guide at bedfordstmartins.com/roarkcompact.

after a handful of battles, the Spanish surrendered on July 17. The war lasted just long enough to elevate Theodore Roosevelt to the status of bona fide war hero. Roosevelt resigned his navy post and formed the Rough Riders, a regiment composed of Ivy League polo players and cowboys Roosevelt knew from his stint as a cattle rancher in the Dakotas. The Rough Riders' charge up Kettle Hill and Roosevelt's role in the decisive battle of San Juan Hill made front-page news. Overnight, Roosevelt became the most famous man in America. By the time he sailed home from Cuba, a coalition of independent Republicans was already plotting his political future.

The Debate over American Imperialism After a few brief campaigns in Cuba and Puerto Rico brought the Spanish-American War to an end, the American people woke up in possession of an empire that stretched halfway around the globe. As part of the spoils of war, the United States acquired Cuba, Puerto Rico, Guam, and the Philippines. Yielding to pressure from American sugar growers, President McKinley expanded the empire further, annexing Hawaii in July 1898. (See "Beyond America's Borders," page 502.)

Contemptuous of the Cubans, whom General William Shafter declared "no more fit for self-government than gun-powder is for hell," the U.S. government dictated a Cuban constitution in 1898. It included the so-called Platt Amendment—a series of provisions that granted the United States the right to intervene to protect Cuba's "independence," as well as the power to oversee Cuban debt so that European creditors would not find an excuse for intervention. For good measure, the United States gave itself a ninety-nine-year lease on a naval base at Guantánamo. In return, McKinley promised to implement an extensive sanitation program to clean up the island, making it more attractive to American investors.

In the formal Treaty of Paris (1898), Spain ceded the Philippines to the United States along with its former colonies of Puerto Rico and Guam (Map 20.4). Empire did not come cheap. When Spain initially balked at these terms, the United States agreed to pay an indemnity of $20 million for the islands. Nor was the cost measured in money alone. Filipino revolutionaries under Emilio Aguinaldo, who had greeted U.S. troops as liberators, bitterly fought the new masters. It would take seven years and 4,000 American dead—almost ten times the number killed in Cuba—not to mention an estimated 20,000

Filipino casualties, to defeat Aguinaldo and secure American control of the Philippines, America's coveted stepping-stone to China.

At home, a vocal minority, mostly Democrats and former Populists, resisted the country's foray into overseas empire, judging it unwise, immoral, and unconstitutional. William Jennings Bryan, who enlisted in the army but never saw action, concluded that American expansionism only distracted the nation from problems at home. Pointing to the central paradox of the war, Representative Bourke Cockran of New York admonished, "We who have been the destroyers of oppression are asked now to become its agents." The anti-imperialists were soon drowned out by cries for empire. As Senator Knute Nelson of Minnesota assured his colleagues,

MAP 20.4 U.S. Overseas Expansion through 1900

The United States extended its interests abroad with a series of territorial acquisitions. Although Cuba was granted independence, the Platt Amendment kept the new nation firmly under U.S. control. In the wake of the Spanish-American War, the United States woke up to find that it held an empire extending halfway around the globe.

Conclusion: Rallying around the Flag

A decade of domestic strife ended amid the blare of martial music and the waving of flags. The Spanish-American War drowned out the calls for social reform that had fueled the Populist politics of the 1890s. During that decade, angry farmers facing hard times looked to the Farmers' Alliance to fight for their vision of economic democracy, workers staged bloody battles across the country to assert their rights, and women attacked drunkenness and the conditions that fostered it and mounted a suffrage movement to secure their basic political rights. In St. Louis in 1892, Frances Willard joined with other disaffected Americans to form a new People's Party to fight for change.

The bitter depression that began in 1893 led to increased labor strife. The Pullman boycott brutally dramatized the power of property and the conservatism of the laissez-faire state. Even the miners' victory in Cripple Creek, Colorado, in 1894 proved short-lived. But workers' willingness to confront capitalism on the streets of Chicago, Homestead, Cripple Creek, and a host of other sites across America eloquently testified to labor's growing determination, unity, and strength.

As the depression deepened, the sight of Coxey's army of unemployed marching on Washington to demand federal intervention in the economy signaled a growing shift in the public mind against the stand-pat politics of laissez-faire. The call for the government to take action to better the lives of workers, farmers, and the dispossessed manifested itself in the fiercely fought presidential campaign of William Jennings Bryan in 1896. With the outbreak of the Spanish-American War in 1898, the decade ended on a harmonious note with patriotic Americans rallying around the flag. Few questioned America's foray into overseas empire. The United States took its place on the world stage, buttressing its hemispheric domination with the Monroe Doctrine and employing the Open Door policy, which promised access to the riches of China. But even though Americans basked in patriotism and contemplated empire, old grievances had not been laid to rest. The People's Party had been beaten, but the Populists' call for greater government involvement in the economy, expanded opportunities for direct democracy, and a more equitable balance of profits and power between the people and the big corporations sounded the themes that would be taken up by a new generation of progressive reformers in the first decades of the twentieth century.

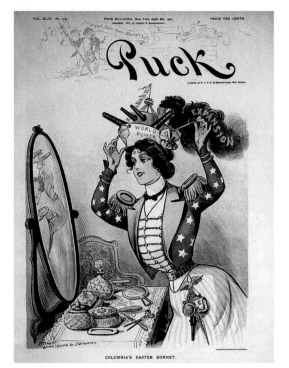

Columbia's Easter Bonnet The United States, symbolized by the female figure of Columbia, tries on "World Power" in this cartoon from *Puck* that appeared in 1901 after the Spanish-American War left the United States in control of Spain's former colonies in Guam, the Philippines, and Puerto Rico. The bonnet, in the shape of an American battleship, indicates the key role the U.S. navy, under the command of Admiral George Dewey, played in the U.S. victory at Manila, which secured the Philippines for the United States. "Expansion," spelled out in the smoke from the ship's smokestack, points to a new overseas direction for American foreign policy at the turn of the twentieth century. Library of Congress.

"We come as ministering angels, not as despots." Fresh from the conquest of Native Americans in the West, the nation largely embraced the heady mixture of racism and missionary zeal that fueled American adventurism abroad. The *Washington Post* trumpeted, "The taste of empire is in the mouth of the people," thrilled at the prospect of "an imperial policy, the Republic renascent, taking her place with the armed nations."

Q: Why did the United States declare war on Spain in 1898?

Reviewing the Chapter

★ KEY TERMS

Explain each term's significance

WHO

Frances Willard (p. 487)

Henry Clay Frick (p. 491)

Alexander Berkman (p. 493)

George M. Pullman (p. 493)

Eugene V. Debs (p. 494)

Elizabeth Cady Stanton (p. 496)

Susan B. Anthony (p. 496)

William McKinley (p. 499)

William Jennings Bryan (p. 499)

Tom Watson (p. 500)

Theodore Roosevelt (p. 506)

WHAT

Farmers' Alliance (p. 489)

Colored Farmers' Alliance (p. 490)

People's Party (Populist Party) (p. 490)

subtreasury (p. 491)

Homestead lockout (p. 492)

Cripple Creek miners' strike of 1894 (p. 493)

American Railway Union (ARU) (p. 494)

Pullman boycott (p. 495)

Coxey's army (p. 497)

Boxer uprising (p. 504)

Monroe Doctrine (p. 504)

Open Door policy (p. 505)

Spanish-American War (p. 506)

yellow journalism (p. 506)

> **FOR PRACTICE QUIZZES AND OTHER STUDY TOOLS,** see the Online Study Guide at **bedfordstmartins.com/roarkcompact.**

★ REVIEW QUESTIONS Q:

Use key terms and dates to support your answer

1. Why did American farmers organize alliances in the late nineteenth century? (pp. 489–91)

2. Why did the strikes of the 1890s fail to produce permanent gains for workers? (pp. 491–95)

3. How did women's temperance activism contribute to the cause of woman suffrage? (pp. 495–97)

4. Why was the People's Party unable to translate national support into victory in the 1896 election? (pp. 497–501)

5. Why did the United States largely abandon its isolationist foreign policy in the 1890s? (pp. 501–05)

6. Why did the United States declare war on Spain in 1898? (pp. 506–09)

★ MAKING CONNECTIONS

Draw on key terms, timeline, and review questions

1. In the late nineteenth century, Americans clashed over the disparity of power brought about by industrial capitalism. Why did many working Americans look to the government to help advance their vision of economic justice? In your answer, discuss specific reforms working-class Americans pursued and the strategies they employed.

2. In the 1890s, workers mounted labor protests and strikes. What circumstances gave rise to these actions? How did they differ from earlier strikes, such as the Great Railroad Strike of 1877? In your answer, discuss specific actions, being sure to consider how local and national circumstances contributed to their ultimate resolution.

3. How did women's activism in the late nineteenth century help advance the cause of woman suffrage? How did women activists in the late nineteenth century differ from their predecessors? In your answer, discuss specific gains made in the late nineteenth century, as well as shifts in reformers' strategies.

4. How did the conquest of Native Americans in the West foreshadow U.S. expansion abroad? In what ways did assumptions of racial superiority evident in U.S. Indian policy affect the treatment of Cubans and Filipinos?

★ SUGGESTED READINGS

Jean H. Baker, *Sisters: The Lives of America's Suffragists* (2005). A lively exploration of the public and private lives of the suffrage leaders.

Elizabeth Jameson, *All That Glitters: Class, Conflict, and Community in Cripple Creek* (1998). A rich history of Cripple Creek and its two strikes, the success of the miners in 1894, and the union's defeat in 1904.

Michael Kazin, *A Godly Hero: The Life of William Jennings Bryan* (2006). A sympathetic portrait of Bryan as an eloquent voice for democracy and anti-imperialism.

Stephen Kinzer, *Overthrow: America's Century of Regime Change from Hawaii to Iraq* (2006). Kinzer vividly portrays the overthrow of Queen Liliuokalani in Hawaii in 1893, arguing that it is the first example of a U.S. penchant for regime change.

Connie L. Lester, *Up from the Mudsills of Hell: The Farmers' Alliance, Populism, and Progressive Agriculture in Tennessee, 1870–1915* (2006). A fascinating account of how Tennessee farmers crossed racial and gender barriers to organize for change.

Paul T. McCartney, *Power and Progress: American National Identity, the War of 1898, and the Rise of American Imperialism* (2006). An exploration of the religious beliefs, national sentiments, and intellectual movements that fueled the U.S. foray into imperialism abroad.

FOR MORE BOOKS ABOUT TOPICS IN THIS CHAPTER, see the Online Bibliography at **bedfordstmartins.com/roarkcompact**.

FOR ADDITIONAL FIRSTHAND ACCOUNTS OF THIS PERIOD, see Chapter 20 in Michael Johnson, ed., *Reading the American Past*, Fourth Edition.

FOR WEB SITES, IMAGES, AND DOCUMENTS RELATED TO TOPICS AND PLACES IN THIS CHAPTER, visit Make History at **bedfordstmartins.com/roarkcompact**.

★ TIMELINE

1884	• Woman's Christian Temperance Union, headed by Frances Willard, calls for woman suffrage.
1889	• Typhoon averts hostilities between German and U.S. ships in Samoan Islands.
1890	• National American Woman Suffrage Association (NAWSA) formed. • Wyoming enters Union with woman suffrage. • Southern Farmers' Alliance numbers three million members.
1892	• People's (Populist) Party founded. • Homestead lockout.
1893	• Stock market crash touches off severe economic depression. • President Grover Cleveland nixes attempt to annex Hawaii.
1894	• Miners' strike in Cripple Creek, Colorado. • Coxey's army marches to Washington, D.C. • Federal troops and court injunction crush Pullman boycott.
1895	• President Grover Cleveland defends Monroe Doctrine in border dispute between British Guiana and Venezuela.
1896	• Democrats and Populists support William Jennings Bryan for president. • Republican William McKinley elected president.
1898	• U.S. battleship *Maine* explodes in Havana harbor. • Congress declares war on Spain. • Admiral George Dewey destroys Spanish fleet in Manila Bay, the Philippines. • U.S. troops defeat Spanish forces in Cuba. • Treaty of Paris ends war with Spain and cedes Philippines, Puerto Rico, and Guam to the United States. • United States annexes Hawaii.
1899–1900	• Secretary of State John Hay enunciates Open Door policy in China. • Boxer uprising in China.
1901	• Boxer Protocol imposed on Chinese government.

PROGRESSIVE PARTY CAMPAIGN SOUVENIR BANDANA This colorful cotton bandana, a campaign novelty from the 1912 presidential race, celebrates the Progressive Party and its candidate, Theodore Roosevelt. The progressive reform movement grew out of the crises of the 1890s to emerge full-blown in the first decades of the twentieth century. Progressives challenged laissez-faire liberalism and argued for government action to counter the power of big business and ensure greater social justice. Theodore Roosevelt, whose presidency set the tone for the era, became so closely associated with progressivism that when he failed to win the Republican nomination in 1912, his followers formed a new Progressive Party proclaiming, as the bandana notes, "We Want Our Teddy Back." The red bandana became the symbol of the new party. Roosevelt, brandishing one, led the crowd in a rousing verse of "Onward, Christian Soldiers." But progressivism was more than one man or one party. A movement that ran from the grass roots to the White House, it included not only members of the short-lived Progressive Party but also insurgent Democrats and Republicans whose belief in government activism would reshape the liberal state of the twentieth century. Collection of Janice L. and David J. Frent.

21

Progressivism from the Grass Roots to the White House

1890–1916

IN THE SUMMER OF 1889, a young woman leased the upper floor of a dilapidated mansion on Chicago's West Side in the heart of a burgeoning immigrant population. Watching as she prepared to move in, neighbors scratched their heads, wondering why the well-dressed woman, who surely could afford a better house in a better neighborhood, chose to live on South Halsted Street. Yet the house, built by Charles Hull, precisely suited the needs of **Jane Addams**.

For Addams, personal action marked the first step in the search for solutions to the social problems fostered by urban industrialism. Her object was twofold: She wanted to help her immigrant neighbors, and she wanted to offer an opportunity for educated women like herself to find meaningful work. As she later wrote in her autobiography, *Twenty Years at Hull-House* (1910), "I gradually became convinced that it would be a good thing to rent a house in a part of the city where many primitive and actual needs are found, in which young women who had been given over too exclusively to study might restore a balance of activity along traditional lines and learn of life from life itself." Addams's emphasis on the reciprocal relationship between the social classes made Hull House different from other philanthropic enterprises. She wished to do things with, not just for, Chicago's poor.

In the next decade, Hull House expanded from one rented floor in the old brick mansion to some thirteen buildings housing a remarkable variety of activities. Addams converted the bathrooms in the basement into public baths, opened a coffee shop and restaurant to sell take-out food to working-women too tired to cook after their long shifts, and sponsored a nursery and kindergarten for neighborhood children. Hull House offered classes, lectures, art exhibits, musical instruction, and college extension courses. It boasted a gymnasium, a theater, a manual training workshop, a labor museum, and the first public playground in Chicago.

But Hull House was more than a group of buildings. From the first, it attracted an extraordinary set of reformers. Some stayed for decades, as did Julia Lathrop before she went to Washington, D.C., in 1912 to head the Children's Bureau. Others, like Gerard Swope, who later became president of the General Electric Company, came for only a short time. Hull House residents pioneered the scientific investigation of urban ills. Armed with statistics, they launched campaigns to improve housing, end child labor, fund playgrounds, mediate between labor and management, and lobby for laws to protect workers.

Addams quickly learned that it was impossible to deal with urban problems without becoming involved in political action. Her determination to clean up the garbage on Halsted Street led her into politics. Piles of decaying garbage overflowed the street's wooden trash bins, breeding flies and disease. Investigation revealed that the local ward boss awarded the contract to pick up the trash as a political plum to one of his henchmen, who felt under no obligation to provide adequate service. To end the graft, Addams got herself appointed garbage inspector. Out on the streets at six in the morning, she rode atop the garbage wagon to make sure it made its rounds. Addams mounted several unsuccessful political campaigns to oust the corrupt ward boss but eventually realized that bossism was a symptom and not the cause of urban blight. Recognizing that bosses stayed in power by providing jobs and services to their constituents, she moved instead to sponsor legislation to help her neighbors. Eventually, her struggle to aid the urban poor led her not only to city hall but on to the state capitol and to Washington, D.C.

Under Jane Addams's leadership, Hull House became a "spearhead for reform," part of a broader movement that contemporaries called progressivism. The transition from personal action to political activism that Addams personified became one of the hallmarks of this reform period, which lasted from the 1890s to World War I.

By the 1890s, it had become clear to many Americans that the laissez-faire approach of government toward business no longer worked. The classical liberalism of the nation's Founders, with its emphasis on opposition to the tyranny of centralized government, had not reckoned on the enormous private wealth and power of the Gilded Age's business giants. As the gap between rich and poor widened in the 1890s, issues of social justice challenged traditional notions of laissez-faire liberalism. The violence and militancy of the 1890s—labor strikes, farmers' revolt, suffrage and antilynching movements—eloquently testified to the growing polarities in society. A laissez-faire state only exacerbated the inequalities of class, race, and gender. A generation of progressive reformers demanded government intervention to guarantee a more equitable society. The willingness to use the government to promote change and to counterbalance the power of private interests redefined liberalism in the twentieth century.

Faith in activism in both the political and the private realms formed a common thread that united an otherwise diverse group of progressive reformers. A sense of Christian mission inspired some. Others, fearing social upheaval, sought to remove some of the worst evils of urban industrialism—tenements, child labor, and harsh working conditions. Progressives shared a growing concern about the power of wealthy individuals and corporations and a strong dislike of the trusts. But often they feared the immigrant poor and sought to control and Americanize them. Along with moral fervor, a belief in technical expertise and scientific management infused progressivism and made the cult of efficiency part and parcel of the movement. All of these elements—uplift and efficiency, social justice and social control—came together in the Progressive Era and characterized the progressive movement both at the grassroots level in the cities and states and in the presidencies of Theodore Roosevelt and Woodrow Wilson. ★

Jane Addams Jane Addams was twenty-nine years old when she founded Hull House on South Halsted Street in Chicago. She and her college roommate, Ellen Gates Starr, established America's premier social settlement. Her desire to live among the poor and her insistence that settlement house work benefited educated women such as herself as well as her immigrant neighbors separated her from the charity workers who had come before her and marked the distance from philanthropy to progressive reform. Her autobiographical *Twenty Years at Hull-House*, published in 1910, is shown in the inset. Photo: Jane Addams Memorial Collection (JAMC neg. 14), Special Collections, University of Illinois at Chicago, photographer: Max Platz; Book: Newberry Library.

Grassroots Progressivism

Much of progressive reform began at the grassroots level and percolated upward into local, state, and eventually national politics as reformers attacked the social problems fostered by urban industrialism. Although reform flourished in many different settings across the country, urban problems inspired the progressives' greatest efforts. In their zeal to "civilize the city," reformers founded settlement houses, professed a new Christian social gospel, and campaigned against vice and crime in the name of "social purity." Allying with the working class, they sought to better the lot of sweatshop garment workers and to end child labor. Their reform efforts often began on the local level but ended up being debated in state legislatures and in the U.S. Congress.

Civilizing the City Progressives attacked the problems of the city on many fronts. The **settlement house** movement attempted to bridge the distance between the classes. The **social gospel** called for the churches to play a new role in social reformation. And the **social purity movement** campaigned to clean up vice, particularly prostitution.

The settlement house movement that began in England came to the United States in 1886 with the opening of the University Settlement House in New York City. The needs of poor urban neighborhoods provided the impetus for these social settlements. In 1893, Lillian Wald, a nurse attending medical school in New York, went to care for a woman living in a dilapidated tenement. The experience led Wald to leave medical school and recruit several other nurses to move to New York City's Lower East Side "to live in the neighborhood as nurses, identify ourselves with it socially, and . . . contribute to it our citizenship." Wald's Henry Street settlement expanded in 1895, pioneering public health nursing. Although Wald herself was Jewish, she insisted that the settlement remain independent of religious ties, making it different from the avowedly religious settlements in England.

Women, particularly college-educated women like Jane Addams and Lillian Wald, formed the backbone of the settlement house movement and stood in the vanguard of the progressive movement. Settlement houses gave college-educated women eager to use their knowledge a place to put their talents to work in the service of society and to champion progressive reform. Largely due to women's efforts, settlements like Hull House grew in number from six in 1891 to more than four hundred in 1911. In the process, settlement house women created a new profession—social work—and stimulated a new reform movement—**progressivism**.

For their part, churches confronted urban social problems by enunciating a new social gospel, one that saw its mission not simply to reform individuals but to reform society. The social gospel offered a powerful corrective to social Darwinism and the gospel of wealth, which fostered the belief that riches somehow signaled divine favor. Washington Gladden, a prominent social gospel minister, challenged that view when he urged Congregationalists to turn down a gift from John D. Rockefeller, arguing that it was "tainted money." In place of the gospel of wealth, progressive clergy exhorted their congregations to put Christ's teachings to work in their daily lives. Charles M. Sheldon's popular book *In His Steps* (1898) called on men and women to Christianize capitalism by asking the question "What would Jesus do?"

Ministers also played an active role in the social purity movement, the campaign to attack vice. The Reverend Charles H. Parkhurst shocked his Madison Square congregation in the 1890s by donning a disguise and touring New York City's brothels to uncover the links between political corruption and urban vice. Armed with eyewitness accounts and affidavits, he demanded reform. To end the "social evil," as reformers euphemistically called prostitution, the social purity movement brought together ministers who wished to stamp out sin, doctors concerned about the spread of venereal disease, and women reformers determined to fight the double standard that made it acceptable for men to engage in premarital and extramarital sex but demanded chastity of women. Advanced progressive reformers linked prostitution to poverty and championed higher wages for women. "Is it any wonder," asked the Chicago vice commission, "that a tempted girl who receives only six dollars per week working with her hands sells her body for twenty-five dollars per week when she learns there is a demand for it and men are willing to pay the price?"

Attacks on alcohol went hand in hand with the push for social purity. The temperance campaign launched by the Woman's Christian Temperance Union (WCTU) heated up in the early twentieth century. The Anti-Saloon League, formed in 1895 under the leadership of Protestant clergy, campaigned for an end to the sale of liquor. Reformers pointed to links between drinking, prostitution, wife and child abuse, unemployment, and industrial accidents. The powerful liquor lobby fought back, spending liberally in election campaigns, fueling the charge that liquor corrupted the political process.

An element of nativism (dislike of foreigners) ran through the movement for prohibition, as it did in a number of progressive reforms. The Irish, the Italians, and the Germans were among the groups stigmatized by temperance reformers for their drinking. Even though most workers toiled six days a week and had only Sunday for recreation and relaxation, some progressives campaigned on the local level to enforce the Sunday closing of taverns, stores, and other commercial establishments. To deny the working class access to alcohol, these progressives pushed for state legislation to outlaw the sale of liquor. By 1912, seven states were "dry."

Progressives' efforts to civilize the city demonstrated their willingness to take action; their belief that environment, not heredity alone, determined human behavior; and their optimism that conditions could be corrected through government action without radically altering America's economy or institutions. All of these attitudes characterized the progressive movement.

Progressives and the Working Class

Day-to-day contact with their neighbors made settlement house workers particularly sympathetic to labor unions. When Mary Kenney O'Sullivan complained that her bookbinders' union met in a dirty, noisy saloon, Jane Addams invited the union to meet at Hull House. And during the Pullman strike in 1894, Hull House residents organized strike relief. "Hull-House has been so unionized," grumbled one Chicago businessman, "that it has lost its usefulness and become a detriment and harm to the community." But to the working class, the support of middle-class reformers marked a significant gain.

Attempts to forge a cross-class alliance became institutionalized in 1903 with the creation of the **Women's Trade Union League (WTUL)**. The WTUL brought together women workers and middle-class "allies." Its goal was to organize workingwomen into unions under the auspices of the American Federation of Labor (AFL). However, as one workingwoman confided, "The men think that the girls should not get as good work as the men and should not make half as much money as a man." Samuel Gompers, president of the AFL, endorsed the principle of equal pay for equal work, shrewdly observing that it would help male workers more than women, since many employers hired women precisely because they could be paid less.

> Clara Lemlich, one of the garment strike's leaders, exclaimed, "They used to say that you couldn't even organize women. They wouldn't come to union meetings. They were 'temporary' workers. Well we showed them!"

Although the alliance between workingwomen, primarily immigrants and daughters of immigrants, and their middle-class allies was not without tension, the WTUL helped workingwomen achieve significant gains. Its most notable success came in 1909 in the "uprising of the twenty thousand," when hundreds of women employees of the Triangle Shirtwaist Company in New York City went on strike to protest low wages, dangerous working conditions, and management's refusal to recognize their union, the International Ladies' Garment Workers Union (ILGWU). An estimated twenty thousand workers, most of them teenage girls and many of them Jewish and Italian immigrants, stayed out on strike through the winter, picketing in the bitter cold. By the time the strike ended in February 1910, the workers had won important demands in many shops. The solidarity shown by the women workers proved to be the strike's greatest achievement. As Clara Lemlich, one of the strike's leaders, exclaimed, "They used to say that you couldn't even organize women. They wouldn't come to union meetings. They were 'temporary' workers. Well we showed them!"

The WTUL made enormous contributions to the strike. It provided volunteers for the picket lines, posted more than $29,000 in bail, protested police brutality, organized a parade of ten thousand strikers, took part in the arbitration conference, appealed for funds, and generated publicity for the strike. Under the leadership of the WTUL, women from every class of society, from J. P. Morgan's daughter Anne to socialists on New York's Lower East Side, joined the strikers in a dramatic display of cross-class alliance.

But for all its success, the uprising of the twenty thousand failed fundamentally to change conditions for women workers, as the tragic Triangle fire dramatized in 1911. A little over a year after the shirtwaist makers' strike ended, fire alarms sounded at the Triangle Shirtwaist factory. The ramshackle building, full of lint and combustible cloth, burned to rubble in half an hour. A WTUL member described the scene below on the street: "Two young girls whom I knew to be working in the vicinity came rushing toward me, tears were running from their eyes and they were white and shaking as they caught me by the arm. 'Oh,' shrieked one of them, 'they are jumping. Jumping from ten stories up! They are going through the air like bundles of clothes.'"

The terrified Triangle workers had little choice but to jump. Flames blocked one exit, and the other door had been locked to prevent workers from pilfering. The flimsy, rusted fire escape

14. Viewing the unfortunates at the Morgue

Triangle Fire Morgue After the Triangle fire on March 26, 1911, New York City set up a makeshift morgue at the end of Manhattan's Charities Pier. There, the remains of more than a hundred young women and two dozen young men were laid out in coffins for their friends and relatives to identify. Victims who had jumped to their deaths from the ninth-floor windows or leaped down the elevator shaft could be easily recognized. Those trapped in the building were burned beyond recognition. A ring, a charred shoe, a melted hair comb often provided the only clues to the identity of a sister, a daughter, or a sweetheart. Artist John Sloan created this illustration to commemorate those who died in the fire. The striking image, with its dark triangle representing the capitalist triumvirate of Rent, Profit, and Interest, features a bloated businessman weeping over his lost profits while a young woman worker lies burning on the pavement and a leering skeleton poses on the left. In the trial that followed the fire, the owners of the Triangle Shirtwaist Company avoided penalty when their skillful lawyer challenged the credibility of witnesses. Photo: United Archives, Kheel Center, Cornell University, Ithaca, NY; Illustration: Granger Collection.

collapsed under the weight of fleeing workers, killing dozens. Trapped, 54 workers jumped from the ninth-floor windows, only to smash to their deaths on the sidewalk. Of 500 workers, 146 died and scores of others were injured. The owners of the Triangle firm went to trial for negligence, but they avoided conviction when authorities determined that the fire had been started by a careless smoker. The Triangle Shirtwaist Company reopened in another firetrap within a matter of weeks.

Outrage and a sense of futility overwhelmed Rose Schneiderman, a leading WTUL organizer, who made a bitter speech at the memorial service for the dead Triangle workers. "I would be a traitor to those poor burned bodies if I came here to talk good fellowship," she told her audience. "We have tried you good people of the public and we have found you wanting. . . . I know from my experience it is up to the working people to save themselves . . . by a strong working class movement." The Triangle fire tested severely the bonds of the cross-class alliance. Along with Schneiderman, WTUL leaders experienced a growing sense of futility. It seemed

not enough to organize and to strike, particularly when the AFL paid so little attention to women workers. Increasingly, the WTUL turned its efforts to lobbying for protective legislation—laws that would limit hours and regulate working conditions for women workers.

Advocates of protective legislation won a major victory in 1908 when the U.S. Supreme Court, in *Muller v. Oregon*, reversed its previous rulings and upheld an Oregon law that limited to ten the hours women could work in a day. A mass of sociological evidence put together by **Florence Kelley** of the National Consumers' League and Josephine Goldmark of the WTUL demonstrated the ill effects of long hours on the health and safety of women. The data convinced the Court that long hours endangered women and therefore the entire human race. The Court's ruling set a precedent, but one that separated the well-being of women workers from that of men by arguing that women's reproductive role justified special treatment. Later generations of women fighting for equality would question the effectiveness of this strategy and argue that it ultimately closed good jobs to women. The WTUL, however, greeted protective legislation as a first step in the attempt to ensure the safety of all workers.

The **National Consumers' League (NCL)**, like the WTUL, fostered cross-class alliance. When Florence Kelley took over the leadership of the NCL in 1899, she urged middle-class women to boycott stores and exert pressure for decent wages and working conditions for women employees, primarily saleswomen. The league published a "white list" of stores that met its standards. Like the WTUL, the NCL increasingly promoted protective legislation to better working conditions for working women. Frustrated by the reluctance of the private sector to respond to the need for reform, progressives turned to government at all levels. Critics would later charge that the progressives assumed too easily that government regulation could best solve social problems.

Reform also fueled the fight for woman suffrage. For women like Jane Addams and Florence Kelley, involvement in social reform led inevitably to support for woman suffrage. These new suffragists emphasized the reforms that could be accomplished if women had the vote. When they talked of the need for the ballot, they often compared it to the broom. Addams insisted that in an urban, industrial society, a good housekeeper could not be sure the food she fed her family or the water and milk they drank were pure unless she became involved in politics and wielded the ballot—and not just the broom—to protect her family. The concept of municipal housekeeping encouraged women to put their talents to work in the service of society.

> **Q:** What types of people were drawn to the progressive movement, and what motivated them?

Progressivism: Theory and Practice

Progressive reformers developed a theoretical basis for their activist approach by countering social Darwinism with a dynamic new reform Darwinism. The progressives emphasized action and experimentation. Dismissing the view that humans should leave progress to the dictates of natural selection, progressive reform Darwinists argued that human intelligence could shape change and improve society. In their zeal for action, progressives often showed an unchecked admiration for speed and efficiency that promoted scientific management and a new cult of efficiency. These varied strands of progressive

theory found practical application in state and local politics, where reformers challenged traditional laissez-faire government.

Reform Darwinism and Social Engineering The active, interventionist approach of the progressives directly challenged social Darwinism, with its insistence that the world operated on the principle of survival of the fittest and that human beings stood powerless in the face of the law of natural selection. Without abandoning the evolutionary framework of Darwinism, a new group of sociologists argued that evolution could be advanced more rapidly if men and women used their intellects to alter the environment. Sociologist Lester Frank Ward put it clearly in his book *Dynamic Sociology* (1883). "I insist that the time must soon come," he wrote, "when control of blind natural forces in society must give way to human foresight." Dubbed **reform Darwinism**, the new sociological theory condemned the laissez-faire approach, insisting that the liberal state should play a more active role in solving social problems.

Efficiency and *expertise* became watchwords in the progressive vocabulary. In *Drift and Mastery* (1914), journalist and critic Walter Lippmann called for skilled "technocrats" to use scientific techniques to control social change, substituting social engineering for aimless drift. Progressive reformers' emphasis on expertise inevitably fostered a kind of elitism. Unlike the Populists, who advocated a greater voice for the masses, progressives, for all their interest in social justice, insisted that experts be put in charge.

At its extreme, the application of expertise and social engineering took the form of **scientific management**, which alienated the working class by elevating productivity and efficiency. Frederick Winslow Taylor pioneered "systematized shop management." After dropping out of Harvard, Taylor went to work as a machinist at Midvale Steel in Philadelphia in the 1880s. Obsessed with making humans and machines produce more and faster, he earned a master's of engineering degree in 1885 and went back to Midvale to restructure the workplace. With his stopwatch, he carefully timed workers and attempted to break down their work into its simplest components, one repetitious action after another, on the theory that productivity would increase if tasks could be simplified. An advocate of piecework, quotas, and pay incentives for productivity, Taylor insisted that unions were unnecessary. As a consulting engineer, he spread his gospel of efficiency and won many converts among corporate managers. Workers hated the monotony of systematized shop management and argued that it led to the speedup—pushing workers to produce more in less time and for less pay. But many progressives applauded the increased productivity and efficiency of Taylor's system.

Progressive Government: City and State The politicians who became premier progressives were generally the followers, not the leaders, in a movement already well advanced at the grassroots level. Yet they left their stamp on the movement. Tom Johnson made Cleveland a model of progressive reform, Robert M. La Follette turned Wisconsin into a laboratory for progressivism, and Hiram Johnson ended the domination of the Southern Pacific Railroad in California politics.

Progressivism burst forth at every level of government in 1900, but nowhere more forcefully than in Cleveland with the election of **Thomas Loftin Johnson** as mayor. A self-made millionaire by age forty, Johnson moved to Cleveland in 1899, where he began his career in politics. During his mayoral campaign, he pledged to reduce the streetcar fare from five cents to three cents. His election touched off a seven-year war between Johnson and the streetcar moguls, who argued that they couldn't meet costs with the lower fare. Reelected four times, Johnson fought for fair taxation and championed greater democracy through the use of the initiative, referendum, and recall—devices that allowed voters to have a direct say in legislative and judicial matters. To get his three-cent fare, he had the city buy the streetcar system, a tactic of municipal ownership progressives called "gas and water socialism." Under Johnson's administration, Cleveland became, in the words of journalist Lincoln Steffens, the "best governed city in America."

In Wisconsin, **Robert M. La Follette** converted to the progressive cause early in the 1900s. An astute politician, La Follette capitalized on the grassroots movement for reform to launch his long political career as governor (1901–1905) and U.S. senator (1906–1925). A graduate of the University of Wisconsin, La Follette brought scientists and professors into his administration and used the university, just down the street from the statehouse in Madison, as a resource in drafting legislation. As governor, he lowered railroad rates, raised railroad taxes, improved education, preached conservation, established factory regulation and workers' compensation, instituted the first direct primary in the country, and inaugurated the first state income tax. Under his leadership, Wisconsin earned the title "laboratory of democracy." A fiery orator, "Fighting Bob" La Follette united his supporters around issues that transcended party loyalties. This emphasis on reform characterized progressivism, which attracted followers from both major parties. Democrats like Tom Johnson and Republicans like Robert La Follette could lay equal claim to the label "progressive." Democrats and Republicans alike crossed party lines to work for reform.

West of the Rockies, progressivism arrived somewhat later and found a champion in **Hiram Johnson** of California, who served as governor from 1911 to 1917 and later as a U.S. senator. Since the 1870s, California politics had been dominated by the Southern Pacific Railroad, a corporation so rapacious that novelist Frank Norris styled it *The Octopus* (1901). Johnson ran for governor in 1910 on the promise to "kick the Southern Pacific out of politics." With the support of the reform wing of the Republican Party and the promise "to return the government to the people," he handily won. As governor, he introduced the direct primary; supported the initiative, referendum, and recall; strengthened the state's railroad commission; supported conservation; and signed an employer's liability law.

Q: How did progressives justify their demand for more activist government?

Progressivism Finds a President: Theodore Roosevelt

On September 6, 1901, President William McKinley was shot by Leon Czolgosz, an anarchist, while attending the Pan-American Exposition in Buffalo, New York. Eight days later, McKinley died. When news of his assassination reached his friend and political mentor Mark Hanna, Hanna is said to have growled, "Now that damned cowboy is president." He was speaking of Vice President Theodore Roosevelt, the colorful hero of the battle of San Juan Hill, who had punched cattle in the Dakotas in the 1880s.

Roosevelt's status as a Spanish-American War hero had propelled him to the governorship of New York in 1898. A moderate reformer, he had clashed with New York's Republican boss, who finagled to get him "kicked upstairs" as a candidate for the vice presidency in 1900. As vice president, the party bosses reasoned, Roosevelt could do little harm. But one bullet proved the error of their logic.

In the first hours of his presidency, Roosevelt reassured the shocked nation that he intended "to continue absolutely unbroken" the policies of McKinley. But Roosevelt was as different from McKinley as the twentieth century was from the nineteenth. An activist and a moralist, imbued with the progressive spirit, Roosevelt would turn the White House into a "bully pulpit" advocating reforms like conservation and championing the nation's emergence as a world power. In the process, Roosevelt would work to shift the nation's center of power from Wall Street to Washington.

The Square Deal At age forty-two, Theodore Roosevelt became the youngest man ever to move into the White House. A patrician by birth and an activist by temperament, Roosevelt brought to the job enormous talent and energy. By the time he graduated from Harvard, he was already an accomplished naturalist, an enthusiastic historian, and a naval strategist. He could have chosen from any of those promising careers; instead, he chose politics, not a bad choice for a man who relished competition and craved power.

Roosevelt was shrewd enough to realize that the path to power did not lie in the good government leagues formed by his well-bred friends. Instead, he apprenticed himself to the local Republican ward boss, who held court in a grimy, smoke-filled club above a Manhattan saloon. Roosevelt's rise in politics was swift and sure. He went from the New York assembly at the age of twenty-three to the presidency in less than twenty years, with time out as a cowboy in the Dakotas, police commissioner of New York City, assistant secretary of the navy, colonel of the Rough Riders, and governor of New York.

As president, Roosevelt would harness his explosive energy to strengthen the power of the federal government, putting business on notice that it could no longer count on a laissez-faire government to give it free rein. The "absolutely vital question" facing the country, Roosevelt wrote to a friend in 1901, was "whether or not the government has the power to control the trusts." The Sherman Antitrust Act of 1890 had been badly weakened by a conservative Supreme Court and by attorneys general more willing to use it against labor unions than against monopolies. To determine whether the law had any teeth left, Roosevelt, in one of his first acts as president, ordered his attorney general to begin a secret antitrust investigation of the Northern Securities Company.

Northern Securities had resulted from one of the most controversial mergers of the era. Two railroad magnates had fought a ruinous rate war that precipitated a panic on Wall Street, bankrupting thousands of small investors. To bring peace to the warring factions, financier J. P. Morgan stepped in and created the Northern Securities Company in 1901, linking three competing railroads under one management. This new behemoth monopolized railroad traffic in the Northwest. Small investors still smarting from their losses, farmers worried about freight rates, and the public in general saw in Northern Securities the symbol of corporate high-handedness.

In February 1902, just five months after Roosevelt took office, Wall Street rocked with the news that the government had filed an antitrust suit against Northern Securities. As one newspaper editor sarcastically observed, "Wall Street is paralyzed at the thought that a President of the United States would sink so low as to try to enforce the law." An indignant J. P. Morgan demanded to know why he had not been consulted. "If we have done anything wrong," he told the attorney general, "send your man to my man and they can fix it up." Roosevelt, amused, later noted that Morgan "could not help regarding me as a big rival operator." Roosevelt's thunderbolt put Wall Street on notice that the new president expected to be treated as an equal and was willing to use government as a weapon to curb business excesses. Perhaps sensing the new mood, the Supreme Court, in a significant turnaround, upheld the Sherman Act and called for the dissolution of Northern Securities in 1904.

Theodore Roosevelt Described aptly by a contemporary observer as "a steam engine in trousers," Theodore Roosevelt, at forty-two, was the youngest president ever to occupy the White House. He brought to the office energy, intellect, and activism in equal measure. Roosevelt boasted that he used the presidency as a "bully pulpit"—a forum from which he advocated reforms ranging from trust-busting to conservation. Library of Congress.

"Hurrah for Teddy the Trustbuster," cheered the papers. Roosevelt went on to use the Sherman Act against forty-three trusts, including such giants as American Tobacco, Du Pont, and Standard Oil. Always the moralist, he insisted on a "rule of reason." He would punish "bad" trusts (those that broke the law) and leave "good" ones alone. In practice, he preferred regulation to antitrust suits. In 1903, he pressured Congress to pass the Elkins Act, outlawing railroad rebates. And he created the new cabinet-level Department of Commerce and Labor with the subsidiary Bureau of Corporations to act as a corporate watchdog.

Observing Roosevelt in action, journalist Joseph Pulitzer remarked, "He has subjugated Wall Street." Pulitzer exaggerated, but Roosevelt had masterfully asserted the moral and political authority of the executive, underscoring, in his words, the "duty of the President to act upon the theory that he is the steward of the people." In his handling of the anthracite coal strike in 1902, Roosevelt again demonstrated his willingness to assert the authority of the presidency, this time to mediate between labor and management.

In May, 147,000 coal miners in Pennsylvania went on strike. The United Mine Workers (UMW) demanded a reduction in the workday from twelve to ten hours, an equitable system of weighing each miner's output, and a 10 percent wage increase, along with recognition of the union. When asked about the appalling conditions in the mines that led to the strike, George Baer, the mine operators' spokesman, scoffed, "The miners don't suffer, why they can't even speak English." Buttressed by social Darwinism, Baer observed that "God in his infinite wisdom" had placed "the rights and interests of the laboring man" in the hands of the capitalists, not "the labor agitators."

The strike dragged on through the summer and into the fall. Hoarding and profiteering drove the price of coal from $2.50 to $6.00 a ton. As winter approached, coal shortages touched off near riots in the nation's big cities. At this juncture, Roosevelt stepped in to mediate, inviting representatives from both sides to meet in Washington in October. His unprecedented intervention served notice that government counted itself an independent force in business and labor disputes. At the same time, it gave unionism a boost by granting the UMW a place at the table.

At the meeting, Baer and the mine owners refused to talk with the union representative—a move that angered the attorney general and insulted the president. The meeting ended in an impasse.

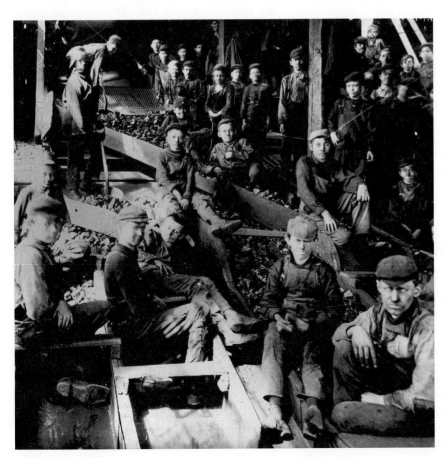

Breaker Boys Child labor in America's mines and mills was common at the turn of the twentieth century, despite state laws that tried to restrict it. Here, "breaker boys," some as young as seven years old, pick over coal in a Pennsylvania mine. Their unsmiling faces bear witness to the difficulty and danger of their work. A committee investigating child labor found more than ten thousand children illegally employed in the Pennsylvania coalfields. Brown Brothers.

Beside himself with anger over the "wooden-headed obstinacy and stupidity" of management, Roosevelt threatened to seize the mines and run them with federal troops. It was a powerful bluff, one that called into question not only the supremacy of private property but also the rule of law. But the specter of federal troops being used to operate the mines quickly brought management around. In the end, the miners won a reduction in hours and a wage increase, but the owners succeeded in preventing formal recognition of the UMW.

Taken together, Roosevelt's actions in the Northern Securities case and the anthracite coal strike marked a dramatic departure from the presidential passivity of his predecessors in the Gilded Age. Roosevelt's actions demonstrated conclusively that government intended to act as a countervailing force to the power of the big corporations. Pleased with his role in the anthracite strike, he announced that all he had tried to do was give labor and capital a square deal.

The phrase **Square Deal** became Roosevelt's campaign slogan in the 1904 election. But to win the presidency in his own right, Roosevelt needed to wrest control of the Republican Party from kingmaker and party boss Mark Hanna. Roosevelt adroitly used patronage to win supporters and weaken Hanna's power. Hanna died of typhoid fever in 1904, leaving Roosevelt the undisputed leader of the party.

In the presidential election of 1904, Roosevelt easily defeated the Democrats, who abandoned their candidate, William Jennings Bryan, to support Judge Alton B. Parker, a "safe" candidate they hoped would lure business votes away from Roosevelt. In the months before the election, the president prudently toned down his criticism of big business. Wealthy Republicans like J. P. Morgan may have grumbled privately, branding Roosevelt a class traitor, but they remained loyal to the party. Roosevelt swept into office with the largest popular majority—57.9 percent—any candidate had polled up to that time.

Roosevelt the Reformer   "Tomorrow I shall come into my office in my own right," Roosevelt is said to have remarked on the eve of his election. "Then watch out for me!" Roosevelt's stunning victory gave him a mandate for reform. He would need all the popularity and political savvy he could muster, however, to guide his reform measures through Congress. The Senate remained controlled by a staunchly conservative Republican "old guard," with many senators on the payrolls of the corporations Roosevelt sought to curb. Roosevelt's pet project remained railroad regulation. The Elkins Act prohibiting rebates had not worked. No one could stop big shippers like Standard Oil from wringing concessions from the railroads. Roosevelt determined that the only solution lay in giving the Interstate Commerce Commission (ICC) real power to set rates and prevent discriminatory practices. But the right to determine the price of goods or services was an age-old prerogative of private enterprise, and one that business had no intention of yielding to government.

To ensure passage of the **Hepburn Act**, which would increase the power of the ICC, Roosevelt worked skillfully behind the scenes. In its final form, the Hepburn Act, passed in May 1906, gave the ICC the power to set rates subject to court review. Committed progressives like La Follette judged the law a defeat for reform. Diehard conservatives branded it a "piece of populism." Both sides exaggerated. The law left the courts too much power and failed to provide adequate means for the ICC to determine rates, but its passage proved a landmark in federal control of private industry. For the first time, a government commission had the power to investigate private business records and to set rates.

Passage of the Hepburn Act marked the high point of Roosevelt's presidency. In a serious political blunder, Roosevelt had announced on the eve of his election in 1904 that he would not run again. By 1906, he had become a "lame duck" at the very moment he enjoyed his greatest public popularity.

Always an apt reader of the public temper, Roosevelt witnessed a growing appetite for reform fed by the revelations of corporate and political wrongdoing and social injustice that filled the papers and boosted the sales of popular periodicals. Roosevelt, who wielded publicity like a weapon in his pursuit of reform, counted many of the new investigative journalists, including Jacob Riis, among his friends. But he warned them against going too far, citing the allegorical character in *Pilgrim's Progress* who was so busy raking muck that he took no notice of higher things. Roosevelt's criticism gave the American vocabulary a new word, *muckraker*, which journalists soon appropriated as a title of honor.

Muckraking, as Roosevelt well knew, provided enormous help in securing progressive legislation. In the spring of 1906, publicity generated by the muckrakers about poisons in patent medicines goaded the Senate, with Roosevelt's backing, into passing a pure food and drug bill. Opponents in the House of Representatives hoped to keep the legislation locked up in committee. There it would have died, were it not for the publication of Upton Sinclair's novel *The Jungle* (1906), with its sensational account of filthy conditions in meatpacking

THE PROMISE OF TECHNOLOGY

Flash Photography The advent of flash photography enabled muckraker Jacob Riis to expose the dark alleys and tenements of New York City. The new technology involved a pistol lamp that fired magnesium cartridges to provide light for instantaneous photography. Armed with the new flash pistols, Riis and a band of amateur photographers set out to shine light in the dark corners of New York. Riis took his camera (much like the one shown here) into a Baxter Street courtyard, pictured here, where he recorded these observations: "I counted the other day the little ones, up to ten years old in a . . . tenement that for a yard has a . . . space in the center with sides fourteen or fifteen feet long, just enough for a row of ill-smelling [water] closets . . . and a hydrant. . . . There was about as much light in the 'yard' as in the average cellar. . . . I counted one hundred twenty eight [children] in forty families." Riis used his photos to campaign for tenement reform. He warned slumlords (some of them prominent New Yorkers) that their greed bred crime and disease and spawned class warfare. Baxter Street courtyard: The Jacob A. Riis Collection, #108 Museum of the City of New York; Camera: George Eastman House.

plants. A massive public outcry led to the passage of the **Pure Food and Drug Act** and the Meat Inspection Act in 1906.

In the waning years of his administration, Roosevelt allied with the more progressive elements of the Republican Party. In speech after speech, he attacked "malefactors of great wealth." Styling himself a "radical," he claimed credit for leading the "ultra conservative" party of McKinley to a position of "progressive conservatism and conservative radicalism."

When an economic panic developed in the fall of 1907, business interests quickly blamed the president. The panic of 1907 proved severe but short. Once again, J. P. Morgan stepped in to avert disaster, this time switching funds from one bank to another to prop up weak institutions. For his services, he claimed the Tennessee Coal and Iron Company, an independent steel business that had long been coveted by the U.S. Steel Corporation. Morgan dispatched his lieutenants to Washington, where they told Roosevelt that the sale of the company would aid the economy "but little benefit" U.S. Steel. Willing to take the word of a gentleman, Roosevelt tacitly agreed not to institute antitrust proceedings against U.S. Steel over the acquisition. Roosevelt later learned that Morgan had been less than candid. U.S. Steel acquired Tennessee Coal and Iron for a price well below market value, doing away with a competitor and undercutting the economy of the Southeast. Roosevelt's promise not to institute antitrust proceedings against U.S. Steel would give rise to the charge that he acted as a tool of the Morgan interests.

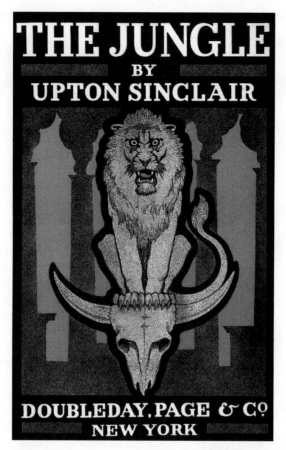

THE JUNGLE
BY
UPTON SINCLAIR

DOUBLEDAY, PAGE & Cº
NEW YORK

The Jungle Novelist Upton Sinclair, a lifelong socialist, wrote *The Jungle* to expose the evils of capitalism. But readers were more horrified by his descriptions of the unsanitary conditions in the meatpacking industry, where the novel's hapless hero sees rats, filth, and diseased animals processed into meat products. It was rumored that after reading the book, President Theodore Roosevelt could no longer stomach sausage for breakfast. The president immediately ordered a thorough study of conditions in the meatpacking industry. The public outcry surrounding *The Jungle* contributed to the enactment of pure food and drug legislation and a federal meat inspection law. Sinclair ruefully remarked, "I aimed at the public's heart, but I hit them in the stomach." Picture Research Consultants, Inc.

The charge of collusion between business and government underscored the extent to which corporate leaders like Morgan found federal regulation preferable to unbridled competition or harsher state measures. During the Progressive Era, enlightened business leaders cooperated with government in the hope of avoiding antitrust prosecution. Convinced that regulation and not trust-busting offered the best way to deal with big business, Roosevelt never acknowledged that his regulatory policies fostered an alliance between business and government that today is called corporate liberalism.

Roosevelt and Conservation In the area of conservation, Roosevelt proved indisputably ahead of his time. When he took office, some 45 million acres of land remained as government reserves. He more than tripled that number to 150 million acres, buying land and creating national parks and wildlife preserves by executive order. To conserve natural resources, he fought western cattle barons, lumber kings, mining interests, and powerful leaders in Congress, including Speaker of the House Joseph Cannon, who was determined to spend "not one cent for scenery."

As the first president to have lived and worked in the West, Roosevelt came to the White House convinced of the need for better management of the nation's rivers and forests. During his presidency he placed the nation's conservation policy in the hands of scientifically trained experts like his chief forester, Gifford Pinchot. Roosevelt and Pinchot preached conservation—the efficient use of natural resources. Willing to permit grazing, lumbering, and the development of hydroelectric power, conservationists fought private interests only when they felt business acted irresponsibly or threatened to monopolize water and electric power. Roosevelt's conservation policies drew criticism from many quarters. Preservationists like John Muir, founder of the Sierra Club, believed the wilderness needed to be protected. Muir soon clashed with Roosevelt, whose policy of managed use led to the destruction of the Hetch Hetchy valley in California's Yosemite National Park. (See "Historical Question," page 526.)

In 1907, Congress put the brakes on Roosevelt's conservation program by passing a law limiting his power to create forest reserves in six western states. In the days leading up to the law's enactment, Roosevelt feverishly created twenty-one new reserves and enlarged eleven more, saving sixteen million acres for posterity. Once again, Roosevelt had outwitted his adversaries. "Opponents of the forest service turned handsprings in their wrath," he wrote, "but the threats . . . were really only a tribute to the efficiency of our action." Worried that private utilities were gobbling up waterpower sites and creating a monopoly of hydroelectric power, he authorized Pinchot to withdraw 2,565 power sites from private use by designating them "ranger stations." Firm in his commitment to conservation, Roosevelt proved willing to stretch the law when it served his ends. Today, the six national parks, sixteen national monuments, and fifty-one wildlife refuges that he created bear witness to his substantial accomplishments as a conservationist (Map 21.1).

MAP 21.1 National Parks and Forests

The national park system in the West began with Yellowstone in 1872. Grand Canyon, Yosemite, Kings Canyon, and Sequoia followed in the 1890s. During his presidency, Theodore Roosevelt added six parks — Crater Lake, Wind Cave, Petrified Forest, Lassen Volcanic, Mesa Verde, and Zion.

READING THE MAP: Collectively, do national parks or national forests encompass more land? According to the map, how many national parks were created before 1910? How many were created after 1910?

CONNECTIONS: How do conservation and preservation differ? Why did Roosevelt believe that conservation was important? What principle guided the national land use policy of the Roosevelt administration?

FOR MORE HELP ANALYZING THIS MAP, see the map activity for this chapter in the Online Study Guide at bedfordstmartins.com/roarkcompact.

The Big Stick Roosevelt's activism extended to his foreign policy, where he worked to buttress the nation's newly won place among world leaders. A fierce proponent of America's interests abroad, he believed that Congress was inept in foreign affairs, and relied on executive power to pursue a vigorous foreign policy, sometimes stretching the powers of the presidency beyond legal limits. In his relations with the European powers, he relied on military strength and diplomacy, a combination he aptly described with the aphorism "Speak softly but carry a big stick."

In the Caribbean, Roosevelt jealously guarded the U.S. sphere of influence defined in the Monroe Doctrine. Roosevelt's proprietary attitude toward the Western Hemisphere became evident in the case of the Panama Canal. Roosevelt had long been a supporter of a canal linking the Carib-

bean and the Pacific. By enabling ships to move quickly from the Atlantic to the Pacific, a canal could effectively double the U.S. navy's power. Having decided on a route across the Panamanian isthmus (a narrow strip of land connecting North and South America), then part of Colombia, Roosevelt in 1902 offered the Colombian government a one-time sum of $10 million and an annual rent of $250,000. When the government in Bogotá refused to accept the offer, Roosevelt became incensed at what he called the "homicidal corruptionists" in Colombia for trying to "blackmail" the United States. At the prompting of a group of New York investors, the Panamanians staged an uprising in 1903, and with unseemly haste the U.S. government recognized the new government within twenty-four hours. The Panamanians promptly accepted the $10 million,

Progressives and Conservation: Should Hetch Hetchy Be Dammed or Saved?

In 1890, President Benjamin Harrison signed into law an act setting aside two million acres in California's Yosemite Valley and designating Yosemite a national park. For naturalist John Muir, the founder of the Sierra Club, the act marked a victory in his crusade to guarantee that "incomparable Yosemite" would be preserved for posterity. But Muir's fight was not yet over.

The growing city of San Francisco needed water and power, and Mayor James Phelan soon sought to obtain water rights in Hetch Hetchy, a spectacular mountain valley within Yosemite's borders. There, the Tuolumne River could easily be dammed and the valley flooded to create a reservoir large enough to ensure the city's water supply for one hundred years.

When Muir heard of the plan, he sprang into action to save Hetch Hetchy. "That any one would try to destroy such a place seems incredible," he wrote, describing the valley as "one of Nature's rarest and most precious mountain temples." All of Yosemite National Park, he argued, should remain sacrosanct. In 1903, the secretary of the interior concurred, denying San Francisco supervisors commercial use of Hetch Hetchy on the grounds that it lay within the national park.

But the San Francisco earthquake and resulting fire in 1906 created a groundswell of sympathy for the devastated city. In this climate, San Francisco renewed its efforts to obtain Hetch Hetchy and in 1907 succeeded in gaining authorization to proceed with plans to dam the river and flood the valley.

Given President Theodore Roosevelt's commitment to conservation, how could his administration have agreed to the destruction of the Hetch Hetchy valley? Historians traditionally have styled the struggle as one that pitted conservationists against preservationists. Roosevelt and his chief forester, Gifford Pinchot, represented the forces of conservation, or managed use. To them, the battle was not over preservation but over public versus private control of water and power.

California progressives, who swept into office with the election of Hiram Johnson as governor in 1910, argued

that if Congress did not grant the city of San Francisco the right to control Hetch Hetchy, the powerful Pacific Gas and Electric Company (PG&E) would monopolize the city's light and power industry. These progressives dismissed Muir and his followers as "nature fakers" and judged them little more than dupes in the machinations of PG&E.

For their part, Muir and the preservationists, although they fought for the integrity of the national parks, did not champion the preservation of wilderness for its own sake. The urban professional men and women who joined the Sierra Club saw nature as a retreat and restorative for city dwellers. The club hosted an annual camping trip to popularize Yosemite and spoke in glowing terms of plans to build new roads and hotels that would make the "healing power of Nature" accessible to "thousands of tired, nerve-shaken, over-civilized people." As historian Robert Righter has pointed out, the battle over Hetch Hetchy represented not so much conservation versus preservation or managed use versus wilderness as it did the victory of water and power over tourism and recreation.

Nevertheless, the engineers and irrigation men who dammed Hetch Hetchy demonstrated a breathtaking arrogance. Speaking for them, Franklin Lane, President Woodrow Wilson's secretary of the interior, proclaimed, "Every tree is a challenge to use, and every pool of water and every foot of soil." Certain of humans' right to dominate nature and bend it to their will, Lane concluded, "The mountains are our enemy. We must pierce them and make them serve. The sinful rivers we must curb."

Lane and the conservationists won the day. In 1913, Congress passed the Raker Act authorizing the building of the O'Shaughnessy Dam, completed a decade later. To build the dam, the Hetch Hetchy valley was first denuded of its trees, then flooded under two hundred feet of water. Muir did not live to see the destruction of Hetch Hetchy. He died in 1914, cursing the "dark damn-dam-damnation." But his fight to save

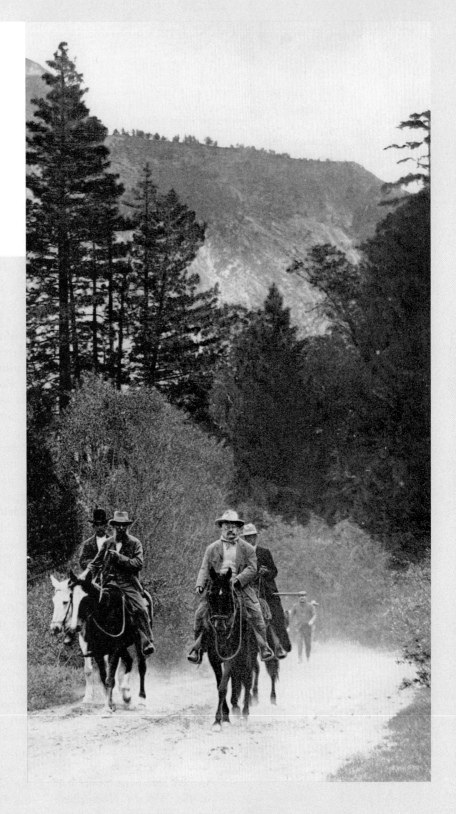

★ **Roosevelt and Muir in Yosemite** This 1903 photograph shows President Theodore Roosevelt on a camping trip in Yosemite National Park with John Muir. Roosevelt and Muir later clashed over the flooding of the Hetch Hetchy valley in Yosemite. Roosevelt and his chief forester, Gifford Pinchot, favored giving San Francisco the right to dam the valley to supply water and power. Muir bitterly noted that Pinchot had never bothered to visit the valley he condemned to a watery grave. Theodore Roosevelt Collection, Harvard College Library.

Hetch Hetchy galvanized the preservation movement and led to the passage of the National Park Service Act in 1916 creating a federal agency to protect the nation's parks.

The last chapter in the battle over Hetch Hetchy may yet be written. In 1987, President Ronald Reagan's secretary of the interior, Donald Hodel, shocked San Francisco by suggesting the removal of the O'Shaughnessy Dam and the restoration of the Hetch Hetchy valley. Although it is unlikely that the dam will be demolished (it supplies San Francisco not only with water but also with revenue from electric power), advocates for the restoration of the Hetch Hetchy valley continue to rally to the cause. As Ken Browner of the Sierra Club wrote, "Waiting in Yosemite National Park, under water, is a potential masterpiece of restoration" and a chance "to correct the biggest environmental mistake ever committed against the National Park System."

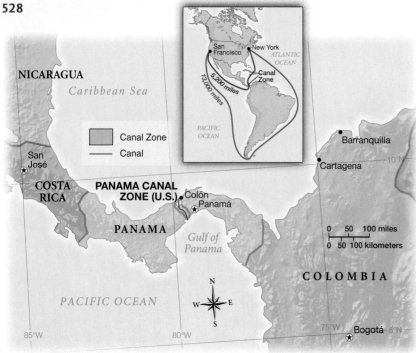

MAP 21.2 **The Panama Canal, 1914**
The Panama Canal, completed in 1914, bisects the isthmus in a series of massive locks and dams. As Theodore Roosevelt had planned, the canal greatly strengthened the U.S. navy by allowing ships to move from the Atlantic to the Pacific in a matter of days.

and the building got under way. The canal would take eleven years and $375 million to complete; it opened in 1914 (Map 21.2).

In the wake of the Panama affair, a confrontation with Germany over Venezuela, and yet another default on a European debt, this time in the Dominican Republic, Roosevelt announced in 1904 what became known as the **Roosevelt Corollary** to the Monroe Doctrine. Couched in the moralistic rhetoric typical of Roosevelt, the corollary declared that the United States would not intervene in Latin America as long as nations there conducted their affairs with "decency." But the United States would step in if any Latin American nation proved guilty of "brutal wrongdoing." The Roosevelt Corollary in effect made the United States the policeman of the Western Hemisphere and served notice to the European powers to keep out.

In Asia, Roosevelt inherited the Open Door policy initiated by Secretary of State John Hay in 1899, designed to

The Roosevelt Corollary in Action

ensure U.S. commercial entry into China. As Britain, France, Russia, Japan, and Germany raced to secure Chinese trade and territory, Roosevelt was tempted to use force to enter the fray and gain economic or possibly territorial concessions. As a result of victory in the Spanish-American War, the United States already enjoyed a foothold in the region by virtue of its control of the Philippines. Realizing that Americans would not support an aggressive Asian policy, Roosevelt sensibly held back.

In his relations with Europe, Roosevelt sought to establish the United States, fresh from its victory over Spain, as a rising force in world affairs. When tensions flared between France and Germany in Morocco in 1905, Roosevelt mediated at a conference in Algeciras, Spain, where he worked to maintain a balance of power that helped neutralize German ambitions. His skillful mediation gained him a reputation as an astute player on the world stage and demonstrated the nation's new presence in world affairs.

Roosevelt earned the Nobel Peace Prize in 1906 for his role in negotiating an end to the Russo-Japanese War, which had broken out when the Japanese invaded Chinese Manchuria, threatening Russia's sphere of influence in the area. Once again, Roosevelt sought to maintain a balance of power, in this case working to curb Japanese expansionism. Roosevelt admired the Japanese, judging them "the most dashing fighters in the world," but he did not want Japan to become too strong in Asia.

When good relations with Japan were jeopardized by discriminatory legislation in California calling for segregated public schools for "Orientals," Roosevelt smoothed over the incident and negotiated the "Gentlemen's Agreement" in 1907, which allowed the Japanese to save face by voluntarily restricting immigration to the United States. To demonstrate America's naval power and counter Japan's growing bellicosity, Roosevelt dispatched the Great White Fleet, sixteen of the navy's most up-to-date battleships, on a "goodwill mission" around the world. U.S. relations with Japan improved, and in the 1908 Root-Takahira agreement, the two nations pledged to maintain the Open Door and support the status quo in the Pacific. Roosevelt's show of American force constituted a classic example of his dictum "Speak softly but carry a big stick."

Q: **How did Roosevelt's foreign policy move the United States onto the world stage?**

THE WORLD'S CONSTABLE.

"The World's Constable" In this political cartoon from 1905, President Theodore Roosevelt, dressed as a constable, wields the club of "The New Diplomacy" in one hand with "Arbitration" tucked under his arm. The Roosevelt Corollary to the Monroe Doctrine made the United States the Western Hemisphere's policeman, a role Roosevelt relished. Granger Collection.

FOR MORE HELP ANALYZING THIS IMAGE, see the visual activity for this chapter in the Online Study Guide at bedfordstmartins.com/roarkcompact.

Progressivism Stalled

Roosevelt retired from the presidency in 1909 at age fifty and removed himself from the political scene by going on safari in Africa. He turned the White House over to his handpicked successor, **William Howard Taft**, a lawyer who had served as governor-general of the Philippines. In the presidential election of 1908, Taft soundly defeated the perennial Democratic candidate, William Jennings Bryan. But Taft's popular majority amounted to only half of Roosevelt's record win in 1904.

Any man would have found it difficult to follow in Roosevelt's footsteps, but Taft proved hopelessly ill suited to the task. A genial man with a talent for law, Taft had no experience in elective office, no feel for politics, and no nerve for controversy. His ambitious wife coveted the office and urged him to seek it. He would have been better off listening to his mother, who warned, "Roosevelt is a good fighter and enjoys it, but the malice of politics would make you miserable." Her words proved prophetic. Taft's presidency was marked by a progressive stalemate, a bitter break with Roosevelt, and a schism in the Republican Party.

The Troubled Presidency of William Howard Taft
Once in office, Taft proved a perfect tool in the hands of Republicans who yearned for a return to the days of a less active executive. A lawyer by training and instinct, Taft believed that it was up to the courts, not the president, to arbitrate social issues. Roosevelt had carried presidential power to a new level, often flouting the separation of powers. Taft the legalist found it difficult to condone Roosevelt's actions. Wary of the progressive insurgents in Congress, Taft relied increasingly on conservatives in the Republican Party. As a progressive senator lamented, "Taft is a ponderous and amiable man completely surrounded by men who know exactly what they want."

> A progressive senator lamented, "Taft is a ponderous and amiable man completely surrounded by men who know exactly what they want."

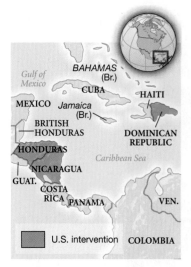

Taft's "Dollar Diplomacy"

Taft's troubles began on the eve of his inaugural, when he called a special session of Congress to deal with the tariff, which had grown inordinately high under Republican rule. Roosevelt had been too politically astute to tackle the troublesome tariff issue, even though he knew that rates needed to be lowered. Taft blundered into the fray. The House of Representatives passed a modest downward revision but the conservative Senate struck down the tax and added more than eight hundred crippling amendments to the tariff. The Payne-Aldrich bill that emerged actually raised the tariff, benefiting big business and the trusts at the expense of consumers. As if paralyzed, Taft neither fought for changes nor vetoed the measure. On a tour of the Midwest in 1909, he was greeted with jeers when he claimed, "I think the Payne bill is the best bill that the Republican Party ever passed." In the eyes of a growing number of Americans, Taft's praise of the tariff made him either a fool or a liar.

Taft's legalism soon got him into hot water in the area of conservation. He undid Roosevelt's work to preserve hydroelectric power sites when he learned that they had been improperly designated as ranger stations. And when Gifford Pinchot publicly denounced Taft's secretary of the interior as a tool of western land-grabbers, Taft fired Pinchot, touching off a storm of controversy that damaged Taft and alienated Roosevelt.

When Roosevelt returned to the United States in June 1910, he received a hero's welcome and attracted a stream of visitors and reporters seeking his advice and opinions. Hurt, Taft kept his distance. By late summer, Roosevelt had taken sides with the progressive insurgents in his party. "Taft is utterly hopeless as a leader," Roosevelt confided to his son as he set out on a speaking tour of the West. Reading the mood of the country, Roosevelt began to sound more and more like a candidate.

With the Republican Party divided, the Democrats swept the congressional elections of 1910. Branding the Payne-Aldrich tariff "the mother of trusts," they captured a majority in the House of Representatives and won several key governorships. The revitalized Democratic Party could look to new leaders, among them the progressive governor of New Jersey, Woodrow Wilson.

The new Democratic majority in the House, working with progressive Republicans in the Senate, achieved a number of key reforms, including legislation to regulate mine and railroad safety, to create the Children's Bureau in the Department of Labor, and to establish an eight-hour day for federal workers.

Two significant constitutional amendments—the Sixteenth Amendment, which provided for a modest graduated income tax, and the Seventeenth Amendment, which called for the direct election of senators (formerly chosen by state legislatures)—went to the states, where they would win ratification in 1913. While Congress rode the high tide of progressive reform, Taft sat on the sidelines.

In foreign policy, Taft continued Roosevelt's policy of extending U.S. influence abroad, but here, too, Taft had a difficult time following in Roosevelt's footsteps. His policy of **dollar diplomacy** championed commercial goals rather than the strategic aims Roosevelt had pursued. Taft naively assumed he could substitute "dollars for bullets." In the Caribbean, he provoked anti-American feeling by attempting to force commercial treaties on Nicaragua and Honduras and by dispatching U.S. Marines to Nicaragua and the Dominican Republic in 1912 pursuant to the Roosevelt Corollary. In Asia, he openly avowed his intent to promote in China "active intervention to secure for . . . our capitalists opportunity for profitable investment." Lacking Roosevelt's understanding of power politics, Taft never recognized that an aggressive commercial policy could not exist without the willingness to use military might to back it up.

Taft faced the limits of dollar diplomacy when revolution broke out in Mexico in 1911. Under pressure to protect American investments, which amounted to more than $4 billion, he mobilized troops along the border. In the end, however, with no popular support for a war with Mexico, he had to fall back on diplomatic pressure to salvage American interests.

Taft hoped to encourage world peace through the use of a world court and arbitration. He unsuccessfully sponsored a series of arbitration treaties that Roosevelt, who prized national honor more than international law, vehemently opposed as weak and cowardly. By 1910, Roosevelt had become a vocal critic of Taft's foreign policy, which he dismissed as "maudlin folly."

The final breach between Taft and Roosevelt came in 1911, when Taft's attorney general filed an antitrust suit against U.S. Steel. In its brief against the corporation, the government cited Roosevelt's agreement with the Morgan interests in the 1907 acquisition of Tennessee Coal and Iron. The incident greatly embarrassed Roosevelt. Thoroughly enraged, he lambasted Taft's "archaic" antitrust policy and hinted that he might be persuaded to run for president again.

Progressive Insurgency and the Election of 1912

In February 1912, Roosevelt challenged Taft for the Republican nomination, announcing, "My hat is in the ring." But for all his popularity, Roosevelt no longer controlled the party machinery. Taft, with uncharacteristic strength, refused to step aside. As he bitterly told a journalist, "Even a rat in a corner will fight." Roosevelt took advantage of newly passed primary election laws and ran in thirteen states, winning 278 delegates to Taft's 48. But at the Chicago convention, Taft's bosses refused to seat the Roosevelt delegates. Fistfights broke out on the convention floor as Taft won nomination on the first ballot. Crying robbery, Roosevelt's supporters bolted the party.

Seven weeks later, in the same Chicago auditorium, the hastily organized Progressive Party met to nominate Roosevelt. Amid a thunder of applause, Jane Addams seconded Roosevelt's nomination. Full of reforming zeal, the delegates chose Roosevelt and Hiram Johnson to head the new party and approved the most ambitious platform since that of the Populists. Planks called for woman suffrage, presidential primaries, conservation of natural resources, an end to child labor, workers' compensation, a minimum wage that would include women workers, social security, and a federal income tax.

Roosevelt arrived in Chicago to accept the nomination and announced that he felt "as strong as a bull moose," giving the new party a nickname and a mascot. But for all the excitement and the cheering, the new Progressive Party was doomed, and the candidate knew it. The people may have supported the party, but the politicians, even progressives like La Follette, stayed within the Republican fold. "I am under no illusion about it," Roosevelt confessed to a friend. "It is a forlorn hope." But he had gone too far to turn back. He led the Bull Moose Party into the fray, exhorting his followers in ringing biblical tones, "We shall not falter, we stand at Armageddon and do battle for the Lord."

The Democrats, delighted at the split in the Republican ranks, smelled victory. Their convention turned into a bitter fight for the nomination. After forty-six ballots, **Woodrow Wilson** became the party's nominee. Wilson's career in politics was nothing short of meteoric. He was elected governor of New Jersey in 1910, and after only eighteen months in office, the former professor of political science and president of Princeton University found himself running for president of the United States.

Voters in 1912 could choose among four candidates who claimed to be progressives. Taft, Roosevelt, and Wilson each embraced the label, and even the Socialist candidate, Eugene V. Debs, styled himself a progressive. That the term *progressive* could stretch to cover these diverse candidates underscored major disagreements in progressive thinking about the relationship between business and government. Taft, in spite of his trust-busting, was generally viewed as the candidate of the old guard. The real contest for the presidency was between Roosevelt and Wilson and the two political philosophies summed up in their respective campaign slogans: **The New Nationalism** and **The New Freedom**.

Wilson Ribbon Woodrow Wilson's political career was meteoric, propelling him from the presidency of Princeton University to the White House in three years. As governor of New Jersey from 1910 to 1912, Wilson turned against the Democratic political machine that had backed him and made a reputation as a champion of progressive reform. With the Republicans divided in 1912, the Democrats turned to Wilson to lead the party, nominating him on the forty-sixth ballot. In those days, prospective candidates generally did not attend the nominating convention. The ribbon in the photograph belonged to a member of the Democratic National Committee, who traveled to Wilson's summer home in Sea Girt, New Jersey, on August 7, 1912, to inform Wilson officially of his nomination. Collection of Janice L. and David J. Frent.

The New Nationalism expressed Roosevelt's belief in federal planning and regulation. He accepted the inevitability of big business but demanded that government act as "a steward of the people" to regulate the giant corporations. Wilson, schooled in the Democratic principles of limited government and states' rights, set a markedly different course with his New Freedom. Wilson promised to use antitrust legislation to get rid of big corporations and to give small businesses and farmers better opportunities in the marketplace.

The energy and enthusiasm of the Bull Moosers made the race seem closer than it was. In the end, the Republican vote split, while the Democrats remained united. No candidate claimed a majority in the race. Wilson captured a bare 42 percent of the popular vote. Roosevelt and his Bull Moose Party won 27 percent, an unprecedented tally for a new party. Taft came in third with 23 percent. The Socialist Party, led by Debs, captured 6 percent. In the electoral college, however, Wilson won a decisive 435 votes, with 88 going to Roosevelt and only 8 to Taft (Map 21.3). The Progressive Party essentially collapsed after Roosevelt's defeat. It had always been, in the words of one astute observer, "a house divided against itself and already mortgaged."

Q: **Why did Roosevelt become the presidential nominee of the Progressive Party in 1912?**

Candidate	Electoral Vote	Popular Vote	Percent of Popular Vote
Woodrow Wilson (Democrat)	435	6,293,454	41.9
Theodore Roosevelt (Progressive)	88	4,119,538	27.4
William H. Taft (Republican)	8	3,484,980	23.2
Eugene V. Debs (Socialist)	0	900,672	6.1

MAP 21.3 The Election of 1912

Woodrow Wilson and Progressivism at High Tide

Born in Virginia and raised in Georgia, Woodrow Wilson became the first southerner to be elected president since 1844 and only the second Democrat to occupy the White House since Reconstruction. Democrats who anticipated a wild celebration when Wilson took office had their hopes dashed. The son of a Presbyterian minister, Wilson was a teetotaler more given to Scripture than to celebration. He called instead for a day of prayer.

This lean, ascetic scholar was, as one biographer conceded, a man whose "political convictions were never as fixed as his ambition." Although he owed his governorship to the Democratic machine, he quickly turned his back on the bosses and, with his eye on the presidency, put New Jersey in the vanguard of progressivism. Always able to equivocate, Wilson proved rarely able to compromise. He brought to the White House a gift for oratory, a stern will, and a set of fixed beliefs. His tendency to turn differences of opinion into personal hatreds would impair his leadership and damage his presidency. Fortunately for Wilson, he came to power with a Democratic Congress eager to do his bidding.

Although he opposed big government in his campaign, Wilson was prepared to work on the base built by Roosevelt to strengthen presidential power, exerting leadership to achieve banking reform and working through his party in Congress to accomplish the Democratic agenda. Before he was finished, Wilson presided over progressivism at high tide and lent his

support not only to the platform of the Democratic Party but also to many of the Progressive Party's social reforms.

Wilson's Reforms: Tariff, Banking, and the Trusts   In March 1913, Wilson showed off his oratorical ability by becoming the first president since John Adams to go to Capitol Hill and speak directly to Congress. With the Democratic Party firmly in control, he called for tariff reform. "The object of the tariff," Wilson told Congress, "must be effective competition." The Democratic House of Representatives hastily passed the Underwood tariff, which lowered rates by 15 percent. To compensate for lost revenue, the House approved a moderate federal income tax, made possible by ratification of the Sixteenth Amendment a month earlier. In the Senate, lobbyists for industries quietly went to work to get the tariff raised, but Wilson rallied public opinion by attacking the "industrious and insidious lobby." In the harsh glare of publicity, the Senate passed the Underwood tariff, which earned praise as "the most honest tariff since the Civil War."

Wilson next turned his attention to banking. The panic of 1907 dramatically testified to the failure of the banking system. That year, Roosevelt, like President Grover Cleveland before him, had to turn to J. P. Morgan to avoid economic catastrophe. But by the time Wilson came to office, Morgan's legendary power had come under close scrutiny. In 1913, a Senate committee investigated the "money trust," calling J. P. Morgan himself to testify. The committee uncovered an alarming concentration of banking power. J. P. Morgan and Company and its affiliates held 341 directorships in 112 corporations, controlling assets of more than $22 billion ($457 billion in today's dollars). The sensational findings created a mandate for banking reform.

The Federal Reserve Act of 1913 marked the most significant piece of domestic legislation of Wilson's presidency. It established a national banking system composed of twelve regional banks, privately controlled but regulated and supervised by the Federal Reserve Board, appointed by the president. It gave the United States its first efficient banking and currency system and, at the same time, provided for a greater degree of government control over banking. The new system made currency more elastic and credit adequate for the needs of business and agriculture. It did not, however, attempt to take control of the boom and bust cycles in the U.S. economy, which would produce the Great Depression of the 1930s.

Wilson, flushed with success, tackled the trust issue next. When Congress reconvened in January 1914, he supported the introduction of the Clayton Antitrust Act to outlaw "unfair competition"—practices such as price discrimination and interlocking directorates (directors from one corporation sitting on the board of another). By spelling out unfair practices, Wilson hoped to guide business activity back to healthy competition without resorting to regulation. In the midst of the fight for the Clayton Act, Wilson changed course and threw his support behind the creation of the **Federal Trade Commission (FTC)**, precisely the kind of federal regulatory agency that Roosevelt had advocated in his New Nationalism platform. The FTC, created in 1914, had not only wide investigatory powers but also the authority to prosecute corporations for "unfair trade practices" and to enforce its judgments by issuing "cease and desist" orders. Despite his campaign promises, Wilson's antitrust program worked to regulate rather than to break up big business.

By the fall of 1914, Wilson had exhausted the stock of ideas that made up the New Freedom. He alarmed progressives by declaring that the progressive movement had fulfilled its mission and that the country needed "a time of healing." Disgruntled progressives also disapproved of Wilson's conservative appointments. Having fought provisions in the Federal Reserve Act that would give bankers control, Wilson promptly named a banker as the first chief of the Federal Reserve Board. Appointments to the new FTC also went to conservative businessmen. The progressive penchant for expertise helps explain Wilson's choices. Believing that experts in the field could best understand the complex issues at stake, Wilson appointed bankers to oversee the banks and businessmen to regulate business.

Wilson, Reluctant Progressive As Wilson repeatedly obstructed or obstinately refused to endorse further progressive reforms, progressives watched in dismay. He failed to support labor's demand for an end to court injunctions against labor unions. He twice threatened to veto legislation providing farm credits for nonperishable crops. He refused to support child labor legislation or woman suffrage. Wilson used the rhetoric of the New Freedom to justify his actions, claiming that his administration would condone "special privileges to none." But, in fact, his stance often reflected the interests of his small-business constituency.

In the face of Wilson's obstinacy, reform might have ended in 1913 had not politics intruded. In the congressional elections of 1914, the Republican Party, no longer split by Roosevelt's Bull Moose faction, won substantial gains. Democratic strategists, with their eyes on the 1916 presidential race, recognized that Wilson needed to pick up support in the Midwest and the West by capturing votes from former Bull Moose progressives. Wilson responded belatedly by lending his support to reform in the months leading up to the election of 1916. In a sharp about-face, he

cultivated union labor, farmers, and social reformers. To please labor, he appointed progressive Louis Brandeis to the Supreme Court. To woo farmers, he threw his support behind legislation to obtain rural credits. And he won praise from labor by supporting workers' compensation and the Keating-Owen child labor law (1916), which outlawed the regular employment of children younger than sixteen. When a railroad strike threatened in the months before the election, Wilson practically ordered Congress to establish an eight-hour day on the railroads. He had moved a long way from his position in 1912 to embrace many of the social reforms championed by Theodore Roosevelt. As Wilson boasted, the Democrats had "opened their hearts to the demands of social justice" and had "come very near to carrying out the platform of the Progressive Party." Wilson's shift toward reform, along with his claim that he had kept the United States out of the war in Europe (see chapter 22), helped him win reelection in 1916.

Q: How and why did Wilson's reform program evolve during his first term?

The Limits of Progressive Reform

While progressivism called for a more active role for the liberal state, at heart it was a movement that sought reforms designed to preserve American institutions and stem the tide of more radical change. Its basic conservatism can be seen by comparing it to the more radical movements of socialism, radical labor, and birth control—and by looking at the groups progressive reform left behind, including women and African Americans.

Radical Alternatives The year 1900 marked the birth of the Social Democratic Party in America, later called simply the Socialist Party. Like the progressives, the socialists were middle-class and native-born. They had broken with the older, more militant Socialist Labor Party precisely because of its dogmatic approach and immigrant constituency. The new group of socialists proved eager to appeal to a broad mass of disaffected Americans.

The Socialist Party chose as its presidential standard-bearer Eugene V. Debs, whose experience in the Pullman strike of 1894 convinced him that "there is no hope for the toiling masses of my countrymen, except by the pathways mapped out by Socialism." Debs would run for president five times, in every election (except 1916) from 1900 to 1920. The socialism Debs advocated preached cooperation over competition and urged men and women to liberate themselves from "the barbarism of private ownership and wage slavery." In the 1912 election, Debs indicted both old parties as "Tweedledee and Tweedledum," each dedicated to the preservation of capitalism and the continuation of the wage system. Only through socialism, he argued, could democracy exist. Styling the Socialist Party the "revolutionary party of the working class," he urged voters to rally to his standard. Debs's best showing came in 1912, when he polled 6 percent of the popular vote, capturing more than 900,000 votes.

Farther to the left of the socialists stood the Industrial Workers of the World (IWW), nicknamed the Wobblies. In 1905, Debs, along with Western Federation of Miners leader **William Dudley "Big Bill" Haywood**, created the IWW, "one big union" dedicated to organizing the most destitute segment of the workforce, the unskilled workers disdained by Samuel Gompers's AFL: western min-

ers, migrant farmworkers, lumbermen, and immigrant textile workers. Haywood, a craggy-faced miner with one eye (he had lost the other in a childhood accident), was a charismatic leader and a proletarian intellectual. Seeing workers on the lowest rung of the social ladder as the victims of violent repression, the IWW advocated direct action, sabotage, and the general strike—tactics designed to trigger a workers' uprising. The IWW never had more than 10,000 members at any one time, although possibly as many as 100,000 workers belonged to the union at one time or another in the early twentieth century. Nevertheless, the IWW's influence on the country extended far beyond its numbers.

In contrast to political radicals like Debs and Haywood, **Margaret Sanger** promoted birth control as a movement for social change. Sanger, a nurse who had worked among the poor on New York's Lower East Side, coined the term *birth control* in 1915 and launched a movement with broad social

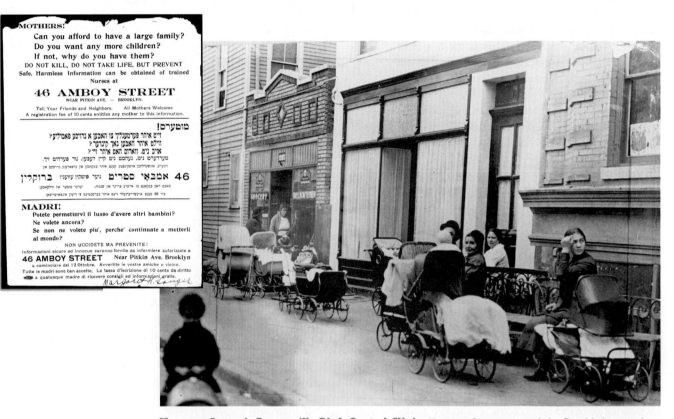

Margaret Sanger's Brownsville Birth Control Clinic Margaret Sanger opened the first birth control clinic in the United States in the Brownsville section of Brooklyn in 1916. During the nine days it operated before police shut it down, more than four hundred women visited the clinic. Here, they are shown waiting patiently in line with their baby carriages. Sanger published her fliers in English, Yiddish, and Italian. Her clinic, located in the heart of an immigrant neighborhood, proved that immigrant women—including Italian Catholics and Russian Jews—wanted information about birth control as much as their middle- and upper-class Protestant counterparts did. Sophia Smith Collection, Smith College.

FOR MORE HELP ANALYZING THIS IMAGE, see the visual activity for this chapter in the Online Study Guide at bedfordstmartins.com/roarkcompact.

implications. Sanger and her followers saw birth control not only as a sexual and medical reform but also as a means to alter social and political power relationships and to alleviate human misery.

The desire for family limitation was widespread, and in this sense, birth control was nothing new. The birthrate in the United States had been falling consistently throughout the nineteenth century. The average number of children per family dropped from 7.0 in 1800 to 3.6 by 1900. But the open advocacy of *contraception*, the use of artificial means to prevent pregnancy, struck many people as both new and shocking. And it was illegal. Anthony Comstock, New York City's commissioner of vice, promoted laws in the 1870s making it a felony not only to sell contraceptive devices like condoms and cervical caps but also to publish information on how to prevent pregnancy.

When Margaret Sanger used her militant feminist newspaper, the *Woman Rebel*, to promote birth control, the Post Office confiscated Sanger's publication and brought charges against her. Facing arrest, she fled to Europe, only to return in 1916 as something of a national celebrity. In her absence, birth control had become linked with free speech and had been taken up as a liberal cause. Under public pressure, the government dropped the charges against Sanger, who undertook a nationwide tour to publicize the birth control cause.

Sanger then turned to direct action, opening the nation's first birth control clinic in the Brownsville section of Brooklyn in October 1916. Located in the heart of a Jewish and Italian immigrant neighborhood, the clinic attracted 464 clients. On the tenth day, police shut down the clinic and threw Sanger in jail. By then, she had become a national figure, and the cause she championed had gained legitimacy, if not legality. After World War I, the birth control movement would become much less radical as Sanger turned to medical doctors for support and mouthed the racist theories of the eugenics movement. But in its infancy, the movement Sanger led was part of a radical vision for reforming the world that made common cause with the socialists and the IWW in challenging the limits of progressive reform.

Progressivism for White Men Only The day before President Woodrow Wilson's inauguration in March 1913, the largest mass march to date in the nation's history took place as more than five thousand demonstrators took to the streets in Washington to demand the vote for women. A rowdy crowd on hand to celebrate the Democrats' triumph attacked the marchers. Men spat at the suffragists and threw lighted cigarettes and matches at their clothing. "If my wife were where you are," a burly cop told one suffragist, "I'd break her head."

But for all the marching, Wilson, who didn't believe that a "lady" should vote, pointedly ignored woman suffrage in his inaugural address the next day.

The march served as a reminder that the political gains of progressivism were not spread equally throughout the population. As the twentieth century dawned, women still could not vote in most states, although they had won major victories in the West. Increasingly, however, woman suffrage had become an international movement. In Great Britain, Emmeline Pankhurst and her daughters Cristabel and Sylvia promoted a new, militant suffragism. They seized the spotlight in a series of marches, mass meetings, and acts of civil disobedience that sometimes escalated into riots, violence, and arson.

Alice Paul, a Quaker social worker who had visited England and participated in suffrage activism there, returned to the United States in 1910 in time to plan the mass march on the eve of Wilson's inauguration and to lobby for a federal amendment to give women the vote. Paul's dramatic tactics alienated many in the National American Woman Suffrage Association (NAWSA). In 1916, Paul founded the militant National Woman's Party (NWP), which became the radical voice of the suffrage movement, advocating direct action such as mass marches and civil disobedience.

Women weren't the only group left out in progressive reform. Progressivism, as it was practiced in the West and South, was tainted with racism and sought to limit the rights of African and Asian Americans. Anti-Asian bigotry in the West led to a renewal of the Chinese Exclusion Act in 1902. At first, California governor Hiram Johnson stood against the strong anti-Asian prejudice of his state. But in 1913, he caved to popular pressure and signed the Alien Land Law, which barred Japanese immigrants from purchasing land in California. The law was largely symbolic—ineffectual in practice because Japanese children born in the United States were U.S. citizens and property could be purchased in their names.

South of the Mason-Dixon line, the progressives' racism targeted African Americans. Progressives preached the disfranchisement of black voters as a "reform." During the bitter electoral fights that had pitted Populists against Democrats in the 1890s, the party of white supremacy held its power by votes purchased or coerced from African Americans. Southern progressives proposed to "reform" the electoral system by eliminating black voters. Beginning in 1890 with Mississippi, southern states curtailed the African American vote through devices such as poll taxes (fees required for voting) and literacy tests. The racist intent of southern voting legislation became especially clear after 1900 when states resorted to the grandfather clause, a legal provision that allowed men who failed a literacy test to vote if their grandfathers had cast a ballot. Grandfathering permitted southern white men to vote while excluding blacks.

The Progressive Era also witnessed the rise of Jim Crow laws to segregate public facilities. The new railroads precipitated segregation in the South where it had rarely existed before, at least on paper. Soon, separate rail cars, separate waiting rooms, separate bathrooms, and separate dining facilities for blacks sprang up across the South. In courtrooms in Mississippi, blacks were required to swear on a separate Bible.

In the face of this growing repression, **Booker T. Washington**, the preeminent black leader of the day, urged caution and restraint. A former slave, Washington had opened the Tuskegee Institute in Alabama in 1881 to teach vocational skills to African Americans. He emphasized education and economic progress for his race and urged African Americans to put aside issues of political and social equality. In an 1895 speech in Atlanta that came to

be known as the **Atlanta Compromise**, he stated, "In all things that are purely social we can be as separate as the fingers, yet one as the hand in all things essential to mutual progress." Washington's accommodationist policy appealed to whites and elevated "the wizard of Tuskegee" to the role of national spokesman for African Americans.

The year after Washington proclaimed the Atlanta Compromise, the Supreme Court upheld the legality of racial segregation, affirming in ***Plessy v. Ferguson*** (1896) the constitutionality of the doctrine of "separate but equal." Blacks could be segregated in separate schools, restrooms, and other facilities as long as the facilities were "equal" to those provided for whites. Of course, facilities for blacks rarely proved equal. In the North, where racism of a different sort led to a clamor for legislation to restrict immigration, support for African American equality found few advocates. And with anti-Asian bigotry strong in the West, the doctrine of "white supremacy" found increasing support in all sections of the country.

Booker T. Washington and Theodore Roosevelt Dine at the White House   When Theodore Roosevelt invited Booker T. Washington to the White House in 1901, he stirred up a hornet's nest of controversy that continued into the election of 1904. This Republican campaign piece gives the meeting a positive slant, showing Roosevelt and a light-skinned Washington sitting under a portrait of Abraham Lincoln, a symbol of the party's historic commitment to African Americans. Democrats portrayed the meeting in a very different light; their campaign buttons pictured Washington with darker skin and implied that Roosevelt favored "race mingling" and had "painted the White House black." Collection of Janice L. and David J. Frent.

When Theodore Roosevelt invited Booker T. Washington to dine at the White House in 1901, a storm of racist criticism erupted. One southern editor fumed that the White House "had been painted black." But Roosevelt summoned Washington to talk politics and patronage, not African American rights. Roosevelt's unquestioned racial prejudice became clear in the Brownsville incident in 1906, when he dishonorably discharged an entire battalion of 167 black soldiers because he suspected (although there was no proof) that they were shielding the murderer of a white saloon-keeper killed in a shoot-out in the Texas town.

Woodrow Wilson brought to the White House southern attitudes toward race and racial segregation. He instituted segregation in the federal workforce, especially the Post Office, and approved segregated drinking fountains and restrooms in the nation's capital. When critics attacked the policy, Wilson insisted that segregation was "in the interest of the Negro."

In 1906 a major race riot in Atlanta called into question Booker T. Washington's strategy of uplift and accommodation. For three days in September, the streets of Atlanta ran red with blood as angry white mobs chased and cornered any blacks they happened upon, pulling passengers from streetcars and invading black neighborhoods to kill and loot. An estimated 250 African Americans died in the riots—members of Atlanta's black middle class along with the poor and derelict. Professor William Crogman of Clark College noted the central irony of the riot: "Here we have worked and prayed and tried to make good men and women of our colored population," he observed, "and at our very doorstep the whites kill these good men." In Dark Town, a working-class neighborhood, blacks fought back to defend their homes, shooting into the white mob and driving off the attackers. In the aftermath of the riot, the city's leaders, black and white, managed to quash any nascent black unity by falling back on the old strategy of allying "the best white people and the best colored people." Yet the riot caused many African Americans to question Washington's strategy of gradualism and accommodation.

Foremost among Washington's critics stood **W. E. B. Du Bois**, a Harvard graduate who urged African Americans to fight for civil rights and racial justice. In *The Souls of Black Folk* (1903), Du Bois attacked the "Tuskegee Machine," comparing Washington to a political boss who used his influence to silence his critics and reward his followers. Du Bois founded the Niagara movement in 1905, calling for universal male suffrage, civil rights, and leadership of a black intellectual elite. The Atlanta riot only bolstered his resolve. In 1909, the Niagara movement helped found the National Association for the Advancement of Colored People (NAACP),

a coalition of blacks and whites that sought legal and political rights for African Americans through the courts. In the decades that followed, the NAACP came to represent the future for African Americans, while Booker T. Washington, who died in 1915, represented the past.

Q: How did race, class, and gender shape the limits of progressive reform?

Conclusion: The Transformation of the Liberal State

Progressivism was never a radical movement. Its goal remained to reform the existing system—by government intervention if necessary, but without uprooting any of the traditional American political, economic, or social institutions. As Theodore Roosevelt, the bellwether of the movement, insisted, "The only true conservative is the man who resolutely sets his face toward the future." Roosevelt was such a man, and progressivism was such a movement. But although progressivism was never radical, neither was it the laissez-faire liberalism of the previous century. Progressives' willingness to use the power of government to regulate business and achieve a measure of social justice redefined liberalism in the twentieth century, tying it to the expanded power of the state.

Progressivism contained many paradoxes. A diverse coalition of individuals and interests, the progressive movement began at the grass roots but left as its legacy a stronger presidency and unprecedented federal involvement in the economy and social welfare. A movement that believed in social justice, progressivism often promoted social control. And while progressives called for greater democracy, they fostered elitism with their worship of experts and efficiency.

Whatever its inconsistencies and limitations, progressivism took action to deal with the problems posed by urban industrialism. Progressivism saw grassroots activists address social problems on the local and state levels and search for national solutions. By increasing the power of the presidency and expanding the power of the state, progressives worked to bring about greater social justice and to achieve a better balance between government and business. Jane Addams and Theodore Roosevelt could lay equal claim to the movement that redefined liberalism and launched the liberal state of the twentieth century. War on a global scale would provide progressivism with yet another challenge even before it had completed its ambitious agenda.

Reviewing the Chapter

★ KEY TERMS

Explain each term's significance

WHO

Jane Addams (p. 513)
Florence Kelley (p. 517)
Thomas Loftin Johnson (p. 519)
Robert M. La Follette (p. 519)
Hiram Johnson (p. 519)
William Howard Taft (p. 529)
Woodrow Wilson (p. 531)
William Dudley "Big Bill" Haywood (p. 534)
Margaret Sanger (p. 534)
Alice Paul (p. 535)
Booker T. Washington (p. 536)
W. E. B. Du Bois (p. 537)

WHAT

settlement house (p. 515)
social gospel (p. 515)
social purity movement (p. 515)
progressivism (p. 515)
Women's Trade Union League (WTUL) (p. 516)
Muller v. Oregon (p. 517)
National Consumers' League (NCL) (p. 518)
reform Darwinism (p. 518)
scientific management (p. 518)
Square Deal (p. 522)
Hepburn Act (p. 522)
muckraking (p. 522)
Pure Food and Drug Act (p. 523)
Roosevelt Corollary (p. 528)
dollar diplomacy (p. 530)
The New Nationalism (p. 531)
The New Freedom (p. 531)
Federal Trade Commission (FTC) (p. 533)
Atlanta Compromise (p. 536)
Plessy v. Ferguson (p. 536)

> **FOR PRACTICE QUIZZES AND OTHER STUDY TOOLS**, see the Online Study Guide at **bedfordstmartins.com/roarkcompact**.

★ REVIEW QUESTIONS Q:

Use key terms and dates to support your answer

1. What types of people were drawn to the progressive movement, and what motivated them? (pp. 515–18)

2. How did progressives justify their demand for more activist government? (pp. 518–19)

3. How did Roosevelt's foreign policy move the United States onto the world stage? (pp. 519–28)

4. Why did Roosevelt become the presidential nominee of the Progressive Party in 1912? (pp. 529–31)

5. How and why did Wilson's reform program evolve during his first term? (pp. 532–33)

6. How did race, class, and gender shape the limits of progressive reform? (pp. 533–37)

★ MAKING CONNECTIONS

Draw on key terms, timeline, and review questions

1. Diverse approaches to reform came under the umbrella of progressivism. Discuss the work of three progressive reformers working at the grassroots or local government level. What do your examples reveal about progressivism? What characteristics connected their reform efforts? What separated them?

2. During the Gilded Age, industrial capitalism concentrated power in the hands of corporations. Americans searched for ways to shift the balance, including strikes, antitrust actions, and regulation. How did Theodore Roosevelt attempt to respond to this problem? How did his approach differ from earlier efforts? Was it effective?

3. Opponents on the campaign stump, Theodore Roosevelt and Woodrow Wilson shared a commitment to domestic reform. Compare their legislative programs, including the evolution of their policies over time and their ability to respond to shifting political circumstances. What do their policies reveal about their understandings of the roles of the executive and the federal government?

4. What contemporary movements lay beyond the limits of progressive reform? Why did progressive reform coincide with the restriction of minority rights? In your answer, discuss how radical movements provide insights into the character of progressivism itself.

★ SUGGESTED READINGS

Victoria Bissell Brown, *The Education of Jane Addams* (2004). Addams's spiritual and political journey from a privileged childhood to activism for the working class.

James Chace, *1912: Wilson, Roosevelt, Taft and Debs — The Election That Changed the Country* (2004). A lively account of one of the most significant elections in U.S. history.

Alan Dawley, *Changing the World: American Progressives in War and Revolution* (2003). A skillful interweaving of foreign policy and domestic issues that demonstrates how progressivism developed in its international context.

David Fort Godshalk, *Veiled Visions: The 1906 Atlanta Race Riot and the Reshaping of American Race Relations* (2005). A detailed look at race relations in the New South that demonstrates how the Atlanta race riot of 1906 radicalized civil rights leaders to challenge the policy of accommodation.

Michael McGerr, *A Fierce Discontent: The Rise and Fall of the Progressive Movement in America, 1870–1920* (2003). A vivid portrait of how middle-class progressives set out to remake America in their own image.

Robert W. Righter, *The Battle over Hetch Hetchy: America's Most Controversial Dam and the Birth of Modern Environmentalism* (2005). A new look at John Muir's struggle to preserve the Yosemite valley and how it pitted water rights against tourism and recreation.

FOR MORE BOOKS ABOUT TOPICS IN THIS CHAPTER, see the Online Bibliography at **bedfordstmartins.com/roarkcompact**.

FOR ADDITIONAL FIRSTHAND ACCOUNTS OF THIS PERIOD, see Chapter 21 in Michael Johnson, ed., *Reading the American Past*, Fourth Edition.

FOR WEB SITES, IMAGES, AND DOCUMENTS RELATED TO TOPICS AND PLACES IN THIS CHAPTER, visit Make History at **bedfordstmartins.com/roarkcompact**.

★ TIMELINE

1889	• Jane Addams opens Hull House.
1895	• Booker T. Washington enunciates Atlanta Compromise.
1896	• *Plessy v. Ferguson.*
1900	• Socialist Party founded.
1901	• William McKinley assassinated; Theodore Roosevelt becomes president.
1902	• Antitrust lawsuit filed against Northern Securities Company. • Roosevelt mediates anthracite coal strike.
1903	• Women's Trade Union League founded. • United States begins construction of Panama Canal. • Elkins Act.
1904	• Roosevelt Corollary to Monroe Doctrine.
1905	• Industrial Workers of the World founded. • W. E. B. Du Bois founds Niagara movement.
1906	• Pure Food and Drug Act and Meat Inspection Act. • Atlanta race riot. • Hepburn Act.
1907	• Panic on Wall Street. • Roosevelt signs "Gentlemen's Agreement" with Japan restricting immigration.
1908	• *Muller v. Oregon.* • Republican William Howard Taft elected president.
1909	• Garment workers' strike in New York City. • National Association for the Advancement of Colored People (NAACP) formed.
1910	• Hiram Johnson elected governor of California.
1911	• Triangle fire in New York City. • Taft launches antitrust suit against U.S. Steel.
1912	• Roosevelt runs for president on Progressive Party ticket. • Democrat Woodrow Wilson elected president.
1913	• Suffragists march in Washington, D.C. • Federal Reserve Act.
1914	• Federal Trade Commission (FTC) created. • Clayton Antitrust Act.
1916	• Alice Paul launches National Woman's Party. • Margaret Sanger opens first U.S. birth control clinic. • Keating-Owen child labor law.

GAS MASK Prior to World War I, the use of poison gas was considered uncivilized, but desperate fighting eroded old moral boundaries. On April 22, 1915, the Germans used poison gas for the first time in battle, and after that soldiers faced death from chemical weapons as well as from artillery, rifles, mortars, machine guns, hand grenades, tanks, airplanes, bayonets, and flamethrowers. The Allies condemned the German innovation as diabolic but quickly developed research programs of their own. Poison gas caused large numbers of casualties early on, then improved gas masks brought a sharp decline in deaths from gas. Despite the crude appearance of this gas mask, filter respirators (using charcoal or antidote chemicals) proved highly effective. Some 50,300 American soldiers were killed in action during the war, but fewer than 1,500 died from gas. Many of those who were gassed and survived, however, were disabled and likely to die young. Collection of Colonel Stuart S. Corning Jr./Picture Research Consultants & Archives.

World War I: The Progressive Crusade at Home and Abroad

1914–1920

WHEN THE UNITED STATES entered World War I against Germany and its allies in 1917, it had neither a grand army nor a commander to lead one. But President Woodrow Wilson quickly tapped Major General John "Black Jack" Pershing, a ramrod-straight West Point graduate, to command the American Expeditionary Force (AEF) on the battlefields of France. Pershing had much to recommend him: He fought Apaches in the West in the 1880s, led a company of African American soldiers up San Juan Hill in Cuba in 1898 (hence his nickname "Black Jack"), overcame fierce resistance in the Philippine jungles in the first decade of the twentieth century, and headed Wilson's Punitive Expedition into Mexico in 1916 and 1917 in pursuit of the revolutionary bandit Pancho Villa.

On June 13, 1917, Pershing and his officer corps arrived in war-weary France, where huge crowds shouting "Vive l'Amérique!" greeted the Americans as saviors. But Pershing knew that it would be months before America's disorganized war effort succeeded in supplying a steady stream of "doughboys," as American troops would be called. Pershing, who was responsible for organizing, training, and supplying this inexperienced force that eventually numbered two million, put his own stamp on the AEF. "The standards for the American Army will be those of West Point," he announced. "The upright bearing, attention to detail, uncomplaining obedience to instruction required of the cadet will be required of every officer and soldier of our armies in France." Hard and relentless, Pershing more than once chewed out an exhausted soldier for having mud on his boots and his collar unbuttoned.

Pershing found himself waging two wars, one against the Germans and the other against America's allies, as he constantly rebuffed French and British efforts to feed his fresh soldiers into their decimated and demoralized armies. Having seen too much of Europe's trench warfare, where enemies dug in, pounded one another with artillery, and squandered thousands of lives in hopeless assaults, Pershing insisted on keeping U.S. soldiers under his own command. He believed that the Americans could break the impasse by relying on the rifle and rapid-movement tactics taught at West Point to create "open warfare," an American style of warfare. But as a disgusted British journalist observed, "After eight months . . . you haven't really fired a damned shot!"

Pershing Button Steely-eyed and determined, General John J. Pershing, surrounded by the flags of the Allied nations, stares out at the viewer. The words circling the button declare that the Allies are "united in the cause of liberty," echoing President Woodrow Wilson's insistence that American democratic ideals were universal and could be achieved internationally through U.S. participation in the war. Collection of Janice L. and David J. Frent.

By the summer of 1918, when the Allied armies began preparing a massive attack against the Germans, Ferdinand Foch, head of the French army, rushed to Pershing's headquarters to "insist" once again that U.S. troops merge with his depleted divisions. Pershing responded: "Marshal Foch, you may insist all you please, but . . . our army will fight . . . only as an independent American Army." Foch stormed out, and Pershing readied his army to strike at the German forces dug in at St.-Mihiel and to begin what he was certain would be a victory march to Berlin. Assembling his officers, Pershing praised them for what they were about to do—break the stalemate of trench warfare. But U.S. troops met a storm of machine-gun and artillery fire, and it took forty days and 100,000 casualties for the Americans to reach the German border, something Pershing had thought his soldiers could do in a few days. Nevertheless, fresh American troops helped destroy the German will to continue the war. In November 1918, Berlin asked for an immediate armistice, and the "Great War," as participants called the conflict, ended.

Pershing's stubborn effort to protect the autonomy of his army was only part of the United States' tortuous struggle to identify its interests in World War I and to maintain its national independence. When Wilson entered the White House, he believed that war was an affliction that modern diplomacy would eventually eradicate. He proclaimed America's absolute neutrality when war erupted in Europe in 1914. By standing apart, Wilson explained, America could offer "impartial mediation" and broker a healing peace. But trade and principle soon entangled the United States in Europe's troubles. When the nation was finally drawn into the war in 1917, Wilson sought to maintain America's grand purpose. Clinging to his battered ideals, he hoped that America's participation would uplift both the United States and the entire world.

At home, the war helped reformers finally achieve their goals of national prohibition and woman suffrage, but it also promoted a vicious attack on Americans' civil liberties. Hyper-patriotism meant intolerance, repression, and vigilante violence. Overseas, after Pershing's troops helped win the war in 1918, in 1919 Wilson sailed for Europe to secure a just peace. Unable to dictate a settlement to the victors, Wilson accepted disappointing compromises. Upon his return to the United States, he met a crushing defeat that marked the end of Wilsonian internationalism. Crackdowns on dissenters, immigrants, racial and ethnic minorities, and unions signaled the end of the Progressive Era at home. ★

Woodrow Wilson and the World

Shortly after winning election to the presidency in 1912, Woodrow Wilson confided to a friend: "It would be an irony of fate if my administration had to deal with foreign affairs." Indeed, Wilson had focused his life and career on domestic concerns, seldom venturing far from home and traveling abroad only on brief vacations. As president of Princeton University and then governor of New Jersey, he had remained rooted in local affairs. In his campaign for the presidency, Wilson spoke passionately about domestic reform but hardly mentioned foreign affairs.

But Wilson could not avoid the world and the rising tide of militarism, nationalism, and violence that beat against American shores. Economic interests compelled the nation outward. Moreover, Wilson was drawn abroad by his own progressive political principles. He believed that the United States had a moral duty to champion national self-determination, peaceful free trade, and political democracy. "We have no selfish ends to serve," he proclaimed. "We desire no conquest, no dominion. . . . We are but one of the champions of the rights of mankind." Yet as president, Wilson revealed he was as ready as any American president to apply military solutions to problems of foreign policy.

Taming the Americas When he took office, Wilson sought to distinguish his foreign policy from that of his Republican predecessors. To Wilson, Theodore Roosevelt's "big stick" and William Howard Taft's "dollar diplomacy" appeared crude flexing of military and economic muscle. To signal a new direction, Wilson appointed **William Jennings Bryan** as secretary of state. A pacifist on religious grounds, Bryan immediately turned his attention to making agreements with thirty nations for the peaceful settlement of disputes.

But Wilson and Bryan, like Roosevelt and Taft, also believed that the Monroe Doctrine gave the United States special rights and responsibilities in the Western Hemisphere. Issued in 1823 to warn Europeans not to attempt to colonize the New World again, the doctrine had become a cloak for U.S. domination. Wilson thus authorized U.S. military intervention in Nicaragua, Haiti, and the Dominican Republic, paving the way for U.S. banks and corporations to take financial control. All the while, Wilson believed that U.S. actions were promoting order and democracy. "I am going to teach the South American Republics to elect good men!" he declared (Map 22.1).

Wilson's most serious involvement in Latin America came in Mexico. When General Victoriano Huerta seized power by violent means, most European nations promptly recognized Mexico's new government, but Wilson refused, declaring that he would not support a "government of butchers." In April 1914, Wilson sent 800 Marines to seize the port of Veracruz to prevent the unloading of a large shipment of arms for Huerta, who was by

MAP 22.1 U.S. Involvement in Latin America and the Caribbean, 1895–1941

Victory against Spain in 1898 made Puerto Rico an American possession and Cuba a protectorate. The United States later gained control of the Panama Canal Zone. The nation was quick to protect expanding economic interests with military force by propping up friendly, though not necessarily democratic, governments.

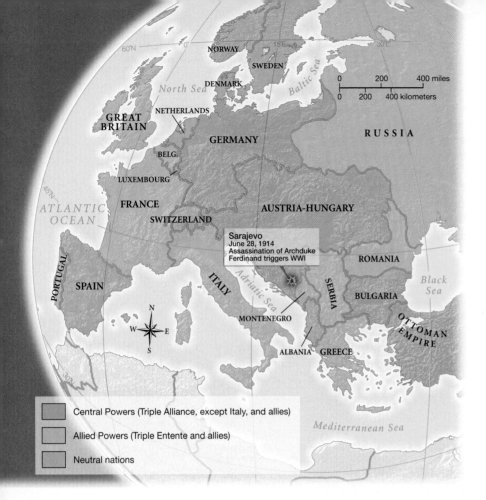

MAP 22.2 European Alliances after the Outbreak of World War I

With Germany and Austria-Hungary wedged between their Entente rivals and all parties fully armed, Europe was poised for war when Archduke Franz Ferdinand of Austria-Hungary was assassinated in Sarajevo in June 1914.

Central Powers (Triple Alliance, except Italy, and allies)

Allied Powers (Triple Entente and allies)

Neutral nations

then involved in a civil war of his own. Huerta fled to Spain, and the United States welcomed a more compliant government.

But a rebellion erupted among desperately poor farmers who believed that the new government of Venustiano Carranza, aided by U.S. business interests, had betrayed the revolution's promise to help the common people. In January 1916, the rebel army, commanded by **Francisco "Pancho" Villa**, seized a train carrying gold to Texas from an American-owned mine in Mexico and killed the 17 American engineers aboard. On March 9, another band of Villa's men crossed the border for a predawn raid on Columbus, New Mexico. They stayed for less than two hours, but they burned much of Columbus and killed 18 Americans. Wilson promptly dispatched 12,000 troops, led by General John J. Pershing. The wily Villa avoided capture, and in January 1917, Wilson recalled Pershing so that he might prepare the army for the possibility of fighting in the Great War.

U.S. Intervention in Mexico, 1916–1917

The European Crisis Before 1914, Europe had enjoyed decades of peace, but just beneath the surface lay the potentially destructive forces of nationalism and imperialism. The consolidation of the German and Italian states into unified nations and the similar ambition of Russia to create a Pan-Slavic union initiated new rivalries throughout Europe. As the conviction spread that colonial possessions were a mark of national greatness, competition expanded onto the world stage. Most ominously, Germany's efforts under Kaiser **Wilhelm II** to challenge Great Britain's world supremacy by creating industrial muscle at home, an empire abroad, and a mighty navy threatened the balance of power and thus the peace.

European nations sought to avoid an explosion with a complex web of military and diplomatic alliances. By 1914, Germany, Austria-Hungary, and Italy (the **Triple Alliance**) stood opposed to Great Britain, France, and Russia (the **Triple Entente**, also known as "the Allies"). But in their effort to prevent war through a balance of power, Europeans had actually magnified the possibility of large-scale conflict by creating trip wires along the boundaries of two heavily armed power blocs (Map 22.2). Treaties, some of them secret, obligated members of the alliances to come to the aid of another member if attacked.

The fatal sequence began on June 28, 1914, in the Bosnian city of Sarajevo, when a Bosnian Serb terrorist assassinated **Archduke Franz Ferdinand**, heir to the Austro-Hungarian throne. On July 18, Austria-Hungary declared war on Serbia, holding it accountable for the killing. The elaborate alliance system meant that the war could not remain local. Russia announced that it would back the Serbs. Compelled by treaty to support Austria-Hungary, Germany on August 3 attacked Russia and France. In response, on August 4, Great Britain, upholding its pact with France, declared war on Germany. Within weeks, Europe was engulfed in war. The conflict became a world war when Japan, seeing an opportunity to rid itself of European competition in China, joined the cause against Germany. The evenly matched alliances would fight a long and bloody war lasting more than four years, at a cost of 8.5 million soldiers' lives — an entire generation of young men. A war that started with a solitary murder proved impossible to stop.

The Ordeal of American Neutrality Woodrow Wilson promptly announced that the war was purely a European matter. Because it engaged no vital American interest and involved no significant principle, he said, the United States would remain neutral and continue normal relations with the warring nations. America had traditionally insisted that "free ships made free goods" — that neutral nations were entitled to trade safely with all nations at war. But more was involved than lofty principle. In the year before Europe went to war, the U.S. economy had slipped into a recession that wartime disruption of European trade could drastically worsen.

Although Wilson proclaimed neutrality, his sympathies, like those of many Americans, lay with Great Britain and France. Americans remembered gratefully crucial French assistance in the American Revolution and shared with the British a language, a culture, and a commitment to liberty. Germany, in contrast, was a monarchy with strong militaristic traditions. The British portrayed the German ruler, Kaiser Wilhelm II, as personally responsible for the war's atrocities, and before long American newspapers were labeling him "the Mad Dog of Europe" and "the Beast of Berlin." Still, Wilson insisted on neutrality, in part because he feared the conflict's effects on the United States as a nation of immigrants, millions of whom had only recently come from countries now at war. As he told the German ambassador, "We definitely have to be neutral, since otherwise our mixed populations would wage war on each other."

Britain's powerful fleet controlled the seas and quickly set up an economic blockade of Germany. The United States vigorously protested, but Britain refused to give up its naval advantage. The blockade actually had little economic impact on the United States. Between 1914 and the spring of 1917, while trade with Germany evaporated, war-related exports to Britain — food, clothing, steel, and munitions — escalated by some 400 percent, enough to pull the American economy out of its prewar slump. Although the British blockade violated American neutrality, the Wilson administration gradually acquiesced, thus beginning the fateful process of alienation from Germany.

Germany retaliated with a submarine blockade of British ports. This terrifying new form of combat by *Unterseebooten*, or **U-boats**, threatened traditional rules of war. Unlike surface warships that could harmlessly stop freighters and prevent them from entering a war zone, submarines relied on sinking their quarry. And once they sank a ship, the tiny U-boats could not possibly pick up survivors. Britain portrayed the submarine as an outlaw weapon that violated notions of "civilized" warfare. Nevertheless, in February 1915, Germany announced that it intended to sink on sight enemy ships en route to the British Isles. On May 7, 1915, a German U-boat torpedoed the British passenger liner *Lusitania*, killing 1,198 passengers, 128 of them U.S. citizens.

Sinking of the *Lusitania*, 1915

American newspapers featured drawings of drowning women and children, and some demanded war. Others pointed out that Germany had warned prospective passengers and that the *Lusitania* carried millions of rounds of ammunition and so was a legitimate target. Secretary of State Bryan resisted the hysteria and declared that a ship carrying war materiel "should not rely on passengers to protect her from attack — it would be like putting women and children in front of an army." He counseled Wilson to warn American citizens that they traveled on ships of belligerent countries at their own risk.

Wilson sought a middle course that would retain his commitment to peace and neutrality without condoning German attacks on passenger ships. On May 10, 1915, he rejected American intervention but also rejected Bryan's position. Any further destruction of ships, Wilson declared, would be regarded as "deliberately unfriendly" and might lead the United States to break diplomatic relations with Germany. Wilson essentially demanded that Germany abandon unrestricted submarine warfare. Bryan resigned, predicting that the president

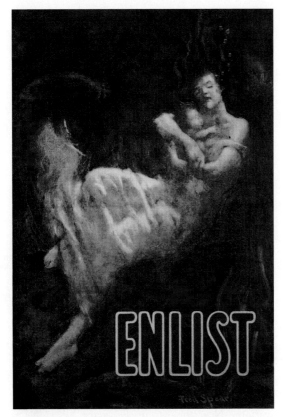

"Enlist" This poster depicting a young mother and her baby sinking beneath the cold waters of the Atlantic Ocean brought home the terrible cost of Germany's sinking of the British passenger liner *Lusitania* in 1915. When a German propagandist in the United States sought to defend the sinking, the American response was so ferocious that the German ambassador was forced to send him back to Germany. Burned into American memory, the *Lusitania* remained a compelling reason to enlist in the armed forces after the United States entered the war in 1917. Library of Congress.

had placed the United States on a collision course with Germany. Wilson's replacement for Bryan, **Robert Lansing**, was far from neutral. He believed that Germany's antidemocratic character and goal of "world dominance" meant that it "must not be permitted to win this war or even to break even."

After Germany apologized for the civilian deaths on the *Lusitania,* tensions subsided. But in 1916, Germany went further, promising no more submarine attacks without warning and without provisions for the safety of civilians. Wilson's supporters celebrated the success of his middle-of-the-road strategy that steered a course between belligerence and pacifism.

Wilson's diplomacy proved helpful in his bid for reelection in 1916. In the contest against Republican Charles Evans Hughes, the Democratic Party ran Wilson under the slogan "He kept us out of war." Wilson felt uneasy with the claim, recognizing that any "little German lieutenant can push us into the war at any time by some calculated outrage." But the Democrats' case for Wilson's neutrality appealed to enough of those in favor of peace to eke out a majority. Wilson won, but only by the razor-thin margins of 600,000 popular and 23 electoral votes.

The United States Enters the War Step by step, the United States backed away from "absolute neutrality" and more forthrightly sided with the Allies (the Triple Entente). The consequence of protesting the German blockade of Great Britain but accepting the British blockade of Germany was that by 1916 the United States was supplying the Allies with 40 percent of their war materiel. When France and Britain ran short of money to pay for U.S. goods and asked for loans, Wilson argued that "loans by American bankers to any foreign government which is at war are inconsistent with the true spirit of neutrality." But rather than jeopardize America's wartime prosperity, Wilson relaxed his objections, and billions of dollars in loans kept American goods flowing to Britain and France.

In January 1917, Germany decided that it could no longer afford to allow neutral shipping to reach Great Britain while Britain's blockade gradually starved Germany. It announced that its navy would resume unrestricted submarine warfare and sink without warning any ship, enemy and neutral, found in the waters off Great Britain. Germany understood that the decision would probably bring the United States into the war but gambled that the submarines would strangle the British economy and allow German armies to win a military victory in France before American troops arrived in Europe.

Resisting demands for war, Wilson continued to hope for a negotiated peace and only broke off diplomatic relations with Germany. Then on February 25, 1917, British authorities informed Wilson of a secret telegram sent by the German foreign secretary, Arthur Zimmermann, to the German minister in Mexico. It promised that in the event of war between Germany and the United States, Germany would see that Mexico regained its "lost provinces" of Texas, New Mexico, and Arizona if Mexico would declare war against the United States. Wilson angrily responded to the **Zimmermann telegram** by asking Congress to approve a policy of "armed neutrality" that would allow merchant ships to fight back against any attackers. Germany's overture to Mexico convinced Wilson that the war was, indeed, a defense of democracy against German aggression.

In March, German submarines sank five American vessels off Britain, killing 66 Americans. On April 2, the president asked Congress to issue a declaration of war. He accused Germany of "warfare against all mankind." Still, he called for a "war without hate" and insisted that the destruction of Germany was not the goal of the United States. Rather, America fought to "vindicate the principles of peace and justice." He promised a world made "safe for democracy." On April 6, 1917, by majorities of 373 to 50 in the House and 82 to 6 in the Senate, Congress voted to declare war.

Wilson feared what war would do at home. He said despairingly, "Once lead this people into war, and they'll forget there ever was such a thing as tolerance. To fight you must be brutal and ruthless, and the spirit of ruthless brutality will infect Congress, the courts, the policeman on the beat, the man in the street."

Q: **Why did President Wilson fail to maintain U.S. neutrality during World War I?**

"Over There"

American soldiers sailed for France with songwriter George M. Cohan's rousing "Over There" ringing in their ears:

> Over there, over there
> Send the word, send the word over there,
> That the Yanks are coming, the Yanks are coming
> The drums rum-tumming ev'rywhere.

Two million American troops eventually reached Europe, by far the largest military venture the United States had ever undertaken on foreign soil. Filled with a sense of democratic mission and trained to be morally upright as well as fiercely effective, some doughboys found the adventure exhilarating and maintained their idealism to the end. The majority, however, saw little that was gallant in rats, lice, and poison gas, and—despite the progressives' hopes—little to elevate the human soul in a landscape of utter destruction and death.

The Call to Arms When America entered the war, Britain and France were nearly exhausted after almost three years of conflict. Hundreds of thousands of soldiers had perished; food and morale were dangerously low. Another Allied power, Russia, was in turmoil. In March 1917, a revolution had forced Czar Nicholas II to abdicate, and eight months later, in a separate peace with Germany, the Bolshevik revolutionary government withdrew Russia from the war.

On May 18, 1917, to meet the demand for fighting men, Wilson signed a sweeping Selective Service Act, authorizing a draft of all young men into the armed forces. Conscription soon transformed a tiny volunteer armed force of 80,000 men into a vast army and navy. Draft boards eventually inducted 2.8 million men into the armed services, in addition to the 2 million who volunteered.

Among the 4.8 million men under arms, 370,000 were black Americans. Although African Americans remained understandably skeptical about President Wilson's war for democracy, most followed W. E. B. Du Bois's advice to "close ranks" and to temporarily "forget our special grievances" until the nation had won the war. During training, black recruits suffered the same prejudices that they encountered in civilian life. Rigidly segregated, they faced crude abuse and miserable conditions, and they were usually assigned to labor battalions, where they shouldered shovels more often than rifles.

Training camps sought to transform raw white recruits into fighting men. Progressives in the government were also determined that the camps turn out soldiers with the highest moral and civic values. Secretary of War Newton D. Baker created the Commission on Training Camp Activities, staffed by YMCA workers and veterans of the settlement house and playground movements. Military training included games, singing, and college extension courses. The army asked soldiers to stop thinking about sex, explaining that a "man who is thinking below the belt is not efficient." The Military Draft Act of 1917 prohibited prostitution and alcohol near training camps. Wilson's choice to command the **American Expeditionary Force (AEF)**, Major General **John "Black Jack" Pershing**, was as morally upright as he was militarily uncompromising. Described by one observer as "lean, clean, keen," he gave progressives perfect confidence.

The War in France At the front, the AEF discovered a desperate situation. The war had degenerated into a stalemate of armies dug defensively into hundreds of miles of trenches across France. Huddling in the mud among the corpses and rats, soldiers were separated from the enemy by only a few hundred yards of "no-man's-land." When ordered "over the top," troops raced desperately toward the enemy's trenches, only to be entangled in barbed wire, enveloped in poison gas, and mowed down by machine guns. The three-day battle of the Somme in 1916 cost the French and British forces 600,000 dead and wounded and the Germans 500,000. The deadliest battle of the war allowed the Allies to advance their trenches only a few meaningless miles across devastated land.

Still, U.S. troops saw almost no combat in 1917. The only exception was the 92nd Division of black troops. When Pershing received an urgent call for troops from the French, he sent the 92nd to the front to be integrated into the French army because he did not want to lose command over the white troops he valued more. In the 191 days they spent in battle — longer than any other American outfit — the 369th Regiment of the 92nd Division won more medals than any other American combat unit. Black soldiers recognized the irony of having to serve with the French to gain respect. German propagandists raised some painful questions. In a leaflet distributed to black troops, the Germans reminded them of their second-class citizenship and asked, "Why, then, fight the Germans, only for the benefit of the Wall Street robbers and to protect the millions they have loaned to the British, French, and Italians?"

White troops continued to train and used their free time to explore places that most of them otherwise could never have hoped to see. True to the crusader image, American officials allowed only uplifting tourism. Paris temptations were off-limits, and French premier Georges Clemenceau's offer to supply U.S. troops with licensed prostitutes was declined with the half-serious remark that if Wilson found out, he would stop the war.

Life in the Trenches One U.S. soldier in a rat-infested trench tensely looks out for danger, while others sprawl in exhausted sleep. They offer a glimpse of the reality of the Great War, minus the noise, stench, and danger. This trench is dry for the moment, but with the rains came mud so deep that wounded men drowned in it. By the time American doughboys arrived in Europe, hostile troops had faced each other for more than three years, burrowed into a double line of trenches that were protected by barbed wire, machine-gun nests, and mortars and backed by heavy artillery. Trenches with millions of combatants stretched from French ports on the English Channel all the way to Switzerland. Nothing could make living in such holes anything better than miserable, but a decent shave with a Gillette safety razor, a pair of dry boots, and a set of checkers offered doughboys temporary relief. Inevitably, however, the whistles would blow, sending the young men "over the top" and rushing toward enemy lines. Photo: Imperial War Museum; Shaving kit and boots: Collection of Colonel Stuart S. Corning Jr./Picture Research Consultants, Inc.

FOR MORE HELP ANALYZING THIS IMAGE, see the visual activity for this chapter in the Online Study Guide at bedfordstmartins.com/roarkcompact.

The sightseeing ended abruptly in March 1918. The Brest-Litovsk treaty signed that month by Germany and the Bolsheviks officially took Russia out of the war, and the Germans launched a massive offensive aimed at French ports on the Atlantic. After 6,000 cannons unleashed the heaviest barrage in history, a million German soldiers smashed a hole in the Allied lines at a cost of 250,000 casualties on each side. Pershing, who believed the right moment for U.S. action had finally come, visited Foch to ask for the "great honor" of becoming "engaged in the greatest battle in history." Foch agreed to Pershing's terms of a separate American command and in May assigned the Americans to the central sector.

In May and June, at Cantigny and then at Château-Thierry, the eager but green Americans checked the German advance with a series of dashing assaults (Map 22.3). Then they headed toward the forest stronghold of Belleau Wood, moving against streams of retreating Allied soldiers who cried defeat: "La guerre est finie!" (The war is over!). A French officer commanded American soldiers to retreat with them, but the American commander replied sharply, "Retreat, hell. We just got here." After charging through a wheat field against withering machine-gun fire, the Marines plunged into hand-to-hand combat. Victory came hard, but a German report praised the enemy's spirit, noting that "the Americans' nerves are not yet worn out." Indeed, it was German morale that was on the verge of cracking.

In the summer of 1918, the Allies launched a massive counteroffensive that would end the war. A quarter of a million U.S. troops joined in the rout of German forces along the Marne River. In September, more than a million Americans took part in the assault that threw the Germans back from positions along the Meuse River. In November, a revolt against the German government sent Kaiser Wilhelm II fleeing to Holland. On November 11, 1918, a delegation from the newly established German republic met with the French high command to sign an armistice that brought the fighting to an end.

The adventure of the AEF was brief, bloody, and victorious. When Germany had resumed unrestricted U-boat warfare in 1917, it had been gambling that it could defeat Britain and France before the Americans could raise and train an army and ship it to France. The German military

MAP 22.3 The American Expeditionary Force, 1918

In the last year of the war, the AEF joined the French army on the western front to respond to the final German offensive and pursue the retreating enemy until surrender.

READING THE MAP: Across which rivers did the Germans advance in 1918? Where did the armistice line of November 11, 1918, lie in relation to the stabilized front of 1915–1917? Through which countries did the armistice line run?

CONNECTIONS: What events paved the way for the American Expeditionary Force to join the combat effort in 1918? What characteristic(s) differentiated American troops from other Allied forces and helped them achieve victory?

FOR MORE HELP ANALYZING THIS MAP, see the map activity for this chapter in the Online Study Guide at bedfordstmartins.com/roarkcompact.

Casualties of the First World War

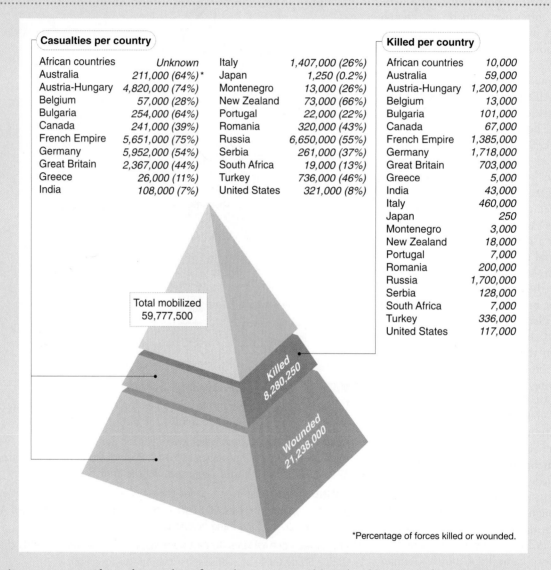

Casualties per country

African countries	*Unknown*	Italy	*1,407,000 (26%)*		
Australia	*211,000 (64%)**	Japan	*1,250 (0.2%)*		
Austria-Hungary	*4,820,000 (74%)*	Montenegro	*13,000 (26%)*		
Belgium	*57,000 (28%)*	New Zealand	*73,000 (66%)*		
Bulgaria	*254,000 (64%)*	Portugal	*22,000 (22%)*		
Canada	*241,000 (39%)*	Romania	*320,000 (43%)*		
French Empire	*5,651,000 (75%)*	Russia	*6,650,000 (55%)*		
Germany	*5,952,000 (54%)*	Serbia	*261,000 (37%)*		
Great Britain	*2,367,000 (44%)*	South Africa	*19,000 (13%)*		
Greece	*26,000 (11%)*	Turkey	*736,000 (46%)*		
India	*108,000 (7%)*	United States	*321,000 (8%)*		

Killed per country

African countries	*10,000*
Australia	*59,000*
Austria-Hungary	*1,200,000*
Belgium	*13,000*
Bulgaria	*101,000*
Canada	*67,000*
French Empire	*1,385,000*
Germany	*1,718,000*
Great Britain	*703,000*
Greece	*5,000*
India	*43,000*
Italy	*460,000*
Japan	*250*
Montenegro	*3,000*
New Zealand	*18,000*
Portugal	*7,000*
Romania	*200,000*
Russia	*1,700,000*
Serbia	*128,000*
South Africa	*7,000*
Turkey	*336,000*
United States	*117,000*

Total mobilized
59,777,500

Killed
8,280,250

Wounded
21,238,000

*Percentage of forces killed or wounded.

There is no agreement about the number of casualties in World War I. Record keeping in many countries was only rudimentary. Moreover, the destructive nature of the war meant that countless soldiers were wholly obliterated or instantly buried. However approximate, these figures make clear that the conflict that raged from 1914 to 1918 was a truly catastrophic world war. Although soldiers came from almost every part of the globe, the human devastation was not evenly distributed. Which country suffered the most casualties? Which country lost the greatest percentage of its soldiers? What do you think was the principal reason the United States lost a smaller percentage of its soldiers than most other nations lost?

had miscalculated badly. Of the 2 million American troops in Europe, 1.3 million saw some action. By the end, 112,000 AEF soldiers perished from wounds and disease, while another 230,000 Americans suffered casualties but survived. Only the Civil War, which lasted much longer, had been more costly in American lives. European nations, however, suffered much greater losses: 2.2 million Germans, 1.9 million Russians, 1.4 million French, and 900,000

Britons. (See "Global Comparison.") Where they had fought, the landscape was as blasted and barren as the moon.

Q: How did the American Expeditionary Force contribute to the defeat of Germany?

The Crusade for Democracy at Home

Many progressives hoped that war would improve the quality of American life as well as free Europe from tyranny and militarism. Mobilization helped propel the crusades for woman suffrage and prohibition to success. Progressives enthusiastically channeled industrial and agricultural production into the war effort. Labor shortages caused by workers' entering the military provided new opportunities for women in the booming wartime economy. With labor at a premium, unionized workers gained higher pay and shorter hours. To instill loyalty in Americans whose ancestry was rooted in the belligerent nations, Wilson launched a campaign to foster patriotism. The campaign included the creation of a government agency to promote official propaganda, indoctrination in the schools, and parades, rallies, and films. But boosting patriotism led to suppressing dissent. When the government launched a harsh assault on civil liberties, mobs gained license to attack those whom they considered disloyal. As Wilson feared, the progressive ideals of rational progress and free expression took a beating at home when the nation undertook its foreign crusade for democracy.

The Progressive Stake in the War The idea of the war as an agent of national improvement fanned the old zeal of the progressive movement. The Wilson administration realized that the federal government would have to assert greater control to mobilize the nation's human and physical resources. The nation's capital soon bristled with agencies charged with managing the war effort. Bernard Baruch headed the War Industries Board (WIB), created to stimulate and direct industrial production. A wealthy Wall Street stockbroker and a reform Democrat, Baruch brought industrial management and labor together into a team that produced everything from boots to bullets and made U.S. troops the best-equipped soldiers in the world.

Herbert Hoover, a self-made millionaire engineer, headed the Food Administration. He led remarkably successful "Hooverizing" campaigns

for "meatless" Mondays and "wheatless" Wednesdays and other ways of conserving resources. Guaranteed high prices, the American heartland not only supplied the needs of U.S. citizens and armed forces but also became the breadbasket of America's allies.

Wartime agencies multiplied: The Railroad Administration directed railroad traffic, the Fuel Administration coordinated the coal industry and other fuel suppliers, the Shipping Board organized the merchant marine, and the National War Labor Policies Board resolved labor disputes. Their successes gave progressives reason to believe that the war promoted harmony between business and labor. Some progressives, however, stubbornly refused to accept the argument that war and reform marched together. Wisconsin senator Robert La Follette attacked the war unrelentingly, claiming that Wilson's promises of peace and democracy were a case of "the blind leading the blind" at home and abroad.

Industrial leaders found that wartime agencies and enforced efficiency helped corporate profits triple. Some working people also had cause to celebrate. Mobilization meant high prices for farmers and plentiful jobs at high wages in the new war industries. Because increased industrial production required peaceful labor relations, the National War Labor Policies Board enacted the eight-hour day, a living minimum wage, and collective bargaining rights in some industries. Wages rose sharply during the war (as did prices), and the American Federation of Labor (AFL) saw its membership soar from 2.7 million to more than 5 million.

The war also provided a huge boost to the stalled moral crusade to ban alcohol. By 1917, prohibitionists had convinced nineteen states to go dry. Liquor's opponents now argued that banning alcohol would make the cause of democracy powerful and pure. At the same time, shutting down the distilleries would save millions of bushels of grain that could feed the United States and its allies. "Shall the many have food or the few drink?" the drys asked. Prohibitionists added a patriotic twist by arguing that closing breweries with German names such as Schlitz, Pabst, and Anheuser-Busch would deal a blow to the German cause. In December 1917, Congress passed the **Eighteenth Amendment**, which banned the manufacture, transportation, and sale of alcohol. After swift ratification by the states, the amendment went into effect on January 1, 1920.

Women, War, and the Battle for Suffrage Women had made real strides during the Progressive Era, but war presented new opportunities. More than 25,000 women served in France. About half were nurses. The others drove ambulances;

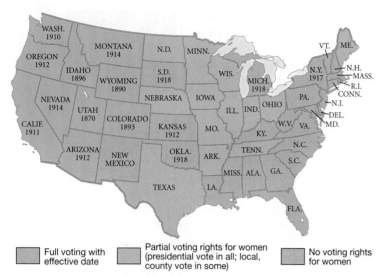

MAP 22.4 Women's Voting Rights before the Nineteenth Amendment
The long campaign for women's voting rights reversed the pioneer epic that moved from east to west. From its first successes in the new democratic West, suffrage rolled eastward toward the entrenched, male-dominated public life of the Northeast and South.

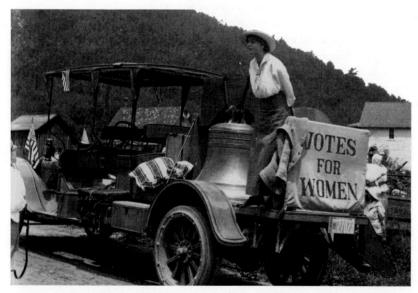

Women's Liberty Bell Suffragists in Pennsylvania made great efforts to get their message out to rural people. This life-size replica of the Liberty Bell in Philadelphia, which suffragists called the Women's Liberty Bell or the Justice Bell, toured country roads on a specially reinforced truck. When rural folks rushed to see this symbol of freedom, suffragists mounted the truck's raised platform to preach the gospel of voting rights for women. Historical Society of Pennsylvania.

ran canteens for the Salvation Army, Red Cross, and YMCA; worked with French civilians in devastated areas; and acted as telephone operators and war correspondents. Like men who joined the war effort, they believed that they were taking part in a great national venture. "I am more than willing to live as a soldier and know of the hardships I would have to undergo," one canteen worker declared when applying to go overseas, "but I want to help my country. . . . I want . . . to do the *real* work." And like men, women struggled against disillusionment in France. One woman explained: "Over in America, we thought we knew something about the war . . . but when you get here the difference is [like the one between] studying the laws of electricity and being struck by lightning."

At home, long-standing barriers against hiring women fell when millions of workingmen became soldiers and few new immigrant workers crossed the Atlantic. Tens of thousands of women found work in defense plants as welders, metalworkers, and heavy machine operators—jobs traditionally reserved for men—and with the railroads. A black woman, a domestic before the war, celebrated her job as a laborer in a railroad yard: "We are making more money at this than any work we can get, and we do not have to work as hard as at housework which requires us to be on duty from six o'clock in the morning until nine or ten at night, with might[y] little time off and at very poor wages."

Other women found white-collar work. Between 1910 and 1920, the number of women clerks doubled. Before the war ended, more than a million women had found work in war industries.

The most dramatic advance for women came in the political arena. Since the Seneca Falls convention of 1848, where women voiced their first formal demand for the ballot, the struggle for woman suffrage had inched forward. Adopting a state-by-state approach, suffragists had achieved some success, but before 1910 only four small western states had adopted woman suffrage (Map 22.4). Elsewhere, voting rights for women met strong hostility and defeat. After 1910, suffrage leaders added a federal campaign to amend the Constitution, targeting Congress and the president, to the traditional state-by-state strategy for suffrage.

The radical wing of the suffragists, led by the indomitable Alice Paul, picketed the White House, where the marchers unfurled banners that proclaimed "America Is Not a Democracy. Twenty Million Women Are Denied the Right to Vote." They chained themselves to fences and went to jail, where many engaged in hunger strikes. "They seem bent on making their cause as obnoxious as possible," Woodrow Wilson declared. His wife, Edith, detested the idea of "masculinized" voting women. But membership in the mainstream organization, the National American Woman Suffrage Association (NAWSA), led by

Carrie Chapman Catt, soared to some two million members. The NAWSA even accepted African American women into its ranks, though not on an equal basis. Seeing the handwriting on the wall, the Republican and Progressive parties endorsed woman suffrage in 1916.

In 1918, Wilson gave his support to suffrage, calling the amendment "vital to the winning of the war." He conceded that it would be wrong not to reward the wartime "partnership of suffering and sacrifice" with a "partnership of privilege and right." By linking their cause to the wartime emphasis on national unity, the advocates of woman suffrage finally triumphed. In 1919, Congress passed the **Nineteenth Amendment**, granting women the vote, and by August 1920, the required two-thirds of the states had ratified it. (See "Documenting the American Promise," page 554.) But rather than being the end of the long road to women's full equality, as some suffragists contended, woman suffrage proved to be only the beginning.

Rally around the Flag—or Else When Congress committed the nation to war, most peace advocates rallied around the flag. The Carnegie Endowment for International Peace adopted new stationery with the heading "Peace through Victory" and issued a resolution saying that "the most effectual means of promoting peace is to prosecute the war against the Imperial German Government."

Only a handful of reformers resisted the tide of patriotism. A group of professional women, led by settlement house leader Jane Addams and economics professor Emily Greene Balch, denounced what Addams described as "the pathetic belief in the regenerative results of war." The Women's Peace Party that emerged in 1915 and its foreign affiliates in the Women's International League for Peace and Freedom (WILPF) led the struggle to persuade governments to negotiate peace and spare dissenters from harsh punishment. After America entered the conflict, advocates for peace were routinely labeled cowards and traitors, their efforts crushed by the steamroller of conformity.

To suppress criticism of the war, Wilson stirred up patriotic fervor. In 1917, the president created the Committee on Public Information (CPI) under the direction of George Creel, who became the nation's cheerleader for war. He sent "Four-Minute Men," a squad of 75,000 volunteers, around the country to give brief pep talks that celebrated successes on the battlefields and in the factories. Posters, pamphlets, and cartoons depicted brave American soldiers and sailors defending freedom and democracy against the evil "Huns," the derogatory nickname applied to German soldiers. America rallied around Creel's campaign. The film industry cranked out melodramas about battle-line and home-front heroes and taught audiences to hiss at the German kaiser. A musical, *The Kaiser: The Beast of Berlin*, opened on Broadway in 1918. Colleges and universities generated war propaganda in the guise of scholarship. When Professor James McKeen Cattell of Columbia University urged that America seek peace with Germany short of victory, university president Nicholas Murray Butler fired him on the grounds that "what had been folly is now treason."

A firestorm of anti-German passion erupted. Across the nation, "100% American" campaigns enlisted ordinary people to sniff out disloyalty. German, the most widely taught foreign language in 1914, practically disappeared from the nation's schools. Targeting German-born Americans, the *Saturday Evening Post* declared that it was time to rid the country of "the scum of the melting pot." Rabid anti-German action reached its extreme with the lynching of Robert Prager, a baker in Collinsville, Illinois. In the eyes of the mob, it was enough that Prager was German-born and had socialist leanings, even though he had not opposed American participation in the war. Persuaded by the defense lawyer who praised what he called a "patriotic murder," the jury at the trial of the killers took only twenty-five minutes to acquit.

As hysteria increased, the campaign reached absurd levels. In Montana, a school board barred a history text that had good things to say about medieval Germany. Menus across the nation changed German toast to French toast and sauerkraut to liberty cabbage. In Milwaukee, vigilantes mounted a machine gun outside the Pabst Theater to prevent the staging of Schiller's *Wilhelm Tell*, a powerful protest against tyranny. One vigilant citizen claimed to see a periscope in the Great Lakes, and the fiancée of one of the war's leading critics, caught dancing on the dunes of Cape Cod, was held on suspicion of signaling to German submarines.

The Wilson administration's zeal in suppressing dissent contrasted sharply with its war aims of defending democracy. In the name of self-defense, the Espionage Act (June 1917), the Trading with the Enemy Act (October 1917), and the Sedition Act (May 1918) gave the government sweeping powers to punish any opinion or activity it considered "disloyal, profane, scurrilous, or abusive." When Postmaster General Albert Burleson blocked mailing privileges for dissenting publications, dozens of journals were forced to close down. Of the fifteen hundred individuals eventually charged with sedition, all but a dozen had merely spoken

The Final Push for Woman Suffrage

By the early twentieth century, the women's movement had mobilized millions, who increasingly concentrated on the passage of an amendment to the U.S. Constitution to ensure women's voting rights. Nothing came easily to the suffragists, but in 1920 their passion and courage were rewarded by the ratification of the Nineteenth Amendment.

DOCUMENT 1
Passing the Baton

Elizabeth Cady Stanton and Susan B. Anthony were best friends and close colleagues in the woman suffrage movement. In this October 1902 letter to Stanton, Anthony acknowledges that neither of them would live to see victory, but she nevertheless remains confident that the campaign will succeed. Stanton died days after receiving this letter, and Anthony died four years later.

My dear Mrs. Stanton

. . . It is fifty-one years since first we met and we have been busy through every one of them, stirring up the world to recognize the rights of women. The older we grow, the more keenly we feel the humiliation of disfranchisement and the more vividly we realize its disadvantages in every department of life and most of all in the labor market.

We little dreamed when we began this contest, optimistic with the hope and buoyancy of youth, that half a century later we would be compelled to leave the finish of the battle to another generation of women. But our hearts are filled with joy to know that they enter upon this task equipped with a college education, with business experience, with the fully admitted right to speak in public—all of which were denied to women fifty years ago. They have practically but one point to gain—the suffrage; we had all. These strong, courageous, capable young women will take our place and complete our work. There is an army of them, where we were but a handful. Ancient prejudice has become so softened, public sentiment so liberalized and women have so thoroughly demonstrated their ability as to

leave not a shadow of doubt that they will carry our cause to victory. . . .

Ever lovingly yours,
Susan B. Anthony

SOURCE: From *The Elizabeth Cady Stanton–Susan B. Anthony Reader: Correspondence, Writings, Speeches,* 298–99, by Ellen Carol DuBois, ed. By permission of Northeastern University Press, 1992.

DOCUMENT 2
Politicking for Suffrage

While radical suffragists chained themselves to the White House fence and went on hunger strikes, other women followed more traditional political channels—methodically gathering petitions, lobbying legislators, building alliances, and rounding up votes. Mary Garrett Hay, vice president of the National American Woman Suffrage Association (NAWSA), reports her efforts with New York state legislators.

New York City, N.Y.
March 13th, 1919

Mrs. Maud Wood Park
1626 Rhode Island Avenue
Washington, D.C.
Dear Mrs. Park,

. . . I kept in very close touch on the telephone and telegraph wire with New York Congressmen and they reported to me, really twice a day what was going on, as far as Speaker, Floor Leader and Suffrage Committee was concerned. I can do more in the House than in the Senate, and I have asked Mr. Hays on the long distance telephone to try and see that things are perfectly straight for our Cause there.

Things will be all right, I believe, but I have made up my mind not to trust either Democrats or Republicans, until the Suffrage Amendment is passed; however, I do not say this to the men[,] only to you, and I shall keep my eyes and ears open and busy, and on the job all I can.

SOURCE: *Women and Social Movements in the United States, 1600–2000,* "How Did Suffragists Lobby to Obtain Congressional Approval of a Woman Suffrage Amendment to the U.S. Constitution, 1917–1920?" Document #10. Courtesy of the Schlesinger Library, Radcliffe Institute, Harvard University (Cambridge, Mass.).

DOCUMENT 3
The President Intervenes

Although some people urged suffragists to muffle their demands during the war so that the nation could concentrate on victory, Carrie Chapman Catt, president of the NAWSA since 1915, pressed on, recognizing that the war offered a special opportunity. Catt prodded President Woodrow Wilson quietly but persistently, and on September 30, 1918, Wilson finally intervened directly, urging the Senate to pass the Nineteenth Amendment. His argument on behalf of democracy mirrored precisely that of radical suffragists who were protesting in front of the White House.

[The Senate's] adoption is, in my judgment, clearly necessary to the successful prosecution of the war and the successful realization of the objects for which the war is being fought.

. . . If we be indeed democrats and wish to lead the world to democracy, we can ask other peoples to accept in proof of our sincerity and our ability to lead them whither they wish to be led, nothing less persuasive and convincing than our actions.

. . . They are looking to the great, powerful, famous democracy of the West to lead them to a new day for which they have so long waited; and they think, in their logical simplicity, that democracy means that women shall play their part in affairs alongside men and upon an equal footing with them.

. . . We have made partners of the women in this war. Shall we admit them only to a partnership of suffering and sacrifice and toil and not to a partnership of privilege and right?

This war could not have been fought, either by the other nations engaged or by America, if it had not been for the services of the women — services rendered in every sphere. . . .

. . . I tell you plainly that this measure which I urge upon you is vital to the winning of the war and to the energies alike of preparation and of battle.

. . . And not to winning the war only. It is vital to the right solution of the great problems which we must settle, and settle immediately, when the war is over. We shall need in our vision of affairs, as we have never needed them before, the sympathy and insight and clear moral instinct of the women of the world. . . . We shall need their moral sense to preserve what is right and fine and worthy in our system of life as well as to discover just what it is that ought to be purified and reformed. Without their counsellings we shall be only half wise.

SOURCE: "Appeal of President Wilson to the Senate of the United States to Submit the Federal Amendment for Woman Suffrage Delivered in Person Sept. 20, 1918," in *History of Woman Suffrage*, Vol. 5: 1900–1920, 760–63.

DOCUMENT 4
Reflections on Victory

Carrie Chapman Catt celebrates the passage of the Nineteenth Amendment in this letter to her staff at the NAWSA on Thanksgiving Day 1920. She reflects on the long road to victory and considers the satisfactions of the journey.

I have kept Thanksgiving sacred to reflections upon the long trail behind us, and the triumph which was its inevitable conclusion. John Adams said long after the Revolution that only about one third of the people were for it, a third being against it, and the remaining third utterly indifferent. Perhaps this proportion applies to all movements. At least a third of the women were for our cause at the end. . . . As I look back over the years . . . I realize that the greatest thing in the long campaign for us was not its crowning victory, but the discipline it gave us all. . . . It was a great crusade, the world has seen none more wonderful. . . . My admiration, love and reverence go out to that band which fought and won a revolution . . . with congratulations that we were permitted to establish a new and good thing in the world.

SOURCE: Carrie Chapman Catt to NAWSA Office Staff, Thanksgiving Day 1920, in Elizabeth Frost and Kathryn Cullen-DuPont, *Women's Suffrage in America: An Eyewitness History* (1992), 335–36.

Questions for Analysis and Debate

1. Why was Susan B. Anthony confident that woman suffrage would soon become a reality?

2. Why do you think some legislators in New York and elsewhere were willing to work closely with suffragists such as Mary Garrett Hay?

3. What, according to Woodrow Wilson, would America's rejection of the Nineteenth Amendment have jeopardized?

4. What do you suppose Carrie Chapman Catt meant when she said that the greatest gain for women in the suffrage campaign was "discipline"?

words the government found objectionable. One of them was Eugene V. Debs, the leader of the Socialist Party, who was convicted under the Espionage Act for speeches condemning the war as a capitalist plot and sent to the Atlanta penitentiary.

The president hoped that national commitment to the war would silence partisan politics, but his Republican rivals used the war as a weapon against the Democrats. The trick was to oppose Wilson's conduct of the war but not the war itself. Republicans outshouted Wilson on the nation's need to mobilize for war but then complained that Wilson's War Industries Board was a tyrannical agency that crushed free enterprise. Such attacks appealed to widely diverse business, labor, and patriotic groups. As the war progressed, Republicans gathered power against the Democrats, who had narrowly reelected Wilson in 1916.

In 1918, Republicans gained a narrow majority in both the House and Senate. The end of Democratic control of Congress not only halted further domestic reform but also meant that the United States would advance toward military victory in Europe with political power divided between a Democratic president and a Republican Congress likely to challenge Wilson's plans for international cooperation.

Q: **How did progressive ideals fare during wartime?**

A Compromised Peace

Wilson decided to reaffirm his noble war ideals by announcing his peace aims before the end of hostilities. He hoped the victorious Allies would adopt his plan for international democracy, but he was sorely disappointed. The leaders of Britain, France, and Italy (which joined the Allies in 1915 in hopes of postwar gains) understood that Wilson's principles jeopardized their own postwar plans for the acquisition of enemy territory, new colonial empires, and reparations. Wilson also faced strong opposition at home from those who feared that his enthusiasm for international cooperation would undermine American sovereignty.

> Disparaging Wilson's Fourteen Points, French premier Georges Clemenceau said, "God himself was content with ten commandments."

Wilson's Fourteen Points On January 8, 1918, President Wilson revealed to Congress his **Fourteen Points**, his blueprint for a new democratic world order. The first five points affirmed basic liberal ideals: an end to secret treaties; freedom of the seas; removal of economic barriers to free trade; reduction of weapons of war; and recognition of the rights of colonized peoples. The next eight points supported the right to self-determination of European peoples who had been dominated by Germany or its allies. Wilson's fourteenth point called for a "general association of nations" — a **League of Nations** — to provide "mutual guarantees of political independence and territorial integrity to great and small states alike." A League of Nations reflected Wilson's lifelong dream of a "parliament of man." Only such an organization of "peace-loving nations," he believed, could justify the war and secure a lasting peace.

Citizens of the United States and of every Allied country greeted the Fourteen Points enthusiastically. Wilson felt confident that he could prevail against undemocratic and selfish forces at the peace table. During the final year of the war, he pressured the Allies to accept the Fourteen Points as the basis of the postwar settlement.

The Paris Peace Conference From January 18 to June 28, 1919, the eyes of the world focused on Paris. There, powerful men wrestled with difficult problems. Although no other American president had ever gone to Europe while in office, Wilson, inspired by his mission, decided to head the U.S. delegation. He said he owed it to the American soldiers. "It is now my duty," he announced, "to play my full part in making good what they gave their life's blood to obtain." A dubious British diplomat retorted that Wilson was drawn to Paris "as a debutante is entranced by the prospect of her first ball." The decision to leave the country at a time when his political opponents challenged his leadership was risky enough, but his stubborn refusal to include prominent Republicans in the delegation proved foolhardy and eventually cost him his dream of a new world order with the United States at its center.

After four terrible years of war, the common people of Europe almost worshipped Wilson, believing that he would create a safer, more decent world. When the peace conference convened at Louis XIV's magnificent palace at Versailles, however, Wilson encountered a different reception. Representing the Allies were the decidedly unidealistic David Lloyd George, prime minister of Britain; Georges Clemenceau, premier of France; and Vittorio Orlando, former prime minister of Italy. To the Allied leaders, Wilson appeared a naive and impractical moralist. His desire to gather former enemies within a new international

Leaders of the Paris Peace Conference The three leaders in charge of putting the world back together after the Great War—from left to right, David Lloyd George, prime minister of Great Britain; Georges Clemenceau, premier of France; and U.S. president Woodrow Wilson—amiably and confidently stride toward the peace conference at the Versailles palace. Clemenceau is caught offering animated instruction to Wilson, whom he considered naively idealistic. Indeed, in an unguarded moment, Clemenceau expressed his contempt for the entire United States as a country that was unique in having passed directly from barbarism to decadence without an intervening period of civilization. Walking silently alongside, Lloyd George maintains the poker face that helped him keep his views carefully guarded throughout the conference. Gamma Liaison.

democratic order showed how little he understood hard European realities. Clemenceau claimed that Wilson "believed you could do everything by formulas" and "empty theory." Disparaging the Fourteen Points, he added, "God himself was content with ten commandments."

The Allies wanted to fasten blame for the war on Germany, totally disarm it, and make it pay so dearly that it would never threaten its neighbors again. The French demanded retribution in the form of territory containing Germany's richest mineral resources. The British made it clear that they were not about to give up the powerful weapon of naval blockade for the vague principle of freedom of the seas.

The Allies forced Wilson to make drastic compromises. In return for France's moderating its territorial claims, he agreed to support Article 231 of the peace treaty, assigning war guilt to Germany. Though saved from permanently losing Rhineland territory to the French, Germany was outraged at being singled out as the instigator of the war and saddled with more than $33 billion in damages. Many Germans felt that their nation had been betrayed. After agreeing to an armistice in the belief that peace terms would be based in Wilson's generous Fourteen Points, they faced hardship and humiliation instead.

Wilson had better success in establishing the principle of self-determination. But from the beginning, Secretary of State Robert Lansing knew that the president's concept of self-determination was "simply loaded with dynamite." Lansing wondered, "What unit has he in mind? Does he mean a race, a territorial area, or a community?" Even Wilson was vague about what self-determination actually meant. "When I gave utterance to those words," he admitted, "I said them without the knowledge that nationalities existed, which are coming to us day after day." Lansing suspected that the notion "will raise hopes which can never be realized. It will, I fear, cost thousands of lives. In the end it is bound to be discredited, to be called the dream of an idealist who failed to realize the danger until it was too late."

Yet partly on the basis of self-determination, the conference redrew the map of Europe and parts of the rest of the world. Portions of Austria-Hungary were ceded to Italy, Poland, and Romania, and the remainder was reassembled into Austria, Hungary, Czechoslovakia, and Yugoslavia — independent republics whose boundaries were drawn with attention to concentrations of major ethnic groups. More arbitrarily, the Ottoman empire was carved up into small mandates (including Palestine) run by local leaders but under the control of France and Great Britain. The conference reserved the mandate system for those regions it deemed insufficiently "civilized" to have full independence. Thus, the reconstructed nations — each beset with ethnic and nationalist rivalries — faced the challenge of making a new democratic government work (Map 22.5). Many of today's bitterest disputes — in the Balkans and Iraq, between Greece and Turkey, between Arabs and Jews — have roots in the decisions made in Paris in 1919.

Wilson hoped that self-determination would also dictate the fate of Germany's colonies in Asia and Africa. But the Allies, who had taken over the colonies during the war, only allowed the League of Nations a mandate to administer them. Technically, the mandate system rejected imperialism, but in reality it allowed the Allies to maintain control. Thus, while denying Germany its colonies, the Allies retained and added to their own far-flung territories.

MAP 22.5 Europe after World War I
The post–World War I settlement redrew boundaries to create new nations based on ethnic groupings. This outcome left within defeated Germany and Russia bitter peoples who resolved to recover the territory taken from them.

Key:
- New and reconstituted nations
- Demilitarized or Allied occupation zone

The cause of democratic equality suffered another setback when the peace conference rejected Japan's call for a statement of racial equality in the treaty. Wilson's belief in the superiority of whites, as well as his apprehension about how white Americans would respond to such a declaration, led him to oppose the clause. To soothe hurt feelings, Wilson agreed to grant Japan a mandate over the Shantung Peninsula in northern China, which had formerly been controlled by Germany. The gesture mollified Japan's moderate leaders, but the military faction preparing to take over the country used bitterness toward racist Western colonialism to build support for expanding Japanese power throughout Asia.

Closest to Wilson's heart was finding a new way to manage international relations. In Wilson's view, war had discredited the old strategy of balance of power. Instead, he proposed a League of Nations that would provide collective security. The league would establish rules of international conduct and resolve conflicts between nations through rational and peaceful means. When the Allies agreed to the league, Wilson was overjoyed. He believed that the league would rectify the errors his colleagues had forced on him in Paris. The league would solidify and extend the noble work he had begun.

To some Europeans and Americans, the **Versailles treaty** came as a bitter disappointment.

Wilson's admirers were shocked that the president dealt in compromise like any other politician. But without Wilson's presence, the treaty that was signed on June 28, 1919, surely would have been more vindictive. Wilson returned home in July 1919 consoled that, despite his frustrations, he had gained what he most wanted—a League of Nations. In Wilson's judgment, "We have completed in the least time possible the greatest work that four men have ever done."

The Fight for the Treaty The tumultuous reception Wilson received when he arrived home persuaded him, probably correctly, that the American people supported the treaty. When the president submitted the treaty to the Senate in July 1919, he warned that failure to ratify it would "break the heart of the world." By then, however, criticism of the treaty was mounting, especially from Americans convinced that their countries of ethnic origin had not been given fair treatment. Irish Americans, Italian Americans, and German Americans launched especially sharp attacks. Others worried that the president's concessions at Versailles had jeopardized the treaty's capacity to provide a generous plan for rebuilding Europe and to guarantee world peace.

"Refusing to Give the Lady a Seat" Woodrow Wilson promised that the League of Nations would usher in an age of international peace. When stiff opposition to American membership in the league developed in the United States, friends of the league mounted a counterattack. This cartoon skewers the three leading Republican opponents of the league—Senators William Borah of Idaho, Henry Cabot Lodge of Massachusetts, and Hiram Johnson of California—who stubbornly refuse to budge an inch for the angel of peace. Clever cartoons could not save the league, however. Only shrewd diplomacy could do that, and Wilson was not able to deliver. Picture Research Consultants & Archives.

Some of the most potent critics were found in the Senate. Bolstered by a slight Republican majority in Congress, a group of Republican "irreconcilables," which included such powerful isolationist senators as Hiram Johnson of California and William Borah of Idaho, condemned the treaty for entangling the United States in world affairs. A larger group of Republicans did not object to American participation in world politics but feared that membership in the League of Nations would jeopardize the nation's ability to act independently. No Republican, in any case, was eager to hand Wilson and the Democrats a foreign policy victory with the 1920 presidential election little more than a year away.

At the center of Republican opposition was Wilson's archenemy, Senator **Henry Cabot Lodge** of Massachusetts. Lodge's hostility was in part personal. "I never thought I could hate a man as much as I hate Wilson," he once admitted. But Lodge also raised cogent objections to the treaty and the league. Lodge was no isolationist, but he thought

that much of the Fourteen Points was a "general bleat about virtue being better than vice." Lodge expected the United States' economic and military power to propel the nation into a major role in world affairs. But he insisted that membership in the League of Nations, which would require collective action to maintain peace, threatened the nation's independence in foreign relations.

Lodge used his position as chairman of the Senate Foreign Relations Committee to air every sort of complaint. Out of the committee hearings came several amendments, or "reservations," that sought to limit the consequences of American membership in the league. For example, several reservations required approval of both the House and Senate before the United States could participate in league-sponsored economic sanctions or military action.

It gradually became clear that ratification of the treaty depended on acceptance of the Lodge reservations. Democratic senators, who overwhelmingly supported the treaty, urged Wilson to accept Lodge's terms, arguing that they left the essentials of the treaty intact. Wilson, however, insisted that the reservations cut "the very heart out of the treaty." He expressed personal hatred as well. "*Lodge* reservations?" he thundered. "Never! I'll never consent to adopt any policy with which that impossible name is so prominently identified."

Wilson decided to take his case directly to the people. On September 3, 1919, he set out by train on the most ambitious speaking tour ever undertaken by a president. On September 25 in Pueblo, Colorado, Wilson collapsed and had to return to Washington. There, he suffered a massive stroke that partially paralyzed him. From his bedroom, Wilson sent messages instructing Democrats in the Senate to hold firm against any and all reservations. Wilson commanded enough loyalty to ensure a vote against the Lodge reservations. But when the treaty without reservations came before the Senate in March 1920, the combined opposition of the Republican irreconcilables and reservationists left Wilson six votes short of the two-thirds majority needed for passage.

The nations of Europe organized the League of Nations at Geneva, Switzerland, but the United States never became a member. Whether American membership could have prevented the world war that would begin in Europe in 1939 is highly unlikely, but the United States' failure to join certainly weakened the league from the start. In refusing to accept relatively minor compromises with Senate moderates, Wilson lost his treaty and American membership in the league. Woodrow Wilson and Henry Cabot Lodge both died in 1924, never seeing international order or security, never knowing the whirlwind of resentment and violence that would eventually follow the Great War's failure to make the world safe for democracy.

Q: **Why did the Senate fail to ratify the Versailles treaty?**

Democracy at Risk

The defeat of Wilson's plan for international democracy proved the crowning blow to progressives who had hoped that the war could boost reform at home. When the war ended, Americans wanted to demobilize swiftly. In the process, servicemen, defense workers, and farmers lost their war-related jobs. The volatile combination—of unemployed veterans returning home, a stalled economy, and leftover wartime patriotism looking for a new cause—threatened to explode. Wartime anti-German passion was quickly followed by anti-radicalism, a fevered campaign that ensnared unionists, socialists, dissenters, and African Americans and Mexicans who had committed no offense but to seek to escape rural poverty. The 1920 election marked the end of Wilson's two terms in the White House and his crusades.

Economic Hardship and Labor Upheaval

Americans greeted peace with a demand that the United States return to a peacetime economy. The government abruptly abandoned its wartime economic controls and canceled war contracts worth millions of dollars. In a matter of months, more than three million soldiers were mustered out of the military and flooded the job market just as war production ceased. Unemployment soared. At the same time, consumers went on a postwar spending spree that drove inflation skyward. In 1919, prices rose 75 percent over prewar levels, and in 1920 prices rose another 28 percent.

Most of the gains workers had made during the war evaporated. Freed from wartime controls, business turned against the eight-hour day and attacked labor unions. With inflation eating up their paychecks, workers fought back. The year 1919 witnessed nearly 3,600 strikes involving 4 million workers. The most spectacular strike occurred in February 1919 in Seattle, where shipyard workers had been put out of work by demobilization. When a coalition of the radical Industrial Workers of the World (IWW, called Wobblies) and the moderate American Federation of Labor (AFL) called a general strike, the largest work stoppage in American history shut down the city.

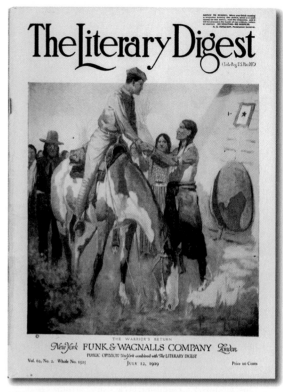

"The Warrior's Return" About sixteen thousand Native Americans served in the U.S. armed forces during World War I. This magazine cover offers a romanticized reconstruction of one homecoming. The young soldier, still in uniform and presumably fresh from France, rides his pony to the tepee of his parents, who proudly welcome their brave warrior. The tepee is decorated with a star, a national symbol that families with sons in the military displayed on their homes. The painting sought to demonstrate that even Americans on the margins of national life were sufficiently assimilated and loyal to join the national sacrifice to defeat the enemy. Picture Research Consultants & Archives.

Newspapers claimed that the walkout was "a Bolshevik effort to start a revolution." The suppression of the **Seattle general strike** by officials cost the AFL many of its wartime gains and contributed to the destruction of the IWW soon afterward.

A strike by Boston policemen in the fall of 1919 underscored postwar hostility toward labor militancy. Although the police were paid less than pick-and-shovel laborers, they won little sympathy. Once the officers stopped walking their beats, looters sacked the city. Massachusetts governor Calvin Coolidge called in the National Guard to restore order. The public, yearning for peace and security in the wake of war, welcomed Coolidge's anti-union assurance that "there is no right to strike against the public safety by anybody, anywhere, any time."

Labor strife climaxed in the grim **steel strike of 1919**. Faced with the industry's plan to revert to seven-day weeks, twelve-hour days, and weekly wages of about $20, Samuel Gompers, head of the AFL, called for a strike. In response, 350,000 workers in fifteen states walked out in September 1919. The steel industry hired 30,000 strikebreakers (many of them African Americans) and convinced the public that the strikers were radicals bent on subverting the Republic. In January 1920, after eighteen striking workers were killed, the strike collapsed. That devastating defeat initiated a sharp decline in the fortunes of the labor movement, a trend that would continue for almost twenty years.

The Red Scare Suppression of labor strikes was one response to the widespread fear of internal subversion that swept the nation in 1919. The **Red scare** ("Red" referred to the color of the Bolshevik flag) had homegrown causes: the postwar recession, labor unrest, and the difficulties of reintegrating millions of returning veterans. But unsettling events abroad also added to Americans' anxieties.

Russian bolshevism became even more menacing in March 1919, when the new Soviet leaders created the Comintern, a worldwide association of Communist leaders intent on fomenting revolution in capitalist countries. A Communist revolution in the United States was extremely unlikely, but edgy Americans faced with a flurry of terrorist acts, most notably thirty-eight bombs mailed to prominent individuals, believed otherwise. Fear, anger, and uncertainty led swiftly to a hunt for terrorists, led by Attorney General **A. Mitchell Palmer**. Targeting men and women who harbored ideas that Palmer believed could lead to violence, even though the individuals may not have done anything illegal, the Justice Department sought to purge the supposed enemies of America.

In January 1920, Palmer ordered a series of raids that netted 6,000 alleged subversives. Finding no revolutionary conspiracies, Palmer nevertheless ordered 500 noncitizen suspects deported. His action came in the wake of a campaign against the most notorious radical alien, Russian-born **Emma Goldman**. Before the war, Goldman's passionate support of labor strikes, women's rights, and birth control had made her a symbol of radicalism. Finally, after a stay in prison for attacking military conscription, she was ordered deported by J. Edgar Hoover, the eager director of the Justice Department's Radical Division. In December 1919, Goldman and 250 others boarded a ship for exile in Russia.

The effort to rid the country of alien radicals was matched by efforts to crush troublesome citizens. Law enforcement officials and vigilante groups joined hands against so-called Reds. In November 1919 in the rugged lumber town of Centralia, Washington, a menacing crowd gathered in front of the IWW hall. Nervous Wobblies inside opened fire, killing three people. Three IWW members were arrested and later convicted of murder, but another, ex-soldier Wesley Everett, was carried off by the mob, which castrated him, hung him from a bridge, and then riddled his body with bullets. His death was officially ruled a suicide.

Public institutions joined the attack on civil liberties. Local libraries removed dissenting books. Schools fired unorthodox teachers. Police shut down radical newspapers. State legislatures refused to seat elected representatives who professed socialist ideas. And in 1919, Congress removed its lone socialist representative, Victor Berger, on the pretext that he was a threat to national safety.

That same year, the Supreme Court provided a formula for restricting free speech. In upholding the conviction of socialist Charles Schenck for publishing a pamphlet urging resistance to the draft during wartime (**Schenck v. United States**), the Court established a "clear and present danger" test. Such utterances as Schenck's during a time of national peril, Justice Oliver Wendell Holmes wrote, were equivalent to shouting "Fire!" in a crowded theater. But Schenck's pamphlet had little power to provoke a public firmly opposed to its message.

In time, the Red scare lost credibility, especially after Attorney General Palmer warned in 1920 that radicals were planning to celebrate the Bolshevik Revolution with a nationwide wave of violence. Officials called out state militias, mobilized bomb squads, and even placed machine-gun nests at major city intersections. When May 1 came and went without a single disturbance, the public mood turned from fear to scorn. The Red scare collapsed as a result of its excesses.

The Great Migrations of African Americans and Mexicans Before the Red scare lost steam, the government raised alarms about the loyalty of African Americans. A Justice Department investigation concluded that Reds were fomenting racial unrest among blacks. Although the report was wrong about Bolshevik influence, it was correct in noticing a new stirring among African Americans, an assertiveness born of participation in the war effort and the massive migration out of the South.

In 1900, nine of every ten blacks still lived in the South, where poverty, disfranchisement,

If You are a Stranger in the City

If you want a job   If you want a place to live
If you are having trouble with your employer
If you want information or advice of any kind
CALL UPON
The CHICAGO LEAGUE ON URBAN
CONDITIONS AMONG NEGROES
3719 South State Street
Telephone Douglas 9098   T. ARNOLD HILL, Executive Secretary
No charges—no fees. We want to help Y O U

SELF-HELP

1. Do not loaf. Get a job at once.
2. Do not live in crowded rooms. Others can be obtained.
3. Do not carry on loud conversations in street cars and public places.
4. Do not keep your children out of school.
5. Do not send for your family until you get a job.
6. Do not think you can hold your job unless you are industrious, sober, efficient and prompt.

Cleanliness and fresh air are necessary for good health. In case of sickness send immediately for a good physician. Become an active member in some church as soon as you reach the city.

Issued by

African Americans Migrate North This southern family arrived in a new home in an unnamed northern city in 1912. Wearing their Sunday best, family members carried the rest of what they owned in two suitcases. Several factors, including World War I, combined to prompt the massive African American migration out of the South. In the 1920s, many rural blacks lost work when boll weevils devoured the cotton crop. Then mechanization and government programs to support crop prices by reducing acreage drove many more people off the land. In Chicago, the League on Urban Conditions among Negroes, which eventually became the Urban League, sought to ease the transition of southern blacks to life in the North by distributing cards such as the one shown here (front and back). Other cards advised hard work, sobriety, cleanliness, finding a church, getting children into school, and speaking softly in public places. Photo: Photographs and Prints Division, Schomburg Center for Research in Black Culture, New York Public Library, Astor, Lenox and Tilden Foundations; Card: Arthur and Graham Aldis Papers (Aldis neg. 1A & 1B), Special Collections, The University Library, University of Illinois at Chicago.

FOR MORE HELP ANALYZING THIS IMAGE, see the visual activity for this chapter in the Online Study Guide at **bedfordstmartins.com/roarkcompact**.

segregation, and violence dominated their lives. A majority of black men continued to toil in agriculture as dirt-poor tenants or sharecroppers or worked for wages of 60 cents a day. Black women worked in the homes of whites as domestics for $2 a week. Whites remained committed to keeping blacks down. "If we own a good farm or horse, or cow, or bird-dog, or yoke of oxen," a black sharecropper in Mississippi observed in 1913, "we are harassed until we are bound to sell, give away, or run away, before we can have any peace in our lives."

The First World War provided African Americans with the opportunity to escape the South's cotton fields and kitchens. War channeled almost 5 million American workers into military service and caused the number of European immigrants to fall from more than a million in 1914 to 31,000 in 1918. Deprived of their traditional sources of laborers just as production demands were increasing, northern industrialists turned to black labor. Young black men, who made up the bulk of the early migrants, found work in steel mills, shipyards, munitions plants, railroad yards, automobile factories, and mines. From 1915 to 1920, a half million blacks (approximately 10 percent of the South's black population) boarded trains bound for Philadelphia, Detroit, Cleveland, Chicago, St. Louis, and other industrial cities.

Thousands of migrants wrote home to tell family and friends about their experiences in the North. One man announced proudly that he had recently been promoted to "first assistant to the head carpenter." He added, "I should have been here twenty years ago. I just begin to feel like a man. . . . My children are going to the same school with the whites and I don't have to [h]umble to no one. I have registered — will vote the next election and there ain't any 'yes sir' — it's all yes and no and Sam and Bill."

But the North was not the promised land. Black men stood on the lowest rungs of the labor ladder. Jobs of any kind proved scarce for black women, and most worked as domestic servants as they did in the South. The existing black middle class sometimes shunned the less educated, less sophisticated rural southerners crowding into northern cities. Many whites, fearful of losing jobs and status, lashed out against the new migrants. Savage race riots ripped through two dozen northern cities. The worst occurred in July 1917 when a mob of whites invaded a section of East St. Louis, Illinois, crowded with blacks who had been recruited to help break a strike. The mob murdered at least 39 people and left most of the black district in flames. In 1918, the nation witnessed 96 lynchings of blacks, some of them returning war veterans still in uniform.

Still, most black migrants stayed in the North and encouraged friends and family to follow. By 1940, more than one million blacks had left the South, profoundly changing their own lives and the course of the nation's history. Black enclaves such as Harlem in New York and the South Side of Chicago, "cities within cities," emerged in the North. These assertive communities provided a foundation for black protest and political organization in the years ahead.

At nearly the same moment that black Americans streamed into northern cities, another migration was under way in the American Southwest. Between 1910 and 1920, the Mexican-born population in the United States soared from 222,000 to 478,000. Mexican immigration resulted from developments on both sides of the border. In Mexico, dictator Porfirio Diaz initiated land policies that decimated poor farmers. When the Mexicans revolted against Diaz in 1910, initiating a ten-year civil war, the trickle of

Mexican Women Arriving in El Paso, 1911 These Mexican women, carrying bundles and wearing traditional shawls, try to get their bearings upon arriving in El Paso, Texas — the Ellis Island for Mexican immigrants. Perhaps they are looking for a family member who preceded them, or perhaps they are alone and calculating their next step. In any case, they were part of the first modern wave of Mexican immigration to the United States. Women like them found work in the cotton and sugar beet fields, canneries, and restaurants of the Southwest, as well as at home taking in sewing, laundry, and boarders. Whatever their work, their journey across the border was life changing. Courtesy of the Rio Grande Historical Collections, New Mexico State University, Las Cruces, New Mexico.

migration became a flood. North of the border, the Chinese Exclusion Act of 1882 and later the disruption of World War I cut off the supply of cheap foreign labor and caused western employers in the expanding rail, mining, construction, and agricultural industries to look south to Mexico for workers.

As a result of Americans' racial stereotyping of Mexicans — a U.S. government economist described them as "docile, patient, usually orderly in camp, fairly intelligent under competent supervision, obedient and cheap" — Mexicans were considered excellent prospects for manual labor but not for citizenship. Employers tried to dampen racial fears by stressing that the immigrants were only temporary residents, not a lasting threat. In 1917, when anti-immigration advocates convinced Congress to do something about foreigners coming into the United States,

> One black man who migrated north announced proudly that he had recently been promoted to "first assistant to the head carpenter." He added, "I should have been here twenty years ago. I just begin to feel like a man."

the restrictive legislation bowed to southwestern industry and exempted Mexicans. By 1920, ethnic Mexicans made up about three-fourths of California's farm laborers. They were also crucial to the Texas economy, accounting for three-fourths of laborers in the cotton fields and in construction there.

Like immigrants from Europe and black migrants from the South, Mexicans in the American Southwest dreamed of a better life. And like the others, they found both opportunity and disappointment. Wages were better than in Mexico, but life in the fields, mines, and factories was hard, and living conditions — in boxcars, labor camps, or urban barrios — often were dismal. Signs warning "No Mexicans Allowed" increased rather than declined. Mexican women nurtured families, but many also worked picking cotton or as domestics. Among Mexican Americans, some of whom had lived in the Southwest for a century or more, *los recien llegados* (the recent arrivals) encountered mixed reactions. One Mexican American expressed this ambivalence: "We are all Mexicans anyway because the *gueros* [Anglos] treat us all alike." But he also called for immigration quotas because the recent arrivals drove down wages and incited white prejudice that affected all ethnic Mexicans.

Despite friction, large-scale immigration into the Southwest meant a resurgence of the Mexican cultural presence, which became the basis for greater solidarity and political action for the ethnic Mexican population. In 1929, Mexican Americans formed the League of United Latin American Citizens (LULAC) in Texas.

Postwar Politics and the Election of 1920 A thousand miles away in Washington, D.C., President Woodrow Wilson, bedridden and paralyzed, stubbornly ignored the mountain of domestic troubles — labor strikes, the Red scare, race riots, immigration backlash — and insisted that the 1920 election would be a "solemn referendum" on the League of Nations. Dutifully, the Democratic nominees for president, James M. Cox of Ohio, and for vice president, Franklin Delano Roosevelt of New York, campaigned on Wilson's international ideals. The Republican Party chose the handsome, gregarious Warren Gamaliel Harding, senator from Ohio. Harding's rise in Ohio politics was a tribute to his amiability, not his mastery of the issues.

Harding found the winning formula when he declared that "America's present need is not heroics, but healing; not nostrums [questionable remedies] but normalcy." But what was "normalcy"?

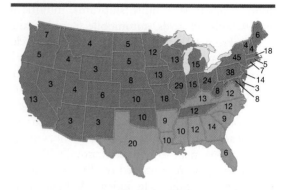

Candidate	Electoral Vote	Popular Vote	Percent of Popular Vote
Warren G. Harding (Republican)	404	16,143,407	60.5
James M. Cox (Democrat)	127	9,130,328	34.2
Eugene V. Debs (Socialist)	0	919,799	3.4

MAP 22.6 The Election of 1920

Harding explained: "By 'normalcy' I don't mean the old order but a regular steady order of things. I mean normal procedure, the natural way, without excess." Eager to put wartime crusades and postwar strife behind them, voters responded by giving Harding the largest presidential victory ever: 60.5 percent of the popular vote and 404 out of 531 electoral votes (Map 22.6). Once in office, Harding and his wife, Florence, threw open the White House gates, which had been closed since the declaration of war in 1917. Their welcome brought throngs of visitors and lifted the national pall, signaling a new, more easygoing era.

Q: **How did the Red scare contribute to the erosion of civil liberties after the war?**

Conclusion: Troubled Crusade

America's experience in World War I was exceptional. For much of the world, the Great War produced great destruction, acres of blackened fields, ruined factories, and millions of casualties. But in the United States, war and prosperity marched hand in hand. America emerged from the war with the strongest economy in the world and a position of international preeminence.

Still, the nation paid a heavy price both at home and abroad. American soldiers and sailors encountered unprecedented horrors — submarines, poison gas, machine guns — and more than 100,000 died. On Memorial Day 1919, at the Argonne Cemetery, where 14,200 Americans lie, General John J. Pershing said: "It is not for us to proclaim what they did, their silence speaks more eloquently than words, but it is for us to uphold the conception of duty, honor and country for which they fought and for which they died. It is for the living to carry forward their purpose and make fruitful their sacrifice." Rather than redeeming their sacrifice, however, as Wilson promised, the peace that followed the armistice tarnished it. At home, rather than permanently improving working conditions, advancing public health, and spreading educational opportunity, as progressives had hoped, the war threatened to undermine the achievements of the previous two decades. Moreover, rather than promoting democracy in the United States, the war bred fear, intolerance, and repression that led to a crackdown on dissent and a demand for conformity. Reformers could count only woman suffrage as a permanent victory.

Woodrow Wilson had promised more than anyone could deliver. Progressive hopes of extending democracy and liberal reform nationally and internationally were dashed. In 1920, a bruised and disillusioned society stumbled into a new decade. The era coming to an end had called on Americans to crusade and sacrifice. The new era promised peace, prosperity, and a good time.

Reviewing the Chapter

★ KEY TERMS

Explain each term's significance

WHO

William Jennings Bryan (p. 543)

Francisco "Pancho" Villa (p. 544)

Wilhelm II (p. 544)

Archduke Franz Ferdinand (p. 545)

Robert Lansing (p. 546)

John "Black Jack" Pershing (p. 547)

Henry Cabot Lodge (p. 559)

A. Mitchell Palmer (p. 561)

Emma Goldman (p. 561)

WHAT

Triple Alliance (p. 544)

Triple Entente (p. 544)

U-boats (p. 545)

Lusitania (p. 545)

Zimmermann telegram (p. 546)

American Expeditionary Force (AEF) (p. 547)

Eighteenth Amendment (p. 551)

Nineteenth Amendment (p. 553)

Fourteen Points (p. 556)

League of Nations (p. 556)

Versailles treaty (p. 558)

Seattle general strike of 1919 (p. 560)

steel strike of 1919 (p. 561)

Red scare (p. 561)

Schenck v. United States (p. 561)

★ REVIEW QUESTIONS Q:

Use key terms and dates to support your answer

1. Why did President Wilson fail to maintain U.S. neutrality during World War I? (pp. 542–47)

2. How did the American Expeditionary Force contribute to the defeat of Germany? (pp. 547–51)

3. How did progressive ideals fare during wartime? (pp. 551–56)

4. Why did the Senate fail to ratify the Versailles treaty? (pp. 556–60)

5. How did the Red scare contribute to the erosion of civil liberties after the war? (pp. 560–64)

★ MAKING CONNECTIONS

Draw on key terms, timeline, and review questions

1. Why did the United States at first resist intervening in World War I? Why did it later retreat from this policy and send troops? In your answer, discuss whether these decisions revised or reinforced earlier U.S. foreign policy.

2. Some reformers were optimistic that World War I would advance progressive ideals at home. Discuss specific wartime domestic developments that displayed progressivism's influence. How did the war contribute to these developments? Did they endure in peacetime? Why or why not?

3. A conservative reaction in American politics followed peace, most vividly in the labor upheaval and Red scare that swept the nation. What factors drove these developments? How did they shape the postwar political spectrum?

4. During World War I, the nation witnessed important demographic changes. What drove African American and Mexican migration north? How did the war facilitate these changes? In your answer, explain the significance of these developments to the migrants and the nation.

FOR PRACTICE QUIZZES AND OTHER STUDY TOOLS, see the Online Study Guide at **bedfordstmartins.com/roarkcompact**.

★ SUGGESTED READINGS

Jean Baker, *Sisters: The Lives of America's Suffragists* (2005). An insightful collective biography of five leaders of the struggle for voting rights for women.

Thomas Fleming, *The Illusion of Victory: America in World War I* (2003). A lively critical account of Wilson's wartime presidential leadership.

James N. Gregory, *Southern Diaspora: How the Great Migrations of Black and White Southerners Transformed America* (2005). A probing discussion of the largest internal migrations in U.S. history.

Jennifer D. Keene, *Doughboys, the Great War, and the Remaking of America* (2001). A thoughtful analysis of how military service transformed ordinary soldiers.

Margaret Olwen Macmillan, *Paris 1919: Six Months That Changed the World* (2002). An eloquent consideration of the Versailles treaty and its global consequences.

Gene Smith, *Until the Last Trumpet Sounds: The Life of General of the Armies John J. Pershing* (1998). A fine biography of the commander of the American Expeditionary Force in Europe.

FOR MORE BOOKS ABOUT TOPICS IN THIS CHAPTER, see the Online Bibliography at **bedfordstmartins.com/roarkcompact**.

FOR ADDITIONAL FIRSTHAND ACCOUNTS OF THIS PERIOD, see Chapter 22 in Michael Johnson, ed., *Reading the American Past,* Fourth Edition.

FOR WEB SITES, IMAGES, AND DOCUMENTS RELATED TO TOPICS AND PLACES IN THIS CHAPTER, visit Make History at **bedfordstmartins.com/roarkcompact**.

★ TIMELINE

1914
- **April**. U.S. Marines occupy Veracruz, Mexico.
- **June 28**. Assassination of Archduke Franz Ferdinand.
- **July 18**. Austria-Hungary declares war on Serbia.
- **August 3**. Germany attacks Russia and France.
- **August 4**. Great Britain declares war on Germany.

1915
- *Lusitania* sunk.
- Women's Peace Party formed.
- Italy joins Allies.

1915–1916
- General Pershing pursues Pancho Villa.

1916
- Wilson reelected.

1917
- Zimmermann telegram intercepted.
- **April 6**. United States declares war on Germany.
- Committee on Public Information created.
- Selective Service Act.
- Espionage Act and Trading with the Enemy Act
- East St. Louis, Illinois, race riot.
- Russia arranges separate peace with Germany.

1918
- **January 8**. President Wilson gives Fourteen Points speech.
- **May**. Sedition Act.
- **May–June**. U.S. Marines see first major combat at Cantigny and Château-Thierry.
- **November 11**. Armistice signed ending World War I.

1919
- **January**. Paris peace conference begins.
- **June**. Treaty of Versailles signed.
- **September**. Wilson undertakes speaking tour.
- Wave of labor strikes.

1920
- **January 1**. Prohibition begins.
- **January**. Palmer raids.
- **March**. Senate votes against ratification of Treaty of Versailles.
- **August 18**. Nineteenth Amendment ratified.
- **November**. Republican Warren G. Harding elected president.

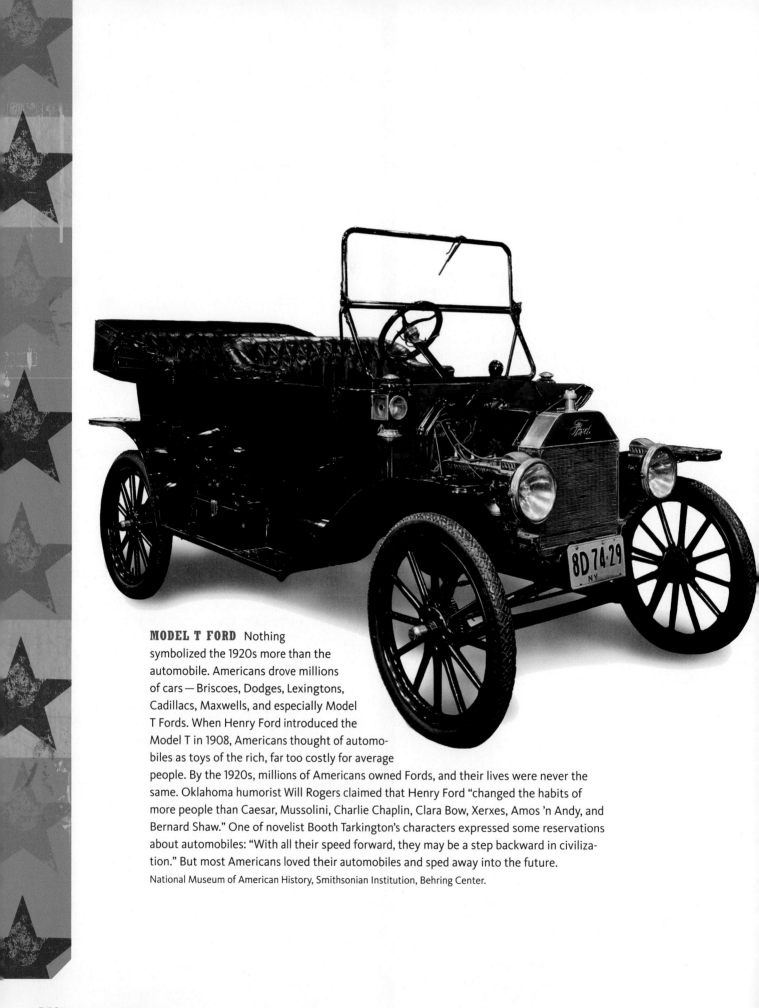

MODEL T FORD Nothing symbolized the 1920s more than the automobile. Americans drove millions of cars — Briscoes, Dodges, Lexingtons, Cadillacs, Maxwells, and especially Model T Fords. When Henry Ford introduced the Model T in 1908, Americans thought of automobiles as toys of the rich, far too costly for average people. By the 1920s, millions of Americans owned Fords, and their lives were never the same. Oklahoma humorist Will Rogers claimed that Henry Ford "changed the habits of more people than Caesar, Mussolini, Charlie Chaplin, Clara Bow, Xerxes, Amos 'n Andy, and Bernard Shaw." One of novelist Booth Tarkington's characters expressed some reservations about automobiles: "With all their speed forward, they may be a step backward in civilization." But most Americans loved their automobiles and sped away into the future.

National Museum of American History, Smithsonian Institution, Behring Center.

From New Era to Great Depression

1920–1932

AMERICANS IN THE 1920s cheered **Henry Ford** as an authentic American hero. When the decade began, he had already produced six million automobiles; by 1927, the figure reached fifteen million. In 1920, one car rolled off the Ford assembly line every minute; in 1925, one appeared every ten seconds. In 1920, a Ford car cost $845; in 1928, the price was less than $300, within range of most of the country's skilled workingmen. Henry Ford put America on wheels, and in the eyes of most Americans, he was an honest man who made an honest car: basic, inexpensive, and reliable. He became the greatest example of free enterprise's promise and achievement. But like the age in which he lived, Henry Ford was many-sided, more complex and contradictory than this simple image suggests.

Born in 1863 on a farm in Dearborn, Michigan, Ford hated the drudgery of farmwork and loved tinkering with machines. At sixteen, he fled rural life for Detroit, where he became a journeyman machinist and experimented with internal combustion engines. In 1893, he put together one of the first successful gasoline-driven carriages in the United States. His ambition, he said, was to "make something in quantity." The product he chose reflected American restlessness, the desire to be on the move. "Everybody wants to be someplace he ain't," Ford declared. "As soon as he gets there he wants to go right back." In 1903, with $28,000 from a few backers, Ford gathered twelve workers in a 250-by-50-foot shed and created the Ford Motor Company.

Ford's early cars were custom-made one at a time. By 1914, his cars were being built along a continuously moving assembly line: Workers bolted on parts brought to them by cranes and conveyor belts. Ford made only one kind of car, the Model T, which became synonymous with mass production. A boxlike black vehicle, it was cheap, easy to drive, and simple to repair. The Model T dominated the market. Throughout the rapid expansion of the automotive industry, the Ford Motor Company remained the industry leader, peaking in 1925, when it outsold all its rivals combined (Map 23.1).

Nobody entertained grander or more contradictory visions of the new America he had helped to create than Henry Ford himself. When he began his rise, progressive critics condemned the industrial giants of the nineteenth century as "robber barons" who lived in luxury while reducing their

Henry and Edsel Ford In this 1924 photograph, Henry Ford looks fondly at his first car while his son, Edsel, stands next to the ten millionth Model T. Edsel, the Fords' only child, remained unspoiled by his father's enormous wealth. Forsaking college, he entered the family business out of high school. Serious, disciplined, and an acute observer, Edsel Ford realized by the mid-1920s that General Motors's more advanced Chevrolet was about to surpass the Model T. Henry Ford stubbornly refused to change his automobile, insisting that the "Model T is the most perfect car in the world." Under Edsel's leadership, however, the Ford Motor Company moved beyond the plain, boxy, black, and fabulously successful Model T. Henry Ford Museum and Greenfield Village.

workers to wage slaves. Ford, however, identified with the common folk and saw himself as the benefactor of Americans yearning to be free and mobile.

Ford's automobile plants made him a billionaire, but their highly regimented assembly lines reduced Ford workers to near robots. On the cutting edge of modern technology, Ford nevertheless remained nostalgic about rural values. He sought to revive the past in Greenfield Village, a museum outside Detroit, where he relocated buildings from a bygone era, including his parents' farmhouse. His museum contrasted sharply with the roaring Ford plant farther along the Detroit River at River Rouge. The African American and immigrant workers who worked there found no place in Greenfield Village. Yet all would be well, Ford insisted, if Americans remained true to their agrarian past and somehow managed to be modern and scientific at the same time.

Tension between traditional values and modern conditions lay at the heart of the conflicted 1920s. For the first time, more Americans lived in urban than in rural areas, yet Americans remained nostalgic about farms and small towns. Although the nation generally prospered, the new wealth widened the gap between rich and poor. While millions admired urban America's sophisticated new style and consumer products, others condemned postwar society for its vulgar materialism. A great outpouring of artistic talent led, ironically, to incessant critiques of America's artistic barrenness. The Ku Klux Klan and other champions of an idealized older America resorted to violence as well as words when they chastised the era's "new woman," "New Negro," and surging immigrant populations.

The public, disillusioned with the outcome of World War I, turned away from the Christian moralism and idealism of the Progressive Era. In the twenties, Ford and businessmen like him replaced political reformers such as Theodore Roosevelt and Woodrow Wilson as the models of progress. The U.S. Chamber of Commerce crowed, "The American businessman is the most influential person in the nation." Social justice gave way to individual advancement. At the center of it all, President Calvin Coolidge spoke in praise of those in power when he declared, "The business of America is business." The fortunes of the era rose, then crashed, according to the values and practices of the business community. ★

The New Era

The 1920s were a time of contradiction and ambivalence. Once Woodrow Wilson left the White House, the energy flowed away from civic reform and toward private economic endeavor. The rise of a freewheeling economy and a heightened sense of individualism caused Secretary of Commerce Herbert Hoover to declare that America had entered a "New Era," one of many labels used to describe the complex 1920s. Some terms focus on the decade's high-spirited energy

and cultural changes: Roaring Twenties, Jazz Age, Flaming Youth, Age of the Flapper. Others echo the rising importance of money—Dollar Decade, Golden Twenties, Prosperity Decade—or reflect the sinister side of gangster profiteering—Lawless Decade. Still others emphasize the lonely confusion of the Lost Generation and the stress and anxiety of the Aspirin Age.

America in the twenties was many things, but there was no getting around the truth of Calvin Coolidge's insight: The business of America *was* business. Politicians and diplomats proclaimed business the heart of American civilization. Average men and women bought into the idea that business and its wonderful products were what made America great, as they snatched up the flood of new consumer items American factories sent forth.

A Business Government   Republicans controlled the White House from 1921 to 1933. The first of the three Republican presidents was **Warren Gamaliel Harding**, the Ohio senator who in his 1920 campaign called for a "return to normalcy," by which he meant the end of public crusades and a return to private pursuits. Harding promised a government run by the best minds, and he appointed a few men of real stature to his cabinet. Herbert Hoover, the energetic and ambitious former head of the wartime Food Administration, became secretary of commerce. But wealth also counted. Andrew Mellon, one of the richest men in America, became secretary of the treasury. And friendship counted, too. Harding handed out jobs to members of his old "Ohio gang," whose only qualification was their friendship. This curious combination of merit and cronyism made for a disjointed administration in which a few men debated national needs, while other men looked for ways to advance their own interests.

When Harding was elected in 1920 in a landslide over Democratic opponent James Cox (see chapter 22, Map 22.6), the unemployment rate hit 20 percent, the highest ever up to that point. Farmers fared the worst; their bankruptcy rate increased tenfold. Harding pushed measures to regain national prosperity—high tariffs to protect American businesses (the Fordney-McCumber tariff in 1922 raised duties to unprecedented heights), price supports for agriculture, and the dismantling of wartime government control over industry in favor of unregulated private business. "Never before, here or anywhere else," the U.S. Chamber of Commerce said proudly, "has a government been so completely fused with business."

Harding's policies to boost American enterprise made him very popular, but ultimately his small-town congeniality and trusting ways did him in. Some of his friends in the Ohio gang were up to their necks in lawbreaking. Three of Harding's appointees would go to jail. Interior Secretary Albert Fall was convicted of accepting bribes of more than $400,000 for leasing oil reserves on public land in Teapot Dome, Wyoming, and "Teapot Dome" became a synonym for political corruption.

On August 2, 1923, when the fifty-eight-year-old Harding died from a heart attack, Vice President **Calvin Coolidge** became president. Coolidge once expressed his belief that "the man who builds a

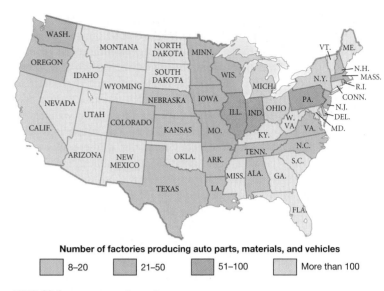

Number of factories producing auto parts, materials, and vehicles

8–20 | 21–50 | 51–100 | More than 100

MAP 23.1   Auto Manufacturing
By the mid-1920s, the massive coal and steel industries of the Midwest had made that region the center of the new automobile industry. A major road-building program by the federal government carried the thousands of new cars produced each day to every corner of the country.

factory builds a temple, the man who works there worships there." Reverence for free enterprise meant that Coolidge continued and extended Harding's policies of promoting business and limiting government. With Coolidge's approval, Secretary of the Treasury Andrew Mellon reduced the government's control over the economy and cut taxes for corporations and wealthy individuals. New rules for the Federal Trade Commission severely limited its power to regulate business. Secretary of Commerce Herbert Hoover limited government authority by encouraging trade associations that would keep business honest and efficient through voluntary cooperation.

Coolidge found a staunch ally in the Supreme Court. For many years, the Court had opposed federal regulation of hours, wages, and working conditions on the grounds that such legislation was the proper concern of the states. With Coolidge, the Court also found ways to curtail a state's ability to regulate business. It ruled against closed shops—businesses where only union members could be employed—while confirming the right of owners to form exclusive trade associations. In 1923, the Court declared unconstitutional the District of Columbia's minimum-wage law for women, asserting that the law interfered with the freedom of employer and

> Coolidge once expressed his belief that "the man who builds a factory builds a temple, the man who works there worships there."

employee to make labor contracts. The Court and the president attacked government intrusion in the free market, even when the prohibition of government regulation threatened the welfare of workers.

The election of 1924 confirmed the defeat of the progressive principle that the state should take a leading role in ensuring the general welfare. To oppose Coolidge, the Democrats nominated John W. Davis, a corporate lawyer whose conservative views differed little from Republican principles. Only the Progressive Party and its presidential nominee, Senator Robert La Follette of Wisconsin, offered a genuine alternative. When La Follette championed labor unions, regulation of business, and protection of civil liberties, Republicans coined the slogan "Coolidge or Chaos." Turning their backs on what they considered labor radicalism and reckless reform, voters chose Coolidge in a landslide. Coolidge was right when he declared, "This is a business country, and it wants a business government." What was true of the government's relationship to business at home was also true abroad.

Promoting Prosperity and Peace Abroad

After orchestrating the Senate's successful effort to block U.S. membership in the League of Nations, Henry Cabot Lodge boasted, "We have torn Wilsonism up by the roots." But repudiation of Wilsonian internationalism and rejection of collective security through the League of Nations did not mean that the United States retreated into isolationism. The United States emerged from World War I with its economy intact and enjoyed a decade of stunning growth. Economic involvement in the world and the continuing chaos in Europe made withdrawal impossible. New York replaced London as the center of world finance, and the United States became the world's chief creditor.

One of the Republicans' most ambitious foreign policy initiatives was the Washington Disarmament Conference, which convened to establish a global balance of naval power. Secretary of State Charles Evans Hughes shaped the **Five-Power Naval Treaty of 1922** committing Britain, France, Japan, Italy, and the United States to a proportional reduction of naval forces. The treaty led to the scrapping of more than two million tons of warships, by far the world's greatest success in disarmament. Americans celebrated President Harding for safeguarding

the peace while remaining outside the League of Nations. By fostering international peace, he also helped make the world a safer place for American trade.

A second major effort on behalf of world peace came in 1928, when Secretary of State Frank Kellogg joined French foreign minister Aristide Briand to produce the **Kellogg-Briand pact**. Nearly fifty nations signed the solemn pledge to renounce war and settle international disputes peacefully. Most Americans considered the nation's signature an affirmation of its commitment to peace rather than to Wilson's foolish notion of a progressive, uplifting war.

But Republican administrations preferred private sector diplomacy to state action. With the blessing of the White House, a team of American financiers led by Chicago banker Charles Dawes swung into action when Germany suspended its war reparation payments in 1923. Impoverished, Germany was staggering under the massive bill of $33 billion presented by the victorious Allies in the Versailles treaty. When Germany failed to meet its annual payment, France occupied Germany's industrial Ruhr Valley, creating the worst international crisis since the war. In 1924, American corporate leaders produced the **Dawes Plan**, which halved Germany's annual reparation payments, initiated fresh American loans to Germany, and caused the French to retreat from the Ruhr. Although the United States failed to join the league, it continued to exercise significant economic and diplomatic influence abroad. These Republican successes overseas helped fuel prosperity at home.

Automobiles, Mass Production, and Assembly-Line Progress

The automobile industry emerged as the largest single manufacturing industry in the nation. Henry Ford shrewdly located his company in Detroit, knowing that key materials for his automobiles were manufactured in nearby states (see Map 23.1). Keystone of the American economy, the automobile industry not only employed hundreds of thousands of workers directly but also brought whole industries into being—filling stations, garages, fast-food restaurants, and "guest cottages" (motels). The need for tires, glass, steel, highways, oil, and refined gasoline for automobiles provided millions of related jobs. By 1929, one American in four found employment directly

Detroit and the Automobile Industry in the 1920s

Main railroads
Centers of iron and steel production
Automobiles and ancillary industries
Oil and gas

Colorado Filling Station and Gas Pump Gulf Oil Company gave away the first free road map in 1914. By 1929, when Conoco (Continental Oil Company) produced this lavish map with Colorado's spectacular mountains looming in the background, nearly every oil company was supplying road maps as part of its campaign to attract the booming tourist trade. This appealing drive-through station is a far cry from the first retail outlets for gas—blacksmith shops and hardware stores, the same places individuals bought kerosene to burn in their lamps. Because motorists did not trust what they could not see, companies in the 1910s introduced glass-cylinder, gravity-flow gas pumps. Courtesy, Colorado Historical Society.

FOR MORE HELP ANALYZING THIS IMAGE, see the visual activity for this chapter in the Online Study Guide at bedfordstmartins.com/roarkcompact.

or indirectly in the automobile industry. "Give us our daily bread" was no longer addressed to the Almighty, one commentator quipped, but to Detroit.

Automobiles altered the face of America. Cars changed where people lived, what work they did, how they spent their leisure, even how they thought. Hundreds of small towns decayed because the automobile enabled rural people to bypass them in favor of more distant cities and towns. In cities, streetcars began to disappear as workers moved to the suburbs and commuted to work along crowded highways. Nothing shaped modern America more than the automobile, and efficient mass production made the automobile revolution possible.

Mass production by the assembly-line technique had become standard in almost every factory, from automobiles to meatpacking to cigarettes. To improve efficiency, corporations reduced assembly-line work to the simplest, most repetitive tasks. They also established specialized divisions—procurement, production, marketing, and employee relations—each with its own team of professionally trained managers. Changes on the assembly line and in management, along with technological advances, significantly boosted overall efficiency. Between 1922 and 1929, productivity in manufacturing increased 32 percent. Average wages, however, increased only 8 percent. As assembly lines became standard, laborers lost many of the skills in which they had once taken pride, but corporations reaped great profits from these changes.

Industries also developed programs for workers that came to be called **welfare capitalism**. Some businesses improved safety and sanitation inside factories and instituted paid vacations and pension plans. Welfare capitalism encouraged loyalty to the company and discouraged traditional labor unions. Not wanting to relive the chaotic strikes of 1919, industrialists sought to eliminate reasons for workers to join unions. One labor organizer in the steel industry bemoaned the success of welfare capitalism. "So many workmen here had been lulled to sleep by the company union, the welfare plans, the social organizations fostered by the employer," he declared, "that they had come to look upon the employer as their protector, and had believed vigorous trade union organization unnecessary for their welfare."

Consumer Culture Mass production fueled corporate profits and national economic prosperity. During the 1920s, per capita income increased by a third, the cost of living stayed the same, and unemployment remained low. But the rewards of the economic boom were not evenly distributed. Americans who labored with their hands inched

ahead, while white-collar workers enjoyed significantly more spending money and more leisure time to spend it. Mass production of a broad range of new products—automobiles, radios, refrigerators, electric irons, washing machines—produced a consumer-goods revolution.

In this new era of abundance, more people than ever conceived of the American dream in terms of the things they could acquire. How the business boom and business values of the 1920s affected average Americans is revealed in *Middletown* (1929), a study of the lives of the inhabitants of Muncie, Indiana. Muncie was, above all, "a culture in which everything hinges on money." Moreover, faced with technological and organizational change beyond their comprehension, many citizens had lost confidence in their ability to play an effective role in civic affairs. More and more they became passive consumers, deferring to the supposed expertise of leaders in politics and economics.

THE PROMISE OF TECHNOLOGY

Household Appliances By the end of the 1920s, most urban homes in America had electricity, and middle-class urban families began acquiring household appliances that transformed women's daily lives. Before electricity, most chores were daylong ordeals. Washing machines saved housewives long hours spent hauling and heating water and hand-washing clothes. Ironing had been one of the most dreaded chores, especially in the summer when the kitchen stove had to be kept hot for heavy irons that needed frequent reheating. Electric irons eased the burden enormously. Vacuum cleaners saved the labor of hauling rugs out of the house to be beaten. Although household appliances relieved women of backbreaking labor, housework did not take less time. With the appearance of appliances, standards of cleanliness rose, and so did the frequency of many household chores. Nevertheless, an advertisement from a leading women's magazine insisted that "the wise woman delegates to electricity all that electricity can do." Ads like this promoted new technologies and reminded prospective buyers that this beautiful Eden washing machine could be theirs through an "easy-payment plan." Picture Research Consultants & Archives.

The pied piper of these disturbing changes was the rapidly expanding business of advertising, which stimulated the desire for new products and hammered away at the traditional values of thrift and saving. Newspapers, magazines, radios, and billboards told Americans what they had to have in order to be popular, secure, and successful. Advertising linked material goods to the fulfillment of every spiritual and emotional need. Americans increasingly defined and measured their social status, and indeed their personal worth, on the yardstick of material possessions. Happiness itself rode on owning a car and choosing the right cigarettes and toothpaste.

By the 1920s, the United States had achieved the physical capacity to satisfy Americans' material wants. The economic problem shifted from production to consumption: Who would buy the goods flying off American assembly lines? One solution was to expand America's markets in foreign countries, and government and business joined in that effort. Another solution to the problem of consumption was to expand the market at home.

Henry Ford realized early on that "mass production requires mass consumption." He understood that automobile workers not only produced cars but would also buy them if they made enough money. "One's own employees ought to be one's own best customers," Ford said. In 1914, he raised wages in his factories to $5 a day, more than twice the going rate. High wages made for workers who were more loyal and more exploitable, and high wages returned as profits when workers bought Fords.

Not all industrialists were as farseeing as Ford. Because the wages of many workers barely edged upward, many people's incomes were too puny to satisfy the growing desire for consumer goods. Business supplied the solution: Americans could realize their dreams through credit. **Installment buying**—a little money down, a payment each month—allowed people to purchase expensive items they could not otherwise afford or purchase items before saving the necessary money. As one newspaper announced, "The first responsibility of an American to his country is no longer that of a citizen, but of a consumer." During the 1920s, America's motto became spend, not save. Old values—"Use it up, wear it out, make it do or do without"—seemed about as pertinent as a horse and buggy. American culture had shifted.

> **Q:** **How did the spread of the automobile transform the United States?**

The Roaring Twenties

By the beginning of the decade, psychoanalyst **Sigmund Freud** had become a household name. Most Americans knew little of the complexity of his pioneering work in the psychology of the unconscious, but people realized that Freud offered a way of looking at the world that was radically different. In the twenties, much to Freud's disgust, the American media turned his ideas about the sexual origins of behavior on its head. If it is wrong to deny that we are sexual beings, some reasoned, then the key to health and fulfillment must lie in following impulse freely. Those who doubted this reasoning were simply "repressed."

The new ethic of personal freedom excited many Americans to seek pleasure without guilt in a whirl of activity that earned the decade the name "Roaring Twenties." Prohibition made lawbreakers of millions of otherwise decent folk. Flappers and "new women" challenged traditional gender boundaries. Other Americans enjoyed the Roaring Twenties through the words and images of vastly expanded mass communication. Motion pictures, radio, and magazines marketed celebrities. In the freedom of America's big cities, particularly New York, a burst of creativity produced the "New Negro," who confounded and disturbed white Americans. The "Lost Generation" of writers, profoundly disillusioned with mainstream America's cultural direction, fled the country.

Prohibition Republicans generally sought to curb the powers of government, but the twenties witnessed a great exception to this rule when the federal government implemented one of the last reforms of the Progressive Era: the Eighteenth Amendment, which banned the manufacture and sale of alcohol and took effect in January 1920 (see chapter 22) and made the United States the world's only society ever to outlaw alcohol. Supporters of **prohibition** believed that stopping consumption would boost production, eliminate crime, and lift the nation's morality. Women were particularly enthusiastic because heavy drinking was closely associated with domestic violence and poverty.

Charged with enforcing prohibition, the Treasury Department smashed more than 172,000 illegal stills in 1925 alone. But Treasury agents faced a staggering task. In 1929, an agent in Indiana reported, "Conditions in most important cities very bad. Lax and corrupt public officials great handicap . . . prevalence of drinking among minor boys and the . . . middle or better class of adults." The "speakeasy," a place where men (and, increasingly, women) drank publicly, became a common feature of the urban landscape. One dealer, trading on common knowledge that whiskey still flowed in the White House, distributed cards advertising himself as the "President's Bootlegger."

Eventually, serious criminals took over the liquor trade. Alphonse "Big Al" Capone became the era's most notorious gang lord by establishing in Chicago a bootlegging empire that reputedly grossed more than $60 million in a single year. During the first four years of prohibition, Chicago witnessed more than two hundred gang-related killings as rival mobs struggled for control of the lucrative liquor trade. The most notorious event came on St. Valentine's Day 1929, when Capone's Italian-dominated mob machine-gunned seven members of a rival Irish gang. Federal authorities finally sent Capone to prison for income tax evasion. "I give the public what the public wants," Capone told a reporter, "and all I get is abuse." Capone was a gangster, but he portrayed himself as a resourceful entrepreneur and successful businessman.

Gang-war slayings prompted demands for the repeal of the Eighteenth Amendment. In 1931, a panel of distinguished experts reported that prohibition, which supporters had defended as "a great social and economic experiment," had failed. The social and political costs of prohibition outweighed the benefits. Prohibition caused ordinary citizens to disrespect the law, corrupted the police, and demoralized the judiciary. In 1933, after thirteen years, the nation ended prohibition, making the Eighteenth Amendment the only constitutional amendment to be repealed.

The New Woman Of all the changes in American life in the 1920s, none sparked more heated debate than the alternatives offered to the traditional roles of women. Increasing numbers of women worked and went to college, defying older gender hierarchies and norms. Even mainstream magazines such as the *Saturday Evening Post* began publishing stories about young, college-educated women who drank gin cocktails, smoked cigarettes, and wore skimpy dresses and dangly necklaces. Before the Great War, the **new woman** dwelt in New York City's bohemian Greenwich Village, but afterward the mass media brought her into middle-class America's living rooms.

When the Nineteenth Amendment, ratified in 1920, granted women the vote, feminists felt liberated and expected women to reshape the political landscape. A Kansas woman declared, "I went to bed last night a *slave*[;] I awoke this morning a *free woman*." Women began pressuring Congress to pass laws that especially concerned women, including measures to protect women in factories and grant federal aid to schools. Black women lobbied particularly for federal courts to assume jurisdiction over the crime of lynching. But women's only significant

"The Girls' Rebellion" The August 1924 cover of *Redbook*, a popular women's magazine, portrays the kind of post-adolescent girl who was making respectable families frantic. Flappers scandalized their middle-class parents by flouting the old moral code. This young woman sports the "badges of flapperhood," including what one critic called an "intoxication of rouge." The cover promises a story inside about girls gone wild. Fictionalized, emotion-packed stories such as this brought the new woman into every woman's home. Picture Research Consultants & Archives.

legislative success came in 1921 when Congress enacted the Sheppard-Towner Act, which extended federal assistance to states seeking to reduce high infant mortality rates. Rather than the beginning of women's political success, the act marked the high tide of women's influence in the 1920s.

A number of factors helped thwart women's political influence. Male domination of both political parties, the rarity of female candidates, and lack of experience in voting, especially among recent immigrants, kept many women away from the polls. In the South, poll taxes, literacy tests, and outright terrorism continued to decimate the vote of African Americans, men and women alike.

Most important, rather than forming a solid voting bloc, feminists divided. Some argued for women's right to special protection; others demanded equal protection. The radical National Woman's Party fought for an Equal Rights Amendment that stated flatly: "Men and women shall have equal rights throughout the United States." The more moderate League of Women Voters feared that the amendment's wording threatened state laws that provided women special protection, such as preventing them from working on certain machines. Put before Congress in 1923, the Equal Rights Amendment went down to defeat, and radical women were forced to work for the causes of birth control, legal equality for minorities, and the end of child labor through other means.

Economically, more women worked for pay—approximately one in four by 1930—but they clustered in "women's jobs." The proportion of women working as secretaries, stenographers, and typists skyrocketed. Women almost monopolized the occupations of librarian, nurse, elementary school teacher, and telephone operator. Women also represented 40 percent of salesclerks by 1930. More female white-collar workers meant fewer women were interested in protective legislation for women; new women wanted salaries and opportunities equal to men's.

Increased earnings gave working women more buying power in the new consumer culture. A stereotype soon emerged of the flapper, so called because of the short-lived fad of wearing unbuckled galoshes. The flapper had short "bobbed" hair and wore lipstick and rouge. She spent freely on the latest styles—dresses with short skirts and drop waists, bare arms, and no petticoats—and she danced all night to wild jazz.

The new woman both reflected and propelled the modern birth control movement. Margaret Sanger, the crusading pioneer for contraception during the Progressive Era, restated her principal conviction in 1920: "No woman can call herself free until she can choose consciously whether she will or will not be a mother." By shifting strategy in the twenties, Sanger courted the conservative American Medical Association; linked birth control with the eugenics movement, which advocated limiting reproduction among "undesirable" groups; and thus made contraception a respectable subject for discussion.

Flapper style and values spread from coast to coast through films, novels, magazines, and advertisements. New women challenged American convictions about separate spheres for women and men, the double standard of sexual conduct, and Victorian ideas of proper female appearance and behavior. Although only a minority of American women became flappers, all women, even those who remained at home, felt the great changes of the era.

The New Negro
The 1920s witnessed the emergence not only of the new woman but also of the **New Negro**. Both new identities riled conservatives and reactionaries. African Americans who challenged the caste system that confined dark-skinned Americans to the lowest levels of society confronted whites who insisted that race relations would not change. Cheers for black soldiers quickly faded after their return from World War I, and African Americans soon faced grim days of economic hardship and race riots (see chapter 22).

The prominent African American intellectual W. E. B. Du Bois and the National Association for the Advancement of Colored People (NAACP) aggressively pursued the passage of a federal anti-lynching law to counter mob violence against blacks in the South. Many poor blacks, however, disillusioned with mainstream politics, turned for new leadership to a Jamaican-born visionary named **Marcus Garvey**. Garvey urged African Americans to rediscover the heritage of Africa, take pride in their own achievements, and maintain racial purity by avoiding miscegenation. In 1917, Garvey launched the Universal Negro Improvement Association (UNIA) to help African Americans gain economic and political independence entirely outside white society. In 1919, the UNIA created its own shipping company, the Black Star Line, to support the "Back to Africa" movement among black Americans. But the business was an economic failure, and in 1927, the federal government pinned charges of illegal practices on Garvey and deported him to Jamaica. Nevertheless, the issues Garvey raised about racial pride, black identity, and the search for equality persisted, and his legacy remains at the center of black nationalist thought.

Still, most African Americans maintained hope in the American promise. In New York City, hope and talent came together. An extraordinary mix of black artists, sculptors, novelists, musicians, and poets poured into Harlem in uptown Manhattan, where they set out to create a distinctive African American culture that drew on their identities as Americans and Africans. As scholar Alain Locke put it in 1925, they introduced to the world the "New Negro," who rose from the ashes of slavery and segregation to proclaim African Americans' creative genius.

The emergence of the New Negro came to be known as the **Harlem Renaissance**. Building on the independence and pride displayed by black soldiers during the war, black artists sought to defeat the fresh onslaught of racial discrimination and violence with poems, paintings, and plays. "We younger Negro artists . . . intend to express our individual dark-skinned selves without fear or shame," poet Langston Hughes said of the Harlem Renaissance. "If white people are pleased, we are glad. If they are not, it doesn't matter. We know we are beautiful. And ugly, too."

The Harlem Renaissance produced dazzling talent. Black writer James Weldon Johnson, who in 1903 had written the Negro national anthem, "Lift Every Voice," wrote "God's Trombones" (1927), in which he expressed the wisdom and beauty of black folktales from the South. The poetry of Langston Hughes, Claude McKay, and Countee Cullen celebrated the vitality of life in Harlem. Zora Neale Hurston's novel *Their Eyes Were Watching God* (1937) explored the complex passions of black people in a southern community. Black painters, led by Aaron Douglas, linked African art, which had recently inspired European modernist artists, to the concept of the New Negro.

Noah's Ark Kansas-born painter Aaron Douglas expressed the Harlem Renaissance visually. When Douglas arrived in New York City in 1925, he quickly attracted the attention of W. E. B. Du Bois, who believed that the arts could manifest the African American soul. At Du Bois's urging, Douglas sought ways of integrating the African cultural heritage with American experience. This depiction of an African Noah commanding the loading of the ark displays a technique that became closely associated with African American art: strong silhouetted figures awash in misty color, indicating a connection between Christian faith and the vital, colorful origins of black Americans in a distant, mythologized African past. Fisk University Art Galleries.

Despite such vibrancy, Harlem for most whites remained a separate black ghetto known only for its lively nightlife. Fashionable whites crowded into Harlem's nightclubs, where they believed they could hear "real" jazz, a relatively new musical form, in its "natural" surroundings. The vigor of the Harlem Renaissance left a powerful legacy for black Americans, but the creative burst did little in the short run to dissolve the prejudice of white society. (See "Seeking the American Promise," page 580.)

Mass Culture In the twenties, popular culture, like consumer goods, was mass-produced and mass-consumed. Since politics was undemanding and uninteresting, Americans looked elsewhere for excitement. The proliferation of movies, radios, music, and sports meant that they found plenty to do, and in doing the same things, they helped create a national culture.

Nothing offered escapist delights like the movies. Hollywood, California, discovered the successful formula of combining opulence, sex, and adventure. By 1929, the movies were drawing more than 80 million people in a single week, as many as lived in the entire country. Rudolph Valentino, described as "catnip to women," and Clara Bow, the "It Girl" (everyone knew what *it* was), became household names. Most loved of all was the comic Charlie Chaplin, whose famous character, the wistful Little Tramp, showed an endearing inability to cope with the rules and complexities of modern life.

Americans also found heroes in sports. Baseball, professionalized since 1869 and segregated into white and black leagues, solidified its place as the national pastime in the 1920s. It remained essentially a game played by and for the working class. In George Herman "Babe" Ruth, baseball had the most cherished free spirit of the time. The "Sultan of Swat" mixed his record-setting home runs with rowdy escapades, demonstrating to fans that sports offered a way to break out of the ordinariness of everyday life. By "his sheer exuberance," one sportswriter declared, Ruth "has lightened the cares of the world."

The public also fell in love with a young boxer from the grim mining districts of Colorado. As a teenager, Jack Dempsey had made his living hanging around saloons betting he could beat anyone in the house. When he took the heavyweight crown just after World War I, he was revered as the people's champ, an American equalizer who was a stand-in for the average American who felt increasingly confined by bureaucracy and machine-made culture.

Football, essentially a college sport, held greater sway with the upper classes. The most famous coach, Knute Rockne of Notre Dame, celebrated football for its life lessons of hard work and teamwork. Let the professors make learning as interesting and significant as football, Rockne advised, and

Heroes and Heroines Two kinds of women look up adoringly at two kinds of 1920s heroes. A wholesome image is seen on the left in a 1927 cover of *People's Popular Monthly* magazine. The healthy outdoor girl, smartly turned out in her raccoon coat and pennant, flatters a naive college football hero. On the right, the pale, sensitive Vilma Banky kneels imploringly before the hypnotic gaze of the movies' greatest heartthrob, Rudolph Valentino. Magazine: Picture Research Consultants & Archives; Poster: Billy Rose Theatre Collection, The New York Public Library at Lincoln Center.

FOR MORE HELP ANALYZING THIS IMAGE, see the visual activity for this chapter in the Online Study Guide at bedfordstmartins.com/roarkcompact.

the problem of getting young people to learn would disappear. But in keeping with the times, football moved toward a more commercial spectacle. Harold "Red" Grange, "the Galloping Ghost," led the way by going from stardom at the University of Illinois to the Chicago Bears in the new professional football league.

The decade's hero worship reached its zenith in the celebration of **Charles Lindbergh**, a young pilot who set out on May 20, 1927, from Long Island in his single-engine plane, *The Spirit of St. Louis*, to become the first person to fly nonstop across the Atlantic. Newspapers tagged Lindbergh "the Lone Eagle"—the perfect hero for an age that celebrated individual accomplishment. "Charles Lindbergh," one journalist proclaimed, "is the stuff out of which have been made the pioneers that opened up the wilderness. His are the qualities

which we, as a people, must nourish." Lindbergh realized, however, that technical and organizational complexity was fast reducing chances for solitary achievement. Consequently, he titled his book about the flight *We* (1927) to include the machine that had made it all possible.

Another machine—the radio—became important to mass culture in the 1920s. The nation's first licensed radio station, KDKA in Pittsburgh, began broadcasting in 1920, and soon American airwaves buzzed with news, sermons, soap operas, sports, comedy, and music. Because they could now reach prospective customers in their own homes, advertisers bankrolled radio's rapid growth. Between 1922 and 1929, the number of radio stations in the United States increased from 30 to 606. In just seven years, homes with radios jumped from 60,000 to a staggering 10.25 million.

A Place of One's Own: The Quest for Home Ownership

Owning a place of one's own has always been important in America. In the nineteenth century, with the rise of industry and cities, the goal of a family farm gave way to the goal of a single-family house. Home ownership has been widely realized today, with roughly two-thirds of Americans (with the assistance of mortgage companies) owning their own homes.

In the 1920s, decent housing was in short supply in Detroit, America's great boomtown, as thousands poured in to work in Henry Ford's automobile factories. Arriving before World War I, blue-collar German, Irish, and Polish immigrants found homes in working-class neighborhoods scattered around the city center. Detroit's black population was tiny when the war began, but the great migration out of the South sent the population soaring by 1925. Tens of thousands of black newcomers frightened white property owners who had worked hard for their modest homes and believed that blacks would drive down property values, cause neighborhood decay, and fill their streets with criminals.

The property owners resolved to keep their neighborhoods all-white by channeling blacks into Black Bottom, the downtown ghetto. Although the U.S. Supreme Court had struck down a law mandating segregated housing in 1917, inventive white homeowners created other means to draw racial boundaries. Real estate agents refused to show blacks houses in white neighborhoods. Banks turned down blacks for mortgages. Whites signed restrictive covenants, promising not to sell their homes to blacks. If a black family managed to slip through their defenses, whites resorted to violence. In Detroit during the 1920s, income, education, occupation, wealth, and respectability meant little compared to race.

Dr. Ossian Sweet, a black physician who had washed dishes and waited tables to pay for his college education at Wilberforce University in Ohio and to attend medical school at Howard University in Washington, D.C., arrived in Detroit in 1921. He set up his medical practice in Black Bottom and prospered. He soon had the down payment for a home, but he refused to settle his wife and baby daughter in the congested, rat-infested ghetto. In 1925, Sweet bought a substantial bungalow at 2905 Garland Avenue, several blocks inside a working-class white neighborhood. His brother said later, "He wasn't looking for trouble. He just wanted to bring up his little girl in good surroundings." But Sweet understood the danger of trying to escape Black Bottom. Whites had recently run other black professionals out of their Detroit neighborhoods. Sweet told a friend, "Well, we have decided we are not going to run. We're not going to look for any trouble, but we're going to be prepared to protect ourselves if trouble arises." When Gladys and Ossian Sweet moved into their home on September 8, 1925, nine friends and family members accompanied them. The moving van that brought their furniture also carried a shotgun, two rifles, six pistols, and four hundred rounds of ammunition.

It did not take long for a crowd to gather. Hundreds of white men filled the streets, greatly outnumbering the few police who hoped to keep the peace. Shouting that they would send the "niggers" back where they belonged, the mob began throwing rocks, breaking windows, and advancing. Suddenly, gunfire erupted from the second story of the Sweet house, and two white men were shot; one was killed. The police kept the mob away long enough for a paddy wagon to haul the eleven blacks to the police station, where they were all indicted for murder.

Asked why he wanted to move to a white neighborhood, where there was likely to be trouble, Sweet said, "Because I bought the house, and it was my house, and I felt I had a right to live in it." The NAACP, which saw the case as a symbol of injustice and an opportunity to strike a legal blow in favor of self-defense against racial violence,

---

Radio added to the spread of popular music, especially jazz. Jazz—with its energy and freedom—provided the sound track for a new, distinct social class of youths. As the traditional bonds of community, religion, and family loosened, the young felt less pressure to imitate their elders and more freedom to develop their own culture. An increasing number of college students helped the "rah-rah" style of college life become a fad promoted in movies, songs, and advertisements. The collegiate set was the vanguard of the decade's "flaming youth."

The Lost Generation Some writers and artists felt alienated from America's mass-culture society, which they found shallow, anti-intellectual,

★ **Dr. Ossian Sweet and His House** Dr. Ossian Sweet's substantial two-story brick home is listed on the National Register of Historic Places. In September 1925, Sweet tried to move his family into the then all-white Detroit suburb where the house is located. Residents reacted violently, determined to uphold "the present high standards of the neighborhood." The Detroit News.

hired Clarence Darrow to defend the accused. Darrow was the most celebrated defense lawyer in the country and fresh from the Scopes trial in Tennessee (see page 584). In the courtroom, Sweet claimed that he had acted in self-defense. Darrow said that the facts were simple: "When they defended their home, they were arrested and charged with murder." He reminded the all-white jury that "every man's home is his castle, which even the king may not enter. Every man has a right to kill to defend himself or his family, or others, either in defense of the home, or in defense of themselves." A split jury caused the judge to declare a mistrial. A second trial ended in not guilty verdicts for all the defendants. "The verdict meant simply that the doctrine that a man's house is his castle applied to the black man as well as the white man," Darrow concluded optimistically.

Over the next several decades, however, housing discrimination became entrenched throughout the nation. Blacks succeeded in breaking out of the inner cities and moving into the suburbs, where today more than one-third of African Americans live, but breaching city boundaries did not mean leaving residential segregation behind. Of all the nation's segregated cities, none was more segregated than Detroit. As late as 1963, Martin Luther King Jr. declared: "I have a dream this afternoon that one day right here in Detroit Negroes will be able to buy a house or rent a house anywhere their money will carry them." As for Sweet, he moved back into his home on Garland Avenue in 1928, but without his wife and daughter, who had both died. He stayed in the bungalow for more than twenty-five years, and when he left, the neighborhood around him was still largely white.

and materialistic. Adoration of silly movie stars disgusted them. Moreover, they believed that business culture blighted American life. To their minds, Henry Ford made a poor hero. Young, white, and mostly college educated, these expatriates, as they came to be called, felt embittered by the war and renounced the progressives who had promoted it as a crusade. For them, Europe—not Hollywood or Harlem—seemed the place to seek their renaissance.

The American-born writer Gertrude Stein, long established in Paris, remarked famously as the young exiles gathered around her, "They are the lost generation." Most of the expatriates, however, believed to the contrary that they had finally found themselves. The **Lost Generation** helped launch the most creative period in American art and literature in the twentieth century. The novelist whose spare, clean style best exemplified the expatriate efforts to make art mirror basic reality was Ernest Hemingway. Hemingway's experience in the Great War convinced him that the world in which he was raised, with its Christian moralism and belief in progress, was bankrupt. Admirers found the terse language and hard lessons of his novel *The Sun Also Rises* (1926) to be perfect expressions of a world stripped of illusions.

Many writers who remained in America were exiles in spirit. Before the war, intellectuals had eagerly joined progressive reform movements. Afterward, they were more likely critics of American cultural vulgarity. Novelist Sinclair Lewis in *Main Street* (1920) and *Babbitt* (1922) satirized his native Midwest as a cultural wasteland. Humorists such as

James Thurber created outlandish characters to poke fun at American stupidity and inhibitions. And southern writers, led by William Faulkner, explored the South's grim class and race heritage. Worries about alienation surfaced as well. Although F. Scott Fitzgerald gained fame as the chronicler of flaming youth, he spoke sadly in *This Side of Paradise* (1920) of a disillusioned generation "grown up to find all Gods dead, all wars fought, all faiths in man shaken."

Q: How did the new freedoms of the 1920s challenge older conceptions of gender and race?

Resistance to Change

Large areas of the country did not share in the wealth of the 1920s and had little confidence that they would anytime soon. By the end of the decade, 40 percent of the nation's farmers were landless, and 90 percent of rural homes had no indoor plumbing, gas, or electricity. Rural America's wariness and distrust of urban America turned to despair in the 1920s when the census reported that the majority of the population had shifted from the country to the city (Map 23.2). Urban domination over the nation's political and cultural life and sharply rising economic disparity drove rural Americans in often ugly, reactionary directions.

Cities seemed to stand for everything rural areas stood against. Rural America imagined itself as solidly Anglo-Saxon (despite the presence of millions of African Americans in the South and Mexican Americans, Native Americans, and Asian Americans in the West), and the cities seemed to be filled with undesirable immigrants. Rural America

was the home of old-time Protestant religion, and the cities teemed with Catholics, Jews, liberal Protestants, and atheists. Rural America championed old-fashioned moral standards—abstinence and self-denial—while the cities spawned every imaginable vice. Once the "backbone of the Republic," rural Americans had become poor country cousins. In the 1920s, frustrated rural people sought to recapture their country by helping to push through prohibition, dam the flow of immigrants, revive the Ku Klux Klan, defend the Bible as literal truth, and defeat an urban Roman Catholic for president.

Rejecting the Undesirables Before the war, when about a million immigrants arrived each year, some Americans warned that unassimilable foreigners were smothering the nation. War against Germany and its allies expanded nativist and anti-radical sentiment. After the war, large-scale immigration resumed (another 800,000 immigrants arrived in 1921) at a moment when industrialists no longer needed new factory laborers. African American and Mexican migration had relieved labor shortages. Moreover, union leaders feared that millions of poor immigrants would undercut their efforts to organize American workers. Rural America's God-fearing Protestants were particularly alarmed that most of the immigrants were Catholic or Jewish. In 1921, Congress responded by severely restricting immigration.

In 1924, Congress very nearly slammed the door shut. The **Johnson-Reid Act** limited the number of immigrants to no more than 161,000 a year and gave each European nation a quota based on 2 percent of the number of people from that country in America in 1890. The act revealed the fear and bigotry that fueled anti-immigration legislation. While it cut immigration by more than 80 percent, it squeezed some nationalities far more than others. Backers of Johnson-Reid openly declared that America had become the "garbage can and the dumping ground of the world," and they manipulated quotas to ensure entry only to "good" immigrants. By basing quotas on the 1890 census, in which western Europeans predominated, the law effectively reversed the trend toward immigration from southern and eastern Europe, which by 1914 had amounted to 75 percent of the yearly total. For example, the Johnson-Reid Act allowed Great Britain 62,458 entries, but Russia could send only 1,992.

The 1924 law reaffirmed the 1880s legislation barring Chinese immigrants and added Japanese and other Asians to the list of the excluded. But it left open immigration from the Western Hemisphere, and during the 1920s, some 500,000 Mexicans crossed the border. Farm interests preserved Mexican

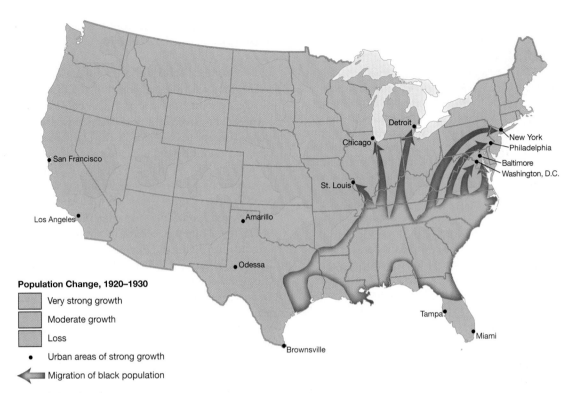

Population Change, 1920–1930

- Very strong growth
- Moderate growth
- Loss
- • Urban areas of strong growth
- ← Migration of black population

MAP 23.2 **The Shift from Rural to Urban Population, 1920–1930**

The movement of whites and Hispanics toward urban and agricultural opportunity made Florida, the West, and the Southwest the regions of fastest population growth. In contrast, large numbers of blacks left the rural South to find a better life in the North. Because almost all migrating blacks went from the countryside to cities in distant parts of the nation, while white and Hispanic migrants tended to move shorter distances toward familiar places, the population shift brought more drastic overall change to blacks than to whites and Hispanics.

READING THE MAP: Which states had the strongest growth? To which cities did southern blacks predominantly migrate?

CONNECTIONS: What conditions in the countryside made the migration to urban areas appealing to many rural Americans? In what social and cultural ways did rural America view itself as different from urban America?

FOR MORE HELP ANALYZING THIS MAP, see the map activity for this chapter in the Online Study Guide at bedfordstmartins.com/roarkcompact.

immigration because of Mexicans' value in southwestern agriculture. Rural Americans strongly supported the law, as did industrialists and labor leaders. The immigration restriction laws of the 1920s marked the end of an era—the denial of the Statue of Liberty's open-arms welcome to Europe's "huddled masses yearning to breathe free."

Antiforeign hysteria climaxed in the trial of two anarchist immigrants from Italy, **Nicola Sacco and Bartolomeo Vanzetti**. Arrested in 1920 for robbery and murder in South Braintree, Massachusetts, the men were sentenced to death by a judge who openly referred to them as "anarchist bastards." In response to doubts about the fairness of the verdict, a blue-ribbon review committee found the trial judge guilty of a "grave breach of official decorum"

but refused to recommend a motion for retrial. When Massachusetts executed Sacco and Vanzetti on August 23, 1927, fifty thousand mourners followed the caskets in the rain, convinced that the men had died because they were immigrants and radicals, not because they were murderers.

The Rebirth of the Ku Klux Klan The nation's sour antiforeign mood struck a responsive chord in members of the **Ku Klux Klan**. The Klan first appeared in the South during Reconstruction to thwart black freedom and expired with the reestablishment of white supremacy. In 1915, the Klan was reborn at Stone Mountain, Georgia, but when the new Klan extended its targets beyond black Americans, it quickly spread beyond the South. Under a banner

WKKK Badge Some half a million women were members of the Women of the Ku Klux Klan (WKKK). Young girls could join the female youth auxiliary, the Tri-K for Girls. Klanswomen fit perfectly within the KKK because the organization proclaimed itself the defender of the traditional virtues of pure womanhood and decent homes. This badge from Harrisburg, Pennsylvania, advertises the local WKKK's support for a home for "orphan and dependent children." Klanswomen also joined in boycotts of businesses owned by Jews and others whom they did not consider "100% American." Collection of Janice L. and David J. Frent.

proclaiming "100 percent Americanism," the Klan promised to defend family, morality, and traditional American values against the threats posed by blacks, immigrants, radicals, feminists, Catholics, and Jews.

Building on the frustrations of rural America, the Klan attracted three million to four million members—women as well as men. By the mid-1920s, the Klan had spread throughout the nation, almost controlling Indiana and influencing politics in Illinois, California, Oregon, Texas, Louisiana, Oklahoma, and Kansas. In 1926, Klan imperial wizard Hiram Wesley Evans described the assault of modernity: "One by one all our traditional moral standards went by the boards or were so disregarded that they ceased to be binding," he explained. "The sacredness of our Sabbath, of our homes, of chastity, and finally even of our right to teach our own children in schools [were] fundamental facts and truth torn away from us." The Klan's uniforms and rituals offered a certain counterfeit dignity to old-stock, Protestant, white Americans who felt passed over, and the hoods allowed members to beat and intimidate their victims with little fear of consequences.

Eventually, social changes, along with lawless excess, crippled the Klan. Immigration restrictions eased the worry about invading foreigners, and sensational wrongdoing by Klan leaders cost it the support of traditional moralists. Grand Dragon David Stephenson of Indiana, for example, went to jail for the kidnapping and rape of a woman who subsequently committed suicide. Yet the social grievances, economic problems, and

religious anxieties of the countryside and small towns remained, ready to be ignited.

The Scopes Trial In 1925 in a Tennessee courtroom, old-time religion and the new spirit of science went head-to-head. The confrontation occurred after several southern states passed legislation against the teaching of Charles Darwin's theory of evolution in the public schools. Fundamentalist Protestants insisted that the Bible's creation story be taught as the literal truth. Scientists and civil liberties organizations clamored for a challenge to the law, and John Scopes, a young biology teacher in Dayton, Tennessee, offered to test his state's ban on teaching evolution. When Scopes came to trial, Clarence Darrow, a brilliant defense lawyer from Chicago, volunteered to defend him. Darrow, an avowed agnostic, took on the prosecution's William Jennings Bryan, three-time Democratic nominee for president, symbol of rural America, and fervent fundamentalist, who was eager to defeat the proposition that humans had evolved from apes.

The **Scopes trial** quickly degenerated into a media circus. The first trial to be covered live on radio, it attracted a nationwide audience. Most of the reporters from big-city newspapers were hostile to Bryan, none more so than the cynical H. L. Mencken, who painted Bryan as a sort of Darwinian missing link ("a sweating anthropoid" and a "gaping primate"). When, under relentless questioning by Darrow, Bryan declared on the witness stand that he did indeed believe that the world had been created in six days and that Jonah had lived in the belly of a whale, his humiliation in the eyes of most urban observers was complete. Nevertheless, the Tennessee court upheld the law and punished Scopes with a $100 fine. Although fundamentalism won the battle, it lost the war. Mencken had the last word in a merciless obituary for Bryan, who died just a week after the trial ended. Portraying the "monkey trial" as a battle between the country and the city, Mencken flayed Bryan as a "charlatan, a mountebank, a zany without shame or dignity," motivated solely by "hatred of the city men who had laughed at him for so long."

As Mencken's acid prose indicated, Bryan's humiliation was not purely a victory of reason and science. It also revealed the disdain urban people felt for country people and the values they clung to. The Ku Klux Klan revival and the Scopes trial dramatized and inflamed divisions between city and country, intellectuals and the uneducated, the privileged and the poor, the scoffers and the faithful.

Al Smith and the Election of 1928 The presidential election of 1928 brought many of the developments of the 1920s—prohibition, immigration, religion, and the clash of rural and urban values—into sharp focus. Republicans emphasized the economic success of their party's pro-business government and turned to Herbert Hoover, the energetic secretary of commerce and leading public symbol of 1920s prosperity. But because both parties generally agreed that the American economy was basically sound, the campaign turned on social issues that divided Americans.

The Democrats nominated four-time governor of New York **Alfred E. Smith**. Smith adopted "The Sidewalks of New York" as a campaign theme song and seemed to represent all that rural Americans feared and resented. A child of immigrants, Smith got his start in politics with the help of Tammany Hall, New York City's Irish-dominated political machine and to many the epitome of big-city corruption. He denounced immigration quotas, signed New York State's anti-Klan bill, and opposed prohibition, believing that it was a nativist attack on immigrant customs. When Smith supposedly asked reporters in 1922, "Wouldn't you like to have your foot on the rail and blow the foam off some suds?" prohibition forces dubbed him "Alcohol Al." Smith's greatest vulnerability in the heartland, however, was his religion. He was the first Catholic to run for president. A Methodist bishop in Virginia denounced Roman Catholicism as "the Mother of ignorance, superstition, intolerance and sin" and begged Protestants not to vote for a candidate who represented "the kind of dirty people that you find today on the sidewalks of New York."

Hoover, who neatly combined the images of morality, efficiency, service, and prosperity, won the election by a landslide (Map 23.3). He received nearly 58 percent of the vote and gained 444 electoral votes to Smith's 87. The only bright spot for Democrats was the nation's cities, which voted Democratic, indicating the rising strength of ethnic minorities, including Smith's fellow Catholics.

Q: **Why did the relationship between urban and rural America deteriorate in the 1920s?**

The Great Crash

At his inauguration in 1929, Herbert Hoover told the American people, "Given a chance to go forward with the policies of the last eight years, we shall soon with the help of God be in sight of the day when poverty will be banished from this nation." Those words came back to haunt Hoover, for within eight months, the Roaring Twenties came to a crashing halt. The prosperity Hoover touted collapsed with the stock market, and the nation ended nearly three decades of barely interrupted economic growth. Like much of the world, the United States fell into the most serious economic depression of all time. Hoover and his reputation were among the first casualties, along with the reverence for business that had been the hallmark of the New Era.

Herbert Hoover: The Great Engineer When **Herbert Hoover** became president in 1929, he seemed the perfect choice to lead a prosperous business nation. He personified America's rags-to-riches ideal, having risen from poor Iowa orphan to one of the world's most celebrated mining engineers by the time he was thirty. His success in managing efforts to feed civilian victims of the fighting during World War I won him acclaim as the "Great Humanitarian" and led Woodrow Wilson to name him head of the Food Administration once the United States entered the war. Hoover's reputation soared even higher as secretary of commerce in the Harding and Coolidge administrations.

Hoover belonged to the progressive wing of his party, and as early as 1909, he declared, "The time when the employer could ride roughshod over his labor is disappearing with the doctrine of 'laissez-faire' on which it is founded." He urged a limited business-government partnership that would manage the sweeping changes Americans experienced. When Hoover entered the White House, he brought a reform agenda: "We want to see a nation built of home owners and farm owners. We want

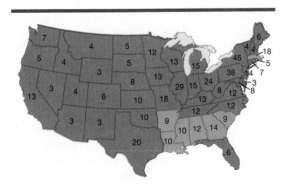

Candidate	Electoral Vote	Popular Vote	Percent of Popular Vote
Herbert Hoover (Republican)	444	21,391,381	57.4
Alfred E. Smith (Democrat)	87	15,016,443	40.3
Norman Thomas (Socialist)	0	881,951	2.3

MAP 23.3 The Election of 1928

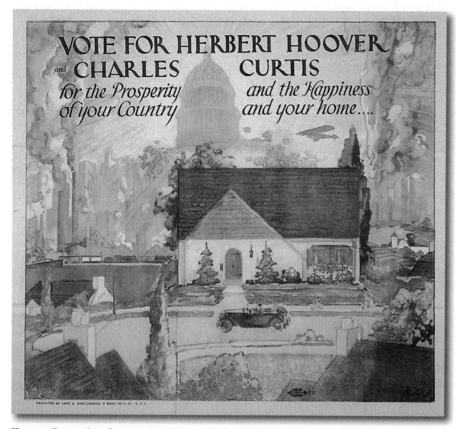

Hoover Campaign Poster This poster effectively illustrates Herbert Hoover's 1928 campaign message: Republican administrations in the 1920s had produced middle-class prosperity, complete with a house in the suburbs and the latest automobile. To remind voters that Hoover as secretary of commerce had promoted industry that made the suburban dream possible, the poster portrays smoking chimneys at a discreet distance. The poster gives no hint that this positive message would give way to outright religious bigotry in the campaign against Democrat (and Catholic) Al Smith. Collection of Janice L. and David J. Frent.

The Distorted Economy In the spring of 1929, the United States enjoyed a fragile prosperity. Although America had become the world's leading economy, it had done little to help rebuild Europe's shattered economy after World War I. Instead, the Republican administrations demanded that Allied nations repay their war loans, creating a tangled web of debts and reparations that sapped Europe's economic vitality. Moreover, to boost American business, the United States enacted tariffs that prevented other nations from selling their goods to Americans. Fewer sales meant that foreign nations had less money to buy American goods, which were pouring out in record abundance. American banks propped up the nation's export trade by extending credit to foreign customers, and fresh debt piled onto existing debt in an absurd pyramid.

The domestic economy was also in trouble. Wealth was badly distributed. Farmers continued to suffer from low prices and chronic indebtedness; the average income of families working the land amounted to only $240 per year. The wages of industrial workers, though rising during the decade, failed to keep up with productivity and corporate profits. Overall, nearly two-thirds of all American families lived on less than the $2,000 per year that economists estimated would "supply only basic necessities." In sharp contrast, the top 1 percent received 15 percent of the nation's income, an amount equal to that received by the bottom 42 percent of the population. The Coolidge administration worsened the deepening inequality by cutting taxes on the wealthy.

By 1929, the inequality of wealth produced a serious problem in consumption. The rich spent lavishly, but they could absorb only a tiny fraction of the nation's output. Ordinary folk, on whom the system ultimately depended, were unable to take up the slack. For a time, the new device of installment buying—buying on credit—kept consumer demand up. By the end of the decade, four out of five cars and two out of three radios were bought on credit.

Signs of economic trouble began to appear at mid-decade. New construction slowed down. Automobile sales faltered. Companies began cutting back production and laying off workers. Between 1921 and 1928, as investment and loan

to see their savings protected. We want to see them in steady jobs. We want to see more and more of them insured against death and accident, unemployment and old age. We want them all secure."

But Hoover also had ideological and political liabilities. Principles that appeared strengths in the prosperous 1920s—individual self-reliance, industrial self-management, and a limited federal government—became straitjackets when economic catastrophe struck. Moreover, Hoover had never held an elected public office, had a poor political touch, and was too thin-skinned to be an effective politician. Even so, most Americans considered him "a sort of superman" able to solve any problem. Prophetically, he confided to a friend his fear that "if some unprecedented calamity should come upon the nation . . . I would be sacrificed to the unreasoning disappointment of a people who expected too much." The distorted national economy set the stage for the calamity Hoover so feared.

opportunities faded, five thousand banks failed, wiping out the life savings of thousands. Still, the boom seemed to roar on, muffling the sounds of economic distress just beneath the surface.

The Crash of 1929 Even as the economy faltered, America's faith in it remained unshaken. Hoping for even bigger slices of the economic pie, Americans speculated wildly in the stock market on Wall Street. Between 1924 and 1929, the values of stocks listed on the New York Stock Exchange increased by more than 400 percent. Buying stocks on margin — that is, putting up only part of the money at the time of purchase — accelerated. Many people got rich this way, but those who bought on credit could finance their loans only if their stocks increased in value. Speculators could not imagine that the market might fall and they would be forced to meet their margin loans with cash they did not have.

Finally, in the autumn of 1929, the market hesitated. Investors nervously began to sell their overvalued stocks. The dip quickly became a panic on October 24, the day that came to be known as Black Thursday. Brokers jammed the stock exchange desperately trying to unload shares. More panic selling came on Black Tuesday, October 29, the day the market suffered a greater fall than ever before. In the next six months, the stock market lost six-sevenths of its total value.

It was once thought that the crash alone caused the Great Depression. It did not. In 1929, the national and international economies were already riddled with severe problems. But the dramatic losses in the stock market crash and the fear of risking what was left acted as a great brake on economic activity. The collapse on Wall Street shattered the New Era's confidence that America would enjoy perpetually expanding prosperity.

Hoover and the Limits of Individualism At first, Americans expressed relief that Herbert Hoover resided in the White House when the bubble broke. Unlike some conservatives who believed that the government should do nothing during economic downturns, Hoover believed that "we should use the powers of government to cushion the situation." Hoover was no do-nothing president, but there were limits to his activism.

In November 1929, to keep the stock market collapse from ravaging the entire economy, Hoover called a White House conference of business and labor leaders and urged them to join in a voluntary plan for recovery: Businesses would maintain production and keep their workers on the job; labor would accept existing wages, hours, and conditions. Within a few months, however, the bargain fell apart. As demand for their products declined, industrialists cut production, sliced wages, and laid off workers. Poorly paid or unemployed workers could not buy much, and their decreased spending led to further cuts in production and further loss of jobs. Thus began the terrible spiral of economic decline.

To deal with the problems of rural America, Hoover got Congress to pass the Agricultural Marketing Act in 1929. The act created the Farm Board, which used its budget of $500 million to buy up agricultural surpluses and thus, it was hoped, raise prices. But prices declined. To help end the decline, Hoover joined conservatives in urging protective tariffs on agricultural goods, and the Hawley-Smoot tariff of 1930 established the highest rates in history. The same year, Congress also authorized $420 million for public works projects to give the unemployed jobs and create more purchasing power. In three years, the Hoover administration nearly doubled federal public works expenditures.

But with each year of Hoover's term, the economy weakened. Tariffs did not end the suffering of farmers because foreign nations retaliated with increased tariffs of their own that crippled American farmers' ability to sell abroad. In 1932, Hoover hoped to help hard-pressed industry with the **Reconstruction Finance Corporation (RFC)**, a federal agency empowered to lend government funds to endangered banks and corporations. The theory was **trickle-down economics**: Pump money into the economy at the top, and in the long run, the people at the bottom would benefit. Or as one wag put it, "Feed the sparrows by feeding the horses." In the end, very little of what critics of the RFC called a "millionaires' dole" trickled down to the poor.

And the poor multiplied. Hundreds of thousands of workers lost their jobs each month. By 1932, an astounding one-quarter of the American workforce — more than twelve million people — were unemployed. There was no direct federal assistance, and state services and private charities were swamped. The depression that began in 1929 devastated much of the world, but no other modern nation provided such feeble support to the jobless. Cries grew louder for the federal government to give hurting people relief.

> The theory was trickle-down economics: Pump money into the economy at the top, and in the long run, the people at the bottom would benefit. Or as one wag put it, "Feed the sparrows by feeding the horses."

In responding, Hoover revealed the limits of his conception of government's proper role. He compared direct federal aid to the needy to the "dole" in Britain, which he thought destroyed the moral fiber of the chronically unemployed. In 1931, he allowed the Red Cross to distribute government-owned agricultural surpluses to the hungry. In 1932, he relaxed his principles further to offer small federal loans, not gifts, to the states to help them in their relief efforts. But Hoover's circumscribed notions of legitimate government action proved vastly inadequate to address the problems of restarting the economy and ending human suffering.

Q: Why did the American economy collapse in 1929?

Life in the Depression

In 1930, suffering on a massive scale set in. Despair settled over the land. Men and women hollow-eyed with hunger grew increasingly bewildered and angry in the face of cruel contradictions. They saw agricultural surpluses pile up in the countryside and knew that their children were going to bed hungry. They saw factories standing idle and knew that they and millions of others were willing to work. The gap between the American people and leaders who failed to resolve these contradictions widened as the depression deepened. By 1932, America's economic problems had created a dangerous social and political crisis.

The Human Toll Statistics only hint at the human tragedy of the Great Depression. When Herbert Hoover took office in 1929, the American economy stood at its peak. When he left in 1933, it had reached its twentieth-century low (Figure 23.1). In 1929, national income was $88 billion. By 1933, it had declined to $40 billion. In 1929, unemployment was 3.1 percent, or 1.5 million workers. By 1933, unemployment stood at 25 percent, or 12.5 million workers. By 1932, more than 9,000 banks had shut their doors, and depositors had lost more than $2.5 billion.

Jobless, homeless victims wandered in search of work, and the tramp, or hobo, became one of the most visible figures of the decade. Riding the rails or hitchhiking, a million vagabonds moved southward and westward looking for seasonal agricultural work. Other unemployed men and women, sick or less hopeful, huddled in doorways, overcome, one man remembered, by "helpless despair and submission." Scavengers haunted alleys behind restaurants in search of food. One writer told of an elderly woman who always took off her glasses to avoid seeing the maggots crawling over the garbage she ate. "I don't want to steal," a Pennsylvania man wrote to the governor in 1931, "but I won't let my wife and boy cry for something to eat. . . . How long is this going to keep up? I cannot stand it any longer."

Rural poverty was most acute. Tenant farmers and sharecroppers, mainly in the South, came to symbolize how poverty crushed the human spirit. Eight and a half million people, three million of them black, crowded into cabins without plumbing,

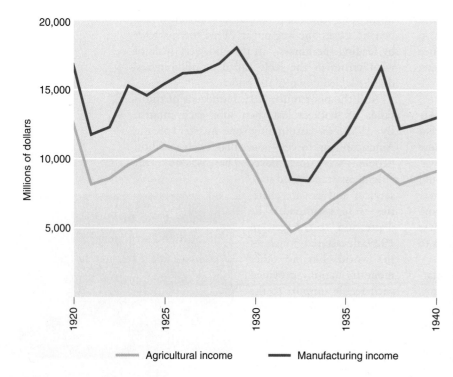

FIGURE 23.1 Manufacturing and Agricultural Income, 1920–1940
After economic collapse, recovery in the 1930s began under New Deal auspices. The sharp declines in 1937–1938, when federal spending was reduced, indicated that New Deal stimuli were still needed to restore manufacturing and agricultural income.

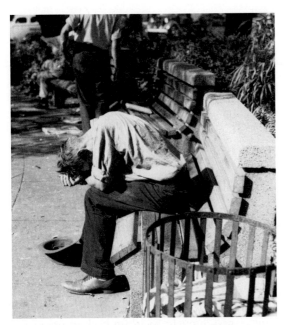

An Unemployed Youth Joblessness was frightening and humiliating. Brought up to believe that if you worked hard, you got ahead, the unemployed had difficulty seeing failure to find work as anything other than personal failure. Many slipped into despair and depression. We can only imagine this young man's story. Utterly alone, sitting on a bench that might be his bed, his hat on the ground and his head in his hands, he looks emotionally battered and perhaps defeated. Whether he found work, joined the throngs of beggars and panhandlers on the streets, or cast his lot with the army of hoboes who rode the rails looking for something better is unknown. Library of Congress.

electricity, or running water. They subsisted—just barely—on salt pork, cornmeal, molasses, beans, peas, and whatever they could hunt or fish. All the diseases of dietary and vitamin deficiencies wracked them. When economist John Maynard Keynes was asked whether anything like this degradation had existed before, he replied, "Yes, it was called the Dark Ages and it lasted four hundred years."

There was no federal assistance to meet this human catastrophe, only a patchwork of strapped charities and destitute state and local agencies. For a family of four without any income, the best the city of Philadelphia could do was provide $5.50 per week. That was not enough to live on but was still comparatively generous. New York City provided only $2.39 per week; and Detroit, devastated by the auto industry's failure, allotted 60 cents a week before the city ran out of money altogether.

The deepening crisis roused old fears and caused some Americans to look for scapegoats. Among the most thoroughly scapegoated were Mexican Americans. During the 1920s, cheap agricultural labor from Mexico flowed legally across the U.S.

border, welcomed by the large farmers. In the 1930s, however, the public denounced the newcomers as dangerous aliens who took jobs from Americans. Government officials, most prominently those in Los Angeles County, targeted Mexican residents for deportation regardless of citizenship status. As many as half a million Mexicans and Mexican Americans were deported or fled to Mexico.

The depression deeply affected the American family. Young people postponed marriage. When they did marry, they produced few children. White women, who generally worked in low-paying service areas, did not lose their jobs as often as men who worked in steel, automobile, and other heavy industries. Idle men suffered a loss of self-esteem. "Before the depression," one unemployed father reported, "I wore the pants in this family, and rightly so." Jobless, he lost "self-respect" and also "the respect of my children, and I am afraid that I am losing my wife." Employers discriminated against married women workers, but necessity continued to drive women into the marketplace. As a result, by 1940 some 25 percent more women were employed for wages than in 1930.

Denial and Escape President Hoover assured the American people that economic recovery was on its way. Contradicting the president's optimism were makeshift shantytowns, called "Hoovervilles," that sprang up on the edges of America's cities. Newspapers used as cover by those sleeping on the streets were "Hoover blankets." An empty pocket turned inside out was a "Hoover flag," and jackrabbits caught for food were "Hoover hogs." Bitter jokes circulated about the increasingly unpopular president. One told of Hoover asking for a nickel to telephone a friend. Flipping him a dime, an aide said, "Here, call them both."

While Hoover practiced denial, other Americans sought refuge from reality at the movies. Throughout the depression, between 60 million and 75 million people (nearly two-thirds of the nation) scraped together enough change to fill the movie palaces every week. Box office hits such as *Forty-second Street* and *Gold Diggers of 1933* capitalized on the hope that prosperity lay just around the corner. But a few filmmakers grappled with hard realities rather than escape them. *The Public Enemy* (1931) taught hard lessons about gangsters' ill-gotten gains. Indeed, under the new production code of 1930, designed to protect public morals, all movies had to find some way to show that crime did not pay.

Despite Hollywood's efforts to keep Americans on the right side of the law, crime increased. Out in the countryside, the plight of people who had lost their farms to bank foreclosures led to the romantic idea that bank robbers were only getting back what banks had stolen from the poor. Woody Guthrie, the populist folksinger from Oklahoma, captured the public's tolerance for outlaws in his tribute to a murderous bank robber with a choirboy face, "The Ballad of Pretty Boy Floyd":

> Yes, as through this world I ramble,
> I see lots of funny men,
> Some will rob you with a six-gun,
> Some will rob you with a pen.
> But as through your life you'll travel,
> Wherever you may roam,
> You won't never see an outlaw drive
> A family from their home.

Working-Class Militancy It was the nation's working class that bore the brunt of the economic collapse. In Chicago, workingwomen received less than twenty-five cents an hour. Sawmill workers in the West got a nickel. By 1931, William Green, head of the American Federation of Labor (AFL), had turned militant. "I warn the people who are exploiting the workers," he shouted, "that they can drive them only so far before they will turn on them and destroy them. They are taking no account of the history of nations in which governments have been overturned. Revolutions grow out of the depths of hunger."

The American people were slow to anger, but on March 7, 1932, several thousand unemployed autoworkers massed at the gates of Henry Ford's River Rouge factory in Dearborn, Michigan, to demand work. Pelted with rocks, Ford's private security forces responded with gunfire, killing four demonstrators. Forty thousand outraged citizens turned out for the unemployed men's funerals.

Farmers mounted uprisings of their own. When Congress refused to guarantee farm prices that would at least equal the cost of production, several thousand farmers created the National Farmers' Holiday Association in 1932, so named because its members planned to take a "holiday" from shipping crops to market. When some farmers persisted, militants barricaded roads and dumped thousands of gallons of milk in ditches. Farm militants also resorted to what they called "penny sales." When

Harlan County Coal Strike, 1931

banks foreclosed and put farms up for auction, neighbors warned others not to bid, bought the foreclosed property for a few pennies, and returned it to the bankrupt owners. Under this kind of pressure, some states suspended debts or reduced mortgages. In California in 1933, when landowners cut their laborers' already substandard wages, more than 50,000 farmworkers, most of them Mexicans, went on strike. Militancy won farmers little in the way of long-term solutions, but one individual observed that "the biggest and finest crop of revolutions you ever saw is sprouting all over the country right now."

The Great Depression—the massive failure of capitalism—brought socialism back to life in the United States and catapulted the Communist Party to its greatest size and influence in American history. Some 100,000 Americans—workers, intellectuals, college students—joined the Communist Party in the belief that only an overthrow of the capitalist system could save the victims of the depression. In 1931, the party, through its National Miners Union, moved into Harlan County, Kentucky, to support a strike by brutalized coal miners. The mine owners unleashed thugs against the strikers and eventually beat the miners down. But the Communist Party gained a reputation as the most dedicated and fearless champion of the union cause.

The left also led the fight against racism. While both major parties refused to challenge segregation in the South, the Socialist Party, led by Norman Thomas, attacked the system of sharecropping that left many African Americans in near servitude. The Communist Party also took action. When nine young black men in Scottsboro, Alabama (the **Scottsboro Boys**), were arrested on trumped-up rape charges in 1931, a team of lawyers sent by the party saved the defendants from the electric chair.

Radicals on the left often sparked action, but protests by moderate workers and farmers occurred on a far greater scale. Breadlines, soup kitchens, foreclosures, unemployment, and cold despair drove patriotic men and women to question American capitalism. "I am as conservative as any man could be," a Wisconsin farmer explained, "but any economic system that has in its power to set me and my wife in the streets, at my age—what can I see but red?"

Q: **How did the depression reshape American politics?**

"Scottsboro Boys" Nine black youths, ranging in age from thirteen to twenty-one, stand in front of rifle-bearing National Guard troops called up by Alabama governor B. M. Miller, who feared a mob lynching after two white women accused the nine of rape in March 1931. In less than two weeks, an all-white jury heard flimsy evidence, convicted the nine of rape, and sentenced them to death. Although none was executed, all nine spent years in jail. Eventually, the state dropped the charges against the youngest four and granted paroles to the others. The last "Scottsboro Boy" left jail in 1950.
© Bettmann/Corbis.

Conclusion: Dazzle and Despair

In the aftermath of World War I, America turned its back on progressive crusades and embraced conservative Republican politics, the growing influence of corporate leaders, and business values. Changes in the nation's economy—Henry Ford's automobile revolution, advertising, mass production—propelled fundamental change throughout society. Living standards rose, economic opportunity increased, and Americans threw themselves into private pleasures—gobbling up the latest household goods and fashions, attending baseball and football games and boxing matches, gathering around the radio, and going to the movies. As big cities came to dominate American life, the culture of youth and flappers became the leading edge of what one observer called a "revolution in manners and morals." At home in Harlem and abroad in Paris, American literature, art, and music flourished.

For many Americans, however, none of the glamour and vitality had much meaning. Instead of seeking thrills at speakeasies, plunging into speculation on Wall Street, or escaping abroad, the vast majority struggled to earn a decent living. Blue-collar America did not participate fully in white-collar prosperity. Rural America was almost entirely left out of the Roaring Twenties. Country folk, deeply suspicious and profoundly discontented, championed

prohibition, revived the Klan, attacked immigration, and defended old-time Protestant religion.

Just as the dazzle of the Roaring Twenties hid deep divisions in society, extravagant prosperity masked structural flaws in the economy. The crash of 1929 and the depression that followed starkly revealed the economy's crises of international trade and consumption. Hard times swept high living off the front pages of the nation's newspapers. Different images emerged: hoboes hopping freight trains, strikers confronting police, malnourished sharecroppers staring blankly into the distance, empty apartment buildings alongside cardboard shantytowns, and mountains of food rotting in the sun while guards with shotguns chased away the hungry.

The depression hurt everyone, but the poor were hurt most. As farmers and workers sank into aching hardship, businessmen rallied around Herbert Hoover to proclaim that private enterprise would get the country moving again. But things fell apart, and Hoover faced increasingly radical opposition. Membership in the Socialist and Communist parties surged, and more and more Americans contemplated desperate measures. By 1932, the depression had nearly brought the nation to its knees. America faced its greatest crisis since the Civil War, and citizens demanded new leaders who would save them from the "Hoover Depression."

Reviewing the Chapter

★ KEY TERMS

Explain each term's significance

WHO

Henry Ford (p. 569)

Warren Gamaliel Harding (p. 571)

Calvin Coolidge (p. 571)

Sigmund Freud (p. 575)

Marcus Garvey (p. 577)

Charles Lindbergh (p. 579)

Nicola Sacco and Bartolomeo Vanzetti (p. 583)

Alfred E. Smith (p. 585)

Herbert Hoover (p. 585)

Scottsboro Boys (p. 590)

WHAT

Five-Power Naval Treaty of 1922 (p. 572)

Kellogg-Briand pact (p. 572)

Dawes Plan (p. 572)

mass production (p. 573)

welfare capitalism (p. 573)

installment buying (p. 575)

prohibition (p. 575)

new woman (p. 576)

New Negro (p. 577)

Harlem Renaissance (p. 577)

Lost Generation (p. 581)

Johnson-Reid Act (p. 582)

Ku Klux Klan (p. 583)

Scopes trial (p. 584)

Reconstruction Finance Corporation (RFC) (p. 587)

trickle-down economics (p. 587)

FOR PRACTICE QUIZZES AND OTHER STUDY TOOLS, see the Online Study Guide at **bedfordstmartins.com/roarkcompact**.

★ REVIEW QUESTIONS Q:

Use key terms and dates to support your answer

1. How did the spread of the automobile transform the United States? (pp. 570–75)

2. How did the new freedoms of the 1920s challenge older conceptions of gender and race? (pp. 575–82)

3. Why did the relationship between urban and rural America deteriorate in the 1920s? (pp. 582–85)

4. Why did the American economy collapse in 1929? (pp. 585–88)

5. How did the depression reshape American politics? (pp. 588–90)

★ MAKING CONNECTIONS

Draw on key terms, timeline, and review questions

1. In the 1920s, Americans' wariness of the concentration of power in the hands of industrial capitalists gave way to unrestrained confidence in American business. What drove this shift in popular opinion? How did it influence Republicans' approach to governance and the development of the American economy in the 1920s?

2. Americans' encounters with the wealth and increased personal freedom characteristic of the 1920s varied greatly. Discuss the impact such variation had on Americans' responses to new circumstances. Why did some embrace the era's changes, while others resisted them? Ground your answer in a discussion of specific political, legal, or cultural conflicts.

3. How did shifting government policy contribute to both the boom of the 1920s and the bust of 1929? In your answer, consider the part domestic and international policy played in these developments, including taxation, tariffs, and international banking.

4. The Great Depression plunged the nation into a profound crisis with staggering personal and national costs. How did Americans attempt to lessen the impact of these circumstances? In your answer, discuss and compare the responses of individual Americans and the federal government.

★ SUGGESTED READINGS

Kristi Anderson, *After Suffrage: Women in Partisan and Electoral Politics before the New Deal* (1996). A thoughtful evaluation of the political impact of the Nineteenth Amendment.

Kevin Boyle, *Arc of Justice: A Saga of Race, Civil Rights, and Murder in the Jazz Age* (2004). The moving story of Dr. Ossian Sweet's struggle to get and keep a home of his own.

Douglas Brinkley, *Wheels for the World: Henry Ford, His Company, and a Century of Progress, 1903–2003* (2003). A lively account of Henry Ford and the Ford Motor Company.

Roger Daniels, *Guarding the Golden Door: American Immigration Policy and Immigrants since 1882* (2004). A probing investigation of changing American attitudes and policies toward immigration.

Steven Fraser, *Every Man a Speculator: A History of Wall Street in American Life* (2006). A fascinating exploration of the nation's evolving perceptions of the stock market.

Nancy MacLean, *Behind the Mask of Chivalry: The Making of the Second Ku Klux Klan* (1994). A perceptive analysis of the second Klan that focuses particularly on the role of women.

FOR MORE BOOKS ABOUT TOPICS IN THIS CHAPTER, see the Online Bibliography at **bedfordstmartins.com/roarkcompact**.

FOR ADDITIONAL FIRSTHAND ACCOUNTS OF THIS PERIOD, see Chapter 23 in Michael Johnson, ed., *Reading the American Past*, Fourth Edition.

FOR WEB SITES, IMAGES, AND DOCUMENTS RELATED TO TOPICS AND PLACES IN THIS CHAPTER, visit Make History at **bedfordstmartins.com/roarkcompact**.

★ TIMELINE

1920
- Eighteenth Amendment goes into effect.
- Nineteenth Amendment ratified.
- Republican Warren G. Harding elected president.

1921
- Sheppard-Towner Act.
- Congress restricts immigration.

1922
- Fordney-McCumber tariff.
- Five-Power Naval Treaty.

1923
- Equal Rights Amendment defeated in Congress.
- Harding dies; Vice President Calvin Coolidge becomes president.

1924
- Dawes Plan.
- Coolidge elected president.
- Johnson-Reid Act.

1925
- Scopes trial.

1927
- Charles Lindbergh flies nonstop across the Atlantic.
- Nicola Sacco and Bartolomeo Vanzetti executed.

1928
- Kellogg-Briand pact.
- Republican Herbert Hoover elected president.

1929
- St. Valentine's Day murders.
- Farm Board created.
- Stock market collapses.

1930
- Congress authorizes $420 million for public works projects.
- Hawley-Smoot tariff.

1931
- Scottsboro Boys arrested.
- Harlan County, Kentucky, coal strike.

1932
- River Rouge factory demonstration.
- Reconstruction Finance Corporation established.
- National Farmers' Holiday Association formed.

FRANKLIN ROOSEVELT'S MICROPHONE
President Roosevelt used this microphone to broadcast his famous fireside chats explaining New Deal programs to ordinary Americans. The chats traveled on airwaves into homes throughout the nation, reassuring listeners that Washington cared about the suffering the Great Depression was spreading across the land. Shortly after the first chat in March 1933, a New Yorker, "a citizen of little or no consequence" as he called himself, wrote to the White House in gratitude for "the President's broadcast. I felt that he walked into my home, sat down and in plain and forceful language explained to me how he was tackling the job I and my fellow citizens gave him. . . . Such forceful, direct and honest action commands the respect of all Americans, it is certainly deserving of it." National Museum of American History, Smithsonian Institution, Behring Center.

The New Deal Experiment

1932–1939

IN THE DEPTHS OF THE GREAT DEPRESSION, a Pennsylvania mother with three small children appealed to the Hoover administration for help for her husband, "who is a world war Veteran and saw active service in the trenches, became desperate and applied for Compensation or a pension from the Government and was turned down." With a weekly income of only $15.60, she and her family were suffering. There ought to be enough, she declared, "to pay all world war veterans a pension . . . and there by relieve a lot of suffering, and banish resentment that causes Rebellions and Bolshevism."

This mother's plea echoed in the demands of tens of thousands of World War I veterans who gathered in Washington, D.C., during June and July 1932 to lobby for immediate payment of the pension (known as a "bonus"). The veterans came from every state and by nearly every means of transportation. They congregated in a huge camp on the outskirts of Washington. They included "a fair cross section" of the nation: immigrants and natives; whites, blacks, and Native Americans, a journalist reported. All of them, one observer wrote, were "down at the heel."

Calling themselves **Bonus Marchers** or the Bonus Army, the veterans hoped their numbers, solidarity, and poverty would persuade Congress to give them the bonus they had been promised in 1924: $1 for every day they had been in uniform and a bit extra for time served overseas. Instead of cash payments, Congress decided to hand out promissory notes that veterans could not convert to cash until 1945. Bonus Marchers condemned this "tombstone bonus," which would not be paid until many of them were dead.

The veterans had supporters in Congress but not in the White House. President Herbert Hoover opposed the payment of an expensive bonus that would require the government to go into debt. Hoover refused to meet with representatives of the Bonus Army, who, his press secretary charged, were "communists or bums." The House of Representatives, controlled by Democrats, voted to pay the promised bonus of $2.4 billion, but the Senate, dominated by Hoover's fellow Republicans, rejected the bonus. Upon hearing of their defeat in the Senate, the Bonus Marchers did not confirm Republican fears of a Communist mob but instead joined in singing "America" before slowly drifting back to their camp.

Attack on the Bonus Marchers Washington police, led by five hundred army soldiers commanded by General Douglas MacArthur, participated in the attack on the Bonus Marchers in July 1932. Soldiers lobbed tear gas grenades toward the marchers, quickly breaking up skirmishes like the one shown here, then advanced into the veterans' camp and torched it. At the head of the mounted cavalry attacking the veterans was George S. Patton, who became a famous general in World War II. MacArthur's chief aide was Dwight D. Eisenhower, who subsequently commanded the Allied assault on Nazi Germany and became president. Eisenhower recalled later that he "told that dumb son-of-a-bitch [MacArthur] he had no business going down there" to destroy the Bonus Marchers' camp in violation of Hoover's orders. Hoover, however, did not discipline MacArthur for his insubordination. National Archives.

FOR MORE HELP ANALYZING THIS IMAGE, see the visual activity for this chapter in the Online Study Guide at bedfordstmartins.com/roarkcompact.

While the Bonus Army hunkered down in shanties, Hoover feared that the disgruntled veterans would riot and spark uprisings throughout the country. He ordered General Douglas MacArthur to evict the Bonus Marchers from the city but not to invade their camp. On July 28, MacArthur led an attack force of five tanks and five hundred soldiers armed with loaded weapons and fixed bayonets through the streets of Washington. Exceeding Hoover's orders, MacArthur pushed the Bonus Marchers back into their camp, where his soldiers torched the veterans' humble dwellings. While their camp burned, the Bonus Marchers raced away. MacArthur boasted that without his attack on the veterans, "the institutions of our Government would have been severely threatened."

MacArthur's expulsion of the Bonus Army undermined public support for the beleaguered, fearful Hoover. When the Democrats' recently nominated presidential candidate, Franklin Delano Roosevelt, heard about the attack, he correctly predicted that it "will elect me." Voters rejected Hoover, who seemed unsympathetic to the suffering caused by the Great Depression. In Roosevelt's inaugural address in March 1933, barely seven months after the expulsion of the Bonus Army, he proclaimed, "The only thing we have to fear is fear itself." Instead of succumbing to fear and suspicion, Roosevelt said, Americans should roll up their sleeves and find some way out of their present difficulties. Roosevelt's confidence that the government could help citizens energized New Deal policies and his presidency, the longest in American history.

When several thousand veterans reassembled in Washington to lobby again for the bonus a few months after Roosevelt's inauguration, the new president's hospitality contrasted with Hoover's hostility. Roosevelt arranged for the veterans to be housed in abandoned military barracks and fed at government expense. He invited a delegation to the White House, where he chatted casually with them, explaining that he could not support the bonus because he considered it too expensive, although he was determined to help them and other victims of the depression. And, to the veterans' surprise and delight, Eleanor Roosevelt slogged through rain and mud to talk personally with them, to express her sympathy, and to lead them in singing their favorite songs. One veteran remarked, "Hoover sent the Army; Roosevelt sent his wife."

Unlike the Bonus Marchers, the tens of millions of other Americans suffering from the Great Depression did not flock to Washington to lobby the government. But like the Bonus Marchers, they appreciated Roosevelt's optimism and expressions of concern. Even more, they welcomed government help from Roosevelt's New Deal initiatives to provide relief for the needy, to speed economic recovery, and to reform basic economic and governmental institutions. Roosevelt's New Deal elicited bitter opposition from critics on the right and left and failed to satisfy fully its own goals of relief, recovery, and reform. But within the Democratic Party, the New Deal energized a powerful political coalition that helped millions of Americans withstand the privations of the Great Depression. In the process, the federal government became a major presence in the daily lives of most American citizens. ★

Franklin D. Roosevelt: A Patrician in Government

Unlike the millions of impoverished Americans, Franklin Roosevelt came from a wealthy and privileged background that contributed to his optimism, self-confidence, and vitality. He constantly drew upon these personal qualities in his political career to bridge the economic, social, and cultural chasm that separated him from the struggles of ordinary people. During the twelve years he served as president (1933–1945), many elites came to hate him as a traitor to his class, while millions more Americans, especially the hard-working poor and dispossessed, revered him because he cared about them and their problems.

The Making of a Politician Born in 1882, **Franklin Delano Roosevelt** grew up on his father's leafy estate at Hyde Park on the Hudson River, north of New York City. Roosevelt was steeped at home and school in high-minded doctrines of public service and Christian duty to help the poor and weak. He prepared for a career in politics, hoping to follow in the political footsteps of his fifth cousin, Theodore Roosevelt.

Unlike cousin Teddy, Franklin Roosevelt sought his political fortune in the Democratic Party. In 1920, he catapulted to the second spot on the national Democratic ticket as the vice presidential candidate of presidential nominee James M. Cox. Although Cox lost the election (see chapter 22), Roosevelt's energetic campaigning convinced Democratic leaders that he had a bright future in national politics.

In the summer of 1921, at the age of thirty-nine, Roosevelt became infected with the polio virus, which paralyzed both his legs. For the rest of his life, he wore heavy steel braces, and he could walk a few steps only by leaning on another person. Tireless physical therapy helped him regain his vitality and intense desire for high political office. But he recaptured his political momentum mostly from a sitting position, although he carefully avoided being photographed in the wheelchair he used routinely.

After his polio attack, Roosevelt frequented a polio therapy facility at Warm Springs, Georgia. There, he combined the health benefits of the soothing waters with political overtures to southern Democrats, which helped make him a rare political creature: a New Yorker from the Democratic Party's urban and immigrant wing with whom whites from the Democratic Party's entrenched southern wing felt comfortable.

By 1928, Roosevelt had recovered sufficiently to campaign to become governor of New York, and he squeaked out a victory. As governor of the nation's most populous state, Roosevelt showcased his leadership and his suitability for a presidential campaign of his own. His activist policies as governor became a dress rehearsal for his presidency.

> Roosevelt proclaimed, "To these unfortunate citizens, aid must be extended by governments. . . . [No one should go] unfed, unclothed, or unsheltered."

Governor Roosevelt believed that government should intervene to protect citizens from economic hardships rather than do nothing but wait for the law of supply and demand to improve the economy. According to the laissez-faire views of

Roosevelt's Common Touch In his reelection as governor of New York in 1930, Franklin Roosevelt boosted his vote total by 700,000 over 1928, and he became the first Democratic candidate for governor to win the vote outside New York City. Sensing that his presentation of himself as a good neighbor was responsible for much of his popularity, Roosevelt arranged to have a friendly chat outside the polls in his hometown of Hyde Park with working-class voter Ruben Appel. In this photograph, Appel seems unaware that Roosevelt's standing was itself a feat of stagecraft. His legs rendered useless by polio, Roosevelt could remain upright only by using the strength he had developed in his arms and shoulders to prop himself up on his cane. Rare photos like this and a taboo against showing Roosevelt in his wheelchair kept the public from thinking of Roosevelt as a "cripple" and unfit for office, or in many cases from even realizing that he was disabled. Franklin D. Roosevelt Library.

many conservatives—especially Republicans, but also numerous Democrats—the depression simply represented market forces separating strong survivors from weak losers. Unlike Roosevelt, conservatives believed that government help for the needy sapped individual initiative and impeded the self-correcting forces of the market by rewarding people for losing the economic struggle to survive. Roosevelt lacked a full-fledged counterargument to these conservative claims, but he sympathized with the plight of poor people. "To these unfortunate citizens," he proclaimed, "aid must be extended by governments. . . . [No one should go] unfed, unclothed, or unsheltered." The highlight of Roosevelt's efforts to relieve the economic hardships of New Yorkers was the Temporary Emergency Relief Administration (TERA), created in 1931. It provided millions in aid for the poor, earning him the gratitude of needy New Yorkers and the attention of national politicians.

To his supporters, Roosevelt seemed to be a leader determined to attack the economic crisis without deviating from democracy—unlike the fascist parties gaining strength in Europe—or from capitalism—unlike Communists in power in the Soviet Union. Roosevelt's ideas about precisely how to revive the economy were vague. But his many supporters appreciated his energy, activism, and conviction that government should do something to help Americans climb out of the economic abyss, propelling him into the front ranks of the national Democratic Party.

The Election of 1932 Democrats knew that Hoover's unpopularity gave them a historic opportunity to recapture the White House in 1932. Since Abraham Lincoln's election, Republicans had occupied the White House three-fourths of the time, a trend Democrats hoped to reverse. Democrats, however, had to overcome warring factions that divided the party by region, religion, culture, and commitment to the status quo. Southern Democrats chaired powerful committees in Congress thanks to their continual reelection in a one-party South devoted to white supremacy. This southern, native-born, white, rural, Protestant, conservative wing of the Democratic Party found little common ground with the northern, immigrant, urban, disproportionately Catholic, liberal wing. Eastern-establishment Democratic dignitaries shared few goals with angry farmers and factory workers. Still, this unruly coalition managed to agree on Franklin Roosevelt as its presidential candidate.

In his acceptance speech, Roosevelt vowed to help "the forgotten man at the bottom of the pyramid"—such as the Bonus Marchers then in Washington—with "bold, persistent experimentation." Highlighting his differences with Hoover and the Republicans, he pledged "a new deal for the American people." Few details about what Roosevelt meant by "a new deal" emerged in the presidential campaign. He declared that "the people of America want more than anything else ... two things: work ... with all the moral and spiritual values that go with work ... and a reasonable measure of security ... for themselves and for their wives and children." Although Roosevelt never explained exactly how the federal government could provide either work or security, voters decided that whatever his new deal might be, it was better than reelecting Hoover.

Roosevelt won the 1932 presidential election in a historic landslide (Map 24.1). He received 57 percent of the nation's votes, the first time a Democrat had won a majority of the popular vote since 1852 (Map 24.2). Roosevelt's coattails swept Democrats into control of Congress by large margins. The popular mandate for change was loud and clear.

Roosevelt's victory represented the emergence of what came to be known as the **New Deal coalition**. Attracting support from farmers, factory workers, immigrants, city folk, African Americans, women, and progressive intellectuals, Roosevelt launched a realignment of the nation's political loyalties. The New Deal coalition dominated American politics throughout Roosevelt's presidency and remained powerful long after his death in 1945. United less by ideology or support for specific policies, voters

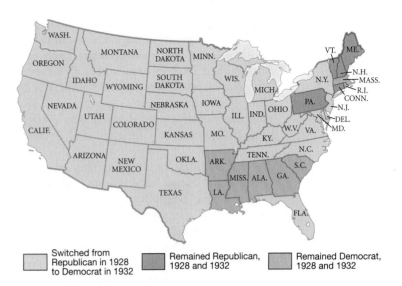

| Switched from Republican in 1928 to Democrat in 1932 | Remained Republican, 1928 and 1932 | Remained Democrat, 1928 and 1932 |

MAP 24.2 Electoral Shift, 1928–1932
The Democratic victory in 1932 signaled the rise of a New Deal coalition within which women and minorities, many of them new voters, made the Democrats the majority party for the first time in the twentieth century.

in the New Deal coalition instead expressed faith in Roosevelt's promise of a government that would, somehow, change things for the better. Nobody, including Roosevelt, knew exactly what the New Deal would change or whether the changes would revive the nation's ailing economy and improve Americans' lives. But Roosevelt and many others knew that the future of American capitalism and democracy was at stake.

Q: Why did Franklin D. Roosevelt win the 1932 presidential election by such a large margin?

Launching the New Deal

At noon on March 4, 1933, Americans gathered around their radios to hear the inaugural address of the newly elected president. Roosevelt began by asserting his "firm belief that the only thing we have to fear is fear itself—nameless, unreasoning, unjustified terror which paralyzes needed efforts to convert retreat into advance." He promised "direct, vigorous action," and the first months of his administration, termed "the Hundred Days," fulfilled that promise in a whirlwind of government initiatives that launched the New Deal.

Roosevelt and his advisers had three interrelated objectives: to provide relief to the destitute, especially the one out of four Americans who were unemployed; to foster the economic recovery of farms and businesses, thereby creating jobs and

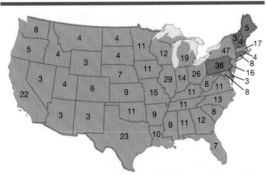

Candidate	Electoral Vote	Popular Vote	Percent of Popular Vote
Franklin D. Roosevelt (Democrat)	472	22,821,857	57.4
Herbert C. Hoover (Republican)	59	15,761,841	39.7
Norman Thomas (Socialist)	0	881,951	2.2
William Z. Foster (Communist)	0	102,991	0.3

MAP 24.1 The Election of 1932

reducing the need for relief; and to reform the government and economy in ways that would reduce the risk of devastating consequences in future economic slumps. The New Deal never fully achieved these goals of relief, recovery, and reform. But by aiming for them, Roosevelt's experimental programs enormously expanded government's role in the nation's economy and society.

The New Dealers To design and implement the New Deal, Roosevelt needed ideas and people. He convened a "Brains Trust" of economists and other leaders to offer suggestions and advice about the problems facing the nation. Among the most important reformers to join the Roosevelt administration were two veterans of Roosevelt's New York governorship: **Harry Hopkins** and **Frances Perkins**. Hopkins, a social worker, administered New Deal relief efforts and served as one of the president's loyal confidants. Perkins, who had extensive experience trying to improve working conditions in shops and factories, served as secretary of labor, making her the first woman cabinet member in American history.

No New Dealers were more important than the president and his wife, Eleanor. The gregarious president radiated charm and good cheer, giving the New Deal's bureaucratic regulations a benevolent human face. **Eleanor Roosevelt** became the New Deal's unofficial ambassador. She served, she said, as "the eyes and ears of the New Deal," traveling throughout the nation meeting Americans of all colors and creeds in church basements, town halls, and front parlors. As Roosevelt's programs swung into action, the millions of beneficiaries of the New Deal became grassroots New Dealers who expressed their appreciation by voting Democratic on election day. In this way, the New Deal created a durable political coalition of Democrats that reelected Roosevelt in 1936, 1940, and 1944.

As Roosevelt and his advisers developed plans to meet the economic emergency, their watchwords were *action, experiment,* and *improvise.* Without a sharply defined template for how to provide relief, recovery, and reform, they moved from ideas to policies as quickly as possible, hoping to identify ways to help people and to boost the economy. Four guiding ideas shaped their policies.

First, Roosevelt and his advisers sought capitalist solutions to the economic crisis. They believed that the depression had resulted from basic imbalances in the nation's capitalist economy—imbalances they wanted to correct. They had no desire to eliminate private property or impose socialist programs, such as public ownership of productive resources. Instead, they hoped to save the capitalist economy by remedying its flaws.

Second, Roosevelt's Brains Trust persuaded him that the greatest flaw of America's capitalist economy was underconsumption, the root cause of the current economic paralysis. Underconsumption, New Dealers argued, resulted from the gigantic productive success of capitalism. Factories and farms produced more than they could sell to consumers, causing factories to lay off workers and farmers to lose money on bumper crops. Workers without wages and farmers without profits shrank consumption and choked the economy. Somehow, the balance between consumption and production needed to be restored.

Third, New Dealers believed that the immense size and economic power of American corporations needed to be counterbalanced by government and by organization among workers and small producers. Unlike progressive trustbusters, New Dealers did not seek to splinter big businesses. Huge businesses had developed for good economic reasons and were here to stay. Roosevelt and his advisers hoped to counterbalance big economic institutions with government programs focused on protecting individuals and the public interest.

Fourth, New Dealers felt that government must somehow moderate the imbalance of wealth created by American capitalism. Wealth concentrated in a few hands reduced consumption by most Americans and thereby contributed to the current economic gridlock. In the long run, government needed to find a way to permit ordinary working people to share more fully in the fruits of the economy. In the short term, New Dealers sought to lend a helping hand to poor people who suffered from the maldistribution of wealth.

Banking and Finance Reform Roosevelt wasted no time making good on his inaugural pledge for "action now." As he took the oath of office on March 4, the nation's banking system was on the brink of collapse. Roosevelt immediately declared a four-day "bank holiday" to devise a plan to shore up banks and restore depositors' confidence. Working round the clock, New Dealers drafted the Emergency Banking Act, which gave the secretary of the treasury the power to decide which banks could be safely reopened and to release funds from the Reconstruction Finance Corporation (RFC) to bolster banks' assets. To secure the confidence of depositors, Congress passed the Glass-Steagall Banking Act, setting up the **Federal Deposit Insurance Corporation (FDIC)**, which guaranteed bank customers that the federal government would reimburse them for deposits if their banks failed.

On Sunday night, March 12, while the banks were still closed, Roosevelt broadcast the first of

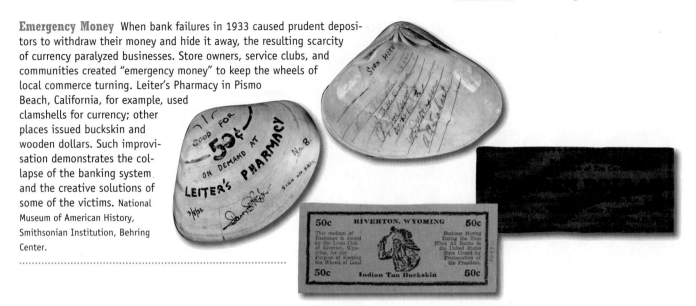

Emergency Money When bank failures in 1933 caused prudent depositors to withdraw their money and hide it away, the resulting scarcity of currency paralyzed businesses. Store owners, service clubs, and communities created "emergency money" to keep the wheels of local commerce turning. Leiter's Pharmacy in Pismo Beach, California, for example, used clamshells for currency; other places issued buckskin and wooden dollars. Such improvisation demonstrates the collapse of the banking system and the creative solutions of some of the victims. National Museum of American History, Smithsonian Institution, Behring Center.

a series of **fireside chats**. Speaking in a friendly, informal manner, he explained the new banking legislation that, he said, made it "safer to keep your money in a reopened bank than under the mattress." With such plain talk, Roosevelt translated complex matters into common sense. This and subsequent fireside chats forged a direct connection—via radio waves—between Roosevelt and millions of Americans, a connection felt by a man from Paris, Texas, who wrote to Roosevelt, "You are the one & only President that ever helped a Working Class of People. . . . Please help us some way I Pray to God for relief."

The banking legislation and fireside chat worked. Within a few days, most of the nation's major banks reopened, and they remained solvent as reassured depositors switched funds from their mattresses to their bank accounts. Some radical critics of the New Deal believed that Roosevelt should have nationalized the banks and made them a cornerstone of economic planning by the federal government. Instead, these first New Deal measures propped up the private banking system with federal funds and subjected banks to federal regulation and oversight.

In his inaugural address, Roosevelt criticized financiers for their greed and incompetence. To prevent the fraud, corruption, and insider trading that had tainted Wall Street and contributed to the crash of 1929, Roosevelt pressed Congress to regulate the stock market. Legislation in 1934 created the Securities and Exchange Commission (SEC) to oversee financial markets by licensing investment dealers, monitoring all stock transactions, and requiring corporate officers to make full disclosures about their companies. To head the SEC, Roosevelt named an abrasive and ambitious Wall Street financier, Joseph P. Kennedy, who had a somewhat shady reputation for stock manipulation. Under Kennedy's leadership, the SEC helped a cleaned-up and regulated Wall Street to recover slowly, although the stock market stayed well below its frothy heights of the 1920s.

Relief and Conservation Programs Patching the nation's financial structure provided little relief for the hungry and unemployed. A poor man from Nebraska asked Eleanor Roosevelt "if the folk who was borned here in America . . . are this Forgotten Man, the President had in mind, [and] if we are this Forgotten Man then we are still Forgotten." Since its founding, the federal government had never assumed responsibility for needy people, except in moments of natural disaster or emergencies such as the Civil War. Instead, churches, private charities, county and municipal governments, and occasionally states assumed the burden of poor relief, usually with meager payments. The depression necessitated unprecedented federal relief efforts, according to Harry Hopkins and other New Dealers. As one New Yorker who still had a job wrote the government, "We work, ten hours a day for six days. In the grime and dirt of a nation [for] . . . low pay [making us] . . . slaves—slaves of the depression!"

Hopkins galvanized support for the **Federal Emergency Relief Administration (FERA)**, which supported four million to five million households with $20 or $30 a month. FERA also created jobs for the unemployed on thousands of public works projects, organized by Hopkins into the Civil Works Administration (CWA), which put paychecks worth more than $800 million into the hands of previously jobless workers. Earning wages between forty and sixty cents an hour, laborers renovated schools, dug sewers, and rebuilt roads and bridges.

The most popular work relief program was the **Civilian Conservation Corps (CCC)**, established

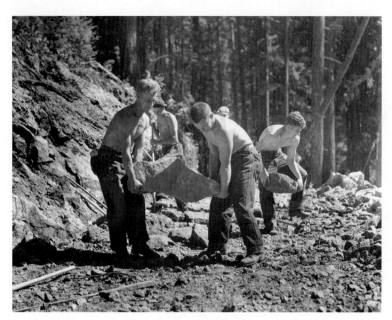

Civilian Conservation Corps Workers The Civilian Conservation Corps employed these young men in 1933 to build a truck trail in a remote region of Snoqualmie National Forest in the state of Washington. Instead of using machinery for the heavy construction work, the CCC intentionally used the muscles of working men in order to maximize employment. Although the truck trail provided emergency relief in the form of badly needed jobs, it contributed minimally to the New Deal goals of recovery and reform among the millions of Americans who could not readily leave their families for jobs in the wilderness. © Bettmann/Corbis.

in March 1933. It offered unemployed young men a chance to earn wages while working to conserve natural resources, a long-standing interest of Roosevelt. Women were excluded from working in the CCC until Eleanor Roosevelt demanded that a token number of young women be hired. By the end of the program in 1942, the three million CCC workers had checked soil erosion, tamed rivers, and planted more than two billion trees. CCC workers left a legacy of vast new recreation areas, along with roads that made those areas accessible to millions of Americans. Just as important, the CCC, CWA, and other work relief efforts replaced the stigma of welfare with the dignity of jobs. As one woman said about her husband's work relief job, "We aren't on relief anymore. My husband is working for the Government."

The New Deal also sought to harness natural resources for hydroelectric power. Continuing a project begun under Hoover, the New Deal completed the colossal Hoover Dam across the Colorado River in Nevada, providing not only electricity but also flood control and irrigation water for Arizona and southern California. Building the dam also provided badly needed jobs and wages for thousands of unemployed workers.

The New Deal's most ambitious and controversial natural resources development project was

the **Tennessee Valley Authority (TVA)**, created in May 1933 to build dams along the Tennessee River to supply impoverished rural communities with cheap electricity (Map 24.3). The TVA planned model towns for power station workers and new homes for the farmers who would benefit from electricity and flood control. The most ambitious example of New Deal enthusiasm for planning, the TVA set out to demonstrate that a partnership between the federal government and local residents could overcome the barriers of state governments and private enterprises to make efficient use of abundant natural resources and break the ancient cycle of poverty. The TVA never fully realized these utopian ends, but it improved the lives of millions in the region with electric power, flood protection, soil reclamation, and jobs.

New sources of hydroelectric power helped the New Deal bring the wonders of electricity to country folk, fulfilling an old progressive dream. When Roosevelt became president, 90 percent of rural Americans lacked electricity. Private electric companies refused to build transmission lines into the sparsely settled countryside when they had a profitable market in more accessible and densely populated urban areas. Beginning in 1935, the Rural Electrification Administration (REA) made low-cost loans available to local cooperatives for power plants and transmission lines to serve rural communities. Within ten years, the REA delivered electricity to nine out of ten farms, giving rural Americans access for the first time to modern conveniences that urban people had enjoyed for decades.

Agricultural Initiatives Farmers had been mired in a depression since the end of World War I. New Dealers diagnosed the farmers' plight as a classic case of overproduction and underconsumption. Following age-old practices, farmers tried to compensate for low crop prices by growing more crops, hoping to boost their earnings by selling larger quantities. Instead, producing more crops pushed prices lower still. Income among farm families plunged to $167 a year, barely one-tenth of the national average.

New Dealers sought to cut agricultural production, thereby raising crop prices and farmers' income. With more money in their pockets, farm families—who made up one-third of all Americans—would then buy more goods and lift consumption in the entire economy. To reduce production, the **Agricultural Adjustment Act (AAA)** authorized the "domestic allotment plan," which paid farmers *not* to grow crops. Individual farmers who agreed not to plant crops on a portion of their fields (their "allotment") would receive a government payment compensating them for the crops they did not plant. Since crops were already in the ground by the time the act was passed in May 1933, drastic measures were necessary to reduce production immediately. While millions of Americans went to bed hungry, farmers slaughtered millions of cattle, hogs, sheep, and other livestock and destroyed millions of acres of crops in order to qualify for their allotment payments.

With the formation of the Commodity Credit Corporation, the federal government allowed farmers to hold their harvested crops off the market and wait for a higher price. In the meantime, the government stored the crop and gave farmers a "commodity loan" based on a favorable price. In effect, commodity loans addressed the problem of underconsumption by making the federal government a major consumer of agricultural goods and reducing farmers' vulnerability to low prices. New Dealers also sponsored the Farm Credit Act (FCA) to provide long-term credit on mortgaged farm property, allowing debt-ridden farmers to avoid foreclosures that were driving thousands off their land.

Crop allotments, commodity loans, and mortgage credit made farmers major beneficiaries of the New Deal. Crop prices rose impressively, farm income jumped 50 percent by 1936, and FCA loans financed 40 percent of farm mortgage debt by the end of the decade. These gains were distributed fairly equally among farmers in the corn, hogs, and wheat region of the Midwest. In the South's cotton belt, however, landlords controlled the distribution of New Deal agricultural benefits and shamelessly rewarded themselves while denying benefits to many sharecroppers and tenant farmers—blacks and whites—by taking the land they worked out of production and assigning it to the allotment program. The president of the Oklahoma Tenant Farmers' Union explained that large farmers who got "Triple-A" payments often used the money to buy tractors and then "forced their tenants and [share]croppers off the land," causing these "Americans to be starved and dispossessed of their homes in our land of plenty."

Industrial Recovery Unlike farmers, industrialists cut production with the onset of the depression. But falling industrial production meant that millions of working people lost their jobs. Unlike farmers, most working people lived in towns and cities and needed jobs to eat. Mass unemployment

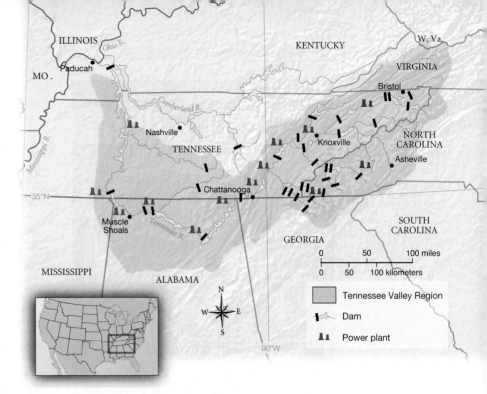

MAP 24.3 The Tennessee Valley Authority
The New Deal created the Tennessee Valley Authority to modernize a vast impoverished region with hydroelectric power dams and, at the same time, to reclaim eroded land and preserve old folkways.

READING THE MAP: How many states were affected by the TVA? How many miles of rivers (approximately) were affected?

CONNECTIONS: What kinds of benefits—economic as well as social and cultural—did TVA programs bring to the region? How might the lives of a poor farming family in Alabama or Tennessee have changed after the mid-1930s owing to these programs?

FOR MORE HELP ANALYZING THIS MAP, see the map activity for this chapter in the Online Study Guide at bedfordstmartins.com/roarkcompact.

also reduced consumer demand for industrial products, contributing to a downward spiral in both production and jobs, with no end in sight. Industries responded by reducing wages for employees who still had jobs, further reducing demand—a trend made worse by competition among industrial producers. New Dealers struggled to find a way to break this cycle of unemployment and underconsumption—a way consistent with corporate profits and capitalism.

The New Deal's National Industrial Recovery Act (NIRA) opted for a government-sponsored form of industrial self-government through the **National Recovery Administration (NRA)**, established in June 1933. The NRA encouraged industrialists in every part of the economy to agree on rules, known as codes, to define fair working conditions, to set prices, and to minimize competition. The idea behind codes was to stabilize existing industries and maintain their workforces while avoiding what both industrialists and New Dealers termed "destructive competition," which forced employers to cut wages and jobs. Industry after industry wrote elaborate codes addressing detailed features of production,

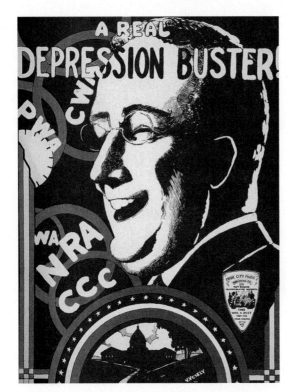

1936 Campaign Poster This campaign poster calls Roosevelt "A Real Depression Buster" and highlights his alphabet soup of New Deal agencies. Roosevelt's face was so well known that the poster does not even mention his name, the Democratic Party, or the New Deal. It exemplifies the political significance of Roosevelt's confident smile, perhaps the most potent symbol of the New Deal. Collection of Janice L. and David J. Frent.

pricing, and competition. In exchange for the relaxation of federal antitrust regulations that prohibited such business agreements, the participating businesses promised to recognize the right of working people to organize and engage in collective bargaining. To encourage consumers to patronize businesses participating in NRA codes, the New Deal mounted a public relations campaign that displayed the NRA's Blue Eagle in shop windows and on billboards throughout the nation.

New Dealers hoped that NRA codes would yield businesses with a social conscience, ensuring fair treatment of workers and consumers and promotion of the general economic welfare. Instead, NRA codes tended to strengthen conventional business practices. Large corporations wrote codes that served primarily their own interests rather than the needs of workers or the welfare of the national economy. (See "Seeking the American Promise," page 606.) The failure of codes to cover agricultural or domestic workers led one woman to complain to Roosevelt that the NRA "never mentioned the robbery of the Housewives" by the privations caused by the depression. Many

business leaders criticized NRA codes as heavy-handed government regulation of private enterprise. In reality, however, compliance with NRA codes was voluntary, and government enforcement efforts were weak to nonexistent. The NRA did little to reduce unemployment, raise consumption, or relieve the depression. In effect, it represented a peace offering to business leaders by Roosevelt and his advisers, conveying the message that the New Deal did not intend to wage war against profits or private enterprise. The peace offering failed, however. Most corporate leaders became active and often bitter opponents of Roosevelt and the New Deal.

Q: How did the New Dealers try to steer the nation toward recovery from the Great Depression?

Challenges to the New Deal

The first New Deal initiatives engendered fierce criticism and political opposition. From the right, Republicans and business people charged that New Deal programs were too radical, undermining private property, economic stability, and democracy. Critics on the left faulted the New Deal for its failure to allay the human suffering caused by the depression and for its timidity in attacking corporate power and greed.

Resistance to Business Reform New Deal programs rescued capitalism, but business leaders lambasted Roosevelt, even though their economic prospects improved more than those of most other Americans during the depression. Republicans and business leaders fulminated against New Deal efforts to regulate or reform what they considered their private enterprises. Although concentrated corporate power avoided reform, business leaders still conducted stridently anti–New Deal campaigns that expressed their resentment and fear of regulations, taxes, and unions. One opponent called the president "Stalin Delano Roosevelt" and insisted that the New Deal was really a "Raw Deal."

By 1935, two major business organizations, the National Association of Manufacturers and the Chamber of Commerce, had become openly anti–New Deal. Their critiques were amplified by the American Liberty League, founded in 1934, which blamed the New Deal for betraying basic constitutional guarantees of freedom and individualism. To them, the AAA was a "trend toward fascist control of agriculture," relief programs marked "the end of democracy," and the NRA was a plunge into the "quicksand of visionary experimentation."

Economists who favored rational planning in the public interest and labor leaders who sought to influence wages and working conditions by organizing unions attacked the New Deal from the left. In their view, the NRA stifled enterprise by permitting monopolistic practices. They pointed out that industrial trade associations twisted NRA codes to suit their aims, thwarted competition, and engaged in price gouging. Labor leaders especially resented the NRA's willingness to allow businesses to form company-controlled unions while blocking workers from organizing genuine grassroots unions to bargain for themselves.

The Supreme Court stepped into this cross fire of criticisms in May 1935 and declared that the NRA unconstitutionally conferred powers reserved to Congress on an administrative agency staffed by government appointees. The NRA codes soon lost the little authority they had. The failure of the NRA demonstrated the depth of many Americans' resistance to economic planning and the stubborn refusal of business leaders to yield to government regulations or reforms.

Casualties in the Countryside

The AAA weathered critical battering by champions of the old order better than the NRA. Allotment checks for keeping land fallow and crop prices high created loyalty among farmers with enough acreage to participate. As a white farmer in North Carolina declared, "I stand for the New Deal and Roosevelt . . . , the AAA . . . and crop control." Agricultural processors and distributors, however, criticized the AAA. They objected that the program reduced the volume of crop production—the only source of their profits—while they paid a tax on processed crops that funded the very program that disadvantaged them. In 1936, the Supreme Court agreed with their contention that they were victims of an illegal attempt to tax one group (processors and distributors) to enrich another (farmers). Down but not out, the AAA rebounded from the Supreme Court ruling by eliminating the offending tax and funding allotment payments from general government revenues.

Protests stirred, however, among those who did not qualify for allotments. The Southern Farm Tenants Union argued passionately that the AAA enriched large farmers and impoverished small farmers who rented rather than owned their land. One black sharecropper explained why only $75 a year from New Deal agricultural subsidies trickled down to her: "De landlord is landlord, de politicians

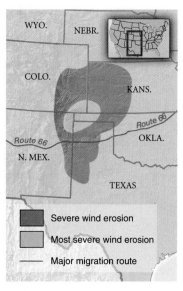

The Dust Bowl

is landlord, de judge is landlord, de shurf [sheriff] is landlord, ever'body is landlord, en we [sharecroppers] ain' got nothin'!" Such testimony showed that the AAA, like the NRA, tended to help most those who least needed help. Roosevelt's political dependence on southern Democrats caused him to avoid confronting such economic and racial inequities in the South's entrenched order.

Displaced tenants often joined the army of migrant workers who straggled across rural America during the 1930s, some to flee Great Plains dust storms. Many migrants came from Mexico to work Texas cotton, Michigan beans, Idaho sugar beets, and California crops of all kinds. But since the number of people willing to take agricultural jobs usually exceeded the number of jobs available, wages fell and native-born white migrants fought to reserve even these low-wage jobs for themselves. Hundreds of thousands of "Okies" streamed out of the Dust Bowl of Oklahoma, Kansas, Texas, and Colorado, where chronic drought and harmful agricultural practices blasted crops and hopes. Parched, poor, and windblown, Okies—like the Joad family immortalized in John Steinbeck's novel *The Grapes of Wrath* (1939)—migrated to the lush fields and orchards of California, congregating in labor camps and hoping to find work and a future. But migrant laborers seldom found steady or secure work. As one Okie said, "When they need us they call us migrants, and when we've picked their crop, we're bums and we got to get out."

Politics on the Fringes

Politically, the New Deal's staunchest opponents were in the Republican Party—organized, well heeled, mainstream, and determined to challenge Roosevelt at every turn. But the New Deal also faced challenges from the political fringes, fueled by the hardship of the depression and the hope for a cure-all.

Socialists and Communists accused the New Deal of being the handmaiden of business elites and of rescuing capitalism from its self-inflicted crisis. Socialist author **Upton Sinclair** ran for governor of California in 1934 on a plan he called "End Poverty in California." Sinclair demanded that the state take ownership of idle factories and unused land and give them to cooperatives of working people, a first step toward what he envisioned as

Textile Workers Strike for Better Wages and Working Conditions

"The 'Stretch-out System' is the cause of the whole trouble," a textile worker declared in 1930, echoing the sentiments of thousands of other mill workers. "There is hundreds of men walking the roads looking for work with wife and kids at home suffering," another mill hand wrote. "The stretch-out is what is wrong."

"The stretch-out" was the term coined by mill workers for the cost-cutting efficiencies implemented by mill owners that led to layoffs and poor working conditions for textile workers during the 1920s and 1930s. Textile manufacturers drastically increased the workload of their employees to cut labor costs and raise productivity. A mill worker who tended thirty looms in 1920 was responsible for ninety to one hundred looms by 1929—if she or he still had a job. "The reason so many people are out of jobs," one mill hand explained in 1933, "is because the mill owners have put two and three men's jobs on one man." A woman who had been working in cotton mills since she was twelve wrote to President Franklin Roosevelt in 1934, "We simply have to fly about our work . . . as if we were putting out a fire or fighting for our life." Layoffs of mill hands in the midst of the Great Depression contributed to further deterioration in wages and working conditions; so many people were desperate for work, no matter what the wage, that manufacturers were able to cut wages in half. If workers complained, mill owners responded, as one mill hand recalled, "If you don't like it there's a barefoot boy waitin' at the gate for your job." The result, as one textile worker wrote Roosevelt, was that "the ones who are Still at Work are Being Treated as Bad or Worse tha[n] the Slaves were in Slavery times."

Like so many other textile workers who faced the tough choice of working with the stretch-out or not working, Icy Norman was relieved to find work in 1929 at Burlington Mills in Piedmont Heights, North Carolina. Icy's father had worked in cotton mills in Virginia and North Carolina, but when he died in 1928, her mother took Icy and her two brothers from mill to mill to find work. For weeks, the family went "hunting jobs," Icy recalled. "We went everywhere. . . . You just couldn't get a job. Every freight train that you seen pass was loaded down with people going from town to town, hoboing." Icy lucked out at Burlington Mills because the supervisor happened to be a friend of her father. He hired Icy to wind thread onto bobbins for weaving. At first, she earned only 15 cents a day, but as she became more skilled, her wages rose to $10 a week, a little over 15 cents an hour. "After I got used to being in there," Icy recalled, "I really loved my work. . . . I got pleasure out of it and it made me happy to do my job." Icy's wages helped support her mother and her siblings. Like thousands of other mill hands, Icy and her family knew that even with the stretch-out, they were lucky to have a job. Still, as one mill worker wrote to Roosevelt, "every textile worker in the South would walk out of the mill today if they were not afraid of starvation."

In September 1934, hundreds of thousands of textile workers throughout the nation overcame their fears and walked out of the mills in the largest strike in American history. Strikers shut down mills from Maine to Alabama. More than half of all textile workers nationwide and about two-thirds of mill hands in the southern heartland of the textile industry walked out, including Icy Norman. Loosely organized by the Textile Workers' Union, the strikers demanded better working conditions and wages through enforcement of the textile code established by the New Deal's National Recovery Administration (NRA).

Like other NRA codes, the textile code was written and administered by the leading textile manufacturers. It provided for a maximum forty-hour workweek, a minimum weekly wage of $12 for southern mill hands and $13 for northern mill workers, and the right of workers to organize unions. Textile workers celebrated the passage of the NRA in June 1933. "It seemed too good to be true," one textile worker observed. A New Deal representative who investigated conditions in mill towns reported, "Every house I visited—mill worker or unemployed—had a picture of the President . . . [in] the place of honor over the mantel." Mill hands told the New Dealer, "We trust in the Supreme Being and Franklin Roosevelt. . . . [We] know that the President will see that [we] have work and proper wages; and that the stretch-out will be abandoned."

But their faith was misplaced, and the code was widely ignored. When workers complained that mill owners continued the stretch-out, cutting wages and firing any mill hands they suspected of union sympathies, their

★ **Striking Mill Workers Jeer Scabs** Textile workers on strike against the Cannon Textile Mills in North Carolina in September 1934 shouted taunts and curses at employees — known as "scabs" — who refused to honor the strikers' picket line. Notice the contrast between the clothing of the strikers and that of the scabs. What might explain this contrast? Although thousands of women like Icy Norman joined the strike, there are no women among the strikers shown here. What might account for the absence of women mill hands in this picket line? © Bettmann/Corbis.

grievances were heard by their bosses, the textile manu-facturers who headed the NRA code authority. In the year before the strike, the textile code authority received nearly 4,000 complaints, investigated 96, and resolved just 1 in favor of a worker. Manufacturers' blatant use of the textile code to bust unions and continue the stretch-out enraged many mill workers who believed they had the support of the New Deal to obtain better wages and working conditions through union organizations. Boiling with frustration over the failure of the textile code, more than 400,000 mill hands went on strike seeking to realize what they viewed as the unfulfilled promises of the New Deal's NRA by organizing a union to bargain with mill own-ers to improve wages and working conditions. But after three weeks and numerous violent confrontations with police and National Guardsmen, the combination of the mill owners' intransigence, the Textile Workers' Union's lack of resources, the mill workers' increasingly desperate financial situation, and Roosevelt's focus on the need for industrial peace to achieve economic recovery brought the strike to an end.

The mill hands achieved virtually nothing as a result of the strike. Mill owners continued to flout the textile codes,

the stretch-out continued without interruption, and work-ing conditions did not improve. Angry mill owners fired and blacklisted strike leaders, succeeding in their efforts to crush workers' organizations. After the strike, a union leader summarized the bitter lesson he had learned: "Many of us did not understand fully the role of the Government in the struggle between labor and industry . . . that the Government protects the strong, not the weak, and that it operates under pressure and yields to that group which is strong enough to assert itself over the other."

Icy Norman went back to work after the strike ended, and since she was not a union activist, she managed to keep her job until she retired in 1976, after forty-seven years at Burlington Mills. Despite working for the company longer than any other employee, Icy was forced to retire six months before she would have received benefits from a profit-sharing plan. "I begged them to let me work on, but they wouldn't," she recalled. "I give the best part of my life to the Burlington Industries. It kind of hurt me to think that as long as I stayed there and as faithful as I worked, that I didn't get none of that profit." Instead, the company gave her a free visit to a local hairdresser, a tour of the Burlington executive suite, and a farewell handshake.

Okie Family This tenant farmer worked land near Eagleton, Oklahoma, but became sick with pneumonia and lost his farm. The county he had lived in for fifteen years refused to give him Works Progress Administration benefits because he briefly left the county after recovering from his illness. Accompanied by his five children, he carted all his possessions in a toy wagon along a highway while looking for work. Such poor, jobless migrants were common along America's roads during the 1930s. Library of Congress.

a "Cooperative Commonwealth" that would put the needs of people above profits. Sinclair lost the election, ending the most serious socialist electoral challenge to the New Deal.

Some intellectuals and artists sought to advance the cause of more radical change by joining left-wing organizations, including the American Communist Party. At its high point in the 1930s, the party had about thirty thousand members, the large majority of them immigrants, especially Scandinavians in the upper Midwest and eastern European Jews in major eastern and midwestern cities. Individual Communists worked to organize labor unions, protect the civil rights of black people, and help the destitute, but the party preached the overthrow of "bourgeois democracy" and the destruction of capitalism in favor of Soviet-style communism. Such talk attracted few followers among the nation's millions of poor and unemployed. They wanted jobs and

economic security within American capitalism and democracy, not violent revolution to establish a dictatorship of the Communist Party.

More powerful radical challenges to the New Deal sprouted from homegrown roots. Many Americans felt overlooked by New Deal programs that concentrated on finance, agriculture, and industry but did little to produce jobs or aid the poor. The merciless reality of the depression also continued to erode the security of people who still had jobs but worried constantly that they, too, might be pushed into the legions of the unemployed and penniless.

A Catholic priest in Detroit named **Charles Coughlin** spoke to and for many worried Americans in his weekly radio broadcasts, which reached a nationwide audience of 40 million. Father Coughlin expressed outrage at the suffering and inequities that he blamed on Communists, bankers, and "predatory capitalists," who, he claimed, were mostly Jews.

In 1932, Coughlin applauded Roosevelt's election and declared, "The New Deal is Christ's deal." But Coughlin became frustrated by Roosevelt's refusal to grant him influence, turned against the New Deal, and in 1935 founded the National Union for Social Justice, or Union Party, to challenge Roosevelt in the 1936 presidential election.

Dr. **Francis Townsend** in Long Beach, California, also criticized the timidity of the New Deal. Angry that many of his retired patients lived in misery, Townsend proposed in 1934 the creation of the Old Age Revolving Pension, which would pay every American over age sixty a pension of $200 a month. To receive the pension, senior citizens had to agree to spend the entire amount within thirty days, thereby stimulating the economy. Townsend organized pension clubs with more than two million paying members and petitioned the federal government to enact his scheme. When the major political parties rebuffed his impractical plan, Townsend merged his forces with Coughlin's Union Party in time for the 1936 election.

A more formidable challenge to the New Deal came from the powerful southern wing of the Democratic Party. **Huey Long**, son of a backcountry Louisiana farmer, was elected governor of the state in 1928 with his slogan "Every man a king, but no one wears a crown." Unlike nearly all other southern white politicians who harped on white supremacy, Long championed the poor over the rich, country people over city folk, and the humble over elites. As governor, "the Kingfish"—as he liked to call himself—delivered on his promises to provide jobs and build roads, schools, and hospitals, but he also behaved ruthlessly to achieve his goals. Journalists routinely referred to him as the "dictator of Louisiana." Swaggering and bullying to get his way, Long delighted his supporters, who elected him to the U.S. Senate in 1932. Senator Long introduced a sweeping "soak the rich" tax bill that would outlaw personal incomes of more than $1 million and inheritances of more than $5 million. When the Senate rejected his proposal, Long decided to run for president, mobilizing more than five million Americans behind his "Share Our Wealth" plan. Like Townsend's scheme, Long's program promised far more than it could deliver. The Share Our Wealth campaign died when Long was assassinated in 1935, but his constituency and the wide appeal of a more equitable distribution of wealth persisted.

The challenges to the New Deal from both Republicans and more radical groups stirred Democrats to solidify their winning coalition. In the midterm congressional elections of 1934—normally a time when a seated president loses support—voters gave New Dealers a landslide victory. Democrats increased their majority in the House of Representatives and gained a two-thirds majority in the Senate.

Q: Why did groups at both ends of the political spectrum criticize the New Deal?

Toward a Welfare State

The popular mandate for the New Deal revealed by the congressional elections persuaded Roosevelt to press ahead with bold new efforts to achieve relief, recovery, and reform. Despite the initiatives of the Hundred Days, the depression still strangled the economy. Rumbles of discontent from Father Coughlin, Huey Long, and their supporters showed that New Deal programs had fallen far short of their goals. In 1935, Roosevelt capitalized on his congressional majorities to enact major new programs that signaled the emergence of an American welfare state.

Taken together, these New Deal efforts stretched a safety net under the lives of ordinary Americans. Although many citizens remained unprotected, New Deal programs helped millions with jobs, relief, and government support. Knitting together the safety net was the idea that when individual Americans suffered because of forces beyond their control, the federal government bore responsibility to support and protect them. The safety net of welfare programs tied the political loyalty of working people to the New Deal and the Democratic Party. As a North Carolina mill worker said, "Mr. Roosevelt is the only man we ever had in the White House who would understand that my boss is a sonofabitch."

Relief for the Unemployed First and foremost, Americans still needed jobs. Since the private economy left eight million people jobless by 1935, Roosevelt and his advisers launched a massive work relief program. Roosevelt believed that direct government handouts crippled recipients with "spiritual and moral disintegration . . . destructive to the human spirit." Jobs, in contrast, bolstered individuals' "self-respect, . . . self-confidence, . . . courage, and determination." With a congressional appropriation of nearly $5 billion—more than all government revenues in 1934—the New Deal created the **Works Progress Administration (WPA)** to give unemployed Americans government-funded jobs on public works projects. The WPA put millions of jobless citizens to work on roads, bridges, parks, public buildings, and more. In addition, Congress passed—over Roosevelt's veto—the bonus long sought by the

California Farmworkers Mural During the 1930s, New Deal agencies employed artists to adorn public buildings with thousands of murals illustrating the variety and vigor of American life. California-born Maxine Albro, one of the first woman muralists commissioned by the WPA, painted this mural, in San Francisco's Coit Tower, depicting farmworkers harvesting the bounty of California's fields. © Corbis. All Rights Reserved.

FOR MORE HELP ANALYZING THIS IMAGE, see the visual activity for this chapter in the Online Study Guide at bedfordstmartins.com/roarkcompact.

Bonus Marchers, giving veterans an average of $580 and further stimulating the economy.

By 1936, WPA funds provided jobs for 7 percent of the nation's labor force. In effect, the WPA made the federal government the employer of last resort, creating useful jobs when the capitalist economy failed to do so. In hiring, WPA officials tended to discriminate in favor of white men and against women and racial minorities. But by the time the WPA ended in 1943—because mobilization for World War II created full employment—it had made major contributions to both relief and recovery. Overall, WPA jobs put thirteen million men and women to work and gave them paychecks worth $10 billion. About three out of four WPA jobs involved construction and renovation of the nation's physical infrastructure. In addition, the WPA gave jobs to thousands of artists, musicians, actors, journalists, poets, and novelists. The WPA reached the most isolated corners of the nation, funding librarians and nurses on horseback to deliver books and health care to remote cabins in Appalachia. Throughout the nation, WPA projects displayed tangible evidence of the New Deal's commitment to public welfare.

Empowering Labor During the Great Depression, factory workers who managed to keep their jobs worried constantly about being laid off while their wages and working hours were cut. When workers tried to organize labor unions to protect themselves, municipal and state governments usually sided with employers. Since the Gilded Age, state and federal governments had been far more effective at busting unions than at busting trusts. The New Deal dramatically reversed the federal government's stance toward unions. With legislation and political support, the New Deal encouraged an unprecedented wave of union organizing among the nation's working people. When the head of the United Mine Workers, John L. Lewis, told coal miners that "the President wants you to join a union," he exaggerated only a little. New Dealers believed that unions would counterbalance the organized might of big corporations by defending working people, maintaining wages, and replacing the bloody violence that often accompanied strikes with economic peace and commercial stability.

Violent battles on the nation's streets and docks showed the determination of militant labor leaders to organize unions that would protect jobs as well as wages. In 1934, striking workers in Toledo, Minneapolis, San Francisco, and elsewhere were beaten and shot by police and the National Guard. In Congress, labor leaders lobbied for the National Labor Relations Act (NLRA), a bill sponsored by Senator Robert Wagner of New York that authorized the federal government to intervene in labor disputes and supervise the organization of labor unions. Justly considered a "Magna Carta for labor," the **Wagner Act**, as it came to be called, guaranteed industrial workers the right to organize unions, putting the might of federal law behind the appeals of labor leaders. The Wagner Act created the National Labor Relations Board (NLRB) to sponsor and oversee elections for union representation. If the majority of workers at a company voted for a union, the union became the sole bargaining agent for the entire workplace, and the employer was required to negotiate with the elected union leaders. Roosevelt signed the Wagner Act in July 1935, providing for the first time federal support for labor organization—the most important New Deal reform of the industrial order.

The achievements that flowed from the Wagner Act and renewed labor militancy were impressive. When Roosevelt became president in 1933, union membership—almost entirely composed of skilled workers in trade unions affiliated with the American Federation of Labor (AFL)—stood at three million, down by half since the end of World War I. With the support of the Wagner Act, union membership expanded almost fivefold, to fourteen million, by the time of Roosevelt's death in 1945. By then, 30 percent of the workforce was unionized, the highest union representation in American history.

Most of the new union members were factory workers and unskilled laborers, many of them immigrants, women, and African Americans. For decades, established AFL unions had no desire to organize factory and unskilled workers, who struggled along without unions. In 1935, under the aggressive leadership of the mine workers' John L. Lewis and the head of the Amalgamated Clothing Workers, Sidney Hillman, a coalition of unskilled workers formed the **Committee for Industrial Organization (CIO**; later the Congress of Industrial Organizations). The CIO, helped by the Wagner Act, mobilized organizing drives in major industries. The exceptional courage and organizing skill of labor militants earned the CIO the leadership role in the campaign to organize the bitterly anti-union automobile and steel industries.

The bloody struggle by the CIO-affiliated United Auto Workers (UAW) to organize workers at General Motors climaxed in January 1937. Striking workers occupied the main assembly plant in Flint, Michigan, in a **sit-down strike** that slashed the plant's production of 15,000 cars a week to a mere 150. Stymied, General Motors eventually surrendered and agreed to make the UAW the sole bargaining agent for all the company's workers and to refrain from interfering with union activity. Having subdued the auto industry's leading producer, the UAW expanded its campaign until, after much violence, the entire industry was unionized when the Ford Motor Company capitulated in 1941.

The CIO hoped to ride organizing success in auto plants to victory in the steel mills. But after unionizing the industry giant U.S. Steel, the CIO ran up against ruthless opposition from smaller steel firms. Following a police attack that killed ten strikers at Republic Steel outside Chicago in May 1937, the battered steelworkers halted their organizing campaign. In steel and other major industries, such as the stridently anti-union southern textile mills, organizing efforts stalled until after 1941, when military mobilization created labor shortages that gave workers greater bargaining power.

Social Security and Tax Reform The single most important feature of the New Deal's emerging welfare state was **Social Security**. An ambitious, far-reaching, and permanent reform, Social Security was designed to provide a modest income to relieve the poverty of elderly people. Prompted by the popular but impractical panaceas of Dr. Townsend, Father Coughlin, and Huey Long, Roosevelt became the first president to advocate protection for the elderly. He told

Your SOCIAL SECURITY ACCOUNT CARD

WHAT it is

WHAT you do with it

& WHY

SOCIAL SECURITY ACT
ACCOUNT NUMBER
944-03-9773
Sidney Pembroke Herbert
12-2-36

LEAVE THIS STUB ATTACHED TO FOLDER

TEAR OFF THIS CARD

FEDERAL SECURITY AGENCY
Social Security Administration
Washington, D.C.

Social Security Card The Social Security Act required each working American who participated in the system to register with the government and obtain a unique number—the "SSN" familiar to every citizen today—inscribed on an identity card, making benefits portable from one job and one state to another. For the first time in the nation's history, millions of ordinary citizens were numbered, registered, and identified by a government bureaucracy, creating a personal, individualized connection between people and the federal government. Administering the massive agency needed to collect, monitor, and regulate this information and distribute the benefits that flowed from it gave government jobs to tens of thousands, providing security for government workers as well as for Social Security beneficiaries. Picture Research Consultants & Archives.

Congress that "it is our plain duty to provide for that security upon which welfare depends . . . and undertake the great task of furthering the security of the citizen and his family through social insurance."

The political struggle for Social Security highlighted class differences among Americans. Support for the measure came from a coalition of advocacy groups for the elderly and the poor, traditional progressives, leftists, social workers, and labor unions. Arrayed against them were economic conservatives, including the American Liberty League, the National Association of Manufacturers, the Chamber of Commerce, and the American Medical Association. Enact the Social Security system, these conservatives and their representatives in the Republican Party warned, and the government will ruin private property, destroy initiative, and reduce proud individuals to spineless loafers.

The large New Deal majority in Congress passed the Social Security Act in August 1935. The act provided that tax contributions from workers and their employers would fund pensions for the elderly, giving contributing workers a personal stake in the system and making it politically invulnerable. When eligible workers reached retirement age, they were not subject to a means test to prove that they were needy. Instead, they had earned benefits based on their contributions and years of work. Social Security also created unemployment insurance that provided modest benefits for workers who lost their jobs.

Not all workers benefited from the Social Security Act. It excluded domestic and agricultural workers, thereby making ineligible about half of all African Americans and more than half of all employed women—about five million people in all. In addition, the law excluded workers employed by religious and nonprofit organizations, such as schools and hospitals, rendering ineligible even more working women and minorities.

In a bow to traditional beliefs about local governments' responsibility for public assistance, Social Security issued multimillion-dollar grants to the states to help support dependent children, public health services, and the blind. After the Supreme Court in 1937 upheld Social Security, the program was expanded to include benefits for dependent survivors of deceased recipients. Although the first Social Security check was not issued until 1940, the system gave millions of working people the assurance that when they became too old to work, they would receive a modest income from the federal government.

> **Bitter critics charged that the New Deal's NRA stood for "Negro Run Around" or "Negroes Ruined Again."**

Fervent opposition to Social Security struck New Dealers as evidence that the rich had learned little from the depression. Roosevelt looked for a way to redistribute wealth that would weaken conservative opposition, advance the cause of social equity, and defuse political challenges from Huey Long and Father Coughlin. In June 1935, as the Social Security Act was being debated, Roosevelt delivered a message to Congress outlining comprehensive tax reform. Charging that large fortunes put "great and undesirable concentration of control in [the hands of] relatively few individuals," Roosevelt urged a graduated tax on corporations, an inheritance tax, and an increase in maximum personal income taxes. Congress endorsed Roosevelt's basic principle by taxing those with higher incomes at a somewhat higher rate.

Neglected Americans and the New Deal The patchwork of New Deal reforms erected a two-tier welfare state. In the top tier, organized workers in major industries were the greatest beneficiaries of New Deal initiatives. In the bottom tier, millions of neglected Americans—women, children, and old folks, along with the unorganized, unskilled, uneducated, and unemployed—often fell through the New Deal safety net. Many working people remained more or less untouched by New Deal benefits. The average unemployment rate for the 1930s stayed high—17 percent. Workers in industries that resisted unions received little help from the Wagner Act or the WPA. Domestic workers—almost all of them women—and agricultural workers—many of them African, Hispanic, or Asian Americans—were neither unionized nor eligible for Social Security.

The New Deal neglected few citizens more than African Americans. About half of black Americans in cities were jobless. In the rural South, where the vast majority of African Americans lived, conditions were worse. New Deal agricultural policies such as the AAA favored landowners and often resulted in black sharecroppers and tenants being pushed off the land they farmed. Disfranchisement by intimidation and legal subterfuge prevented southern blacks from protesting their plight at the ballot box. Protesters risked vicious retaliation from local whites. After years of decline, lynching increased during the 1930s. In 1935, a riot in Harlem focused on white-owned businesses, dramatizing blacks' resentment and despair. Bitter critics charged that the New Deal's NRA stood for "Negro Run Around" or "Negroes Ruined Again."

Roosevelt responded to such criticisms with great caution, since New Deal reforms required the political support of powerful conservative, segregationist, southern white Democrats who would be alienated by programs that aided blacks. Stymied by the political clout of entrenched white racism, New Dealers still tried to attract political support from black leaders. Roosevelt's overtures to African Americans prompted northern black voters in the 1934 congressional elections to shift from the Republican to the Democratic Party, helping elect New Deal Democrats.

Eleanor Roosevelt sponsored the appointment of **Mary McLeod Bethune**—the energetic cofounder of the National Council of Negro Women—as head of the Division of Negro Affairs in the National Youth Administration. The highest-ranking black official in Roosevelt's administration,

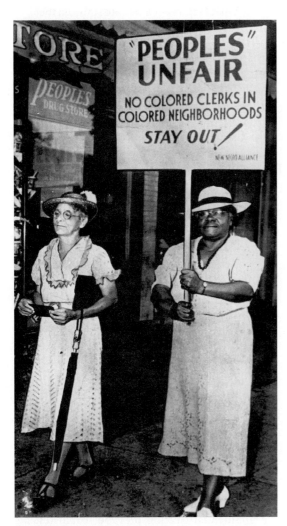

Mary McLeod Bethune At the urging of Eleanor Roosevelt, Mary McLeod Bethune, a southern educational and civil rights leader, became director of the National Youth Administration's Division of Negro Affairs. The first black woman to head a federal agency, Bethune used her position to promote social change. Here, Bethune takes her mission to the streets to protest the discriminatory hiring practices of the Peoples Drug Store chain in the nation's capital.
Moorland-Spingarn Research Center, Howard University.

Bethune used her position to guide a small number of black professionals and civil rights activists to posts within New Deal agencies. Nicknamed the "Black Cabinet," these men and women composed the first sizable representation of African Americans in white-collar posts in the federal government, and they ultimately helped about one in four African Americans get access to New Deal relief programs.

Despite these gains, by 1940 African Americans still suffered severe handicaps. Most of the thirteen million black workers toiled at low-paying menial jobs, unprotected by the New Deal safety net. Making a mockery of the "separate but equal" doctrine, segregated black schools had less money and worse facilities than white schools, and only 1 percent of black students earned college degrees. In southern states, there were no black police officers or judges and hardly any black lawyers, and vigilante violence against blacks went unpunished. For these problems of black Americans, the New Deal offered few remedies.

Hispanic Americans fared no better. About a million Mexican Americans lived in the United States in the 1930s, most of them first- or second-generation immigrants who worked crops throughout the West. During the depression, field workers saw their low wages plunge lower still to about a dime an hour. Ten thousand Mexican American pecan shellers in San Antonio, Texas, earned only a nickel an hour. To preserve scarce jobs for U.S. citizens, the federal government choked off immigration from Mexico, while state and local officials prohibited the employment of aliens on work relief projects and deported tens of thousands of Mexican Americans, many with their American-born children. Local white administrators of many New Deal programs throughout the West discriminated against Hispanics and other people of color. A New Deal study concluded that "the Mexican is . . . segregated from the rest of the community as effectively as the Negro . . . [by] poverty and low wages."

Asian Americans had similar experiences. Asian immigrants were still excluded from U.S. citizenship and in many states were not permitted to own land. By 1930, more than half of Japanese Americans had been born in the United States, but they were still liable to discrimination. One young Asian American expressed the frustration felt by many others: "I am a fruit-stand worker. I would much rather it were doctor or lawyer . . . but my aspirations [were] frustrated long ago by circumstances [and] I am only what I am, a professional carrot washer."

Native Americans also suffered neglect from New Deal agencies. As a group, they remained the poorest of the poor. Since the Dawes Act of 1887 (see chapter 17), the federal government had encouraged Native Americans to assimilate—to abandon their Indian identities and adopt the cultural norms of the majority society. Under the leadership of the New Deal's commissioner of Indian affairs, John Collier, the New Deal's **Indian Reorganization Act (IRA)** of 1934 largely reversed that policy. Collier claimed that "the most interesting and important fact about Indians" was that they "do not expect much, often they expect nothing at all; yet they are able to be happy." Given such views, the IRA provided little economic aid to Native Americans, but it did restore their right to own land communally and to have greater control over their own affairs. The IRA brought little immediate benefit to Native Americans and remained a divisive issue for decades, but it provided an important foundation for Indians' economic, cultural, and political resurgence a generation later.

The troubadour of working people, singer and songwriter Woody Guthrie, traveled the nation for eight years during the 1930s and heard other rambling men tell him "the story of their life," giving voice to experiences common among Americans neglected by the New Deal: "how the home went to pieces, how . . . the crops got to where they wouldn't bring nothing, work in factories would kill a dog . . . and—always, always [you] have to fight and argue and cuss and swear . . . to try to get a nickel more out of the rich bosses."

Q: **What features of a welfare state did the New Deal create and why?**

The New Deal from Victory to Deadlock

To accelerate the sputtering economic recovery, Roosevelt shifted the emphasis of the New Deal in the mid-1930s. Instead of seeking cooperation from conservative business leaders, he decided to rely on the growing New Deal coalition to enact reforms over the strident opposition of the Supreme Court, Republicans, and corporate interests.

Added to New Deal strength in farm states and big cities were some new allies on the left. Throughout Roosevelt's first term, socialists and Communists denounced the slow pace of change and accused the New Deal of failing to serve the interests of the workers who produced the nation's wealth. But in 1935, the Soviet Union, worried about the threat of fascism in Europe, instructed Communists throughout the world to join hands with non-Communist progressives in a "Popular Front" to advance the fortunes of the working class. With varying degrees of enthusiasm, many radicals switched from opposing the New Deal to supporting its relief programs and encouragement of labor unions.

The Election of 1936 Roosevelt believed that the presidential election of 1936 would test his leadership and progressive ideals. The depression still had a stranglehold on the economy. Conservative leaders believed that the New Deal's failure to lift the nation out of the depression indicated that Americans were ready for a change. Left-wing critics insisted that the New Deal had missed the opportunity to displace capitalism with a socialist economy and that voters would embrace candidates who recommended more radical remedies.

John Collier Meets with Navajo Representatives Commissioner of Indian Affairs John Collier receives a Navajo delegation protesting restrictions in the Indian Reorganization Act of 1934. The Navajos display a blanket made from the wool of their own sheep to protest limits on the number of sheep they could raise. Collier had crafted the act to revive Native American society by granting tribes an independent land base and many self-governing powers. However, his attempt to make the reservations economically viable through conservation measures, including restrictions on grass-devouring sheep, roused resistance by Indians who chose traditional ways of using resources. The tension between federal benevolence and Indian views of their own way of life has remained a painful issue. AP Images.

Republicans turned to the Kansas heartland to select Governor Alfred (Alf) Landon as their presidential nominee. A moderate who had supported some New Deal measures, Landon stressed mainstream Republican proposals to achieve a balanced federal budget and to ease the perils of illness and old age with old-fashioned neighborliness instead of faceless government bureaucracies such as Social Security.

Roosevelt believed the growing coalition of New Deal supporters would help him liberate the nation from a long era of privilege and wealth for a few and "economic slavery" for the rest. He triumphed spectacularly. He won 60.8 percent of the popular vote, making it the widest margin of victory in a presidential election to date. Third parties—including the Socialist and Communist parties—fell pitifully short of the support they expected and never again mounted a significant challenge to the New Deal. Congressional results were equally lopsided, with Democrats outnumbering Republicans more than three to one in both houses. In his inaugural address, Roosevelt pledged to use his mandate to help all citizens achieve a decent standard of living. He announced, "I see one third of a nation ill-housed, ill-clad, [and] ill-nourished," and he promised to devote his second term to alleviating their hardship.

Court Packing In the afterglow of his reelection triumph, Roosevelt pondered how to remove the remaining obstacles to New Deal reforms. He decided to target the Supreme Court. Laden with conservative justices appointed by Republican presidents, the Court had invalidated eleven New Deal measures as unconstitutional interferences with free enterprise. Now, Social Security, the Wagner Act, the Securities and Exchange Commission, and other New Deal innovations were about to be considered by justices.

To ensure that the Supreme Court's "horse and buggy" notions did not dismantle the New Deal, Roosevelt proposed a **court-packing** plan that added one new justice for each existing judge who had served for ten years and was over the age of seventy. In effect, the proposed law would give Roosevelt the power to pack the Court with up to six New Dealers who could outvote the elderly, conservative, Republican justices. But the president had not reckoned with Americans' deeply rooted deference to the independent authority of the Supreme Court. More than two-thirds of Americans believed that the Court should be free from political interference. Even New Deal supporters were disturbed by the "court-packing" scheme. The suggestion that individuals over age seventy had diminished mental capacity offended

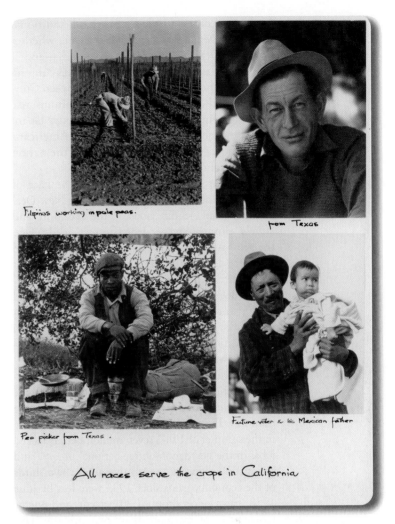

"All Races Serve the Crops in California" New Deal agencies dispatched dozens of photographers to document the lives of Americans during the 1930s. This page from the 1935 journal of New Deal photographer Dorothea Lange documents migrant workers from the Philippines, Texas, and Mexico whom she encountered in California fields. Library of Congress.

many elderly members of Congress, which defeated the bill in 1937.

Although Roosevelt's court-packing plan failed, Supreme Court justices got the message. After the furor abated, Chief Justice Charles Evans Hughes and fellow moderate Owen Roberts changed their views enough to keep the Court from invalidating the Wagner Act and Social Security. Then the most conservative of the elderly justices—the "four horsemen of reaction," one New Dealer called them—retired. Roosevelt eventually named eight justices to the Court—more than any other president, ultimately giving New Deal laws safe passage through the Court.

Reaction and Recession Emboldened by their defeat of the court-packing plan, Republicans and southern Democrats rallied around their common conservatism to obstruct additional reforms. Democrats' arguments over whether the New Deal needed to be expanded—and if so, how—undermined the consensus among reformers and sparked antagonism between Congress and the White House. The ominous rise of belligerent regimes in Germany, Italy, Japan, and elsewhere slowed reform as some Americans began to worry more about defending the nation than changing it.

Roosevelt himself favored slowing the pace of the New Deal. He believed that existing New Deal measures had steadily boosted the economy and largely eliminated the depression crisis. In fact, the gross national product in 1937 briefly equaled the 1929 level before dropping lower for the rest of the decade. Unemployment declined to 14 percent in 1937 but quickly spiked upward and stayed higher until 1940. Roosevelt's unwarranted optimism about the economic recovery persuaded him that additional deficit spending by the federal government was no longer necessary.

Roosevelt's optimism failed to consider the stubborn realities of unemployment and poverty, and the reduction in deficit spending reversed the improving economy. Even at the high-water mark of recovery in the summer of 1937, seven million people lacked jobs. In the next few months, national income and production slipped so steeply that almost two-thirds of the economic gains since 1933 were lost by June 1938. Farm prices dropped 20 percent, and unemployment rose by more than two million. This economic reversal hurt the New Deal politically. Conservatives argued that this recession proved that New Deal measures produced only an illusion of progress. The way to weather the recession was to tax and spend less and wait for the natural laws of supply and demand to restore prosperity. Many New Dealers insisted instead that the continuing depression demanded that Roosevelt revive federal spending and redouble efforts to stimulate the economy. In 1938, Congress heeded such pleas and enacted a massive new program of federal spending.

The recession scare of 1937–1938 taught the president the lesson that economic growth had to be carefully nurtured. The English economist John Maynard Keynes, in a theory that became known as **Keynesian economics**, argued in his influential work *The General Theory of Employment, Interest, and Money* (1936) that only government intervention could pump enough money into the economy to restore prosperity. Roosevelt never had the inclination or time to master Keynesian theory. But in a commonsense way, Roosevelt understood that escape from the depression required a plan for large-scale spending to alleviate distress and stimulate economic growth. (See "Global Comparison.")

The Last of the New Deal Reforms From the moment he was sworn in, Roosevelt sought to expand the powers of the presidency. He believed that the president needed more authority to meet emergencies such as the depression and to administer the sprawling federal bureaucracy. In September 1938, Congress passed the Administrative Reorganization Act, which gave Roosevelt (and future presidents) new influence over the bureaucracy. Combined with a Democratic majority in Congress, a now-friendly Supreme Court, and the revival of deficit spending, the newly empowered White House seemed to be in a good position to move ahead with a revitalized New Deal.

Resistance to further reform was also on the rise, however. Conservatives argued that the New Deal had pressed government centralization too far. Even the New Deal's friends became weary of one emergency program after another while economic woes continued to shadow New Deal achievements. By the midpoint of Roosevelt's second term, restive members of Congress balked at new initiatives. Clearly, the New Deal was losing momentum, but enough support remained for one last burst of reform.

Agriculture still had strong claims on New Deal attention in the face of drought, declining crop prices, and impoverished sharecroppers and tenants. In 1937, the Agriculture Department created the Farm Security Administration (FSA) to provide housing and loans to help tenant farmers become independent. A black tenant farmer in North Carolina who received an FSA loan told a New Deal interviewer, "I wake up in the night sometimes and think I must be half-dead and gone to heaven." But relatively few tenants received loans, because the FSA was starved for funds and ran up against major farm organizations intent on serving their own interests. For those who owned farms, the New Deal offered renewed prosperity with a second Agricultural Adjustment Act (AAA) in 1938. To moderate price swings by regulating supply, the plan combined production quotas on five staple crops—cotton, tobacco, wheat, corn, and rice—with storage loans through its Commodity Credit Corporation. The most prosperous farmers benefited most, but the act's Federal Surplus Commodities Corporation added an element of charity by issuing food stamps so that the poor could obtain surplus food. The AAA of 1938 brought stability to American agriculture and ample food to most—but not all—tables.

Advocates for the urban poor also made modest gains after decades of neglect. New York senator Robert Wagner convinced Congress to pass the **National Housing Act** in 1937. By 1941, some 160,000 residences had been made available to

National Populations and Economies, ca. 1938

	Population (millions)	Gross Domestic Product (millions of dollars)
United States	𝝰𝝰𝝰𝝰𝝰𝝰𝝰𝝰𝝰𝝰𝝰𝝰𝝰	(large block of money-bag symbols)
Britain	𝝰𝝰𝝰𝝰𝝰	(money-bag symbols)
British Colonies	(many people symbols)	(money-bag symbols)
France	𝝰𝝰𝝰𝝰	(money-bag symbols)
French Colonies	𝝰𝝰𝝰𝝰	𝕊𝕊𝕊𝕊𝕊
Italy	𝝰𝝰𝝰𝝰	(money-bag symbols)
Italian Colonies	𝝰	𝕊
Netherlands	𝝰	𝕊𝕊𝕊𝕊
Dutch Colonies	𝝰𝝰𝝰𝝰𝝰	𝕊𝕊𝕊𝕊𝕊𝕊𝕊
USSR	(many people symbols)	(money-bag symbols)
Japan	𝝰𝝰𝝰𝝰𝝰𝝰𝝰	(money-bag symbols)
Japanese Colonies	𝝰𝝰𝝰𝝰𝝰	𝕊𝕊𝕊𝕊𝕊𝕊
Germany	𝝰𝝰𝝰𝝰𝝰𝝰	(money-bag symbols)
Austria	𝝰	𝕊𝕊
Czechoslovakia	𝝰	𝕊𝕊𝕊
Poland	𝝰𝝰𝝰𝝰	𝕊𝕊𝕊𝕊𝕊𝕊𝕊𝕊
Hungary	𝝰	𝕊𝕊
Yugoslavia	𝝰𝝰	𝕊𝕊
Romania	𝝰𝝰	𝕊𝕊

𝝰 = 10 million people
𝕊 = 10 million dollars

Throughout the Great Depression, the United States remained more productive than any other nation in the world. Despite the lingering effects of the depression, by 1938 the United States produced more than twice as much as Germany and the Soviet Union, nearly three times as much as Britain, more than four times as much as France and Japan, and more than five times as much as Italy. From the viewpoint of Germany, if the European nations listed here could be brought under German control, its economy would be greater than that of the United States and the mightiest in the world. Economically, how important were colonies to the major powers? In general, do these data suggest a relationship between population and gross domestic product?

617

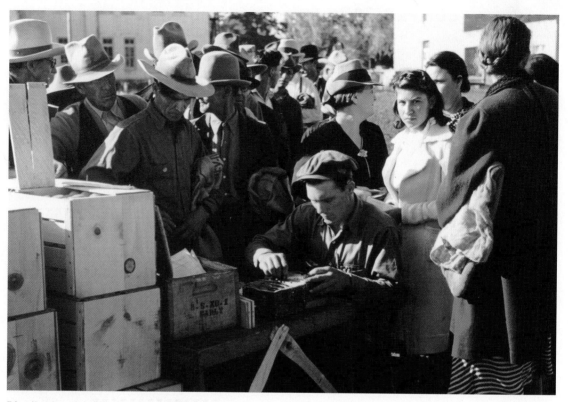

Distributing Surplus Food to the Needy When bountiful harvests produced surplus crops that would depress prices if they were sent to market, the New Deal arranged to distribute some of them to needy Americans. Here, farmworkers near the New Mexico border in east-central Arizona line up to receive a ration of potatoes authorized by the New Deal agent checking the box of index cards. Surplus commodity distribution represented New Dealers' attempt to provide relief for the hungry with crops that otherwise would rot or need to be destroyed in order to limit supply and thereby maintain agricultural prices. Library of Congress.

poor people at affordable rents. The program did not come close to meeting the need for affordable housing, but for the first time, the federal government took an active role in providing decent urban housing.

The last major piece of New Deal labor legislation, the **Fair Labor Standards Act** of June 1938, reiterated the New Deal pledge to provide workers with a decent standard of living. After lengthy haggling and compromise that revealed the waning strength of the New Deal, Congress finally agreed to intervene in the long-sacrosanct realm of worker contracts. The new law set wage and hours standards and at long last curbed the use of child labor. The minimum-wage level was modest—twenty-five cents an hour for a maximum of forty-four hours a week. In order to attract enough conservative votes, the act exempted merchant seamen, fishermen, domestic help, and farm laborers—relegating most women and African Americans to lower wages. Enforcement of the minimum-wage standards was weak and haphazard. Nevertheless, the Fair Labor Standards Act slowly advanced Roosevelt's inaugural promise

to improve the living standards of the poorest Americans.

The final New Deal reform effort failed to make much headway against the hidebound system of racial injustice. Although Roosevelt denounced lynching as murder, he would not jeopardize his vital base of southern political support by demanding antilynching legislation, and Congress voted down attempts to make lynching a federal crime. Laws to eliminate the poll tax—used to deny blacks the opportunity to vote—encountered the same overwhelming resistance. The New Deal refused to confront racial injustice with the same vigor it brought to bear on economic hardship.

By the end of 1938, the New Deal had lost steam and encountered stiff opposition. In the congressional elections of 1938, Republicans made gains that gave them more congressional influence than they had enjoyed since 1932. New Dealers could claim unprecedented achievements since 1933, but nobody needed reminding that those achievements had not ended the depression. In his annual message to Congress in January 1939, Roosevelt signaled a halt to New Deal reforms by speaking about preserving the progress already achieved rather than extending it. Roosevelt pointed to the ominous threats posed by fascist aggressors in Germany and Japan, and he proposed defense expenditures that surpassed New Deal appropriations for relief and economic recovery.

Q: **Why did political support for New Deal reforms decline?**

Conclusion: Achievements and Limitations of the New Deal

The New Deal replaced the fear symbolized by Hoover's expulsion of the Bonus Army with Roosevelt's confidence, optimism, and energetic pragmatism. A growing majority of Americans agreed with Roosevelt that the federal government should help those in need, thereby strengthening the political coalition that propelled the New Deal. In the process of seeking relief for victims of the depression, recovery of the general economy, and basic reform of major economic institutions, the New Deal vastly expanded the size and influence of the federal government and changed the way the American people viewed Washington. New Dealers achieved significant victories, such as Social Security, labor's right to organize, and guarantees that farm prices would be maintained through controls on production and marketing. New Deal measures marked the emergence of a welfare state, but the New Deal's limited, two-tier character left many needy Americans with little aid.

Full-scale relief, recovery, and reform eluded New Deal programs. Even though millions of Americans benefited directly from the alphabet soup of agencies and programs, both relief and recovery were limited and temporary. In 1940, the depression still plagued the economy. The most durable New Deal achievements were reforms that stabilized agriculture, encouraged the organization of labor unions, and created the safety net of Social Security and fair labor standards. Perhaps the most impressive achievement of the New Deal was what did not happen. Although authoritarian governments and anticapitalist policies were common outside the United States during the 1930s, they were shunned by the New Deal coalition. The greatest economic crisis the nation had ever faced did not cause Americans to abandon democracy, as happened in Germany, where Adolf Hitler seized dictatorial power. Nor did the nation turn to radical alternatives such as socialism or communism.

Republicans and other conservatives claimed that the New Deal amounted to a form of socialism that threatened democracy and capitalism. But rather than attack capitalism, Franklin Roosevelt sought to save it, and he succeeded. That success also marked the limits of the New Deal's achievements. Franklin Roosevelt believed that a strengthened national government was necessary to curb the destructive tendencies of concentrated economic power. A shift of authority toward the federal government would allow capitalist enterprises to be balanced by the nation's democratic tradition. The New Deal stopped far short of challenging capitalism either by undermining private property or by imposing strict national planning.

New Dealers repeatedly described their programs as a kind of warfare against the economic adversities of the 1930s. In the next decade, with the depression only partly vanquished, the Roosevelt administration had to turn from the New Deal's war against economic crisis at home to participate in a worldwide conflagration to defeat the enemies of democracy abroad.

Reviewing the Chapter

★ KEY TERMS

Explain each term's significance

WHO

Franklin Delano Roosevelt (p. 597)
Harry Hopkins (p. 600)
Frances Perkins (p. 600)
Eleanor Roosevelt (p. 600)
Upton Sinclair (p. 605)
Charles Coughlin (p. 608)
Francis Townsend (p. 609)
Huey Long (p. 609)
Mary McLeod Bethune (p. 613)

WHAT

Bonus Marchers (p. 595)
New Deal coalition (p. 599)
Federal Deposit Insurance Corporation (FDIC) (p. 600)
fireside chats (p. 601)
Federal Emergency Relief Administration (FERA) (p. 601)
Civilian Conservation Corps (CCC) (p. 601)
Tennessee Valley Authority (TVA) (p. 602)
Agricultural Adjustment Act (AAA) (p. 602)
National Recovery Administration (NRA) (p. 603)
Works Progress Administration (WPA) (p. 609)
Wagner Act (p. 611)
Committee for Industrial Organization (CIO) (p. 611)
sit-down strike (p. 611)
Social Security (p. 611)
Indian Reorganization Act (IRA) (p. 614)
court packing (p. 615)
Keynesian economics (p. 616)
National Housing Act (p. 616)
Fair Labor Standards Act (p. 618)

> **FOR PRACTICE QUIZZES AND OTHER STUDY TOOLS**, see the Online Study Guide at **bedfordstmartins.com/roarkcompact**.

★ REVIEW QUESTIONS Q:

Use key terms and dates to support your answer

1. Why did Franklin D. Roosevelt win the 1932 presidential election by such a large margin? (pp. 597–99)

2. How did the New Dealers try to steer the nation toward recovery from the Great Depression? (pp. 599–604)

3. Why did groups at both ends of the political spectrum criticize the New Deal? (pp. 604–09)

4. What features of a welfare state did the New Deal create and why? (pp. 609–14)

5. Why did political support for New Deal reforms decline? (pp. 614–19)

★ MAKING CONNECTIONS

Draw on key terms, timeline, and review questions

1. Franklin Roosevelt's landslide victory in 1932 changed the political landscape. How did Roosevelt build an effective interregional political coalition for the Democratic Party? How did the challenges of balancing interests within the coalition shape the policies of the New Deal? In your answer, discuss the character of the coalition and specific reforms.

2. New Dealers experimented with varied solutions to the economic disorder of the 1930s. Compare reform efforts targeting rural and industrial America. Were they effective? Why or why not? What do they reveal about how the Roosevelt administration understood the underlying causes of the Great Depression?

3. Although the New Deal enjoyed astonishing popularity, some Americans were consistently critical of Roosevelt's reforms. Why? In your answer, discuss three opponents of the New Deal, being attentive to changes over time in their opinions. Were they able to influence the New Deal? If so, how?

4. Although the New Deal extended help to many Americans, all did not benefit equally from the era's reforms. Who remained outside the reach of New Deal assistance? Why? In your answer, consider how politics shaped the limits of reform, both in constituents' ability to demand assistance and in the federal government's response to their demands.

★ SUGGESTED READINGS

Lizbeth Cohen, *Making a New Deal: Industrial Workers in Chicago, 1919–1939* (1990). An insightful case study of Chicago industrial workers and New Deal policies.

Alonzo Hamby, *For the Survival of Democracy: Franklin Roosevelt and the World Crisis of the 1930s* (2004). The story of the global challenges confronted by the New Deal.

David M. Kennedy, *Freedom from Fear: The American People in Depression and War, 1929–1945* (1999). A Pulitzer Prize–winning survey of Americans during Roosevelt's administrations.

Jennifer Klein, *For All These Rights: Business, Labor, and the Shaping of America's Public-Private Welfare State* (2003). A deeply researched account of the influence of the insurance industry and labor on the shaping of the welfare state.

Sarah Phillips, *This Land, This Nation: Conservation, Rural America, and the New Deal* (2007). A revealing analysis of the impact of the New Deal on rural America.

Amity Shlaes, *The Forgotten Man: A New History of the Great Depression* (2008). A compelling narrative history of economic crisis and the New Deal's efforts to overcome it.

FOR MORE BOOKS ABOUT TOPICS IN THIS CHAPTER, see the Online Bibliography at **bedfordstmartins.com/roarkcompact**.

FOR ADDITIONAL FIRSTHAND ACCOUNTS OF THIS PERIOD, see Chapter 24 in Michael Johnson, ed., *Reading the American Past*, Fourth Edition.

FOR WEB SITES, IMAGES, AND DOCUMENTS RELATED TO TOPICS AND PLACES IN THIS CHAPTER, visit Make History at **bedfordstmartins.com/roarkcompact**.

★ TIMELINE

1932
- Bonus Army marches on Washington.

1933
- Democrat Franklin D. Roosevelt becomes president.
- **March–June.** Legislation of the Hundred Days establishes the New Deal.
- Roosevelt closes the nation's banks for a four-day "bank holiday."
- Federal Emergency Relief Administration (FERA) established.

1934
- Securities and Exchange Commission (SEC) created.
- Upton Sinclair loses bid for governorship of California.
- American Liberty League founded.
- Dr. Francis Townsend devises Old Age Revolving Pension scheme.
- Indian Reorganization Act.

1935
- Legislation creates Works Progress Administration (WPA).
- Wagner Act.
- Committee for Industrial Organization (CIO) founded.
- Social Security Act.
- Father Charles Coughlin begins National Union for Social Justice.

1936
- John Maynard Keynes publishes *The General Theory of Employment, Interest, and Money*.
- Franklin Roosevelt elected to a second term by a landslide.

1937
- United Auto Workers stages successful sit-down strike at General Motors plant in Flint, Michigan.
- Roosevelt's court-packing legislation defeated in the Senate.
- Economic recession slows recovery from depression.

1938
- Second Agricultural Adjustment Act and Fair Labor Standards Act.
- Congress rejects administration's antilynching bill.
- Administrative Reorganization Act.

NORDEN
BOMBSIGHT
American pilots depended on the Norden bombsight
to hit targets in both the European and Pacific theaters throughout World
War II. Invented by Carl Norden, a Dutch immigrant raised in Indonesia and
educated in Switzerland, the sight combined an analog computer with gyroscopes,
gears, and optics to calculate the path of bombs to a target, adjusting for the speed
and altitude of the aircraft and the prevailing winds. In ideal conditions, the sight allowed
pilots to deliver bombs within a 50-foot radius of a target from an altitude of 20,000 feet, making
it possible for American bombers to aim for industrial plants, transportation hubs, bridges, and
other high-value enemy targets. In combat, however, the bombsight was less precise. Two-thirds
of American bombs unleashed from 20,000 feet actually fell more than 1,000 feet from their targets. Still, the Norden bombsight permitted American bombers to conduct effective high-altitude
daytime raids. By contrast, British bombers, which lacked an accurate sighting mechanism, were
forced to fly low-altitude, saturation bombing runs at night, when the danger from artillery on the
ground was less. To prevent this valuable technology from falling into enemy hands, American
bombardiers were trained to destroy the bombsight—by shooting it or by igniting an intense fire
that would melt the mechanism into a lump of useless metal—if they were forced down in enemy
territory. The Nazis purchased plans for the sight from a disgruntled Norden employee in 1937,
but they never used it, focusing instead on dive-bombing tactics in support of ground forces. Paul
Tibbets used the Norden bombsight to drop the atomic bomb on Hiroshima, Japan, in August 1945.
Museum of World War II, Natick, Mass.

CHAPTER 25

The United States and the Second World War

1939–1945

ON A SUN-DRENCHED FLORIDA AFTERNOON in January 1927, twelve-year-old **Paul Tibbets** cinched on a leather helmet and clambered into the front seat of the open cockpit of a biplane for his first airplane ride. While the pilot sitting behind him brought the plane in low over the Hialeah race-track in Miami, Tibbets pitched Baby Ruth candy bars tethered to small paper parachutes to racing fans in the grandstands below. After two more candy-bar drops over the racetrack, the pilot raced to the beach, and Tibbets tossed out the remaining candy bars and watched the bathers scramble for chocolate from heaven. After this stunt, sales of Baby Ruths soared, and Tibbets was hooked on flying.

In 1937, Tibbets joined the Army Air Corps and become a military pilot. Shortly after the Japanese attack on Pearl Harbor in December 1941, Tibbets led a squadron of airplanes flying antisubmarine patrol against German U-boats lurking along the East Coast. When the heavily armored B-17 Flying Fortress bombers began to come off American assembly lines early in 1942, he took a squadron of the new planes from the United States to England. On August 17, 1942, he led the first American daytime bombing raid on German-occupied Europe, releasing 1,100 pounds of bombs from his B-17, the first of some 700,000 tons of explosives dropped by American bombers during the air war in Europe.

After numerous raids over Europe, Tibbets was reassigned to the North African campaign, where his duties included ferrying the American commander, General Dwight D. Eisenhower, into the battle zone. After eight months of combat missions, Tibbets returned to the United States and was ordered to test the new B-29 Super Fortress being built in Wichita, Kansas. The B-29 was much bigger than the B-17 and could fly higher and faster, making it ideal for the campaign against Japan. Tibbets's mastery of the B-29 caused him to be singled out in September 1944 to command a top-secret unit training for a special mission.

The mission was to be ready to drop on Japan a bomb that was so powerful it might bring the war to an end. No such bomb yet existed, but American scientists and engineers were working around the clock to build one.

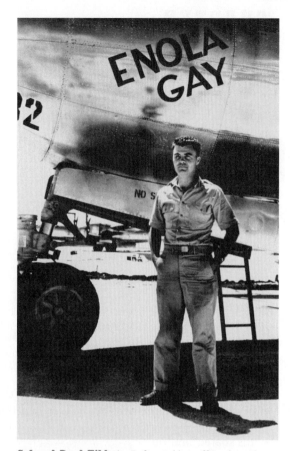

Colonel Paul Tibbets Before taking off to drop the world's first atomic bomb on Hiroshima, Tibbets posed on the tarmac next to his customized B-29 Super Fortress bomber, named *Enola Gay* in honor of his mother. A crew of eleven handpicked airmen accompanied Tibbets on the top-secret mission. After the war, President Harry S. Truman invited Tibbets to the White House and told him, "Don't you ever lose any sleep over the fact that you planned and carried out that mission. It was my decision. You had no choice."
© Bettmann/Corbis.

Tibbets kept this secret from his men but took them and his B-29s to Utah to develop a way to drop such a powerful weapon without getting blown up by it. In May 1945, Tibbets and his men went to Tinian Island in the Pacific, where they trained for their secret mission by flying raids over Japanese cities and dropping ordinary bombs. The atomic bomb arrived on Tinian on July 26, just ten days after the successful test explosion in the New Mexico desert. Nicknamed "Little Boy," the bomb packed the equivalent of 40 million pounds of TNT, or 200,000 of the 200-pound bombs Tibbets and other American airmen had dropped on Europe.

At 2:30 a.m. on August 6, 1945, Tibbets, his crew, and their atomic payload took off in the B-29 bomber *Enola Gay* and headed for Japan. Less than seven hours later, over the city of Hiroshima, Tibbets and his men released Little Boy from the *Enola Gay*'s bomb bay. The plane bucked upward after dropping the 4.5-ton explosive, while Tibbets struggled to maintain control as the shock wave from the explosion blasted past and a purple cloud mushroomed nearly ten miles into the air. Three days later, Tibbets's men dropped a second atomic bomb on Nagasaki, and within five days, Japan surrendered.

Paul Tibbets's experiences traced an arc followed by millions of Americans during World War II, from the innocence of bombarding Miami with candy bars to the deadly nuclear firestorms that rained down on Japan. Like Tibbets, Americans joined their allies to fight the Axis powers in Europe and Asia. Like his *Enola Gay* crewmen—who hailed from New York, Texas, California, New Jersey, New Mexico, Maryland, North Carolina, Pennsylvania, Michigan, and Nevada—Americans from all regions united to defeat the fascist aggressors. American industries mobilized to produce advanced bombers—like the ones Tibbets piloted—along with enough other military equipment to supply the American armed forces and their allies. At enormous cost in human life and suffering, the war brought employment and prosperity to most Americans at home, ending the depression, providing new opportunities for women, and ushering the nation into the postwar world as a triumphant economic and—on the wings of Paul Tibbets's *Enola Gay*—atomic superpower. ★

Peacetime Dilemmas

The First World War left a dangerous and ultimately deadly legacy. The victors—especially Britain, France, and the United States—sought to avoid future wars at almost any cost. The defeated nations, as well as those that felt humiliated by the Versailles peace settlement—particularly Germany, Italy, and Japan—aspired to reassert their power and avenge their losses by means of renewed warfare. Japan invaded the northern Chinese province of Manchuria in 1931 with ambitions to expand throughout Asia. Italy, led by the fascist Benito Mussolini since 1922, hungered for an empire in Africa. In Germany, National Socialist **Adolf Hitler** rose to power in 1933 in a quest to dominate Europe and the world. These aggressive, militaristic, antidemocratic regimes seemed a smaller threat to most people in the United States during the 1930s than did the economic crisis at home. Shielded from external threats by the Atlantic and Pacific oceans, Americans hoped to avoid entanglement in foreign woes and to concentrate on climbing out of the nation's economic abyss.

Roosevelt and Reluctant Isolation Like most Americans during the 1930s, Franklin Roosevelt believed that the nation's highest priority was to attack the domestic causes and consequences of the depression. But unlike most Americans, Roosevelt had long advocated an active role for the United States in international affairs. After World War I, Roosevelt embraced Woodrow Wilson's vision that the United States should take the lead in making the world "safe for democracy," and he continued to advocate American membership in the League of Nations during the isolationist 1920s.

The depression forced Roosevelt to retreat from his previous internationalism. He came to believe that energetic involvement in foreign affairs diverted resources and political support from domestic recovery. During his 1932 presidential campaign, he pulled back from his endorsement of the League of Nations and reversed his previous support for forgiving European war debts. Once in office, Roosevelt sought to combine domestic economic recovery with a low-profile foreign policy that encouraged free trade and disarmament.

Roosevelt's pursuit of international amity was constrained by economic circumstances and American popular opinion. After an opinion poll demonstrated popular support for recognizing the Soviet Union — an international pariah since the Bolshevik Revolution in 1917 — Roosevelt established formal diplomatic relations in 1933. But when the League of Nations condemned Japanese and German aggression, Roosevelt did not support the league's attempts to keep the peace because he feared jeopardizing isolationists' support for New Deal measures in Congress. America watched from the sidelines when Japan withdrew from the league and ignored the limitations on its navy imposed after World War I. The United States also looked the other way when Hitler rearmed Germany and recalled its representative to the league in 1933, declaring that the international organization sought to thwart Germany's national ambitions. Roosevelt worried that German and Japanese violations of league sanctions and the Versailles settlement threatened world peace. But

he reassured Americans that the nation would not "use its armed forces for the settlement of any [international] dispute anywhere."

The Good Neighbor Policy In his 1933 inaugural address, Franklin Roosevelt announced that the United States would pursue "the policy of the good neighbor" in international relations. A few weeks later, he emphasized that this policy applied specifically to Latin America, where U.S. military forces had often intervened in local affairs. In December 1933, Secretary of State Cordell Hull formalized the good neighbor pledge that no nation had the right to intervene in the internal or external affairs of another.

The good neighbor policy did not indicate a U.S. retreat from empire in Latin America. Instead, it declared that the United States would not depend on military force to exercise its influence in the region. When Mexico nationalized American oil holdings and revolution boiled over in Nicaragua, Guatemala, and Cuba during the 1930s, Roosevelt refrained from sending troops to defend the interests of American corporations. In 1934, Roosevelt even withdrew American Marines from Haiti, which they had occupied since 1916. While nonintervention honored the principle of national self-determination, it also permitted the rise of dictators, such as Anastasio Somoza in Nicaragua and Fulgencio Batista in Cuba, who exploited and terrorized their nations with private support from U.S. businesses and the hands-off policy of Roosevelt's administration.

> After World War I, Roosevelt embraced Wilson's vision that the United States should take the lead in making the world "safe for democracy."

Military nonintervention also did not prevent the United States from exerting its economic influence in Latin America. In 1934, Congress passed the Reciprocal Trade Agreements Act, which gave the president the power to reduce tariffs on goods imported into the United States from nations that agreed to lower their own tariffs on U.S. exports. By 1940, twenty-two nations had agreed to reciprocal tariff reductions, helping U.S. exports to Latin America to double and contributing to the New Deal's goal of boosting the domestic economy through free trade. Although the economic power of the United States continued to overshadow that of its neighbors, the nonintervention policy planted seeds of friendship and hemispheric solidarity.

The Price of Noninvolvement In Europe, Hitler rebuilt Germany's military strength, openly defying the terms of the Versailles peace treaty. Britain and France only made verbal protests.

Emboldened, Hitler plotted to avenge defeat in World War I by recapturing territories with German inhabitants, all the while accusing Jews of polluting the purity of the Aryan master race. The virulent anti-Semitism of Hitler and his Nazi Party unified non-Jewish Germans and attracted sympathizers among many other Europeans, even in France and Britain, thereby weakening support for opposing Hitler or defending Jews.

In Japan, a stridently militaristic government planned to follow the invasion of Manchuria in 1931 with conquests extending throughout Southeast Asia. The Manchurian invasion bogged down in a long and vicious war when Chinese Nationalists rallied around their leader, **Chiang Kai-shek**, to fight against the Japanese. Preparations for new Japanese conquests continued, however. In 1936, Japan openly violated naval limitation treaties it had agreed to and began to build a battle-ready fleet to achieve naval superiority in the Pacific.

In the United States, the hostilities in Asia and Europe reinforced isolationist sentiments. Popular disillusionment with the failure of Woodrow Wilson's idealistic goals caused many Americans to question the nation's participation in World War I. In 1933, Gerald Nye, a Republican from North Dakota, chaired a Senate committee that investigated why the United States had gone to war in 1917. The Nye committee concluded that greedy "merchants of death"—American weapons makers, bankers, and financiers—dragged the nation into the war to line their own pockets. The Nye committee persuaded many Americans that war profiteers might once again push the nation into a world war. International tensions and the Nye committee report prompted Congress to pass a series of neutrality acts between 1935 and 1937 designed to avoid entanglement in foreign wars. The neutrality acts prohibited making loans and selling arms to nations at war.

By 1937, the growing conflicts overseas caused some Americans to call for a total embargo on all trade with warring countries. Roosevelt and Congress worried that such an embargo would hurt the nation's economy by reducing production and boosting unemployment. The Neutrality Act of 1937 attempted to reconcile the nation's desire for both peace and foreign trade with a "cash-and-carry" policy that required warring nations to pay cash for nonmilitary goods and to transport them in their own ships. This policy supported foreign trade and thereby benefited the nation's economy, but it also helped foreign aggressors by supplying them with goods and thereby undermining peace.

The desire for peace in France, Britain, and the United States led Germany, Italy, and Japan to launch offensives on the assumption that the Western democracies lacked the will to oppose them. In March 1936, Nazi troops marched into the industry-rich Rhineland on Germany's western border, in blatant violation of the Treaty of Versailles. One month later, Italian armies completed their conquest of Ethiopia, projecting fascist power into Africa. In December 1937, Japanese invaders captured Nanking and celebrated their triumph in the "Rape of Nanking," a deadly rampage of murder, rape, and plunder that killed 200,000 Chinese civilians.

In Spain, a bitter civil war broke out in July 1936 when fascist rebels led by General Francisco Franco attacked the democratically elected Republican government. Both Germany and Italy reinforced Franco with soldiers, weapons, and aircraft, while the Soviet Union provided much less aid to the Republican Loyalists. The **Spanish civil war** seemed to many observers a dress rehearsal for a coming worldwide conflict, but it did not cause European democracies or the U.S. government to help the Loyalists, despite sympathizing with their cause. More than 3,000 individual Americans enlisted in the Russian-sponsored Abraham Lincoln Brigade to fight for the Loyalists. But, abandoned by the Western nations, the Loyalists and their allies were defeated in 1939, and Franco built a fascist bulwark in southwestern Europe.

Spanish Civil War, 1936–1939

Hostilities in Europe, Africa, and Asia alarmed Roosevelt and other Americans. The president sought to persuade most Americans to moderate their **isolationism** (the desire to retreat from the world's conflicts) and find a way to support the victims of fascist aggression. Speaking in Chicago in October 1937, Roosevelt declared that the "epidemic of world lawlessness is spreading" and warned that "mere isolation or neutrality" offered no remedy for the "contagion" of war. Instead, he proposed that the United States "quarantine" aggressor nations and stop the spread of war's contagion.

Roosevelt's speech ignited a storm of protest from isolationists. The *Chicago Tribune* accused the president of seeking to replace "Americanism" with "internationalism." Disappointed by the strength of isolationism and the absence of congressional support for his quarantine policy, Roosevelt remarked, "It's a terrible thing to look over your shoulder when you are trying to lead and find no one there." The popularity of isolationist sentiment convinced Roosevelt that he needed to maneuver carefully if the United States were to help prevent fascist aggressors from conquering Europe and Asia, leaving the United States an isolated and imperiled island of democracy.

Q: Why did isolationism during the 1930s concern Roosevelt?

The Onset of War

Between 1939 and 1941, fascist victories overseas eventually eroded American isolationism. Continuing German and Japanese aggression caused more and more Americans to believe that it was time for the nation to take a stand. At first, taking a stand was limited to providing material support to the enemies of Germany and Japan, principally Britain, China, and the Soviet Union. But Japan's surprise attack on Pearl Harbor eliminated that restraint, and the nation began to mobilize for an all-out assault on foreign foes.

Nazi Aggression and War in Europe Under the spell of isolationism, Americans passively watched Hitler's relentless campaign to dominate Europe. Hitler bullied Austria in 1938 into accepting incorporation—*Anschluss*—into the Nazi Third Reich. Next, Hitler turned his attention to the German-speaking Sudetenland, granted to Czechoslovakia by the Versailles treaty. Hoping to avoid war, British prime minister Neville Chamberlain went to Munich, Germany, in September 1938 and offered Hitler terms of **appeasement** that would give the Sudetenland to Germany if Hitler agreed to leave the rest of Czechoslovakia alone. Hitler accepted Chamberlain's offer and promised that he would make no more territorial claims in Europe. But Hitler never intended to honor his promise. In March 1939, Hitler boldly marched the German army into Czechoslovakia and conquered it without firing a shot (Map 25.1).

In April 1939, Hitler demanded that Poland return the German territory it had been awarded after World War I. Recognizing that appeasement had failed, Britain and France assured Poland that they would go to war with Germany if Hitler launched an attack across the Polish border. In turn, Hitler negotiated with his bitter enemy, Soviet premier **Joseph Stalin**, offering him concessions in order to prevent the Soviet Union from joining Britain and France in opposing a German attack on Poland. Despite the enduring hatred between fascist Germany and the Communist Soviet Union, the two powers signed the Nazi-Soviet treaty of nonaggression in August 1939, exposing Poland to an onslaught by both the German Wehrmacht (army) and the Soviet Red Army.

At dawn on September 1, 1939, Hitler unleashed his *blitzkrieg* (literally, "lightning war") on Poland. The attack triggered Soviet attacks on eastern Poland and declarations of war from France and Britain two days later, igniting a conflagration that raced around the globe. When it finally ended after Paul Tibbets's historic flight in August 1945, more than 60 million people were dead and untold millions more maimed.

After the Nazis overran Poland, Hitler paused for a few months before launching a westward blitzkrieg. In April 1940, German forces smashed through Denmark and Norway. In May, Germany invaded the Netherlands, Belgium, Luxembourg, and France. The French believed that their Maginot Line, a concrete fortification built after

German Invasion of Poland In 1940, German infantry reserves marched to the eastern front led by two officers on horseback. Although the German blitzkrieg massed thousands of tanks and aircraft at the front, German forces lacked sufficient trucks and other motorized vehicles to move soldiers and military supplies. When Hitler invaded the Soviet Union in June 1941, his armies included some 3,300 tanks and more than 650,000 horses. The Germans' dependence on horse and foot travel limited the mobility of their troops compared with the more thoroughly motorized Allied armies.
© Bettmann/Corbis.

MAP 25.1 Axis Aggression through 1941

For different reasons, Hitler and Mussolini launched a series of surprise military strikes before 1942. Mussolini sought to re-create the Roman empire in the Mediterranean. Hitler struck to reclaim German territories occupied by France after World War I and to annex Austria. When the German dictator began his campaign to rule "inferior" peoples beyond Germany's border by attacking Poland, World War II broke out.

World War I, would halt the German attack (see Map 25.1). But the Maginot Line proved little more than a detour for Hitler's mechanized divisions, which wheeled around it and raced south toward Paris.

The speed of the German attack trapped more than 300,000 British and French soldiers, who retreated to the port of Dunkirk, where an improvised armada of British vessels hurriedly ferried them to safety across the English Channel. By mid-June 1940, France had surrendered the largest army in the world, signed an armistice that gave Germany control of the entire French coastline and nearly two-thirds of the countryside, and installed a collaborationist government at Vichy in southern France. With an empire that stretched across Europe from Poland to France, Hitler seemed invincible as he poised to attack Britain.

The new British prime minister, **Winston Churchill**, vowed that Britain, unlike France, would never surrender to Hitler. "We shall fight on the seas and oceans [and] . . . in the air," he proclaimed, "whatever the cost may be, we shall fight on the beaches, . . . and in the fields and in the streets." Churchill's defiance stiffened British resolve for a defense against Hitler's attack, which began in mid-June 1940 when wave after wave of German bombers targeted British military installations and cities, killing tens of thousands of civilians. The undermanned and outgunned Royal Air Force fought as doggedly as Churchill had predicted and finally won the **Battle of Britain** by November, clearing German bombers from British skies and handing Hitler his first defeat. Advance knowledge of German plans made possible by British use of the new technology of radar and the ability to decipher Germany's top-secret military codes aided British pilots. Battered and exhausted, Britain could not hold out forever without American help, as Churchill repeatedly wrote Roosevelt in private.

From Neutrality to the Arsenal of Democracy

When the Nazi attack on Poland ignited the war in Europe, Roosevelt issued an official proclamation of American neutrality. Most Americans condemned German aggression and favored Britain and France, but isolationism remained powerful. Roosevelt feared that if Congress did not repeal the arms embargo mandated by the Neutrality Act of 1937, France and Britain would soon succumb to the Nazi onslaught. After heated debate, Congress voted in November 1939 to revise the neutrality legislation and allow belligerent nations to buy arms, as well as nonmilitary supplies, on a cash-and-carry basis.

In practice, the revised neutrality law permitted Britain and France to purchase American war materiel and carry it across the Atlantic in their own ships, thereby shielding American vessels from attack by German submarines lurking in the Atlantic. Roosevelt wrote a friend, "What worries me is that public opinion . . . is patting itself on the back every morning and thanking God for the Atlantic Ocean (and the Pacific Ocean)" and underestimating "the serious implications" of the European war "for our own future." Roosevelt searched for a way to aid Britain short of entering a formal alliance or declaring war against Germany. Churchill pleaded for American destroyers, aircraft, and munitions, but he had no money to buy them under the prevailing cash-and-carry neutrality law. By late summer in 1940, as the Battle of Britain raged in the skies over Britain, Roosevelt concocted a scheme to deliver fifty old destroyers to Britain in exchange for American access to British bases in the Western Hemisphere. Claiming the constitutional power to strengthen America's defenses by swapping destroyers for bases, Roosevelt took the first steps toward building a firm Anglo-American alliance against Hitler.

While German Luftwaffe (air force) pilots bombed Britain, Roosevelt decided to run for an unprecedented third term as president in 1940. He hoped to woo voters away from their complacent isolationism to back the nation's international interests as well as New Deal reforms. But the presidential election, which Roosevelt won handily, provided no clear mandate for American involvement in the European war. The Republican candidate, Wendell Willkie, a former Democrat who generally favored New Deal measures and Roosevelt's foreign policy, attacked Roosevelt as a warmonger. Willkie's accusations caused the president to promise voters, "Your boys are not going to be sent into any foreign wars," a pledge counterbalanced by his repeated warnings about the threats to America posed by Nazi aggression.

Empowered by the voters for another presidential term, Roosevelt maneuvered to support Britain in every way short of war. In a fireside chat shortly after Christmas 1940, he proclaimed that it was incumbent on the United States to become "the great arsenal of democracy" and send "every ounce and every ton of munitions and supplies that we can possibly spare to help the defenders who are in the front lines."

In January 1941, Roosevelt proposed the **Lend-Lease Act**, which allowed the British to obtain arms from the United States without paying cash but with the promise to reimburse the United States when the war ended. The purpose of Lend-Lease, Roosevelt proclaimed, was to defend democracy and human rights throughout the world, specifically the Four Freedoms: "freedom of speech and expression . . . freedom of every person to worship God in his own way . . . freedom from want . . . [and] freedom from fear." Congress passed the Lend-Lease Act in March 1941 and started a flow of support to Britain that totaled more than $50 billion during the war, far more than all federal expenditures combined since Roosevelt had become president in 1933.

Stymied in his plans for an invasion of England, Hitler turned his massive army eastward and on June 22, 1941, sprang a surprise attack on the Soviet Union, his erstwhile ally in the 1939 Nazi-Soviet nonaggression pact. Neither Roosevelt nor Churchill had any love for Joseph Stalin or communism, but they both welcomed the Soviet Union to the anti-Nazi cause. Both Western leaders understood that Hitler's attack on Russia would provide relief for the hard-pressed British. Roosevelt quickly persuaded Congress to extend Lend-Lease to the Soviet Union, beginning the shipment of millions of tons of trucks, jeeps, and other equipment that, in all, supplied about 10 percent of Russian war materiel.

MAP 25.2 Japanese Aggression through 1941
Beginning with the invasion of Manchuria in 1931, Japan sought to extend its imperialist control over most of East Asia. Japanese aggression was driven by the need for raw materials for the country's expanding industries and by the military government's devotion to martial honor.

As Hitler's Wehrmacht raced across the Russian plains and Nazi U-boats tried to choke off supplies to Britain and the Soviet Union, Roosevelt met with Churchill aboard a ship near Newfoundland to cement the Anglo-American alliance. In August 1941, the two leaders issued the **Atlantic Charter**, pledging the two nations to freedom of the seas and free trade as well as the right of national self-determination.

Japan Attacks America Hitler exercised a measure of restraint in directly provoking America. In contrast, Japanese ambitions in Asia clashed more openly with American interests and commitments, especially in China and the Philippines. And unlike Hitler, the Japanese high command planned to attack the United States if necessary to pursue Japan's aspirations to rule an Asian empire it termed the Greater East Asia Co-Prosperity Sphere. Appealing to widespread Asian bitterness toward such white colonial powers as the British in India and Burma, the French in Indochina (now Vietnam), and the Dutch in the East Indies (now Indonesia), the Japanese campaigned to preserve "Asia for the Asians." Japan's invasion of China—which had lasted for ten years by 1941—proved that its true goal was Asia for the Japanese (Map 25.2). Japan coveted the raw materials available from China and Southeast Asia and ignored American demands to stop its campaign of aggression.

In 1940, Japan signaled a new phase of its imperial designs by entering a defensive alliance with Germany and Italy—the Tripartite Pact. In 1941, U.S. naval intelligence cracked the Japanese secret code and learned that Tokyo also planned to invade the resource-rich Dutch East Indies. To thwart these plans, in July 1941 Roosevelt announced a trade embargo that denied Japan access to oil, scrap iron, and other goods essential for its war machines. Roosevelt hoped the embargo would strengthen factions within Japan that opposed the militarists and sought to restore relations with the United States.

The American embargo played into the hands of Japanese militarists headed by General Hideki Tojo, who seized control of the government in October 1941 and persuaded other leaders, including Emperor Hirohito, that swift destruction of American naval bases in the Pacific would leave Japan free to follow its destiny. On December 7, 1941, 183 attack aircraft lifted off six Japanese carriers and attacked the U.S. Pacific Fleet at **Pearl Harbor** on the Hawaiian island

of Oahu. The devastating surprise attack sank or disabled eighteen ships, including all of the fleet's battleships; killed more than 2,400 Americans; and wounded more than 1,000, almost crippling U.S. war-making capacity in the Pacific. Luckily for the United States, Japanese pilots failed to destroy the vital machine shops and oil storage facilities at Pearl Harbor, and none of the nation's aircraft carriers happened to be in port at the time of the attack.

The Japanese scored a stunning tactical victory at Pearl Harbor, but in the long run, the attack proved a colossal blunder. The victory made many Japanese commanders overconfident about their military prowess. Worse for the Japanese, Americans instantly united in their desire to fight and avenge the attack, which Roosevelt termed "dastardly and unprovoked." On December 8, Congress endorsed the president's call for a declaration of war. Neither Hitler nor Mussolini knew about the Japanese attack

Bombing of Pearl Harbor, December 7, 1941

Pearl Harbor Attack Brothers Wesley and Edward Heidt from Los Angeles were one of thirty-four pairs of brothers killed when Japanese warplanes sank the battleship *Arizona* at Pearl Harbor. This pennant was salvaged from the ship's wreckage. Also included here is the official telegram informing the Heidt brothers' mother that her sons "lost their life in the service of their country," a heartbreaking message received by hundreds of thousands of American families over the next four years. U.S.S. *Arizona* Memorial, Hawaii, National Park Service/photos by Douglas Peebles.

in advance, but they both declared war against America on December 11, bringing the United States into all-out war with the Axis powers in both Europe and Asia.

> **Q:** How did Roosevelt attempt to balance American isolationism with the increasingly ominous international scene of the late 1930s?

Mobilizing for War

The time had come, Roosevelt announced, for the prescriptions of "Dr. New Deal" to be replaced by the stronger medicines of "Dr. Win-the-War." Military and civilian leaders rushed to secure the nation against possible attacks, causing Americans of Japanese descent to be stigmatized and sent to internment camps. Roosevelt and his advisers lost no time enlisting millions of Americans in the armed forces to bring the isolationist-era military to fighting strength for a two-front war. The war emergency also required economic mobilization unparalleled in the nation's history. As Dr. Win-the-War, Roosevelt set aside the New Deal goal of reform and plunged headlong into transforming the American economy into the world's greatest military machine, thereby achieving full employment and economic recovery, goals that had eluded the New Deal.

Home-Front Security Shortly after declaring war against the United States, Hitler dispatched German submarines to hunt American ships along the Atlantic coast from Maine to Florida, where Paul Tibbets and other American pilots tried to destroy them. The U-boats had devastating success for about eight months, sinking hundreds of U.S. ships and threatening to disrupt the Lend-Lease lifeline to Britain and the Soviet Union. But by mid-1942, the U.S. navy had chased German submarines away from the East Coast and into the mid-Atlantic, reducing the direct threat to the nation.

Within the continental United States, Americans remained sheltered from the chaos and destruction the war was bringing to hundreds of millions in Europe and Asia. Nevertheless, the government worried constantly about espionage and internal subversion. Billboards and posters warned Americans that "Enemy agents are always near; if you don't talk, they won't hear." The campaign for patriotic vigilance focused on German and Japanese foes, but Americans of Japanese descent became targets of official and popular persecution because of Pearl Harbor and

long-standing racial prejudice against people of Asian descent.

About 320,000 people of Japanese descent lived in U.S. territory in 1941, two-thirds of them in Hawaii, where they largely escaped wartime persecution because they were essential and valued members of society. On the mainland, however, Japanese Americans were a tiny minority—even along the West Coast, where most of them worked on farms and in small businesses—subject to frenzied wartime suspicions and persecution. Although an official military survey concluded that Japanese Americans posed no danger, popular hostility fueled a campaign to round up all mainland Japanese Americans—two-thirds of them U.S. citizens. "A Jap's a Jap. . . . It makes no difference whether he is an American citizen or not," one official declared.

On February 19, 1942, Roosevelt issued Executive Order 9066, which authorized sending all Americans of Japanese descent to ten makeshift **internment camps**—euphemistically termed "relocation centers"—located in remote areas of the West (Map 25.3). Allowed little time to secure or sell their property, Japanese Americans lost homes and businesses worth about $400 million and lived out the war penned in by barbed wire and armed guards. Although several thousand Japanese Americans served with distinction

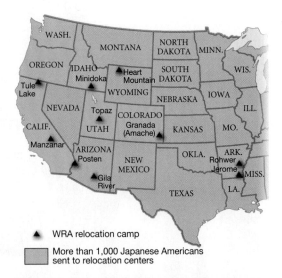

▲ WRA relocation camp

More than 1,000 Japanese Americans sent to relocation centers

MAP 25.3 Western Relocation Authority Centers
Responding to prejudice and fear of sabotage, President Roosevelt authorized the roundup and relocation of all Americans of Japanese descent in 1942. Taken from their homes in the cities and fertile farmland of the far West, Japanese Americans were confined in desolate camps scattered as far east as the Mississippi River.

in the U.S. armed forces and no case of subversion by a Japanese American was ever uncovered, the Supreme Court, in its 1944 *Korematsu* decision, upheld Executive Order 9066's blatant violation of constitutional rights as justified by "military necessity."

Building a Citizen Army In 1940, Roosevelt encouraged Congress to pass the **Selective Service Act** to register men of military age who would be subject to a draft if the need arose. More than 6,000 local draft boards registered more than 30 million men and, when war came, rapidly inducted them into military service. In all, more than 16 million men and women served in uniform during the war, two-thirds of them draftees, mostly young men. Women were barred from combat duty, but they worked at nearly every noncombatant task, eroding traditional barriers to women's military service.

The Selective Service Act prohibited discrimination "on account of race or color," and almost a million African American men and women donned uniforms, as did half a million Mexican Americans, 25,000 Native Americans, and 13,000 Chinese Americans. The racial insults and discrimination suffered by all people of color made some soldiers ask, as a Mexican American GI did on his way to the European front, "Why fight for America when you have not been treated as an American?" Only black Americans were trained in segregated camps, confined in segregated barracks, and assigned to segregated units. Most black Americans were consigned to manual labor, and relatively few served in combat until late in 1944, when the need for military manpower in Europe intensified. Then, as General George Patton told black soldiers in a tank unit in Normandy, "I don't care what color you are, so long as you go up there and kill those Kraut sonsabitches."

Homosexuals also served in the armed forces, although in much smaller numbers than black Americans. Allowed to serve as long as their sexual preferences remained covert, gay Americans, like other minorities, sought to demonstrate their worth under fire. As a gay GI remarked, "Who in the hell is going to worry about [homosexuality]" in the midst of the life-or-death realities of war?

Conversion to a War Economy In 1940, the American economy remained mired in the depression. Nearly one worker in seven was still without a job, factories operated far below their productive capacity, and the total federal budget was under $10 billion. Shortly after the attack on Pearl Harbor, Roosevelt announced the goal of converting the economy to produce "overwhelming . . . , crushing superiority of equipment in any theater

African American Machine Gunners These African American soldiers prepare their machine gun for action on the side of a road near Pisa, Italy, in September 1944. They and other black soldiers who served in combat in segregated units repeatedly earned praise from their commanders for gallantry and courage under fire. As a Mississippi-born African American veteran of the Pacific theater recalled, "We had two wars to fight: prejudice . . . and those Japs." © Bettmann/Corbis.

of the world war." Factories were converted from making passenger cars to assembling tanks and airplanes, and production soared to record levels. By the end of the war, jobs exceeded workers, plants operated at full capacity, and the federal budget topped $100 billion.

To organize and oversee this tidal wave of military production, Roosevelt called upon business leaders to come to Washington and, for the token payment of a dollar a year, head new government agencies such as the War Production Board, which, among other things, set production priorities and pushed for maximum output. Contracts flowed to large corporations, often on a basis that guaranteed their profits. During the first half of 1942, the government issued contracts worth more than the entire gross national product in 1941.

Booming wartime employment swelled union membership. To speed production, the government asked unions to pledge not to strike. Despite the relentless pace of work, union members kept their no-strike pledge, with the important exception of members of the United Mine Workers, who walked

Weapons Production by the Axis and Allied Powers during World War II

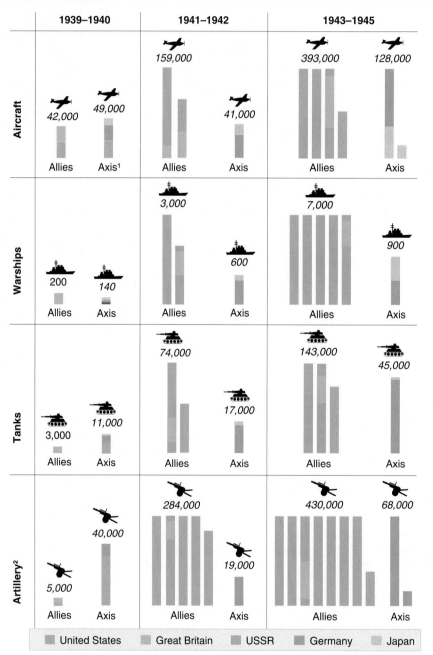

	1939–1940	1941–1942	1943–1945

Aircraft
Allies 42,000 | Axis[1] 49,000 | Allies 159,000 | Axis 41,000 | Allies 393,000 | Axis 128,000

Warships
Allies 200 | Axis 140 | Allies 3,000 | Axis 600 | Allies 7,000 | Axis 900

Tanks
Allies 3,000 | Axis 11,000 | Allies 74,000 | Axis 17,000 | Allies 143,000 | Axis 45,000

Artillery[2]
Allies 5,000 | Axis 40,000 | Allies 284,000 | Axis 19,000 | Allies 430,000 | Axis 68,000

■ United States ■ Great Britain ■ USSR ■ Germany ■ Japan

[1] The USSR was allied with Germany 1939–1940.
[2] No reliable data exist for Japan.

This chart demonstrates the massive contribution of the United States to Allied weapons production during World War II. In the air and on the sea, U.S. weapons predominated, after 1940 accounting for more aircraft and many more warships than Britain and the Soviet Union combined. Together, the three Allied powers produced about three times as many aircraft and five to eight times as many warships as the two Axis powers. On the ground, the Soviet Union led the other Allies in the production of tanks and artillery, an outgrowth of the colossal battles on the eastern front. Overall, the Allies produced almost three times as many tanks as the Axis powers and more than seven times as many artillery pieces as Germany (no figures are available for Japan). What do these data suggest about the significance of America's entry into the war in December 1941? What do they suggest about the kind of warfare emphasized by each of the belligerents? What do they suggest about the chronology of weapons production during the war?

out of the coal mines in 1943, demanding a pay hike and earning the enmity of many Americans.

Overall, conversion to war production achieved Roosevelt's ambitious goal of "crushing superiority" in military goods. At a total cost of $304 billion during the war, the nation produced an avalanche of military equipment, more than double the combined production of Germany, Japan, and Italy. (See "Global Comparison.") This outpouring of military goods supplied not only U.S. forces but also America's allies, giving tangible meaning to Roosevelt's pledge to make America the "arsenal of democracy."

Q: How did the Roosevelt administration mobilize the human and industrial resources necessary to fight a two-front war?

Fighting Back

The United States confronted a daunting military challenge in December 1941. The attack on Pearl Harbor destroyed much of its Pacific Fleet, crippling the nation's ability to defend against Japan's offensive throughout the southern Pacific. In the Atlantic, Hitler's U-boats sank American ships, while German armies occupied most of western Europe and relentlessly advanced eastward into the Soviet Union. Roosevelt and his military advisers believed that defeating Germany took top priority. To achieve that victory required preventing Hitler from defeating America's allies, Britain and the Soviet Union. If they fell, Hitler would command all the resources of Europe in a probable assault on the United States. To fight back effectively against Germany and Japan, the United States had to coordinate military and political strategy with its allies and muster all its human and economic assets. But in 1941, nobody knew whether that would be enough.

Turning the Tide in the Pacific In the Pacific theater, Japan's leading military strategist, Admiral Isoroku Yamamoto, believed that if his forces did not quickly conquer and secure the territories they targeted, Japan would eventually lose the war as a result of America's far greater resources. Swiftly, the Japanese assaulted American airfields in the Philippines and captured U.S. outposts on Guam and Wake Island. Singapore, the great British naval base in Malaya, surrendered to the Japanese in February 1942, and most of Burma had fallen by March. All that stood in the way of Japan's domination of the southern Pacific was the American stronghold in the Philippines.

Japanese Pilot's Flag Japanese pilots often carried small flags covered with admonitions to fight hard and well. This flag belonged to a pilot named Imano, whose relatives sent him aloft with an inscription that read, "Let your divine plane soar in the sky. We who are left behind pray only for your certain success in sinking an enemy ship." Notably, the inscription emphasized harming Japan's enemies rather than returning home safely. U.S. Naval Academy Museum/photo by Richard D. Bond Jr.

The Japanese unleashed a withering assault against the Philippines in January 1942 (see Map 25.5, page 643). American defenders surrendered to the Japanese in May, and the Japanese victors marched captured American and Filipino soldiers to a concentration camp. Thousands died during the Bataan Death March, and 16,000 more perished in the camp. By the summer of 1942, the Japanese war machine had conquered the oil-rich Dutch East Indies and was poised to strike Australia and New Zealand.

In the spring of 1942, U.S. forces launched a major two-pronged counteroffensive that military officials hoped would reverse the Japanese advance. Forces led by General Douglas MacArthur, commander of the U.S. Armed Forces in the Pacific Theater, moved north from Australia and attacked the Japanese in the Philippines. Far more decisively, Admiral Chester W. Nimitz sailed his battle fleet west from Hawaii to retake Japanese-held islands in the mid-Pacific. On May 7–8, 1942, in the Coral

Sea just north of Australia, the American fleet and carrier-based warplanes defeated a Japanese armada that was sailing around the coast of New Guinea.

Nimitz then learned from an intelligence intercept that the Japanese were massing an invasion force aimed at Midway Island, an outpost guarding the Hawaiian Islands. Nimitz maneuvered his carriers and cruisers into the Central Pacific to surprise the Japanese. In a furious battle that raged on June 3–6, American ships and planes delivered a devastating blow to the Japanese navy.

The **Battle of Midway** reversed the balance of naval power in the Pacific and put the Japanese at a disadvantage for the rest of the war. Japan managed to build only six more large aircraft carriers during the war, while the United States launched dozens, proving the wisdom of Yamamoto's prediction. But the Japanese still occupied and defended the many places they had conquered.

The Campaign in Europe In the dark months after Pearl Harbor, Hitler's eastern-front armies marched ever deeper into the Soviet Union while his western-front forces prepared to invade Britain. As in World War I, the Germans attempted to starve the British into submission by destroying their seaborne lifeline. In 1941 and 1942, they sank Allied ships faster than new ones could be built. Overall, the U-boat campaign sank 4,700 merchant vessels and nearly 200 warships and killed 40,000 Allied seamen.

Until mid-1943, the outcome of the war in the Atlantic remained in doubt. Then, newly invented radar detectors and production of sufficient destroyer escorts for merchant vessels allowed the Allies to prey upon the lurking U-boats. After suffering a 75 percent casualty rate among U-boat crews, Hitler withdrew German submarines from the North Atlantic in late May 1943, allowing thousands of American supply ships to cross the Atlantic unimpeded. Winning the battle of the Atlantic allowed the United States to continue to supply its British and Soviet allies for the duration of the war and to reduce the imminent threat of a German invasion of Britain.

The most important strategic questions confronting the United States and its allies were when and where to open a second front against the Nazis. Stalin demanded that America and Britain mount an immediate and massive assault across the English Channel into western France. A cross-Channel invasion would force Hitler to divert his armies from the eastern front and relieve the pressure on the Soviet Union. Churchill and Roosevelt instead delayed opening a second front, allowing the Germans and the Soviets to slug it out. This weakened both the Nazis and the Communists and made an eventual Allied attack on western France more likely to succeed. Churchill and Roosevelt promised Stalin that they would open a second front, but they decided to strike first in southern Europe and the Mediterranean, a region of long-standing British influence.

In October and November 1942, British forces at El-Alamein in Egypt halted German general Erwin Rommel's drive to capture the Suez Canal, Britain's lifeline to the oil of the Middle East and to British colonies in India and South Asia (Map 25.4). In November, an American army under General Dwight D. Eisenhower landed far to the west, in French Morocco. Propelled by American tank units commanded by General George Patton, the Allied armies had defeated the Germans in North Africa by May 1943. The **North African campaign** killed and captured 350,000 Axis soldiers, pushed the Germans out of Africa, made the Mediterranean safe for Allied shipping, and opened the door for an Allied invasion of Italy.

In January 1943, while the North African campaign was still underway, Roosevelt traveled to the Moroccan city of Casablanca to confer with Churchill and other Allied leaders. Stalin did not attend but urged his allies to keep their promise of opening a major second front in western Europe. Roosevelt and Churchill announced that they would accept nothing less than the "unconditional surrender" of the Axis powers, ruling out peace negotiations. But Churchill and Roosevelt concluded that they needed more time to amass sufficient forces for the cross-Channel invasion of France that Stalin demanded. In the meantime, they planned to capitalize on their success in North Africa and strike against Italy, consigning the Soviet Union to bear the brunt of the Nazi war machine for another year.

On July 10, 1943, combined American and British amphibious forces landed 160,000 troops in Sicily. The badly equipped Italian defenders quickly withdrew to the mainland. Soon afterward, Mussolini was deposed in Italy, ending the reign of Italian fascism. Quickly, the Allies invaded the mainland, and the Italian government surrendered unconditionally. The Germans responded by rushing reinforcements to Italy and seizing control of Rome, turning the Allies' **Italian campaign** into a series of battles to liberate Italy from German occupation.

German troops dug into strong fortifications and fought to defend every inch of Italy's rugged terrain. Only after a long, deadly, and frustrating campaign up the Italian peninsula did the Allies finally liberate Rome in June 1944. Allied forces continued to push into northern Italy against stubborn German defenses for the remainder of the war, making the Italian campaign the war's deadliest for American infantrymen. One soldier wrote that his buddies "died like butchered swine." The Italian campaign

MAP 25.4 The European Theater of World War II, 1942–1945

The Russian reversal of the German offensive at Stalingrad and Leningrad, combined with Allied landings in North Africa and Normandy, trapped Germany in a closing vise of Allied armies on all sides.

READING THE MAP: By November 1942, which nations or parts of nations in the European theater were under Axis control? Which had been absorbed by the Axis powers before the war? Which nations remained neutral? Which ones were affiliated with the Allies?

CONNECTIONS: What were the three fronts in the European theater? When did the Allies initiate actions on each front, and why did Churchill, Stalin, and Roosevelt disagree on the timing of the opening of these fronts?

FOR MORE HELP ANALYZING THIS MAP, see the map activity for this chapter in the Online Study Guide at bedfordstmartins.com/roarkcompact.

occupied numerous German divisions that Hitler might otherwise have deployed on the Russian front, but no German forces were actually taken away from the ongoing attack against the Soviet Union.

Stalin denounced the Allies' Italian campaign because it left "the Soviet Army, which is fighting not only for its country, but also for its Allies, to do the job alone, almost single-handed." The Italian campaign exacted a high cost from the Americans and British, bringing the Nazis no closer to surrender and consuming men and materiel that might have been reserved for a second front in France.

Q: How did the United States seek to counter the Japanese in the Pacific and the Germans in Europe?

The Wartime Home Front

The war effort mobilized Americans as never before. Factories churned out ever more bombs, bullets, tanks, ships, and airplanes, which workers rushed to assemble, leaving their farms and small towns and congregating in cities. Women took jobs with wrenches and welding torches, boosting the nation's workforce and fraying traditional notions that a woman's place was in the home rather than on the assembly line. Despite rationing and shortages, unprecedented government expenditures for war production brought prosperity to many Americans after years of depression-era poverty. Although Americans in uniform risked their lives on battlefields in Europe and Asia, Americans on the U.S. mainland enjoyed complete immunity from foreign attack—in sharp contrast to their Soviet and British allies. The wartime ideology of human rights provided justification for the many sacrifices Americans were required to make in support of the military effort. It also established a standard of basic human equality that became a potent weapon in the campaign for equal rights at home and against the horrifying atrocities of the Holocaust perpetrated by the Nazis.

Women and Families, Guns and Butter

Millions of American women gladly took their places on assembly lines in defense industries. At the start of the war, about a quarter of adult women worked outside the home, most as teachers, nurses, social workers, and domestic servants. Few women worked in factories, except for textile mills and sewing industries, because employers and male workers often discriminated against them. But wartime mobilization of the economy and the siphoning of millions of men into the armed forces left factories begging for women workers.

Pitching in at Home This poster encourages women and children to contribute to the war effort by collecting scrap metal for recycling into weaponry. The poster highlights the middle-class prosperity of the war years, a sharp contrast to the hard times of the 1930s. Chicago Historical Society.

FOR MORE HELP ANALYZING THIS IMAGE, see the visual activity for this chapter in the Online Study Guide at **bedfordstmartins.com/roarkcompact**.

Government advertisements urged women to take industrial jobs by assuring them that their household chores had prepared them for work on the "Victory Line." One billboard proclaimed, "If you've sewed on buttons, or made buttonholes, on a [sewing] machine, you can learn to do spot welding on airplane parts." Millions of women responded, and by the end of the war, women working outside the home numbered 18 million, 50 percent more than in 1939. Contributing to the war effort also paid off in wages. A Kentucky woman remembered her job at a munitions plant, where she earned "the fabulous sum of $32 a week. To us it was an absolute miracle." Although men were paid an average of $54 for comparable wartime work, women accepted the pay differential and welcomed their chance to earn wages and help win the war at the same time.

The majority of married women remained at home, occupied with domestic chores and child care. But they, too, supported the war effort, planting Victory Gardens to provide homegrown vegetables, saving tin cans and newspapers for recycling into war materiel, and hoarding pennies and nickels to buy war bonds. Many families scrimped to cope with the 30 percent inflation during the war, but families supported by men and women in manufacturing industries enjoyed wages that grew twice as fast as inflation.

The war influenced how all families spent their earnings. Buying a new washing machine or car was out of the question, since factories that formerly built them now made military goods. Many other consumer goods—such as tires, gasoline, shoes, and meat—were rationed at home to meet military needs overseas. But most Americans had more money in their pockets than ever before, and they readily found things to buy, including movie tickets, cosmetics, and music recordings.

The wartime prosperity and abundance enjoyed by most Americans contrasted with the experiences of their hard-pressed allies. Personal consumption fell by 22 percent in Britain, and food output plummeted to just one-third of prewar levels in the Soviet Union, creating widespread hunger and even starvation. Few went hungry in the United States. New Deal restraints on agricultural production were lifted, and farm output grew by 25 percent each year during the war, providing a cornucopia of food to be exported to the Allies.

The Double V Campaign Fighting against Nazi Germany and its ideology of Aryan racial supremacy, Americans were confronted with the extensive racial prejudice in their own country. The *Pittsburgh Courier*, a leading black newspaper, asserted that the wartime emergency called for a **Double V campaign** seeking "victory over our enemies at home and victory over our enemies on the battlefields abroad." It was time, the *Courier* proclaimed, "to persuade, embarrass, compel and shame our government and our nation . . . into a more enlightened attitude."

In 1941, black organizations demanded that the federal government require companies receiving defense contracts to integrate their workforces. **A. Philip Randolph**, head of the Brotherhood of Sleeping Car Porters, promised that 100,000 African American marchers would descend on Washington if the president did not eliminate discrimination in defense industries. Roosevelt decided to risk offending his white allies in the South and in unions and issued Executive Order 8802 in mid-1941. It authorized the Committee on Fair Employment Practices to investigate and prevent racial discrimination in employment. Civil rights champions hailed the act, and Randolph triumphantly called off the march.

Progress came slowly, however. In 1940, nine out of ten black Americans lived below the federal poverty line, and those who worked earned an average of just 39 percent of whites' wages. In search of better jobs and living conditions, 5.5 million black Americans migrated from the South to centers of industrial production in the North and West, making a majority of African Americans city dwellers for the first time in U.S. history. Many discovered that unskilled jobs were available but that unions and employers often barred blacks from skilled trades. At least eighteen major unions explicitly prohibited black members. Severe labor shortages and government fair employment standards opened assembly-line jobs in defense plants to African Americans, causing black unemployment to drop by 80 percent during the war. But more jobs did not mean equal pay for blacks. The average income of black families rose during the war, but by the end of the conflict, it still stood at only half of what white families earned.

Blacks' migration to defense jobs intensified racial antagonisms, which boiled over in the hot summer of 1943, when 242 race riots erupted in 47 cities. In the "zoot suit riots" in Los Angeles, hundreds of white servicemen, claiming they were punishing draft dodgers, chased and beat young Mexican American men who dressed in distinctive broad-shouldered, peg-legged zoot suits. The worst mayhem occurred in Detroit, where a long-simmering conflict between whites and blacks over racially segregated housing ignited into a race war. Whites with clubs smashed through black neighborhoods, and blacks retaliated by destroying and looting white-owned businesses. In two days of violence, twenty-five blacks and nine whites were killed, and scores more were injured.

Racial violence created the impetus for the Double V campaign, officially supported by the National Association for the Advancement of Colored People (NAACP), which asserted black Americans' demands for the rights and privileges enjoyed by all other Americans—demands reinforced by the Allies' wartime ideology of freedom and democracy. While the NAACP focused on court challenges to segregation, a new organization founded in 1942, the Congress of Racial Equality (CORE), organized picketing and sit-ins against Jim Crow restaurants and theaters. The Double V campaign greatly expanded membership in the NAACP but achieved only limited success against racial discrimination during the war.

Wartime Politics and the 1944 Election Americans rallied around the war effort in unprecedented unity. Despite the consensus on war aims, the strains and stresses of the nation's massive wartime mobilization made it difficult for Roosevelt to maintain his political coalition. Whites often resented blacks who migrated to northern cities, took jobs, and made themselves at home. Many Americans complained about government price controls and the rationing of scarce goods while the war dragged on. Republicans seized the opportunity to roll back New Deal reforms. A conservative coalition of Republicans and southern Democrats succeeded in abolishing several New Deal agencies in 1942 and 1943, including the Work Projects Administration and the Civilian Conservation Corps.

In June 1944, Congress recognized the sacrifices made by millions of veterans, unanimously passing the landmark **GI Bill of Rights** that gave GIs government funds for education, housing, and health care and provided loans to help them start businesses and buy homes. The GI Bill put the financial resources of the federal government behind the abstract goals of freedom and democracy for which veterans were fighting, and it empowered millions of GIs to better themselves and their families after the war.

After twelve turbulent years in the White House, Roosevelt was exhausted and gravely ill with heart disease, but he was determined to remain president until the war ended. His poor health made the selection of a vice presidential candidate unusually important. Convinced that many Americans had soured on liberal reform, Roosevelt chose Senator Harry S. Truman of Missouri as his running mate. A reliable party man from a southern border state, Truman satisfied urban Democratic leaders while not worrying white southerners who were nervous about challenges to racial segregation.

The Republicans, confident of a strong conservative upsurge in the nation, nominated as their presidential candidate the governor of New York, Thomas E. Dewey, who had made his reputation as a tough crime fighter. In the 1944 presidential campaign, Roosevelt's failing health alarmed many observers, but his frailty was outweighed by Americans' unwillingness to change presidents in the midst of the war and by Dewey's failure to persuade most voters that the New Deal was a creeping socialist menace. Voters gave Roosevelt a 53.5 percent majority, his narrowest presidential victory, ensuring his continued leadership as Dr. Win-the-War.

Reaction to the Holocaust Since the 1930s, the Nazis had persecuted Jews in Germany and every German-occupied territory, causing many Jews to seek asylum beyond Hitler's reach. Roosevelt sympathized

The Holocaust, 1933–1945

with the refugees' pleas for help, but he did not want to jeopardize his foreign policy or offend American voters. After Hitler's Anschluss in 1938, thousands of Austrian Jews sought to immigrate to the United States, but 82 percent of Americans opposed admitting them, and they were turned away. Roosevelt tried to persuade countries in Latin America and Africa to accept Jewish refugees, but none would do so.

In 1942, numerous reports that Hitler was implementing a "final solution" filtered out of German-occupied Europe. Jews and other "undesirables"—such as Gypsies, religious and political dissenters, and homosexuals—were being sent to concentration camps. Old people, children, and others deemed too weak to work were systematically slaughtered and cremated, while the able-bodied were put to work at slave labor until they died of starvation and abuse. Despite such reports, skeptical U.S. State Department officials refused to grant asylum to Jewish refugees. Most Americans, including top officials, believed that reports of the killing camps were exaggerated. Only 152,000 of Europe's millions of Jews managed to gain refuge in the United States prior to America's entry into the war. Afterward, the number of refugees admitted dropped steadily, to just 2,400 by 1944.

Desperate to stem the killing, the World Jewish Congress appealed to the Allies to bomb the death camps and the railroad tracks leading to them in order to hamper the killing and block further shipments of victims. Intent on achieving military victory as soon as possible, the Allies repeatedly turned down bombing requests, arguing that the air forces could not spare resources from their military missions.

The nightmare of the **Holocaust** was all too real. When Russian troops arrived at Auschwitz in Poland in February 1945, they found emaciated prisoners, skeletal corpses, gas chambers, pits filled with human ashes, and loot the Nazis had stripped from the dead, including hair, gold fillings, and false teeth. At last, the truth about the Holocaust began to be known beyond the Germans who had perpetrated and tolerated these atrocities and the men, women, and children who had succumbed to the genocide. By then, it was too late for the 9 million victims—mostly Jews—of the Nazis' crimes against humanity.

Q: **How did the war influence American society?**

Toward Unconditional Surrender

By February 1943, Soviet defenders had finally defeated the massive German offensive against Stalingrad, turning the tide of the war in Europe. After gargantuan sacrifices in fighting that had lasted for eighteen months and killed more than 95 percent of the Russian soldiers and noncommissioned officers engaged at Stalingrad, the Red Army forced Hitler's Wehrmacht to turn back toward the west. Now the Soviets and their Western allies faced the task of driving the Nazis out of eastern and western Europe and forcing them to surrender. Stalin continued to urge Britain and the United States to open a second front in France, but that offensive was postponed for more than a year after the victory at Stalingrad. In the Pacific, the Allies had halted the expansion of the Japanese empire but now had the deadly task of dislodging Japanese defenders from the far-flung outposts they still occupied. Allied military planners devised a strategy to annihilate Axis resistance by taking advantage of America's industrial superiority.

From Bombing Raids to Berlin While the Allied campaigns in North Africa and Italy were under way, British and American pilots flew bombing missions from England to German territories as an airborne substitute for the delayed second front on the ground. During night raids, British bombers targeted general areas, hoping to hit civilians, create terror, and undermine morale. Beginning with Paul Tibbets's flight in August 1942, American pilots flew heavily armored B-17s from English airfields in daytime raids on industrial targets vital for the German war machine, especially oil refineries and ball bearing factories.

German air defenses took a fearsome toll on Allied pilots and aircraft. In 1943, two-thirds of American airmen did not survive to complete their twenty-five-mission tours of duty. In all, 85,000 American airmen were killed in the skies over Europe. Many others were shot down and held as prisoners of war. In February 1944, the arrival of America's durable and deadly P-51 Mustang fighter gave Allied bombers superior protection. The Mustangs slowly began to sweep the Luftwaffe from the skies, allowing bombers to penetrate deep into Germany and pound civilian and military targets around the clock. In April 1944, the Allies began to target bridges and railroads in northwestern Europe in preparation for their cross-Channel invasion.

In November 1943, Churchill, Roosevelt, and Stalin met in Teheran to discuss wartime strategy and the second front. Roosevelt conceded to Stalin that the Soviet Union would exercise de facto control of the eastern European countries that the Red Army occupied as it rolled back the still-potent German Wehrmacht. Stalin agreed to enter the war against Japan once Germany finally surrendered, in effect promising to open a second front in the Pacific theater. Roosevelt and Churchill promised that they would at last launch a massive second-front assault in northern France. Code-named Overlord, the offensive was scheduled to begin in May 1944.

General Eisenhower was assigned overall command of Allied forces and stockpiled mountains of military supplies in England. German defenders, directed by General Erwin Rommel, fortified the cliffs and mined the beaches of northwestern France. But the huge deployment of Hitler's armies in the east, which were trying to halt the Red Army's westward offensive, left too few German troops to stop the millions of Allied soldiers waiting to attack. More decisive, years of Allied air raids had decimated the German Luftwaffe, which could send aloft only 300 fighter planes against 12,000 Allied aircraft.

> Naval officer Tracy Sugarman recalled, "What I thought were piles of cordwood [on the beach] I later learned were the bodies of 2,500 men killed by withering fire from the Nazi gun emplacements."

After frustrating delays caused by stormy weather, Eisenhower launched the largest amphibious assault in world history on **D Day**, June 6, 1944. Rough seas and deadly fire from German machine guns slowed the assault, but Allied soldiers finally succeeded in securing the beachhead. As naval officer Tracy Sugarman recalled, "What I thought were piles of cordwood [on the beach] I later learned were the bodies of 2,500 men killed by withering fire from the Nazi gun emplacements." Sugarman reported that he and the other GIs who made the landing "were exhausted and we were exultant. We had survived D Day!"

Within a week, a flood of soldiers, tanks, and other military equipment swamped the Normandy beaches and propelled Allied forces toward Germany. On August 25, the Allies liberated Paris from four years of Nazi occupation. As the giant pincers of the Allied and Soviet armies closed on Germany in December 1944, Hitler ordered a counterattack to capture the Allies' essential supply port at Antwerp, Belgium. In the Battle of the Bulge (December 16, 1944, to January 31, 1945), as the Allies termed it, German forces drove fifty-five miles into Allied lines before being stopped at Bastogne. More than 70,000 Allied soldiers were killed, including more Americans than in any other battle of the war. The Nazis lost more than 100,000 men and hundreds of tanks, fatally depleting Hitler's reserves.

In February 1945, while Allied armies relentlessly pushed German forces backward, Churchill, Stalin, and Roosevelt met secretly at the **Yalta Conference** (named for the Russian resort town where it was held) to discuss their plans for the postwar world. Seriously ill and noticeably frail, Roosevelt managed

D Day Invasion "Taxi to Hell—and Back" is what Robert Sargent called his photograph of the D Day invasion of Normandy on June 6, 1944. Amid a dense fleet of landing craft, men lucky enough to have made it through rough seas and enemy fire struggle onto the beach to open a second front in Europe. Most of the soldiers in this first wave were cut down by enemy fire from the cliffs beyond the beach. Library of Congress.

to secure Stalin's promise to permit votes of self-determination in the eastern European countries occupied by the Red Army. The Allies pledged to support Chiang Kai-shek as the leader of China. The Soviet Union obtained a role in the postwar governments of Korea and Manchuria in exchange for entering the war against Japan after the defeat of Germany.

The "Big Three" also agreed on the creation of a new international peacekeeping organization, the United Nations (UN). All nations would have a place in the UN General Assembly, but the Security Council would wield decisive power, and its permanent representatives from the Allied powers—China, France, Great Britain, the Soviet Union, and the United States—would possess a veto over UN actions. The Senate ratified the United Nations Charter in July 1945 by a vote of 89 to 2, reflecting the triumph of internationalism during the nation's mobilization for war.

While Allied armies sped toward Berlin, Allied warplanes dropped more bombs after D Day than in all the previous European bombing raids combined. By April 11, Allied armies sweeping in from the west reached the banks of the Elbe River, the agreed-upon

rendezvous with the Red Army, and paused while the Soviets smashed into Berlin. In three weeks of vicious house-to-house fighting, the Red Army captured Berlin on May 2. Hitler had committed suicide on April 30, and the provisional German government surrendered unconditionally on May 7. The war in Europe was finally over, with the sacrifice of 135,576 American soldiers, nearly 250,000 British troops, and 9 million Russian combatants. (See "Historical Question," page 644.)

Roosevelt did not live to witness the end of the war. On April 12, while resting in Warm Springs, Georgia, he suffered a fatal stroke. Americans grieved for the man who had led them through years of depression and world war, and they worried aloud about his successor, Vice President Harry Truman, who would have to steer the nation to victory over Japan and protect American interests in the postwar world.

The Defeat of Japan After the punishing defeats in the Coral Sea and at Midway, Japan had to fend off Allied naval and air attacks. In 1943, British and American forces, along with Indian and Chinese allies, launched an offensive against Japanese outposts

MAP 25.5 The Pacific Theater of World War II, 1941–1945

To drive the Japanese from their far-flung empire, the Allies launched two combined naval and military offensives—one to recapture the Philippines and then attack Japanese forces in China, the other to hop from island to island in the Central Pacific toward the Japanese mainland.

in southern Asia, pushing through Burma and into China, where the armies of Chiang Kai-shek continued to resist conquest. In the Pacific, Americans and their allies attacked Japanese strongholds by sea, air, and land, moving island by island toward the Japanese homeland (Map 25.5).

The island-hopping campaign began in August 1942, when American marines landed on Guadalcanal in the southern Pacific. For the next six months, a savage battle raged for control of the strategic area. Finally, during the night of February 8, 1943,

Japanese forces withdrew. The terrible losses on both sides indicated to the Marines how costly it would be to defeat Japan. After the battle, Joseph Steinbacher, a twenty-one-year-old from Alabama, sailed from San Francisco to New Guinea, where, he recalled, "all the cannon fodder waited to be assigned" to replace the killed and wounded.

In mid-1943, Allied forces launched offensives in New Guinea and the Solomon Islands that gradually secured the South Pacific. In the Central Pacific, amphibious forces conquered the Gilbert

Why Did the Allies Win World War II?

Tens of millions of people around the globe contributed to the outcome of World War II. Battlefield and home-front sacrifices, determination, perseverance, resilience, mistakes, and luck combined with brains, courage, leadership, and material resources to bring about the Allied victory. One indispensable factor in the Allied victory was the alliance among the major powers: the United States, Great Britain, and the Soviet Union. Fighting alone, none of the Allies could have prevailed against Nazi Germany. Together, they were able to defeat what had been the strongest military power in the world.

The major Axis nations—Germany and Japan—did almost nothing to help each other. In the Pacific, Japan fought alone against the United States and its other allies, especially Australia and China. Britain and the Soviet Union contributed relatively little to Allied efforts in the Pacific.

In Europe, Germany enjoyed the support of Hungary, Romania, Bulgaria, and Italy, but none of these nations had the resources and industrial might to field a fully modern army. As late as August 1942, for example, Italian cavalry on horseback brandished sabers and charged Russian lines bristling with tanks. Germany conscripted tens of thousands of men from the territories it occupied as its armies swept east, but such coerced recruits made poorly motivated soldiers.

In contrast, the Allies had a single galvanizing purpose: to defeat Hitler. That goal focused their attention on the European theater. The United States devoted only about 15 percent of its effort to the war against Japan; the remaining 85 percent was directed against Germany. Little else united the Allies. Political and ideological differences between the capitalist democracies and a Communist dictatorship produced suspicion and mistrust, fed by Joseph Stalin's alliance with Adolf Hitler between 1939 and 1941. Nonetheless, the Allies collaborated to force the unconditional surrender of Germany. Three militarily significant consequences of the wartime alliance stand out as decisive ingredients of Allied victory: American material support for Britain and the Soviet Union; American and British bombing campaigns and the D Day invasion of Europe; and the Red Army's success in stopping the eastward advance of the German army at Stalingrad, then relentlessly driving it back to Berlin.

The flood of military supplies that poured out of American factories during the war made Allied victory possible. In total, the United States produced two-thirds of all Allied military equipment. The American auto industry, for example, rapidly converted to war production. By 1944, one Ford plant could assemble the 1.5 million parts of a B-24 bomber in just over an hour and repeat the feat hour after hour, month after month. In addition to shipping hundreds of millions of tons of supplies to Britain and stockpiling equipment for the D Day invasion, the United States sent more than half a million military vehicles to the Soviet Union, accounting for the bulk of the Red Army's motorized transportation. By 1944, American refineries supplied 90 percent of the Allies' high-octane gasoline, prompting Stalin to raise a toast at the Teheran conference "to the American auto industry and the American oil industry," which met the needs of "this . . . war of engines and octanes." American food shipments provided the equivalent of one meal a day for each Russian soldier. The American canned meat Spam was distributed so widely that Soviet troops called it "The Second Front," a sarcastic reference to the Americans' delay in opening a second front in western Europe.

The British and American bombing campaign against German targets in western Europe served as a crucial second-front surrogate until D Day, and it eventually allowed Allied pilots to rule the skies. The bombing campaign reduced the production of tanks, airplanes, and trucks by more than a third and diverted two-thirds of Germany's aircraft and three-quarters of its antiaircraft weapons from supporting the infantry on the eastern front to protecting German cities from Allied air attacks. In addition, improvements in Allied fighter planes allowed British and American pilots to decimate the Luftwaffe. By D Day, the Allies in the west sent aloft more than 12,000 aircraft against only 300 Nazi warplanes. Similarly, 13,000 Soviet aircraft confronted just 500 German fighter planes in the east. Although both the German civilian population and Allied air crews suffered huge casualties as a result

and Marshall islands, which served as forward bases for air assaults on the Japanese home islands. As the Allies attacked island after island, Japanese soldiers were ordered to refuse to surrender no matter how hopeless their plight. The fierce Japanese resistance spurred remorseless Allied bombing attacks on Japanese-occupied islands, followed by amphibious landings by Marines and grinding, inch-by-inch combat to root Japanese fighters out of bunkers and caves.

МЫ ЗЛОМУ ВРАГУ ВСЕ ОТРЕЖЕМ ПУТИ,
ИЗ ПЕТЛИ, ИЗ ЭТОЙ ЕМУ НЕ УЙТИ!

★ **The Eastern Front and the Allied War Effort** The Russian poster shown here illustrates the combined efforts of the Allies, declaring, "We won't let the evil enemy escape the noose. He will not evade it." Photo: Museum of World War II, Natick, Mass.

FOR MORE HELP ANALYZING THIS IMAGE, see the visual activity for this chapter in the Online Study Guide at bedfordstmartins.com/roarkcompact.

of the air campaign, it decisively aided the Soviets' battle against the Germans on the eastern front.

But neither the bombing campaign nor the mountains of American supplies would have won the war if the Soviet Union had not stopped the seemingly unstoppable advance of the German Wehrmacht in the east. Within six months of Hitler's surprise attack on the Soviet Union in June 1941, Stalin's army had lost 4 million soldiers and nearly all its tanks and airplanes, and German armies threatened Moscow. President Franklin Roosevelt's military advisers expected Stalin to capitulate within two or three months. Instead, the Red Army regrouped and managed to halt the Germans' eastward advance by early 1943.

This amazing turn of events required colossal sacrifices by the people of the Soviet Union. As the German army swept east during 1941, Russians frantically dismantled more than 1,500 major industrial plants about to be captured by the Nazis, shipped them east of the Ural Mountains, and reassembled them there. They also built new plants and soon began producing thousands of new tanks, aircraft, and artillery to rearm the Soviet military. Through sheer hard work, the productivity of Soviet war industries more than doubled during the war (see "Global Comparison"). Meanwhile, food production plummeted, allowing the average Russian only one-fourth the amount of food available to the average German. Nearly every able-bodied man not working in a vital war industry was conscripted into the Red Army, which finally crushed the German attackers in the long, merciless battle of Stalingrad and forced the Nazis to begin their retreat west. By the end of the war, about 20 million Soviet civilians and soldiers had been killed, casualties that dwarfed the losses of the other Allies. For every American killed during the war, 45 Soviets died. No contribution to Allied victory was more important than the monumental success of the Soviet Union on the eastern front.

While the island-hopping campaign kept pressure on Japanese forces, the Allies invaded the Philippines in the fall of 1944. In the four-day **Battle of Leyte Gulf**, the greatest naval encounter in world history, the American fleet crushed the Japanese armada, clearing the way for Allied victory in the Philippines. While the Philippine campaign was underway, American forces captured two crucial islands—Iwo Jima and Okinawa—from which they planned to launch an attack on the Japanese homeland. To

Hiroshima Bombing This rare shot taken by a news photographer in Hiroshima immediately after the atomic bomb exploded on August 6, 1945, suggests the shock and incomprehension that survivors later described as their first reactions. On August 9, another atomic bomb created similar devastation in Nagasaki. UN photo.

defend Okinawa and prevent the American invaders from getting within close bombing range of their home islands, Japanese leaders ordered thousands of suicide pilots, known as *kamikaze*, to crash their bomb-laden planes into Allied ships. But instead of destroying the American fleet, they demolished the last vestige of the Japanese air force. By June 1945, the Japanese were nearly defenseless on the sea and in the air. Still, their leaders prepared to fight to the death for their homeland.

Joseph Steinbacher and other GIs who had suffered "horrendous" casualties in the Philippines were now told by their commanding officer, "Men, in a few short months we are going to invade [Japan]. . . . We will be going in on the first wave and are expecting ninety percent casualties the first day. . . . For the few of us left alive the war will be over." Steinbacher later recalled his mental attitude at that moment: "I know that I am now a walking dead man and will not have a snowball's chance in hell of making it through the last great battle to conquer the home islands of Japan."

Atomic Warfare In mid-July 1945, as Allied forces prepared for the final assault on Japan, American scientists tested a secret weapon at an isolated desert site near Los Alamos, New Mexico. In 1942, Roosevelt had authorized the top-secret **Manhattan Project** to find a way to convert nuclear energy into a super-bomb before the Germans added such a weapon to their arsenal. More than 100,000 Americans, led by scientists, engineers, and military officers at Los Alamos, worked frantically to win the race for an atomic bomb. Germany surrendered two and a half months before the test on July 16, 1945, when scientists first witnessed an awesome explosion that sent a mushroom cloud of debris eight miles into the atmosphere.

A delegation of scientists and officials, troubled by the bomb's destructive force, secretly proposed that the United States give a public demonstration of the bomb's cataclysmic power, hoping to persuade Japan's leaders to surrender. But U.S. government officials quickly rejected such a demonstration. Despite numerous defeats, Japan still had more than 6 million reserves at home, fortified by more than

5,000 kamikaze aircraft stockpiled for a last-ditch defense against the anticipated Allied assault, which U.S. military advisers estimated would cost the lives of at least 250,000 Americans.

President Truman heard about the successful bomb test when he was in Potsdam, Germany, negotiating with Stalin about postwar issues. Truman realized that the atomic bomb could hasten the end of the war with Japan, perhaps before the Russians could attack the Japanese, as Stalin had pledged at Yalta. Within a few months after the defeat of Germany, Truman also recognized that the bomb gave the United States a devastating atomic monopoly that could be used to counter Soviet ambitions and advance American interests in the postwar world.

Truman saw no reason not to use the atomic bomb against Japan if doing so would save American lives. But first he issued an ultimatum: Japan must surrender unconditionally or face utter ruin. When the Japanese failed to respond by the deadline, Truman ordered that a bomb be dropped on a Japanese city not already heavily damaged by American raids. On August 6, Colonel Paul Tibbets piloted the *Enola Gay* over Hiroshima and released an atomic bomb, leveling the city and incinerating 78,000 people. Three days later, after the Japanese government still refused to surrender, Tibbets-trained airmen dropped a second atomic bomb on Nagasaki, killing more than 100,000 civilians.

With American assurance that the emperor could retain his throne after the Allies took over, Japan surrendered on August 14. On a troop ship departing from Europe for what would have been the final assault on Japan, an American soldier spoke for millions of others when he heard the wonderful news that the killing was over: "We are going to grow to adulthood after all."

Q: Why did Truman elect to use the atomic bomb against Japan?

Conclusion: Allied Victory and America's Emergence as a Superpower

Shortly after Pearl Harbor, Hitler pronounced America "a decayed country" without "much future"; a country "half Judaized, and the other half Negrified"; a country "where everything is built on the dollar" and bound to fall apart. American mobilization for World War II disproved Hitler's arrogant prophecy, as Paul Tibbets's historic flight dramatized. At a cost of 405,399 American lives, the nation united with its allies to battle Axis aggressors in Europe and Asia and eventually to crush them into unconditional surrender. Almost all Americans believed they had won a "good war" against totalitarian evil. The Allies saved Asia and Europe from enslavement and finally halted the Nazis' genocidal campaign against Jews and others whom the Nazis considered inferior. To secure human rights and protect the world against future wars, the Roosevelt administration took the lead in creating the United Nations.

Wartime production lifted the nation out of the Great Depression. The gross national product soared to four times what it had been when Roosevelt became president in 1933. Jobs in defense industries eliminated chronic unemployment, provided wages for millions of women workers and African American migrants from southern farms, and boosted Americans' prosperity. Ahead stretched the challenge of maintaining that prosperity while reintegrating millions of uniformed men and women.

By the end of the war, the United States had emerged as a global superpower. Wartime mobilization made the American economy the strongest in the world, buttressed by the military clout of the nation's nuclear monopoly. Although the war left much of the world a rubble-strewn wasteland, the American mainland had enjoyed immunity from attack. The Japanese occupation of China had left 50 million people without homes and millions more dead, maimed, and orphaned. The German offensive against the Soviet Union had killed more than 20 million Russian soldiers and civilians. Germany and Japan lay in ruins, their economies as shattered as their military forces. The Allies had killed more than 4 million Nazi soldiers and more than 1.2 million Japanese combatants, as well as hundreds of thousands of civilians. But in the gruesome balance sheet of war, the Axis powers had inflicted far more grief, misery, and destruction upon the global victims of their aggression than they had suffered in return.

As the dominant Western nation in the postwar world, the United States asserted its leadership in the reconstruction of Europe while occupying Japan and overseeing its economic and political recovery. America soon confronted new challenges in the tense aftermath of the war, as the Soviets seized political control of eastern Europe, a Communist revolution swept China, and national liberation movements emerged in the colonial empires of Britain and France. The surrender of the Axis powers ended the battles of World War II, but the forces unleashed by the war would shape the United States and the rest of the world for decades to come.

Reviewing the Chapter

★ KEY TERMS

Explain each term's significance

WHO
Paul Tibbets (p. 623)
Adolf Hitler (p. 625)
Chiang Kai-shek (p. 626)
Joseph Stalin (p. 627)
Winston Churchill (p. 628)
A. Philip Randolph (p. 639)

WHAT
Spanish civil war (p. 626)
isolationism (p. 626)
appeasement (p. 627)
Battle of Britain (p. 629)
Lend-Lease Act (p. 629)
Atlantic Charter (p. 630)
Pearl Harbor (p. 631)
internment camps (p. 632)
Selective Service Act (p. 633)
Battle of Midway (p. 636)
North African campaign (p. 636)
Italian campaign (p. 636)
Double V campaign (p. 639)
GI Bill of Rights (p. 640)
Holocaust (p. 640)
D Day (p. 641)
Yalta Conference (p. 641)
Battle of Leyte Gulf (p. 645)
Manhattan Project (p. 646)

FOR PRACTICE QUIZZES AND OTHER STUDY TOOLS, see the Online Study Guide at **bedfordstmartins.com/roarkcompact**.

★ REVIEW QUESTIONS Q:

Use key terms and dates to support your answer

1. Why did isolationism during the 1930s concern Roosevelt? (pp. 624–27)

2. How did Roosevelt attempt to balance American isolationism with the increasingly ominous international scene of the late 1930s? (pp. 627–32)

3. How did the Roosevelt administration mobilize the human and industrial resources necessary to fight a two-front war? (pp. 632–35)

4. How did the United States seek to counter the Japanese in the Pacific and the Germans in Europe? (pp. 635–38)

5. How did the war influence American society? (pp. 638–40)

6. Why did Truman elect to use the atomic bomb against Japan? (pp. 641–47)

★ MAKING CONNECTIONS

Draw on key terms, timeline, and review questions

1. Did isolationism bolster or undermine national security and national economic interests? Discuss Roosevelt's evolving answer to this question as revealed in his administration's policies toward Europe. In your answer, consider how other constraints (such as politics, history, and ethics) affected administration policies.

2. World War II brought new prosperity to many Americans. Why did war succeed in creating the full economic recovery that the New Deal had pursued with more limited success? In your answer, discuss both the objectives of specific New Deal economic reforms and the needs of the wartime economy.

3. Japan's attack on Pearl Harbor plunged the United States into war with the Axis powers. How did the United States recover from this attack to play a decisive role in the Allies' victory? Discuss three American military or diplomatic actions and their contribution to the defeat of the Axis powers.

4. As the United States battled racist regimes abroad, the realities of discrimination at home came sharply into focus. How did minorities' contributions to the war effort as soldiers and laborers draw attention to these problems? What were the political implications of these developments? In your answer, consider both grassroots political action and federal policy.

★ SUGGESTED READINGS

Elizabeth Borgwardt, *A New Deal for the World: America's Vision for Human Rights* (2005). The story of the Allies' efforts to uphold human rights in the context of wartime devastation.

John Dower, *War without Mercy: Race and Power in the Pacific War* (1986). A powerful exploration of racial attitudes among belligerents in the Pacific theater.

Max Hastings, *Armageddon: The Battle for Germany, 1944–45* (2005). A compelling analysis of the Allied attacks from east and west that finally defeated Germany.

Max Hastings, *Retribution: The Battle for Japan, 1944–45* (2008). A penetrating account of the defeat of Japan.

Richard Rhodes, *The Making of the Atomic Bomb* (1986). The fascinating history of the industrial, scientific, and military mobilization to build the atomic bomb.

E. B. Sledge, *With the Old Breed at Peleliu and Okinawa* (1981). A Marine's classic firsthand account of brutal combat in the Pacific island-hopping campaign.

FOR MORE BOOKS ABOUT TOPICS IN THIS CHAPTER, see the Online Bibliography at **bedfordstmartins.com/roarkcompact**.

FOR ADDITIONAL FIRSTHAND ACCOUNTS OF THIS PERIOD, see Chapter 25 in Michael Johnson, ed., *Reading the American Past*, Fourth Edition.

FOR WEB SITES, IMAGES, AND DOCUMENTS RELATED TO TOPICS AND PLACES IN THIS CHAPTER, visit Make History at **bedfordstmartins.com/roarkcompact**.

★ TIMELINE

1935–1937	• Congress passes neutrality acts.
1936	• Nazi Germany occupies Rhineland. • Mussolini conquers Ethiopia. • Spanish civil war begins.
1937	• Japanese troops capture Nanking. • Roosevelt introduces his quarantine policy.
1938	• Hitler annexes Austria.
1939	• German troops occupy Czechoslovakia. • Nazi-Soviet nonaggression pact. • **September 1.** Germany's attack on Poland begins World War II.
1940	• Germany invades Denmark, Norway, France, Belgium, Luxembourg, and the Netherlands. • British and French evacuation from Dunkirk. • Vichy government installed in France. • Battle of Britain. • Tripartite Pact signed by Japan, Germany, and Italy.
1941	• Lend-Lease Act. • **June.** Germany invades Soviet Union. • **August.** Atlantic Charter issued. • **December 7.** Japanese attack Pearl Harbor.
1942	• Roosevelt authorizes internment of Japanese Americans. • Japan captures Philippines. • Congress of Racial Equality (CORE) founded. • Battles of Coral Sea and Midway. • Roosevelt authorizes Manhattan Project. • **November.** U.S. forces invade North Africa.
1943	• Allied leaders demand unconditional surrender of Axis powers. • Zoot suit riots. • U.S. and British forces invade Sicily.
1944	• **June 6.** D Day.
1945	• **February.** Yalta Conference. • **April 12.** Roosevelt dies; Vice President Harry Truman becomes president. • **April 30.** Hitler commits suicide. • **May 7.** Germany surrenders. • **July.** United States joins United Nations. • **August 6.** United States drops atomic bomb on Hiroshima. • **August 9.** United States drops atomic bomb on Nagasaki. • **August 14.** Japan surrenders, ending World War II.

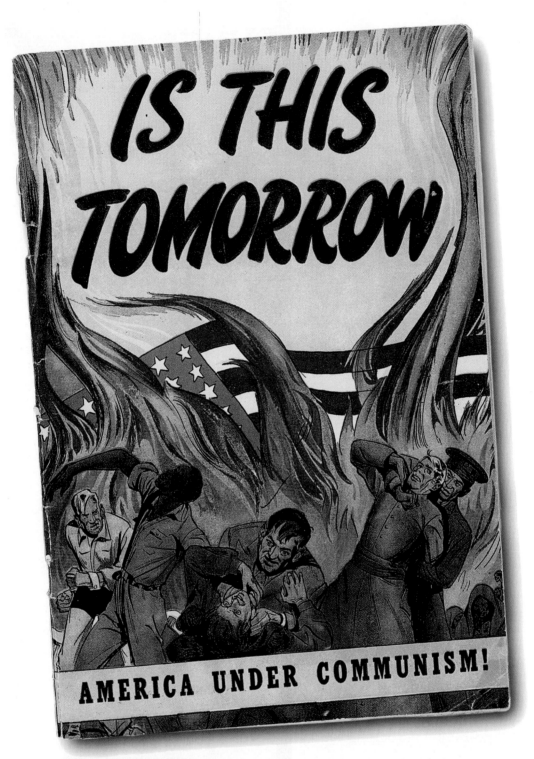

COLD WAR COMIC BOOK Americans barely had time to celebrate the Allied victory in World War II when they perceived a new threat, posed by the Soviet Union. Fear of communism dominated much of postwar American life and politics, even invading popular culture. Four million copies of this comic book, published by a religious organization in 1947, painted a terrifying picture of what would happen to Americans if the Soviets took over the country. Such takeover stories appeared in movies, cartoons, and magazines as well as in other comic books. Collection of Charles H. Christensen.

Cold War Politics in the Truman Years

1945–1953

HEADS TURNED WHEN Congresswoman **Helen Gahagan Douglas** walked through the U.S. Capitol. When she served there from 1945 to 1951, she had no more than 10 female colleagues at any one time in the 435-member House of Representatives. Not only did she stand out as a woman in a thoroughly male institution, but she also drew attention as a strikingly attractive former Broadway star and opera singer. She served in Congress when the fate of the New Deal was up for grabs and the nation charted a dramatic new course in foreign policy.

Helen Gahagan was born to prosperous parents in 1900 and grew up in Brooklyn, New York. Drawn to the theater as a child, she defied her father and left Barnard College for the stage after her sophomore year. She quickly won fame on Broadway, starring in show after show until she fell in love with one of her leading men, Melvyn Douglas. They married in 1931, and she followed him to Hollywood, where he hoped to advance his movie career. During the 1930s, she bore two children. She continued to appear in theater productions and concerts as well as in one movie, but her career was on the wane.

Helen Gahagan Douglas abandoned the staunch Republicanism of her parents during the depression, when Franklin D. Roosevelt's leadership captured her admiration. As Hollywood became a hotbed of liberal and radical politics, the Douglases were drawn in. Both were shaken by the anti-Semitism and militarism that they witnessed on a visit to Germany in 1937, vowing never to perform there again and subsequently joining the Anti-Nazi League in California. But it was the plight of poor migrant farmworkers moving to California from Oklahoma and other states that pushed Helen Douglas into politics. Visiting migrant camps, she saw "faces stamped with poverty and despair," a "human calamity" that prompted her to head the John Steinbeck Committee to Aid Migratory Workers.

Douglas's work on behalf of migrant farmworkers connected her to the White House. She testified before Congress and became a friend of Eleanor Roosevelt and a campaigner for the president in 1940. In California, she rose fast in party politics, becoming vice chairman of the state Democratic Party and head of the Women's Division. In 1944, she won election to

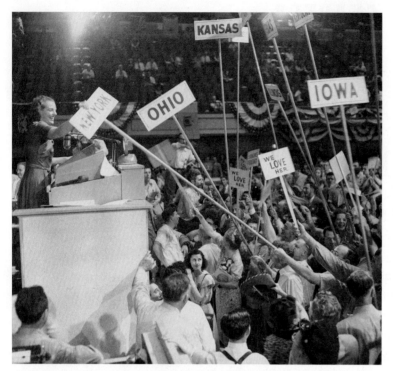

Helen Gahagan Douglas at the Democratic National Convention Long accustomed as an actress to appearing before an audience, the congresswoman from California was a popular campaigner for the Democrats and a featured speaker at the Democratic National Conventions of 1944 and 1948. Her appeal, shown in this photo from the 1948 convention, sparked interest in her for higher office. The *Washington Post* called it the "first genuine boom in history for a woman for vice-president," but she made it clear that she was not in the running. © Bettmann/Corbis.

Congress. There she represented not the posh Hollywood district where she lived, but the Fourteenth Congressional District in downtown Los Angeles, with its multiethnic, multiracial population, which helped shape her progressive politics.

Like many liberals who were devoted to Roosevelt, Douglas was devastated by his death and unsure of his successor, Harry S. Truman. "Who was Harry Truman anyway?" she said. "None of us knew much about him." A compromise choice for the vice presidency, this "accidental president" lacked the charisma and political skills with which Roosevelt had transformed foreign and domestic policy, won four presidential elections, and forged a Democratic Party coalition that dominated national politics. Truman faced a resurgent Republican Party, which had gained strength in Congress during World War II, as well as revolts from within his own party. Besides confronting domestic problems that the New Deal had not solved — how to sustain economic growth and avoid another depression without the war to fuel the economy — Truman faced new international challenges that threatened to undermine the nation's security.

By 1947, a new term had been coined to describe the intense rivalry that grew between the United States and the Soviet Union superpowers — Cold War. Truman and his advisers became convinced that the Soviet Union posed a major threat to the United States, and they gradually shaped a policy to contain Soviet power wherever it threatened to spread. As a member of the House Foreign Affairs Committee, Douglas urged cooperation with the Soviet Union, and she voted against aid to Greece and Turkey, the first step in the new containment policy. Thereafter, she was Truman's loyal ally, supporting the Marshall Plan, the creation of the North Atlantic Treaty Organization (NATO), and the war in Korea. The containment policy achieved its goals in Europe, but communism spread in Asia, and at home a wave of anti-Communist hysteria — a second Red scare — harmed many Americans and stifled dissent and debate about U.S. policies.

Douglas's earlier links with leftist and liberal groups and her advocacy of civil rights, women's rights, and social welfare programs made her and other liberals easy targets for conservative politicians seeking to capitalize on anti-Communist fervor. When she decided to run for the U.S. Senate in 1950, she faced Republican Richard M. Nixon, who had gained national attention as a member of the House Un-American Activities Committee, which sought to expose Communists in government and whose funding Douglas had voted to cut. Nixon's campaign labeled her as "pink right down to her underwear" and telephoned thousands of homes on election eve with the anonymous message, "I think you should know Helen Douglas is a Communist." Nixon won a decisive victory but carried throughout his life the appellation Douglas gave him, "Tricky Dick." Douglas's political career ended in defeat, just as much of Truman's domestic agenda fell victim to the Red scare. ★

From the Grand Alliance to Containment

With Japan's surrender in August 1945, Americans besieged the government for the return of their loved ones. Baby booties arrived at the White House with a note, "Please send my daddy home." Americans wanted to dismantle the large military establishment and expected the Allies, led by the United States and working within the United Nations, to cooperate in the management of international peace. Postwar realities quickly dashed these hopes. New threats arose as the wartime alliance forged by the United States, Great Britain, and the Soviet Union crumbled, and the United States began to develop the means to contain the spread of Soviet power around the globe.

The Cold War Begins "The guys who came out of World War II were idealistic," reported Harold Russell, a young paratrooper who had lost both hands in a training accident. "We felt the day had come when the wars were all over." Public opinion polls echoed the veterans' confidence in the promise of peace. But political leaders were less optimistic. Once the Allies had overcome a common enemy, the prewar mistrust and antagonism between the Soviet Union and the West resurfaced over their very different visions of the postwar world.

The Western Allies' delay in opening a second front in Western Europe aroused Soviet suspicions during the war. The Soviet Union made supreme wartime sacrifices, losing more than twenty million citizens and vast portions of its agricultural and industrial capacity. Soviet leader Joseph Stalin wanted to make Germany pay for Soviet economic reconstruction and to expand Soviet influence in the world. Above all, he wanted friendly governments on the Soviet Union's borders in Eastern Europe. A ruthless dictator, he also wanted to maintain his own power.

In contrast to the Soviet devastation, enemy fire had never touched the mainland of the United States, and its 405,000 dead amounted to just 2 percent of the Soviet loss. With a vastly expanded economy and a monopoly on atomic weapons, the United States was the most powerful nation on the planet. That sheer power, along with U.S. economic interests, policymakers' views about how the recent war might have been avoided, and a belief in the superiority of American institutions and intentions, all affected how American leaders approached the Soviet Union.

Fearing a return of the depression, U.S. officials believed that a healthy economy depended on opportunities abroad. American companies needed access to raw materials, markets for their goods, and security for their investments overseas. These needs could be met best in countries with similar economic and political systems, not in those where government controls interfered with the free flow of products and dollars. As Truman put it in 1947, "The American system can survive in America only if it becomes a world system." Yet both leaders and citizens regarded their foreign policy not as a self-interested campaign to guarantee economic interests, but as the means to preserve national security and bring freedom, democracy, and capitalism to the rest of the world. Laura Briggs spoke for many Americans who believed "it was our destiny to

prove that we were the children of God and that our way was right for the world."

Recent history also shaped postwar foreign policy. Americans believed that World War II might have been avoided had Britain and France resisted rather than appeased Hitler's initial aggression. Navy Secretary James V. Forrestal argued against trying to "buy [the Soviets'] understanding and sympathy. We tried that once with Hitler." This "appeasement" analogy would be invoked repeatedly when the United States faced challenges to the international status quo.

The man with ultimate responsibility for U.S. policy was a keen student of history but came to the White House with little international experience. **Harry S. Truman** envisioned Soviet-American cooperation, as long as the Soviet Union conformed to U.S. plans for the postwar world and restrained its expansionist impulses. Proud of his ability to make quick decisions, Truman determined to be firm with the Soviets, knowing well that America's nuclear monopoly gave him the upper hand.

Soviet and American interests clashed first in Eastern Europe. Stalin insisted that the Allies' wartime agreements gave him a free hand in the countries defeated or liberated by the Red Army, just as the United States was unilaterally reconstructing governments in Italy and Japan. The Soviet dictator used harsh methods to install Communist governments in neighboring Poland and Bulgaria. Elsewhere, the Soviets initially tolerated non-Communist governments in Hungary and Czechoslovakia. In the spring of 1946, Stalin responded to pressure from the West and removed troops from Iran on the Soviet Union's southwest border, allowing U.S. access to the rich oil fields there.

Stalin considered U.S. officials hypocritical in demanding democratic elections in Eastern Europe while supporting dictatorships friendly to U.S. interests in Latin America. The United States clung to its sphere of influence while opposing Soviet efforts to create its own. But the Western Allies were unwilling to match tough words with military force against the largest army in the world. They issued sharp protests but failed to prevent the Soviet Union from establishing satellite countries throughout Eastern Europe.

In 1946, the wartime Allies contended over Germany's future. Both sides wanted to demilitarize Germany, but American policymakers sought rapid industrial revival there to foster European economic recovery and thus America's own long-term prosperity. By contrast, the Soviet Union wanted Germany weak militarily and economically, and Stalin demanded heavy reparations to help rebuild the devastated Soviet economy. Unable to settle their differences, the Allies divided Germany. The Soviet

MAP 26.1 The Division of Europe after World War II
The "iron curtain," a term coined by Winston Churchill to refer to the Soviet grip on Eastern and central Europe, divided the continent for nearly fifty years. Communist governments controlled the countries along the Soviet Union's western border. The only exception was Finland, which remained neutral.

Union installed a puppet Communist government in the eastern section, and in December 1946, Britain, France, and the United States unified their occupation zones, beginning the process that established the Federal Republic of Germany—West Germany—in 1949 (Map 26.1).

The war of words escalated early in 1946. Boasting of the superiority of the Soviet system, Stalin told a Moscow audience in February that capitalism inevitably produced war. One month later, Truman accompanied Winston Churchill to Fulton, Missouri, where the former prime minister denounced Soviet interference in Eastern and central Europe. "From Stettin in the Baltic to Trieste in the Adriatic, an **iron curtain** has descended across the Continent," Churchill said. (See "Documenting the American Promise," page 656.) Stalin saw Churchill's proposal for joint British-American action to combat Soviet aggression as "a call to war against the USSR."

In February 1946, **George F. Kennan**, a career diplomat and expert on Russia, wrote a comprehensive rationale for hard-line foreign policy. Downplaying the influence of Communist ideology in Soviet policy, he instead stressed the Soviets' insecurity and Stalin's need to maintain authority at home, which he believed prompted Stalin to exaggerate threats from abroad and to expand Soviet power. Kennan believed that the Soviet Union would retreat from its expansionist efforts "in the face of superior force," recommending that the United States respond with "unalterable counterforce." He predicted that this approach, which came to be called **containment**, would eventually end in "either the breakup or the gradual mellowing of Soviet power."

Kennan later expressed dismay when his ideas were used to justify what he considered an indiscriminate American response wherever communism seemed likely to arise. Nonetheless, his analysis marked a critical turning point in the development of the Cold War, providing a compelling rationale for wielding U.S. power throughout the world.

Not all public figures accepted the toughening line. In September 1946, Secretary of Commerce **Henry A. Wallace** urged greater understanding of the Soviets' concerns about their nation's security, insisting that "we have no more business in the political affairs of Eastern Europe than Russia has in the political affairs of Latin America." (See "Documenting the American Promise," page 656.) State Department officials were furious, and Truman fired Wallace.

The Truman Doctrine and the Marshall Plan

In 1947, the United States began to implement the doctrine of containment that would guide foreign policy for the next four decades. It was not an easy transition; Americans approved taking a hard line against the Soviet Union, but they wanted to keep their soldiers and tax dollars at home. In addition to selling containment to the public, Truman had to gain the support of a Republican-controlled Congress, which included a forceful bloc opposed to a strong U.S. presence in Europe.

Crises in two Mediterranean countries triggered the implementation of containment. In February 1947, Britain informed the United States that its crippled economy could no longer sustain military assistance either to Greece, where the autocratic government faced a leftist uprising, or to Turkey, which was trying to resist Soviet pressures. Truman promptly sought congressional authority to send the two countries military and economic missions, along with $400 million in aid. Meeting with congressional leaders, Undersecretary of State Dean Acheson predicted that if Greece and Turkey fell, communism would soon consume three-fourths of the world. After a stunned silence, Michigan senator Arthur Vandenberg, the Republican foreign policy leader and a recent convert from isolationism, warned that to get approval, Truman would have to "scare hell out of the country."

Truman did just that. Outlining what would later be called the domino theory, he warned that if Greece fell to the rebels, "confusion and disorder might well spread throughout the entire Middle East" and then create instability in Europe. Failure to act, he said, "may endanger the peace of the world—and shall surely endanger the welfare of the nation." According to what came to be called the **Truman Doctrine**, the United States would not only resist Soviet military power but also "support free peoples who are resisting attempted subjugation by armed minorities or by outside pressures." The president failed to convince Helen Gahagan Douglas and some of her colleagues in Congress, who wanted the United States to work through the United Nations before acting unilaterally and who opposed propping up the authoritarian Greek

government. But the administration won the day, setting a precedent for forty years of Cold War interventions that would aid any kind of government if the only alternative appeared to be communism.

A much larger assistance program for Europe followed aid to Greece and Turkey. In May 1947, Acheson described a war-ravaged Western Europe, with "factories destroyed, fields impoverished, transportation systems wrecked, populations scattered and on the borderline of starvation." American citizens were sending generous amounts of private aid, but Europe needed large-scale assistance. European economic recovery, Acheson argued, was essential to halt the growth of socialist and Communist parties in France and Italy.

In March 1948, Congress approved the **European Recovery Program**—known as the **Marshall Plan**, after retired general George C. Marshall, who as secretary of state proposed the plan. Over the next five years, the United States spent $13 billion to restore the economies of sixteen Western European nations. Marshall invited all European nations and the Soviet Union to cooperate in a request for aid, but as administration officials expected, the Soviets objected to the American terms of free trade and financial disclosure and ordered their Eastern European satellites likewise to reject the offer.

The Marshall Plan marked the first step toward the European Union. Humanitarian impulses as well as the goal of keeping Western Europe free of communism drove the adoption of this enormous aid program. But the Marshall Plan also helped boost the U.S. economy because the European nations spent most of the dollars to buy American products and Europe's economic recovery created new markets and opportunities for American investment.

In February 1948, the Soviets staged a brutal coup and installed a Communist regime in Czechoslovakia, the last democracy left in Eastern Europe. Next, Stalin threatened Western access to Berlin. That former capital of Germany lay within Soviet-controlled East Germany, but all four Allies jointly occupied Berlin, dividing it into separate administrative units. As the Western Allies moved to organize West Germany as a separate nation, the Soviets retaliated by blocking roads and rail lines between West Germany and the Western-held sections of Berlin, cutting off food, fuel, and other essentials to two million inhabitants.

Berlin Divided, 1948

The Emerging Cold War

Although antagonism between the Soviet Union and the West stretched back to the Russian Revolution of 1917, the United States, the Soviet Union, Britain, and other powers had cooperated to win World War II. Early in 1946, however, Soviet and Western leaders publicly expressed distrust and attributed hostile motivations to each other. Within the United States, disagreement arose about how to deal with the Soviet Union.

DOCUMENT 1
Joseph Stalin Addresses a Rally in Moscow, February 9, 1946

In early 1946, Premier Joseph Stalin called on the Soviet people to support his program for economic development. Although Stalin did not address Cold War issues, leaders in the West viewed his comments about communism and capitalism and his boasts about the strength of the Red Army as a threat to peace.

The [Second World War] arose as the inevitable result of the development of the world economic and political forces on the basis of monopoly capitalism. . . .

. . . The uneven development of the capitalist countries leads in time to sharp disturbances in their relations, and the group of countries which consider themselves inadequately provided with raw materials and export markets try usually to change this situation and to change the position in their favor by means of armed force. As a result of these factors, the capitalist world is split into two hostile camps and war follows. . . . The Soviet social system has proved to be more capable of life and more stable than a non-Soviet social system. . . .

. . . The Red Army heroically withstood all the adversities of the war, routed completely the armies of our enemies and emerged victoriously from the war. This is recognized by everybody—friend and foe.

[Stalin talks about his new Five-Year Plan.] Apart from the fact that in the very near future the rationing system will be abolished, special attention will be focused on expanding the production of goods for mass consumption, on raising the standard of life of the working people by consistent

and systematic reduction of the costs of all goods, and on wide-scale construction of all kinds of scientific research institutes to enable science to develop its forces. I have no doubt that if we render the necessary assistance to our scientists they will be able not only to overtake but also in the very near future to surpass the achievements of science outside the boundaries of our country.

SOURCE: Excerpts from Joseph Stalin, *Vital Speeches of the Day*, February 9, 1946.

DOCUMENT 2
Winston Churchill Delivers His "Iron Curtain" Speech at Westminster College in Fulton, Missouri, March 5, 1946

With Truman sitting on the podium, Winston Churchill, former prime minister of Great Britain, assessed Soviet actions in harsh terms. In response, Stalin equated Churchill with Hitler, as a "firebrand of war."

The United States stands at this time at the pinnacle of world power. It is a solemn moment for the American democracy. With primacy in power is also joined an awe-inspiring accountability to the future. [Churchill then speaks of the need to support the United Nations.]

It would nevertheless be wrong and imprudent to intrust the secret knowledge or experience of the atomic bomb, which the United States, Great Britain and Canada now share, to the world organization [the United Nations], while it is still in its infancy. It would be criminal madness to cast it adrift in this still agitated and ununited world. . . .

. . . I have a strong admiration and regard for the valiant Russian people and for my war-time comrade, Marshal Stalin. . . . We understand the Russians need to be secure on her western frontiers from all renewal of German aggression. . . . It is my duty, however, to place before you certain facts. . . .

From Stettin in the Baltic to Trieste in the Adriatic, an iron curtain has descended across the Continent. Behind that line lie all the capitals of the ancient states of central and eastern Europe. Warsaw, Berlin, Prague, Vienna, Budapest, Belgrade, Bucharest and Sofia, all these famous

"We stay in Berlin, period," Truman vowed. To avoid a confrontation with Soviet troops, for nearly a year U.S. and British pilots airlifted 2.3 million tons of goods to sustain the West Berliners. Stalin hesitated to shoot down these cargo planes, and

in 1949 he lifted the blockade. The city was then divided into East Berlin, under Soviet control, and West Berlin, which became part of West Germany. For many Americans, the **Berlin airlift** confirmed the wisdom of containment: When challenged, cities and the populations around them lie in the Soviet sphere and all are subject in one form or another, not only to Soviet influence but to a very high and increasing measure of control from Moscow. . . . The Communist parties, which were very small in all these eastern states of Europe, have been raised to preeminence and power far beyond their numbers and are seeking everywhere to obtain totalitarian control. Police governments are prevailing in nearly every case. . . .

. . . In a great number of countries, far from the Russian frontiers and throughout the world, Communist fifth columns are established and work in complete unity and absolute obedience to the directions they receive from the Communist center.

I do not believe that Soviet Russia desires war. What they desire is the fruits of war and the indefinite expansion of their power and doctrines. . . . Our difficulties and dangers will not be removed by . . . mere waiting to see what happens; nor will they be relieved by a policy of appeasement. . . . I am convinced that there is nothing [the Russians] admire so much as strength, and there is nothing for which they have less respect than for military weakness.

SOURCE: Excerpts from Winston Churchill, *Vital Speeches of the Day*, March 5, 1946.

DOCUMENT 3
Henry A. Wallace Addresses an Election Rally at Madison Square Garden, New York, September 12, 1946

Throughout 1946, Henry A. Wallace, Truman's secretary of commerce and predecessor as vice president, urged the president to take a more conciliatory approach toward the Soviet Union, a position reflected in a speech Wallace gave to a rally of leftist and liberal groups in New York City. Truman believed that Wallace's words undermined his foreign policy and asked for Wallace's resignation.

We cannot rest in the assurance that we invented the atom bomb—and therefore that this agent of destruction will work best for us. He who trusts in the atom bomb will sooner or later perish by the atom bomb—or something worse. . . .

To achieve lasting peace, we must study in detail just how the Russian character was formed—by invasions of Tartars, Mongols, Germans, Poles, Swedes, and French; by the czarist rule based on ignorance, fear and force; by the intervention of the British, French and Americans in Russian affairs from 1919 to 1921; by the geography of the huge

Russian land mass situated strategically between Europe and Asia; and by the vitality derived from the rich Russian soil and the strenuous Russian climate. Add to all this the tremendous emotional power which Marxism and Leninism gives to the Russian leaders—and then we can realize that we are reckoning with a force which cannot be handled successfully by a "Get tough with Russia" policy. "Getting tough" never bought anything real and lasting—whether for schoolyard bullies or businessmen or world powers. The tougher we get, the tougher the Russians will get. . . .

. . . We want cooperation. And I believe that we can get cooperation once Russia understands that our primary objective is neither saving the British Empire nor purchasing oil in the Near East with the lives of American soldiers. . . .

On our part we should recognize that we have no more business in the political affairs of Eastern Europe than Russia has in the political affairs of Latin America, Western Europe and the United States. . . . We have to recognize that the Balkans are closer to Russia than to us—and that Russia cannot permit either England or the United States to dominate the politics of that area. . . .

. . . Under friendly peaceful competition the Russian world and the American world will gradually become more alike. The Russians will be forced to grant more and more of the personal freedoms; and we shall become more and more absorbed with the problems of social-economic justice.

SOURCE: Excerpts from Henry A. Wallace, *Vital Speeches of the Day*, September 12, 1946. Reprinted with permission.

Questions for Analysis and Debate

1. What lessons did these three leaders draw from World War II? What did they see as the most critical steps to preventing another war?

2. What differences did these men see between the political and economic systems of the Soviet Union on the one hand and the United States and Western Europe on the other? How do their predictions about these systems differ?

3. What motives did these three men ascribe to Soviet actions? How do Churchill's and Wallace's proposals for the Western response to the Soviet Union differ?

4. Which leader do you think was most optimistic about the prospects for good relationships between Russia and the West? Which was most correct? Why?

the Russians backed down, as George Kennan had predicted.

Building a National Security State
During the Truman years, advocates of the new containment

policy fashioned a six-pronged defense strategy: (1) development of atomic weapons, (2) strengthening of traditional military power, (3) military alliances with other nations, (4) military and economic aid to friendly nations, (5) an espionage

Marshall Plan Bread for Greek Children Greece was one of sixteen European nations that participated in the European Recovery Program. In this photograph taken in 1949, Greek children receive loaves of bread made from the first shipment of Marshall Plan flour from the United States. © Bettmann/Corbis.

network and secret means to subvert Communist expansion, and (6) a propaganda offensive to win popular admiration for the United States around the world.

In September 1949, the United States lost its nuclear monopoly when the Soviet Union detonated its own atomic bomb. To keep the United States ahead, in January 1950 Truman approved the development of a **hydrogen bomb**, equivalent to five hundred atomic bombs, rejecting the arguments of several scientists who had worked on the atomic bomb and of George Kennan, who warned of an endless arms race. The "super bomb" was ready by 1954, but the U.S. advantage was brief. In November 1955, the Soviets exploded their own hydrogen bomb.

From the 1950s through the 1980s, deterrence formed the basis of American nuclear strategy. To deter the Soviet Union from attacking, the United States strove to maintain a nuclear force more powerful than the Soviets'. Because the Russians pursued a similar policy, the superpowers became locked in an ever-escalating nuclear weapons race.

Albert Einstein, whose mathematical discoveries had laid the foundations for nuclear weapons, commented grimly on the enormous destructive force now possessed by the superpowers. The war that came after World War III, he warned, would "be fought with sticks and stones."

Implementing the second component of its containment strategy, the United States beefed up its conventional military power to deter Soviet threats that might not warrant nuclear retaliation. The National Security Act of 1947 united the military branches under a single secretary of defense and created the National Security Council (NSC) to advise the president. During the Berlin crisis in 1948, Congress hiked military appropriations and enacted a peacetime draft. In addition, Congress granted permanent status to the women's military branches, though it limited their numbers and rank and banned them from combat. With 1.5 million men and women in uniform in 1950, the military strength of the United States had quadrupled since the 1930s, and defense expenditures claimed one-third of the federal budget.

Collective security, the third prong of containment strategy, marked a sharp reversal of the nation's traditional foreign policy. In 1949, the United States joined Canada and Western European nations in its first peacetime military alliance, the **North Atlantic Treaty Organization (NATO)**, designed to counter a Soviet threat to Western Europe (see Map 26.1). For the first time in its history, the United States pledged to go to war if one of its allies was attacked.

The fourth element of defense strategy involved foreign assistance programs to strengthen friendly countries, such as aid to Greece and Turkey and the Marshall Plan. In addition, in 1949 Congress approved $1 billion of military aid to its NATO allies, and the government began economic assistance to nations in other parts of the world.

The fifth ingredient of containment improved the government's espionage capacities and ability to thwart communism through covert activities. The National Security Act of 1947 created the **Central Intelligence Agency (CIA)** not only to gather information but also to perform any activities "related to intelligence affecting the national security" that the NSC might authorize. Such functions included propaganda, sabotage, economic warfare, and support for "anti-communist elements in threatened countries of the free world." In 1948, secret CIA operations helped defeat Italy's Communist Party. Subsequently, CIA agents would intervene even more actively, helping to topple legitimate foreign governments and violating the rights of U.S. citizens.

Finally, the U.S. government sought, through cultural exchanges and propaganda, to win "hearts and minds" throughout the world. The government expanded the Voice of America, created during World War II to broadcast U.S. propaganda abroad. In addition, the State Department sent books, exhibits, jazz musicians, and other performers to foreign countries as "cultural ambassadors."

By 1950, the United States had abandoned age-old tenets of foreign policy. Isolationism and neutrality had given way to a peacetime military alliance and efforts to control events far beyond U.S. borders. Short of war, the United States could not stop the descent of the iron curtain, but it aggressively and successfully promoted economic recovery and a military shield for the rest of Europe.

Superpower Rivalry around the Globe

Efforts to implement containment moved beyond Europe. In Africa, Asia, and the Middle East, World War II accelerated a tide of national liberation movements against war-weakened imperial powers. By 1960, forty countries, with more than a quarter of the world's people, had won

Cold War Spying
"Intelligence," the gathering of information to determine the capabilities and intentions of the enemy, is as old as human warfare, but it took on new importance with the onset of the Cold War. Created by the National Security Act of 1947, the Central Intelligence Agency (CIA) became one of the most important tools for obtaining Soviet secrets, deceiving the enemy about U.S. plans, countering subversive activities by Communists, and assisting local forces against leaders whom the United States wanted to oust. While much of the CIA's intelligence work took place in Washington, where analysts combed through Communist newspapers, official reports, and leaders' speeches, secret agents operating behind the iron curtain gathered information with bugs and devices such as these cameras hidden in cigarette packs. Spying soon gained a prominent place in popular culture, most notably in more than a dozen movies featuring James Bond, British agent 007. The character first appeared in the 1952 novel *Casino Royale* by former British naval intelligence agent Ian Fleming. Bond made his screen debut in 1962 in the movie *Dr. No.* Jack Naylor Collection.

their independence. These nations, along with Latin America, came to be referred to collectively as the **third world**, a term denoting countries outside the Western (first world) and Soviet (second world) orbits that had not yet developed industrial economies.

Like Woodrow Wilson during World War I, Roosevelt and Truman promoted the ideal of self-determination. The United States granted independence to the Philippines in 1946 and applauded the British withdrawal from India. At the same time, both the United States and the Soviet Union cultivated governments in emerging nations that were friendly to their own interests.

Leaders of many liberation movements, impressed with Russia's rapid economic growth, adopted socialist or Communist ideas. Although few had formal ties with the Soviet Union, American leaders saw these movements as a threatening extension of Soviet power. Seeking to hold communism at bay by fostering economic development and political stability, the Truman administration initiated the Point IV Program in 1949, providing technical aid to developing nations.

In Asia, civil war raged in China, where the Communists, led by **Mao Zedong** (Mao Tse-tung), fought the official Nationalist government under Chiang

Kai-shek. While the Communists gained support among the peasants for their land reforms and valiant stand against the Japanese, Chiang's corrupt and incompetent government alienated much of the population. Failing to promote negotiations between Chiang and Mao, the United States provided almost $3 billion in aid to the Nationalists during the civil war. Yet, recognizing the ineptness of Chiang's government, Truman and his advisers refused to divert further resources from Europe to China.

In October 1949, Mao established the People's Republic of China (PRC), and the Nationalists fled to the island of Taiwan. Fearing a U.S.-supported invasion to recapture China for the Nationalists, Mao signed a mutual defense treaty with the Soviet Union in which each nation pledged to defend the other in case of attack. The United States refused to recognize the PRC, blocked its admission to the United Nations, and supported the Nationalist government in Taiwan. Only a massive U.S. military commitment could have stopped the Chinese Communists, yet some Republicans cried that Truman and "the pro-Communists in the State Department" had "lost" China. China became a political albatross for the Democrats, who resolved never again to be vulnerable to charges of being soft on communism.

With China in turmoil, the administration reconsidered its plans for postwar Japan. U.S. policy shifted to helping Japan rapidly reindustrialize and secure access to natural resources and markets in Asia. In a short time, the Japanese economy was flourishing, and the official military occupation ended when the two nations signed a peace treaty and a mutual security pact in September 1951. Like West Germany, Japan now sat squarely within the American orbit, ready to serve as an economic hub in a vital area.

The one place where Cold War considerations did not control American policy was Palestine. In 1943, then-Senator Harry Truman spoke passionately about Nazi Germany's annihilation of the Jews, asserting, "This is not a Jewish problem, it is an American problem—and we must . . . face it squarely and honorably." As president, he made good on his words. Jews had been migrating to Palestine, their biblical homeland, since the nineteenth century, resulting in tension and hostilities with the Palestinian Arabs. After World War II, as hundreds of thousands of European Jews sought refuge and the creation of a national homeland in Palestine, fighting escalated into brutal terrorism on both sides.

Truman's foreign policy experts sought American-Arab friendship as a barrier against Soviet influence in the Middle East and as a means to secure access to Arabian oil. Uncharacteristically defying his advisers,

Haganah Troops Mobilize in Palestine Haganah originated in the 1910s as a paramilitary group to defend Jewish settlers in Palestine against Arabs who opposed the Zionists' expressed desire to build a Jewish state there. After World War I, Palestine was governed by the British under a League of Nations mandate. During that time, Haganah was an illegal underground organization, but by the end of World War II, it had gathered a substantial number of members and weapons. After Israel declared itself a nation in 1948, Haganah became the core of the Israel Defense Forces, Israel's main military organization. In this photo, Haganah troops are mobilizing in July 1948 to defend the new state from the armies of the surrounding nations of Syria, Jordan, Egypt, Lebanon, and Iraq. The Israelis won the war, but the declaration of the state of Israel created 700,000 Arab refugees and an issue that would fuel turmoil in the area for decades to come.
© Bettmann/Corbis.

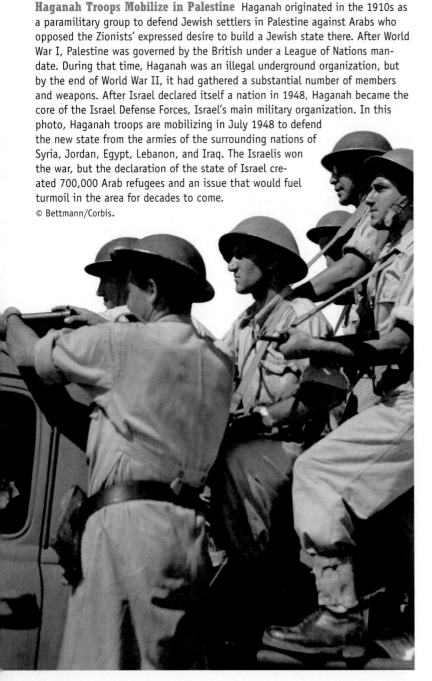

the president responded instead to pleas from Jewish organizations, his moral commitment to Holocaust survivors, and his interest in the American Jewish vote for the 1948 election. When Jews in Palestine declared the state of Israel in May 1948, Truman quickly recognized the new country and made its defense the cornerstone of U.S. policy in the Middle East.

> **Q:** Why did relations between the United States and the Soviet Union deteriorate after World War II?

Truman and the Fair Deal at Home

Referring to the Civil War general who coined the phrase "War is hell," Truman said in December 1945, "Sherman was wrong. I'm telling you I find peace is hell." Challenged by crises abroad, Truman also faced shortages, strikes, inflation, and other problems as the economy shifted to peacetime production. At the same time, he tried to expand New Deal reform with his own **Fair Deal** agenda of initiatives in civil rights, housing, education, and health care—efforts hindered by the wave of anti-Communist hysteria sweeping the country. In sharp contrast to his success with Congress in foreign policy, Truman achieved but a modest slice of his domestic agenda.

Reconverting to a Peacetime Economy

Despite scarcities and deprivations during World War II, most Americans had enjoyed a higher standard of living than ever before. Economic experts as well as ordinary citizens worried about sustaining that standard and providing jobs for millions of returning soldiers. Truman wasted no time unveiling his plan, asking Congress to enact a twenty-one-point program of social and economic reforms. He wanted to maintain the government's power to regulate the economy while it adjusted to peacetime production, and he sought government programs to provide basic essentials such as housing and health care to those in need, programs that had been on the drawing board during the New Deal. "Not even President Roosevelt ever asked for as much at one sitting," exploded Republican leader Joseph W. Martin Jr.

Congress approved one of Truman's key proposals—full-employment legislation—but even that was watered down. The Employment Act of 1946 invested the federal government with the responsibility "to promote maximum employment, production, and purchasing power," thereby formalizing what had been implicit in Roosevelt's anti-depression measures—government's responsibility

for maintaining a healthy economy. The law created the Council of Economic Advisors to assist the president, but it authorized no new powers to translate the government's obligation into effective action.

Inflation, not unemployment, turned out to be the most severe problem in the early postwar years. Consumers had $30 billion in wartime savings to spend, but shortages of meat, automobiles, housing, and other items persisted. Until industry could convert fully to civilian production and make more goods available, consumer demand would continue to drive up prices. With a basket of groceries on her arm to dramatize rising costs, Helen Gahagan Douglas urged Congress to support Truman's efforts to maintain price and rent controls. Those efforts fell, however, to pressures from business groups and others determined to trim government powers.

Labor relations were another thorn in Truman's side. Organized labor survived the war stronger than ever, its 14.5 million members making up 35 percent of the civilian workforce. Yet union members feared the erosion of wartime gains and launched an intense struggle to preserve them. Turning to the weapon they had set aside during the war, 5 million workers went out on strike in 1946, affecting nearly every major industry. Workers saw corporate executives profiting at their expense. Shortly before voting to strike, a former Marine and his coworkers calculated that a lavish party given by a company executive had cost more than they would earn in a whole year at the steel mill. "That sort of stuff made us realize, hell we had to bite the bullet . . . the bosses sure didn't give a damn for us." Although most Americans approved of unions in principle, they became fed up with strikes, blamed unions for shortages and rising prices, and called for government restrictions on organized labor. When the wave of strikes subsided, workers had won wage increases of about 20 percent, but the loss of overtime pay along with rising prices left their purchasing power only slightly higher than in 1942.

Women workers fared even less well. Polls indicated that as many as 68 to 85 percent wanted to keep their wartime jobs, but most who remained in the workforce had to settle for relatively low-paying jobs in light industry or the service sector. Displaced from her shipyard work, Marie Schreiber took a cashier's job, lamenting, "You were back to women's wages, you know . . . practically in half." With the backing of women's organizations and union women, Congresswoman Douglas sponsored bills to require equal pay

Israel, 1948

Women's Role in Peacetime Like many manufacturers forced to convert to war production during World War II, Proctor Electric Company, which had switched from making appliances to producing bomb fuses, cartridges, and airplane wing flaps, hoped to profit after the war from pent-up consumer demand. Even before the company had fully reconverted its plants, ads tempted consumers with products soon to come and asked them to be patient until Proctor could meet their needs, as this 1946 ad indicates. Picture Research Consultants & Archives.

FOR MORE HELP ANALYZING THIS IMAGE, see the visual activity for this chapter in the Online Study Guide at **bedfordstmartins.com/roarkcompact.**

for equal work, to provide child care for employed mothers, and to create a government commission to study the status of women. But at a time when women were viewed primarily as wives and mothers and a strong current of opinion resisted further expansion of federal powers, these initiatives got nowhere.

By 1947, the economy had stabilized, avoiding the postwar depression that so many had feared. Wartime profits enabled businesses to expand. Consumers could now spend their wartime savings on houses, cars, and appliances that had lain

> "I spent four years in the army to free a bunch of Frenchmen and Dutchmen," an African American corporal declared, "and I'm hanged if I'm going to let the Alabama version of the Germans kick me around when I get home."

beyond their reach during the depression and war. Defense spending and foreign aid that enabled war-stricken countries to purchase American products also stimulated the economy. A soaring birthrate further sustained consumer demand. Although prosperity was far from universal, the United States entered into a remarkable economic boom that lasted through the 1960s (see chapter 27).

Another economic boost came from the only large welfare measure passed after the New Deal. The **Servicemen's Readjustment Act (GI Bill)**, enacted in 1944, offered 16 million veterans job training and education; unemployment compensation while they looked for jobs; and low-interest loans to purchase homes, farms, and small businesses. By 1948, some 1.3 million veterans had bought houses with government loans. Helping 2.2 million ex-soldiers attend college, the subsidies sparked a boom in higher education. A drugstore clerk before his military service, Don Condren was able to get an engineering degree and buy his first house. "I think the GI Bill gave the whole country an upward boost economically," he said.

Condren overlooked the disparate ways in which the GI Bill operated. Like key New Deal programs such as unemployment insurance and aid to mothers with dependent children, GI programs were administered at the state and local levels, which especially in the South routinely discriminated against African Americans. Black veterans who sought jobs for which the military had trained them were shuttled into menial labor. One decorated veteran said that the GI Bill "draws no color line," yet "my color bars me from most decent jobs, and if, instead of accepting menial work, I collect my $20 a week readjustment allowance, I am classified as a 'lazy nigger.'" Thousands of black veterans did benefit from the GI Bill, but it did not help all ex-soldiers equally.

Blacks and Mexican Americans Push for Their Civil Rights "I spent four years in the army to free a bunch of Frenchmen and Dutchmen," an African American corporal declared, "and I'm hanged if I'm going to let the Alabama version of the Germans kick me around when I get home." Black veterans as well as civilians resolved that the return to peace would not be a return to the racial injustices of prewar America. Their political clout had grown with the migration of two million African Americans to northern and western cities, where they could vote. Pursuing civil rights through the courts and Congress, the National Association for the Advancement of Colored People (NAACP) counted half a million members.

In the postwar years, individual African Americans broke through the color barrier, achieving several "firsts." Jackie Robinson integrated major league baseball, playing for the Brooklyn

Dodgers and braving abuse from fans and players to win the Rookie of the Year Award in 1947. In 1950, Ralph J. Bunche received the Nobel Peace Prize for his United Nations work, and Gwendolyn Brooks won the Pulitzer Prize for poetry.

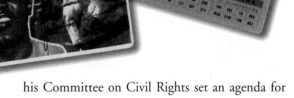

Still, for most African Americans, little had changed, especially in the South, where violence greeted their attempts to assert their rights. Armed white men turned back Medgar Evers (who would become a key civil rights leader in the 1960s) and four other veterans trying to vote in Mississippi. A mob lynched Isaac Nixon for voting in Georgia, and an all-white jury acquitted the men accused of his murder. In the South, political leaders and local vigilantes routinely intimidated potential black voters with threats of economic retaliation and violence.

The Cold War heightened American leaders' sensitivity to racial issues, as the superpowers vied for the allegiance of newly independent nations with nonwhite populations. Soviet propaganda repeatedly highlighted racial injustice in the United States. Republican senator Henry Cabot Lodge called race relations "our Achilles' heel before the world," while Secretary of State Dean Acheson noted that systematic segregation and discrimination endangered "our moral leadership of the free and democratic nations of the world."

"My very stomach turned over when I learned that Negro soldiers just back from overseas were being dumped out of army trucks in Mississippi and beaten," wrote Truman. Wrestling with the Democrats' need for northern black and liberal votes as well as southern white votes, Truman spoke more boldly on civil rights than any previous president. In 1946, he created the President's Committee on Civil Rights, and in February 1948 he asked Congress to enact the committee's recommendations. The first president to address the NAACP, Truman asserted that all Americans should have equal rights to housing, education, employment, and the ballot.

As with much of his domestic program, the president failed to act aggressively on his bold words. Congress rebuffed Truman's proposals for civil rights legislation, but some northern and western states passed laws against discrimination in employment and public accommodations. Running for reelection in 1948, Truman issued an executive order to desegregate the armed services, but it lay unimplemented until the Korean War. Despite the gap between Truman's words and what his administration actually accomplished, desegregation of the military and the administration's support of civil rights cases in the Supreme Court contributed to far-reaching changes, while

his Committee on Civil Rights set an agenda for years to come.

Although discussion of race and civil rights usually focused on African Americans, Mexican Americans endured similar injustices. In 1929, they had formed the League of United Latin-American Citizens (LULAC) to combat discrimination and segregation in the Southwest. Like black soldiers after World War II, Mexican American veterans believed, as one of them insisted, that "we had earned our credentials as American citizens. We had paid our dues." Problems with getting their veterans' benefits spurred a group in Corpus Christi, Texas, led by Dr. Héctor

Segregation The segregation visible on this bus was a feature of life in the South from the late nineteenth century until the 1960s. State and local laws mandated separation from the cradle to the grave. African Americans could not use white hospitals, cemeteries, schools, libraries, swimming pools, restrooms, or drinking fountains. They were relegated to balconies in movie theaters and kept apart from whites in all public meetings. Segregated buses would become the target of the first large-scale civil rights protest, in Montgomery, Alabama, in 1955–1956. Stan Wayman/Time Life Pictures/Getty Images.

Peréz García, a combat surgeon who had earned the Bronze Star, to form the American GI Forum in 1948. It went on to become a key national organization battling discrimination against Latinos and electing sympathetic officials.

"Education is our freedom," read the GI Forum's motto, yet Mexican American children were routinely segregated in public schools. Parents filed a class action suit in Orange County, California, winning a federal court decision in 1947 that outlawed the practice of separating Mexican American and white children. In 1948, LULAC and the GI Forum achieved a similar victory over segregation in Texas schools. Such projects paralleled the efforts of the NAACP on behalf of African Americans that would culminate in the *Brown* decision in 1954 (see chapter 27). These efforts, along with challenges to discrimination in employment and efforts for political representation, demonstrated a growing mobilization of Mexican Americans in the Southwest.

The Fair Deal Flounders Republicans capitalized on public frustrations with economic reconversion in the 1946 congressional election. Helen Gahagan Douglas hung on to her seat, but the Republicans captured control of Congress for the first time in fourteen years. Many had campaigned against New Deal "bureaucracy" and "radicalism" in 1946, and they succeeded in the Eightieth Congress to weaken some reform programs and enact tax cuts favoring higher-income groups.

Organized labor took the most severe blow when Congress passed the Taft-Hartley Act over Truman's veto in 1947. The law reduced the power of organized labor and made it more difficult to organize workers. For example, states could now pass "right-to-work" laws, which banned the practice of requiring all workers to join a union once a majority had voted for it. Many states, especially in the South and West, rushed to enact such laws, encouraging industries to relocate there. Taft-Hartley maintained the New Deal principle of government protection for collective bargaining, but it put the government more squarely between labor and management.

As the 1948 elections approached, Truman faced not only a resurgent Republican Party headed by its nominee, Thomas E. Dewey, but also two revolts within his own party. On the left, Henry A. Wallace, whose foreign policy views had cost him his cabinet seat, led the new Progressive Party. On the right, South Carolina governor J. Strom Thurmond headed the States' Rights Party—the Dixiecrats—formed by southern Democrats who had walked out of the 1948 Democratic Party convention when it passed a liberal civil rights plank.

Almost alone in believing he could win, Truman crisscrossed the country by train, answering

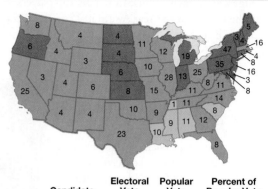

Candidate	Electoral Vote	Popular Vote	Percent of Popular Vote
Harry S. Truman (Democrat)	303	24,105,695	49.5
Thomas E. Dewey (Republican)	189	21,969,170	45.1
J. Strom Thurmond (States' Rights)	39	1,169,021	2.4
Henry A. Wallace (Progressive)	0	1,156,103	2.4

MAP 26.2 The Election of 1948

supporters' cries of "Give 'em hell, Harry." So bleak were Truman's prospects that on election night, the *Chicago Daily Tribune* printed its next day's issue with the headline "DEWEY DEFEATS TRUMAN." But Truman took 303 electoral votes to Dewey's 189, and his party regained control of Congress (Map 26.2). His unexpected victory attested to the broad support for his foreign policy and the enduring popularity of New Deal reform.

Truman failed to turn his victory into success for his Fair Deal agenda. Congress made modest improvements in Social Security and raised the minimum wage, but it passed only one significant reform measure. The **Housing Act of 1949** authorized 810,000 units of government-constructed housing over the next six years and represented a landmark commitment by the government to address the housing needs of the poor. Yet it fell far short of actual need—just 61,000 units had been built when Truman left office—and slum clearance frequently displaced the poor without providing decent alternatives.

With southern Democrats often joining the Republicans, Congress rejected Truman's proposals for civil rights, a universal health care program, and federal aid to education. His efforts to revise immigration policy were mixed. The McCarran-Walter Act of 1952 ended the outright ban on immigration and citizenship for Japanese and other Asians, but it also authorized the government to bar suspected Communists and homosexuals and maintained the discriminatory quota system established in the 1920s. Truman denounced that provision as "unworthy of our traditions and our ideals," but Congress overrode his veto.

Truman's Whistle-Stop Campaign Harry Truman rallies a crowd from his campaign train at a stop in Bridgeport, Pennsylvania, in October 1948. His campaign theme song, "I'm Just Wild about Harry," was borrowed, with the words slightly changed, from the 1921 musical *Shuffle Along*. This was the last presidential election in which pollsters predicted the wrong winner. They stopped taking polls in mid-October, after which many voters apparently changed their minds. One commentator praised the American citizenry, who "couldn't be ticketed by the polls, knew its own mind and had picked the rather unlikely but courageous figure of Truman to carry on its banner." Photo: Truman Library; Sheet music: Collection of Janice L. and David J. Frent.

FOR MORE HELP ANALYZING THIS IMAGE, see the visual activity for this chapter in the Online Study Guide at **bedfordstmartins.com/roarkcompact.**

Truman's concentration on foreign policy rather than domestic proposals contributed to the failure of his Fair Deal. Moreover, by late 1950, the Korean War embroiled the president in controversy and depleted his power as a legislative leader. Truman's failure to make good on his domestic proposals set the United States apart from most European nations, which by the 1950s had in place comprehensive health, housing, and employment security programs to underwrite the material well-being of their populations.

The Domestic Chill: McCarthyism Truman's domestic program also suffered from a wave of anticommunism that weakened liberal and leftist forces. "Red-baiting" (attempts to discredit individuals or ideas by associating them with communism) and official retaliation against leftist critics of the government had flourished during the Red scare at the end of World War I (see chapter 22). A second Red scare followed World War II, born of partisan political

maneuvering, collapse of the Soviet-American alliance, setbacks in U.S. foreign policy, and disclosures of Soviet espionage.

Republicans who had attacked the New Deal as a plot of radicals now jumped on such Cold War events as the Soviet takeover of Eastern Europe and the Communist triumph in China to accuse Democrats of fostering internal subversion. Wisconsin senator **Joseph R. McCarthy** avowed that "the Communists within our borders have been more responsible for the success of Communism abroad than Soviet Russia." McCarthy's charges—such as the allegation that retired general George C. Marshall belonged to a Communist conspiracy—were reckless and often ludicrous, but the press covered him avidly, and **McCarthyism** became a term synonymous with the anti-Communist crusade.

Revelations of Soviet espionage gave some credibility to fears of internal communism. For example, a number of ex-Communists, including Whittaker

Chambers and Elizabeth Bentley, testified that they and others had provided secret documents to the Soviets. Most alarming of all, in 1950 a British physicist working on the atomic bomb project confessed that he was a spy and implicated several Americans, including **Ethel and Julius Rosenberg**. The Rosenbergs pleaded innocent but were convicted of conspiracy to commit espionage and electrocuted in 1953.

Records opened in the 1990s showed that the Soviet Union did receive secret documents from Americans that probably hastened its development of nuclear weapons by a year or two. Yet the vast majority of individuals hunted down in the Red scare had done nothing more than at one time joined the Communist Party, associated with Communists, or supported radical causes. And most of those activities had taken place long before the Cold War had made the Soviet Union an enemy. Investigators often cared little for such distinctions, however.

The hunt for subversives was conducted by both Congress and the executive branch. Stung by charges of communism in the 1946 midterm elections, Truman issued Executive Order 9835 in March 1947, establishing loyalty review boards to investigate every federal employee. "A nightmare from which there [was] no awakening" was how State Department employee Esther Brunauer described it when she and her husband, a chemist in the navy, both lost their jobs because he had joined a Communist youth organization in the 1920s and associated with suspected radicals. Government investigators routinely violated the Bill of Rights by allowing anonymous informers to make charges and by placing the burden of proof on the accused. More than two thousand civil service employees lost their jobs, and another ten thousand resigned as **Truman's loyalty program** continued into the mid-1950s. Years later, Truman admitted that the loyalty program had been a mistake.

Congressional committees, such as the House Un-American Activities Committee (HUAC), also investigated individuals' past and present political associations. When those under scrutiny refused to name names, investigators charged that silence was tantamount to confession, and these "unfriendly witnesses" lost their jobs and suffered public ostracism. In 1947, HUAC investigated radical activity in Hollywood. Frank Sinatra protested, wondering if someone called for "a square deal for the underdog, will they call you a Commie? . . . Are they going to scare us into silence?" Some actors and directors cooperated, but ten refused, citing their First Amendment rights. The "Hollywood Ten" served jail sentences for contempt of Congress, a punishment that Helen Gahagan Douglas fought, and then found themselves blacklisted in the movie industry.

The Truman administration went after the Communist Party directly, prosecuting its leaders under the Smith Act of 1940, which made it a crime to "advocate the overthrow and destruction of the Government of the United States by force and violence." Although civil libertarians argued that the guilty verdicts violated First Amendment rights of freedom of speech, press, and association, the Supreme Court ruled in 1951 (*Dennis v. United States*) that the Communist threat overrode constitutional guarantees.

The domestic Cold War spread beyond the nation's capital. State and local governments investigated citizens, demanded loyalty oaths, fired employees suspected of disloyalty, banned books from public libraries, and more. College professors and public school teachers lost their jobs in New York, California, and elsewhere. Because the Communist Party had helped organize unions and championed racial justice, labor and civil rights activists fell prey to McCarthyism as well. African American activist Jack O'Dell remembered that segregationists pinned the tag of Communist on "anybody who supported the right of blacks to have civil rights." McCarthyism caused untold harm to individuals innocent of breaking any law. Thousands of people were humiliated and discredited, hounded from their jobs, even in some cases imprisoned. The anti-Communist crusade violated fundamental constitutional rights of freedom of speech and association, stifled expression of dissenting ideas, and removed unpopular causes from public contemplation.

Q: **Why did Truman have limited success in implementing his domestic agenda?**

The Cold War Becomes Hot: Korea

The Cold War erupted into a shooting war in June 1950 when troops from Communist North Korea invaded South Korea. For the first time, Americans went into battle to implement containment. Confirming the global reach of the Truman Doctrine, U.S. involvement in Korea also marked the militarization of American foreign policy. The United States, in concert with the United Nations, ultimately held the line in Korea, but at a great cost in lives, dollars, and domestic unity.

Korea and the Military Implementation of Containment The war grew out of the artificial division of Korea after World War II. Having expelled the Japanese, who had controlled Korea since 1904, the United States and the Soviet Union created two occupation zones separated by the thirty-eighth parallel (Map 26.3). With Moscow and Washington unable to agree on a unification plan, the United Nations sponsored elections in South Korea in July 1948. The American-favored candidate, Syngman Rhee, was elected president, and the United States withdrew most of its troops. In fall 1948, the Soviets established the People's Republic of North Korea under Kim Il-sung and also withdrew. Although doubting that Rhee's repressive government could sustain popular support, U.S. officials appreciated his staunch anticommunism and provided small amounts of economic and military aid to South Korea.

North and South Korean troops at the thirty-eighth parallel had engaged in skirmishes since 1948, but in June 1950, 90,000 North Koreans swept into South Korea. Assuming that the Soviet Union or China had instigated the attack (scholars learned later that they had not), Truman decided to intervene, viewing Korea as "the Greece of the Far East." With the Soviet Union boycotting the UN Security Council to protest its refusal to seat a representative from the People's Republic of China, the United States obtained UN sponsorship of a collective effort to repel the attack. Authorized to appoint a commander for the UN force, Truman named General **Douglas MacArthur**, World War II hero and head of the postwar occupation of Japan.

Sixteen nations, including many NATO allies, sent troops to Korea, but the United States furnished most of the personnel and weapons, deploying almost 1.8 million troops and dictating military strategy. By failing to ask Congress for a declaration of war, Truman violated the spirit if not the letter of the Constitution. Moreover, although Congress appropriated funds to fight the war, the president's political opponents called it "Truman's war" when the military situation worsened.

The first American soldiers rushed to Korea unprepared and ill equipped, enduring severe defeats in the first three months of the war. The North Koreans took the capital of Seoul and drove deep into South Korea, forcing UN troops to retreat to Pusan by September. General MacArthur then launched a bold counteroffensive at Inchon, 180 miles behind North Korean lines. By mid-October, UN forces had pushed the North Koreans back to the thirty-eighth parallel. Then came the momentous decision of whether to invade North Korea and seek to unify the country.

From Containment to Rollback to Containment

"Troops could not be expected . . . to march up to a surveyor's line and stop," remarked Secretary of State Dean Acheson, reflecting popular and official support for transforming the military objective from containment to elimination of the enemy and unification of Korea. Thus, for the only time during the Cold War, the United States tried to roll back communism by force. With UN approval, on September 27, 1950, Truman authorized MacArthur to cross the thirty-eighth parallel. Concerned

MAP 26.3 The Korean War, 1950–1953

Although each side had plunged deep into enemy territory, the war ended in 1953 with the dividing line between North and South Korea nearly where it had been before the fighting began.

READING THE MAP: How far south did the North Korean forces progress at the height of their invasion? How far north did the UN forces get? What countries border Korea?

CONNECTIONS: What dangers did the forays of MacArthur's forces to within forty miles of the Korean-Chinese border pose? Why did Truman forbid MacArthur to approach that border? What political considerations on the home front influenced Truman's policy and military strategy regarding Korea?

FOR MORE HELP ANALYZING THIS MAP, see the map activity for this chapter in the Online Study Guide at bedfordstmartins.com/roarkcompact.

> "Troops could not be expected . . . to march up to a surveyor's line and stop," remarked Secretary of State Dean Acheson.

about possible intervention by China or the Soviet Union, the president directed him to keep UN troops away from the Korean-Chinese border. Disregarding the order, MacArthur sent UN forces to within forty miles of China, whereupon 300,000 Chinese soldiers crossed the Yalu River into Korea. With Chinese help, the North Koreans recaptured Seoul.

After three months of grueling battle, UN forces fought their way back to the thirty-eighth parallel. At that point, Truman decided to seek a negotiated settlement. MacArthur was furious when the goal of the war reverted to containment, which to him represented defeat. Taking his case to the public challenged both the president's authority to conduct foreign policy and the principle of civilian control of the military. Fed up with MacArthur's insubordination, Truman fired him in April 1951. Many Americans, however, sided with MacArthur. "Quite an explosion. . . . Letters of abuse by the dozens," Truman recorded in his diary. The adulation for MacArthur reflected American frustrations with containment. Why should Americans die simply to preserve the status quo? Why not destroy the enemy once and for all? In siding with MacArthur, Americans assumed that the United States was all-powerful and that stalemate in Korea resulted from the government's ineptitude or willingness to shelter subversives.

When Congress investigated MacArthur's firing, all of the top military leaders supported the president. According to the chairman of the Joint Chiefs of Staff, MacArthur wanted to wage "the wrong war, at the wrong place, at the wrong time, with the wrong enemy." Yet Truman never recovered from the political fallout. Nor was he able to end the war. Negotiations began in July 1951, but peace talks dragged on for two more years while twelve thousand more U.S. soldiers died.

Korea, Communism, and the 1952 Election

Popular discontent with President Truman's war boosted Republican candidates in the 1952 election. The Republicans' presidential nominee, General **Dwight D. Eisenhower**, had emerged from World War II with immense popularity. Reared in modest circumstances in Abilene, Kansas, Eisenhower attended West Point and rose steadily through the army ranks. As supreme commander in Europe, he won widespread acclaim for leading the Allied armies to victory over Germany. After the war, he served as army chief of staff, and in 1950 Truman appointed Eisenhower the first supreme commander of NATO forces.

Although Eisenhower believed that professional soldiers should stay out of politics, he found compelling reasons to run in 1952. The general largely agreed with Democratic foreign policy, but he deplored the Democrats' propensity to solve domestic problems with costly new federal programs. He equally disliked the foreign policy views of the leading Republican presidential contender, Senator Robert A. Taft, who attacked containment and sought to cut defense spending. Eisenhower defeated Taft for the nomination, but the old guard wrote a party platform that excoriated containment as "negative, futile, and immoral" and charged the Truman administration with shielding "traitors to the Nation in high places." By choosing thirty-nine-year-old Senator **Richard M. Nixon** for his running mate, Eisenhower helped to appease the right wing of the party and ensured that anticommunism would be a major theme of the campaign.

Richard Milhous Nixon grew up in southern California, worked his way through college and law school, served in the navy, and briefly practiced law. In 1946, he helped the Republicans recapture Congress by defeating a liberal incumbent for a seat in the House of Representatives. Nixon quickly made a name for himself as a member of HUAC and a key anti-Communist, moving to the Senate with his victory over Helen Gahagan Douglas in 1950.

With his public approval ratings sinking, Truman decided not to run for reelection. The Democrats nominated Adlai E. Stevenson, the popular governor of Illinois, who was acceptable to both liberals and southerners. Stevenson could not escape the domestic fallout from the Korean War, however, nor could he match the widespread appeal of Eisenhower. The Republican campaign stumbled just once, over the last item of its "Korea, Communism, and Corruption" policy. When the press reported that Nixon had accepted money from a private political fund supported by wealthy Californians, Democrats jumped to the attack, even though such gifts were common and legal. While Eisenhower deliberated about whether to dump Nixon from the ticket, Nixon saved himself by making an emotional nationwide appeal on the new medium of television. He disclosed his finances and documented his modest standard of living. Conceding that the family pet, Checkers, might be considered an illegal gift, Nixon refused to break his daughters' hearts by returning the cocker spaniel. The overwhelmingly positive response to the "Checkers speech" kept Nixon on the ticket.

Shortly before the election, Eisenhower announced dramatically, "I shall go to Korea," and voters registered their confidence in his ability to end the war. Cutting sharply into traditional Democratic territory, Eisenhower won several southern states and garnered 55 percent of the popular vote overall. His coattails carried a narrow Republican majority to Congress.

An Armistice and the War's Costs

Eisenhower made good on his pledge to end the Korean War. In July 1953, the two sides reached an armistice that left Korea divided, again roughly at the thirty-eighth parallel, with North and South separated by a two-and-one-half-mile-wide demilitarized zone (see Map 26.3). The war took the lives of 36,000 Americans and wounded more than 100,000. South Korea lost more than 1 million people to war-related causes, and more than 1.8 million North Koreans and Chinese were killed or wounded.

The Truman administration judged the war a success for containment, since the United States had backed up its promise to help nations that were resisting communism. Both Truman and Eisenhower managed to contain what amounted to a world war—involving twenty nations altogether—within a single country and to avoid the use of nuclear weapons.

The Korean War had an enormous effect on defense policy and spending. In April 1950, two months before the war began, the National Security Council completed a top-secret report, known as **NSC 68**, on the United States' military strength. It warned that the survival of the nation required a massive military buildup and a tripling of the defense budget. Truman took no immediate action on these recommendations, but the Korean War brought about nearly all of the military expansion called for in NSC 68, vastly increasing U.S. capacity to act as a global power. Military spending shot up from $14 billion in 1950 to $50 billion in 1953 and remained above $40 billion thereafter. By 1953, defense spending claimed 60 percent of the federal budget, and the size of the armed forces had tripled.

To General Matthew Ridgway, MacArthur's successor as commander of the UN forces, Korea taught the lesson that U.S. forces should never again fight a land war in Asia. Nevertheless, the Korean War induced the Truman administration to expand its role in Asia by increasing aid to the French, who were fighting to hang on to their colonial empire in Indochina. As U.S. Marines retreated from a battle against Chinese soldiers in 1950, they sang, prophetically, "We're Harry's police force on call, / So put back your pack on, / The next step is Saigon, / Cheer up, me lads, bless 'em all."

Q: How did the Korean War shape American foreign policy in the 1950s?

Conclusion: The Cold War's Costs and Consequences

Helen Gahagan Douglas initially resisted designating the Soviet Union as an enemy and opposed the implementation of containment with aid to Greece and Turkey in 1947. By 1948, however, she had gotten behind Truman's decision to fight communism throughout the world, which marked the most momentous foreign policy initiative in the nation's history. More than any development in the postwar world, the Cold War defined American politics and society for decades to come. It transformed the federal government, shifting its priorities from domestic to external affairs, greatly expanding its budget, and substantially increasing the power of the president. Military spending helped transform the nation itself, as defense contracts encouraged economic and population booms in the West and Southwest. The nuclear arms race put the people of the world at risk, consumed resources that might have been used to improve living standards, and skewed the economy toward dependence on military projects.

In sharp contrast to foreign policy, the domestic policies of the postwar years reflected continuity with the past. Most of the New Deal reforms remained in place despite Republicans' promises to turn back the clock. Helen Gahagan Douglas came to Congress hoping to expand the New Deal, to help find "a way by which all people can live out their lives in dignity and decency." She avidly supported Truman's proposals for new programs in education, health, and civil rights, but a majority of her colleagues did not. Consequently, the poor and minorities suffered even while a majority of Americans enjoyed a higher standard of living in an economy boosted by Cold War spending and the reconstruction of Western Europe and Japan.

Many Americans, not accustomed to paying sustained attention to foreign policy or to fighting wars without total defeat of the enemy, had difficulty accepting the terms of the Cold War. Consequently, another high cost of the Cold War was the anti-Communist hysteria that swept the nation, costing Douglas a Senate seat and more generally stifling debate and narrowing the range of ideas acceptable for political discussion. Partisan politics and Truman's warnings about the Communist menace fueled McCarthyism, but the obsession with subversion also fed on popular frustrations over the failure of containment to produce clear-cut victories. Convulsing the nation in bitter disunity, McCarthyism reflected a loss of confidence in American power. That frustration grew with the Korean War, which ended in stalemate rather than the defeat of communism. It would be a major challenge of the next administration to restore national unity and confidence.

Reviewing the Chapter

Explain each term's significance

WHO

Helen Gahagan Douglas (p. 651)

Harry S. Truman (p. 653)

George F. Kennan (p. 654)

Henry A. Wallace (p. 655)

Mao Zedong (p. 660)

Joseph R. McCarthy (p. 665)

Ethel and Julius Rosenberg (p. 666)

Douglas MacArthur (p. 667)

Dwight D. Eisenhower (p. 668)

Richard M. Nixon (p. 668)

WHAT

iron curtain (p. 654)

containment (p. 654)

Truman Doctrine (p. 655)

Marshall Plan (European Recovery
   Program) (p. 655)

Berlin airlift (p. 656)

hydrogen bomb (p. 658)

North Atlantic Treaty Organization
   (NATO) (p. 659)

Central Intelligence Agency (CIA) (p. 659)

third world (p. 659)

Fair Deal (p. 661)

Servicemen's Readjustment Act
   (GI Bill) (p. 662)

Housing Act of 1949 (p. 664)

McCarthyism (p. 665)

Truman's loyalty program (p. 666)

NSC 68 (p. 669)

★ REVIEW QUESTIONS Q:

Use key terms and dates to support your answer

1. Why did relations between the United States and the Soviet Union deteriorate after World War II? (pp. 652–61)

2. Why did Truman have limited success in implementing his domestic agenda? (pp. 661–66)

3. How did the Korean War shape American foreign policy in the 1950s? (pp. 666–69)

★ MAKING CONNECTIONS

Draw on key terms, timeline, and review questions

1. Containment shaped American actions abroad for almost half a century. Why did it become the dominant feature of American foreign policy after World War II? In your answer, discuss both proponents and opponents of the policy.

2. How did returning American servicemen change postwar domestic life in the areas of education and civil rights? In your answer, discuss how wartime experiences influenced their demands.

3. Why did anti-Communist hysteria sweep the country in the early 1950s? How did it shape domestic politics? In your answer, be sure to consider the influence of developments abroad and at home.

FOR PRACTICE QUIZZES AND OTHER STUDY TOOLS, see the Online Study Guide at **bedfordstmartins.com/roarkcompact**.

★ SUGGESTED READINGS

Greg Behrman, *The Most Noble Adventure: The Marshall Plan and the Time When America Helped Save Europe* (2007). A highly readable story told through the lives of several key actors in the Marshall Plan.

Alonzo L. Hamby, *Man of the People: A Life of Harry S. Truman* (1995). A thorough biography that focuses on Truman's presidency.

Melvyn P. Leffler, *For the Soul of Mankind: The United States, the Soviet Union, and the Cold War* (2007). A balanced account of the Cold War from its start to finish with a focus on four key episodes.

Brenda Gayle Plummer, *Rising Wind: Black Americans and U.S. Foreign Affairs, 1935–1960* (1996). An examination of the connections between civil rights in the United States and Cold War foreign policy.

Ellen W. Schrecker, *Many Are the Crimes: McCarthyism in America* (1998). An assessment of the roots, varieties, longevity, and effects of the Red scare on individuals, politics, and culture.

William Stueck, *The Korean War: An International History* (1995). A narrative of the diplomatic and military events of the Korean War in a world context.

FOR MORE BOOKS ABOUT TOPICS IN THIS CHAPTER, see the Online Bibliography at **bedfordstmartins.com/roarkcompact**.

FOR ADDITIONAL FIRSTHAND ACCOUNTS OF THIS PERIOD, see Chapter 26 in Michael Johnson, ed., *Reading the American Past,* Fourth Edition.

FOR WEB SITES, IMAGES, AND DOCUMENTS RELATED TO TOPICS AND PLACES IN THIS CHAPTER, visit Make History at **bedfordstmartins.com/roarkcompact**.

★ TIMELINE

1945
- Roosevelt dies; Vice President Harry S. Truman becomes president.

1946
- Postwar labor unrest.
- President's Committee on Civil Rights created.
- George F. Kennan drafts a containment policy.
- United States grants independence to Philippines.
- Employment Act.
- Republicans gain control of Congress.

1947
- National Security Act: National Security Council (NSC) and Central Intelligence Agency (CIA) created.
- Truman asks for aid to Greece and Turkey and announces Truman Doctrine.
- Truman establishes loyalty program.

1948
- Congress approves Marshall Plan.
- Women become permanent part of armed services.
- Truman orders desegregation of armed services.
- American GI Forum founded.
- United States recognizes state of Israel.
- Truman elected president.

1948–1949
- Berlin crisis and airlift.

1949
- Communists take over mainland China; Nationalists retreat to Taiwan.
- North Atlantic Treaty Organization (NATO) formed.
- Point IV technical aid program begins.
- Soviet Union explodes atomic bomb.

1950
- Senator Joseph McCarthy begins to accuse U.S. government of harboring Communists.
- Truman approves development of hydrogen bomb.
- United States sends troops to South Korea.

1951
- Truman relieves General Douglas MacArthur of command in Korea.
- United States ends occupation of Japan and signs peace treaty and mutual security pact.

1952
- Republican Dwight D. Eisenhower elected president.

1953
- Armistice halts Korean War.

1956 CADILLAC CONVERTIBLE The automobile reflected both corporate and family prosperity in the 1950s. By the end of the decade, three out of every four households had a car, and the automotive industry generated one out of every six jobs. This car was manufactured by General Motors, the biggest and richest corporation in the world and the first to sell a billion dollars' worth of products. Costing about $5,000, the Cadillac was GM's top-of-the-line car and one of the first purchases the McDonald brothers made when they struck it rich with their hamburger stand in California. Even the cheaper models that average Americans bought by the millions featured the gas-guzzling size and the space-age design of this Cadillac. A massive interstate highway system begun in 1956 boosted automobile travel, and widespread car ownership went hand in hand with Americans' move to the suburbs and their devotion to consumption. Ron Kimball Photography.

The Politics and Culture of Abundance

1952–1960

TRAILED BY REPORTERS, U.S. vice president Richard M. Nixon led Soviet premier Nikita Khrushchev through the American National Exhibition in Moscow in July 1959. The display of American consumer goods followed an exhibition of Soviet products in New York, part of a cultural exchange between the two superpowers that reflected a slight thaw in the Cold War after Khrushchev replaced Stalin. Both Khrushchev and Nixon seized on the propaganda potential of the moment. As they made their way through the display, their verbal sparring turned into a slugfest of words and gestures that reporters dubbed the **kitchen debate**. Showing off a new color television set, Nixon said the Soviet Union "may be ahead of us . . . in the thrust of your rockets for . . . outer space," but he assured Khrushchev that the United States outstripped the Soviets in consumer goods. "Any steelworker could buy this house," Nixon boasted, as they walked through a six-room ranch-style model. Khrushchev retorted that in the Soviet Union, "you are entitled to housing," whereas in the United States the homeless slept on pavements.

While the two men inspected household appliances, Nixon declared, "These are designed to make things easier for our women." Khrushchev responded that his country did not have "the capitalist attitude toward women" and appreciated women's contributions to the economy, not their domesticity. The Soviet leader found many of the items on display interesting, but, he said, "they are not needed in life. . . . They are merely gadgets." In reply, Nixon insisted, "Isn't it far better to be talking about washing machines than machines of war?" Khrushchev agreed, yet Cold War tensions surfaced when he later blustered, "We too are giants. You want to threaten — we will answer threats with threats."

The Eisenhower administration (1953–1961) in fact had begun with threats to the Soviet Union. During the 1952 campaign, Republicans had vowed to roll back communism and liberate "enslaved" peoples under Soviet rule. In practice, however, President Dwight D. Eisenhower settled for a containment policy much like that of his predecessor, Harry S. Truman, though Eisenhower relied more on nuclear weapons and on secret actions by the Central Intelligence Agency (CIA) against left-leaning governments. Yet, as

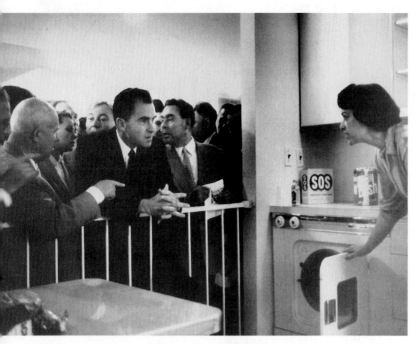

The Kitchen Debate Soviet premier Nikita Khrushchev (left) and Vice President Richard M. Nixon (center) debate the relative merits of their nations' economies at the American National Exhibition held in Moscow in 1959. "You are a lawyer for capitalism and I am a lawyer for communism," Khrushchev told Nixon as each tried to outdo one another. Howard Sochurek/TimePix/Getty.

Nixon's visit to Moscow demonstrated, Eisenhower seized on political changes in the Soviet Union to reduce tensions in Soviet-American relations.

Continuity with the Truman administration also characterized domestic policy. Although Eisenhower favored corporations with tax cuts and opposed strong federal efforts in health care, education, and race relations, he did not propose to roll back New Deal programs. He even extended the federal government with a massive highway program, and he remained immensely popular through his two terms in office.

Although poverty clung stubbornly to some 20 percent of the population, the Moscow display testified to the unheard-of material gains savored by most Americans in the postwar era. Cold War weapons production spurred the economy, whose vitality stimulated suburban development, contributed to the burgeoning population and enterprise in the West and Southwest (the Sun Belt), and enabled millions of Americans to buy a host of new products. As new homes, television sets, and household appliances transformed living patterns, Americans took part in a consumer culture that celebrated marriage, family, and traditional gender roles, even as more and more married women took jobs outside the home. Also challenging dominant norms were an emerging youth culture and dissenting writers known as the Beats.

The Cold War and the economic boom helped African Americans mount the most dramatic challenge of the 1950s, a struggle against the system of segregation and disfranchisement that had replaced slavery. Large numbers of African Americans took direct action against the institutions of injustice, developing the organizations, leadership, and strategies to mount a civil rights movement of unprecedented size and influence. ★

Eisenhower and the Politics of the "Middle Way"

Moderation was the guiding principle of Eisenhower's domestic agenda and leadership style. In 1953, he pledged a "middle way between untrammeled freedom of the individual and the demands for the welfare of the whole Nation," promising that his administration would "avoid government by bureaucracy as carefully as it avoids neglect of the helpless." Eisenhower generally resisted expanding the federal government's power, he acted reluctantly when the Supreme Court ordered schools to desegregate, and his administration terminated the federal trusteeship of dozens of Indian tribes.

As a moderate Republican, however, Eisenhower supported the continuation, and in some cases the expansion, of New Deal programs. He signed key legislation establishing a national highway system and enlarged the federal bureaucracy with a new

Department of Health, Education, and Welfare. Nicknamed "Ike," the confident war hero remained popular, but he was not able to lift the Republican Party to national dominance.

Modern Republicanism In contrast to the old guard conservatives in his party who criticized containment and wanted to repeal much of the New Deal, Eisenhower preached "modern Republicanism." This meant resisting additional federal intervention in economic and social life, but it did not mean turning the clock back to the 1920s. Democratic control of Congress after the elections of 1954 further contributed to Eisenhower's moderate approach, which overall maintained the course charted by Roosevelt and Truman.

The new president attempted to distance himself from the anti-Communist fervor that had plagued the Truman administration. Yet Eisenhower intensified Truman's loyalty program,

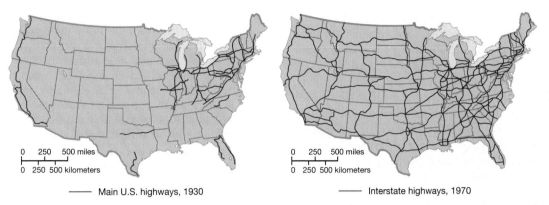

MAP 27.1 The Interstate Highway System, 1930 and 1970
Built with federal funds authorized in the Interstate Highway and Defense System Act of 1956, superhighways soon crisscrossed the nation. Trucking, construction, gasoline, and travel were among the industries that prospered, but railroads suffered from the subsidized competition.

allowing federal executives to dismiss thousands of employees on grounds of loyalty, security, or "suitability." Reflecting his disinclination to involve himself in controversial issues, Eisenhower refused to denounce Senator Joseph McCarthy publicly. In 1954, McCarthy began to destroy himself when he went after the army. As he hurled reckless charges of communism against military personnel during weeks of televised hearings, public opinion turned against him. When the army's lawyer demanded of McCarthy, "Have you left no sense of decency?" those in the hearing room applauded. A Senate vote to condemn McCarthy in December 1954 marked the end of his influence.

Eisenhower sometimes echoed the conservative Republicans' conviction that government was best left to the states and economic decisions to private business. "If all Americans want is security, they can go to prison," Eisenhower commented about social welfare in 1949. Yet the welfare state grew somewhat during his administration, and Eisenhower signed laws bringing ten million more workers into Social Security, increasing the minimum wage, and continuing the federal government's modest role in financing public housing. He created a new Department of Health, Education, and Welfare, appointing as its head former Women's Army Corps commander Oveta Culp Hobby, the second woman to hold a cabinet post. And when the spread of polio neared epidemic proportions, Eisenhower obtained funds from Congress to distribute a vaccine, even though conservatives wanted to leave that responsibility to the states.

Eisenhower's greatest domestic initiative was the **Interstate Highway and Defense System Act of 1956** (Map 27.1). Promoted as essential to national defense and an impetus to economic growth, the

act authorized the construction of a national highway system, with the federal government paying most of the costs through increased fuel and vehicle taxes. The new highways accelerated the mobility of Americans and goods and spurred suburban expansion, shopping malls, and growth in the fast-food and motel industries. The trucking, construction, and automobile industries had lobbied hard for the law and benefited substantially from it. Eventually, the monumental highway project exacted unforeseen costs in the form of air pollution, energy consumption, declining railroads and mass transportation, and decay of central cities.

In other areas, Eisenhower restrained federal activity in favor of state governments and private enterprise. His large tax cuts directed most benefits to business and the wealthy, and he stubbornly resisted national health insurance, federal aid to primary and secondary education, and White House leadership on behalf of civil rights. Moreover, whereas Democrats sought to keep nuclear power in government hands, Eisenhower signed legislation authorizing the private manufacture and sale of nuclear energy.

Termination and Relocation of Native Americans Eisenhower's efforts to limit the federal government were consistent with a new direction in Indian policy, which reversed the emphasis on strengthening tribal governments and preserving Indian culture that had been established in the 1930s (see chapter 24). After World War II, when some 25,000 Indians had left their homes for military service and another 40,000 for work in defense industries, policymakers began to favor assimilating Native Americans and ending their special relationships with the government.

To some officials, who reflected the Cold War emphasis on conformity to dominant American values, the communal practices of Indians resembled socialism and stifled individual initiative. Eisenhower's commissioner of Indian affairs, Glenn Emmons, did not believe that tribal lands could produce income sufficient to lift Indians from poverty, but he also revealed the ethnocentrism of policymakers when he insisted that Indians wanted to "work and live like Americans."

By 1960, the government had implemented a three-part program of compensation, termination, and relocation. In 1946, Congress established the Indian Claims Commission to discharge outstanding claims by Native Americans for land taken by the government. When it closed in 1978, the commission had settled 285 cases, with compensation exceeding $800 million. Yet the awards were based on land values at the time the land was taken and did not include interest.

The second policy, termination, also originated in the Truman administration, where Commissioner Dillon S. Myer asserted that his Bureau of Indian Affairs should do "nothing for Indians which Indians can do for themselves." Beginning in 1953, Eisenhower signed bills transferring jurisdiction over tribal land to state and local governments and ending the trusteeship relationship between Indians and the federal government. The loss of federal hospitals, schools, and other special arrangements devastated Indian tribes. As had happened after passage of the Dawes Act in 1887 (see chapter 17), some corporate interests and individuals took advantage of the opportunity to purchase Indian land cheaply. For many Indians, termination was "like the strike of doom." The government abandoned termination in the 1960s after some 13,000 Indians and more than one million acres of their land had been affected. Decades later, the Menominee and Klamath tribes fought to reverse termination and secured restoration of their tribal status.

Relocation, the third piece of Native American policy, began in 1948 and involved more than 100,000 Native Americans by 1973. The government encouraged Indians to move to cities, where relocation centers were supposed to help with housing, job training, and medical care. Even though government officials made it difficult to return home by sending Indians far away from their reservations, about one-third returned to the reservation. Most who stayed in cities

Major Indian Relocations, 1950–1970

Indian Relocation As part of its new emphasis on assimilation in the late 1940s and 1950s, the Bureau of Indian Affairs distributed this leaflet to entice Native Americans to move from their reservations to cities. Either with government assistance or on their own, thousands of Indians relocated in the years after World War II. In 1950, just 13.4 percent of Indians lived in urban areas. By 1970, 44 percent did so, and by 1990 the figure had reached 63 percent. National Archives.

FOR MORE HELP ANALYZING THIS IMAGE, see the visual activity for this chapter in the Online Study Guide at bedfordstmartins.com/roarkcompact.

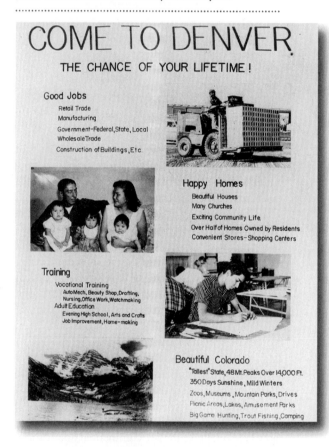

faced racism, lack of adequately paying jobs for which they had skills, poor housing, and the loss of their traditional culture. "I wish we had never left home," said one woman whose husband was out of work. "It's dirty and noisy, and people all around, crowded. . . . It seems like I never see the sky or trees."

Reflecting long-standing disagreements among Indians themselves, some who overcame these obstacles applauded the program. But most urban Indians remained in or near poverty, and even many who had welcomed relocation began to worry that "we would lose our identity as Indian people, lose our culture and our [way] of living." Within two decades, a national pan-Indian movement emerged to resist assimilation and demand much more for Indians. The new militancy and connections across tribal lines that arose were a by-product of the urbanization of Native Americans (see chapter 28).

The 1956 Election and the Second Term Not all citizens were living the American dream, but with the nation at peace and the economy booming, Eisenhower easily defeated Adlai Stevenson in 1956, doubling his margin of 1952. Yet Democrats kept control of Congress, and in the midterm elections two years later, they all but wiped out the Republican Party, gaining a 64–34 majority in the Senate and a 282–135 advantage in the House. Although Ike captured voters' hearts, a majority of Americans remained wedded to the programs and policies of the Democrats.

Eisenhower faced more serious leadership challenges in his second term. When the economy plunged into a recession in late 1957, Eisenhower fought with Congress over the budget and vetoed bills to expand housing, urban development, and public works projects. The president and Congress did reach agreement in two key areas: enacting the first, though largely symbolic, civil rights legislation in a century and establishing a new role for the government in education.

In the end, the first Republican administration after the New Deal left the size and functions of the federal government intact, though it tipped policy somewhat more in favor of corporate interests. Unparalleled prosperity graced the Eisenhower years, and inflation was kept low. The economy weathered two recessions without putting to the test the president's aversion to substantial federal intervention. Eisenhower celebrated what he called the "wide diffusion of wealth and incomes" across the United States. Yet neglected amid the remarkable abundance were some forty million Americans who lived below the poverty level. Rural deprivation was particularly pronounced, as was poverty among African Americans and other minorities.

Q: **How did Eisenhower's domestic policies reflect his moderate political vision?**

Liberation Rhetoric and the Practice of Containment

At his 1953 inauguration, Eisenhower warned that "forces of good and evil are massed and armed and opposed as rarely before in history." Like Truman, he saw communism as a threat to the nation's security and economic interests. Eisenhower's foreign policy differed from Truman's, however, in three areas: its rhetoric, its means, and—after Stalin's death in 1953—its movement toward accommodation with the Soviet Union.

Republican rhetoric, voiced most prominently by Secretary of State John Foster Dulles, deplored containment as "negative, futile, and immoral" because it accepted the existing Soviet sphere of control. Yet despite promises to roll back Soviet power, the Eisenhower administration continued the containment policy. The United States intervened at the margins of Communist power—in Asia, the Middle East, and Latin America—but not at its core in Europe. Eisenhower assigned nuclear weapons and CIA secret operations larger roles in defense strategy, and he took steps to ease tensions between the two superpowers.

The "New Look" in Foreign Policy To meet his goals of balancing the budget and cutting taxes, Eisenhower was determined to control military expenditures. Moreover, he feared that massive defense spending would threaten the nation's economic strength. As he declared in 1953, "Every gun that is made, every warship launched, every rocket fired signifies, in the final sense, a theft from those who hunger and are not fed, those who are cold and not clothed."

Reflecting Americans' confidence in technology and opposition to a large peacetime army, Eisenhower's defense strategy concentrated U.S. military strength in nuclear weapons and the planes and missiles to deliver them. Instead of maintaining large ground forces of its own, the United States would give friendly nations American weapons and back them up with an ominous nuclear arsenal. This was Eisenhower's "New Look" in foreign policy. Secretary of State Dulles believed that America's willingness to "go to the brink" of war with its intimidating nuclear weapons—a strategy called **brinksmanship**—would block any Soviet efforts to expand.

Nuclear weapons could not stop a Soviet nuclear attack, but in response to one, they could inflict enormous destruction. This certainty of "massive retaliation" was meant to deter the Soviets from launching an attack. Because the Soviet Union could respond similarly to an American first strike, this nuclear standoff became known as **mutually assured destruction**, or **MAD**. Yet leaders of each nation sought not just balance but nuclear superiority, and they pursued an ever-escalating arms race.

Nuclear weapons, however, could not roll back the iron curtain. When a revolt against the Soviet-controlled government began in Hungary in 1956, Dulles's liberation rhetoric proved to be empty. A radio plea from Hungarian freedom fighters cried, "SOS! They just brought us a rumor that the American troops will be here within one or two hours." But help did not come. Eisenhower was unwilling to risk U.S. soldiers and possible nuclear war, and Soviet troops soon suppressed the insurrection, killing thirty thousand Hungarians.

Applying Containment to Vietnam A major challenge to the containment policy came in Southeast Asia. During World War II, Ho Chi Minh, a Vietnamese nationalist, had founded a coalition called the Vietminh to fight both the occupying Japanese forces and the French colonial rulers. In 1945, the Vietminh declared Vietnam's independence from France, and when France fought to maintain its colony, the area plunged into war (see Map 29.2, page 728). Because Ho declared himself a Communist, the Truman administration quietly began to provide aid to the French. American principles of national self-determination took a backseat to the battle against communism.

Eisenhower viewed communism in Vietnam much as Truman had regarded it in Greece and Turkey, a view that became known as the **domino theory**. "You have a row of dominoes," Eisenhower explained, and "you knock over the first one, and what will happen to the last one is the certainty that it will go over very quickly." A Communist victory in Southeast Asia, he warned, could trigger the fall of Japan, Taiwan, and the Philippines. By 1954, the United States was contributing 75 percent of the cost of France's war, but Eisenhower resisted a larger role. When the French asked for troops and airplanes from the United States to avert almost certain defeat at Dien Bien Phu, Eisenhower, conscious of U.S. losses in the Korean War, said no.

Dien Bien Phu fell in May 1954 and with it the French colony of Vietnam. Two months later in Geneva, France signed a truce. The **Geneva accords** temporarily partitioned Vietnam at the seventeenth parallel, separating the Vietminh in the north from the puppet government established by the French in the south. Within two years, the Vietnamese people were to vote in elections for a unified government. Some officials warned against U.S. involvement in Vietnam. Defense Secretary Charles Wilson saw "nothing but grief in store for us if we remained in that area." Eisenhower nonetheless began to send weapons and military advisers to South Vietnam and put the CIA to work infiltrating and destabilizing North Vietnam. Fearing a Communist victory in the elections mandated by the Geneva accords, the United States supported South Vietnamese prime minister Ngo Dinh Diem's refusal to hold the vote.

Between 1955 and 1961, the United States provided $800 million to the South Vietnamese army

Geneva Accords, 1954

(the Army of the Republic of Vietnam, or ARVN). Yet the ARVN proved grossly unprepared for the guerrilla warfare that began in the late 1950s. With military assistance from Ho Chi Minh's government in Hanoi, Vietminh rebels in the south stepped up their guerrilla attacks on the Diem government. The insurgents gained support from the largely Buddhist peasants who were outraged by the repressive regime of the Catholic, Westernized Diem. Unwilling to abandon containment, Eisenhower left his successor with the deteriorating situation and a firm commitment to defend South Vietnam against communism.

Interventions in Latin America and the Middle East While supporting friendly governments in Asia, the Eisenhower administration worked secretly to topple unfriendly ones in Latin America and the Middle East. Officials saw internal civil wars in terms of the Cold War conflict between the superpowers and tended to view nationalist uprisings as Communist threats to democracy. They acted against governments that not only seemed too leftist but also threatened U.S. economic interests. The Eisenhower administration took this course of action out of sight of Congress and the public, making the CIA an important arm of foreign policy.

The government of Guatemala, under the popularly elected reformist president Jacobo Arbenz, was not Soviet controlled, but it accepted support from the local Communist Party (see Map 29.1). In 1953, Arbenz moved to help landless, poverty-stricken peasants by nationalizing land owned but not cultivated by the United Fruit Company, a U.S. corporation whose annual profits were twice the size of the Guatemalan government's budget. United Fruit refused Arbenz's offer to compensate it at the value of the land the company had declared for tax purposes. Then, in response to the nationalization program, the CIA organized and supported an opposition army that overthrew the elected government and installed a military dictatorship in 1954. United Fruit kept its land, and Guatemala succumbed to a series of destructive civil wars that lasted through the 1990s.

When Cubans' desire for political and economic autonomy erupted in 1959, a CIA agent promised "to take care of Castro just like we took care of Arbenz." American companies had long controlled major Cuban resources, and decisions made in Washington directly influenced the lives of the Cuban people. An uprising in 1959 led by **Fidel Castro** drove out the U.S.-supported dictator Fulgencio Batista and led the CIA to warn Eisenhower that "Communists and other extreme radicals appear to have penetrated the Castro movement." When the United States denied Castro's requests for loans, he turned to the Soviet Union. And when U.S. companies refused Castro's offer to purchase them at their assessed value, he began to nationalize their property. Many anti-Castro Cubans fled to the United States and reported his atrocities, including the execution of hundreds of Batista's supporters. (See "Seeking the American Promise," page 680.) Before leaving office, Eisenhower broke off diplomatic relations with Cuba and authorized the CIA to train Cuban exiles for an invasion.

In the Middle East, the CIA intervened to oust an elected government, support an unpopular dictatorship, and maintain Western access to Iranian oil (see Map 30.3, page 759). **Mohammed Mossadegh,** the left-leaning democratic prime minister of Iran, accepted support from the Iranian Communist Party and challenged the power of Shah Mohammad Reza Pahlavi, Iran's hereditary leader, who favored foreign oil interests and the Iranian wealthy classes. In 1951, the Iranian parliament nationalized the oil fields and refineries, then held mostly by the British.

Advisers convinced Eisenhower that Mossadegh's government left Iran vulnerable to communism, and the president wanted to keep oil-rich areas "under the control of people who are friendly." With his authorization, CIA agents instigated a coup by bribing army officers and financing demonstrations against the government. In August 1953, Iranian army officers captured Mossadegh and reestablished the shah's power, whereupon Iran renegotiated its oil concessions, giving U.S. companies a 40 percent share. Resentment over this use of force would poison U.S.-Iranian relations into the twenty-first century.

Elsewhere in the Middle East, the Eisenhower administration continued Truman's support of Israel but also sought to foster friendships with Arab nations to secure access to oil and build a bulwark against communism. Yet U.S. officials demanded that smaller nations take the American side in the Cold War, even when those nations preferred neutrality. In 1955, as part of the U.S. effort to win Arab allies, Secretary of State Dulles began talks with Egypt about American support to build the Aswan Dam on the Nile River. The following year, Egypt's leader, Gamal Abdel Nasser, sought arms from Communist Czechoslovakia, formed a military alliance with other Arab nations, and recognized the People's Republic of China. Unwilling to tolerate such independence, Dulles called off the deal for the dam.

On July 26, 1956, Nasser responded by seizing the Suez Canal, then owned by Britain and France but scheduled to revert to Egypt within seven years. In response to the seizure, Israel, whose forces had been skirmishing with Egyptian troops along their common border since 1948, attacked Egypt with military help from Britain and France. Eisenhower opposed the intervention, recognizing that the Egyptians had claimed their own territory and that Nasser "embodie[d] the emotional demands of the people . . . for independence." He put economic pressure on Britain and France while calling on the United Nations to arrange a truce. The French and British soon pulled back, forcing Israel to retreat.

Despite staying out of the **Suez crisis,** Eisenhower made it clear that the United States would actively combat communism in the Middle East. In March 1957, Congress passed a joint resolution approving aid to any Middle Eastern nation "requesting assistance against armed aggression from any country controlled by international communism." The president invoked this **Eisenhower Doctrine** to send aid to Jordan in 1957 and troops to Lebanon in 1958 to counter anti-Western pressures on those governments.

The Suez Crisis, 1956

The Nuclear Arms Race While Eisenhower moved against perceived Communist inroads abroad, he also sought to reduce superpower tensions. After Stalin's death in 1953, a more moderate leadership under **Nikita Khrushchev** emerged. Like Eisenhower, who remarked privately that the arms race would lead "at worst to atomic warfare, at best to robbing every people and nation on earth of the fruits of their own toil," Khrushchev wanted to reduce defense spending and the threat of nuclear devastation. Eisenhower and Khrushchev met in Geneva in 1955 at the first summit conference since the end of World War II. Although the meeting produced no new agreements, it symbolized what Eisenhower called "a new spirit of conciliation and cooperation."

In August 1957, the Soviets test-fired their first intercontinental ballistic missile (ICBM) and two months later beat the United States into space by launching ***Sputnik,*** the first artificial satellite to circle the earth. The United States launched a successful satellite of its own in January 1958, but *Sputnik* raised fears that the United States lagged behind the USSR not only in missile development and space exploration but also

> Eisenhower remarked privately that the arms race would lead "at worst to atomic warfare, at best to robbing every people and nation on earth of the fruits of their own toil."

Operation Pedro Pan: Young Political Refugees Take Flight

Six-year-old María was awakened before dawn one summer day in Cuba in 1962. Her parents drove her to the Havana airport, with one suitcase and her favorite doll. A paper pinned to her gingham dress gave her name and the phone number of the family friends in Miami who planned to meet her. She traveled with a six-year-old boy whose father in Miami had obtained the visa waivers the children would need to enter the United States. María, excited but anxious, had never been away from her parents before; she would not see them for four months.

On a different flight that summer, a ten-year-old boy named Carlos flew to Miami with his older brother, leaving behind a father they would never see again. Because of their age difference, the boys were separated on arrival and sent to different refugee camps in rural Florida. Through the help of a family acquaintance—a Cuban lawyer working as a janitor in Miami—both boys soon gained temporary placement with foster families just ten blocks apart. A few months later, they were transferred to a juvenile delinquent facility that provided only one meal a day. Finally, a Cuban uncle arrived and took them with him to a small midwestern town where no one spoke Spanish. After three years of traumatic separation, their mother fled Cuba and joined them.

María and Carlos were just two of the more than fourteen thousand unaccompanied children, ages six to eighteen, who left Cuba as part of a special U.S. government–facilitated program called Operation Pedro Pan, which functioned for twenty-two months from December 1960 to October 1962. With little money, no knowledge of English, and often no friends or relatives to receive them, the children faced at the minimum daunting loneliness and possibly neglect. What drove the parents of these children to take such an extraordinary step?

The U.S. government had already made unusual accommodation for the large exodus of adult refugees who fled Cuba after Fidel Castro came to power in 1959. No U.S. law yet defined political asylum, but the government relaxed immigration restrictions for Cubans, allowing indefinite entry on tourist visas. Most of the refugees came with little money: Just $5 and thirty pounds of luggage per person were all the Cuban government allowed. Those with U.S. bank accounts had resources to draw on, but the rest needed income, so visa restrictions were relaxed to enable the refugees to work. Additionally, in late 1960, President Dwight D. Eisenhower authorized $1 million in relief and resettlement funds under a little-known provision of the Mutual Security Act, which authorized aid for people "subjected to the captivity of Communist despotism." Shortly thereafter, the new president, John F. Kennedy, released $4 million more and established the Cuban Refugee Program in the Department of Health, Education, and Welfare, which provided job training, health services, and food distribution along with monthly relief checks.

The U.S. government provided special assistance to Cuban refugees for several reasons. First, the refugees considered themselves exiles, not immigrants. They intended to return to Cuba as soon as Castro's government fell. The U.S. government shared that expectation (and was taking active steps to help it happen) and thus did not anticipate that the exiles would become permanent residents. Second, the U.S. government felt an obligation to shelter Cubans who had worked in the government or military of deposed dictator Fulgencio Batista, a close U.S. ally. In addition, many Cubans fleeing in the first two years after the revolution had worked for U.S.-owned businesses. Others were wealthy merchants and professionals—doctors, lawyers, university professors. In December 1960, well over a thousand of these upper- and middle-class exiles were arriving each week. By the fall of 1962, 248,000 Cubans had chosen to flee communism, furnishing the United States with a powerful symbolic statement of Cold War politics.

An even more potent symbol was Operation Pedro Pan, with its implication that Castro's Cuba had to be truly

in science and education. In response, Eisenhower established the National Aeronautics and Space Administration (NASA) and signed the National Defense Education Act, providing support for students in math, foreign languages, and science.

Eisenhower assured the public that the United States possessed nuclear superiority. In fact, during his presidency, the stockpile of nuclear weapons more than quadrupled, and the United States had installed ICBMs in the United States and Britain and was prepared to deploy more in Italy and Turkey. The first Polaris submarine carrying nuclear missiles was launched in November 1960. Yet these weapons could not guarantee security, because both superpowers terrible for parents to part with their children. It recalled the dramatic *kindertransport* of ten thousand Jewish children sent out of Germany and Austria to Britain in 1938 and 1939. But mass death was not impending; Cuban parents fully expected to see their children soon, either in Florida or in Cuba after Castro's regime collapsed. Even so, no one could be sure that it would be possible for parents to follow their children to America. Exit permits and transport were not easy to arrange, and after the U.S.-Soviet showdown in the Cuban missile crisis of October 1962 (see chapter 29), air travel was completely suspended, blocking parental exits for several years.

Cuban parents who opposed Castro feared not for their children's lives, but for their minds. Public schools in Cuba reportedly taught an escalating rhetoric of revolution, while private schools were shut down. Compulsory military service for boys and summer programs relocating teenagers to jobs teaching literacy in the rural countryside threatened parental rights to determine their children's activities. Relatively prosperous Cuban families did not benefit from Castro's reforms, which focused on improving health and education for the impoverished masses. Their fears of socialized child rearing were reinforced by a program of disinformation allegedly broadcast from a CIA radio station located on the U.S. mainland, which warned parents that "the Revolutionary Government will take [your children] away from you when they turn five and will keep them until they are eighteen." Rumors of Communist indoctrination ran rampant.

Fear of communism gripped the United States in the 1950s, and the Pedro Pan exodus both demonstrated and heightened that fear. The belief that Communists brainwashed children and turned them against their parents led some Cuban parents to try to save their children by sending them to a country that celebrated freedom. This positive view of Operation Pedro Pan is still held by some people today. In a 2002 speech, President George W. Bush praised Cuban parents of the early 1960s who "were willing to give up their children so they could grow up in a free society." But some of the children themselves, as adults, have questioned whether coming to America was worth the trauma they endured and have speculated that Cold War politics might have shaped the operation more than humanitarian concerns.

María de los Angeles Torres and Carlos Eire, two among the thousands, grew up to become university professors in the United States. Like the majority of Pedro Pan children, they are now glad they came here, but they also wonder about the choices their families made. Professor Torres's research for her scholarly study of the children's exodus, *The Lost Apple*, led her to archives in Cuba and Washington, D.C., and to interviews with parents, children, and clandestine workers involved in the program. She realized that she had long avoided discussing the subject with her mother because of their different political outlooks, but she came to understand her mother's perspective. Professor Eire produced a different type of book—a memoir of his childhood titled *Waiting for Snow in Havana: Confessions of a Cuban Boy*. Unlike Torres, he has refused to return to Cuba while Castro remains in power, and he writes, "The world that exists in my memory is so vivid perhaps because I have given up on the idea of ever reclaiming it."

★ **Leaving Havana** A family camera captures María de los Angeles Torres (far left) at the airport in Havana, before her flight to Miami in July 1961. AP Images.

possessed sufficient nuclear capacity to devastate each other. Most Americans did not follow Civil Defense Administration recommendations to construct home bomb shelters, but they did realize how precarious nuclear weapons had made their lives.

In the midst of the arms race, the superpowers continued to talk. In 1959, Khrushchev visited the United States, and Nixon went to the Soviet Union, where he engaged in the famous kitchen debate. By 1960, the two sides were close to a ban on nuclear testing. But just before an agreed upon summit in Paris, a Soviet missile shot down a U-2 spy plane over Soviet territory. The State Department first denied that U.S. planes had been

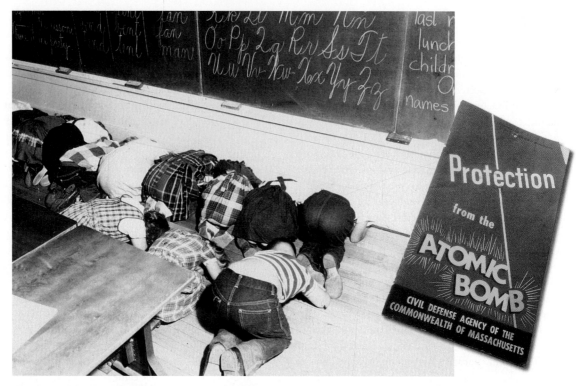

The Age of Nuclear Anxiety Within just five years after World War II, state and local governments were educating the American people about the nuclear threat. As schools routinely held drills to prepare for possible Soviet attacks, children experienced directly the anxiety and insecurity of the 1950s nuclear arms race. This pamphlet about how to protect oneself from an atomic attack was published by the federal government and distributed to the general public. Photo: Archive Photos/Getty Images; Pamphlet: Lynn Historical Society.

FOR MORE HELP ANALYZING THIS IMAGE, see the visual activity for this chapter in the Online Study Guide at bedfordstmartins.com/roarkcompact.

violating Soviet airspace, but the Soviets produced the pilot and the photos taken on his flight. Eisenhower and Khrushchev met briefly in Paris, but the U-2 incident dashed all prospects for a nuclear arms agreement.

As Eisenhower left office, he warned about the growing influence of the **military-industrial complex** in American government and life. Eisenhower had struggled against persistent pressures from defense contractors, who, in tandem with the military, sought more dollars for newer, more powerful weapons systems. In his farewell address, he warned that the "conjunction of an immense military establishment and a large arms industry . . . exercised a total influence . . . in every city, every state house, every office of the federal government." The Cold War had created a warfare state.

Q: **Where and how did Eisenhower practice containment?**

New Work and Living Patterns in an Economy of Abundance

Stimulated in part by American military spending, economic productivity increased enormously in the 1950s. A multitude of new items came on the market, and consumption became the order of the day. Millions of Americans enjoyed new homes in the suburbs, and higher education enrollments skyrocketed. Although every section of the nation enjoyed the new abundance, the West and Southwest especially boomed in production, commerce, and population.

Work itself changed. Fewer people labored on farms, service sector employment overtook manufacturing jobs, and women's employment grew. These economic shifts disadvantaged some Americans, and they did little to help the forty million who lived in poverty. Most Americans, however, enjoyed a higher standard of living, leading economist John Kenneth Galbraith to call the United States "the affluent society."

Technology Transforms Agriculture and Industry Between 1940 and 1960, agricultural output mushroomed while the number of farmworkers declined by almost one-third. Farmers achieved nearly miraculous productivity through greater crop specialization, intensive use of fertilizers, and, above all, mechanization. A single mechanical cotton picker, for example, replaced fifty people and cut the cost of harvesting a bale of cotton from $40 to $5.

The decline of family farms and the growth of large commercial farming, or agribusiness, were both causes and consequences of mechanization. Benefiting handsomely from federal price supports begun in the New Deal, larger farmers could afford technological improvements, whereas smaller producers lacked capital to invest in the machinery necessary to compete. Consequently, average farm size more than doubled between 1940 and 1964, and the number of farms fell by more than 40 percent.

Many small farmers who hung on constituted a core of rural poverty often overlooked in the celebration of affluence. Southern landowners replaced sharecroppers with machines, forcing them off the land. Hundreds of thousands of African Americans joined an exodus to cities, where racial discrimination and a lack of jobs for which they could qualify mired many in urban poverty. A Mississippi mother whose family had worked on a plantation since slavery reported that most of her relatives headed for Chicago when they realized that "it was going to be machines now that harvest the crops." Worrying that "it might be worse up there" for her children, she agonized, "I'm afraid to leave and I'm afraid to stay."

Industrial production also benefited from new technologies. Between 1945 and 1960, for example, the number of labor-hours needed to manufacture a car fell by 50 percent. Technology transformed industries such as electronics, chemicals, and air transportation and promoted the growth of television, plastics, computers, and other newer industries. American businesses enjoyed access to cheap oil, ample markets abroad, and little foreign competition. Moreover, even with Eisenhower's conservative fiscal policies, government spending reached $80 billion annually and created new jobs.

Labor unions enjoyed their greatest success during the 1950s, and real earnings for production workers shot up 40 percent. The merger in 1955 of the American Federation of Labor (AFL) and the Congress of Industrial Organizations (CIO) improved labor's bargaining position. As one worker put it, "We saw continual improvement in wages, fringe benefits like holidays, vacation, medical plans . . . all sorts

of things that provided more security for people." In most industrial nations, government programs underwrote their citizens' security, but the United States developed a mixed system in which company-funded programs won by unions through collective bargaining played a much larger role in providing for retirement, health care, and the like. This system resulted in wide disparities among workers, severely disadvantaging those not represented by unions and those with irregular employment.

While the absolute number of organized workers continued to grow, union membership peaked at 27.1 percent of the labor force in 1957. Technological advances eliminated jobs in heavy industry, reducing the number of workers in the steel, copper, and aluminum industries by 17 percent. "You are going to have trouble collecting union dues from all of these machines," commented a Ford manager to union leader Walter Reuther. Moreover, the economy as a whole was shifting from production to service as more workers distributed goods, performed services, provided education, and carried out government work. Unions made some headway in these fields, especially among government employees, but most service industries resisted unionization.

The growing clerical and service occupations swelled the demand for female workers. By the end of the 1950s, women held nearly one-third of all jobs. The vast majority of them worked in offices, light manufacturing, domestic service, teaching, and nursing; because these were female occupations, wages were relatively low. In 1960, the average full-time female worker earned just 60 percent of the average male worker's wages. At the bottom of the employment ladder, black women took home only 42 percent of what white men earned.

Burgeoning Suburbs and Declining Cities Although suburbs had existed since the nineteenth century, nothing symbolized the affluent society more than their tremendous expansion in the 1950s. Eleven million new homes went up in the suburbs, and by 1960 one in four Americans lived there. As Nixon boasted to Khrushchev during the kitchen debate, the suburbs were accessible to families with modest incomes. Builder William J. Levitt adapted the factory assembly-line process, planning nearly identical units so that individual construction workers could move from house to house and perform the same single operation in each one. In 1949, families could purchase mass-produced houses in his 17,000-home development, called **Levittown**, on Long Island, New York, for just under $8,000 each. Developments similar to Levittown, as well as

HOMEOWNERS GUIDE

• SOME INFORMATION FOR RESIDENTS OF LEVITTOWN TO HELP THEM ENJOY THEIR NEW HOMES more luxurious ones, quickly went up throughout the country. The government underwrote home ownership with low-interest mortgage guarantees through the Federal Housing Administration and the Veterans Administration and by making interest on mortgages tax deductible. Thousands of miles of interstate highway running through urban areas indirectly subsidized suburban development.

The growing suburbs helped polarize society, especially along racial lines. Each Levittown home-owner signed a contract pledging not to rent or sell to a non-Caucasian. The Supreme Court declared such covenants unenforceable in 1948, but sub-urban America remained dramatically segregated. Levitt commented, "We can solve a housing prob-lem, or we can try and solve a racial problem, but we cannot combine the two." Social critic Lewis Mumford blasted the suburbs as "a multitude of uniform, unidentifiable houses in a treeless com-munal wasteland, inhabited by people of the same class, the same income, the same age group."

Although some African Americans joined the suburban migration, most moved to cities in search of economic opportunity, increasing their numbers in most cities by 50 percent during the 1950s. These migrants, however, came to cities that were already in decline, losing not only population but also com-merce and industry to the suburbs or to southern and western states. Shoppers gradually chose new suburban malls over downtown department stores.

Many of the new jobs lay beyond the reach of the recent black arrivals to the inner cities.

The Rise of the Sun Belt No regions experienced the postwar economic and population booms more intensely than the West and Southwest. Architect Frank Lloyd Wright quipped, "Everything loose will land in Los Angeles." California overtook New York as the most populous state. Sports franchises followed fans: In 1958, the Brooklyn Dodgers moved to Los Angeles, joined by the Minneapolis Lakers three years later.

A pleasant natural environment drew new resi-dents to the West and Southwest, but no magnet proved stronger than the promise of economic oppor-tunity (Map 27.2). As railroads had fueled western growth in the nineteenth century, so the automobile and airplane spurred the post–World War II surge. The technology of air-conditioning facilitated indus-trial development and by 1960 cooled nearly eight million homes in the so-called **Sun Belt**, which stretched from Florida to California.

So important was the defense industry to the South and West that the area was later referred to as the "Gun Belt." The aerospace industry boomed in Seattle–Tacoma, Los Angeles, and Dallas–Fort Worth, and military bases helped underwrite pros-perity in cities such as San Diego and San Antonio. Although defense dollars benefited other regions, the Sun Belt captured the lion's share of Cold War

THE PROMISE OF TECHNOLOGY

Air-Conditioning In 1902, Willis Haviland Carrier, a twenty-six-year-old American engineer, designed the first system to control temperature and humidity and installed it in a Brooklyn printing plant. Room air conditioners began to appear in the 1930s and spread rapidly in the 1950s. By cooling homes, businesses, factories, and hotels, air-conditioning made possible the industrial and population explosion in the Sun Belt. While this ad promised consumers clean as well as cool air inside the house, it failed to note that air-conditioning consumed large amounts of energy and contributed to out-door air pollution. Hotpoint/General Electric Company.

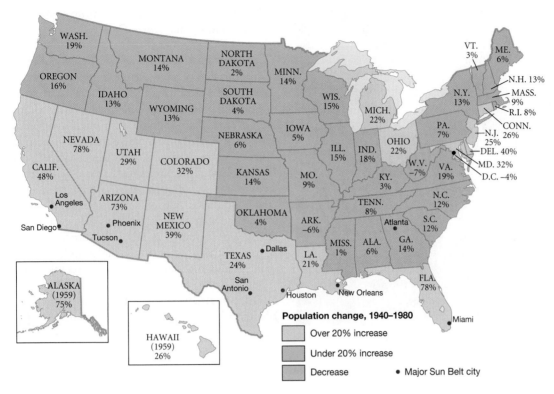

MAP 27.2 The Rise of the Sun Belt, 1940–1980

The growth of defense industries, a non-unionized labor force, and the spread of air-conditioning all helped spur economic development and population growth, which made the Sun Belt the fastest-growing region of the country between 1940 and 1980.

READING THE MAP: What states experienced population growth of more than 20 percent? What states experienced the largest population growth?

CONNECTIONS: What stimulated the population boom in the Southwest? What role did the Cold War play in this expansion? What role did African Americans play in the western population boom?

FOR MORE HELP ANALYZING THIS MAP, see the map activity for this chapter in the Online Study Guide at bedfordstmartins.com/roarkcompact.

....

spending. By the 1960s, nearly one of every three California workers held a defense-related job.

The surging populations and industries soon threatened the environment. Providing sufficient water and power to cities and to agribusiness meant building dams and reservoirs on free-flowing rivers. Native Americans lost fishing sites on the Columbia River, and dams on the Upper Missouri displaced nine hundred Indian families. Sprawling urban and suburban settlement without efficient public transportation contributed to blankets of smog over Los Angeles and other cities.

The high-technology basis of postwar economic development drew well-educated, highly skilled workers to the West, but the economic promise also attracted the poor. "We see opportunity all around us here. . . . We smell freedom here, and maybe soon we can taste it," commented a black

mother in California. Between 1945 and 1960, more than one-third of the African Americans who left the South moved west.

The Mexican American population also grew, especially in California and Texas. To supply California's vast agribusiness industry, the government continued the *bracero* program begun during World War II. Until the program ended in 1964, more than 100,000 Mexicans entered the United States each year to labor in the fields—and many of them stayed, legally or illegally. But permanent Mexican immigration was not as welcome as Mexicans' low-wage labor. In 1954, the government launched a series of raids called "Operation Wetback," resulting in deportation of more than one million Mexicans. Even Mexicans with legal status felt unwelcome and vulnerable to incidents of mistaken identity.

Rounding Up Undocumented Migrants Not all Mexican Americans who wanted to work in the United States were accommodated by the bracero program. In 1953, Los Angeles police arrested these men who did not have legal documents and were hiding in a freight train. Some Americans used the crude term "wetback" to refer to illegal Mexican immigrants because many of them swam across the Rio Grande, which forms part of the border between the United States and Mexico. © Bettmann/Corbis.

At the same time, Mexican American citizens gained a small victory in their ongoing struggle for civil rights in *Hernandez v. Texas*. When a Texas jury convicted Pete Hernandez of murder, lawyers from the American GI Forum and the League of United Latin-American Citizens (see chapter 26) appealed on the grounds that persons of Mexican origin had been routinely excluded from jury service. In 1954, the Supreme Court decided the first Mexican American civil rights case of the post–World War II era, ruling unanimously that Mexican Americans constituted a distinct group and that their systematic exclusion from juries violated the constitutional guarantee of equal protection.

Free of the discrimination faced by minorities, white Americans enjoyed the fullest prosperity in the West. In April 1950, when California developers opened Lakewood, a large housing development in Los Angeles County, thirty thousand people lined up to buy houses at prices ranging from $68,000 to $85,000 in 2007 dollars. Many of the new home-owners were veterans, blue-collar, and lower-level white-collar workers whose defense-based jobs at aerospace corporations enabled them to fulfill the American dream of the 1950s. A huge shopping mall, Lakewood Center, offered myriad products of the consumer culture, and the workers' children

lived within commuting distance from community colleges and six state universities.

The Democratization of Higher Education

California's university system exemplified a spectacular transformation of higher education. Between 1940 and 1960, college enrollments in the United States more than doubled. More than 40 percent of young Americans attended college by the mid-1960s, up from 15 percent in the 1940s. Prosperity enabled more families to keep their children in school longer, and the federal government subsidized the education of more than two million veterans. The Cold War also sent millions of federal dollars to universities for defense-related research. And state governments vastly expanded the number of public colleges and universities, while municipalities began to build two-year community colleges.

All Americans did not benefit equally from the democratization of higher education. Although their college enrollments surged from 37,000 in 1941 to 90,000 in 1961, African Americans constituted only about 5 percent of all college students. Black men and women attended college in nearly equal numbers, but for a time, the educational gap between white men and women grew. In 1940, women had earned 40 percent of undergraduate degrees, but as veterans flocked to college campuses, women's proportion fell to 25 percent in 1950 and rebounded to only 33 percent by 1960. The large veteran enrollments moved colleges to relax rules that had forbidden students to marry. Unlike men, however, women tended to drop out of college after marriage and to take jobs so their husbands could stay in school. Reflecting gender norms of the 1950s, most college women agreed that "it is natural for a woman to be satisfied with her husband's success and not crave personal achievement."

Q: How did technology contribute to changes in the economy, suburbanization, and the growth of the Sun Belt?

The Culture of Abundance

Prosperity in the 1950s intensified the transformation of the nation into a consumer society, changing the way Americans lived and converting the traditional work ethic into an ethic of consumption. People married at earlier ages, the birthrate soared, and dominant values celebrated family life and traditional gender roles. Religious observance expanded even as Americans sought satisfaction in material possessions. Television entered the homes of most Americans, both reflecting and helping to promote a consumer culture. Undercurrents of rebellion, especially among young people, and women's increasing employment defied some of the dominant norms but did not greatly disrupt the complacency of the 1950s.

Consumption Rules the Day In the 1950s, Robert Samuelson remembered, "you were a daily witness to the marvels of affluence . . . a seemingly endless array of new gadgets and machines." Scorned by Khrushchev during the kitchen debate as unnecessary gadgets, consumer items flooded American society. Although the purchase and display of consumer goods was not new (see chapter 23), by the 1950s, consumption had become a reigning value, vital for economic prosperity and essential to individuals' identity and status. In place of the traditional emphasis on work and savings, the consumer culture encouraged satisfaction and happiness through the purchase and use of new products.

The consumer culture rested on a firm material base. Between 1950 and 1960, both the gross national product (the value of all goods and services produced) and median family income grew by 25 percent in constant dollars. Economists claimed that 60 percent of Americans enjoyed middle-class incomes in 1960. Referring to the popular ranch-style houses in the new suburbs, *House Beautiful* magazine boasted, "Our houses are all on one level, like our class structure." Though ignoring the one in five Americans who still lived in poverty, the statement did reflect the increasing ability of people to consume products that made class differences less visible. By 1960, four out of every five families owned a television set, nearly all had a refrigerator, and most owned at least one car. The number of shopping centers quadrupled between 1957 and 1963.

Several forces spurred this unparalleled abundance. A population surge—from 152 million in 1950 to 180 million in 1960—expanded the demand for products and boosted industries ranging from housing to baby goods. Consumer borrowing also fueled the economic boom, as people increasingly made purchases on installment plans and began to use credit cards. In what *Life* magazine referred to as a "revolution in consumer purchasing," Americans now enjoyed their possessions while they paid for them instead of saving their money for future purchases.

Although the sheer need to support themselves and their families explained most women's employment, a desire to secure some of the new abundance sent growing numbers of women to work. In fact, married women's employment rose more than that of any other group in the 1950s. As one remarked, "My Joe can't put five kids through college . . . and the washer had to be replaced, and Ann was ashamed to bring friends home because

the living room furniture was such a mess, so I went to work." The standards for family happiness imposed by the consumer culture increasingly required a second income.

The Revival of Domesticity and Religion Despite married women's growing employment, a dominant ideology celebrated traditional family life and conventional gender roles. Both popular culture and public figures defined the ideal family as a male breadwinner, a full-time homemaker, and three or four children. Writer and feminist **Betty Friedan** gave a name to the idealization of women's domestic roles in her 1963 book *The Feminine Mystique*. Friedan criticized scholars, advertisers, and public officials for assuming that biological differences dictated different roles for men and women. According to the feminine mystique that they promulgated, women should find fulfillment in devotion to their homes, families, and serving others. Not many women directly challenged these ideas, but Edith Stern, a college-educated writer, maintained that "many arguments about the joys of housewifery have been advanced, largely by those who have never had to work at it."

Although the glorification of domesticity clashed with women's increasing employment, many Americans' lives did embody the family ideal. Postwar prosperity enabled people to marry earlier and to have more children. The American birthrate soared between 1945 and 1965, peaking in 1957 with 4.3 million births and producing the **baby boom** generation. (See "Global Comparison" and appendix II, page A-22.) Experts encouraged mothers to devote even more attention to child rearing, while they also urged fathers to cultivate family "togetherness" by spending more time with their children.

The 1950s also witnessed a surge of interest in religion. From 1940 to 1960, membership in churches or synagogues rose from 50 to 63 percent of all Americans. Polls reported that 95 percent of the population believed in God. Evangelism took on new life, most notably in the nationwide crusades of Baptist minister **Billy Graham**. Congress linked religion more closely to the state by adding "under God" to the pledge of allegiance and by requiring that "In God We Trust" be printed on all currency.

Religion helped to calm anxieties in the nuclear age, while ministers such as Graham made the Cold War a holy war, labeling communism "a great sinister anti-Christian movement masterminded by Satan." Some critics questioned the depth of the religious revival, attributing the growth in church membership to a desire for conformity and a need for social outlets. One commentator, for example,

The Baby Boom in International Perspective

	Live Births per 1,000
Brazil	🚶🚶🚶🚶🚶🚶🚶🚶🚶🚶🚶🚶🚶🚶🚶🚶🚶🚶🚶🚶🚶🚶🚶🚶🚶🚶🚶🚶🚶🚶🚶🚶🚶🚶🚶
Canada	🚶🚶🚶🚶🚶🚶🚶🚶🚶🚶🚶🚶🚶🚶🚶🚶🚶🚶🚶🚶🚶🚶🚶
China	🚶🚶🚶🚶🚶🚶🚶🚶🚶🚶🚶🚶🚶🚶🚶🚶🚶🚶🚶🚶🚶🚶🚶🚶🚶🚶🚶🚶🚶🚶🚶🚶🚶
Cuba	🚶🚶🚶🚶🚶🚶🚶🚶🚶🚶🚶🚶🚶🚶🚶🚶🚶🚶🚶🚶🚶🚶
Egypt	🚶🚶🚶🚶🚶🚶🚶🚶🚶🚶🚶🚶🚶🚶🚶🚶🚶🚶🚶🚶🚶🚶🚶🚶🚶🚶🚶🚶🚶🚶🚶
West Germany	🚶🚶🚶🚶🚶🚶🚶🚶🚶🚶🚶🚶🚶🚶🚶🚶
Great Britain	🚶🚶🚶🚶🚶🚶🚶🚶🚶🚶🚶🚶🚶🚶🚶🚶
Iran	🚶🚶🚶🚶🚶🚶🚶🚶🚶🚶🚶🚶🚶🚶🚶🚶🚶🚶🚶🚶🚶🚶🚶🚶🚶🚶🚶🚶🚶🚶🚶🚶🚶
Israel	🚶🚶🚶🚶🚶🚶🚶🚶🚶🚶🚶🚶🚶🚶🚶🚶🚶🚶🚶🚶🚶🚶🚶
Mexico	🚶🚶🚶🚶🚶🚶🚶🚶🚶🚶🚶🚶🚶🚶🚶🚶🚶🚶🚶🚶🚶🚶🚶🚶🚶🚶🚶🚶🚶🚶🚶🚶🚶🚶🚶🚶
Sweden	🚶🚶🚶🚶🚶🚶🚶🚶🚶🚶🚶🚶🚶
United States	🚶🚶🚶🚶🚶🚶🚶🚶🚶🚶🚶🚶🚶🚶🚶🚶🚶🚶🚶🚶🚶🚶🚶🚶
USSR	🚶🚶🚶🚶🚶🚶🚶🚶🚶🚶🚶🚶🚶🚶🚶🚶🚶🚶🚶🚶🚶🚶🚶🚶🚶

Live Births per 1,000

The United States was not alone in welcoming bumper crops of babies in the 1950s. High fertility continued in nonindustrialized countries, while in Europe, as in the United States, birthrates rebounded from low levels during the Great Depression and World War II. Which countries had birthrates comparable to those of the United States? What might explain why countries such as Brazil, China, Iran, and Mexico had birthrates so much higher than those in the United States? What might explain why birthrates in Europe were lower than those in the United States?

noted that 53 percent of Americans could not name any book of the Christian Bible's New Testament.

Television Transforms Culture and Politics

Just as family life and religion offered a respite from Cold War anxieties, so too did the new medium of television. By 1960, close to 90 percent of American homes boasted a television set, and the average viewer spent more than five hours each day in front of the screen. Audiences were especially attracted to situation comedies, which projected the family ideal and the feminine mystique into millions of homes. On TV, married women did not have paying jobs, and they deferred to their husbands, though they often got the upper hand through subtle manipulation. In the most popular television show of the early

1950s, *I Love Lucy*, the husband-and-wife team of Lucille Ball and Desi Arnaz played the couple Lucy and Ricky Ricardo. Ricky would not let Lucy get a job, and many plots depicted her zany attempts to get around him.

Television also began to affect politics. Eisenhower's 1952 presidential campaign used TV ads for the first time, although he was not happy that "an old soldier should come to this." By 1960, television played a key role in election campaigns. Reflecting on his narrow victory in 1960, president-elect John F. Kennedy remarked, "We wouldn't have had a prayer without that gadget."

Television transformed politics in other ways. Money played a much larger role in elections because candidates needed to pay for expensive TV spots. The ability to appeal directly to voters in their living rooms put a premium on personal attractiveness and encouraged candidates to build their own campaign organizations, relying less on political parties. The declining strength of parties and the growing power of money in elections were not new trends, but TV helped accelerate them.

Unlike government-financed television in Europe, American TV was paid for by private enterprise. What NBC called a "selling machine in every living room" became the major vehicle for hawking the products of the affluent society and creating a consumer culture. In the mid-1950s, advertisers spent $10 billion to push their goods on TV. Television programs also tantalized viewers with things to buy. On *Queen for a Day*, for example, the women with the most pitiful personal stories won fur coats, vacuum cleaners, and other merchandise.

In 1961, Newton Minow, chairman of the Federal Communications Commission, called television a "vast wasteland." While acknowledging some of TV's great achievements, particularly documentaries and drama, Minow depicted it as "a procession of game shows, . . . formula comedies about totally unbelievable families, blood and thunder, mayhem, violence, sadism, murder . . . and cartoons." But viewers kept tuning in. In little more than a decade, television came to dominate Americans' leisure time, influence their consumption patterns, and shape their perceptions of the nation's leadership.

Countercurrents Pockets of dissent underlay the complacency of the 1950s. Some intellectuals took exception to the materialism and conformity of the era. In *The Lonely Crowd* (1950), sociologist David Riesman lamented a shift from the "inner-directed" to the "other-directed" individual, as Americans replaced independent thinking with an eagerness to adapt to external standards of behavior and belief. Sharing that distaste for the importance of "belonging," William H. Whyte Jr., in his popular book *The Organization Man* (1956), blamed the modern corporation for making employees tailor themselves to the group. Vance Packard's 1959 best seller, *The Status Seekers*, decried "the vigorous merchandising of goods as status-symbols" and argued that "class lines . . . appear to be hardening."

Implicit in much of the critique of consumer culture was concern about the loss of traditional masculinity. Consumption itself was associated with women and their presumed greater susceptibility to manipulation. Men, required to conform in order to get ahead, moved farther away from the nineteenth-century masculine ideals of individualism and aggressiveness. Moreover, the increase in married women's employment compromised the male ideal of breadwinner.

The Made-for-TV Family *The Adventures of Ozzie and Harriet* began as a radio program in the 1940s and ran on television from 1952 to 1966. Along with other family sitcoms, it idealized white family life, in which no one got divorced or became gravely ill, no one took drugs or seriously misbehaved, fathers held white-collar jobs, mothers did not work outside the home, and husbands and wives slept in twin beds. Following the 1950s norm, Ozzie sought to fulfill his role as head of the household, but the impeccably dressed and high-heeled Harriet more often appeared as the wise and sensible one who rescued Ozzie and the teenage boys, David and Ricky, from their misadventures. In what ways do today's sitcoms differ from those of the 1950s? Picture Research Consultants & Archives.

Into this gender confusion came *Playboy*, which began publication in 1953 and quickly gained a circulation of one million. The new magazine idealized masculine independence in the form of bachelorhood and assaulted the reigning middle-class norms of domesticity and respectability. By associating the sophisticated bachelor with good wine, music, furnishings, and the like, the magazine made consumption more masculine while promoting sexual freedom, at least for men.

In fact, new research on Americans' sexual behavior disclosed that it often departed from the postwar family ideal. Two books published by **Alfred Kinsey** and other researchers at Indiana University — *Sexual Behavior in the Human Male* (1948) and *Sexual Behavior in the Human Female* (1953) — uncovered a surprising range of sexual conduct. In a large survey, Kinsey found that 85 percent of the men and 50 percent of the women had had sex before marriage, half of the husbands and a quarter of the wives had engaged in adultery, and one-third of the men and one-seventh of the women reported homosexual experiences. Although Kinsey's sampling procedures later cast doubt on his ability to generalize across the population, the books became best sellers. They also drew a firestorm of outrage, especially because Kinsey insisted on the natural variability of human sexuality and refused to make moral judgments.

Less direct challenges to mainstream standards appeared in the everyday behavior of young Americans. "Roll over Beethoven and tell Tchaikovsky the news!" belted out Chuck Berry in his 1956 hit record celebrating a new form of music that combined country sounds and black rhythm and blues — rock and roll. White teenagers lionized Elvis Presley, who shocked their parents with his tight pants, hip-rolling gestures, and sensuous rock-and-roll music. "Before there was Elvis . . . I started going crazy for 'race music,'" recalled a white man of his teenage years. "That got me into trouble with my parents and the schools." His recollection underscored African Americans' contributions to rock and roll, as well as the rebellion expressed by white youths' attraction to black music.

The most blatant revolt against conventionality came from the self-proclaimed **Beat generation**, a small group of primarily male literary figures based in New York City and San Francisco. Rejecting nearly everything in mainstream culture — patriotism, consumerism, technology, conventional family life, discipline — the Beats celebrated spontaneity and absolute personal freedom, including drug consumption and freewheeling sex. In his landmark poem *Howl* (1956), Allen Ginsberg denounced the social forces that "frightened me out of my natural ecstasy!" Jack Kerouac, who gave the Beat generation its name, published the best-selling novel *On the Road* (1957), whose energetic, stream-of-consciousness, bebop-style prose narrated the impetuous cross-country travels of two young men. The Beats' lifestyles shocked "square" Americans, but they would provide a model for a much larger movement of youthful dissidents in the 1960s.

Bold new styles in the visual arts also showed the 1950s to be more than a decade of bland conventionality. In New York City, an artistic revolution known as "action painting" or "abstract expressionism" flowered, rejecting the idea that painting should represent recognizable forms. Jackson Pollock and other abstract expressionists, emphasizing spontaneity, poured, dripped, and threw paint on canvases or substituted sticks and other implements for brushes. The new form of painting so captivated and redirected the Western art world that New York replaced Paris as its center.

Q: Why did American consumption expand so dramatically in the 1950s, and what aspects of society and culture did it influence?

Emergence of a Civil Rights Movement

Building on the civil rights initiatives begun during World War II, African Americans posed the most dramatic challenge to the status quo of the 1950s as they sought to overcome the political and social barriers that had replaced the literal bonds of slavery. Every southern state mandated rigid segregation in public settings ranging from hospitals and schools to drinking fountains and restrooms. Voting laws and practices in the South disfranchised the vast majority of African Americans; employment discrimination kept them at the bottom of the economic ladder throughout the country.

Although black protest was as old as American racism, in the 1950s a grassroots movement arose that attracted national attention and the support of white liberals. Pressed by civil rights groups, the Supreme Court delivered significant institutional reforms, but the most important changes of all occurred among blacks themselves. Ordinary African Americans in substantial numbers sought their own liberation, building a movement that would transform race relations in the United States.

African Americans Challenge the Supreme Court and the President Several factors spurred black protest in the 1950s. Between 1940 and 1960, more than three million African Americans moved from the South into areas where they had a political voice. Black leaders made sure that foreign policy officials realized how racist practices at home handicapped the United States in its competition with the Soviet Union. In the South, the very system of segregation meant that African Americans controlled certain organizational resources, such as churches and colleges, where leadership skills could be honed and networks developed.

The legal strategy of the major civil rights organization, the National Association for the Advancement of Colored People (NAACP), reached its crowning achievement with the Supreme Court decision in **Brown v. Board of Education** in 1954. *Brown* consolidated five separate suits that reflected the growing determination of black Americans to fight for their rights. Oliver Brown, a World War II veteran in Topeka, Kansas, filed suit because his daughter had to pass by a white school just seven blocks from their home to attend a black school more than a mile away. In Virginia, sixteen-year-old Barbara Johns initiated a student strike over wretched conditions in her black high school, leading to another of the suits joined in *Brown*. The NAACP's lead lawyer, future Supreme Court justice Thurgood Marshall, urged the Court to overturn the "separate but equal" precedent established in *Plessy v. Ferguson* in 1896 (see chapter 21). A unanimous Court, headed by Chief Justice Earl Warren, declared, "Separate educational facilities are inherently unequal" and thus violated the Fourteenth Amendment.

Ultimate responsibility for enforcement of the decision lay with President Eisenhower, but he refused to endorse *Brown*. He also kept silent in 1955 when whites murdered Emmett Till, a fourteen-year-old black boy who had allegedly whistled at a white woman in Mississippi. Reflecting his own prejudice, his preference for limited federal intervention in the states, and a leadership style that favored consensus and gradual progress, Eisenhower kept his distance from civil rights issues. Such inaction fortified southern resistance to school desegregation and contributed to the gravest constitutional crisis since the Civil War.

The crisis came in Little Rock, Arkansas, in September 1957, when Governor Orval Faubus sent Arkansas National Guard troops to block the enrollment of nine black students in **Little Rock's Central High School**. Later, he allowed them to enter but withdrew the National Guard, leaving the students to face an angry white mob. "During

School Integration in Little Rock, Arkansas The nine African American teenagers who integrated Central High School in Little Rock, Arkansas, endured nearly three weeks of threats and hateful taunts before they even got through the doors. Here Elizabeth Eckford tries to ignore angry students and adults as she approaches the entrance to the school, only to be blocked by Arkansas National Guardsmen. Even after President Eisenhower intervened to enable the "Little Rock Nine" to attend school, they were called names, tripped, spat upon, and otherwise harassed by some white students. When Minnijean Brown, one of the black students, could take no more, she dumped a bowl of chili on a white boy who had taunted her. After she was expelled for that act, cards circulated among white students reading "One Down . . . Eight to Go." Francis Miller/TimePix/Getty.

those years when we desperately needed approval from our peers," Melba Patillo Beals remembered, "we were victims of the most harsh rejection imaginable." As television cameras transmitted the ugly scene, Eisenhower was forced to send regular army troops to Little Rock, the first federal military intervention in the South since Reconstruction. Paratroopers escorted the "Little Rock Nine" into the school; other southern cities avoided integration by closing public schools and using tax dollars to support private ones.

Eisenhower did order the integration of public facilities in Washington, D.C., and on military bases, and he supported the first federal civil rights legislation since Reconstruction. Yet Southern Democrats made sure that the Civil Rights Acts of 1957 and 1960 were little more than symbolic. Baseball star Jackie Robinson spoke for many African Americans when he wired Eisenhower in 1957, "We disagree that half a loaf is better than none. Have waited this long for a bill with meaning—can wait a little longer." Eisenhower appointed the first black professional to the White House staff, E. Frederick Morrow, but Morrow confided in his diary, "I feel ridiculous . . . trying to defend the administration's record on civil rights."

Montgomery and Mass Protest What set the civil rights movement of the 1950s and 1960s apart from earlier acts of black protest was the large number of people involved, their willingness to confront white institutions directly, and the use of nonviolent protest and civil disobedience to bring about change. The Congress of Racial Equality (CORE) and other groups had experimented with these tactics in the 1940s, and African Americans had boycotted the segregated bus system in Baton Rouge, Louisiana, in 1953, but the first sustained protest to claim national attention began in Montgomery, Alabama, on December 1, 1955.

That day, police arrested **Rosa Parks** for violating a local segregation ordinance. Riding a crowded bus home from her job as a seamstress in a department store, she refused to give up her seat so that a white man could sit down. "People always say that I didn't give up my seat because I was tired, but that isn't true," Parks recalled. "I was not tired physically. . . . I was not old. . . . I was forty-two. No, the only tired I was, was tired of giving in." The bus driver called the police, who promptly arrested her.

> "People always say that I didn't give up my seat because I was tired, but that isn't true," Rosa Parks recalled. "I was not tired physically. . . . I was . . . tired of giving in."

Parks had long been active in the local NAACP, headed by E. D. Nixon. They had already talked about challenging bus segregation. So had the Women's Political Council (WPC), composed of black professional women and led by Jo Ann Robinson, an English professor at Alabama State. Such local individuals and organizations, long committed to improving conditions for African Americans, laid critical foundations for the black freedom struggle throughout the South.

When word came that Parks would fight her arrest, WPC leaders mobilized teachers and students to distribute fliers calling for blacks to stay off the buses. E. D. Nixon called a mass meeting at the Holt Street Baptist Church, where those assembled founded the Montgomery Improvement Association (MIA) to organize a bus boycott. The MIA arranged volunteer car pools and marshaled more than 90 percent of the black community to sustain the year-long **Montgomery bus boycott**.

Elected to head the MIA was twenty-six-year-old Martin Luther King Jr., a young Baptist pastor with a doctorate in theology from Boston University. A captivating speaker, King addressed mass meetings at churches throughout the boycott, inspiring blacks' courage and commitment by linking racial justice to Christianity. He promised, "If you will protest courageously and yet with dignity and Christian love . . . historians will have to pause and say, 'There lived a great people—a black people—who injected a new meaning and dignity into the veins of civilization.'"

Montgomery blacks summoned their courage and determination in abundance. They walked miles to get to work, contributed their meager financial resources, and stood up with dignity to intimidation and police harassment. An older woman insisted, "I'm not walking for myself, I'm walking for my children and my grandchildren." Authorities arrested several leaders, and whites firebombed King's house. Yet the movement persisted until November 1956, when the Supreme Court declared unconstitutional Alabama's laws requiring bus segregation. African Americans had demonstrated that they could sustain a lengthy protest and would not be intimidated.

King's face on the cover of *Time* magazine in February 1957 marked his rapid rise to national and international fame. In January, black clergy from across the South had chosen King to head the **Southern Christian Leadership Conference (SCLC)**, newly established to coordinate local protests against segregation and disfranchisement. The prominence of King and other ministers obscured the substantial numbers and critical importance of

Martin Luther King Jr. In February 1957, *Time* magazine featured the leader of the Montgomery bus boycott, Martin Luther King Jr., on its cover. Seven years later, in 1964, he appeared on the cover again, this time as the magazine's "Man of the Year." That year, at the age of thirty-five, King was awarded the Nobel Peace Prize. He was the youngest person ever to be so honored. Time Life Pictures/Getty Images.

black women in the movement. In fact, the SCLC owed much of its success to Ella Baker, a seasoned activist who came from New York to manage its office in Atlanta.

Q: **What were the goals and strategies of civil rights activists in the 1950s?**

Conclusion: Peace and Prosperity Mask Unmet Challenges

At the American National Exhibition in Moscow in 1959, the consumer goods that Nixon proudly displayed to Khrushchev and the Cold War competition that crackled through their dialogue reflected two dominant themes of the 1950s: the prosperity of the U.S. economy and the superpowers' success in keeping their antagonism within the bounds of peace. The tremendous economic growth of the 1950s, which raised the standard of living for most Americans, resulted in part from the Cold War: One of every ten American jobs depended directly on defense spending.

Affluence changed the very landscape of the United States. Suburban housing developments sprang up, interstate highways began to divide cities and connect the country, farms declined in number but grew in size, and population and industry moved south and west. Daily habits and even values of ordinary people shifted as the economy became more service oriented and the appearance of a host of new products intensified the growth of a consumer culture.

The prosperity, however, masked a number of developments and problems that Americans would face head-on in later years: rising resistance to racial injustice, a 20 percent poverty rate, married women's movement into the labor force, and the emergence of a self-conscious youth generation. Although the federal government's defense spending and housing, highway, and education subsidies helped to sustain the economic boom, in general Eisenhower tried to curb domestic programs and let private enterprise have its way. His administration maintained the welfare state inherited from the Democrats but resisted substantial further reforms.

In global affairs, Eisenhower exercised restraint on large issues, recognizing the limits of U.S. power. In the name of deterrence, he promoted the development of more destructive atomic weapons, but he withstood pressures for even larger defense budgets. Still, Eisenhower took from Truman the assumption that the United States must fight communism everywhere, and when movements in Iran, Guatemala, Cuba, and Vietnam seemed too radical, too friendly to communism, or too inimical to American economic interests, he tried to undermine them, often with secret operations and severe consequences for native populations.

Although Eisenhower presided over eight years of peace and prosperity, his foreign policy inspired anti-Americanism, established dangerous precedents for the expansion of executive power, and forged commitments and interventions that future generations would deem unwise. As Eisenhower's successors took on the struggle against communism and grappled with the domestic challenges of race, poverty, and urban decay that he had avoided, the tranquility and consensus of the 1950s would give way to the turbulence and conflict of the 1960s.

Reviewing the Chapter

★ KEY TERMS

Explain each term's significance

WHO

Fidel Castro (p. 678)

Mohammed Mossadegh (p. 679)

Nikita Khrushchev (p. 679)

Betty Friedan (p. 687)

Billy Graham (p. 687)

Alfred Kinsey (p. 690)

Rosa Parks (p. 692)

WHAT

kitchen debate (p. 673)

Interstate Highway and Defense System Act of 1956 (p. 675)

brinksmanship (p. 677)

mutually assured destruction (MAD) (p. 677)

domino theory (p. 678)

Geneva accords (p. 678)

Suez crisis (p. 679)

Eisenhower Doctrine (p. 679)

***Sputnik* (p. 679)**

military-industrial complex (p. 682)

Levittown (p. 683)

Sun Belt (p. 684)

***Hernandez v. Texas* (p. 686)**

baby boom (p. 687)

Beat generation (p. 690)

***Brown v. Board of Education* (p. 691)**

Little Rock's Central High School (p. 691)

Montgomery bus boycott (p. 692)

Southern Christian Leadership Conference (SCLC) (p. 692)

> **FOR PRACTICE QUIZZES AND OTHER STUDY TOOLS,** see the Online Study Guide at **bedfordstmartins.com/roarkcompact**.

★ REVIEW QUESTIONS Q:

Use key terms and dates to support your answer

1. How did Eisenhower's domestic policies reflect his moderate political vision? (pp. 674–77)

2. Where and how did Eisenhower practice containment? (pp. 677–82)

3. How did technology contribute to changes in the economy, suburbanization, and the growth of the Sun Belt? (pp. 682–86)

4. Why did American consumption expand so dramatically in the 1950s, and what aspects of society and culture did it influence? (pp. 686–90)

5. What were the goals and strategies of civil rights activists in the 1950s? (pp. 690–93)

★ MAKING CONNECTIONS

Draw on key terms, timeline, and review questions

1. Both President Truman and President Eisenhower perceived a grave threat in the Soviet Union and the spread of communism around the world. How did these two presidents approach foreign policy during the Cold War? In your answer, consider their similarities and differences.

2. The 1950s brought significant changes to the everyday lives of many Americans. Discuss the economic and demographic changes that contributed to the growth of suburbs and the Sun Belt. How did these trends shape the culture of abundance? In your answer, consider both Americans who participated in these trends and those who did not.

3. During the 1950s, actions by the federal government and the courts had a significant impact on African Americans, Native Americans, and Mexican Americans. Discuss how new policies and court actions came about and how laws affected these groups for better and for worse.

4. Eisenhower was the first Republican president since the New Deal had transformed the federal government. How did his "modern Republicanism" address Roosevelt's legacy? How did the shape and character of government change or not change during Eisenhower's administration?

★ SUGGESTED READINGS

Taylor Branch, *Parting the Waters: America in the King Years, 1954–1963* (1988). A dramatic narrative of the life of Martin Luther King Jr. within the context of civil rights activism.

Lizabeth Cohen, *A Consumers' Republic: The Politics of Mass Consumption in Postwar America* (2003). An exploration of how consumption and consumer movements shaped American politics, economy, and culture.

David Halberstam, *The Fifties* (1993). A history of American life that ranges across topics from politics and foreign policy to popular culture.

Stephen Kinzer, *All the Shah's Men: An American Coup and the Roots of Middle East Terror* (2003). A fast-paced account of the U.S. intervention in Iran in 1953 and an appraisal of its aftereffects.

James Miller, *Flowers in the Dustbin: The Rise of Rock and Roll, 1947–1977* (1999). An engaging and critical history of the music that defined a generation.

Bruce J. Schulman, *From Cotton Belt to Sunbelt: Federal Policy, Economic Development, and the Transformation of the South, 1938–1980* (1994). The classic account of the development of the Sun Belt.

FOR MORE BOOKS ABOUT TOPICS IN THIS CHAPTER, see the Online Bibliography at **bedfordstmartins.com/roarkcompact**.

FOR ADDITIONAL FIRSTHAND ACCOUNTS OF THIS PERIOD, see Chapter 27 in Michael Johnson, ed., *Reading the American Past*, Fourth Edition.

FOR WEB SITES, IMAGES, AND DOCUMENTS RELATED TO TOPICS AND PLACES IN THIS CHAPTER, visit Make History at **bedfordstmartins.com/roarkcompact**.

★ TIMELINE

1952
- Republican Dwight D. Eisenhower elected president.

1953
- Termination of special status of American Indians and relocation of thousands off reservations.
- CIA engineers coup against government of Iran.

1954
- CIA stages coup against government of Guatemala.
- France signs Geneva accords, withdrawing from Vietnam.
- United States begins aid to South Vietnam.
- Government launches Operation Wetback.
- *Hernandez v. Texas*.
- *Brown v. Board of Education*.
- Senate condemns Senator Joseph McCarthy.

1955
- Eisenhower and Khrushchev meet in Geneva.

1955–1956
- Montgomery, Alabama, bus boycott.

1956
- Interstate Highway and Defense System Act.
- Eisenhower reelected by landslide to second term.
- *Howl* published.

1957
- Southern Christian Leadership Conference (SCLC) founded.
- Soviets launch *Sputnik*.
- Labor union membership peaks at 27.1 percent of labor force.
- *On the Road* published.

1958
- National Aeronautics and Space Administration (NASA) established.

1959
- Kitchen debate between Nixon and Khrushchev.

1960
- Soviets shoot down U.S. U-2 spy plane.
- One-quarter of Americans live in suburbs.

"COUNTRY JOE" McDONALD'S GUITAR Music was an indispensable element of protest movements in the 1960s. Civil rights demonstrators sang "We Shall Overcome," antiwar rallies featured folk and rock singers, and hippies turned on to acid rock. The guitar was the central musical instrument for each kind of music: traditional African American, folk, and rock. This wooden acoustic guitar, adorned with a peace symbol, belonged to "Country Joe" McDonald, who started his band, Country Joe and the Fish, at a draft protest in Oakland, California, in 1965. The band was one of many that originated in the San Francisco Bay area, but its popularity soon spread across the country. The Oakland Museum of California.

Reform, Rebellion, and Reaction

1960–1974

ON AUGUST 31, 1962, <u>Fannie Lou Hamer</u> boarded a bus carrying eighteen African Americans from Ruleville, Mississippi, to the county seat in Indianola, where they intended to register to vote. Blacks accounted for more than 60 percent of Sunflower County's population but only 1.2 percent of registered voters. Before civil rights activists arrived in Ruleville to start a voter registration drive, Hamer recalled, "I didn't know that a Negro could register and vote." Her forty-five years of poverty, exploitation, and political disfranchisement typified the lives of most blacks in the rural South. The daughter of sharecroppers, Hamer began work in the cotton fields at age six, attending school in a one-room shack from December to March and only until she was twelve. She later married Perry Hamer and moved onto a plantation, where both she and her husband worked in the fields and she did domestic work for the owner and recorded the cotton that sharecroppers harvested.

At the Indianola County courthouse, Hamer and her companions had to pass through a hostile, white, gun-carrying crowd. Using a common practice to deny blacks the vote, the registrar tested Hamer on an obscure section of the state constitution. She failed the test but resolved to try again. When the plantation owner ordered Hamer to withdraw her registration application or get off his land, she left the plantation. Ten days later, bullets flew into the home of friends who had taken her in. Refusing to be intimidated, she registered to vote on her third attempt, attended a civil rights leadership training conference, and began to mobilize others to vote. In 1963, she and other activists were arrested in Winona, Mississippi, and brutally beaten. Hamer went from jail to the hospital, where her sister could not recognize her battered face.

Fannie Lou Hamer's courage and determination made her a prominent figure in the black freedom struggle. Such activists shook the nation's conscience, provided a protest model for other groups, and pushed the government to enact not only civil rights legislation but also a host of other liberal policies. Although the federal government often tried to curb civil rights protest, the two Democratic presidents of the 1960s favored using government to ameliorate social and economic problems. After John F. Kennedy was assassinated in November 1963, Lyndon B. Johnson launched

Mississippi Freedom Democratic Party Rally Fannie Lou Hamer (left foreground) and other activists sing at a rally outside the Democratic National Convention hall in 1964, supporting the Mississippi Freedom Democratic Party (MFDP) in its challenge to the all-white delegation sent by the regular Mississippi Democratic Party. Next to Hamer is Eleanor Holmes Norton, a civil rights lawyer, and Ella Baker (far right), who helped organize the Southern Christian Leadership Conference and later managed MFDP headquarters in Washington, D.C. Matt Herron/Take Stock.

the **Great Society** — a multitude of efforts to promote racial justice, education, medical care, urban development, environmental and economic health, and more. Those who struggled for racial justice lost property and sometimes their lives, but by the end of the decade, American law had caught up with the American ideal of equality.

Yet strong civil rights legislation and pathbreaking Supreme Court decisions did little to mitigate the deplorable economic conditions of African Americans nationwide, on which Hamer and others increasingly focused after 1965. Nor were liberal politicians reliable supporters, as Hamer found out in 1964 when President Johnson and his allies rebuffed black Mississippi Democrats' efforts to be represented at the Democratic National Convention. "We followed all the laws," she said, only to find that "the white man is not going to give up his power to us. . . . We have to take [it] for ourselves." By 1966, a minority of African American activists were demanding black power; the movement soon splintered, and white support sharply declined. The war in Vietnam stifled liberal reform, while a growing conservative movement protested that the Great Society went too far and condemned the challenge to American traditions and institutions mounted by blacks, students, and others.

Though disillusioned and often frustrated, Fannie Lou Hamer remained an activist until her death in 1977, participating in new social movements stimulated by the black freedom struggle. In 1969, she supported students at Mississippi Valley State College who demanded black studies courses and a voice in campus decisions. In 1972, she attended the first conference of the National Women's Political Caucus, established to achieve greater representation for women in government. The caucus was part of a diverse feminist movement that transformed women's legal status as well as everyday relationships between women and men.

Feminists and other groups, including ethnic minorities, environmentalists, and gays and lesbians, carried the tide of reform into the 1970s. They pushed Richard M. Nixon's Republican administration to sustain the liberalism of the 1960s, with its emphasis on a strong government role in regulating the economy, guaranteeing the welfare and rights of all individuals, and improving the quality of life. Despite its conservative rhetoric, the Nixon administration implemented school desegregation and affirmative action and adopted pathbreaking measures in environmental regulation, equality for women, and justice for Native Americans. The years between 1960 and 1974 contained the greatest efforts to reconcile America's promise with reality since the New Deal. ★

Liberalism at High Tide

At the Democratic National Convention in 1960, John F. Kennedy announced "a New Frontier" that would confront "unsolved problems of peace and war, unconquered pockets of ignorance and prejudice, unanswered questions of poverty and surplus." Four years later, Lyndon B. Johnson invoked the ideal of a "Great Society, [which] rests on abundance and liberty for all [and] demands an end to poverty and racial injustice." Acting under the liberal faith that government should use its power to solve social and economic problems, end injustice, and promote the welfare of all citizens, the Democratic administrations of the 1960s won legislation on civil rights, poverty, education, medical care, housing, consumer protection, and environmental protection. These measures took up the unfulfilled agendas of the New Deal and Fair Deal, responded to demands for rights from African Americans and other groups, and addressed problems arising from rapid economic growth.

The Unrealized Promise of Kennedy's New Frontier

John F. Kennedy grew up in privilege, the child of an Irish Catholic businessman who served as ambassador to Great Britain and nourished political ambitions for his sons. Helped by a distinguished World War II navy record, Kennedy won election to the House of Representatives in 1946 and the Senate in 1952. With a powerful political machine, his family's fortune, and a dynamic personal appeal, Kennedy won the Democratic presidential nomination in 1960. He stunned many Democrats by choosing as his running mate Lyndon B. Johnson of Texas, a rival for the presidential nomination whom liberals disparaged as a typical southern conservative.

Kennedy defeated his Republican opponent, Vice President Richard M. Nixon, in an excruciatingly close election. African American voters contributed to his victory, helping to offset the 52 percent of the white vote cast for Nixon and contributing to Kennedy's 118,550-vote margin overall. Lyndon Johnson helped carry most of the South, and a rise in unemployment in 1960 also favored the Democrats. Finally, Kennedy benefited from the nation's first televised presidential debates, during which he appeared cool and confident beside a nervous and pale Nixon.

The Kennedy administration projected energy, idealism, and glamour, although Kennedy was in most ways a cautious, pragmatic politician. The first president to hold televised press conferences, Kennedy charmed the audience with his grace and wit. Journalists kept from the public Kennedy's serious health problems and extramarital affairs, instead projecting warm images of a vigorous president with his chic and cultured wife, Jacqueline.

At his inauguration, the forty-three-year-old Kennedy called on Americans to serve the common good. "Ask not what your country can do for you," he implored, "ask what you can do for your country." Although Kennedy's idealism inspired many, he failed to redeem campaign promises to expand the welfare state with federal education and health care programs. Moreover, he resisted leadership on behalf of racial justice until civil rights activists gave him no choice.

Moved by the desperate conditions he observed while campaigning in Appalachia, Kennedy pushed poverty onto the national agenda. In 1962, he read Michael Harrington's *The Other America*, which described the poverty that left more than one in five Americans "maimed in body and spirit, existing at levels beneath those necessary for human decency." By 1962, Kennedy had won support for a $2 billion urban renewal program, legislation that offered incentives to businesses to locate in economically depressed areas, and a training program for the unemployed. In the summer of 1963, Kennedy asked aides to plan a full-scale attack on poverty, and he issued a dramatic call for a comprehensive civil rights bill, marking a turning point in his domestic agenda.

Kennedy had promised to make economic growth a key objective. "A rising tide lifts all boats" expressed his belief that economic growth could eradicate poverty. To that end, he asked Congress to pass an enormous tax cut in 1963, arguing that reducing taxes would infuse money into the economy and thus increase demand, boost production, and reduce unemployment. Passed in February 1964, the law contributed to an economic boom, as unemployment dropped to 4.1 percent, and the gross national product shot up by 7 to 9 percent annually between 1964 and 1966. Some liberal critics of the tax cut, however, pointed out that it favored the well-off and that economic growth alone would not eliminate poverty. They argued instead for increased spending on social programs.

Kennedy's economic efforts were in their infancy when he fell victim to an assassin's bullet on November 22, 1963. Within minutes of the shooting—which occurred as Kennedy's motorcade passed through Dallas, Texas—radio and television broadcast the unfolding horror to the nation. Millions watched the return of *Air Force One* to Washington bearing the president's coffin, his widow in a bloodstained suit, and the new president, Lyndon Baines Johnson.

Stunned Americans struggled to understand what had happened. Soon after the assassination, police arrested Lee Harvey Oswald and concluded that he had fired the shots from a nearby building. Two days later, while officers were transferring Oswald from one jail to another, a local nightclub operator, Jack Ruby, killed him. Suspicions arose that Ruby murdered Oswald to cover up a conspiracy by ultraconservatives who hated Kennedy, or by Communists who supported Castro's Cuba. To get at the truth, President Johnson appointed a commission headed by Chief Justice Earl Warren, which concluded that both Oswald and Ruby had acted alone. Although some contested the lone-killer explanation, most scholars agreed that no conspiracy had existed.

Debate continued over how to assess Kennedy's domestic record. It had been unremarkable in his first two years, but his proposals on taxes, civil rights, and poverty in 1963 suggested an important shift. Whether Kennedy could have persuaded Congress to enact them remained in question. In the words of journalist James Reston, "What was killed was not only the president but the promise. . . . He never reached his meridian: We saw him only as a rising sun."

Johnson Fulfills the Kennedy Promise

Lyndon B. Johnson assumed the presidency with a wealth of political experience. A self-made man from the Texas hill country, he had won election to the House of Representatives in 1937 and to the Senate in 1948. Although his Texas base required caution on civil rights and issues affecting oil and other big businesses, Johnson's presidential aspirations led him to take more liberal stands. His own modest upbringing in an impoverished area, his admiration for Franklin Roosevelt, and his fierce ambition to outdo the New Deal president all spurred his commitment to reform. Equally compelling were external pressures generated by the black freedom struggle and the host of movements it helped inspire.

Johnson's coarse wit and vanity repulsed those who preferred the sophisticated Kennedy style. Lacking his predecessor's eloquence, Johnson excelled behind the scenes, where he could entice, maneuver, or threaten legislators to support his objectives. The famous "Johnson treatment" became legendary. In his ability to achieve consensus around his goals, he had few peers in American history.

Johnson entreated Congress to act so that "John Fitzgerald Kennedy did not live or die in vain." He signed Kennedy's tax cut bill in February 1964. More remarkable was passage of the **Civil Rights Act of 1964**, which Kennedy had proposed in response to black protest. The strongest such measure since Reconstruction, the law required every ounce of Johnson's political skill to pry sufficient votes from Republicans to balance the "nays" of southern Democrats. Senate Republican leader Everett Dirksen's aide reported that Johnson "never left him alone for thirty minutes."

Antipoverty legislation followed fast on the heels of the Civil Rights Act. Just two months after Johnson announced "an unconditional war on poverty" in his January 1964 State of the Union message, the

The "Johnson Treatment" Abe Fortas, a distinguished lawyer who had argued a major criminal rights case, *Gideon v. Wainwright* (1963), before the Supreme Court, was a close friend of and adviser to President Johnson. This photograph of the president and Fortas taken in July 1965 illustrates how Johnson used his body as well as his voice to bend people to his will. Yoichi R. Okamoto/LBJ Library Collection.

administration rushed a draft bill to Congress, which responded with equal haste in August. The Economic Opportunity Act of 1964 authorized ten new programs, allocating $800 million—about 1 percent of the federal budget—for the first year. Many provisions targeted children and youths, including Head Start for preschoolers, work-study grants for college students, and the Job Corps for unemployed young people. The Volunteers in Service to America (VISTA) program paid modest wages to volunteers working with the disadvantaged, and a legal services program provided lawyers for the poor.

The most novel and controversial part of the law, the Community Action Program (CAP), required "maximum feasible participation" of the poor themselves in antipoverty projects. Poor people began to organize community action programs to take control of their neighborhoods and to make welfare agencies, school boards, police departments, and housing authorities more accountable to the people they served. When mayors complained that activists were challenging local governments and "fostering class struggle," Johnson backed off from pushing genuine representation for the poor. Nonetheless, CAP gave people usually excluded from government an opportunity to act on their own behalf and develop leadership skills.

Policymaking for a Great Society As the 1964 election approached, Johnson projected stability and security in the midst of a booming economy. Few voters wanted to risk the dramatic change promised by his Republican opponent, Arizona senator Barry M. Goldwater, who attacked the welfare state and suggested using nuclear weapons if necessary to crush communism in Vietnam. Although Goldwater captured five southern states, Johnson achieved a record-breaking landslide of 61 percent of the popular vote, and Democrats won resounding majorities in the House (295–140) and Senate (68–32). Still, Goldwater's campaign aroused considerable grassroots support, and a movement on the right grew alongside the more noticeable left and liberal movements (see chapter 30).

"I want to see a whole bunch of coonskins on the wall," Johnson told his aides, using a hunting analogy to stress his ambitious legislative goals for what he called the "Great Society." The large Democratic majorities in Congress, his own political skills, and pressure from the black freedom struggle enabled Johnson to succeed mightily. He persuaded Congress to act on discrimination, poverty, education, medical care, housing, consumer and environmental protection, and more. Reporters called the legislation of the Eighty-ninth Congress (1965–1966) "a political miracle."

The Economic Opportunity Act of 1964 was the opening shot in the **War on Poverty**. Congress doubled the program's funding in 1965, enacted new economic development measures for depressed regions, and authorized more than $1 billion to improve the nation's slums. Direct aid included a new food stamp program, giving poor people greater choice in obtaining food, and rent supplements that provided alternatives to public housing projects for some poor families. Moreover, a movement of welfare mothers, the National Welfare Rights Organization, assisted by antipoverty lawyers, pushed administrators of Aid to Families with Dependent Children (AFDC) to ease restrictions on welfare recipients. The number of families receiving assistance jumped from less than one million in 1960 to three million by 1972, benefiting 90 percent of those eligible.

Central to Johnson's War on Poverty were efforts to equip the poor with the skills necessary to find jobs. His Elementary and Secondary Education Act of 1965 marked a turning point by involving the federal government in K–12 education. The measure sent federal dollars to local school districts based on the number of poor children they enrolled, and provided equipment and supplies to private and parochial schools serving the poor. That same year, Congress passed the Higher Education Act, vastly expanding federal assistance to colleges and universities for buildings, programs, scholarships, and loans.

The federal government's responsibility for health care marked an even more significant watershed. Faced with a powerful medical lobby that opposed national health insurance as "socialized medicine," Johnson pared down Truman's proposal for government-sponsored universal care. Instead, he focused on the elderly, who constituted a large portion of the nation's poor. Congress responded with the **Medicare** program, providing the elderly with universal compulsory medical insurance financed largely through Social Security taxes. A separate program, **Medicaid**, authorized federal grants to supplement state-paid medical care for poor people.

Whereas programs such as Medicare fulfilled New Deal and Fair Deal promises, the Great Society's civil rights legislation represented a break with tradition and an expansion of liberalism. Racial minorities were neglected or discriminated against in many New Deal programs, and Truman's civil rights proposals bore few results. By contrast, the Civil Rights Act of 1964 made discrimination in

A Tribute to Johnson for Medicare George Niedermeyer, who lived in Hollywood, Florida, and received a Social Security pension, painted pieces of wood and glued them together to create this thank-you to President Johnson for establishing Medicare. Niedermeyer entrusted his congressional representative, Claude Pepper, known for his support of the interests of the elderly, to deliver the four-foot-tall tribute to Johnson in 1967. LBJ Library, photo by Henry Groskinsky.

employment, education, and public accommodations illegal. The **Voting Rights Act of 1965** banned literacy tests like the one that stymied Fannie Lou Hamer and authorized federal intervention to ensure access to the voting booth.

Another form of bias fell with the **Immigration and Nationality Act of 1965**, which abolished fifty-year-old quotas based on national origins that discriminated against immigrants from areas outside northern and western Europe. The law maintained caps on the total number of immigrants and for the first time limited those from the Western Hemisphere; preference was now given to immediate relatives of U.S. citizens and to those with desirable skills. Senator Edward Kennedy predicted that "our cities will not be flooded with a million citizens annually," but the measure's unanticipated consequences did nearly that, triggering a surge of immigration near the end of the century (see chapter 31).

Great Society benefits reached well beyond victims of discrimination and the poor. Medicare, for example, covered the elderly, regardless of income.

> Johnson insisted that the Great Society meet "not just the needs of the body but the desire for beauty and hunger for community."

A groundswell of consumer activism fueled by Ralph Nader's exposé of the auto industry, *Unsafe at Any Speed* (1965), won legislation making cars safer and raising standards for the food, drug, and cosmetics industries.

Johnson himself insisted that the Great Society meet "not just the needs of the body but the desire for beauty and hunger for

community." In 1965, he sent Congress the first presidential message on the environment, obtaining measures to control water and air pollution and to preserve the natural beauty of the American landscape. In addition, the National Arts and Humanities Act of 1965 funded artists, musicians, writers, and scholars and brought their work to public audiences.

The flood of reform legislation dwindled after 1966, when Democratic majorities in Congress diminished and a backlash against government programs arose. Some Americans expressed their opposition with buttons reading "I fight poverty—I work." The Vietnam War dealt the largest blow to Johnson's ambitions, diverting his attention, spawning an antiwar movement that crippled his leadership, and devouring tax dollars that might have been used for reform (see chapter 29).

Against these odds, in 1968 Johnson pried out of Congress one more civil rights law, which banned discrimination in housing and jury service. He also signed the National Housing Act of 1968, which authorized an enormous increase in low-income housing—1.7 million units over three years—and, by leaving construction and ownership in private hands, a new way of providing it.

Assessing the Great Society Measured by statistics, the reduction in poverty in the 1960s was considerable. The number of poor Americans fell from more than 20 percent of the population in 1959 to around 13 percent in 1968. Those who Johnson had said "lived on the outskirts of hope" gained more control of their circumstances and a sense of their right to a fairer share of America's bounty. To Rosemary Bray, what turned her family of longtime welfare recipients into tax-paying workers "was the promise of the civil rights movement and the war on poverty." A Mexican American who learned to be a sheet metal worker through a jobs program reported that his children "will finish high school and maybe go to college. . . . I see my family and I know the chains are broken."

Certain groups fared better than others. Many of the aged and many male-headed families rose out of poverty, while impoverishment among female-headed families actually increased. Whites escaped poverty at a faster rate than racial and ethnic minorities. Great Society programs contributed to a burgeoning black middle class, and the proportion of African Americans who were poor fell by 10 percentage points between 1966 and 1974. Still, one out of three remained poverty-stricken.

Conservative critics charged that Great Society programs discouraged initiative by giving the poor "handouts." Liberal critics claimed that focusing on training and education unjustly blamed the poor themselves for their poverty rather than an economic system that could not provide enough adequately paying jobs. Most government training programs prepared graduates for low-skilled labor and could not guarantee employment. In contrast to the New Deal, the Great Society avoided structural reform of the economy and spurned public works projects as a means of providing jobs for the disadvantaged.

Who reaped the greatest advantages from Great Society programs? Programs such as Medicare and those addressing consumer safety and environmental reform benefited Americans across the board. Funds for economically depressed areas built highways, benefiting the construction industry. Real estate developers, investors, and moderate-income families benefited most from the National Housing Act of 1968. Urban renewal often relied on slum clearance programs, which displaced the poor and caused blacks to refer to it as "Negro removal." Physicians' fees and hospital costs soared after the enactment of Medicare and Medicaid, resulting in advantages for both health care providers and the elderly and poor.

Some critics argued that ending poverty required a redistribution of income—raising taxes and using those funds to create jobs, overhaul welfare systems, and rebuild slums. Great Society programs did invest more heavily in the public sector, but they were funded from economic growth rather than from new taxes on the rich or middle class. There was no significant redistribution of income, despite large increases in subsidies for food stamps, housing, medical care, and AFDC. Economic prosperity allowed spending for the poor to rise and improved the lives of millions, but that spending never approached the amounts necessary to claim victory in the War on Poverty.

The Judicial Revolution

A key element of liberalism's ascendancy emerged in the Supreme Court under Chief Justice Earl Warren (1953–1969), which often moved out in front of Congress and public opinion. Expanding the Constitution's promise of equality and individual rights, the Court's decisions supported an activist government to prevent injustice and provided new protections to disadvantaged groups and accused criminals.

Following the pathbreaking *Brown v. Board of Education* school desegregation decision of 1954 (see chapter 27), the Court ruled against all-white public facilities and struck down southern states' educational plans to avoid integration. In addition, a unanimous Court in *Loving v. Virginia* (1967) struck down state laws banning interracial marriage. The justices' declaration that marriage was one of the "basic civil rights of man" would later be repeated by gay men and lesbians seeking the right to marry.

Chief Justice Warren considered *Baker v. Carr* (1963) his most important decision. The case grew out of a complaint that Tennessee electoral districts were drawn so inequitably that sparsely populated rural districts had far more representatives than densely populated urban areas. Using the Fourteenth Amendment guarantee of "equal protection of the laws," *Baker* established the principle of "one person, one vote" for both state legislatures and the House of Representatives. As states redrew electoral districts, legislatures became more responsive to metropolitan interests.

The **Warren Court** also reformed the criminal justice system, using the Fourteenth Amendment to overturn a series of convictions on the grounds that the accused had been deprived of "life, liberty, or property, without due process of law." In decisions that dramatically altered law enforcement practices and the treatment of individuals accused of crimes, the Court declared that states, as well as the federal government, were subject to the Bill of Rights. *Gideon v. Wainwright* (1963) ruled that when an accused criminal could not afford to hire a lawyer, the state had to provide one without charge. In 1966, *Miranda v. Arizona* required police officers to inform suspects of their rights upon arrest. The Court also overturned convictions based on evidence obtained by unlawful arrest, by electronic surveillance, or without a search warrant. Critics accused the justices of obstructing law enforcement and letting criminals go free; liberals argued that these rulings promoted equal treatment in the criminal justice system.

The Court's decisions on religion provoked even greater outrage. *Abington School District v. Schempp* (1963) ruled that requiring Bible reading and prayer in the schools violated the First Amendment principle of separation of church and state. Later decisions ruled against official prayer in public schools even if students were not required to participate. These decisions left students free to pray on their own, but an infuriated Alabama legislator complained, "They put Negroes in the schools and now they've driven God out." The Court's supporters, however, declared that the religion cases protected the rights of non-Christians and atheists.

Critics of the Court, part of a larger backlash mounting against Great Society liberalism, worked to pass laws or constitutional amendments that would upset despised decisions, and billboards demanded, "Impeach Earl Warren." Nonetheless, the Court's major decisions withstood the test of time.

Q: **How did the Kennedy and Johnson administrations exemplify a liberal vision of the federal government?**

The Second Reconstruction

Before the Great Society reforms—and, in fact, contributing to them—African Americans had mobilized a movement that struck down legal separation and discrimination in the South. Whereas the first Reconstruction reflected the power of northern Republicans in the aftermath of the Civil War, the second Reconstruction depended heavily on the courage and determination of black people themselves. Sheyann Webb, one of the thousands of marchers in the 1965 Selma, Alabama, campaign for voting rights, recalled, "We were just people, ordinary people, and we did it."

The early black freedom struggle focused on legal rights in the South and won widespread acceptance. But when African Americans began attacking racial injustice in the rest of the country and challenging the economic deprivation that equal rights left untouched, a strong backlash developed as the movement itself lost cohesion.

The Flowering of the Black Freedom Struggle

The Montgomery bus boycott of 1955–1956 gave racial issues national visibility and produced a leader in **Martin Luther King Jr**. In the 1960s, protest expanded dramatically, mobilizing blacks into direct confrontation with the people and institutions that segregated and discriminated against them: retail establishments, public parks and libraries, buses and depots, voting registrars, and police forces.

Massive direct action began in February 1960, when four African American college students in Greensboro, North Carolina, requested service at the whites-only Woolworth's lunch counter. Within days, hundreds of young people joined them, and others launched sit-ins in thirty-one southern cities. From Southern Christian Leadership Conference (SCLC) headquarters, Ella Baker telephoned her young contacts at various colleges: "What are you going to do? It's time to move."

Baker organized a meeting of student activists in April 1960 and supported their decision to

Lunch Counter Sit-in John Salter Jr., a professor at Tougaloo College, and students Joan Trumpauer and Anne Moody take part in a 1963 sit-in at the Woolworth's lunch counter in Jackson, Mississippi. Shortly before this photograph was taken, whites had thrown two students to the floor, and police had arrested one student. Salter was spattered with mustard and ketchup. In 1968, Moody published *Coming of Age in Mississippi,* a popular book about her experiences in the black freedom struggle. State Historical Society of Wisconsin.

FOR MORE HELP ANALYZING THIS IMAGE, see the visual activity for this chapter in the Online Study Guide at bedfordstmartins.com/roarkcompact.

form a new organization, the **Student Nonviolent Coordinating Committee (SNCC)**, pronounced "snick." Embracing civil disobedience and the nonviolence principles of Martin Luther King Jr., activists would confront their oppressors and stand up for their rights, but they would not respond if attacked. In the words of SNCC leader James Lawson, "Nonviolence nurtures the atmosphere in which reconciliation and justice become actual possibilities." SNCC, however, rejected the top-down leadership of King and the established civil rights organizations, adopting a decentralized structure that fostered decision making and the development of leadership at the grassroots level.

The activists' optimism and commitment to nonviolence soon underwent severe testing. Although some cities quietly met student demands, more typically activists encountered violence. Hostile whites poured food over demonstrators, burned them with cigarettes, called them "niggers," and pelted them with rocks. Local police attacked protesters with dogs, clubs, fire hoses, and tear gas; they arrested more than 3,600 demonstrators in the year following the Greensboro sit-in.

Another wave of protest occurred in May 1961, when the Congress of Racial Equality (CORE) organized Freedom Rides to integrate interstate transportation in the South. When a group of six whites and seven blacks reached Alabama, whites bombed their bus and beat them with baseball bats so fiercely that an observer "couldn't see their faces through the blood." CORE rebuffed President Kennedy's pleas to call off the rides. But after a huge mob attacked the riders in Montgomery, Alabama, Attorney General Robert Kennedy dispatched federal marshals to restore order. Although violence against the riders abated, Freedom Riders arriving in Jackson, Mississippi, were promptly arrested, and several hundred spent part of the summer in jail. All told, more than four hundred blacks and whites participated in the Freedom Rides, which typified the black freedom struggle: administration efforts to stop the protests, officials' reluctance to intervene to protect demonstrators, and the steely courage of African Americans in the face of tremendous violence.

Civil Rights Freedom Rides, May 1961

Encouraged by Kennedy administration officials who preferred voter registration to civil disobedience, SNCC and other groups began the Voter Education Project in summer 1961. They, too, met violence. Whites bombed black churches, threw tenant farmers out of their homes, and beat and jailed activists such as Fannie Lou Hamer. In June 1963, a white man gunned down Mississippi NAACP leader Medgar Evers in front of his house in Jackson. Similar violence met King's 1963 campaign in Birmingham, Alabama, to integrate public facilities and open jobs to blacks. The police attacked demonstrators with dogs, cattle prods, and fire hoses—brutalities that television broadcast around the world.

The largest demonstration drew 250,000 blacks and whites to the nation's capital in August 1963 in the **March on Washington** for Jobs and Freedom, inspired by the strategy of A. Philip Randolph in 1941 (see chapter 25). Speaking from the Lincoln Memorial, King put his indelible stamp on the day, drawing on all the passion and skills that made him the greatest orator of his day. "I have a dream," he repeated again and again, imagining the day "when all of God's children . . . will be able to join hands and sing . . . 'Free at last, free at last; thank God Almighty, we are free at last.'"

The euphoria of the March on Washington faded as activists returned to continued violence in the South. In 1964, the **Mississippi Freedom Summer Project** mobilized more than a thousand northern black and white college students to conduct voter registration drives. Resistance was fierce, intensified by the sight of white activist women working alongside black men. By the end of the summer, only twelve hundred new voters had been allowed to register. Southern whites had killed several activists, beaten eighty, arrested more than a thousand, and burned thirty-five black churches. Hidden resistance came from the federal government itself, as the FBI spied on King and other leaders and expanded its activities to "expose, disrupt, misdirect, discredit, or otherwise neutralize" black protest.

Still, the movement persisted. In March 1965, Alabama state troopers used such fierce force to turn back a voting rights march from Selma to the state capitol in Montgomery that the incident earned the

The Selma March for Voting Rights In 1963, the Student Nonviolent Coordinating Committee (SNCC) began a campaign for voting rights in Selma, Alabama, where white officials had registered only 335 of the 15,000 African Americans of voting age. As often happened, after younger activists got things started, Martin Luther King Jr. came to Selma in January 1965. He planned a fifty-four-mile march from Selma to Montgomery, the state capital, to insist that blacks be registered to vote. Warned of a serious threat on his life, however, he did not lead the march. In this photo, young African Americans carrying the flag march with nuns, priests, and other supporters. During the march, Juanita Williams wore out her shoes (shown here), which are now displayed at the National Museum of History in Washington, D.C. What do you think motivated the marchers to carry the American flag? Photo: Steve Shapiro/TimePix/ Getty; Shoes: Smithsonian Institution, Washington, D.C.

name "Bloody Sunday" and compelled President Johnson to call up the Alabama National Guard to protect the marchers. Battered and hospitalized on Bloody Sunday, John Lewis, chairman of SNCC (and later a congressman), managed to make the final stretch of the **Selma march** to the capitol, which he counted as one of his most meaningful experiences: "In October of that year the Voting Rights bill was passed and we all felt we'd had a part in it."

The Response in Washington Civil rights leaders would have to wear sneakers, Lyndon Johnson said, if they were going to keep up with him. But both Kennedy and Johnson, reluctant to alienate southern voters and their congressional representatives, tended to move only when events gave them little choice. Kennedy sent federal marshals to protect the Freedom Riders, dispatched troops to enable air force veteran James H. Meredith to enroll in the all-white University of Mississippi in 1962, and called up the Alabama National Guard during the Birmingham demonstrations. But, aware of the political costs of deploying federal force, he told activists pleading for more protection that law enforcement was a local matter.

In June 1963, Kennedy finally made good on his promise to seek strong antidiscrimination legislation. Pointing to the injustice suffered by blacks, Kennedy asked white Americans, "Who among us would then be content with the counsels of patience and delay?" Johnson took up Kennedy's commitment with passion, as scenes of violence against peaceful demonstrators appalled many television viewers across the nation. The resulting public support, the "Johnson treatment," and the president's appeal to memories of the martyred Kennedy all produced the most important civil rights law since Reconstruction.

The Civil Rights Act of 1964 guaranteed access for all Americans to public accommodations, public education, employment, and voting, thus sounding the death knell for the South's system of segregation and discrimination. The law also extended constitutional protections to Indians on reservations. Title VII of the measure, banning discrimination in employment, not only attacked racial discrimination, but also outlawed job discrimination against women. Because Title VII applied to every aspect of employment, including wages, hiring, and promotion, it represented a giant step toward equal employment opportunity for white women as well as for racial minorities.

Responding to black voter registration drives in the South, Johnson demanded legislation to remove "every remaining obstacle to the right and the opportunity to vote." In August 1965, he signed the Voting Rights Act, empowering the federal government to intervene directly to enable African Americans to register and vote, thereby launching a major transformation in southern politics. Black voting rates shot up dramatically (Map 28.1). In turn, the number of African Americans holding political office in the South increased from a handful in 1964 to more than a thousand by 1972. Such gains translated into tangible benefits as black officials upgraded public facilities, police protection, and other basic services for their constituents.

Johnson also declared the need to realize "not just equality as a right and theory, but equality as fact and result." To this end, he issued an executive order in 1965 to require employers holding government contracts (affecting about one-third of the labor force) to take affirmative action to ensure equal opportunity. Extended to cover women in 1967, the affirmative action program was called "reverse discrimination" by people who incorrectly thought that it required quotas and the hiring of unqualified candidates. In fact, it required employers to counter the effects of centuries of oppression by acting forcefully to align their labor force with

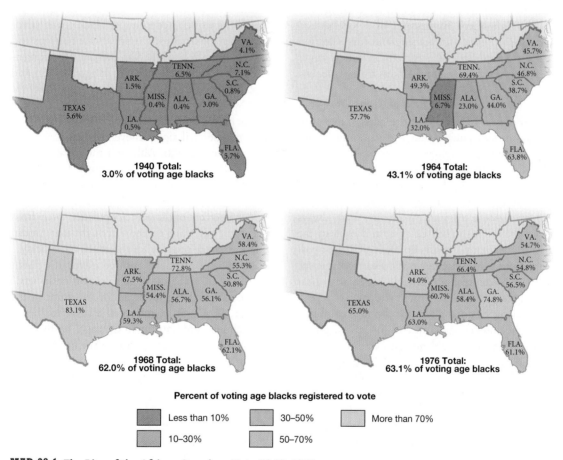

MAP 28.1 The Rise of the African American Vote, 1940–1976
Voting rates of southern blacks increased gradually in the 1940s and 1950s but shot up dramatically in the deep South after the Voting Rights Act of 1965 provided for federal agents to enforce African Americans' right to vote.

READING THE MAP: When did the biggest change in African American voter registration occur in the South? Which states had the highest and which had the lowest voter registration rates in 1968?

CONNECTIONS: What role did African American voters play in the 1960 election? What were the targets of three major voting drives in the 1960s?

FOR MORE HELP ANALYZING THIS MAP, see the map activity for this chapter in the Online Study Guide at bedfordstmartins.com/roarkcompact.

the available pool of qualified candidates. Most corporations came to see affirmative action as a good employment practice.

In 1968, Johnson pried one final bill from a Congress increasingly resistant to reform. Opposition to civil rights outside the South had already appeared in 1963, when California voters rejected a law passed by the legislature banning discrimination in housing; a majority of voters were more concerned with their right to do as they pleased with their property than with the rights of minorities to be free of discrimination. And when Martin Luther King Jr. launched a campaign against de facto segregation in Chicago in 1966, demonstrators were met by jeers and stones thrown by thousands of whites. Johnson's efforts to get a federal open-housing law succeeded only in the wake of King's assassination in 1968. The Civil Rights Act of 1968 banned racial discrimination in housing and jury selection and authorized federal intervention when states failed to protect civil rights workers from violence.

Black Power and Urban Rebellions

By 1966, black protest engulfed the entire nation, demanding not just legal equality but also economic justice and abandoning nonviolence as its basic principle. These developments were not entirely new. African Americans had waged campaigns for decent jobs and housing outside the South since the 1930s. Moreover, some African Americans had always armed themselves in self-defense, and even in the early 1960s, many activists doubted that their passive suffering would change the hearts of racists. Still, the black freedom struggle began to appear more threatening to the white majority.

The new emphases resulted from a combination of heightened activism and unrealized promise. Legal equality could not quickly improve the material conditions of blacks, and black rage at oppressive conditions erupted in waves of urban uprisings from 1965 to 1968. The Watts district of Los Angeles in August 1965, Newark and Detroit in July 1967, and the nation's capital in April 1968 saw the most looting and destruction of property, but violence visited hundreds of cities, usually after an incident between white police and local blacks. The Detroit riots ended in 43 deaths (30 at the hands of law enforcement officers, with most of the victims black), 7,000 arrests, and 1,300 destroyed buildings.

In the North, Malcolm X posed a powerful challenge to the ethos of nonviolence. In 1952, he went to work for the Nation of Islam, which drew on the long tradition of black nationalism and whose adherents called themselves Black Muslims. Calling for black pride and autonomy, separation from the "corrupt [white] society," and self-defense

against white violence, Malcolm X attracted a large following, especially in urban ghettos.

At a June 1966 rally in Greenwood, Mississippi, SNCC chairman **Stokely Carmichael** gave the ideas espoused by Malcolm X a new name when he shouted, "We want black power." Those words quickly became the rallying cry in SNCC and CORE, and the black power movement riveted national attention in the late 1960s. Carmichael called integration "a subterfuge for the maintenance of white supremacy" and rejected assimilation because it implied white superiority. African Americans were encouraged to develop independent businesses and control their own schools, communities, and political organizations. "Black is beautiful" emphasized pride in African American culture and connections to dark-skinned people around the world. According to black power advocates, nonviolence brought only more beatings and killings. After police killed an unarmed black teenager in San Francisco in 1966, Huey Newton and Bobby Seale organized the Black Panther Party for Self-Defense to guard against police brutality.

The press paid inordinate attention to black radicals, and the civil rights movement encountered a severe white backlash. Although the urban riots of the mid-1960s erupted spontaneously, triggered by specific incidents of alleged police mistreatment, horrified whites blamed black power militants. By 1966, 85 percent of the white population—up from 34 percent two years earlier—thought that African Americans were pressing for too much too quickly.

Agreeing with black power advocates about the need for "a radical reconstruction of society," Martin Luther King Jr. expanded the scope of the struggle. In 1965, he mounted a drive for better jobs, schools, and housing in Chicago. Yet he clung to nonviolence and integration as the means to this end. In April 1968, the thirty-nine-year-old leader went to Memphis to support striking municipal sanitation workers. There, on April 4, he was murdered by an escaped white convict.

Although black power organizations captured the headlines, they failed to gain the massive support from African Americans that King and other leaders had attracted. Nor could they alleviate the poverty and racism entrenched in the urban North and West. Black militants were harassed by the FBI and jailed; some encounters left both black militants and police dead. Yet black power's emphasis on racial pride and its critique of American institutions resonated loudly and helped shape the protest activities of other groups.

Q: **How did the civil rights movement change in the mid-1960s?**

A Multitude of Movements

The civil rights movement's undeniable moral claims helped make protest more respectable, while its successes encouraged other groups with grievances. Native Americans, Latinos, college students, women, gay men and lesbians, environmentalists, and others drew on the black freedom struggle for inspiration and models of activism. Many of these groups engaged in direct-action protests, expressed their own cultural nationalism, and challenged dominant institutions and values. Like participants in the black freedom struggle, they met strong resistance, and their accomplishments fell far below their aims. Still, their grievances gained attention in the political arena, and they expanded justice and opportunity for many of their constituents.

Native American Protest The cry "red power" reflected the influence of black radicalism on Native Americans, whose activism took on fresh militancy and goals in the 1960s. The assimilationist programs of the 1940s and 1950s, contrary to their intent, stirred a sense of Indian identity across tribal lines and a determination to preserve traditional culture. Native Americans demonstrated and occupied land and public buildings, claiming rights to natural resources and territory they had owned collectively before European settlement.

In 1969, Native American militants captured world attention when several dozen seized Alcatraz Island, an abandoned federal prison in San Francisco Bay, claiming their right of "first discovery" of this land. They remained on the island for nineteen months, using the occupation to publicize injustices against Indians, promote pan-Indian cooperation, and celebrate traditional cultures. One of the organizers, Dr. LaNada Boyer, the first Native American to attend the University of California, Berkeley, said of Alcatraz, "We were able to reestablish our identity as Indian people, as a culture, as political entities."

In Minneapolis in 1968, two Chippewa Indians, Dennis Banks and George Mitchell, founded the **American Indian Movement (AIM)** to attack problems in cities, where about 300,000 Indians lived. AIM sought to protect Indians from police harassment, secure antipoverty funds, and establish "survival schools" to teach Indian history and values. The movement's appeal quickly spread and filled many Indians with a new sense of purpose. AIM members did not have "that hangdog reservation look I was used to," Lakota activist and author Mary Crow Dog wrote, and their visit to her South Dakota reservation

"loosened a sort of earthquake inside me." AIM leaders helped organize the "Trail of Broken Treaties" caravan to the nation's capital in 1972, when activists occupied the Bureau of Indian Affairs to express their outrage at the bureau's policies and bureaucratic interference in Indians' lives.

Although these dramatic occupations failed to achieve their specific goals, Indians won the end of relocation and termination policies, greater tribal sovereignty and control over community services, protection of Indian religious practices, and a measure of respect and pride. A number of laws and court decisions restored rights to ancestral lands and compensated tribes for land seized in violation of treaties.

Latino Struggles for Justice The fastest-growing minority group in the 1960s was Latino, or Hispanic American, an extraordinarily varied population encompassing people of Mexican, Puerto Rican, Caribbean, and other Latin American origins. (The term *Latino* stresses their common bonds as a minority group in the United States. The older, less political term *Hispanic* also includes people with origins in Spain.) People of Puerto Rican and Caribbean descent flocked to East Coast cities, but more than half of the nation's Latino population—including some six million Mexican Americans—lived in the Southwest. In addition, thousands illegally crossed the two-thousand-mile border between Mexico and the United States yearly in search of economic opportunity.

Political organization of Mexican Americans dated back to the League of United Latin-American Citizens (LULAC), founded in 1929, which fought segregation and discrimination through litigation (see chapter 26). In the 1960s, however, young Mexican Americans increasingly rejected traditional politics in favor of direct action. One symbol of this generational challenge was young activists' adoption of the term *Chicano* (from *mejicano*, the Spanish word for "Mexican").

Chicano protest drew national attention to California, where **Cesar Chavez** and **Dolores Huerta** organized a movement to improve the wretched conditions of migrant agricultural workers. As a child moving from farm to farm with his family, living in soggy tents and exploited by labor contractors, Chavez changed schools frequently and encountered indifference and discrimination. One teacher, he recalled, "hung a sign on me that said, 'I am a clown, I speak Spanish.'" After serving in World War II, Chavez began to organize voter registration drives among Mexican Americans.

In contrast to Chavez, Dolores Huerta grew up in an integrated urban neighborhood where she avoided the farmworkers' grinding poverty but

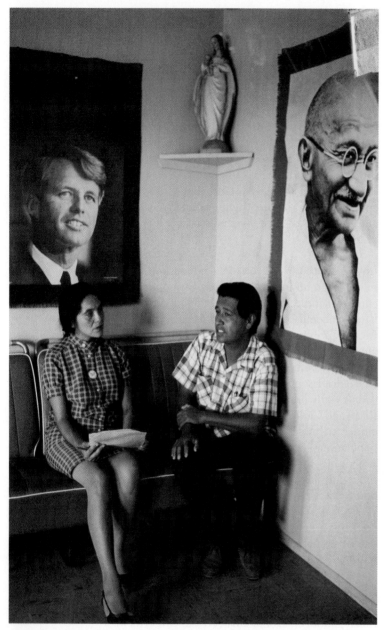

Cesar Chavez and Dolores Huerta Chavez and Huerta confer in Delano, California, in early 1968 during the United Farm Workers' five-year struggle with grape growers for better wages and working conditions and union recognition. The symbols surrounding them reflect the UFW's origins and connections. Chavez was a devout Catholic, as were many of the farmworkers, and his commitment to reform was nourished by liberal Catholicism. Reading about Mahatma Gandhi's leadership in the movement for India's independence also had a profound impact on him. He adopted Gandhi's ideas about civil disobedience and nonviolence, and, like Gandhi, he undertook fasting to demonstrate his determination to obtain social justice. People from across the country supported the UFW's strike and grape boycott, including Senator Robert Kennedy before his assassination in June 1968. Huerta left her teaching job to organize workers, saying, "I thought I could do more by organizing farm workers than by trying to teach their hungry children." She raised eleven children of her own while leading the UFW. Arthur Schatz/TimePix/Getty Images.

witnessed subtle forms of discrimination. Once, a high school teacher challenged her authorship of an essay because it was so well written. Believing that a labor union was the key to progress, she and Chavez founded the United Farm Workers (UFW) in 1962. Although Chavez headed the union until his death in 1993, Huerta was indispensable to its vitality. To gain leverage for striking workers, the UFW mounted a nationwide boycott of California grapes, which drew support from millions of Americans and helped win a wage increase for the workers in 1970. Although the UFW struggled and lost membership during the 1970s, it helped politicize Mexican Americans and improve farmworkers' lives.

Other Chicanos mobilized to force the Equal Employment Opportunity Commission (EEOC), the enforcement agency of Title VII of the Civil Rights Act of 1964, to act against job discrimination against Mexican Americans. LULAC, the American GI Forum (see chapter 26), and other groups picketed government offices. President Johnson responded in 1967 by appointing Vicente T. Ximenes as the first Mexican American EEOC commissioner and by creating a special committee on Mexican American affairs.

Claiming "brown power," Chicanos organized to end discrimination in education, gain political power, and combat police brutality. In Denver, Rodolfo "Corky" Gonzales set up "freedom schools" where Chicano children studied the Spanish language and Mexican American history. The nationalist strains of Chicano protest were evident in La Raza Unida (the United Race), a political party founded in 1970 in Texas and based on cultural pride and brotherhood. Along with blacks and Native Americans, Chicanos continued to be disproportionately represented among the poor, but they gradually won more political offices, more effective enforcement of antidiscrimination legislation, and greater respect for their culture.

Student Rebellion, the New Left, and the Counterculture Although materially and legally more secure than their African American, Indian, and Latino counterparts, white youths also expressed dissent, supporting the black freedom struggle and launching student protests, the antiwar movement, and the new feminist and environmental movements. Challenging establishment institutions and traditional values, young activists helped change higher education, the family, the national government, and other key institutions. They were part of a larger international phenomenon, as student movements arose in Mexico, Germany, Turkey, Czechoslovakia, Japan, and other nations around the globe.

The central organization of white protest was **Students for a Democratic Society (SDS)**, formed in 1960. In 1962, the organizers wrote in their statement of purpose, "We are people of this generation, bred in at least modest comfort, housed now in universities, looking uncomfortably at the world we inherit." The idealistic students criticized the complacency of their elders, the remoteness of decision makers, and the powerlessness and alienation generated by a bureaucratic society. SDS aimed to mobilize a "New Left" around the goals of civil rights, peace, and universal economic security. Other forms of student activism soon followed.

The first large-scale white student protest arose at the University of California, Berkeley, in 1964, when university officials banned students from setting up tables to recruit support for various causes. Led by whites back from civil rights work in the South, the students claimed the right to freedom of expression and political action. The "free speech" movement occupied the administration building, and more than seven hundred students were arrested before the California Board of Regents overturned the new restrictions.

Hundreds of student rallies and building occupations followed on campuses across the country, especially after 1965, when opposition to the Vietnam War mounted and students protested against universities' links to the military (see chapter 29). Students also changed the collegiate environment. Women at the University of Chicago, for example, charged in 1969 that all universities "discriminate against women, impede their full intellectual development, deny them places on the faculty, exploit talented women and mistreat women students." At Howard University, African American students called for a "Black Awareness Research Institute" and demanded that academic departments "place more emphasis on how these disciplines may be used to effect the liberation of black people." Across the country, students won curricular reforms such as black studies and women's studies programs, more financial aid for minority and poor students, independence from paternalistic rules, and a larger voice in campus decision making.

Student protest bewildered and angered older Americans, even more so when it blended into a cultural revolution against nearly every conventional standard of behavior. Drawing on the ideas of the Beats of the 1950s, the "hippies," as they were called, rejected mainstream values such as materialism, order, and sexual control. Seeking personal rather than political change, they advocated "Do your own thing" and drew attention with their long hair, wildly colorful clothing, and use of marijuana, LSD, and other illegal drugs. Across the country, thousands of radicals established communes in cities or on farms, where they renounced private property and shared everything, often including sexual partners.

Rock and folk music defined both the counterculture and the political left. English groups such as the Beatles and the Rolling Stones and homegrown performers such as Bob Dylan, Janis Joplin, and the Grateful Dead took American youth by storm. Music during the 1960s often carried insurgent political and social messages that reflected radical youth culture. "Eve of Destruction," a top hit of 1965, reminded young men, "You're old enough to kill but not for votin'." The Woodstock Music Festival, which featured the greatest rock and folk musicians of the era and drew 400,000 young people to a farm in Bethel, New York, in 1969, epitomized the centrality of music to the youth rebellion.

> SDS organizers wrote in their statement of purpose, "We are people of this generation, bred in at least modest comfort, housed now in universities, looking uncomfortably at the world we inherit."

WOODSTOCK MUSIC and ART FAIR
SUNDAY
AUGUST 17, 1969
10:00 A. M.
$8.00   Good For One Admission Only
03721 M   NO REFUNDS GLOBE TICKET COMPANY
SUN.
AUG. 17
1969
03721 M

The hippies faded away in the 1970s, but many elements of the counterculture—rock music, jeans, and long hair, as well as new social attitudes—filtered into the mainstream. More tolerant approaches to sexual behaviors spawned what came to be called the "sexual revolution," with help from the birth control pill, which became available in the 1960s. Self-fulfillment became a dominant concern of many Americans, and questioning of authority became more widespread.

Gay Men and Lesbians Organize

More permissive sexual norms did not stretch easily to include tolerance of homosexuality. Gay men and lesbians avoided discrimination and ridicule only by concealing their very identities. Those who couldn't or wouldn't found themselves fired from jobs, arrested for their sexual activities, deprived of their children, or accused of being "perverted." While most kept their sexuality hidden, in the 1950s, some gays and lesbians began to organize.

Some of the first gay activism challenged the government's aggressive efforts to keep homosexuals out of the civil service. In October 1965, a picket line formed outside the White House with signs calling discrimination against homosexuals

The Pill Longtime birth control advocate Margaret Sanger believed that the pill was "the key to liberty" for women. In 1960, the Food and Drug Administration approved the first birth control pill, and it soon became the leading form of contraception for American women. To help women remember to take the daily tablet, Ortho Pharmaceutical introduced the Dialpak, shown here. At that time, federal law prohibited direct advertising of prescription drugs to consumers, so drug companies appealed to doctors. This 1965 ad shows doctors how the Ortho-Novin Dialpak will tell "her" when she has taken her last pill and when to take the next one. And, typical of the way drugs are marketed in the United States, it promises "for you," the doctor, a gift — in this case, a calendar that can be attached to a watchband. National Museum of American History, Smithsonian Institution, Behring Center.

FOR MORE HELP ANALYZING THIS IMAGE, see the visual activity for this chapter in the Online Study Guide at **bedfordstmartins.com/roarkcompact**.

THE PROMISE OF TECHNOLOGY

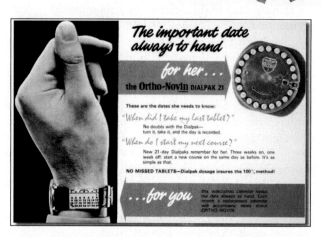

"as immoral as discrimination against Negroes and Jews." Not until ten years later, however, did the Civil Service Commission formally end its antigay policy.

The spark that ignited a larger movement was struck in 1969 when police raided a gay bar, the Stonewall Inn, in New York City's Greenwich Village, and gay men and lesbians fought back. "Suddenly, they were not submissive anymore," a police officer remarked. Energized by the defiance shown at the **Stonewall riots**, gay men and lesbians founded a host of new groups, such as the Gay Liberation Front. A more reformist organization, the National Gay and Lesbian Task Force, was founded in 1973 to ensure that sustained national attention was given to gay issues.

The gay rights movement struggled much longer and harder to win recognition than did other social movements. In 1972, Ann Arbor, Michigan, passed the first antidiscrimination ordinance, and two years later, Elaine Noble's election to the Massachusetts legislature marked the first time an openly gay candidate won state office. In 1973, gay activists persuaded the American Psychiatric Association to remove its designation of homosexuality as a mental disease. It would take decades for these initial gains to improve conditions for most homosexuals, but by the mid-1970s, gay men and lesbians had established a movement through which they could claim equal rights and express pride in their identities.

A New Movement to Save the Environment

Unlike other social movements, environmentalism was organized around a cause rather than around the identity of its members. One aspect of the new environmental movement resembled the conservation movement born in the Progressive Era to preserve portions of nature for recreational and aesthetic purposes and conserve it for future use (see chapter 21). Especially in the West, the post–World War II explosion of economic growth and mushrooming population, with the resulting demands for electricity and water, made such efforts seem even more critical. Environmental groups began mobilizing in the 1950s to stop the construction of dams that would disrupt national parks and wilderness areas.

The new environmentalists, however, went beyond conservationism. Polluted air and water and the use of deadly chemicals threatened the delicate ecological balance that sustained human life itself. To the leaders of a new organization, Friends of the Earth, unlimited economic growth was "no longer healthy, but a cancer." Biologist Rachel Carson drew national attention in 1962 with her best seller *Silent Spring*, which described the harmful effects of toxic chemicals such as the pesticide DDT. The Sierra Club and other older conservation organizations expanded their agendas, and a host of new groups arose. Millions of Americans expressed environmental concerns on the first observation of Earth Day in April 1970.

Responding to these concerns, the federal government staked out a new role in environmental regulation. Lyndon Johnson sent Congress the first presidential message on the environment and signed laws controlling air and water. Richard Nixon's 1970 State of the Union message called "clean air, clean water, open spaces . . . the birthright of every American," and that year he created the **Environmental Protection Agency (EPA)** to enforce clean air and water policies and regulate pesticides. Congress also passed the Occupational Safety and Health Act (OSHA), protecting workers against workplace accidents and disease, and the Clean Air Act of 1970, setting national standards for air quality and restricting factory and automobile emissions of carbon dioxide and other pollutants.

Nevertheless, the desire for economic growth often trumped environmental concerns. Corporations seeking to expand, apply new technologies, or exploit natural resources resisted restrictions. "If you're hungry and out of work, eat an environmentalist," read a union bumper sticker reflecting fears that regulations threatened jobs. Many Americans who wanted to protect the environment also valued economic expansion, personal acquisition, and convenience. Despite these conflicts, the environmental movement achieved cleaner air and water, a reduction in toxic wastes, and some preservation of endangered species and wilderness.

Q: **How did the black freedom struggle influence other reform movements of the 1960s and 1970s?**

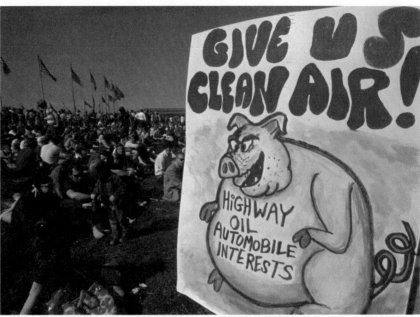

Earth Day in the Nation's Capital Building on the success of the teach-ins about the Vietnam War, Democratic senator Gaylord Nelson of Wisconsin came up with the idea of Earth Day "to shake up the political establishment and force this issue [environmentalism] onto the national agenda." As a result, on April 22, 1970, some twenty million people participated in grassroots demonstrations all over the country. This banner displayed on the Mall in Washington, D.C., focused on clean air. Other activists dramatized oil spills, toxic dumps, pesticides, polluted rivers and lakes, the loss of wilderness, and the extinction of wildlife. Dennis Brack/Black Star/Stockphoto.com.

The New Wave of Feminism

On August 26, 1970, fifty years after women won the right to vote, tens of thousands of women across the country—from radical women in jeans to conservatively dressed suburbanites, peace activists, and politicians—took to the streets. They carried signs reading "Sisterhood Is Powerful" and "Don't Cook Dinner—Starve a Rat Today." Some of the banners opposed the war in Vietnam, others demanded racial justice, but women's own liberation stood at the forefront.

Becoming visible by the late 1960s, the women's movement reached its high tide in the 1970s and persisted into the twenty-first century. By that time, despite a powerful countermovement, women had experienced tremendous transformations in their legal status, public opportunities, and personal and sexual relationships, and popular expectations about appropriate gender roles had shifted dramatically.

A Multifaceted Movement Emerges Beginning in the 1940s, large demographic changes laid the preconditions for a resurgence of feminism. As more women took jobs, the importance of their paid work to the economy and their families belied the idea of women as dependent, domestic beings and awakened many women workers, especially labor union women, to the inferior conditions of their employment. The democratization of higher education brought more women to college campuses, where their aspirations exceeded the confines of domesticity and of routine, subordinate jobs.

Policy initiatives in the early 1960s reflected both these larger transformations and the efforts of women's rights activists. In 1961, Assistant Secretary of Labor Esther Peterson persuaded President Kennedy to create the President's Commission on the Status of Women (PCSW). Though not challenging women's domestic roles, in 1963, the commission reported widespread discrimination against women and recommended remedies. Counterparts of the PCSW sprang up in every state, filled with women eager for action. One of the PCSW's concerns was addressed even before it issued its report, when Congress passed the Equal Pay Act of 1963, making it illegal to pay women less than men for the same work.

Like other movements, the rise of feminism owed much to the black freedom struggle. Women gained the ban against sex discrimination in Title VII of the Civil Rights Act of 1964 and the extension of affirmative action to women by piggyback-ing onto civil rights measures. They soon grew impatient when the government failed to take these new policies seriously. Outraged by the gov-ernment's slowness in enforcing Title VII, Betty Friedan, civil rights activist Pauli Murray, several union women, and others founded the **National Organization for Women (NOW)** in 1966.

Simultaneously, a more radical feminism grew among civil rights and New Left activists. In 1965, two white women, Mary King and Casey Hayden, wrote that their work in SNCC had awakened them to sex discrimina-tion. Although most black women did not consider themselves to be marginalized in the movement, King and Hayden presented their ideas to white male radicals in the New Left, who responded with indifference or ridicule. By contrast, their message invigorated other white women who shared their frustration with subordi-nate roles. Many women walked out of New Left organizations and created an independent women's liberation movement composed of small groups across the nation.

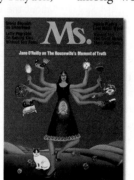

Women's liberation began to gain public atten-tion, especially when dozens of women picketed the Miss America beauty pageant in 1968, pro-testing against being forced "to compete for male approval [and] enslaved by ludicrous 'beauty' stan-dards." Women began to speak publicly about per-sonal experiences that had always been shrouded in secrecy, such as rape and abortion. Throughout the country, women joined consciousness-raising groups, where they discovered that what they had considered "personal" problems reflected an entrenched system of discrimination against and devaluation of women.

Radical feminists, who called their movement "women's liberation," differed from feminists in NOW and other more mainstream groups in sev-eral ways. NOW focused on equal treatment for women in the public sphere; women's liberation emphasized ending women's subordination in fam-ily and other personal relationships. Groups such as NOW wanted to integrate women into existing institutions; radical groups insisted that women's liberation required a total transformation of eco-nomic, political, and social institutions. Differences between these two strands of feminism blurred in the 1970s, as NOW and other mainstream groups embraced many of the issues raised by radicals.

Although NOW elected a black president, Aileen Hernandez, in 1970, the new feminism's leadership and constituency were predominantly white and middle-class. Women of color criticized white femi-nists for their inadequate attention to the dispro-portionate poverty experienced by minority women and to the additional layers of discrimination based on race or ethnicity. One black woman said, "My mother took care of rich white kids. I didn't think they were oppressed." To black women, much more frequently compelled to work in the lowest-paying jobs for their families' survival, employment did not necessarily look like liberation.

In addition to struggling with vast differences among women, feminism also contended with the refusal of the mass media to take women's grievances seriously. When the House of Representatives passed an equal rights amendment to the U.S. Constitution in 1970, the *New York Times* criticized it in an editorial titled "The Henpecked House." After Gloria Steinem founded *Ms: The New Magazine for Women* in 1972, femi-nists had their own mass-circulation periodical controlled by women and featuring articles on a broad range of feminist issues.

Ms. reported on a movement that was exceed-ingly multifaceted. Most African American women worked through their own groups, such as the older National Council of Negro Women and the National Black Feminist Organization, founded in 1973. Similarly, in the early 1970s, American Indian women and Mexican American women founded national organizations, and Asian Ameri-can women formed local movements. Labor union women, who had long struggled for workplace gender justice, organized the National Coalition of Labor Union Women in 1974. Lesbians estab-lished collectives throughout the country, as well as their own caucuses in organizations such as NOW. Welfare mothers formed the National Wel-fare Rights Organization, and religious women mobilized in the National Council of Churches of Christ to "place the question of women's libera-tion in the main stream of the church's concern." Other new groups focused on single issues such as health, abortion rights, education, and violence against women. In addition, U.S. feminists inter-acted with women abroad, joining a movement that crossed national boundaries. (See "Beyond America's Borders," page 716.)

Common threads underlay the great diversity of organizations, issues, and activities. Above all, feminism represented the belief that women were barred from, unequally treated in, or poorly served by the male-dominated public arena, encompassing politics, medicine, law, education, and religion. Many feminists also sought equality in the private sphere, challenging traditional norms that identified women primarily as wives and mothers or sex objects, subservient to men.

Feminist Gains Spark a Countermovement

Although more an effect than a cause of women's rising employment, feminism lifted female aspirations and helped lower barriers to posts monopolized by men. Between 1970 and 2000, their share of law degrees shot up from 5 percent to nearly 50 percent, and their proportion of medical degrees from less than 10 percent to more than 35 percent. Women gained political offices very slowly; yet by 2008, they constituted about 16 percent of Congress and more than 20 percent of all state executives and legislators.

Feminists also encountered frustrations along with achievements. Despite some inroads into male-dominated occupations, women still tended to concentrate in low-paying, traditionally female jobs. Employed women continued to bear primary responsibility for their homes and families, thereby working a "double day."

By the mid-1970s, feminism faced a powerful countermovement, organized around opposition to an **Equal Rights Amendment (ERA)** for women that would outlaw differential treatment of men and women under all state and federal laws. After Congress passed the ERA in 1972, Phyllis Schlafly, a conservative activist in the Republican Party, mobilized thousands of women at the grassroots level who feared that the ERA would devalue their own God-given roles as wives and mothers. These women, marching on state capitols, persuaded some male legislators to block ratification. When the time limit ran out in 1982, only thirty-five states had ratified the amendment, three short of the necessary three-fourths majority.

Powerful opposition likewise arose to feminists' quest for the right to abortion. "Without the full capacity to limit her own reproduction," abortion rights activist Lucinda Cisler insisted, "a woman's other 'freedoms' are tantalizing mockeries that cannot be exercised." In 1973, the Supreme Court issued the landmark *Roe v. Wade* decision, ruling that the Constitution protects the right to abortion, which states cannot prohibit in the early stages of pregnancy. This decision galvanized many

Americans who believed that human life begins with conception and equated abortion with murder. Like ERA opponents, with whom they often overlapped, activists in the right-to-life movement mobilized thousands of women who believed that abortion disparaged motherhood. Beginning in 1977, abortion foes got Congress to restrict the right to abortion by denying coverage under Medicaid and other government-financed health programs, and the Supreme Court allowed states to impose additional obstacles.

Despite resistance, feminists won other lasting gains. **Title IX** of the Education Amendments Act of 1972 banned sex discrimination in all aspects of education, such as admissions, athletics, and hiring. Congress also outlawed sex discrimination in credit in 1974, opened U.S. military academies to women in 1976, and prohibited discrimination against pregnant workers in 1978. Moreover, the Supreme Court struck down laws that treated men and women differently in Social Security, welfare and military benefits, and workers' compensation.

At the state and local levels, women saw reforms in areas that radical feminists had first brought attention to. They won laws forcing police departments and the legal system to treat rape victims more justly and humanely. Activists also pushed domestic violence onto the public agenda, obtaining government financing for shelters for battered women and laws ensuring both greater protection for victims of domestic violence and more effective prosecution of abusers.

Q: **Why did a strong countermovement emerge to oppose feminist reform?**

Liberal Reform in the Nixon Administration

Opposition to civil rights measures, Great Society reforms, and protest groups—along with frustrations surrounding the war in Vietnam (see chapter 29)—delivered the White House to Republican **Richard M. Nixon** in 1968. Nixon attacked the Great Society for "pouring billions of dollars into programs that have failed," and he promised to represent the "forgotten Americans, the non-shouters, the non-demonstrators." Yet despite Nixon's desire to capitalize on the backlash against civil rights and the Great Society, the Nixon administration either promoted or accepted substantially greater federal assistance to the poor, new protections for minorities and women, major environmental regulations, and financial policies deviating sharply from traditional Republican economics.

Transnational Feminisms

When American women began to protest sex discrimination in the 1960s, most were unaware that they belonged to a movement stretching back more than a century and across oceans. In 1850, Polish-born Ernestine Rose told a women's rights convention in Massachusetts, "We are not contending here for the rights of the women of New England, or of old England, but of the world." Her statement affirmed the connections among women from European countries and the United States who wrote and visited each other and exchanged ideas and inspiration in the first international women's movement.

By the early twentieth century, women had formalized such connections. For example, the International Alliance of Women, founded in 1904 to promote global woman suffrage, expanded its agenda to include equal pay and employment, peace, married women's citizenship, and more. By 1929, the alliance claimed national organizations in fifty-one countries, including the United States and most of Europe, China, Egypt, India, Japan, Palestine, and several Latin American nations.

Alliance women struggled to create a "universal sisterhood." White Christian women from the United States and Europe dominated the organization and blithely assumed that they could speak for all women. But oppression and discrimination looked quite different to women in other parts of the world. In colonized countries such as India and Egypt, feminism arose alongside movements for independence from the very imperial nations that were home to most alliance leaders. Egyptian feminist and nationalist Huda Sha'arawi was the only Muslim among the international leadership. She worked closely with the alliance on many issues, but she realized the need to address the particular interests of Arab women overlooked or opposed by Euro-American feminists, and she established the Arab Feminist Union in 1945.

Global connections among women increased dramatically in 1945 with the creation of the United Nations. Its charter affirmed "the equal rights of men and women" and "fundamental freedoms for all without distinction as to race, sex, language, or religion." Two years later, the UN established the Commission on the Status of Women, creating a forum for women from around the globe to meet and be heard. In 1948, it adopted the Universal Declaration of Human Rights, which enumerated an extensive set of rights and explicitly rejected sex discrimination. These and other international commitments to justice for women went far beyond any rights guaranteed to women by the U.S. legal system or by the laws of most other nations, thereby setting standards and raising expectations. The UN, for example, asserted women's right to equal pay in 1951, twelve years before the U.S. Congress did so, and the international body attacked discrimination in education a decade before Congress passed Title IX.

The UN helped launch a global feminist movement of unparalleled size and diversity when it declared 1975 International Women's Year and sponsored a conference in Mexico City. Six thousand women came to Mexico City on their own; official delegates from 125 nations approved the World Plan of Action for Women and prompted the UN to declare 1976 to 1985 the UN Decade for Women.

In response to the call for action in individual countries, the U.S. government funded the National Women's Conference in Houston, Texas, in 1977. More than two thousand state delegates attended, representing a cross section of American womanhood. They adopted the National Plan of Action, not only supporting ratification of the ERA and reproductive freedom but also addressing the needs of specific groups of women, including the elderly, lesbians, racial minorities, rural women, and homemakers. For the first time, the U.S. women's movement had a comprehensive national agenda setting goals for decades to come.

The three themes of the UN Decade for Women—equality, development, and peace—reflected an effort to address the enormously diverse needs of women throughout the world. Feminists from Western nations who focused on equal rights met criticism from women who represented impoverished third world countries and

Extending the Welfare State and Regulating the Economy A number of factors shaped the liberal policies of the Nixon administration. Not only did the Democrats continue to control Congress, but Nixon also saw political advantages in accepting some liberal programs. He could not entirely ignore grassroots movements, and several of his advisers were sympathetic to particular concerns, such as environmentalism and Native American rights. Serious economic problems also compelled new approaches, and although Nixon's real passion lay in foreign policy, he knew that history's approving gaze would depend in part on his domestic record.

★ **International Women's Year Tribune** A majority of delegates at the UN International Women's Year Conference in Mexico City in July 1975 were women, but men provided the leadership, and delegates frequently took positions mandated by their governments but not necessarily reflecting the interests of women. In contrast, nongovernmental organizations associated with the UN sponsored a tribune on the other side of the city, where six thousand women attended workshops that they or their organizations designed. There participants expressed the conflicting priorities of Western women and women from developing countries, and they argued over whether issues such as apartheid in South Africa and self-government for Palestinians were women's issues. Despite their disagreements, most women left Mexico City enlightened and energized. © Bettye Lane.

insisted that women's issues must include economic development and anticolonialism. Ever larger UN-sponsored meetings followed Mexico City—Copenhagen in 1980, Nairobi in 1985, and Beijing in 1995, where twenty thousand women gathered. These global exchanges taught American feminists that to participate in a truly international movement, they would have to revise their Western-centered perspective on women's needs.

American feminists also learned that theirs was not always the most advanced nation when it came to women's welfare and status. Most industrialized countries provided paid maternity leave and public child care. By 2008, women had headed governments in more than thirty countries, including India, Israel, Britain, and Germany. Many nations, such as Argentina, Egypt, and the European Union, had some form of affirmative action to increase the numbers of women in government. And whereas American women held 16 percent of the seats in the House of Representatives, women constituted 20 percent of the lower house in South Korea, 30 percent in Germany, and more than 35 percent in Norway, Denmark, and Sweden.

Despite enormous differences among women around the world, internationally minded feminists continued to seek common ground. As Gertrude Mongella, secretary general of the Beijing conference, insisted in 1995, "A revolution has begun and there is no going back. . . . This revolution is too just, too important, and too long overdue."

Under Nixon, government assistance programs grew. Congress resisted his attempts to eliminate the Office of Economic Opportunity. Key programs such as Medicaid, Head Start, and Legal Services remained intact. Social Security benefits—now required to rise with the cost of living—increased; subsidies for low-income housing tripled; a new billion-dollar program provided Pell grants for low-income students to attend college; and the food stamp program expanded to benefit 12.5 million recipients. Noting the disparity between what Nixon said and what he did, his speechwriter, the archconservative Pat Buchanan, grumbled, "Vigorously did

Nixon's 1968 Campaign Seeking the presidency in 1968 — a turbulent year of protests, riots, and assassinations — Richard Nixon tried to appeal to a broad spectrum of voters, reflected in this campaign poster. Prominent Republicans of all stripes appear in the poster, including the liberal Nelson Rockefeller and the conservative Barry Goldwater. While his slogan "Champion of Forgotten America" spoke to white Americans alienated by the Great Society's programs for minorities and the poor, the appearance on the poster of the black Republican senator Edward Brooke and basketball player Wilt Chamberlain of the Los Angeles Lakers gave a nod to African Americans. Nixon also appealed to youths by supporting the vote for eighteen-year-olds and promising to end the draft. Collection of Janice L. and David J. Frent.

we inveigh against the Great Society, enthusiastically did we fund it."

Nixon also acted contrary to his antigovernment rhetoric when economic crises and energy shortages induced him to increase the federal government's power in the marketplace. By 1970, both inflation and unemployment had surpassed 6 percent, an unprecedented combination dubbed "stagflation." Domestic troubles were compounded by the decline of American dominance in the international economy. With the economies of Japan and Western Europe fully recovered from World War II, foreign cars, electronic equipment, and other products now competed favorably with American goods. In 1971, for the first time in decades, the United States imported more than it exported. Because the amount of dollars in foreign hands exceeded U.S. gold reserves, the nation could no longer back up its currency with gold.

In 1971, Nixon abandoned the convertibility of dollars into gold and devalued the dollar to increase exports. To protect domestic manufacturers, he imposed a 10 percent surcharge on most imports, and he froze wages and prices, thus enabling the government to stimulate the economy without fueling inflation. In the short run, these policies worked, and Nixon was resoundingly reelected in 1972. Yet by 1974, unemployment had crept back up and inflation soared, leaving to Nixon's successor the most severe economic crisis since the 1930s.

Soaring energy prices intensified stagflation. Throughout the post–World War II economic boom, the nation's abundant oil deposits and access to cheap Middle Eastern oil had encouraged the building of large cars and skyscrapers with no concern for fuel efficiency. In the fall of 1973, the United States faced its first energy crisis. Arab nations, furious at the administration's support of Israel during the Yom Kippur War (see chapter 29), cut off oil shipments to the United States. Long lines formed at gas stations, where prices had nearly doubled, and many homes were cold. In response, Nixon authorized temporary emergency measures allocating petroleum and establishing a national 55-mile-per-hour speed limit to save gasoline. The energy crisis eased, but the nation had yet to come to grips with its seemingly unquenchable demand for fuel and dependence on foreign oil.

More permanently, Nixon expanded the government's regulatory role with a host of environmental protection measures. He proclaimed in 1970 that the nation must make "reparations for the damage we have done to our air, to our land and to our water." In addition to establishing the Environmental Protection Agency, he signed strong clean air legislation and measures to regulate noise pollution, oil spill cleanup, and the dumping of pesticides into the oceans. Environmentalists criticized Nixon's veto of the Clean Water Act of 1972, which Congress overrode. Yet his environmental initiatives surpassed those of previous administrations.

Responding to Demands for Social Justice

Nixon's 1968 campaign had exploited hostility to black protest and new civil rights policies to appeal to southern Democrats and white workers, but his administration had to answer to the courts and to Congress. In 1968, fourteen years after the *Brown* decision, school desegregation had barely touched the South. Like Eisenhower, Nixon was reluctant to use federal power to compel integration, but the Supreme Court overruled the administration's efforts to delay court-ordered desegregation and compelled it to enforce the law. By the time Nixon left office, fewer than one in ten southern black children attended totally segregated schools.

Nixon also began to implement affirmative action among federal contractors and unions and awarded more government contracts and loans to minority businesses. Congress took the initiative in other areas. In 1970, it extended the Voting Rights Act of 1965, and in 1972, it strengthened the Civil Rights Act of 1964 by enlarging the powers of the Equal Employment Opportunity Commission.

Women as well as minority groups benefited from the implementation of affirmative action and the strengthened EEOC, but several measures of the Nixon administration also specifically attacked sex discrimination. The president privately expressed patronizing attitudes about women. "Thank God we don't have any in the Cabinet," he told aides. Yet again, he confronted a growing movement that included Republican feminists. Nixon vetoed a child care bill and publicly opposed abortion, but he signed the pathbreaking Title IX, guaranteeing equality in all aspects of education, and allowed his Labor Department to push affirmative action.

President Nixon gave more public support for justice to Native Americans than to any other protest group. While not bowing to radical demands, the administration dealt cautiously with extreme protests, such as the occupation of the Bureau of Indian Affairs in Washington, D.C. Nixon signed measures recognizing claims of Alaskan and New Mexican Indians and set in motion legislation restoring tribal lands and granting Indians more control over their schools and other service institutions.

Q: Why and how did Republican president Richard Nixon expand the liberal reforms of previous administrations?

Conclusion: Achievements and Limitations of Liberalism

Senate majority leader Mike Mansfield was not alone in concluding that Lyndon Johnson "has done more than FDR ever did, or ever thought of doing." The Great Society had expanded the New Deal's focus on economic security, refashioning liberalism to embrace individual rights and to extend material well-being to groups neglected by or discriminated against in New Deal programs. Yet opposition to Johnson's leadership grew so strong by 1968 that he abandoned hopes for reelection. As his liberal vision lay in ruins, he asked, "How was it possible that all these people could be so ungrateful to me after I have given them so much?"

Fannie Lou Hamer could have provided a number of reasons. Support from the federal government was minimal when efforts to help southern blacks obtain their rights met with violence. The failure of Hamer's attempts to use Johnson's antipoverty programs to help poor blacks in Mississippi resulted in part from internal problems, but it also reflected some of the more general shortcomings of the War on Poverty. Hastily planned and inadequately funded, many antipoverty programs benefited industry more than they did the poor. The War on Poverty focused more on remediating individual shortcomings than on economic and political reforms that would ensure adequately paying jobs for all. Because Johnson launched an all-out war in Vietnam and refused to ask for sacrifices from prosperous Americans, the Great Society never commanded the resources necessary for victory over poverty.

Furthermore, black aspirations exceeded white Americans' commitment to genuine equality. When the civil rights movement attacked racial barriers long entrenched throughout the nation and sought equality in fact as well as in law, it faced a powerful backlash. By the end of the 1960s, the revolution in the legal status of African Americans was complete, but the black freedom struggle had lost momentum, and African Americans remained, with Native Americans and Chicanos, at the bottom of the economic ladder.

Johnson's critics overlooked the Great Society's more successful and lasting elements. Medicare and Medicaid provided access to health care for the elderly and the poor and contributed to a sharp decline in poverty among aged Americans. Federal aid for education and housing became permanent elements of national policy. Moreover, Richard Nixon's otherwise conservative administration implemented school desegregation in the South and affirmative action, initiated substantial environmental regulations, and secured new rights for Native Americans and women. Women especially benefited from the decline of discrimination, and significant numbers of African Americans and other minority groups began to enter the middle class.

Yet the perceived shortcomings of government programs contributed to social turmoil and fueled the resurgence of conservative politics. Young radicals launched direct confrontations with the government and universities that, together with racial conflict, escalated into political discord and social disorder. The war in Vietnam polarized American society as much as did racial issues or the behavior of young people, and it devoured resources that might have been used for social reform and undermined faith in presidential leadership.

Reviewing the Chapter

★ KEY TERMS

Explain each term's significance

WHO

Fannie Lou Hamer (p. 697)

John F. Kennedy (p. 699)

Lyndon B. Johnson (p. 700)

Martin Luther King Jr. (p. 704)

Malcolm X (p. 708)

Stokely Carmichael (p. 708)

Cesar Chavez (p. 709)

Dolores Huerta (p. 709)

Richard M. Nixon (p. 715)

WHAT

Great Society (p. 698)

Civil Rights Act of 1964 (p. 700)

War on Poverty (p. 701)

Medicare and Medicaid (p. 701)

Voting Rights Act of 1965 (p. 702)

Immigration and Nationality Act of 1965 (p. 702)

Warren Court (p. 703)

Student Nonviolent Coordinating Committee (SNCC) (p. 705)

March on Washington (p. 705)

Mississippi Freedom Summer Project (p. 705)

Selma march (p. 706)

Civil Rights Act of 1968 (p. 708)

American Indian Movement (AIM) (p. 709)

Students for a Democratic Society (SDS) (p. 711)

Stonewall riots (p. 712)

Environmental Protection Agency (EPA) (p. 713)

National Organization for Women (NOW) (p. 714)

Equal Rights Amendment (ERA) (p. 715)

Roe v. Wade (p. 715)

Title IX (p. 715)

> **FOR PRACTICE QUIZZES AND OTHER STUDY TOOLS,** see the Online Study Guide at **bedfordstmartins.com/roarkcompact**.

★ REVIEW QUESTIONS Q:

Use key terms and dates to support your answer

1. How did the Kennedy and Johnson administrations exemplify a liberal vision of the federal government? (pp. 699–703)

2. How did the civil rights movement change in the mid-1960s? (pp. 704–08)

3. How did the black freedom struggle influence other reform movements of the 1960s and 1970s? (pp. 709–13)

4. Why did a strong countermovement emerge to oppose feminist reform? (pp. 713–15)

5. Why and how did Republican president Richard Nixon expand the liberal reforms of previous administrations? (pp. 715–19)

★ MAKING CONNECTIONS

Draw on key terms, timeline, and review questions

1. Both Franklin Roosevelt's New Deal and Lyndon Johnson's Great Society attacked poverty. How was Johnson's approach different from Roosevelt's? Which was more successful, and what contributed to the relative successes and failures of each approach?

2. During the 1960s, African Americans made substantial gains in asserting their freedoms and rights. Discuss how the civil rights movement produced significant social change. Were there limits to its success? What part did government play in this process?

3. Women participated in various ways in the feminism that emerged in the 1960s. How can we explain the rise of this movement? What assumptions and goals were held in common in this diverse movement?

4. Most of the reform movements of the 1960s sought equality as one of their key priorities, but significant differences existed among Americans in general about what equality meant. Should equality be limited to equal treatment under the law, or should it extend to economic welfare, education, sexual relations, and other aspects of life? Examining two reform movements, discuss how different ideas of equality contributed to the accomplishments and disappointments of each movement.

★ SUGGESTED READINGS

Terry H. Anderson, *The Movement and the Sixties* (1995). A detailed look at student protests throughout the country.

Sara Evans, *Tidal Wave: How Women Changed America at Century's End* (2003). A balanced and vivid portrayal of the multifaceted women's movement.

Maurice Isserman and Michael Kazin, *America Divided: The Civil War of the 1960s* (2000). A highly readable account covering all aspects of the 1960s.

Charles Payne, *I've Got the Light of Freedom: The Organizing Tradition and the Mississippi Freedom Struggle* (1995). A close look at how ordinary people participated in and led the black freedom struggle.

Peter Chaat Smith and Robert Allen Warrior, *Like a Hurricane: The Indian Movement from Alcatraz to Wounded Knee* (1996). A detailed and often gripping account of Native American protests.

Thomas J. Sugrue, *Sweet Land of Liberty: The Forgotten Struggle for Civil Rights in the North* (2009). A captivating history of the long and multifaceted freedom struggle in the North.

Randall Woods, *LBJ: Architect of American Ambition* (2006). A masterful and engaging biography.

FOR MORE BOOKS ABOUT TOPICS IN THIS CHAPTER, see the Online Bibliography at **bedfordstmartins.com/roarkcompact**.

FOR ADDITIONAL FIRSTHAND ACCOUNTS OF THIS PERIOD, see Chapter 28 in Michael Johnson, ed., *Reading the American Past,* Fourth Edition.

FOR WEB SITES, IMAGES, AND DOCUMENTS RELATED TO TOPICS AND PLACES IN THIS CHAPTER, visit Make History at **bedfordstmartins.com/roarkcompact**.

★ TIMELINE

1960
- Lunch counter sit-ins.
- Democrat John F. Kennedy elected president.
- Student Nonviolent Coordinating Committee (SNCC) established.
- Students for a Democratic Society (SDS) founded.

1961
- Congress of Racial Equality (CORE) sponsors Freedom Rides.

1962
- United Farm Workers (UFW) founded.

1963
- President's Commission on the Status of Women issues report.
- Equal Pay Act.
- *Baker v. Carr.*
- *Abington School District v. Schempp.*
- March on Washington.
- President Kennedy assassinated; Lyndon B. Johnson becomes president.

1964
- Civil Rights Act.
- Mississippi Freedom Summer Project.
- Economic Opportunity Act.
- Tax cuts enacted.

1965
- Selma-to-Montgomery march.
- Voting Rights Act.

1965–1966
- Congress passes most of Johnson's Great Society domestic programs.

1966
- Black Panther Party for Self-Defense founded.
- *Miranda v. Arizona.*
- National Organization for Women (NOW) founded.

1967
- Detroit riots.
- *Loving v. Virginia.*

1968
- Martin Luther King Jr. assassinated.
- American Indian Movement (AIM) founded.
- Republican Richard M. Nixon elected president.

1969
- Stonewall riots.

1970
- First Earth Day celebrated.
- Occupational Safety and Health Act.
- Environmental Protection Agency established.
- Clean Air Act.

1971
- Nixon takes United States off gold standard and freezes prices and wages.

1972
- Title IX of Education Amendments Act.
- Congress passes Equal Rights Amendment; sends it to states for ratification.
- American Indians' "Trail of Broken Treaties" caravan to Washington, D.C.

1973
- *Roe v. Wade.*

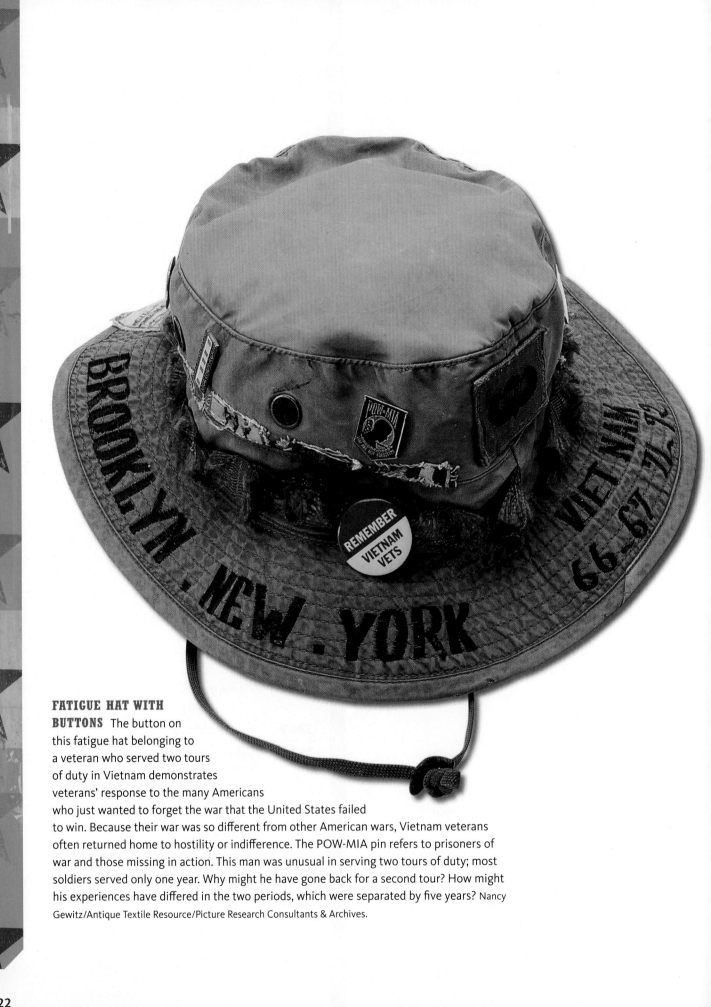

FATIGUE HAT WITH BUTTONS The button on this fatigue hat belonging to a veteran who served two tours of duty in Vietnam demonstrates veterans' response to the many Americans who just wanted to forget the war that the United States failed to win. Because their war was so different from other American wars, Vietnam veterans often returned home to hostility or indifference. The POW-MIA pin refers to prisoners of war and those missing in action. This man was unusual in serving two tours of duty; most soldiers served only one year. Why might he have gone back for a second tour? How might his experiences have differed in the two periods, which were separated by five years? Nancy Gewitz/Antique Textile Resource/Picture Research Consultants & Archives.

Vietnam and the Limits of Power

1961–1975

AS A PLANELOAD OF SOLDIERS prepared to land, the pilot announced, "Gentlemen, we'll be touching down in Da Nang, Vietnam, in about ten minutes. . . . On behalf of the entire crew and staff, I'd like to say we've enjoyed having you with us . . . and we hope to see all of you again next year on your way home. Goodbye and good luck." As the number of U.S. soldiers fighting in Vietnam soared, after 1966 most went to war on commercial airliners, complete with stewardesses (as they were called then) in miniskirts.

The picture of military personnel traveling to battle like business executives or tourists only hints at how different the Vietnam War was from America's previous wars. Marine infantry officer Philip Caputo landed at Da Nang in March 1965 confident, as were soldiers in previous wars, that the enemy "would be quickly beaten and that we were doing something altogether noble and good." But in just a few months, what had begun as an "adventurous expedition" became "an exhausting, indecisive war of attrition in which we fought for no other cause than our own survival."

Another soldier discovered even more quickly that "something was wrong." Wondering about the wire mesh that wrapped the military bus he boarded just after landing, he was told, "The gooks will throw grenades through the windows." Soldiers in Vietnam initially used the racist word *gook* to refer to the enemy—the North Vietnamese or their supporters in the South—but it soon became a term used for any Vietnamese. One American reported on the "changes coming over guys on our side—decent fellows, who wouldn't dream of calling an Oriental a 'gook' back home." The problem was that "they couldn't tell who was their friend and who wasn't. Day after day, out on patrol we'd come to . . . a shabby village, and the elders would welcome us and the children come running with smiles on their faces, waiting for the candy we'd give them. But . . . just as we were leaving the village behind, the enemy would open up on us, and there was bitterness among us that the villagers hadn't given us warning."

Americans' horrifying and bewildering experiences in Vietnam grew out of Cold War commitments made in the 1940s and 1950s by Presidents Harry S. Truman and Dwight D. Eisenhower. John F. Kennedy wholeheartedly took on those commitments, promising more flexible and vigorous efforts to thwart

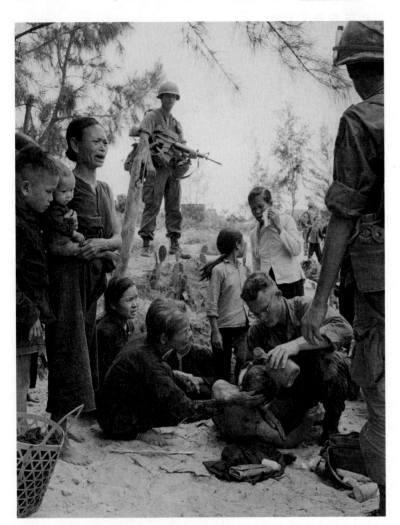

American Soldiers Confront the South Vietnamese The unconventional nature of the Vietnam War often resulted in U.S. soldiers harming the very people they were sent to save. There were no fixed battle lines, soldiers could not tell which South Vietnamese civilians were supporting the North Vietnamese, and U.S. troops destroyed villages and farmland in an effort to seek and eliminate North Vietnamese soldiers and their civilian allies. In this photo, a trooper of the U.S. First Cavalry stands guard while a medic treats South Vietnamese civilians who had been wounded during a search-and-destroy mission near Da Nang in October 1967. The mission destroyed their hamlet. © Bettmann/Corbis.

communism. The most memorable words of his 1961 inaugural address declared that the United States would "pay any price, bear any burden, meet any hardship, support any friend, oppose any foe to assure the survival and the success of liberty." Marine Philip Caputo recalled being "seduced into uniform by Kennedy's challenge . . . and by the missionary idealism he had awakened in us."

Vietnam became the foremost test of John F. Kennedy's anticommunism. He sent increasing amounts of American arms and personnel to sustain the South Vietnamese government, but it was Lyndon B. Johnson who dramatically escalated that commitment in 1965 and turned a civil war among the Vietnamese into America's war. At peak strength in 1968, 543,000 U.S. military personnel served in Vietnam; all told, some 2.6 million saw duty there. Yet this massive intervention not only failed to defeat North Vietnam but also created intense discord at home. It cost President Johnson another term in office and contributed to the demise of his Republican successor, Richard M. Nixon. Some Americans supported the government's goal in Vietnam and decried only its failure to pursue it effectively. Others believed that preserving a non-Communist South Vietnam was neither in the best interests of the United States nor within its capacity or moral right to achieve.

But none could deny the war's enormous costs. Lieutenant Caputo lamented that "our idealism was lost, our morals corrupted, and the purpose forgotten." Martin Luther King Jr. mourned "the promises of the Great Society . . . shot down on the battlefield of Vietnam." In addition to derailing domestic reform, the war exacted a heavy toll in American lives and dollars, disrupted the economy, kindled internal conflict, and led to the violation of protesters' rights, leaving a lasting mark on the nation.

As the United States fought communism in Vietnam and, on a much smaller scale, in other third world countries, American leaders moved to ease Cold War tensions with the major Communist powers. After a dramatic standoff with the Soviet Union during the Cuban missile crisis, the United States began to cooperate with its Cold War enemy to limit the spread of nuclear weapons. In addition, Nixon's historic visit to China in 1972 marked the abandonment of the policy of isolating China and paved the way for normal diplomatic relations by the end of the 1970s. ★

New Frontiers in Foreign Policy

John F. Kennedy moved quickly to pursue containment more aggressively and with more flexible means. In contrast to the Eisenhower administration's emphasis on nuclear weapons, Kennedy expanded not only the nation's nuclear capacity but also its ability to fight conventional battles and to engage in guerrilla warfare. To ensure U.S. superiority over the Soviet Union in every domain, Kennedy accelerated the nation's space exploration program and increased attention to the third world. To deny the Soviets a nuclear outpost in the Western Hemisphere, he took the United States to the brink of war during the 1962 **Cuban missile crisis**. Less dramatically but no less resolutely, Kennedy sent increasing amounts of American arms and personnel to save the South Vietnamese government from Communist insurgents.

Meeting the "Hour of Maximum Danger"

Underlying Kennedy's foreign policy was an assumption that the United States had "gone soft—physically, mentally, spiritually soft," as he put it in 1960. Calling the Eisenhower era "years of drift and impotency" and criticizing the Eisenhower administration for relying too heavily on nuclear weapons, Kennedy built up conventional ground forces to provide a flexible response to Communist expansion. He also charged that limits on defense spending had caused the United States to fall behind even in nuclear capability. In January 1961, Kennedy warned that the nation faced a grave peril: "Each day the crises multiply. . . . Each day we draw nearer the hour of maximum danger."

Although the president exaggerated the threat to national security, several developments in 1961 heightened the sense of crisis and provided a rationalization for his military buildup. Shortly before Kennedy's inauguration, Khrushchev publicly encouraged "wars of national liberation," thereby aligning the Soviet Union with independence movements in the third world that were often anti-Western. His statement reflected in part the Soviet competition with China for the allegiance of emerging nations, but U.S. officials saw in his words a threat to the status quo of containment.

Cuba, just ninety miles off the Florida coast, posed the most immediate threat to the United States. Fidel Castro's revolution had already moved Cuba into the Soviet orbit, and Eisenhower's CIA had been planning an invasion of the island by Cuban exiles living in Florida. Kennedy ordered the invasion to proceed even though his military advisers gave it only a fair chance of success.

On April 17, 1961, about 1,400 anti-Castro exiles trained and armed by the CIA landed at the **Bay of Pigs** on the south shore of Cuba (Map 29.1). Contrary to U.S. expectations, no popular uprising materialized to support the anti-Castro brigade. Kennedy refused to provide direct military support, and the invaders quickly fell to

MAP 29.1 U.S. Involvement in Latin America and the Caribbean, 1954–1994
During the Cold War, the United States frequently intervened in Central American and Caribbean countries to suppress Communist or leftist movements.

Castro's forces. The disaster humiliated Kennedy and the United States, posing a stark contrast to the president's inaugural promise of a new, more effective foreign policy. The attempted invasion evoked memories of Yankee imperialism among Latin Americans and aligned Cuba even more closely with the Soviet Union.

Days before the Bay of Pigs invasion, the Soviet Union delivered a psychological blow when a Soviet astronaut became the first human being to orbit the earth. In May 1961, Kennedy called for a huge new commitment to the space program, with the goal of sending a man to the moon by 1970. Congress authorized the Apollo program and boosted appropriations for space exploration. John H. Glenn orbited the earth in 1962, and in July 1969, two U.S. astronauts landed on the moon.

> One Peace Corps volunteer spoke of his service as a way to ease his guilt at having been "born between clean sheets when others were issued into the dust with a birthright of hunger."

Early in his presidency, Kennedy determined to show Khrushchev "that we can be as tough as he is." But when the two met in June 1961 in Vienna, Austria, Khrushchev was belligerent and shook the president's confidence. The stunned Kennedy reported privately, "He just beat [the] hell out of me. . . . If he thinks I'm inexperienced and have no guts . . . we won't get anywhere with him." Khrushchev demanded an agreement recognizing the existence of two Germanys and made veiled threats about America's occupation rights in and access to West Berlin.

Khrushchev was concerned about the massive exodus of East Germans into West Berlin, a major embarrassment for the Communists. To stop these escapees from behind the iron curtain, in August 1961 East Germany shocked the world by erecting a wall between East and West Berlin. With the **Berlin Wall** stemming the tide of migration and Kennedy insisting that West Berlin was "the great testing place of Western courage and will," Khrushchev backed off from his threats. But not until 1972 did the superpowers recognize East and West Germany as separate nations and guarantee Western access to West Berlin.

Kennedy used the Berlin crisis to add $3.2 billion to the defense budget. He increased draft calls and mobilized the reserves and National Guard, adding 300,000 troops to the military. This buildup of conventional forces provided for a "flexible response," offering "a wider choice than humiliation or all-out nuclear action." Still, Kennedy also pushed for the development of new nuclear weapons and delivery systems, more than doubling the nation's nuclear force within three years.

New Approaches to the Third World Complementing Kennedy's hard-line policy toward the Soviet Union were fresh approaches to the nationalist movements that had arisen since the end of World War II. In 1960 alone, seventeen African nations gained their independence. Much more than his predecessors, Kennedy publicly supported third world aspirations, believing that the United States could win the hearts and minds of people in developing nations by helping to fulfill hopes for autonomy and democracy. To that end, in 1961 Kennedy created the Alliance for Progress, pledging $20 billion in aid for Latin America over the next decade. Like the Marshall Plan (see chapter 26), the Alliance for Progress was designed to thwart communism and hold nations within the American sphere by fostering economic development. Yet, by 1969, the United States had provided only half of the promised $20 billion, much of which went to military projects or corrupt ruling elites.

Kennedy launched his most dramatic third world initiative in 1961 with an idea borrowed from Senator Hubert H. Humphrey: the **Peace Corps**. The program recruited young people to work in developing countries, attracting many who had been moved by Kennedy's appeal for idealism and sacrifice in his inaugural address. One volunteer's service eased his guilt at having been "born between clean sheets when others were issued into the dust with a birthright of hunger." After studying a country's language and culture, Peace Corps volunteers went to work directly with its people, opening schools, providing basic health care, and assisting with agriculture and small economic enterprises. By the mid-1970s, more than 60,000 volunteers had served in Latin America, Africa, and Asia. Peace Corps projects were generally welcomed, but they did not address the receiving countries' larger economic and political structures.

Kennedy also used direct military means to bring political stability to the third world. He rapidly expanded the elite special forces corps established under Eisenhower to aid groups sympathetic to the United States and fighting against Communist-leaning movements. These counterinsurgency forces, including the army's Green Berets and the navy's SEALs, were trained to wage guerrilla warfare and equipped with the latest technology. They would get their first test in Vietnam.

The Arms Race and the Nuclear Brink The final piece of Kennedy's defense strategy was to strengthen American nuclear dominance. He upped the number of nuclear weapons based in Europe from 2,500 to 7,200 and multiplied fivefold the supply of **intercontinental ballistic missiles (ICBMs)**. Concerned that this buildup would enable the United States to launch a first strike and wipe out Soviet missile sites before they could respond, the Soviet Union stepped up its own ICBM program. Thus began the most intense arms race in history.

The superpowers came perilously close to using their weapons in 1962, when Khrushchev decided to install nuclear missiles in Cuba, while insisting to Kennedy that he had no intention of doing so. Khrushchev wanted to protect Cuba from further U.S. attempts at intervention and to balance the U.S. missiles aimed at the Soviet Union from Britain, Italy, and Turkey. On October 16, the CIA showed Kennedy aerial photographs of missile launching sites under construction in Cuba. Considering this an intolerable threat to the United States, the president decided to react. On October 22, he announced to a television audience that the military was on full alert and that the navy would turn back any Soviet vessel suspected of carrying offensive missiles to Cuba. Kennedy warned that any attack launched from Cuba would trigger a full nuclear assault against the Soviet Union.

Projecting the appearance of toughness was paramount to President Kennedy. Although the missiles did not "alter the strategic balance in fact," according to one of his aides, "that balance would have been substantially altered in appearance; and in matters of national will and world leadership such appearances contribute to reality." Kennedy feared that "Communism and Castroism are going to be spread . . . as governments frightened by this new evidence of power [fall]."

But if Kennedy risked nuclear war for appearances, he also exercised caution, refusing advice from the military to bomb the missile sites. On October 24, Russian ships carrying nuclear warheads toward Cuba suddenly turned back. When one ship crossed the blockade line, Kennedy ordered the navy to follow the ship rather than attempt to stop it.

While Americans experienced the Cold War's most dangerous days, Kennedy and Khrushchev negotiated an agreement. The Soviets removed the missiles and pledged not

Cuban Missile Crisis, 1962

□ U.S. blockade zone
— Range of Soviet missiles
▲ Soviet missile and jet bomber base

to introduce new offensive weapons into Cuba. The United States promised not to invade the island. Secretly, Kennedy also agreed to remove the U.S. missiles from Turkey. The Cuban crisis led to Khrushchev's fall from power two years later, and Kennedy emerged triumphant. The image of an inexperienced president fumbling the Bay of Pigs invasion gave way to that of a strong leader bearing the United States through its "hour of maximum danger."

Having proved his toughness, Kennedy worked with Khrushchev to prevent future confrontations by installing a special "hot line" to speed top-level communication. In a major speech at American University in June 1963, Kennedy called for a reexamination of Cold War assumptions, asking Americans "not to see conflict as inevitable." Acknowledging the superpowers' differences, Kennedy stressed what they had in common: "We all breathe the same air. We all cherish our children's future and we are all mortal." In August 1963, the United States, the Soviet Union, and Great Britain signed a limited nuclear test ban treaty, reducing the threat of radioactive fallout from nuclear testing and raising hopes for further superpower accord.

Preparing for the Worst during the Cuban Missile Crisis Waiting out the tense days after President Kennedy issued the ultimatum to the Soviet Union to halt shipments of missile materials to Cuba, many Americans tried to prepare for the worst possible outcome. Owners of Chalet Suzanne, a hotel in Lake Wales, Florida, canned several thousand cases of well water, labeled "NASK" for Nuclear Attack Survival Kit. Courtesy Chalet Suzanne Foods, Inc., Lake Wales, Florida. Photo by David Woods.

A Growing War in Vietnam In his American University speech, Kennedy criticized the idea of "a Pax Americana enforced on the world by American weapons of war," but in 1961 he began to increase the flow of those weapons into South Vietnam. Kennedy's strong anticommunism and attachment to a vigorous foreign policy prepared him to expand the commitment in Vietnam that he had inherited from Eisenhower. Convinced that China and the Soviet Union were behind Ho Chi Minh's efforts to unify Vietnam under communism, Kennedy's key military adviser, General Maxwell Taylor, argued that holding firm in Vietnam would show the Soviets and Chinese that wars of national liberation were "costly, dangerous, and doomed to failure."

By the time Kennedy took office, more than $1 billion in aid and seven hundred U.S. military advisers had failed to stabilize South Vietnam. Two major obstacles stood in the way. First, the South Vietnamese insurgents—whom Americans called Vietcong, short for *Vietnam Cong-san* ("Vietnamese Communists")—were an indigenous force whose initiative came from within, not from the Soviet Union or China. Because the Saigon government refused to hold elections, the rebels saw no choice but to take up arms. Increasingly, Ho Chi Minh's Communist government in North Vietnam supplied them with weapons and soldiers.

Second, the South Vietnamese government and army (ARVN) refused to satisfy the demands of the insurgents but could not defeat them militarily. Ngo Dinh Diem, South Vietnamese premier from 1954 to 1963, chose self-serving military leaders for their personal loyalty rather than for their effectiveness.

Many South Vietnamese, the majority of whom were Buddhists, saw the Catholic Diem as a corrupt and brutal tool of the West. Even Secretary of State Dean Rusk called him "an oriental despot."

The growing intervention by North Vietnam made matters worse. In 1960, the Hanoi government established the National Liberation Front (NLF), composed of South Vietnamese rebels but directed by the northern army. In addition, Hanoi constructed a network of infiltration routes, called the **Ho Chi Minh Trail**, in neighboring Laos and Cambodia, through which it sent people and supplies to help liberate the South (Map 29.2).

MAP 29.2 The Vietnam War, 1964–1975
The United States sent 2.6 million soldiers to Vietnam and spent more than $150 billion on the longest war in American history, but it was unable to prevent the unification of Vietnam under a Communist government.

READING THE MAP: What accords divided Vietnam into two nations? When were these accords signed, and where was the line of division drawn? Through what countries did the Ho Chi Minh Trail go?

CONNECTIONS: What was the Gulf of Tonkin incident, and how did the United States respond? What was the Tet Offensive, and how did it affect the war?

FOR MORE HELP ANALYZING THIS MAP, see the map activity for this chapter in the Online Study Guide at bedfordstmartins.com/roarkcompact.

Violence escalated between 1960 and 1963, bringing the Saigon government close to collapse.

Kennedy responded to the deteriorating situation with measured steps. Some advisers called for using any force necessary to save South Vietnam from communism. Others questioned whether such a victory was either necessary or possible. Undersecretary of State Chester Bowles, for example, warned that the American effort was "headed full blast up a dead end street," while another foreign policy expert warned that the United States should not "stake its prestige" on an unsalvageable government.

Taking the middle ground, Kennedy gradually escalated the U.S. commitment. By the spring of 1963, military aid had doubled, and the 9,000 Americans serving in Vietnam as military advisers occasionally participated in actual combat. The South Vietnamese government promised reform but never made good on its promises.

Reflecting racist attitudes of American superiority over nonwhite populations, officials assumed that U.S. technology and sheer power could win in Vietnam. Soldiers such as Philip Caputo carried to Vietnam "the pride and overpowering self-assurance" that victory was inevitable. Yet advanced weapons were ill suited to the guerrilla warfare practiced by the enemy, whose surprise attacks were designed to weaken support for the South Vietnamese government. In addition, U.S. weapons and strategy harmed the very people they were intended to save. Thousands of peasants were uprooted and resettled in "strategic hamlets," supposedly secure from the Communists. Those left in the countryside fell victim to bombs—containing the highly flammable substance napalm—dropped by the South Vietnamese air force to quell the Vietcong. In January 1962, U.S. planes began to spray herbicides such as **Agent Orange** to destroy the Vietcong's jungle hideouts and food supply.

With tacit permission from Washington, South Vietnamese military leaders executed a coup against Diem and his brother, who headed the secret police, on November 2, 1963. Kennedy expressed shock that the two were murdered but indicated no change in policy. In a speech to be given on the day he was assassinated, he referred specifically to Southeast Asia and warned, "We dare not weary of the task." At his death, 16,700 Americans were stationed in Vietnam, and 100 had died there.

Q: **Why did Kennedy believe that engagement in Vietnam was crucial to his foreign policy?**

Lyndon Johnson's War against Communism

The Cold War assumptions that had shaped Kennedy's foreign policy underlay his successor's approach to Southeast Asia and Latin America. Retaining Kennedy's key advisers—Secretary of State Rusk, Secretary of Defense Robert McNamara, and National Security Adviser McGeorge Bundy—**Lyndon B. Johnson** continued the massive buildup of nuclear weapons and conventional and counterinsurgency forces. In 1965, Johnson made the fateful decisions to order U.S. troops into combat and to initiate sustained bombing of the North. That same year, Johnson sent U.S. Marines to the Dominican Republic to crush a leftist rebellion.

An All-Out Commitment in Vietnam The president who wanted to make his mark on domestic policy was compelled to deal with the commitments his predecessors had made to stopping communism in Vietnam. Early in Johnson's administration, the public paid little attention to Vietnam and seemed willing to follow the administration's lead. Yet some advisers, politicians, and international leaders raised questions about the wisdom of a greater commitment in Vietnam, viewing the situation there as a civil war rather than Communist aggression. Most U.S. allies did not consider Vietnam crucial to containing communism and were not prepared to share the military burden in more than token ways. Senate majority leader Mike Mansfield wondered whether Vietnam could be won with a "limited expenditure of American lives and resources somewhere commensurate with our national interests." Senate Armed Services Committee member Richard Russell warned, "It'd take a half million men. They'd be bogged down there for ten years."

Johnson disregarded the opportunity for disengagement that these critics saw in 1964 and expanded the United States' military involvement. Along with most of his advisers, he believed that American credibility was on the line. Moreover, the president's own credibility also came into play. Like Kennedy, he feared the domestic political repercussions of disengagement without victory. His own insecurities and fear of being compared unfavorably with Kennedy precluded a course that might make him appear soft or cowardly.

Johnson understood the ineffectiveness of his South Vietnamese allies and agonized over sending young men into combat. Yet he continued to dispatch more military advisers, weapons, and economic aid and, in August 1964, seized an opportunity to increase the pressure on North Vietnam.

During a routine espionage mission in the Gulf of Tonkin, off the coast of North Vietnam, two U.S. destroyers reported that North Vietnamese gunboats had fired on them (see Map 29.2). Johnson quickly ordered air strikes on North Vietnamese torpedo bases and oil storage facilities. Concealing the uncertainty about whether the second attack had even occurred and the provocative U.S. operations along the North Vietnamese coast, he won from Congress the **Gulf of Tonkin Resolution**, granting him authority to take "all necessary measures to repel any armed attacks against the forces of the United States and to prevent further aggression."

The president's tough stance only two months before the 1964 election helped counter the charges made by his opponent, Arizona senator Barry Goldwater, that he was "soft on communism." Yet Johnson also presented himself as the peace candidate, assuring Americans that "we are not going to send American boys nine or ten thousand miles away from home to do what Asian boys ought to be doing for themselves."

Soon after winning reelection, however, Johnson did widen the war. He rejected peace overtures from North Vietnam, which insisted on American withdrawal and a coalition government in South Vietnam as steps toward ultimate unification of the country. Instead, in February 1965, Johnson authorized **Operation Rolling Thunder**, a strategy of gradually intensified bombing of North Vietnam. Less than a month later, Johnson ordered the first U.S. combat troops to South Vietnam, and in July he shifted U.S. troops from defensive to offensive operations, dispatching 50,000 more soldiers. Although the administration downplayed the import of these decisions, they marked a critical turning point. Now it was genuinely America's war.

Preventing Another Castro in Latin America

Closer to home, Johnson faced persistent problems in Latin America. Thirteen times during the 1960s, military coups toppled Latin American governments, and local insurgencies grew apace. The administration's response varied from case to case but centered on the determination to prevent any more Castro-type revolutions.

In 1964, riots erupted in the Panama Canal Zone, which the United States had seized and made a U.S. territory early in the century (see chapter 21). Instigated by Panamanians who viewed the United States as a colonial power, the riots left four U.S. soldiers and more than twenty Panamanians dead. Johnson sent troops to quell the disturbance, but he also initiated negotiations that eventually returned the canal to Panamanian authority in 2000.

Elsewhere, Johnson's Latin American policy generated new cries of "Yankee imperialism." In 1961, voters in the Dominican Republic ousted a longtime dictator and elected a constitutional government headed by reformist Juan Bosch, who was overthrown by a military coup two years later. In 1965, when Bosch supporters launched an uprising against the military government, Johnson sent more than 20,000 soldiers to quell what he perceived to be a leftist revolt and to take control of the island. A truce was arranged, and in 1966 Dominicans voted in a constitutional government under a moderate rightist.

This first outright show of Yankee force in Latin America in four decades damaged the administration at home and abroad. Although it had justified intervention on the grounds that Communists were among the rebels, it quickly became clear that they had played no significant role, and U.S. actions kept the reform-oriented Boschists from returning to power. Moreover, the president had not consulted the Dominicans or the Organization of American States (OAS), to which the United States had pledged that it would respect national sovereignty in Latin America.

The Americanized War The military success in the Dominican Republic no doubt encouraged the president to press on in Vietnam. From 1965 to early 1968, the United States gradually escalated attacks against the North Vietnamese and their Vietcong allies, endeavoring to break their will without provoking intervention by the Chinese, as had occurred in Korea. Johnson himself scrutinized military plans, boasting, "They can't even bomb an outhouse without my approval."

Over the course of the war, U.S. pilots dropped 3.2 million tons of explosives, more than the United States had dropped in all of World War II. Claiming monthly death tolls of more than 2,000 North Vietnamese, the intensive bombing nonetheless failed to dampen the Hanoi government's commitment. (See "Historical Question," page 732.) In the South, the United States rained down more than twice the tonnage of bombs dropped on North Vietnam.

On the ground, General William Westmoreland's strategy of attrition was designed to seek out and kill the Vietcong and North Vietnamese regular army. The military used helicopters extensively to conduct offensives all over South Vietnam. Because there was no battlefront as in previous wars, officials calculated progress not in territory seized but in "body counts" and "kill ratios"—the number of enemies killed relative to the cost in American and ARVN lives. In this situation, American soldiers did not always distinguish between military combatants and civilians; according to Lieutenant Philip Caputo, the operating rule was "If it's dead and Vietnamese, it's VC [Vietcong]."

what to do. . . . But their sons don't end up in the swamps over there, in Vietnam."

The antiwar movement outraged millions of Americans who supported the war. Some members of the generation who had fought against Hitler could not understand younger men's refusal to support their government. They expressed their anger at war protesters with bumper stickers that read "America: Love It or Leave It."

By 1967, the administration realized that "discontent with the war is now wide and deep." President Johnson used various means to silence critics. He equated opposition to the war with communism and assistance to the enemy. To avoid focusing attention on the war's costs, he eschewed measures to control inflation and delayed asking for a tax increase to pay for the war. Not until June 1968 did Congress pass a 10 percent income tax surcharge. Great Society programs suffered, and the surcharge failed to check inflation.

The administration deceived the public by making optimistic statements and concealing officials' ever-graver doubts about the possibility of success in Vietnam. Johnson ordered the CIA to spy on peace advocates, and without the president's specific authorization, the FBI infiltrated the peace movement, disrupted its work, and spread false information about activists. Even the resort to illegal measures failed to subdue the opposition.

1968: Year of Upheaval

The year 1968 was marked by violent confrontations around the world. Protests against governments erupted from Mexico City to Paris to Tokyo, usually led by students in collaboration with workers. American society also became increasingly polarized. On one side, the so-called hawks charged that the United States was fighting with one hand tied behind its back and called for intensification of the war. The doves wanted de-escalation or withdrawal. As U.S. troop strength neared half a million and military deaths approached 20,000 by the end of 1967, most people were torn between weariness with the war and a desire to fulfill the U.S. commitment. As one woman said, "I want to get out but I don't want to give up."

Grave doubts penetrated the administration itself in 1967. Secretary of Defense Robert McNamara, a principal architect of U.S. involvement, now believed that the North Vietnamese "won't quit no matter how much bombing we do." He feared for the image of the United States, "the world's greatest superpower, killing or seriously injuring 1,000 noncombatants a week, while trying to pound a tiny, backward nation into submission on an issue whose merits are hotly disputed." McNamara did not publicly oppose the war, but in early 1968 he left the administration.

A critical turning point came with the **Tet Offensive**. On January 30, 1968, the North Vietnamese and Vietcong launched attacks on key cities and every major American base in South Vietnam. This was the biggest surprise of the war, and not simply because both sides had customarily observed a truce during Tet, the Vietnamese New Year holiday. The offensive displayed the Communists' vitality and refusal to be intimidated by the presence of half a million American soldiers. Militarily, the enemy suffered a defeat, losing ten times as many soldiers as ARVN and U.S. forces. Psychologically, however, Tet was devastating to the United States.

The Tet Offensive underscored the credibility gap between official statements and the war's actual progress. TV anchorman Walter Cronkite wondered, "What the hell is going on? I thought we were winning the war." The attacks created a million more South Vietnamese refugees as well as widespread destruction. Explaining how he had defended a village, a U.S. army official said, "We had to destroy the town to save it." The statement epitomized for more and more Americans the brutality and senselessness of the war. Public approval of Johnson's handling of it dropped to 26 percent.

In the aftermath of Tet, Johnson conferred with advisers in the Defense Department and an unofficial group of foreign policy experts who had been key architects of Cold War policies for two decades. Dean Acheson, Truman's secretary of state, summarized their conclusion: "We can no longer do the job we set out to do in the time we have left and we must begin to take steps to disengage."

On March 31, 1968, Lyndon Johnson announced in a televised speech that the United States would reduce its bombing of North Vietnam and that he was prepared to begin peace talks. He added the stunning declaration that he would not run for reelection. The gradual escalation of the war was over, and military strategy shifted from "Americanization" to "Vietnamization" of the war. But this was not a shift in policy. The goal remained a non-Communist South Vietnam; the United States would simply rely more heavily on the South Vietnamese to achieve it.

Negotiations began in Paris in May 1968. The United States would not agree to recognition of the Hanoi government's National Liberation Front, to a coalition government, or to American withdrawal. The North Vietnamese would agree to nothing less. Although the talks continued, so did the fighting.

Meanwhile, violence escalated at home. Protests occurred on two hundred college campuses in the spring of 1968. In the bloodiest action, students occupied buildings at Columbia University in New York City, making demands connected to the university's war-related research and to its treatment of African Americans. When negotiations failed, university officials called in the city police, who cleared the buildings, injuring scores of demonstrators and arresting hundreds. An ensuing student strike prematurely ended the academic year.

In June, two months after the murder of Martin Luther King Jr. and the riots that followed, another assassination shook the nation. Antiwar candidate Senator Robert F. Kennedy, campaigning in California for the Democratic Party's presidential nomination, was shot by a Palestinian Arab refugee who was outraged by Kennedy's support for Israel.

In August, protesters battled the police in Chicago, where the Democratic Party had convened to nominate its presidential ticket. Several thousand demonstrators came to the city, some to support the peace candidate Senator Eugene McCarthy, others to cause disruption. The Youth International Party (Yippies), a splinter group of SDS, urged protesters to demonstrate their hatred of the establishment by provoking the police and creating chaos. On August 25, when demonstrators jeered at orders to disperse, police attacked them with tear gas and clubs. Street battles continued for three days, culminating in a police riot on the night of August 28.

Taunted by the crowd, the police used mace and nightsticks, clubbing not only those who had come to provoke violence but also reporters, peaceful demonstrators, and convention delegates.

Although the bloodshed in Chicago horrified those who saw it on television, it had little effect on the convention's outcome. An assassin had ended Robert Kennedy's promising campaign in June, and Vice President **Hubert H. Humphrey** trounced the remaining antiwar candidate, McCarthy, by nearly three to one for the Democratic nomination.

In contrast to the turmoil around the Democratic convention, the Republican convention met peacefully and nominated former vice president Richard Nixon on the first ballot. For his running mate, Nixon chose Maryland governor Spiro T. Agnew, hoping to gather southern support. A strong third candidate entered the electoral scene when the American Independent Party nominated former Alabama governor and staunch segregationist **George C. Wallace**. Wallace appealed to Americans' dissatisfaction with the reforms and rebellions of the 1960s and outrage at the assaults on traditional values. Nixon guardedly played on resentments that fueled the Wallace campaign, calling for "law and order" and attacking liberal Supreme Court decisions, busing for school desegregation, and protesters.

Nixon and Humphrey differed little on the central issue of Vietnam. Nixon promised "an honorable end" to the war but did not indicate how he would do it. Humphrey had strong reservations about U.S. policy in Vietnam, yet as vice president he was tied to Johnson's policies. With nearly 13 percent of the total popular vote, the American Independent Party produced the strongest third-party finish since 1924. Nixon edged out Humphrey by just half a million popular votes but garnered 301 electoral college votes to Humphrey's 191 and Wallace's 46. The Democrats maintained control of Congress.

The 1968 election revealed deep cracks in the coalition that had kept the Democrats in power for most of the previous thirty years. Johnson's liberal policies on race shattered a century of Democratic Party dominance in the South, which delivered all its electoral votes to Wallace and Nixon. Elsewhere, large numbers of blue-collar workers broke union ranks to vote for Wallace and Nixon, as did other groups that associated the Democrats with racial turmoil, poverty programs, changing sexual mores, and failure to turn the tide in Vietnam. These resentments would soon be mobilized into a resurging right in American politics (see chapter 30).

Protest in Chicago The worst violence surrounding the 1968 Democratic National Convention in Chicago came on August 28 when protesters decided to assemble in Grant Park and march to the convention site. Near the Hilton Hotel, where most of the delegates stayed, some 3,000 protesters came up against a line of police. The police attacked not only the demonstrators but also reporters, hotel guests, and bystanders with nightsticks and mace, driving a crowd through the plate-glass window of the hotel and injuring hundreds. Here a policeman sprays Mace on the crowd. AP Images/Michael Boyer.

Q: How did the Vietnam War shape the election of 1968?

Nixon, Détente, and the Search for Peace in Vietnam

Richard M. Nixon took office with ambitious foreign policy goals, hoping to make his mark on history by applying his broad understanding of international relations to a changing world. Diverging from Republican orthodoxy, he made dramatic overtures to the Soviet Union and China. Yet anticommunism remained central to U.S. policy. In Latin America, Africa, and the Middle East, Nixon backed repressive regimes when the alternatives suggested victories for the left. Relying on public deception, secrecy, and silencing of opponents even more than his predecessor, Nixon aggressively pursued the war in Vietnam, expanding the conflict into Cambodia and Laos and ferociously bombing North Vietnam. Yet in the end, he was forced to settle for peace without victory.

Moving toward Détente with the Soviet Union and China In Nixon's view, the "rigid and bipolar world of the 1940s and 1950s" was giving way to "the fluidity of a new era of multilateral diplomacy." Well aware of the increasing conflict between the Soviet Union and China, he worked with National Security Adviser **Henry A. Kissinger**, his key foreign policy adviser, to exploit the situation. This Soviet-Chinese hostility, according to Nixon, "served our purpose best if we maintained closer relations with each side than they did with each other." In addition, these two nations might be used to help the United States extricate itself from Vietnam.

Following two years of secret negotiations, in February 1972 Nixon became the nation's first president to set foot on Chinese soil—an astonishing act by a man whose career had rested on fervent anticommunism. In fact, his anti-Communist credentials enabled him to conduct this shift in U.S.-Chinese relations with no significant domestic repercussions. Although his visit was largely symbolic, cultural and scientific exchanges followed, and American manufacturers began to find markets in China—small steps in the process of globalization that would take giant strides in the 1990s (see chapter 31).

As Nixon and Kissinger had hoped, the warming of U.S.-Chinese relations furthered their strategy of **détente**, their term for easing conflict with the Soviet Union. Détente did not mean abandoning containment but instead focusing on issues of common concern, such as arms control and trade. Containment would be achieved not only by military threat but also by ensuring that the Soviets and Chinese had stakes in a stable international order. Nixon's goal was "a stronger healthy United States, Europe, Soviet Union, China, Japan, each balancing the other."

Arms control, trade, and stability in Europe were three areas where the United States and the Soviet Union had common interests. In May 1972, Nixon visited Moscow, signing several agreements on trade and cooperation in science and space. Most significantly, Soviet and U.S. leaders concluded arms limitation treaties that had grown out of the **Strategic Arms Limitation Talks (SALT)** begun in 1969, agreeing to limit antiballistic missiles (ABMs) to two each. Giving up pursuit of a defense against nuclear weapons was a crucial move, because it prevented either nation from building so secure an ABM defense against a nuclear attack that it would risk a first strike.

Although the policy of détente made little progress after 1974, U.S., Soviet, and European leaders signed a historic agreement in 1975 in Helsinki, Finland, that formally recognized the post–World War II boundaries in Europe. The **Helsinki accords** were controversial because they acknowledged Soviet domination over Eastern Europe—a condition that had triggered the Cold War thirty years earlier. Yet, they also contained a clause committing the

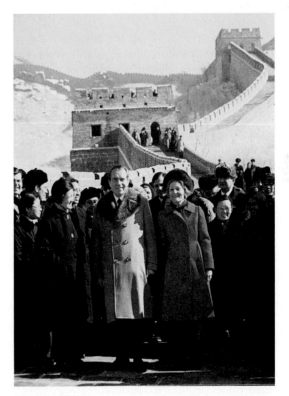

Nixon in China "This was the week that changed the world," proclaimed President Nixon in February 1972, emphasizing the stunning turnaround in relations with America's former enemy, the People's Republic of China. Nixon's trip was meticulously planned to dramatize the event on television and, aside from criticism from some conservatives, won overwhelming support from Americans. The Great Wall of China forms the setting for this photograph of Nixon and his wife, Pat. Nixon Presidential Materials Project, National Archives and Record Administration.

signing countries to recognize "the universal significance of human rights and fundamental freedoms." Dissidents in the Soviet Union and its Eastern European satellites used this official promise of rights to challenge the Soviet dictatorship and help force its overthrow fifteen years later.

Shoring Up Anticommunism in the Third World

Nixon promised in 1973 that "The time has passed when America will make every other nation's conflict our own . . . or presume to tell the people of other nations how to manage their own affairs." Yet in Vietnam and elsewhere, Nixon and Kissinger continued to view left-wing movements as threats to U.S. interests and actively resisted social revolutions that might lead to communism.

Consequently, the Nixon administration helped to overthrow Salvador Allende, a self-proclaimed Marxist who was elected president of Chile in 1970. Since 1964, the Central Intelligence Agency (CIA) and U.S. corporations concerned about nationalization of their Chilean properties had assisted Allende's opponents. After Allende became president, Nixon ordered the CIA director to destabilize his government by making the Chilean economy "scream." In 1973, the CIA helped the Chilean military engineer a coup, killing Allende and establishing a brutal dictatorship under General Augusto Pinochet. Representative government did not return until 1990.

In other parts of the world, too, the Nixon administration stood by repressive regimes. In southern Africa, it eased pressures on white minority governments that tyrannized blacks. In the Middle East, the United States sent massive arms shipments to support the shah of Iran's harsh regime because Iran had enormous petroleum reserves and seemed a stable anti-Communist ally. Unnoticed by most Americans, the administration cemented a relationship that turned many Iranians against the United States and would ignite a new crisis when the

Chile

shah was overthrown in 1979 (see chapter 30).

Like his predecessors, Nixon pursued a delicate balance between defending Israel's security and seeking the goodwill of Arab nations strategically and economically important to the United States. Conflict between Israel and the Arab nations had escalated into the **Six-Day War** in 1967, when Israel attacked Egypt after that nation had massed troops on its border and cut off the sea passage to Israel's southern port. Although Syria and Jordan joined the war on Egypt's side, Israel won a stunning victory, seizing territory that amounted to twice its original size. Israeli forces took control of the Sinai Peninsula and the Gaza Strip from Egypt, the Golan Heights from Syria, and the West Bank (which included the Arab sector of Jerusalem, a city sacred to Jews, Christians, and Muslims alike) from Jordan.

That decisive victory did not quell Middle Eastern turmoil. In October 1973, on the Jewish holiday Yom Kippur, Egypt and Syria surprised Israel with a full-scale attack. When the Nixon administration sided with Israel in the **Yom Kippur War**, Arab nations retaliated with an oil embargo that created severe shortages in the United States. After Israel repulsed the attack, Kissinger attempted to mediate between Israel and the Arab nations, but with very limited success. The Arab countries refused to recognize Israel's right to exist, Israel began to settle its citizens in territories occupied during the Six-Day War, and no solution could be found for the Palestinian refugees who had been displaced by the creation of Israel in the late 1940s. The simmering conflict contributed to anti-American sentiment among Arabs who viewed the United States as Israel's supporter.

Israeli Territorial Gains in the Six-Day War, 1967

Vietnam Becomes Nixon's War

"I'm not going to end up like LBJ, holed up in the White House afraid to show my face on the street," the new president asserted. "I'm going to stop that war. Fast." Nixon gradually withdrew U.S. ground troops, but he was no more willing than Eisenhower, Kennedy, or Johnson to be the president who allowed South Vietnam to fall to the Communists. That goal was tied to the larger objective of maintaining American credibility. Regardless of the wisdom of the initial intervention, Kissinger asserted, "the commitment of 500,000 Americans has settled the importance of Vietnam. For what is involved now is confidence in American promises."

From 1969 to 1972, Nixon and Kissinger pursued a four-pronged approach. First, they tried to strengthen the South Vietnamese military and government. Second, to disarm the antiwar movement at home, Nixon gradually replaced U.S. forces with South Vietnamese soldiers and American technology and bombs. Third, the United States negotiated with both North Vietnam and the Soviet Union. Fourth, the military applied intensive bombing to persuade Hanoi to accept American terms at the bargaining table.

As part of the Vietnamization of the war, ARVN forces grew to more than a million, and the South Vietnamese air force became the fourth largest in the world. The United States also promoted land reform, village elections, and the building of schools, hospitals, and transportation facilities. Meanwhile, U.S. forces withdrew, decreasing from 543,000 in 1968 to 140,000 by the end of 1971, a move that critics called merely "changing the color of the corpses." Even with the reduction of U.S. forces, however, more than 20,000 Americans perished in Vietnam between 1969 and 1973.

In the spring of 1969, Nixon began a ferocious air war in Cambodia, carefully hiding it from Congress and the public for more than a year. Seeking to knock out North Vietnamese sanctuaries in Cambodia, Americans dropped more than 100,000 tons of bombs but succeeded only in sending the North Vietnamese to other hiding places. Echoing Johnson, Kissinger believed that a "fourth-rate power like North Vietnam" had to have a "breaking point," but the massive bombing failed to find it. (See "Historical Question," page 732.)

To support a new, pro-Western Cambodian government installed through a military coup in 1970 and "to show the enemy that we were still serious about our commitment in Vietnam," Nixon ordered a joint U.S.-ARVN invasion of Cambodia in April 1970. That order made Vietnam

Pro-War Demonstrators Advocates as well as opponents of the war in Vietnam took to the streets, as these New Yorkers did in support of the U.S. invasion of Cambodia in May 1970. Construction workers — called "hard hats" — and other union members marched with American flags and posters championing President Nixon's policies and blasting New York mayor John Lindsay for his antiwar position. Following the demonstration, sympathetic union leaders presented Nixon with an honorary hard hat. Paul Fusco/Magnum Photos, Inc.

FOR MORE HELP ANALYZING THIS IMAGE, see the visual activity for this chapter in the Online Study Guide at **bedfordstmartins.com/roarkcompact**.

U.S. Invasion of Cambodia, 1970

"Nixon's war" and provoked outrage at home. Nixon made a belligerent speech defending his move and emphasizing the importance of U.S. credibility: "If when the chips are down, the world's most powerful nation acts like a pitiful helpless giant, the forces of totalitarianism and anarchy will threaten free nations" everywhere. Upon reading a draft of the speech, a cabinet member predicted, "This will make the students puke."

They did more. In response, more than 100,000 people protested in Washington, D.C., and students boycotted classes on hundreds of campuses. At **Kent State University** in Ohio, National Guard troops were dispatched after protesting students burned an old ROTC building. Then, at a rally there on May 4, when some students threw rocks at the troops, they fired at the students, killing four and wounding ten others. "They're starting to treat their own children like they treat us," commented a black woman in Harlem. In a confrontation at **Jackson State College**

Students Killed at Kent State On May 4, 1970, John Filo, a photojournalism student at Kent State University in Ohio, decided to take pictures of students demonstrating against President Nixon's recently announced decision to invade Cambodia. He observed several hundred protesters, some of whom threw rocks at National Guardsmen, who in turn sprayed tear gas toward the students. Suddenly, some guardsmen opened fire, killing four students and wounding ten. Filo took this photograph of fourteen-year-old runaway Mary Ann Vecchio sobbing over the dead body of Kent State student Jeffrey Miller. He sent his photographs to the Associated Press; this one was published around the world and won Filo a Pulitzer Prize. John Filo.

FOR MORE HELP ANALYZING THIS IMAGE, see the visual activity for this chapter in the Online Study Guide at **bedfordstmartins.com/ roarkcompact**.

in Mississippi on May 14, police shot into a dormitory, killing two black students. And in August, police in Los Angeles used tear gas and clubs against Chicano antiwar protesters.

Congressional reaction to the invasion of Cambodia revealed increasing concern about abuses of presidential power. In the name of national security, presidents since Franklin Roosevelt had conducted foreign policy without the consent or sometimes even the knowledge of Congress — for example, Eisenhower in Iran and Johnson in the Dominican Republic. But in their determination to win the war in Vietnam, Johnson and Nixon had taken extreme measures to deceive the public and silence their critics. The bombing and invasion of Cambodia infuriated enough legislators that the Senate voted to terminate the Gulf of Tonkin Resolution, which had given the president virtually a blank check in Vietnam, and to cut off funds for the Cambodian operation. The House refused to go along, but by the end of June, Nixon had pulled all U.S. troops out of Cambodia.

The Cambodian invasion failed to break the will of North Vietnam, but it set in motion a terrible tragedy for the Cambodian people. The North Vietnamese moved farther into Cambodia and strengthened the Khmer Rouge, Communist insurgents attempting to overthrow the U.S.-supported government of Lon Nol. A brutal civil war raged

until 1975, when the Khmer Rouge triumphed and imposed a savage rule, slaughtering millions of Cambodians and giving the name "killing fields" to the land of a historically peaceful people.

In 1971, Vietnam veterans became a visible part of the peace movement, the first men in U.S. history to protest a war in which they had fought. Veterans held a public investigation of "war crimes" in Vietnam, rallied in front of the Capitol, and cast away their war medals. In May 1971, veterans numbered among the 40,000 protesters who engaged in civil disobedience in an effort to shut down Washington. Officials made more than 12,000 arrests, which courts later ruled violations of protesters' rights.

After the spring of 1971, there were fewer massive antiwar demonstrations, but protest continued. Public attention focused on the court martial of Lieutenant William Calley, which began in November 1970. During the trial, Americans learned that in March 1968, Calley's company had systematically killed every inhabitant of the hamlet of **My Lai**, even though they had encountered no enemy forces there. These four hundred villagers were nearly all old men, women, and children. The military covered up the atrocity for more than a year before a journalist exposed it. Eventually, twelve officers and enlisted men were charged with murder or assault to commit murder, but only Calley was convicted.

Administration policy suffered another blow in June 1971 when the *New York Times* published the **Pentagon Papers**, secret government documents consisting mostly of an internal study of the war begun in 1967. Even though the study did not cover the Nixon administration, government lawyers went to court to stop further publication, in part out of fear that other information would be leaked. The Supreme Court, however, ruled that the attempt to stop publication was a "flagrant, indefensible" violation of the First Amendment. Subsequent circulation of the *Pentagon Papers*, which revealed considerable pessimism among officials even as they made rosy promises, heightened disillusionment with the war by casting doubts on the government's credibility. More than 60 percent of Americans polled in 1971 considered it a mistake to have sent American troops to Vietnam; 58 percent believed the war to be immoral.

Military morale sank in the last years of the war. Having been exposed to the antiwar movement at home, many of the remaining soldiers had less faith in the war than their predecessors had had. Racial tensions among soldiers mounted, many soldiers sought escape in illegal drugs, and enlisted men committed hundreds of "fraggings," attacks on officers. In a 1971 report, "The Collapse of the Armed Forces," a retired Marine Corps colonel described the lack of discipline: "Our army that now remains in Vietnam [is] near mutinous."

The Peace Accords and the Legacy of Defeat Nixon and Kissinger continued to believe that intensive firepower could bring the North Vietnamese to their knees. In March 1972, responding to a strong North Vietnamese offensive, the United States resumed sustained bombing of the North, mined Haiphong and other harbors for the first time, and announced a naval blockade. With peace talks stalled, in December Nixon ordered the most devastating bombing of North Vietnam yet.

The intense bombing, called "jugular diplomacy" by Kissinger, was costly to both sides, but it brought renewed negotiations. On January 27, 1973, representatives of the United States, North Vietnam, South Vietnam, and the Vietcong (now called the People's Revolutionary Government) signed a formal peace accord in Paris. The agreement required removal of all U.S. troops and military advisers but allowed North Vietnamese forces to remain. Both sides agreed to return prisoners of war. Nixon called the agreement "peace with honor," but in fact it allowed only a face-saving withdrawal for the United States.

Fighting resumed immediately among the Vietnamese. Nixon's efforts to support the South Vietnamese government, and indeed his ability to

govern at all, were increasingly eroded by what came to be known as the Watergate scandal (see chapter 30). Nixon had been forced to give up his office by 1975, when North Vietnam launched a new offensive. On April 30, it occupied Saigon and renamed it Ho Chi Minh City to honor the Communist leader. The Americans hastily evacuated, along with 150,000 of their South Vietnamese allies.

Confusion, humiliation, and tragedy marked the rushed departure. The United States lacked sufficient transportation capabilities and time to evacuate all the South Vietnamese who had supported the South Vietnamese government and were desperate to leave. Former lieutenant Philip Caputo, who had returned to South Vietnam as a journalist, reported that his departing helicopter "took some ground fire from

Evacuating South Vietnam As Communist troops rolled south toward Saigon in the spring of 1975, desperate South Vietnamese attempted to flee along with the departing Americans. These South Vietnamese, carrying little or nothing, attempt to scale the wall of the U.S. Embassy to reach evacuation helicopters. Thousands of Vietnamese who wanted to be evacuated were left behind. Even though space for evacuees was desperately limited, South Vietnamese president Nguyen Van Thieu fled to Taiwan on a U.S. plane, taking with him fifteen tons of baggage. AP Images.

South Vietnamese soldiers who probably felt that the Americans had betrayed them."

During the four years it took Nixon to end the war, he had expanded the conflict into Cambodia and Laos and had launched massive bombing campaigns. Although increasing numbers of legislators criticized the war, Congress never denied the president the funds to fight it. Only after the peace accords did the legislative branch stiffen its constitutional authority in the making of war, passing the War Powers Act in November 1973. The law required the president to report to Congress within forty-eight hours of deploying military forces abroad. If Congress failed to endorse the president's action within sixty days, the troops would have to be withdrawn. The new law, however, did little to dispel the distrust of and disillusionment with the government that resulted from Americans' realization that their leaders had not told the truth about Vietnam.

The disorder that had accompanied antiwar protests and bitter divisions among Americans were other legacies of the war. Vietnam diverted money from domestic programs and sounded the death knell of Johnson's Great Society. It created federal budget deficits and triggered inflation that contributed to ongoing economic crises throughout the 1970s (see chapter 30).

Four presidents had declared that the survival of South Vietnam was essential for U.S. containment policy, but their dire predictions that a Communist victory in South Vietnam would set the dominoes cascading did not materialize. Although Vietnam, Laos, and Cambodia all fell within the Communist camp in the spring of 1975, Thailand, Burma, Malaysia, and the rest of Southeast Asia did not. When China and Vietnam reverted to their historically hostile relationship, the myth of a monolithic Communist power overrunning Asia evaporated.

The long pursuit of victory in Vietnam complicated the United States' relations with other nations, as even its staunchest ally, Britain, doubted the wisdom of the war. The spectacle of terrifying American power used against a small Asian country alienated many in the third world and compromised efforts to win the hearts and minds of people in developing nations through initiatives such as the Peace Corps and the Alliance for Progress.

The cruelest legacy of Vietnam fell on those who had served. "We would not return to cheering crowds, parades, and the pealing of great cathedral bells," wrote Philip Caputo. The failure of the United States to win the war, its unpopularity at home, and its character as a guerrilla war denied veterans the traditional soldiers' homecoming. Veterans themselves expressed different reactions to the defeat. Many believed in the war's purposes and felt betrayed by the government for not letting them win it. Other veterans blamed the government for sacrificing the nation's youth in an immoral, unnecessary, or useless war, expressing their sense of the war's futility by referring to their dead comrades as having been "wasted." Some veterans belonging to minority groups had more reason to doubt the nobility of their purpose. A Native American soldier assigned to resettle Vietnamese civilians found it to be "just like when they moved us to the rez [reservation]. We shouldn't have done that."

Because the Vietnam War was a civil war involving guerrilla tactics, combat was especially brutal (Table 29.1). The terrors of conventional warfare were multiplied, and so were the motivations to commit atrocities. The massacre in March 1968 at My Lai of over four hundred villagers by the men of Charlie Company was only the most widely publicized war crime. To demonstrate the immorality of the war, peace advocates stressed the atrocities, contributing to a distorted image of the Vietnam veteran as dehumanized and violent.

Most veterans came home to public neglect; some faced harassment from antiwar activists who failed to distinguish the war from the warriors. A veteran remembered the "feelings of rejection and scorn that a bunch of depressed and confused young men experienced when they returned home from doing what their country told them to do." Government benefits were less generous to Vietnam veterans than they had been to those of the past two wars. Yet two-thirds of Vietnam veterans said that they would serve again, and most veterans readjusted well to civilian life.

> The cruelest legacy of Vietnam fell on those who had served. "We would not return to cheering crowds, parades, and the pealing of great cathedral bells," wrote Philip Caputo.

★ TABLE 29.1 Vietnam War Casualties

United States	
Battle deaths	47,434
Other deaths	10,786
Wounded	153,303
South Vietnam	
Killed in action	110,357
Military wounded	499,026
Civilians killed	415,000
Civilians wounded	913,000
Communist Regulars and Guerrillas	
Killed in action	66,000

Source: U.S. Department of Defense.

Nonetheless, some suffered long after the war ended. The Veterans Administration (VA) estimated that nearly one-sixth of the veterans suffered from post-traumatic stress disorder, with its symptoms of recurring nightmares, feelings of guilt and shame, violence, drug and alcohol abuse, and suicidal tendencies. Thirty years after performing army intelligence work in Saigon, Doris Allen "still hit the floor sometimes when [she heard] loud bangs." Many of those who had served in Vietnam began to produce deformed children and fell ill themselves with cancer, severe skin disorders, and other ailments. Veterans claimed a link between those illnesses and Agent Orange, a herbicide that contained the deadly poison dioxin, which the military had sprayed over Vietnam. Not until 1991 did Congress provide assistance to veterans with diseases linked to the poison.

By then, the climate had changed. The war began to enter the realm of popular culture, with novels, TV shows, and hit movies depicting a broad range of military experience—from soldiers reduced to brutality to men and women serving with courage and integrity. The incorporation of the Vietnam War into the collective experience was symbolized most dramatically in the Vietnam Veterans Memorial unveiled in Washington, D.C., in November 1982. Designed by Yale architecture student Maya Lin, the black, V-shaped wall inscribed with the names of 58,200 men and women lost in the war became one of the most popular sites in the nation's capital. In an article describing the memorial's dedication, a Vietnam combat veteran spoke to and for his former comrades: "Welcome home. The war is over."

Q: How did Nixon try to bring American involvement in Vietnam to a close?

Conclusion: An Unwinnable War

Vietnam was America's longest war. The United States spent more than $150 billion (nearly $600 billion in 2007 dollars) and sent 2.6 million young men and women to Vietnam. Of those, 58,200 never returned, and 150,000 suffered serious injury. The war shattered consensus at home, increased presidential power at the expense of congressional authority and public accountability, weakened the economy, and contributed to the downfall of two presidents.

Even as Nixon and Kissinger took steps to ease Cold War tensions with the major Communist powers—the Soviet Union and China,

which were also the main suppliers of the North Vietnamese—they also acted vigorously throughout the third world to install or prop up anti-Communist governments. They embraced their predecessors' commitment to South Vietnam as a necessary Cold War engagement: To do otherwise would threaten American credibility and make the United States appear weak. Defeat in Vietnam did not make the United States the "pitiful helpless giant" predicted by Nixon, but it did mark a relative decline of U.S. power and the impossibility of containment on a global scale.

One of the constraints on U.S. power was the tenacity of revolutionary movements determined to achieve national independence. Marine lieutenant Philip Caputo was surprised to discover "that the men we had scorned as peasant guerrillas were, in fact, a lethal, determined enemy." Overestimating the effectiveness of American technological superiority, U.S. officials badly underestimated the sacrifices that the enemy was willing to make and failed to realize how easily the United States could be perceived as a colonial intruder.

A second constraint on Eisenhower, Kennedy, Johnson, and Nixon was their resolve to avoid a major confrontation with the Soviet Union or China. For Johnson, who conducted the largest escalation of the war, caution was especially critical so as not to provoke direct intervention by the Communist superpowers. After China exploded its first atomic bomb in 1964, the potential heightened for the Vietnam conflict to escalate into worldwide disaster.

Third, in Vietnam the United States sought to prop up an extremely weak ally engaged in a civil war. The South Vietnamese government failed to win the support of its people, and the intense devastation the war brought to civilians only made things worse. Short of taking over the South Vietnamese government and military, the United States could do little to strengthen South Vietnam's ability to resist communism.

Finally, domestic opposition to the war, which by 1968 had spread to mainstream America, constrained the options of Johnson and Nixon. As the war dragged on, with increasing American casualties and growing evidence of the damage being inflicted on innocent Vietnamese, more and more civilians wearied of the conflict. Even some who had fought in the war joined the movement, including Philip Caputo, who sent his military ribbons and a bitter letter of protest to the White House. In 1973, Nixon and Kissinger bowed to the resolution of the enemy and the limitations of U.S. power. As the war wound down, passions surrounding it contributed to a rising conservative movement that would substantially alter the post–World War II political order.

Reviewing the Chapter

★ KEY TERMS

Explain each term's significance

WHO

John F. Kennedy (p. 724)

Lyndon B. Johnson (p. 729)

Hubert H. Humphrey (p. 736)

George C. Wallace (p. 736)

Richard M. Nixon (p. 737)

Henry A. Kissinger (p. 737)

WHAT

Cuban missile crisis (p. 725)

Bay of Pigs (p. 725)

Berlin Wall (p. 726)

Peace Corps (p. 726)

intercontinental ballistic missiles (ICBMs) (p. 727)

Ho Chi Minh Trail (p. 728)

Agent Orange (p. 729)

Gulf of Tonkin Resolution (p. 730)

Operation Rolling Thunder (p. 730)

Tet Offensive (p. 735)

détente (p. 737)

Strategic Arms Limitation Talks (SALT) (p. 737)

Helsinki accords (p. 737)

Six-Day War (p. 738)

Yom Kippur War (p. 738)

Kent State University and Jackson State College (p. 739)

My Lai (p. 740)

***Pentagon Papers* (p. 741)**

★ REVIEW QUESTIONS **Q:**

Use key terms and dates to support your answer

1. Why did Kennedy believe that engagement in Vietnam was crucial to his foreign policy? (pp. 724–29)

2. How did American troops serving in Vietnam differ from those who served in World War II, and how were their experiences different? (pp. 729–34)

3. How did the Vietnam War shape the election of 1968? (pp. 734–36)

4. How did Nixon try to bring American involvement in Vietnam to a close? (pp. 737–43)

★ MAKING CONNECTIONS

Draw on key terms, timeline, and review questions

1. Cuba featured prominently in the most dramatic foreign policy actions of the Kennedy administration. Citing specific events, discuss why Cuba was an area of great concern to the administration. How did Cuba figure into Kennedy's Cold War policies? Were his actions in regard to Cuba effective?

2. Explain the Gulf of Tonkin incident and its significance to American foreign policy. How did President Lyndon Johnson respond to the incident? What considerations, domestic and international, contributed to his course of action?

3. The United States' engagement in Vietnam divided the nation. Discuss the range of American responses to the war. How did they change over time? How did domestic political concerns shape the country's response to the war? How did the war shape domestic politics in the 1960s and early 1970s?

4. What was détente, and how did it affect the United States' Cold War foreign policy? What were its achievements and limitations? In your answer, discuss how Nixon's approach to communism built on and departed from the approaches of the previous two administrations.

FOR PRACTICE QUIZZES AND OTHER STUDY TOOLS, see the Online Study Guide at **bedfordstmartins.com/roarkcompact**.

★ SUGGESTED READINGS

Philip Caputo, *A Rumor of War* (1977). A gripping narrative by an infantry officer who served in Vietnam in 1965 and 1966.

Charles DeBenedetti, with Charles Chatfield, *An American Ordeal: The Antiwar Movement in the Vietnam Era* (1990). A comprehensive account of antiwar protest.

Michael Dobbs, *One Minute to Midnight: Kennedy, Khrushchev, and Castro on the Brink of Nuclear War* (2008). A dramatic account of the Cuban missile crisis.

Elizabeth Cobbs Hoffman, *All You Need Is Love: The Peace Corps and the Spirit of the 1960s* (1998). An engaging history of the policy behind the Peace Corps, its impact, and the volunteers' experiences.

A. J. Langguth, *Our Vietnam/Nuoc Viet Ta: A History of the War, 1954–1975* (2000). A compelling narrative of the entire war by a former journalist.

Jeremi Suri, *Power and Protest: Global Revolution and the Rise of Détente* (2003). A history of the global protest movements of 1968 and their impact on policy.

FOR MORE BOOKS ABOUT TOPICS IN THIS CHAPTER, see the Online Bibliography at **bedfordstmartins.com/roarkcompact**.

FOR ADDITIONAL FIRSTHAND ACCOUNTS OF THIS PERIOD, see Chapter 29 in Michael Johnson, ed., *Reading the American Past*, Fourth Edition.

FOR WEB SITES, IMAGES, AND DOCUMENTS RELATED TO TOPICS AND PLACES IN THIS CHAPTER, visit Make History at **bedfordstmartins.com/roarkcompact**.

★ TIMELINE

1961
- Bay of Pigs invasion.
- Berlin Wall erected.
- Kennedy administration increases military aid to South Vietnam.
- Alliance for Progress established.
- Peace Corps created.

1962
- Cuban missile crisis.

1963
- Limited nuclear test ban treaty signed.
- President Kennedy assassinated; Lyndon B. Johnson becomes president.

1964
- Anti-American rioting in Panama Canal Zone.
- Gulf of Tonkin Resolution.

1965
- First major demonstration against Vietnam War.
- Operation Rolling Thunder begins.
- Johnson orders first combat troops to Vietnam.
- U.S. troops invade Dominican Republic.

1967
- Arab-Israeli Six-Day War.

1968
- Demonstrations against Vietnam War increase.
- Tet Offensive.
- Johnson decides not to seek second term.
- Police and protesters clash near Democratic convention in Chicago.
- Republican Richard Nixon elected president.

1969
- American astronauts land on moon.
- Nixon orders secret bombing of Cambodia.

1970
- Nixon orders invasion of Cambodia.
- Students killed during protests at Kent State and Jackson State.

1971
- *New York Times* publishes *Pentagon Papers*.

1972
- Nixon becomes first U.S. president to visit China.
- Nixon visits Moscow to sign arms limitation treaties with Soviets.

1973
- Paris Peace Accords.
- War Powers Act.
- CIA-backed military coup in Chile.
- Arab oil embargo following Yom Kippur War.

1975
- North Vietnam takes over South Vietnam, ending the war.
- Helsinki accords.

MAKING AMERICA "REAGAN COUNTRY" This delegate badge from the 1980 Republican National Convention played on themes that would characterize Ronald Reagan's presidential campaigns and the politics and policies of the 1980s. Just as the badge appealed to patriotic sentiments with the flag, the Statue of Liberty, and the space program, Reagan encouraged Americans to take pride in their nation and celebrate its achievements instead of focusing on its shortcomings. His image as a cowboy brought to mind some of the movies he had acted in and his favorite recreation — working on his ranch in California — as well as the independence and rugged individualism of the West, where he had made his home since the 1940s. The West housed key elements in the surge of conservatism that ensured Reagan's victory in 1980, shaped his administration's antigovernment, anti-Communist agenda, and helped reverse the liberal direction that national politics had taken in the 1960s. National Museum of American History, Smithsonian Institution, Behring Center.

America Moves to the Right

1969–1989

PHYLLIS SCHLAFLY called it "one of the most exciting days of my life" when she heard conservative Republican Barry Goldwater address the National Federation of Republican Women in 1963. Like Goldwater, **Phyllis Schlafly** opposed the moderate stance of the Eisenhower administration and current Republican leadership. Both Schlafly and Goldwater wanted the United States to go beyond merely containing communism and to eliminate that threat entirely. They also wanted to cut back the federal government, especially its role in providing social welfare and enforcing civil rights. Goldwater's loss to Lyndon Johnson in 1964 did not diminish Schlafly's conservative commitment. She assailed the policy innovations and turmoil of the 1960s, adding new issues to the conservative agenda and helping to build a grassroots movement that would redefine the Republican Party and American politics into the twenty-first century.

Phyllis Stewart was born in St. Louis in 1924, attended Catholic schools, and worked her way through Washington University testing ammunition at a World War II defense plant. She earned an M.A. in government from Radcliffe College in 1945 and went to work at the American Enterprise Institute, where she imbibed the think tank's conservatism. Returning to the Midwest, she married Fred Schlafly, an Alton, Illinois, attorney whose anticommunism and antigovernment passions equaled hers. The mother of six children, Schlafly claimed, "I don't think there's anything as much fun as taking care of a baby," and she asserted that she would "rather scrub bathroom floors" than write political articles.

Yet while insisting that caring for home and family was women's most important career, Schlafly spent much of her time on the road—writing, speaking, leading Republican women's organizations, and testifying before legislative committees. She lost two bids for Congress in her heavily Democratic district in Illinois, in 1952 and again in 1970. Her book, *A Choice Not an Echo*, pushed Barry Goldwater for president and sold more than a million copies. In 1967, she began publishing *The Phyllis Schlafly Report*, a monthly newsletter about current political issues. Throughout the 1950s and 1960s, Schlafly called for stronger efforts to combat communism at home and abroad, a more powerful military, and a less active government in domestic affairs—all traditional conservative goals.

The Phyllis Schlafly Report

VOL. 5, NO. 10, SECTION 2 　 Box 618, ALTON, ILLINOIS 62002 　 MAY, 1972

The Fraud Called The Equal Rights Amendment

If there ever was an example of how a tiny minority can cram its views down the throats of the majority, it is the Equal Rights Amendment, called ERA. A noisy ciaque of women's lib agitators rammed ERA through Congress, intimidating the men into voting for it so they would not be labeled "anti-woman."

The ERA passed Congress with big majorities on March 22, 1972 and was sent to the states for ratification. When it is ratified by 38 states, it will become the law of the land. Within two hours of Senate passage, Hawaii ratified it. New Hampshire and Nebraska, both anxious to be second, rushed their approval the next day. Then in steady succession came Iowa, Idaho, Delaware, Kansas, Texas, Maryland, Tennessee, Alaska, Rhode Island, and New Jersey. As this goes to press, 13 states have ratified it and others are on the verge of doing so.

Three states have rejected it: Oklahoma, Vermont and Connecticut.

What is ERA? The Amendment reads: "Equality of rights under the law shall not be denied or abridged by the United States or by any state on account of sex."

Does that sound good? Don't kid yourself. This innocuous-sounding amendment will take away far more important rights than it will ever give. This was made abundantly clear by the debate in Congress. Senator Sam Ervin (D., N.C.) called it "the most drastic measure in Senate history." He proved this by putting into the *Congressional Record* an article from the *Yale Law Journal* of April 1971.

The importance of this *Yale Law Journal* article is that both the proponents and the opponents of ERA agree that it is an accurate analysis of the consequences of ERA. Congresswoman Martha Griffiths, a leading proponent of ERA, sent a copy of this article to every member of Congress, stating that "It will understand the purposes and effe Rights Amendment.... The artic ERA will work in

the most important of all women's rights.

"In all states husbands are primarily liable for the support of their wives and children.... The child support sections of the criminal nonsupport laws ... could not be sustained where only the male is liable for support." (YLJ, pp. 944-945)

"The Equal Rights Amendment would bar a state from imposing greater liability for support on a husband than on a wife merely because of his sex." (YLJ, p. 945)

"Like the duty of support during marriage and the obligation to pay alimony in the case of separation or divorce, nonsupport would have to be eliminated as a ground for divorce against husbands only...." (YLJ, p. 951)

"The Equal Rights Amendment would not require that alimony be abolished but only that it be available equally to husbands and wives." (YLJ, p. 952)

2. ERA will wipe out the laws which protect only women against sex crimes such as rape.

"Courts faced with criminal laws which do not apply equally to men and women would be likely to invalidate the laws rather than extending or rewriting them to apply to women and men alike." (YLJ, p. 966)

"Seduction laws, statutory rape laws, laws prohibiting obscene language in the presence of women, prostitution and 'manifest danger' laws ... The Equal Rights Amendment would not permit such laws, which base their sex discriminatory classification on social stereotypes." (YLJ, p. 954)

"The statutory rape laws, which punish men for having sexual intercourse with any wom under an age specified by law ... suffer from fect under the Equal Rights Amendmen

"To ngling out

The Phyllis Schlafly Report Phyllis Schlafly began her monthly newsletter for members of her conservative Eagle Forum in 1967 with articles attacking federal social programs and calling for stronger measures and weapons to fight communism. When Congress passed the Equal Rights Amendment in 1972, the *Report* began to add antifeminism and other concerns of the New Right to its agenda, including opposition to abortion rights, to sex education in the schools, and to protections for gays and lesbians. Schlafly's attacks on feminism appealed to many people; subscribers to her newsletter numbered more than 35,000 in the mid-1970s. Feminist leader Betty Friedan told Schlafly, "I consider you a traitor to your sex. I consider you an Aunt Tom." Courtesy of Phyllis Schlafly.

In the 1970s, Schlafly began to address new issues, including feminism and the Equal Rights Amendment, abortion, gay rights, busing for racial integration, and religion in the schools. Her positions resonated with many Americans who were fed up with the expansion of government, the protest movements, the challenges to authority, and the loosening of moral standards that seemed to define the 1960s. The votes of those Americans began to reshape American politics — in Richard Nixon's victories in 1968 and 1972; in the presidency of Jimmy Carter, whose policies stood substantially to the right of his Democratic predecessors; and in conservative Ronald Reagan's capture of the Republican Party, the presidency, and the political agenda in 1980.

Although Richard Nixon did not embrace the entire conservative agenda, he sought to make the Republicans the dominant party by appealing to disaffected blue-collar and southern white Democrats. The Watergate revelations forced Nixon to leave the presidency in 1974, and his Republican successor, Gerald Ford, occupied the Oval Office for little more than two years, but the shift of the political spectrum to the right continued even when Democrat Jimmy Carter captured the White House in 1976.

Antigovernment sentiment grew out of the deceptions of the Johnson administration, Nixon's abuse of presidential powers, and the inability of Presidents Ford and Carter to resolve domestic and foreign crises. As Americans saw their incomes shrink from an unprecedented combination of unemployment and inflation — called stagflation — their confidence in government and willingness to pay taxes eroded.

In 1980, Phyllis Schlafly's call for "a choice not an echo" was realized when Ronald Reagan won the presidency. Cutting taxes and government regulations, attacking social programs, expanding the nation's military capacity, and pressuring the Soviet Union and communism in the third world, Reagan addressed the hopes of traditional conservatives. Like Schlafly, he also championed the concerns of the New Right, opposing abortion and sexual permissiveness and supporting a larger role for religion in public life.

Reagan's goals encountered resistance from feminists, civil rights groups, environmentalists, and others who fought to keep what they had won in the 1960s and 1970s. Although Reagan failed to enact the entire conservative agenda, enormously increased the national debt, and engaged in illegal activities to thwart communism in Latin America, his popularity helped send his vice president, George H. W. Bush, to the White House at the end of his second term. And Reagan's determined optimism and spirited leadership contributed to a revival in national pride and confidence.　★

Nixon and the Rise of Postwar Conservatism

As we saw in chapter 28, Nixon acquiesced in the continuation of most Great Society programs and even approved pathbreaking environmental and minority and women's rights measures. Yet his public rhetoric and some of his actions signaled the country's rightward move in both politics and sentiment. Whereas Kennedy had appealed to Americans to contribute to the common good, Nixon invited Americans to "let each of us ask—not just what will government do for me, but what can I do for myself?" His words invoked individualism and reliance on the market and private enterprise rather than on government, preferences that would grow stronger in the nation during the 1970s and beyond.

During Nixon's presidency, a new strand of conservatism joined the older movement that focused on anticommunism, a strong national defense, and a limited federal role in domestic affairs. New conservatives, whom Phyllis Schlafly helped mobilize, wanted to restore what they considered traditional moral values by increasing the presence of Christianity in public life and opposing sex education, feminism, abortion, homosexuality, and sexual permissiveness.

Emergence of a Grassroots Movement

Hidden beneath Lyndon Johnson's landslide victory over Barry Goldwater in 1964 lay a rising conservative movement. Defining his purpose as "enlarging freedom at home and safeguarding it from the forces of tyranny abroad," Arizona senator Goldwater echoed the ideas of conservative intellectuals who argued that government intrusions into economic life hindered prosperity, stifled personal responsibility, and interfered with individuals' rights to determine their own values. Conservatives assailed big government in domestic affairs but demanded a strong military to eradicate "Godless communism."

Behind Goldwater's nomination was a growing grassroots movement. Vigorous especially in the South and West, it included middle-class suburban women and men, members of the rabidly anti-Communist John Birch Society, and college students in the new Young Americans for Freedom (YAF). They did not give up when he lost the election. In California, newly energized conservatives helped Ronald Reagan defeat the incumbent liberal governor, Edmund Brown, in 1966,

another sign of the right's rising strength. Reagan linked Brown with the Watts riot and student disruptions at the University of California at Berkeley (see chapter 28), exploiting popular fears about rising taxes, student rebellion, and black demands for justice.

Grassroots conservatism was not limited to the West and South, but a number of Sun Belt characteristics made it especially strong in places such as Orange County, California; Dallas, Texas; and Scottsdale, Arizona. Such predominantly white areas contained relatively homogeneous, skilled, and economically comfortable populations, as well as military bases and defense production facilities. The West harbored a long-standing tradition of Protestant morality, individualism, and opposition to interference by a remote federal government. That tradition continued with the emergence of the New Right, even though it was hardly consistent with the Sun Belt's economic dependence on defense spending and on huge federal projects providing water and power for the burgeoning population and its economy.

The South, which also benefited from military bases and the space program, shared the West's antipathy toward the federal government. Hostility to racial change, however, was much more central to the South's conservatism. After signing the Civil Rights Act of 1964, President Lyndon Johnson remarked privately, "I think we just delivered the South to the Republican Party." Indeed, Barry Goldwater carried five southern states in 1964.

Grassroots movements proliferated around what conservatives believed marked the "moral decline" of their nation. For example, in 1962, Mel and Norma Gabler succeeded in getting the Texas board of education to drop books that they found not in conformity with "the Christian-Judeo morals, values, and standards as given to us by God through . . . the Bible." Sex education roused the ire of Eleanor Howe in Anaheim, California, who felt that "nothing [in the sex education curriculum] depicted my values. . . . It wasn't so much the information. It was the shift in values." The Supreme Court's liberal decisions on issues such as school prayer, obscenity, and birth control also galvanized conservatives to restore "traditional values" to the nation.

In the 1970s, grassroots protests against taxes grew alongside concerns about morality. As Americans struggled with inflation and unemployment, many also found themselves paying higher taxes, especially higher property taxes as the value of their homes increased. In 1978, Californians revolted in a popular referendum, reducing property taxes by more than one-half and limiting the state legislature's ability to raise taxes. What a newspaper called a "primal scream by the People against Big Government" spread to similar antitax crusades in other states.

Nixon Courts the Right In his 1968 presidential campaign, Richard Nixon exploited hostility to black protest and new civil rights policies, wooing white southerners and a considerable number of northern voters away from the Democratic Party. As president, he used this "southern strategy" to make further inroads into traditional Democratic strongholds in the 1972 election.

The Nixon administration reluctantly enforced court orders to achieve high degrees of integration in southern schools, but it resisted efforts to deal with segregation outside the South. In northern and western cities, where segregation resulted from discrimination in housing and in the drawing of school district boundaries, half of all African American children attended nearly all black schools. After courts began to order the transfer of students between schools in white and black neighborhoods to achieve desegregation, busing became "political dynamite," according to a Gallup poll. "We've had all we can take of judicial interference with local schools," Phyllis Schlafly railed in 1972.

Children had been riding buses to school for decades, but busing for racial integration provoked fury. Violence erupted in Boston in 1974 when a district judge found that school officials had maintained what amounted to a dual system based on race and ordered busing "if necessary to achieve a unitary school system." When black students began to attend the formerly all-white South Boston High School, white students boycotted classes and angry whites threw rocks at black students disembarking from buses. As was true elsewhere, the whites most affected by busing came from working-class families who remained in cities abandoned by the more affluent and whose children often rode buses to predominantly black, overcrowded schools with deficient facilities. Clarence McDonough decried the liberal officials who bused his "kid half way around Boston so that a bunch of politicians can end up their careers with a clear conscience." African Americans themselves

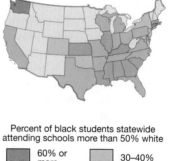

Percent of black students statewide attending schools more than 50% white

60% or more	30–40%
50–60%	20–30%
40–50%	20% or less

Integration of Public Schools, 1968

were conflicted about sending their children on long rides to schools where white teachers might not welcome or respect them.

White parents and students eventually became more accepting of integration, especially after the creation of magnet schools and other new mechanisms for desegregation offered more choice. Nonetheless, integration propelled white flight to the suburbs. The number of white students in Boston public schools by 1987 was just one-third of what it had been in 1974. Nixon failed to persuade Congress to end court-ordered busing, but after he had appointed four new justices, the Supreme Court imposed strict limits on the use of that tool to achieve racial balance.

Nixon's judicial appointments also reflected the southern strategy. He criticized the Supreme Court under Chief Justice Earl Warren for being "unprecedentedly politically active . . . using their interpretation of the law to remake American society according to their own social, political, and ideological precepts." When Warren resigned in 1969, Nixon replaced him with **Warren E. Burger**, a federal appeals court judge who was a strict constructionist—someone inclined to interpret the Constitution narrowly and to limit government intervention on behalf of individual rights. The Burger Court proved more sympathetic than the Warren Court to the president's agenda, restricting somewhat the protections of individual rights established by the previous Court, but continuing to uphold many of the liberal programs of the 1960s. For example, the Court limited the range of affirmative action in *Regents of the University of California v. Bakke* (1978), but it allowed affirmative action programs to attack the results of past discrimination if they avoided strict quotas or racial classifications.

Nixon's southern strategy and other repercussions of the civil rights revolution of the 1960s ended the Democratic hold on the "solid South." In 1964, Senator Strom Thurmond of South Carolina, leader of the Dixiecrat challenge to Truman in 1948, changed his party affiliation to Republican. North Carolina senator Jesse Helms followed suit in 1971, and politicians throughout the South began to realize that the future for Democratic candidates had darkened there. By 2005, Republicans held the majority of southern seats in Congress and governorships in seven southern states.

In addition to exploiting racial fears, Nixon aligned himself with those anxious about women's changing roles and new demands. In 1971, he vetoed a bill providing federal funds for day care centers with a message that combined the old and new conservatism. Parents should purchase child care services "in the private, open market," he insisted, not through government programs. He appealed to social conservatives by warning about the measure's "family-weakening implications." In response to the movement to liberalize abortion laws, Nixon sided with "defenders of the right to life of the unborn." He did not comment publicly on *Roe v. Wade* (1973), but his earlier stance against abortion anticipated the Republican Party's eventual embrace of this as a key issue for the New Right.

Q: How did Nixon's policies reflect the increasing influence of conservatives on the Republican Party?

Constitutional Crisis and Restoration

Nixon's ability to attract Democrats resulted in his resounding victory in the 1972 election. Two years later, however, the so-called Watergate scandal caused him to abandon his office. Nixon's abuse of power and efforts to cover up crimes committed by subordinates betrayed the public trust and forced the first presidential resignation in history. His handpicked successor, Gerald Ford, helped restore confidence in the presidency, but the aftermath of Watergate and severe economic problems returned the White House to the Democrats in 1976. Nonetheless, the rising conservative tide not only survived the temporary setback when Nixon resigned the presidency but also quickly challenged the Democratic administration that followed.

The Election of 1972 Nixon's ability to appeal to concerns about Vietnam, race, law and order, and traditional morality heightened his prospects for reelection in 1972. Although the war in Vietnam continued, antiwar protests diminished with the decrease in American ground forces and casualties. Nixon's economic initiatives had temporarily checked inflation and unemployment (see chapter 28), and his attacks on busing and antiwar protesters had appealed to the right, positioning him favorably for the 1972 election.

A large field of contenders vied for the Democratic nomination, including New York representative **Shirley Chisholm**, the first African American

to make a serious bid for the presidency. On the right, Governor George Wallace of Alabama captured a series of southern primaries as well as those of Michigan and Maryland, but his campaign was cut short when a shot fired by a deranged man left him paralyzed below the waist. South Dakota senator George S. McGovern came to the Democratic convention as the clear leader, and the new makeup of the convention delegates made his position even stronger.

After the bitter 1968 convention in Chicago (see chapter 29), the Democrats reformed their rules, requiring delegations to represent the proportions of minorities, women, and young people in their states. These newcomers displaced many regular Democrats—officeholders, labor leaders, and representatives of older ethnic groups. One labor leader grumbled that "the Democratic party was taken over by the kooks," referring to the considerable numbers of young people and women who were to the left of party regulars. Though easily nominated, McGovern struggled against Nixon from the outset. Republicans portrayed him as a left extremist, and his support for busing, a generous welfare program, and immediate withdrawal from Vietnam alienated conservative Democrats.

Nixon achieved a landslide victory, winning 60.7 percent of the popular vote and every state except Massachusetts. Although the Democrats maintained control of Congress, Nixon won majorities among traditional Democrats—southerners, Catholics, urbanites, and blue-collar workers. The president, however, had little time to savor his triumph, as revelations began to emerge about crimes committed to ensure the victory.

Watergate During the early-morning hours of June 17, 1972, five men working for Nixon's reelection campaign crept into Democratic Party headquarters in the Watergate complex in Washington, D.C. Intending to repair a bugging device installed in an earlier break-in, they were discovered and arrested. Nixon and his aides then tried to cover up the intruders' connection to administration officials, setting in motion the most serious constitutional crisis since the Civil War. Reporters dubbed the scandal **Watergate**.

Over the next two years, Americans learned that Nixon and his associates had engaged in other abuses, such as accepting illegal campaign contributions and unlawfully attempting to silence critics of the Vietnam War. Nixon was not the first president to lie to the public or to misuse power. Every president since Franklin D. Roosevelt had enlarged the powers of his office, justifying his actions as necessary to protect national security. This expansion of executive powers, often called the "imperial

The Gap in the Watergate Tapes Franklin Roosevelt installed the first recording apparatus in the White House under his desk in 1940, but neither he, Truman, nor Eisenhower recorded conversations extensively. John F. Kennedy was the first president to put in a complete taping network, and Richard Nixon was the first to use a voice-activated system. This system taped about 2,800 hours of conversations, which most participants did not know were being recorded. When Nixon was compelled to turn over the tapes during the Watergate investigation, an eighteen-and-a-half-minute gap was discovered in a conversation between Nixon and his chief of staff, H. R. Haldeman, just three days after the Watergate break-in. Nixon's secretary, Rose Mary Woods, said that her foot must have slipped on the controls while she was transcribing the tape, using the transcription machine pictured here. Others, noting that the gap contained several separate erasings, suggested that the clumsiness of the deed linked it to Nixon. Nixon Presidential Materials Project, National Archives and Records Administration.

presidency," weakened the traditional checks and balances on the executive branch and opened the door to abuses.

No president, however, had dared go as far as Nixon, who saw opposition to his policies as a personal attack and was willing to violate the Constitution to stop it. The Watergate scandal began when White House adviser Charles Colson established a secret unit nicknamed the "plumbers" to stop the kinds of "leaks" that had led to publication of the *Pentagon Papers* in 1971 (see chapter 29). These men soon turned to projects to disrupt and discredit Democrats, and in 1972 they broke into Watergate to bug the Democratic Party's phones.

Upon their arrest, Nixon plotted to conceal links between the burglars and the White House while publicly denying any connection. In April 1973, after investigations by a grand jury and the Senate suggested that White House aides had been involved, Nixon accepted official responsibility for Watergate but denied any knowledge of the break-in or cover-up. He also announced the resignations of three White House aides and the attorney general. In May, he authorized the appointment of an independent special prosecutor, Archibald Cox, to conduct an investigation.

Meanwhile, sensational revelations exploded in the Senate investigating committee, headed by Democrat Samuel J. Ervin of North Carolina. White House counsel John Dean described projects to harass "enemies" through tax audits and other illegal means and implicated the president in efforts to cover up the Watergate break-in. A White House aide struck the most damaging blow when he disclosed that all conversations in the Oval Office were taped. Both Cox and the Ervin

committee immediately asked for the tapes related to Watergate. When Nixon refused, citing executive privilege and separation of powers, Cox and Ervin took their case to court.

Additional disclosures exposed Nixon's misuse of federal funds and tax evasion. In August 1973, Vice President Spiro Agnew resigned after an investigation revealed that he had taken bribes while governor of Maryland. Although Nixon's choice of House minority leader Gerald Ford of Michigan to succeed Agnew won widespread approval, Agnew's resignation further tarnished the administration, and Nixon's popular support plummeted to 27 percent.

In February 1974, the House of Representatives voted to begin an impeachment investigation. In April, Nixon began to release edited transcripts of the tapes. As the public read passages sprinkled with "expletive deleted," House Republican leader Hugh Scott of Pennsylvania abandoned his support of the president, calling the transcripts a "deplorable, shabby, disgusting, and immoral performance by all." The transcripts revealed Nixon's orders to aides in March 1973: "I don't give a shit what happens. I want you all to stonewall it, let them plead the Fifth Amendment, cover up or anything else, if it'll save it—save the plan."

In July 1974, the House Judiciary Committee considered specific charges for impeachment: (1) obstruction of justice, (2) abuse of power, (3) contempt of Congress, (4) unconstitutional waging of war by the secret bombing of Cambodia, and (5) tax evasion and the selling of political favors. The committee voted to take the first three charges to the House, where a vote of impeachment seemed certain. Ordered by a unanimous Supreme Court to hand over the remaining tapes, Nixon released transcripts on August 5 that contained his conversations about how to hinder the FBI's investigation of the break-in. This was sufficient evidence to seal his fate.

Nixon announced his resignation to a national television audience on August 8, 1974. Acknowledging some incorrect judgments, he insisted that he had always tried to do what was best for the nation. The next morning, Nixon ended a rambling, emotional farewell to his staff with some advice: "Always give your best, never get discouraged, never get petty; always remember, others may hate you, but those who hate you don't win unless you hate them, and then you destroy yourself." Had he practiced that advice, he might have saved his presidency.

The Ford Presidency and the 1976 Election

Gerald R. Ford, who had represented Michigan in the House of Representatives since 1948, had built a reputation as a conservative party loyalist. Not a brilliant thinker, he was known for his integrity, humility, and dedication to public office. "I'm a Ford, not a Lincoln," he acknowledged. Most of official Washington and the American public looked favorably on his succession as president.

Upon taking office, Ford announced, "Our long nightmare is over." But he shocked many Americans one month later when he granted Nixon a pardon "for all offenses against the United States which he . . . has committed or may have committed or taken part in" during his presidency. This sweeping pardon saved Nixon from nearly certain indictment and trial, and it provoked a tremendous outcry from Congress and the public. Democrats made impressive gains in the November congressional elections, while Ford's action gave Nixon a new political life. Having gained a pardon without having to admit that he had violated the law and betrayed the public trust, he rebuilt his image over the next two decades into that of an elder statesman. Thirty of his associates ultimately pleaded guilty to or were convicted of crimes related to Watergate.

Congress's efforts to guard against the types of abuses revealed in the Watergate investigations had only limited effects. The **Federal Election Campaign Act of 1974** established public financing of presidential campaigns and imposed some restrictions on contributions to help prevent the selling of political favors. Yet politicians found other ways of raising money—for example, through political action committees (PACs). Moreover, in the 1976 case *Buckley v. Valeo*, the Supreme Court struck down limitations on campaign spending as violations of freedom of speech. Ever-larger campaign donations flowed to candidates from interest groups, corporations, labor unions, and wealthy individuals.

Special investigating committees in Congress discovered a host of illegal FBI and CIA activities stretching back to the 1950s, including harassment of political dissenters and plots to assassinate Fidel Castro and other foreign leaders. In response to these revelations, President Ford established new controls on covert operations, and Congress created permanent committees to oversee the intelligence agencies. Yet these measures did little to diminish the public's cynicism about their government.

Disillusionment grew as the Ford administration struggled with serious economic problems: a low growth rate, high unemployment, a foreign trade deficit, and soaring energy prices. Ford carried these burdens into the election campaign of 1976, while contending with a major challenge from the Republican right. Blasting Nixon's and Ford's foreign policy of détente for causing the "loss of U.S. military supremacy," California governor Ronald Reagan came close to capturing the nomination.

> Not a brilliant thinker, Ford was known for his integrity, humility, and dedication to public office. "I'm a Ford, not a Lincoln," he acknowledged.

The Democrats nominated **James Earl "Jimmy" Carter Jr.**, former governor of Georgia. A graduate of the U.S. Naval Academy, Carter spent seven years as a nuclear engineer in the navy before returning to Plains, Georgia, to run the family peanut farming business. Carefully prepared on policy issues, Carter appealed to the rise of evangelical religion and alienation from government by stressing his faith as a "born-again Christian" and his distance from the government in Washington. Although he selected liberal senator **Walter F. Mondale** of Minnesota as his running mate, Carter's nomination nonetheless marked a rightward turn in the party.

Carter had considerable appeal as a candidate who carried his own bags, lived modestly, and taught a Bible class at his Baptist church. He also benefited from Ford's failure to solve the country's economic problems, which helped him win the traditional Democratic coalition of blacks, organized labor, and ethnic groups, and even recapture some of the white southerners who had voted for Nixon in 1972. Yet although Democrats retained substantial margins in Congress, Carter received just 50 percent of the popular vote to Ford's 48 percent (Map 30.1).

Q: Why did Nixon resign the presidency in August 1974?

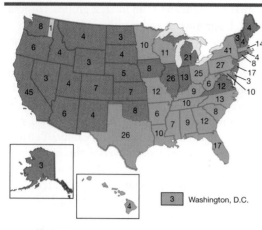

Candidate	Electoral Vote	Popular Vote	Percent of Popular Vote
Jimmy Carter (Democrat)	297	40,830,763	50.1
Gerald R. Ford (Republican)	240	39,147,793	48.0
Ronald Reagan (Independent Republican)	1	n/a	n/a

MAP 30.1 The Election of 1976

The "Outsider" Presidency of Jimmy Carter

Carter promised a government that was "competent" as well as "decent, open, fair, and compassionate." He also warned Americans "that even our great Nation has its recognized limits, and that we can neither answer all questions nor solve all problems." Carter's humility and personal integrity helped revive trust in the presidency, but he faltered in the face of domestic and foreign crises.

Energy shortages and stagflation worsened, exposing Carter's deficiencies in working with Congress and rallying the public to his objectives. His administration achieved notable advances in environmental and energy policies, and he oversaw foreign policy successes concerning the Panama Canal, China, and the Middle East. Yet near the end of his term, Soviet-American relations deteriorated, new crises emerged in the Middle East, and the economy plummeted, all costing him a second term.

Retreat from Liberalism Jimmy Carter vowed "to help the poor and aged, to improve education, and to provide jobs," but at the same time "not to waste money." When these goals conflicted, reform took second place to budget balancing. Increasing numbers of Americans unhappy about their tax

dollars being used to benefit the disadvantaged while stagflation eroded their own material status welcomed Carter's approach. But his fiscal stringency frustrated liberal Democrats pushing for major welfare reform and a national health insurance program. They accused him of deserting the Democratic reform tradition stretching back to Franklin D. Roosevelt.

A number of factors hindered Carter's ability to lead. His outsider status contributed to his election but left him without strong ties to party leaders in Congress. Democrats complained of inadequate consultation and Carter's tendency to flood them with comprehensive proposals when they were more accustomed to incremental reforms. In addition, Carter refused to offer simple solutions to the American people, who had a short attention span and were impatient for quick action against the forces that were squeezing their pocketbooks.

Even if he had possessed Lyndon Johnson's political skills, Carter might not have done much better. The economic problems he inherited—unemployment, inflation, and sluggish economic growth—confounded economic doctrine. Usually, rising prices accompanied a humming economy with a strong demand for labor. Now, however, the nation faced steep inflation and high unemployment at the same time, a combination called stagflation.

Carter first targeted unemployment. Although liberals complained that his programs did not do enough, Carter signed bills pumping $14 billion into the economy through public works and public service jobs programs and cutting taxes by $34 billion. Unemployment receded, but then inflation surged. Working people, wrote one journalist, "winced and ached" as their paychecks bought less and less. To curb inflation, Carter curtailed federal spending, and the Federal Reserve Board tightened the money supply. Not only did these measures fail to halt inflation, which surpassed 13 percent in 1980, but they also contributed to rising unemployment, reversing the gains made in Carter's first two years.

Carter's commitment to holding down the federal budget frustrated Democrats pushing for comprehensive welfare reform, national health insurance, and a substantial jobs program that would make government the employer of last resort. Carter did sign legislation to ensure solvency in the Social Security system, but the measure increased both employer and employee contributions, thereby increasing the tax burden on lower- and middle-income Americans.

By contrast, corporations and wealthy individuals gained from new legislation, such as a sharp cut in the capital gains tax. When the Chrysler

Jimmy Carter's Inauguration After his inauguration in January 1977, Jimmy Carter shunned the customary presidential limousine and instead walked with his wife, daughter, and two sons and their wives down Pennsylvania Avenue from the Capitol to the White House. Carter wanted to emphasize his opposition to some of the trappings of office that separated government from the people. Ordering cabinet heads to drive their own cars, he told the American people, "Government officials can't be sensitive to your problems if we are living like royalty here." Jimmy Carter Presidential Library.

Corporation approached bankruptcy in 1979, Congress provided $1.5 billion in loan guarantees to bail out the tenth-largest corporation in the country. Congress also acted on Carter's proposals to deregulate airlines in 1978 and the banking, trucking, and railroad industries in 1980. Carter's successor would move much further, implementing conservatives' attachment to a free market and unfettered private enterprise.

Energy and Environmental Reform Complicating the government's efforts to deal with stagflation was the nation's enormous consumption of energy and its dependence on foreign nations to fill one-third of its energy demands. Consequently, Carter proposed a comprehensive program to conserve energy, and he elevated its importance by establishing the Department of Energy. Beset with competing demands among energy producers and consumers, Congress picked Carter's program apart. The **National Energy Act of 1978** penalized manufacturers of gas-guzzling automobiles and provided other incentives for conservation and development of alternative

fuels, but the act fell far short of a long-term, comprehensive program.

In 1979, a new upheaval in the Middle East, the Iranian revolution, created the most severe energy crisis yet. In midsummer, shortages caused 60 percent of gasoline stations to close down; frustrated drivers waited in long lines and paid unprecedentedly high prices for gas. "We are struggling with a profound transition from a time of abundance to a time of growing scarcity in energy," Carter told the nation, asking Congress for additional measures to address the shortages. Congress reduced controls on oil and gas to stimulate American production and imposed a windfall profits tax on producers to redistribute some of the profits they would reap from deregulation.

Carter's energy measures failed to reduce American dependence on foreign oil. European nations shared that dependence but more successfully controlled consumption. They levied high taxes on gasoline, causing people to rely more on public transportation and manufacturers to produce more energy-efficient cars. In the automobile-dependent United States, however,

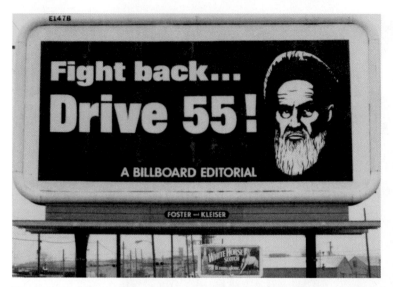

The Fuel Shortage This billboard was sponsored by the Outdoor Advertising Association of America in 1980, while Iran held Americans hostage in Teheran (see page 759) and gasoline shortages and rising gas prices vexed motorists all over the country. The shortages and high prices were sparked by the Iranian revolution, which brought to power Ayatollah Ruholla Khomeini, pictured on the billboard. The ad appeals to drivers to observe the 55-mile-per-hour national speed limit imposed in 1974 during the first oil crisis. John W. Hartman Center/Duke University Special Collections Library.

FOR MORE HELP ANALYZING THIS IMAGE, see the visual activity for this chapter in the Online Study Guide at bedfordstmartins.com/roarkcompact.

with inadequate public transit, people accustomed to driving long distances, and an aversion to taxes, politicians dismissed that approach. By the end of the century, the United States, with 6 percent of the world's population, would consume more than 25 percent of global oil production. (See "Global Comparison" and Map 30.2.)

One alternative fuel, nuclear energy, aroused opposition from a vigorous environmental movement. Activists warned of radiation leakage, potential accidents, and the hazards of radioactive wastes from nuclear power plants, which provided about 10 percent of the nation's electricity in the 1970s. In 1976, hundreds of members of the Clamshell Alliance went to jail for attempting to block construction of a nuclear power plant in Seabrook, New Hampshire; other groups sprang up across the United States to demand an environment safe from nuclear radiation and waste. The perils of nuclear energy claimed international attention in March 1979, when a meltdown of the reactor core was narrowly averted at the **Three Mile Island** nuclear facility near Harrisburg, Pennsylvania. Popular opposition and the great expense of building nuclear power plants stalled further development of the industry. The explosion of a nuclear reactor in Chernobyl, Ukraine,

in 1986 further solidified antinuclear concerns as part of the environmental movement.

A disaster at Love Canal in Niagara Falls, New York, advanced other environmental goals by underscoring the human costs of unregulated development. Residents suffering high rates of serious illness noted that their homes sat amid highly toxic waste products from a nearby chemical company. Finally responding to the residents' claims in 1978, the State of New York agreed to help families relocate, and the Carter administration sponsored legislation in 1980 that created the so-called Superfund, $1.6 billion for cleanup of hazardous wastes left by the chemical industry.

Carter's environmental legislation did not stop there. He signed bills to improve clean air and water programs; to expand the Arctic National Wildlife Refuge (ANWR) preserve in Alaska; and to control strip-mining, which left destructive scars on the land. During the 1979 gasoline crisis, Carter attempted to balance the development of domestic fuel sources with environmental concerns, winning legislation to conserve energy and to provide incentives for the development of solar energy and environmentally friendly alternative fuels.

Promoting Human Rights Abroad Jimmy Carter charged that his predecessors' foreign policy violated the nation's principles of freedom and human dignity. "We're ashamed of what our government is as we deal with other nations around the world," he said. Carter promised to reverse the cynical support of dictators, secret diplomacy, interference in the internal affairs of other countries, and excessive reliance on military solutions.

Human rights formed the cornerstone of his approach. The Carter administration applied economic pressure on governments that denied their citizens basic rights, refusing aid or trading privileges to nations such as Chile and El Salvador, as well as to the white minority governments of Rhodesia and South Africa, which brutally violated the rights of their black majorities. Yet in other instances, Carter sacrificed human rights ideals to strategic and security considerations. He invoked no sanctions against repressive governments in Iran, South Korea, and the Philippines, for example, and he established formal diplomatic relations with the People's Republic of China in 1979, even though its government blatantly withheld democratic rights.

Carter's human rights principles faced another test when a popular movement overthrew an oppressive dictatorship in Nicaragua. U.S. officials were uneasy about the leftist Sandinistas

MAP 30.2 Worldwide Oil Reserves, 1980

Data produced by geologists and engineers enable experts to estimate the size of "proved oil reserves," quantities that are recoverable with existing technology and costs. In 1980, the total worldwide reserves were estimated at 645 billion barrels. The recovery of reserves depends on many factors, including the precise location of the oil. Large portions of the U.S. reserves, for example, lie under deep water in the Gulf of Mexico, where it is expensive to drill and where operations can be disrupted by hurricanes. But the U.S. government is much more generous than most nations in allowing oil companies to take oil from public land, imposing relatively low taxes and royalty payments.

who led the rebellion and had ties to Cuba. Once they assumed power in 1979, however, Carter recognized the new government and sent economic aid, signaling that the way a government treated its citizens was as important as how anti-Communist and friendly to American interests it was.

Applying moral principles to relations with Panama, Carter sped up negotiations over control of the Panama Canal and in 1977 signed a treaty providing for Panama's takeover of the canal in 2000. Supporters viewed the treaty as recompense for the barefaced use of U.S. power to obtain the canal in 1903. Opponents insisted on retaining the vital waterway. "We bought it, we paid for it, it's ours," claimed Ronald Reagan during the presidential primaries of 1976. It took a massive effort by the administration to get Senate ratification of the **Panama Canal treaty**.

Seeking to promote peace in the Middle East, Carter seized on the courage of Egyptian president Anwar Sadat, the first Arab leader to risk his political career by talking directly with Israeli officials. In 1979, Carter invited Sadat and Israeli prime minister Menachem Begin to the presidential retreat at Camp David, Maryland, where he applied his tenacious diplomacy for thirteen days. These talks led to the **Camp David accords**, whereby Egypt became the first Arab state to recognize Israel, and Israel agreed to gradual withdrawal from the Sinai Peninsula, which it had seized in the 1967 Six-Day War (Map 30.3). Although the issues of Palestinian self-determination in other Israeli-occupied territories (the West Bank and Gaza) and the plight of Palestinian refugees remained unresolved, Carter had nurtured the first meaningful steps toward peace in the Middle East.

The Cold War Intensifies Consistent with his human rights approach, Carter preferred to pursue national security through nonmilitary means and initially sought accommodation with the

Energy Consumption per Capita, 1980

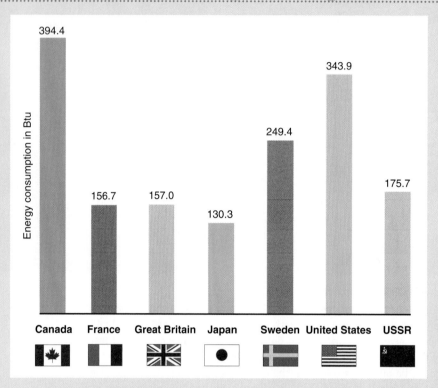

Relative to most other industrialized nations, the United States consumed energy voraciously, with a per capita rate of consumption in 1980 that was more than twice as high as that of Britain, France, and Japan and nearly twice as high as that of the Soviet Union. A number of factors influence a nation's energy consumption (shown here in British thermal units, or Btu), including standard of living, climate, size of landmass and dispersal of population, availability and price of energy, and government policies such as support for public transportation. What country had a per capita rate of consumption even higher than that of the United States?

Soviet Union. But in 1979, Carter decided to pursue a military buildup when the Soviet Union invaded neighboring Afghanistan, whose recently installed Communist government was threatened by Muslim opposition (see Map 30.3). Carter also imposed economic sanctions on the Soviet Union, barred U.S. participation in the 1980 Summer Olympic Games in Moscow, and obtained legislation requiring all nineteen-year-old men to register for the draft.

Claiming that Soviet actions jeopardized oil supplies from the Middle East, the president announced the "Carter Doctrine," threatening the use of any means necessary to prevent an outside force from gaining control of the Persian

Gulf. His human rights policy fell by the wayside as the United States stepped up aid to the military dictatorship in Afghanistan's neighbor, Pakistan. Carter authorized the CIA to funnel secret aid through Pakistan to the Afghan rebels. Finally, Carter called for hefty increases in defense spending.

Events in Iran also encouraged this hard-line approach. All the U.S. arms and aid had not enabled the shah to crush Iranian dissidents who still resented the CIA's role in the overthrow of the Mossadegh government in 1953 (see chapter 27), condemned the shah's savage attempts to silence opposition, and detested his adoption of Western culture and values. These grievances erupted into a

The following labels appear on the map:

LEBANON (inset box): U.S. aids pro-American government, 1958; Israel invades, 1982; U.S. Marine barracks bombed, 1983

YUGOSLAVIA BULGARIA 30°E Black Sea Caspian Sea SOVIET UNION

ITALY ALBANIA GREECE

Ankara TURKEY 60°E

SOVIET UNION (box): Soviet troops invade. U.S. imposes economic sanctions on Soviet Union and aids Muslim guerrillas, 1979; Gradual withdrawal of Soviet troops; civil war continues, 1988

(box near Turkey/Iran): At war with Iran, 1980–1988; Chemical attacks on Kurds, 1988

LEBANON Beirut Damascus SYRIA Tel Aviv Jerusalem Amman ISRAEL JORDAN

War of Independence, 1948; Sinai War, 1956; Six-Day War, 1967; Yom Kippur War, 1973; Palestinian uprising begins, 1987

CYPRUS Mediterranean Sea

Tehran IRAN AFGHANISTAN

SYRIA Beirut Damascus Baghdad IRAQ LEBANON ISRAEL Jerusalem Amman JORDAN Cairo EGYPT Suez Canal Sinai See inset map

(box, Iran): CIA stages coup against Mossadegh government, 1953; Shah overthrown, 1979; U.S. hostage crisis, 1979–1981; Secret U.S. arms sales to Iran; proceeds diverted to Nicaraguan Contras, 1985–1986

PAKISTAN

OMAN Strait of Hormuz

LIBYA 0 250 500 miles 0 250 500 kilometers

(box, Egypt): Suez crisis, 1956; Egypt and Israel agree to Camp David accords, 1978; Egypt and Israel sign peace treaty, 1979; Sadat assassinated, 1981

KUWAIT BAHRAIN Riyadh SAUDI ARABIA QATAR Abu Dhabi Gulf of Oman Persian Gulf

(box): Arab oil embargo against U.S., 1973

UNITED ARAB EMIRATES OMAN

Red Sea SUDAN

P.D.R. OF YEMEN YEMEN Arabian Sea

ETHIOPIA

Legend:
- OPEC member
- Israel before 1967
- Land gained by Israel in Six-Day War
- Land returned to Egypt, 1973–1981
- Oil field

MAP 30.3 The Middle East, 1948–1989

Determination to preserve access to the rich oil reserves of the Middle East and commitment to the security of Israel were the fundamental—and often conflicting—principles of U.S. foreign policy in that region.

READING THE MAP: Where did the United States become involved diplomatically or militarily in the Middle East between 1948 and 1989? Which countries are members of OPEC?

CONNECTIONS: What role did U.S. foreign policy regarding the Middle East and events in Israel play in provoking the 1973 Arab oil embargo against the United States? What precipitated the taking of U.S. hostages in Iran in 1979? Was U.S. intervention in the country a factor? If so, why?

FOR MORE HELP ANALYZING THIS MAP, see the map activity for this chapter in the Online Study Guide at bedfordstmartins.com/roarkcompact.

revolution in 1979 that forced the shah out of Iran and brought to power Shiite Islamic fundamentalists led by Ayatollah Ruholla Khomeini, whom the shah had exiled in 1964.

Carter's decision to allow the shah into the United States for medical treatment enraged Iranians, who believed that the United States would put the shah back in power as it had done in 1953. Anti-American demonstrations escalated in the capital city of Teheran. On November 4, 1979, a crowd broke into the U.S. Embassy and seized sixty-six U.S. diplomats, CIA officers, citizens, and military attachés. Refusing the captors' demands that the shah be returned to Iran for trial, Carter froze Iranian assets in U.S. banks and placed an embargo on Iranian oil. In April 1980, he sent a small military operation into Iran, but the rescue mission failed.

The disastrous rescue attempt and scenes of blindfolded U.S. citizens paraded before TV cameras fed Americans' feelings of impotence, simmering since the defeat in Vietnam. These frustrations in turn increased support for a more militaristic foreign policy. Opposition to Soviet-American détente, combined with the Soviet invasion of Afghanistan, nullified the thaw in superpower relations that had begun in the 1960s. The **Iran hostage crisis** dominated the news during the 1980 presidential campaign and contributed to Carter's defeat. Iran freed the hostages the day he left office, but relations with the United States remained tense.

Q: How did Carter attempt to balance his commitment to human rights and anticommunism in his foreign policy?

Ronald Reagan and the Conservative Ascendancy

Ronald Reagan's election in 1980 marked the most important turning point in politics since Franklin D. Roosevelt won the presidency in 1932. Eisenhower and Nixon were middle-of-the-road Republicans, but Reagan's victory established conservatism's dominance in the Republican Party. Since the 1930s, the Democrats had defined the major issues. In the 1980s, the Republicans assumed that initiative, while Democrats searched for voter support by moving toward the right. The United States was not alone in this political shift. Conservatives rose to power in Britain with Prime Minister Margaret Thatcher, and they led governments in Germany, Canada, and Sweden, while socialist and social democratic governments elsewhere trimmed their welfare states.

On the domestic front, the Reagan administration embraced the conservative Christian values of the New Right, but it left its most important mark on the economy: victory over inflation, deregulation of industry, enormous tax cuts, and a staggering federal budget deficit. Economic expansion, which took off after 1983, helped the middle class and brought great wealth to some, but the percentage of poor Americans increased, and income inequality grew. Although the Reagan era did not see a policy revolution comparable to that of the New Deal, it dealt a sharp blow to the liberalism that had informed American politics since the 1930s.

Ronald Reagan Nominated for President Nancy and Ronald Reagan respond to cheers at the 1980 Republican National Convention, where he was nominated for president. Reagan became one of the most popular presidents of the twentieth century. Lester Sloan/Woodfin Camp & Associates.

Appealing to the New Right and Beyond

Sixty-nine-year-old **Ronald Reagan** was the oldest candidate ever nominated for the presidency. Born in Tampico, Illinois, Reagan attended a small religious college and worked as a sportscaster before becoming a movie actor. He initially shared the politics of his staunchly Democratic father but moved to the right in the 1940s and 1950s and campaigned for Goldwater in 1964.

Reagan's political career took off when he was elected governor of California in 1966. He ran as a conservative, but in office he displayed considerable flexibility, approving a major tax increase, a strong water pollution bill, and a liberal abortion law. Displaying similar agility in the 1980 presidential campaign, he softened earlier attacks on programs such as Social Security and chose the moderate George H. W. Bush as his running mate.

Nonetheless, some Republicans balked at his nomination and at the party platform, which reflected the concerns of the party's right wing. For example, after Phyllis Schlafly persuaded the party to reverse its forty-year support for the Equal Rights

Amendment, moderate and liberal Republican women protested outside the convention hall. (See "Historical Question," page 762.) Some Republicans found a more acceptable presidential candidate in Illinois representative John B. Anderson, who deserted his party to run as an independent.

Reagan's campaign capitalized on the economic recession and the international challenges symbolized by the Americans held hostage in Iran. Repeatedly, Reagan asked voters, "Are you better off now than you were four years ago?" He promised to "take government off the backs of the people" and to restore Americans' morale and other nations' respect. Fifty-one percent of voters responded favorably to Reagan's upbeat message, while Carter won 41 percent, and 7 percent went to Anderson. Republicans won control of the Senate for the first time since the 1950s.

While the economy and Iran sealed Reagan's victory, he also benefited from the burgeoning grassroots conservative movements. An extraordinarily adept politician, Reagan appealed to a wide spectrum of groups and sentiments: free-market advocates, militant anti-Communists, fundamentalist Christians, white southerners, and white working-class Democrats—the so-called Reagan Democrats disenchanted with the Great Society and suffering from the stagflation of the 1970s.

Reagan's support from religious conservatives, predominantly Protestants, constituted a relatively new phenomenon in politics known as the New Right or New **Christian Right**. During the 1970s, evangelical and fundamentalist Christianity claimed thousands of new adherents. Evangelical ministers such as **Pat Robertson** preached to huge television audiences, attacking feminism, abortion, and homosexuality and calling for the restoration of old-fashioned "family values." They wanted prayer back in the schools and sex education out of them. A considerable number of Catholics, such as Phyllis Schlafly, shared the fundamentalists' goal of a return to "Christian values."

Conservatives created political organizations, such as the Moral Majority founded by minister Jerry Falwell in 1979, to fight "left-wing, social-welfare bills, . . . pornography, homosexuality, [and] the advocacy of immorality in school textbooks." The Christian Coalition, founded by Pat Robertson in 1989, claimed 1.6 million members and control of the Republican Party in more than a dozen states. The instruments of more traditional conservatives, who stressed limited government at home and militant anticommunism abroad, likewise flourished. These included publications such as the *National Review*, founded in the 1950s, and conservative think tanks such as the American Enterprise Institute. The monthly *Phyllis Schlafly Report* merged the sentiments of the old and new right.

Reagan embraced the full spectrum of conservatism, but he actually delivered more to the traditional right. He spoke for the New Right on such issues as abortion and school prayer, but he did not push hard for so-called moral or social policies. Instead, his major achievements fulfilled goals of the older right—strengthening the nation's anti-Communist posture and reducing taxes and government restraints on free enterprise. "In the present crisis," Reagan declared, "government is not the solution to our problem, government is the problem."

Reagan's admirers stretched far beyond conservatives. The extraordinarily popular president was liked even by Americans who opposed his policies and even when he made glaring mistakes. Reagan's optimism, confidence, and easygoing humor formed a large part of his appeal. Ignoring the darker moments of the American past, he presented a version of history that Americans could feel good

about. Listeners understood his declaration that it was "morning in America" as a promise that the best was yet to come. Reagan also gained public sympathy after being shot by a would-be assassin in March 1981. Just before surgery to remove the bullet, Reagan joked to physicians, "I hope you're Republicans." His tremendous popularity helped him withstand serious charges of executive branch misconduct in his second term.

Unleashing Free Enterprise Reagan's first domestic objective was a massive tax cut. Although tax cuts in the face of a large budget deficit contradicted traditional Republican economic doctrine, Reagan relied on a new theory called **supply-side economics**, which held that cutting taxes would actually increase revenue by enabling businesses to expand, encouraging individuals to work harder because they could keep more of their earnings, and increase the production of goods and services—the supply—which in turn would boost demand. Reagan promised that the economy would grow so much that the government would recoup the lost taxes, but instead it incurred a galloping deficit.

In the summer of 1981, Congress passed the **Economic Recovery Tax Act**, the largest tax reduction in U.S. history. Rates were cut from 14 percent to 11 percent for the lowest-income individuals and from 70 percent to 50 percent for the wealthiest. The law gave corporations tax breaks and reduced levies on capital gains, gifts, and inheritances. A second measure, the Tax Reform Act of 1986, went even further, lowering the maximum rate on individual income to 28 percent and on business income to 35 percent. Although the 1986 law narrowed loopholes used primarily by the wealthy, affluent Americans saved far more on their tax bills than did average taxpayers, and the distribution of wealth tipped further in favor of the rich.

> "In the present crisis," Reagan declared, "government is not the solution to our problem, government is the problem."

"Hack, chop, crunch!" were *Time* magazine's words for Reagan's efforts to free private enterprise from government restraints. Carter had confined deregulation to particular industries, such as air transportation and banking, while increasing health, safety, and environmental regulations. The Reagan administration, by contrast, pursued across-the-board deregulation. It declined to enforce the Sherman Antitrust Act's limits on monopolies (see chapter 18) against an unprecedented number of business mergers and takeovers. Reagan also loosened regulations protecting employee health

Why Did the ERA Fail?

The proposed Equal Rights Amendment to the U.S. Constitution guaranteed simply that women and men would be treated equally under the law: "Equality of rights under the law shall not be denied or abridged by the United States or by any State on account of sex." Two more short sections gave Congress enforcement powers and provided that the ERA would take effect two years after ratification. By the 1970s, it had become the symbol of the late-twentieth-century women's movement.

Members of a small, militant feminist organization, the National Woman's Party, first proposed an equal rights amendment to the Constitution in 1923, but it won little support either in Congress or among the public before the resurgence of feminism in the mid-1960s. In 1968, the National Organization for Women (NOW) made it a key objective and, armed with support from traditional women's organizations and liberal groups, began to pressure Congress. The pressure took many forms, including civil disobedience. In early 1970, for example, NOW members disrupted a Senate subcommittee hearing on extending the vote to eighteen-year-olds, demanding Senate hearings on the ERA. Feminists and their allies, including women in both political parties, lobbied Congress and flooded some congressional offices with fifteen hundred letters a month.

Despite opposition in committee hearings, both houses of the Democratic-controlled Congress passed the amendment by overwhelming margins, 354 to 23 in the House and 84 to 8 in the Senate. Within three hours of Senate passage in March 1972, Hawaii rushed to become the first state to ratify. By the end of 1972, twenty-three states had done so. Public opinion heavily favored ratification, peaking at 74 percent in favor in 1974 and never falling below 52 percent, while the opposition never topped 31 percent. Yet even after Congress extended the time period for ratification until 1982, the ERA failed. The Constitution requires approval of amendments by three-fourths of the states, and only thirty-five states ratified, three short of the minimum needed (see the map on page 766). Why did a measure with so much congressional and popular support fail?

The ERA encountered well-organized and passionate opposition linked to the growing conservative forces in the 1970s. Opponents ranged from religious organizations, such as the National Council of Catholic Women, to local groups such as HOTDOGS

(Humanitarians Opposed to the Degradation of Our Girls), sponsored by the John Birch Society in Utah. Leading the resistance was Phyllis Schlafly. Conservatives' opposition to the ERA reflected in part their distaste for big government and their demand for a strong defense system to counter communism. Schlafly predicted that the amendment would transfer power from state legislatures and even from families to the federal government. The ERA would put women in foxholes alongside men, she warned, weakening the military and making the nation more vulnerable to communism. To these arguments, the New Right added claims that the ERA would destroy the American family.

ERA opponents raised fears about the amendment by suggesting extravagant ways in which courts might interpret it. Senator Samuel J. Ervin Jr., nationally known for his chairing of the Watergate hearings, claimed that the ERA would eliminate laws against rape, require male and female prisoners to be housed together, and deprive women of alimony and child support. Others claimed that it would legalize homosexual marriage. Overall, the anti-ERA forces emphasized sex differences. By destroying the distinct sex roles on which the family was based, Ervin claimed, the ERA would destroy the family and produce "increased rates of alcoholism, suicide, and possible sexual deviation."

Anti-ERA arguments spoke to many women's religious beliefs and understandings of their own self-interest. In contrast to feminists, who viewed traditional sex roles as constructed by society, anti-ERA men and women believed that they were God given. Evangelical minister and politician Jerry Falwell declared the ERA "a definite violation of holy Scripture [and its] mandate that 'the husband is the head of the wife.'" Many ERA opponents were full-time housewives who had no stake in equal treatment in the marketplace and who feared that the amendment would eliminate the duty of men to support their families. Women in both camps recognized the precariousness of economic security, but whereas feminists wanted to render women self-sustaining, antifeminists wanted men to bear responsibility for their support.

Schlafly and other conservative leaders skillfully mobilized women who saw their traditional roles threatened. In October 1972, she established a national movement called STOP (Stop Taking Our Privileges) ERA, which was so highly organized that it could

★ **Phyllis Schlafly Derails the ERA in Illinois** Illinois was one of the most hotly contested states in the battle over ratification of the Equal Rights Amendment. Here Schlafly rallies ERA opponents in the state capitol in 1975. Schlafly's STOP ERA movement succeeded in Illinois, her home state and the only northern state that failed to ratify. Despite time-consuming and energetic political activities that involved traveling and speaking across the country, Schlafly insisted on calling herself a housewife. © Bettmann/Corbis.

respond immediately when action was necessary. For instance, when a state legislature began to consider ratification, STOP ERA members deluged legislators with letters and lobbied them personally in state capitols. In Illinois, they gave lawmakers apple pies with notes attached that read, "My heart and my hand went into this dough / For the sake of the family please vote 'no.'" Opponents also brought baby girls to the legislature wearing signs that pleaded, "Please don't draft me."

Another opposition group, Happiness of Womanhood (HOW), presented California legislators with mice bearing the message, "Do you want to be a man or a mouse?"

ERA opponents had an easier task than supporters, because the framers of the Constitution had stacked the odds against revision. All opponents had to do was to convince a minority of legislators in a minority of states to preserve the status quo. Supporters, by contrast, had to persuade a majority of lawmakers in three-quarters of the states that the need to guarantee women equal rights was urgent and could not be accomplished without a constitutional amendment. In addition, ERA forces had concentrated on winning Congress and were not prepared for the state campaigns. The intensity of the opposition took them by surprise.

Feminists had to overcome the tendency of men to trivialize women's rights. For example, when the House initially passed the ERA in 1970, the *New York Times* printed a critical editorial under the title "The Henpecked House." The conservative columnist James J. Kilpatrick called the ERA "the contrivance of a gang of professional harpies" that congressmen had voted for simply to "get these furies off their backs." The very gains feminists made in the 1960s and 1970s also worked against approval of the ERA. Congress had already banned sex discrimination in employment, education, credit, and other areas, and the Supreme Court had struck down several state and federal laws that treated men and women differently. Even though the Court did not ban all distinctions based on sex, its decisions made it harder for ERA advocates to demonstrate the urgency of constitutional revision.

So why did the ERA fail? It failed because a handful of men in a handful of state legislatures voted against it. The shift of only a few votes in states such as Illinois and North Carolina would have meant ratification. Phyllis Schlafly's forces played a key role in the defeat, because men could vote "no" and take cover behind the many women who opposed it. And those women proved willing to commit time, energy, and money to block ratification because conservative leaders convinced them that the ERA threatened their very way of life.

Feminists did not leave the ERA battle empty-handed, however. The National Organization for Women grew enormously during the struggle for ratification. Thousands of women were mobilized across the political spectrum and participated in the political arena for the first time. Fourteen states passed their own equal rights amendments after 1970. And feminists continued to struggle in the legislative and judicial arenas for the expansion of women's rights, struggles that continue to bear fruit in the twenty-first century.

and safety, and he weakened labor unions. When members of the Professional Air Traffic Controllers Organization (PATCO) struck in 1981, Reagan fired them, destroying their union and intimidating organized labor.

Ronald Reagan loved the outdoors and his remote ranch in southern California, where altogether he spent nearly one-eighth of his two-term presidency. Yet he blamed environmental laws for the nation's sluggish economic growth and targeted them for deregulation. His first secretary of the interior, James Watt, declared, "We will mine more, drill more, cut more timber," releasing federal lands to private exploitation. Meanwhile, the head of the Environmental Protection Agency relaxed enforcement of air and water pollution standards. Of environmentalists, Reagan wisecracked, "I don't think they'll be happy until the White House looks like a bird's nest," but their numbers grew in opposition to his policies. Popular support for environmental protection forced several officials to resign and blocked full realization of Reagan's deregulatory goals.

Deregulation of the banking industry, begun under Carter with bipartisan support, created a crisis in the savings and loan industry. Some of the newly deregulated savings and loan institutions (S&Ls) extended enormous loans to real estate developers and invested in other high-yield but risky ventures. S&L owners reaped lavish profits, and their depositors enjoyed high interest rates. But when real estate values began to plunge, hundreds of S&Ls went bankrupt. After Congress voted to bail out the S&L industry in 1989, American taxpayers bore the burden of the largest financial scandal in U.S. history, estimated at more than $100 billion.

The **S&L crisis** deepened the federal deficit. The administration cut funds for food stamps, job training, student aid, and other social welfare programs, and hundreds of thousands of people lost benefits. Yet increases in defense spending far exceeded the budget cuts, and the deficit climbed from $74 billion in 1981 to a high of $220 billion in 1986. Under Reagan, the nation's debt tripled to $2.3 trillion, and interest on the debt consumed one-seventh of all federal expenditures. Despite Reagan's antigovernment rhetoric, the number of federal employees increased from 2.9 million to 3.1 million during his presidency.

It took the severest recession since the 1930s to squeeze inflation out of the U.S. economy. Unemployment approached 11 percent late in 1982, and record numbers of banks and businesses closed. The threat of unemployment further undermined organized labor, forcing unions to make concessions that management insisted were necessary for industry's survival. In 1983, the economy recovered and entered a period of unprecedented growth.

That economic upswing and Reagan's own popularity posed a formidable challenge to the Democrats in the 1984 election. They nominated Carter's vice president, Walter F. Mondale, to head the ticket, but even his precedent-breaking move in choosing a woman as his running mate — New York representative Geraldine A. Ferraro — did not save the Democrats from a humiliating defeat. Reagan charged his opponents with concentrating on America's failures, while he emphasized success and possibility. Democrats, he claimed, "see an America where every day is April 15th [the due date for income tax returns] . . . we see an America where every day is the Fourth of July."

Voters responded to the president's sunny vision and the economic comeback, giving him a landslide victory with 59 percent of the popular vote and every state but Minnesota. Stung by Republican charges that the Democratic Party was captive to "special interests" such as labor, women, and minorities, some Democratic leaders, including the young Arkansas governor, Bill Clinton, urged the party to shift more toward the right.

Winners and Losers in a Flourishing Economy After the economy took off in 1983, some Americans won great fortunes. Popular culture celebrated making money and displaying wealth. Books by business wizards topped best seller lists, the press described lavish million-dollar parties, and a new television show, *Lifestyles of the Rich and Famous*, drew large audiences. College students listed making money as their primary ambition.

Participating conspicuously in the new affluence were members of the baby boom generation, known popularly as "yuppies," short for "young urban professionals." These mostly white, well-educated young men and women lived in urban condominiums and consumed lavishly — fancy cars, health clubs, expensive vacations, and electronic gadgets. Though definitely a minority, they established consumption standards that many tried to emulate. And, in fact, millions of Americans enjoyed larger houses that they filled with such new products as VCRs, microwave ovens, and personal computers.

Many of the newly wealthy got rich from moving assets around rather than from producing goods. Notable exceptions included Steven Jobs, who invented the Apple computer in his garage; Bill Gates, who transformed the software industry; and Liz Claiborne, who created a billion-dollar fashion enterprise. But many others made money by manipulating debt and restructuring corporations through mergers and takeovers. Most financial wizards operated within the law, but greed sometimes led to criminal convictions.

Older industries faced increasing international pressures. Americans bought more Volkswagens and Hondas and fewer Fords and Chevrolets, as German and Japanese corporations overtook U.S. manufacturing in steel, automobiles, and electronics. International competition forced the collapse of some older companies. Others moved factories and jobs abroad to be closer to foreign markets or to benefit from the low wages in countries such as Mexico and Korea. Service industries expanded and created new jobs at home, but these jobs paid substantially lower wages. When David Ramos was laid off in 1982 from his $12.75-an-hour job in a steel plant, his wages fell to $5 an hour as a security guard, forcing his family to rely on food stamps. The number of full-time workers earning wages below the poverty level ($12,195 for a family of four in 1990) rose from 12 percent to 18 percent of all workers in the 1980s.

The weakening of organized labor combined with the decline in manufacturing to erode the position of blue-collar workers. Chicago steelworker Ike Mazo, who contemplated the $6-an-hour jobs available to him, fumed, "It's an attack on the living standards of workers." Increasingly, a second income was needed to stave off economic decline. By 1990, nearly 60 percent of married women with young children worked outside the home. Yet even with two incomes, families struggled. Speaking of her children, Mazo's wife confessed, "I worry about their future every day. Will we be able to put them through college?" The average $10,000 gap between men's and women's annual earnings made things even harder for the nearly 20 percent of families headed by women.

In keeping with conservative philosophy, Reagan adhered to trickle-down economics, insisting that a booming economy would benefit everyone. Average personal income did rise during his tenure, but the trend toward greater economic inequality that had begun in the 1970s intensified in the 1980s, encouraged in part by his tax policies. Personal income shot up sharply for the wealthiest 20 percent of Americans, while it fell for the poorest by 9.8 percent between 1979 and 1987. During Reagan's presidency, the percentage of Americans living in poverty increased from 11.7 to 13.5, the highest poverty rate in the industrialized world. Social Security and Medicare helped to stave off destitution among the elderly. Less fortunate were other groups that the economic boom had bypassed: racial minorities, female-headed families, and children. One child in five lived in poverty.

Q: **Why did economic inequality increase during the Reagan administration?**

Continuing Struggles over Rights

The rise of conservatism put liberal social movements on the defensive, as the Reagan administration moved away from the national commitment to equal opportunity undertaken in the 1960s and the president's federal court appointments reflected that shift. Feminists and minority groups fought to keep protections they had recently won, and they achieved some limited gains. The gay and lesbian rights movement actually grew in numbers, edging attitudes toward greater tolerance and winning important protections in some states and cities.

Battles in the Courts and Congress Ronald Reagan agreed with conservatives that the nation had moved too far in guaranteeing rights to minority groups. Crying "reverse discrimination," they maintained that affirmative action unfairly hurt whites. Instead they called for "color-blind" policies, ignoring statistics showing that minorities and white women still lagged far behind white men in opportunities and income. Intense mobilization by civil rights groups, educational leaders, and even corporate America prevented the administration from abandoning affirmative action, and the Supreme Court upheld important antidiscrimination policies. Moreover, against Reagan's wishes, Congress voted to extend the Voting Rights Act with veto-proof majorities. The administration did, however, put the brakes on civil rights enforcement by appointing conservatives to the Justice Department, the Civil Rights Commission, and other agencies and by slashing their budgets.

Congress stepped in to defend antidiscrimination programs after the Justice Department persuaded the Supreme Court to severely weaken Title IX of the Education Amendments Act of 1972, a key law promoting equal opportunity in education. *Grove City v. Bell* (1984) allowed the Justice Department to abandon dozens of civil rights cases against schools and colleges, which in turn galvanized a coalition of civil rights organizations and groups representing women, the aged, and the disabled, along with their allies. In 1988, Congress passed the Civil Rights Restoration Act, which reversed the administration's victory in *Grove City* and banned any organization that practiced discrimination on the basis of race, color, national origin, sex, disability, or age from receiving government funds.

The *Grove City* decision reflected a rightward movement in the federal judiciary, upon which liberals had counted as a powerful ally. With the opportunity to appoint half of the 761 federal court judges and three new Supreme Court justices, President Reagan encouraged this trend by carefully selecting conservative candidates. Thus, he turned the tide back toward strict construction—the literal interpretation of the Constitution that narrowly adheres to the words of its authors, thereby limiting judicial power to protect individual rights. The full impact of these appointments became clear after Reagan left office, as the Court allowed states to impose restrictions that weakened access to abortion for poor and uneducated women, reduced protections against employment discrimination, and whittled down legal safeguards against the death penalty.

Feminism on the Defensive A signal achievement of the New Right was capturing the Republican Party's position on women's rights. For the first time in its history, the Republican Party took an explicitly antifeminist tone, opposing both the **Equal Rights Amendment (ERA)** and a woman's right to abortion, key goals of women's rights activists. When the time limit for ratification of the ERA ran out in 1982, Phyllis Schlafly celebrated victory on the issue that had first galvanized her antifeminist campaign, while amendment supporters looked for the silver lining. Sonia Johnson, who was excommunicated by the Mormon Church for her feminism in 1979, exaggerated only somewhat when she called the ratification struggle "the greatest political training ground for women in the history of the world." (See chapter 28 and "Historical Question," page 762.)

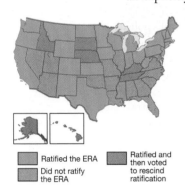

Ratified the ERA
Did not ratify the ERA
Ratified and then voted to rescind ratification

The Fight for the Equal Rights Amendment

Cast on the defensive, feminists focused more on women's economic and family problems, where they found some common ground with the Reagan administration. The Child Support Enforcement Amendments Act helped single and divorced mothers collect court-ordered child support payments from absent fathers. The Retirement Equity Act of 1984 benefited divorced and older women by strengthening their claims to their husbands' pensions and enabling women to qualify more easily for private retirement pensions.

The Reagan administration had its own concerns about women, specifically about the gender gap—women's tendency to vote for liberal and Democratic candidates in larger numbers than men did. Reagan eventually appointed three women to cabinet posts and, in 1981, selected the first woman, **Sandra Day O'Connor**, a moderate conservative, for the Supreme Court, despite the Christian Right's objection to her support of abortion. But these actions accompanied a general decline in the number of women and minorities in high-level government positions. And with higher poverty rates than men, women suffered most from Reagan's cuts in social programs.

Although court decisions placed restrictions on women's ability to obtain abortions, feminists fought successfully to retain the basic principles of *Roe v. Wade*. Moreover, they won a key decision from the Supreme Court ruling that sexual harassment in the workplace constituted sex discrimination. Feminists also made some gains at the state level in such areas as pay equity, rape, and domestic violence.

The Gay and Lesbian Rights Movement In contrast to feminism and other social movements, gay and lesbian rights activism grew during the 1980s, galvanized in part by the discovery in 1981 of a devastating disease, **acquired immune deficiency syndrome (AIDS)**. Because initially the disease disproportionately affected male homosexuals in the United States, activists mobilized to promote public funding for AIDS education, prevention, and treatment.

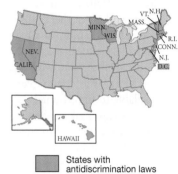

States with antidiscrimination laws

Antidiscrimination Laws for Gays and Lesbians, 1982–2000

The gay and lesbian rights movement helped closeted homosexuals experience the relief of "coming out," and their visibility increased awareness, if not always acceptance, of homosexuality among the larger population. Beginning with the election of Elaine Noble to the Massachusetts legislature in 1974, several openly gay politicians won offices ranging from mayor to member of Congress, and the Democrats began to include gay rights in their party platforms. Activists organized gay rights marches throughout the country, turning out half a million people in New York City in 1987.

Popular attitudes about homosexuality moved toward greater tolerance but remained complex, leading to uneven changes in policies. Dozens of cities banned job discrimination against homosexuals, and beginning with Wisconsin in 1982, eleven states made sexual orientation a protected category under civil rights laws. Local governments and large corporations began to offer health insurance and other benefits to same-sex domestic partners.

Yet a strong countermovement challenged the drive for recognition of gay rights. The Christian

Right targeted gays and lesbians as symbols of national immorality and succeeded in overturning some homosexual rights measures, which already lagged far behind antidiscrimination guarantees for minorities and women. Many states removed antisodomy laws from the books, but in 1986 the Supreme Court upheld the constitutionality of such laws. Until the Court reversed that opinion in 2003, more than a dozen states retained statutes that left homosexuals vulnerable to criminal charges for private consensual behavior.

Q: What gains and setbacks did minorities, feminists, and gays and lesbians experience during the Reagan years?

Ronald Reagan Confronts an "Evil Empire"

Campaigning for president in the wake of the Soviet invasion of Afghanistan and the Iranian hostage crisis, Reagan accused Carter of weakening the military and losing the confidence of the nation's allies and the respect of its enemies. As president, he accelerated Carter's arms buildup and harshly censured the Soviet Union, calling it "an evil empire." Yet despite the new aggressiveness—or, as some argued, because of it—Reagan presided over the most impressive thaw in superpower conflict since the Cold War had begun. On the periphery of the Cold War, however, Reagan practiced militant anticommunism, assisting antileftist movements in Asia, Africa, and Central America and dispatching troops to the Middle East and the Caribbean. When Congress blocked Reagan's efforts to help overthrow the leftist government in Nicaragua, administration officials resorted to secret and illegal means to effect their agenda.

Militarization and Interventions Abroad

Reagan expanded the military with new bombers and missiles, an enhanced nuclear force in Europe, a larger navy, and a rapid-deployment force. Despite the growing budget deficit, Congress approved most of these programs, and military expenditures shot up by one-third in the first half of the 1980s. Throughout Reagan's presidency, defense spending averaged $216 billion a year, up from $158 billion in the Carter years and higher even than in the Vietnam era.

Reagan justified the military buildup as a means to negotiate with the Soviets from a position of strength, but it provoked an outburst of pleas to halt the arms race. A rally demanding a freeze on additional nuclear weapons drew 700,000 people in New York City in 1982. Hundreds of thousands demonstrated across Europe, stimulated by fears of new U.S. missiles scheduled for deployment there in 1983.

Reagan startled many of his own advisers in March 1983 by announcing plans for research on the Strategic Defense Initiative (SDI). Immediately dubbed "Star Wars" by critics who doubted its feasibility, the project would deploy lasers in space to destroy enemy missiles before they could reach their targets. Reagan conceded that SDI could appear as "an aggressive policy" allowing the United States to strike first and not fear retaliation. The Soviets reacted angrily because SDI violated the 1972 Antiballistic Missile Treaty and because they would require huge investments to develop their own Star Wars technology. Subsequent administrations continued to spend billions on SDI research without producing a working system.

The U.S. military buildup could not extinguish the growing threat of terrorism by nonstate organizations that sought political objectives by attacking civilian populations. Terrorism had a long history throughout the world, but in the 1970s and 1980s, Americans saw it escalate in the Middle East, used by Palestinians after the Israeli occupation of the West Bank and by other groups hostile to Western policies. The terrorist organization Hezbollah, composed of Shiite Muslims and backed by Iran and Syria, arose in Lebanon in 1982 after Israeli forces invaded that country to stop the Palestine Liberation Organization (PLO) from using sanctuaries in Lebanon to launch attacks on Israel.

Reagan's effort to stabilize Lebanon by sending 2,000 Marines to join an international peacekeeping mission failed. In April 1983, a suicide attack on the U.S. Embassy in Beirut killed 63 people, and in October a Hezbollah fighter drove a bomb-filled truck into a U.S. barracks there, killing 241 marines (see Map 30.3). The attack prompted the withdrawal of U.S. troops, and Lebanon remained in chaos, while incidents of murder, kidnapping, and hijacking by various Middle Eastern extremist groups continued.

Following a Cold War pattern begun under Eisenhower, the Reagan administration sought to contain leftist movements across the globe. In October 1983, 5,000 U.S. troops invaded Grenada, a small island nation in the Caribbean that had succumbed to a Marxist coup. In Asia, the United States moved more quietly, aiding the Afghan rebels' war against Afghanistan's Soviet-backed government. In the African nation of Angola, the United States armed rebel forces against the government supported by both the Soviet Union and Cuba. Reagan also sided with the South African government, which was brutally suppressing black protest against apartheid, forcing Congress to override his veto in order to impose economic sanctions against South Africa.

El Salvador and Nicaragua

Administration officials were most fearful of left-wing movements in Central America, which Reagan claimed could "destabilize the entire region from the Panama Canal to Mexico." When a leftist uprising occurred in El Salvador in 1981, the United States sent money and military advisers to prop up the authoritarian government even though it had committed murderous human rights violations. In neighboring Nicaragua, the administration aided the Contras (literally, "opposers"), an armed coalition seeking to unseat the left-wing Sandinistas, who had toppled a long-standing dictatorship.

The Iran-Contra Scandal The Reagan administration's commitment to the Contras highlighted the issue of presidential versus congressional authority in using force abroad. Fearing another Vietnam, many Americans opposed aligning the United States with reactionary forces not supported by the majority of Nicaraguans. Congress repeatedly instructed the president to stop aiding the Contras, but the administration continued to secretly provide them with weapons and training and helped wreck the Nicaraguan economy. With support for his government undermined, Nicaragua's president, Daniel Ortega, agreed to a political settlement, and when he was defeated by a coalition of all the opposition groups, he stepped aside.

Secret aid to the Contras was part of a larger project that came to be known as the **Iran-Contra scandal**. It began in 1985 when officials of the National Security Council and CIA arranged to sell arms to Iran, then in the midst of an eight-year war with neighboring Iraq, even while the United States supplied Iraq with funds and weapons. The purpose was to get Iran to pressure Hezbollah to release seven American hostages being held in Lebanon (see Map 30.3). Funds from the arms sales were then channeled through Swiss bank accounts to aid the Nicaraguan Contras. Over the objections of his secretary of state and secretary of defense, Reagan approved the arms sales, but the three subsequently denied knowing that the proceeds were diverted to the Contras.

When news of the affair surfaced in November 1986, the Reagan administration faced serious charges. The president's aides had defied Congress's express ban on military aid for the Contras. Investigations by an independent prosecutor appointed by Reagan led to a trial in which seven individuals pleaded guilty or were convicted of lying to Congress

and destroying evidence. One felony conviction was later overturned on a technicality, and President George H. W. Bush pardoned the other six officials in December 1992. The independent prosecutor's final report found no evidence that Reagan had broken the law, but it concluded that he had known about the diversion of funds to the Contras and had "knowingly participated or at least acquiesced" in covering up the scandal—the most serious case of executive branch misconduct since Watergate.

A Thaw in Soviet-American Relations A momentous reduction in Cold War tensions soon overshadowed the Iran-Contra scandal. The new Soviet-American accord depended both on Reagan's flexibility and on an innovative Soviet head of state who recognized that his country's domestic problems demanded an easing of Cold War antagonism. **Mikhail Gorbachev** assumed power in 1985 determined to revitalize an inefficient Soviet economy incapable of delivering basic consumer goods. Hoping to stimulate production and streamline distribution, Gorbachev introduced some elements of free enterprise and proclaimed a new era of *glasnost* (greater freedom of expression), eventually allowing contested elections and challenges to Communist rule.

Nuclear Freeze Campaign Sixteen-year-old Justin Martino made this mask to wear in a 1985 march on the Pentagon in support of disarmament and world peace. Martino wanted to express his belief that "the arms race has no end except the end of life," and he later donated the mask to the Smithsonian Museum of American History. Worldwide demonstrations for nuclear disarmament achieved limited success when the United States and Soviet Union signed arms limitation agreements in 1987. Smithsonian Institution, Washington, D.C.

Concerns about immense defense budgets moved both Reagan and Gorbachev to the negotiating table. Enormous military expenditures stood between the Soviet premier and his goal of economic revival. With growing popular support for arms reductions, along with a push from his wife, Nancy, Reagan made disarmament a major goal in his last years in office and readily responded when Gorbachev took the initiative. A positive personal chemistry developed between them, and they met four times between 1985 and 1988. Although Reagan's insistence on proceeding with SDI nearly killed the talks, by December 1987 the superpowers had completed an **intermediate-range nuclear forces (INF) agreement**. The treaty eliminated all short- and medium-range missiles from Europe and provided for on-site inspection for the first time. This was also the first time either nation had pledged to eliminate weapons already in place.

In 1988, Gorbachev further reduced tensions by announcing a gradual withdrawal from Afghanistan, which had become the Soviet equivalent of America's Vietnam. In addition, the Soviet Union, the United States, and Cuba agreed on a political settlement of the civil war in the African nation of Angola. In the Middle East, both superpowers supported a cease-fire and peace talks in the eight-year war between Iran and Iraq. Within three years, the Cold War that had defined the world for nearly half a century would be history.

Q: **How did anticommunism shape Reagan's foreign policy?**

Conclusion: Reversing the Course of Government

"Ours was the first revolution in the history of mankind that truly reversed the course of government," boasted Ronald Reagan in his farewell address in 1989. The word *revolution* exaggerated the change, but his administration did mark the slowdown or reversal of expanding federal budgets, programs, and regulations that had taken off in the 1930s. Although he did not deliver on the social or moral issues dear to the heart of the New Right, Reagan represented the "choice not an echo" that Phyllis Schlafly had called

for in 1964, as he used his skills as "the Great Communicator" to cultivate antigovernment sentiment and undo the liberal assumptions of the New Deal.

Antigovernment sentiment grew along with the backlash against the reforms of the 1960s and the conduct of the Vietnam War. Watergate and other misdeeds of the Nixon administration further disillusioned Americans. Presidents Ford and Carter restored morality to the White House, but neither could solve the gravest economic problems since the Great Depression—slow economic growth, stagflation, and an increasing trade deficit. Even the Democrat Carter gave higher priority to fiscal austerity than to social reform, and he began the government's retreat from regulation of key industries.

A new conservative movement helped Reagan win the presidency and flourished during his administration. Reagan's tax cuts, combined with hefty increases in defense spending, created a federal deficit crisis that justified cuts in social welfare spending and made new federal initiatives unthinkable. Many Americans continued to support specific federal programs—especially those, such as Social Security and Medicare, that reached beyond the poor—but public sentiment about the government in general had taken a U-turn from the Roosevelt era. Instead of seeing the government as a helpful and problem-solving institution, many believed that not only was it ineffective at solving national problems, but it also often made things worse. As Reagan appointed new justices, the Supreme Court retreated from liberalism, curbing the government's authority to protect individual rights and regulate the economy.

With the economic recovery that set in after 1982 and his optimistic rhetoric, Reagan lifted the confidence of Americans about their nation and its promise—confidence that had eroded with the economic and foreign policy blows of the 1970s. Beginning his presidency with harsh rhetoric against the Soviet Union and a huge military buildup, Reagan helped move the two superpowers to the highest level of cooperation since the Cold War began. Although that accord was not welcomed by strong anti-Communist conservatives like Phyllis Schlafly, it signaled developments that would transform American-Soviet relations—and the world—in the next decade.

Reviewing the Chapter

★ KEY TERMS

Explain each term's significance

WHO

Phyllis Schlafly (p. 747)

Warren E. Burger (p. 750)

Shirley Chisholm (p. 751)

Gerald R. Ford (p. 753)

James Earl "Jimmy" Carter Jr. (p. 753)

Walter F. Mondale (p. 753)

Ronald Reagan (p. 760)

Pat Robertson (p. 761)

Sandra Day O'Connor (p. 766)

Mikhail Gorbachev (p. 768)

WHAT

Watergate (p. 751)

Federal Election Campaign Act of 1974 (p. 753)

National Energy Act of 1978 (p. 755)

Three Mile Island (p. 756)

Panama Canal treaty (p. 757)

Camp David accords (p. 757)

Iran hostage crisis (p. 759)

Christian Right (p. 761)

supply-side economics (p. 761)

Economic Recovery Tax Act (p. 761)

S&L crisis (p. 764)

Equal Rights Amendment (ERA) (p. 766)

acquired immune deficiency syndrome (AIDS) (p. 766)

Iran-Contra scandal (p. 768)

glasnost (p. 768)

intermediate-range nuclear forces (INF) agreement (p. 769)

FOR PRACTICE QUIZZES AND OTHER STUDY TOOLS, see the Online Study Guide at **bedfordstmartins.com/roarkcompact**.

★ REVIEW QUESTIONS Q:

Use key terms and dates to support your answer

1. How did Nixon's policies reflect the increasing influence of conservatives on the Republican Party? (pp. 749–51)

2. Why did Nixon resign the presidency in August 1974? (pp. 751–53)

3. How did Carter attempt to balance his commitment to human rights and anticommunism in his foreign policy? (pp. 754–59)

4. Why did economic inequality increase during the Reagan administration? (pp. 760–65)

5. What gains and setbacks did minorities, feminists, and gays and lesbians experience during the Reagan years? (pp. 765–67)

6. How did anticommunism shape Reagan's foreign policy? (pp. 767–69)

★ MAKING CONNECTIONS

Draw on key terms, timeline, and review questions

1. What was Watergate's legacy for American politics in the following decade? In your answer, explain what led to Nixon's resignation. How did Congress try to prevent such abuses of power in the future?

2. Both the left and the right ends of the American political spectrum changed significantly in the 1970s and 1980s. Describe these changes, and discuss how they shaped contemporary American politics. In your answer, be sure to cite specific political developments.

3. Recent experiences in Vietnam hung over the foreign policy decisions of Presidents Carter and Reagan. How did each president try to reconcile the lessons of that conflict and the ongoing Cold War? In your answer, be sure to discuss the legacy of the Vietnam War in the United States in the 1970s and 1980s.

4. American regional politics shifted in significant ways during the 1970s and 1980s. Why was grassroots conservatism particularly strong in the Sun Belt? What was its relationship to the civil rights and equal opportunity developments of the 1960s?

★ SUGGESTED READINGS

Douglas Little, *American Orientalism: The United States and the Middle East since 1945* (2002). An overview of American relations with this troubled region.

J. Anthony Lukas, *Common Ground: A Turbulent Decade in the Lives of Three American Families* (1986). A riveting narrative of race relations in Boston, culminating with the school busing crisis.

Donald G. Mathews and Jane Sherron De Hart, *Sex, Gender, and the Politics of the ERA* (1990). An exploration of the experiences and emotions of feminists and antifeminists in the ERA ratification struggle.

Lisa McGirr, *Suburban Warriors: The Origins of the New American Right* (2001). An account of the complex forces behind the rise of conservatism in Orange County, California.

Sean Wilentz, *The Age of Reagan: A History, 1974–2008* (2008). A lively history of Reagan's place in conservatism and his impact on American history.

FOR MORE BOOKS ABOUT TOPICS IN THIS CHAPTER, see the Online Bibliography at **bedfordstmartins.com/roarkcompact**.

FOR ADDITIONAL FIRSTHAND ACCOUNTS OF THIS PERIOD, see Chapter 30 in Michael Johnson, ed., *Reading the American Past,* Fourth Edition.

FOR WEB SITES, IMAGES, AND DOCUMENTS RELATED TO TOPICS AND PLACES IN THIS CHAPTER, visit Make History at **bedfordstmartins.com/roarkcompact**.

★ TIMELINE

1966	• Republican Ronald Reagan elected governor of California.
1968	• Republican Richard Nixon elected president.
1969	• Warren E. Burger appointed chief justice of U.S. Supreme Court.
1971	• Nixon vetoes comprehensive child care bill.
1972	• Nixon campaign aides arrested at Watergate complex.
1974	• Nixon resigns; Gerald Ford becomes president. • Ford pardons Nixon of any crimes he may have committed while president.
1976	• Democrat Jimmy Carter elected president.
1977	• United States signs Panama Canal Treaty.
1978	• *Regents of University of California v. Bakke.* • Congress deregulates airlines.
1979	• Camp David accords signed. • Carter establishes formal diplomatic relations with China. • Soviet Union invades Afghanistan. • Hostage crisis in Iran begins. • Moral Majority founded.
1980	• Congress deregulates banking, trucking, and railroad industries. • Congress passes Superfund legislation. • Republican Ronald Reagan elected president.
1981	• Researchers discover AIDS virus. • Economic Recovery Tax Act.
1982	• Large demonstrations against nuclear weapons.
1983	• Terrorist bomb kills 241 U.S. Marines in Beirut, Lebanon. • Reagan announces plans for Strategic Defense Initiative ("Star Wars").
1986	• Iran-Contra scandal.
1987	• INF agreement signed.
1988	• Civil Rights Restoration Act.

A SHRINKING WORLD The cellular telephone was one of the new technologies contributing to the intensifying globalization that occurred with the end of the Cold War in 1990. Wireless phones began to be used in Tokyo in 1979, and the first American system began in 1983. Cellular systems have improved communication for people in countries that lack good wire-based telephone systems, facilitating commerce as well as connecting far-flung family members and other individuals. The terrorists who struck the World Trade Center towers and the Pentagon on September 11, 2001, used mobile devices to coordinate the attacks, and many victims of the terror spoke their last words to loved ones on cell phones. By 2008, there were 233 million wireless subscribers in the United States and 3 billion around the world. Rapid development of cell phone technology has enabled people not only to call friends and business associates but also to connect to the Internet, take photographs, download music and movies, and send and receive e-mail.

The End of the Cold War and the Challenges of Globalization

SINCE 1989

IN HIS MOSCOW HOTEL ROOM on April 22, 1988, Ronald Reagan's national security adviser, army general **Colin L. Powell**, contemplated the plans that Premier Mikhail Gorbachev had just announced, which would dramatically alter the Soviet Union's government and economy. "Lying there in bed," Powell recalled, "I realized that one phase of my life had ended, and another was about to begin. Up until now, as a soldier, my mission had been to confront, contain, and, if necessary, combat communism. Now I had to think about a world without a Cold War." For the next sixteen years, Powell would have a central place in redefining his country's role in a world transformed.

Colin Powell was born in Harlem in 1937 and grew up in the Bronx, the son of parents who had emigrated from Jamaica in 1920. His father headed the shipping department in a garment factory, where his mother worked as a seamstress. After attending public schools, Powell enrolled in City College of New York. There he joined the army's Reserve Officers Training Corps (ROTC) program, the defining experience of his college years. "The discipline, the structure, the camaraderie, the sense of belonging," he said, "were what I craved." Commissioned as a lieutenant when he graduated in 1958, Powell began a lifelong career in military and public service, rising to the highest rank of four-star general. He chose to stay in the army primarily because "I loved what I was doing." But he also recognized that "for a black, no other avenue in American society offered so much opportunity." Powell's two tours of duty in Vietnam taught him that "you do not squander courage and lives without clear purpose, without the country's backing, and without full commitment." In his subsequent capacities as national security adviser to Ronald Reagan, chairman of the Joint Chiefs of Staff in the George H. W. Bush and Bill Clinton administrations, and secretary of state under George W. Bush, Powell endeavored to keep his country out of "halfhearted warfare for half-baked reasons that the American people could not understand or support."

Powell's sense that Gorbachev's reforms would bring about the end of the Cold War became a reality more quickly than anyone anticipated. Eastern Europe broke free from Communist control in 1989, and the Soviet Union disintegrated in 1991. Throughout the 1990s, as the lone superpower,

Secretary of State Colin Powell Among the many characteristics that helped Colin Powell rise through the ranks of the army and serve in four presidential administrations were his loyalty and discretion. The decision by George W. Bush to invade Iraq in March 2003 ran counter to Powell's commitment to acting through the international community and sacrificing American lives only when a vital interest was at stake and a plan for ending the intervention had been established. Although Secretary of State Powell's position lost to that of the more hawkish Vice President Dick Cheney and Secretary of Defense Donald Rumsfeld, Powell stayed in his job until 2005 and defended administration policy. In this photo taken at the White House in February 2003, he listens to Rumsfeld. National Security Adviser Condoleezza Rice stands behind them. Charles Ommanney/Contact Press Images for *Newsweek*.

the United States deployed both military and diplomatic power during episodes of instability in Latin America, the Middle East, eastern Europe, and Asia, almost always in concert with the major nations of Europe and Asia. In 1991, in its first full-fledged war since Vietnam, the United States led a United Nations–authorized force of twenty-eight nations to repel Iraq's invasion of Kuwait.

During his temporary retirement from public service in the 1990s, Powell remarked that "neither of the two major parties fits me comfortably." Many Americans seemed to agree: They turned Republican George H. W. Bush out of office in 1992 but elected Republican Congresses during Democrat Bill Clinton's administration. When Republican George W. Bush (son of George H. W. Bush) entered the White House in 2001, he faced a nearly evenly divided Congress. Between 1989 and 2000, domestic policies reflected a slight retreat from the conservatism of the Reagan years. The first Bush administration approved tighter environmental protections and new rights for people with disabilities, and President Clinton signed measures strengthening gun control and aiding low-wage earners. But the pendulum swung back to the right in the second Bush presidency.

All three presidents shared a commitment to hastening the globalization processes that were linking nations together in an increasingly connected economy. As capital, products, information, and people crossed national boundaries at greater speed, the United States experienced a surge of immigration rivaling the stream of a century earlier that had brought Powell's parents to the United States. Powell cheered globalization, predicting that the world would become "defined by trade relations, by the flow of information, capital, technology, and goods, rather than by armies glaring at each other across borders."

Powell was not so naive as to anticipate a world "without war or conflict," recognizing challenges such as nuclear proliferation, nationalist passions in areas of former Soviet dominance, civil wars in

Africa, and Islamic fundamentalism. But he shared other Americans' shock when in September 2001 deadly terrorist attacks in New York City and Washington, D.C., exposed American vulnerability to new and horrifying threats and sent U.S. soldiers into Afghanistan to overthrow the government that harbored the attackers. Subsequently, the administration's response to terrorism overwhelmed Secretary of State Powell's commitments to internationalism, multilateralism, and military restraint as George W. Bush began a second war against Iraq, implementing a distinct shift to a foreign policy based on preemptive attacks against presumed threats and going it alone if necessary. The unpopularity of that war and a severe financial crisis helped the Democrats regain power and elect Barack Obama as the first African American president. ★

The Presidency of George H. W. Bush

Vice President **George H. W. Bush** announced his bid for the presidency in the 1988 election, declaring, "We don't need radical new directions." Generally satisfied with the agenda set by Ronald Reagan and facing a Democratic-controlled Congress, Bush proposed few domestic initiatives. His dispatch of troops to oust the corrupt dictator of Panama, Manuel Noriega, represented a much longer continuity, following a century of U.S. intervention in Latin America.

Yet as the most dramatic changes since the 1940s swept through the world, Bush confronted situations that did not fit the simpler free world versus communism framework that had guided foreign policy since World War II. Most Americans approved of Bush's handling of two challenges to U.S. foreign policy: the disintegration of the Soviet Union and its hold over Eastern Europe, and Iraq's invasion of neighboring Kuwait. But voters' concern over a sluggish economy limited Bush to one term in the White House.

Gridlock in Government The son of a wealthy New England senator, George Herbert Walker Bush fought in World War II, earned a Yale degree, and then settled in Texas to make his own way in the oil industry and politics. He served in Congress during the 1960s and headed the CIA during the Nixon and Ford years. When Ronald Reagan achieved a commanding lead in the 1980 presidential primaries, Bush adjusted his more moderate policy positions to fit Reagan's conservative agenda and accepted second place on the Republican ticket. At the end of Reagan's second term, Republicans rewarded him with the presidential nomination.

Several candidates competed for the Democratic nomination in 1988. The Reverend Jesse Jackson—whose Rainbow Coalition campaign centered on the needs of minorities, women, the working class, and the poor—made an impressive bid,

winning several primaries and seven million votes. But a more centrist candidate, Massachusetts governor Michael Dukakis, won the nomination. On election day, half the eligible voters stayed home, indicating their disgust with the negative campaigning or their satisfaction with the Republican record on peace and prosperity. Divided government would remain, however, as Bush won 54 percent of the vote but the Democrats gained seats in Congress.

Although President Bush saw himself primarily as guardian and beneficiary of the Reagan legacy, he promised "a kinder, gentler nation" and was more inclined than Reagan to approve government activity in the private sphere. For example, he signed the **Clean Air Act of 1990**, the strongest, most comprehensive environmental law in history. Some forty million Americans reaped the benefits of a second regulatory measure, the **Americans with Disabilities Act** in 1990. Job discrimination against people with disabilities was now illegal, and private businesses and public facilities had to be made handicapped accessible. Cynthia Jones, publisher of a magazine on disability politics, noticed a breeze that stirred over the White House lawn at the signing of the bill. She said, "It was kind of like a new breath of air was sweeping across America. . . . People knew they had rights. That was wonderful." (See "Seeking the American Promise," page 776.)

Yet Bush also needed to satisfy party conservatives. His most famous campaign pledge had been "Read my lips: No new taxes," and he opposed most proposals requiring additional federal funds. Bush vetoed thirty-six bills, including those lifting abortion restrictions, extending unemployment benefits, raising taxes, and mandating family and medical leave for workers. Press reports increasingly used the words *stalemate, gridlock,* and *divided government.*

Continuing a trend begun during the Reagan years, states tried to compensate for this paralysis, becoming more innovative than Washington. States passed bills to block corporate takeovers, establish parental leave policies, improve food labeling, and protect the environment. In the

Suing for Access: Disability and the Courts

When the Americans with Disabilities Act (ADA) passed in 1990, Beverly Jones was elated. "For me, the passage of the ADA was like opening a door that had been closed to me for so long," she said. The ADA promised to protect people with disabilities from discrimination by private employers, public agencies, and state and local governments in employment, public services, public transportation, public accommodations, and telecommunications. A civil rights act, the ADA aimed to provide equal opportunity and access for people with disabilities and followed in a long tradition of Americans fighting for their rights.

Jones, a single mother with two children, joined the ranks of the 2.2 million Americans who use a wheelchair after an automobile accident in 1984 resulted in paraplegia. Determined not to "allow what I wanted in life to be denied because of . . . physical limitations," she trained as a court reporter and in 1990, the year the ADA passed, went to work to support herself and her kids. But Jones found that despite the ADA's promise to make facilities accessible for disabled people, she was not always able to do her job: In Tennessee, where she worked, seven out of ten courthouses were not wheelchair accessible. "I could not even get in the front door or the side or back door," Jones recalled. "I was often forced to ask complete strangers to carry me up the stairs." She found the experiences "humiliating and frightening."

Motivated by her anger, Jones became a national adult representative for Easter Seals Disability Services in 1997 and worked tirelessly to promote rights for the disabled. "I spoke to local, state, and federal officials. I talked to anyone who would listen. But I could not get anyone's attention," she stated. "The door that I thought had been opened was still closed and my freedom to live my dream was still a dream, and turning into a nightmare."

So in 1998, Jones filed a lawsuit against the state of Tennessee, joining five other plaintiffs who alleged that the state was in violation of Title II of the ADA, which prohibits governmental entities from denying public services, programs, and activities to individuals because of a disability. George Lane, another plaintiff in the suit, had injured his hip and pelvis in a car accident. Cited for reckless driving, he went to court in a wheelchair, and when he found the second-floor courtroom inaccessible, he crawled up the stairs. When the court adjourned for lunch, he crawled back down. That afternoon, he refused to crawl upstairs again and was arrested and jailed for failing to appear in court. Lane said that he would never forget the humiliation of having to drag his body up the thirty tile steps of the Polk County Courthouse. For Beverly Jones, the decision to file the suit came after she had to ask a judge to carry her to a restroom. "I was forced to turn down jobs, or face humiliating experiences," she testified. Lane, Jones, and the four other plaintiffs sought legal redress and damages of $250,000 each.

The case dragged on for six years without a ruling on the substance of their claims. Tennessee immediately countersued, challenging the constitutionality of the ADA's requirement that states make public facilities accessible to people with disabilities. Finally, in 2004, the case of *Tennessee v. Lane* reached the Supreme Court. In the fourteen years since the passage of the ADA, the legal landscape in America had changed markedly. Conservatives on the bench showed a revived interest in states' rights, espousing a "new federalism" that challenged the right of Congress to tell the states what

1980s, a few states began to pass measures guaranteeing gay and lesbian rights. In the 1990s, dozens of cities passed ordinances requiring businesses receiving tax abatements or other city benefits to pay wages well above the federal minimum wage. And in 1999, California passed a gun control bill with much tougher restrictions on assault weapons than reformers had been able to get through Congress.

A huge federal budget deficit inherited from the Reagan administration impelled the president in 1990 to abandon his "no new taxes" pledge, outraging conservatives. The new law, which Bush depended on Democrats to pass, authorized modest tax increases for high-income Americans and higher taxes on gasoline, cigarettes, alcohol, and luxury items. Yet it had little effect on the massive tax reductions of the early 1980s, leaving intact a key element of Reagan's legacy. Neither the new revenues nor controls on spending curbed the deficit, which was boosted by rising costs for Social Security, Medicare, and Medicaid and spending on war and natural disasters.

to do. Citing sovereign immunity (protection from lawsuits), granted to states by the Eleventh Amendment to the Constitution, courts began to question the right of Congress to make federal laws binding on the states. In 2001, in a dramatic example of the trend to limit Congress's power, the Supreme Court held that Congress lacked a constitutional basis for permitting states to be sued under Title I of the ADA, which applies to state employment.

In *Tennessee v. Lane*, the state cited this decision, claiming sovereign immunity and challenging the constitutionality of the ADA. The state's solicitor general argued that the law "imposes obligations on the states that go far beyond what the Constitution itself requires." Carol Westlake, executive director of the Tennessee Disability Coalition, pointed out that Tennessee's claim of states' rights was the same argument used to deny civil rights to African Americans in the 1950s and 1960s. In January 2004, as the Supreme Court heard arguments in the case, activists demonstrated outside the Court, chanting, "Justice for all; we won't crawl."

At stake was not only the right of people with disabilities to sue a state when denied access to public facilities but also the right of Congress to make federal laws binding on the states. In May 2004, in a five-to-four decision, the Supreme Court ruled that states that failed to make their courthouses accessible to people with disabilities could be sued for damages under federal disability law. But rather than validate, or even address, Congress's attempt to force states to make public services and programs accessible to the disabled, the Court confined its ruling to the specific context presented in the case: access to courts. By the narrowest possible margin, with the crucial fifth vote cast by Justice Sandra Day O'Connor, the Court focused on one narrow application of the ADA and upheld it in the face of Tennessee's claim of constitutional immunity.

"My case is over," Jones acknowledged. "We have accomplished what we wanted to be achieved." But she worried that the Court's fragile majority might be at risk with the appointment of Justice John Roberts to replace retiring Justice O'Connor in 2005. "Without the protections that Congress guaranteed in the Americans with Disabilities Act," Jones testified at Roberts's confirmation hearing in the Senate, "my life and the lives of millions of other people with disabilities would be a lot harder." At present, her fears have not been borne out. In a 2006 decision involving the ADA, the new Roberts Court ruled unanimously that a Georgia prisoner could sue the state for failing to accommodate his disability.

★ **Beverly Jones** Beverly Jones is shown here in her wheelchair next to one of the Tennessee courthouse stairways that made her job as a court reporter so difficult. "As a single mom supporting myself and two kids," she said, "I could not afford to quit my job or strictly limit my work to accessible courthouses." In 1998, Jones filed suit under the Americans with Disabilities Act. Six years later, in 2004, the Supreme Court upheld her right to enforce the protections the ADA granted to the disabled. AP Images.

Bush also continued Reagan's efforts to create a more conservative Supreme Court. His first nominee, federal appeals court judge David Souter, was a moderate. But in 1991, when the only African American on the Court, Justice Thurgood Marshall, retired, Bush set off a national controversy. He nominated Clarence Thomas, a conservative black appeals court judge who had opposed affirmative action as head of the Equal Employment Opportunity Commission (EEOC) under Reagan. Charging that Thomas would not protect minority rights,

civil rights groups and other liberal organizations fought the nomination. Then Anita Hill, a black law professor and former EEOC employee, shook the confirmation process by accusing Thomas of sexual harassment.

Before the Senate Judiciary Committee, Thomas angrily denied the charges, claiming that he was the victim of a "high-tech lynching for uppity blacks." Hill's testimony failed to sway the Senate, which voted narrowly to confirm Thomas. The hearings angered many women, who noted that only

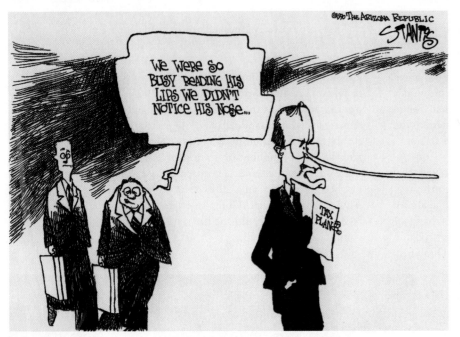

Bush and Taxes When George H. W. Bush accepted the Republican nomination for president in 1988, he addressed an issue central to conservative politics. "Read my lips," he told convention delegates: "No new taxes." Yet the federal budget deficit he had inherited from Ronald Reagan grew even larger, and Bush decided that fiscal responsibility required him to curb the accelerating debt with a package of both budget cuts and tax cuts. Many Republicans were outraged, and Bush had to depend on Democrats' votes in Congress to pass the measure. Editorial cartoonists had a field day with the controversy. Here, conservative cartoonist Scott Stantis, then at the *Arizona Republic* in Phoenix, likens Bush to Pinocchio, whose nose grew when he lied. Scott Stantis/Copley News Service.

FOR MORE HELP ANALYZING THIS IMAGE, see the visual activity for this chapter in the Online Study Guide at **bedfordstmartins.com/roarkcompact**.

two women sat in the Senate and denounced the male senators for failing to take sexual harassment seriously. Feminists complained that men "still don't get it" and redirected their anger to electoral politics, making 1992 a banner year for female candidates. Thomas's confirmation solidified the Supreme Court's shift to the right.

Going to War in Central America and the Persian Gulf

President Bush won greater support for his actions abroad, and he twice sent U.S. soldiers into battle. In Central America, the United States had tolerated and, in fact, paid Panamanian dictator Manuel Noriega for helping the Contras in Nicaragua and providing the CIA with information about Communist activities in the region. But in 1989, after Noriega was indicted for drug trafficking by an American grand jury and after his troops killed an American Marine, President Bush ordered 25,000 military personnel into Panama. In **Operation Just Cause**, U.S. forces quickly overcame Noriega's troops, sustaining 23 deaths, while

hundreds of Panamanians, including many civilians, died. Chairman of the Joint Chiefs of Staff Colin Powell noted that "our euphoria over our victory in Just Cause was not universal." Both the United Nations and the Organization of American States censured the unilateral action by the United States.

If the invasion of Panama fit within the century-old tradition of Yankee imperialism, Bush's second military engagement rested solidly on international approval. Considering Iran to be America's major enemy in the Middle East, U.S. officials had quietly assisted the Iraqi dictator **Saddam Hussein** in the Iran-Iraq war, which began in 1980 and ended inconclusively in 1988. In August 1990, Hussein sent troops into the small, oil-rich country of Kuwait to the south (Map 31.1), and within days the invasion neared the Saudi Arabian border, threatening the world's largest oil reserves. President Bush quickly ordered a massive mobilization of American forces and assembled an international coalition to stand up to Iraq. He invoked principles of national self-determination and international law, but long-standing interests in Middle Eastern oil also drove the U.S. response. As the largest importer of oil, the United States consumed one-fourth of the world's supply, 20 percent of which came from Iraq and Kuwait.

Reflecting the easing of Cold War tensions, the Soviet Union condemned Hussein and cut off arms shipments to Iraq. The UN declared an embargo on Iraqi oil and authorized the use of force if Iraq did not withdraw from Kuwait by January 15, 1991. By then, the United States had deployed 400,000 soldiers to Saudi Arabia, joined by 265,000 troops from some two dozen other nations, including several Arab states. "The community of nations has resolutely gathered to condemn and repel lawless aggression," Bush announced. "With few exceptions, the world now stands as one."

With Iraqi forces still in Kuwait, in January 1991 Bush asked Congress to approve war. Considerable sentiment favored waiting to see if the embargo and other means would force Hussein to back down, a position quietly urged within the administration by Colin Powell. Linking the crisis to the failure of U.S. energy conservation, Democratic senator Edward M. Kennedy insisted, "Not a single American life should be sacrificed in a war for the price of oil." Congress debated for three days and then authorized war by a margin of five votes in the Senate and sixty-seven in the House. On January 17, 1991, the U.S.-led coalition launched Operation Desert Storm, a forty-day bombing campaign against Iraqi military targets, power plants, oil refineries, and transportation networks. Having severely crippled Iraq by air, the coalition then stormed into Kuwait with massive ground forces, forcing Iraqi troops to withdraw (see Map 31.1).

"By God, we've kicked the Vietnam syndrome once and for all," President Bush exulted on March 1. Most Americans found no moral ambiguity in the **Persian Gulf War** and took pride in

the display of military prowess. In contrast to the loss of 58,000 American lives in Vietnam, 270 U.S. service members perished in Desert Storm. The United States stood at the apex of global leadership, steering a coalition in which Arab nations fought beside their former colonial rulers.

Some Americans criticized the Bush administration for ending the war without deposing Hussein. But Bush pointed to the UN mandate that limited the mission to driving Iraqi forces out of Kuwait and to Middle Eastern leaders' concern that an invasion

MAP 31.1 Events in the Middle East, 1989–2009

During the Persian Gulf War of 1991, Egypt, Syria, and other Middle Eastern nations joined the coalition against Iraq, and the twenty-two-member Arab League supported the war as a means to liberate Kuwait. After September 11, 2001, the Arab League approved of U.S. military operations in Afghanistan because the attacks "were an attack on the common values of the world, not just on the United States." Yet, except for the countries where the United States had military bases — Bahrain, Kuwait, Qatar, and Saudi Arabia — no Arab country supported the American invasion and occupation of Iraq in 2003. Arab hostility toward the United States also reflected the deterioration of Israeli-Palestinian relations after 1999, as Arabs charged that the United States allowed Israel to deny Palestinians land and liberty.

READING THE MAP: In what countries are the sources of oil located? In what countries does the United States have military bases?

CONNECTIONS: What conditions prompted the U.S. military interventions in Iraq and Afghanistan in 1991, 2001, and 2003? What were the U.S. goals in each of these interventions? To what extent were those goals realized?

FOR MORE HELP ANALYZING THIS MAP, see the map activity for this chapter in the Online Study Guide at bedfordstmartins.com/roarkcompact.

MAP 31.2 Events in Eastern Europe, 1989–2002
The overthrow of Communist governments throughout Eastern Europe and the splintering of the Soviet Union into more than a dozen separate nations were among the most momentous changes in world history since World War II.

of Iraq would destabilize the region. His secretary of defense Richard Cheney doubted that coalition forces could secure a stable government to replace Hussein and considered the price of a long occupation too high. Administration officials counted on economic sanctions and Hussein's pledges not to rearm or develop weapons of mass destruction, secured by a system of UN inspections, to contain the dictator.

Yet Middle Eastern stability remained elusive. Israel, which had endured Iraqi missile attacks, was more secure, but the Israeli-Palestinian conflict remained intractable. Despite military losses, Saddam Hussein remained in power and turned his war machine on Iraqi Kurds and Shiite Muslims whom the United States had encouraged to rebel. And he found ways to conceal arms from UN weapons inspectors before he threw them out in 1998.

The End of the Cold War Soviet support in the Persian Gulf War marked a momentous change in relations between the United States and the USSR. The progressive forces that Gorbachev had encouraged in the Communist world (see chapter 30) swept through Eastern Europe in 1989, when popular uprisings demanded an end to state repression and inefficient economic bureaucracies. Communist

governments toppled like dominoes (Map 31.2), virtually without bloodshed, because Gorbachev refused to prop them up with Soviet armies. East Germany opened its border with West Germany, and in November 1989, ecstatic Germans danced on the Berlin Wall and struck sledgehammers to demolish that dominant symbol of the Cold War, which had separated East and West since 1961.

Encouraged by President Bush, unification of East and West Germany sped to completion in 1990, and former iron curtain countries such as Hungary and Poland lined up to join NATO. Although U.S. military forces remained in Europe as part of NATO, Europe no longer depended on the United States for its security. Its economic clout also grew as Western Europe formed a common economic market in 1992. The destiny of Europe, to which the United States and the Soviet Union had held the key for forty-five years, now lay in European hands.

Inspired by the liberation of Eastern Europe, republics within the Soviet Union soon sought their own independence. In December 1991, Boris Yeltsin, president of the Russian Republic, announced that Russia and eleven other republics had formed a new entity, the Commonwealth of Independent States (CIS), and other former Soviet states declared their

Fall of the Berlin Wall After 1961, the Berlin Wall stood as the prime symbol of the Cold War and the iron grip of communism over Eastern Europe and the Soviet Union. More than four hundred Eastern Europeans were killed trying to flee to the West. After Communist authorities opened the wall on November 9, 1989, permitting free travel between East and West Germany, Berliners from both sides gathered at the wall to celebrate. Eric Bouvet/GAMMA/ZUMA.

FOR MORE HELP ANALYZING THIS IMAGE, see the visual activity for this chapter in the Online Study Guide at bedfordstmartins.com/roarkcompact.

independence. With nothing left to govern, Gorbachev resigned. The Soviet Union had dissolved, and with it the Cold War tensions that had defined U.S. foreign policy for decades.

China and North Korea resisted the liberalizing tides sweeping the world. In 1989, Chinese soldiers killed hundreds of pro-democracy demonstrators in Tiananmen Square in Beijing, and the Communist government arrested some ten thousand reformers. North Korea remained under a Communist dictatorship committed to developing nuclear weapons. "The post–Cold War world is decidedly not post-nuclear," declared one U.S. official. In 1990, the United States and Soviet Union had signed the Strategic Arms Reduction Talks (START) treaty, which cut about 30 percent of each superpower's nuclear arsenal. And in 1996, the UN General Assembly overwhelmingly approved a total nuclear test ban treaty. Yet India and Pakistan, hostile neighbors, refused to sign the treaty, and both exploded atomic devices in 1998, increasing the nuclear risk in South Asia. Moreover, the Republican-controlled Senate defeated U.S. ratification of the test ban treaty in October 1999, halting a decade of progress on nuclear weapons control. The potential for rogue nations and terrorist groups to develop nuclear weapons posed an ongoing threat to international peace and security.

The 1992 Election In March 1991, Bush's chances for reelection in 1992 looked golden. The Gulf War victory catapulted his approval rating to 88 percent, causing the most prominent Democrats to opt out of the presidential race. But that did not deter **William Jefferson "Bill" Clinton**, who at age forty-five had served as governor of Arkansas for twelve years. Like Carter in 1976, Clinton and his running mate, Tennessee senator Albert Gore Jr., presented themselves as "New Democrats" and sought to rid the party of its liberal image.

Clinton promised to work for the "forgotten middle class," who "do the work, pay the taxes, raise the kids, and play by the rules." Disavowing the "tax and spend" label that Republicans pinned on his party, he promised a tax cut for the middle class, pledged to reinvigorate government and the economy, and vowed "to put an end to welfare as we know it." Bush was vulnerable

> Clinton promised to work for the "forgotten middle class," who "do the work, pay the taxes, raise the kids, and play by the rules."

to voters' concerns about the ailing economy, as unemployment reached 7 percent, and to the Clinton campaign's emphasis on bread-and-butter issues. The popularity of a third candidate, self-made Texas billionaire H. Ross Perot, revealed Americans' frustrations with government and the major parties. Perot's ability to mobilize a sizable grassroots movement with his appeals to voters' disgust with Washington hurt the president more than it hurt Clinton, and it established the federal budget deficit as a key campaign issue.

Fifty-five percent of those eligible voted, just barely reversing the thirty-year decline in voter turnout. Clinton won 43 percent of the popular vote, Bush 38 percent, and Perot 19 percent — the strongest third-party finish in eighty years. By casting two-thirds of their votes against Bush, voters suggested a mandate for change but not the direction that change should take.

Q: Why did George H. W. Bush lose the presidency in 1992?

The Clinton Administration's Search for the Middle Ground

Bill Clinton's assertion that "the era of big government is over" reflected the Democratic Party's move to the right that had begun with Jimmy Carter in the 1970s. Clinton did not completely abandon liberal principles. He extended benefits for the working poor; delivered incremental reforms to feminists, environmentalists, and other groups; and spoke out in favor of affirmative action and gay rights. Yet his administration attended more to the concerns of middle-class Americans than to the needs of the disadvantaged.

Clinton's eight-year presidency witnessed the longest economic boom in history and ended with a budget surplus. Although various factors generated the prosperity, many Americans identified Clinton with the buoyant economy, elected him to a second term, and continued to support him even when his reckless sexual behavior resulted in impeachment. The Senate did not find sufficient cause to remove him from office, but the scandal crippled Clinton's leadership in his last years in office.

Clinton's Promise of Change Clinton wanted to restore confidence in government as a force for good but also to avoid alienating antigovernment voters. The huge budget deficit that he inherited — $4.4 trillion in 1993 — further precluded substantial federal initiatives. Moreover, Perot's challenges denied Clinton a majority of the popular

vote in both 1992 and 1996, and the Republicans controlled Congress for all but his first two years in office. Throughout most of his presidency, Clinton was burdened by investigations into past financial activities and private indiscretions. While the president had an extraordinary knack for making voters feel that he liked and understood them, he struggled to translate that appeal into gains for his party.

Despite these obstacles, Clinton achieved a number of incremental reforms. He used his executive authority to ease restrictions on abortion and signed several bills that Republicans had previously blocked. In 1993, Congress enacted gun control legislation and the Family and Medical Leave Act, which entitled workers in larger companies to unpaid leave for childbirth, adoption, and family medical emergencies. The Violence against Women Act of 1994 authorized $1.6 billion and new remedies for combating sexual assault and domestic violence. Clinton won stricter air pollution controls and greater protection for national forests and parks. Other liberal measures included a minimum-wage increase, expansion of aid for college students, and the creation of AmeriCorps, which enabled students to pay for their education with community service.

Most significantly, Clinton pushed through a substantial increase in the **Earned Income Tax Credit (EITC)** for low-wage earners, a program begun in 1975. The EITC gave tax cuts to people who worked full-time at meager wages or, if they paid no taxes, a subsidy to lift their family income above the poverty line. By 2003, some fifteen million low-income families were benefiting from the EITC, almost half of them minorities. One expert called it "the largest antipoverty program since the Great Society."

Shortly before Clinton took office, the economy had begun to rebound, and the boom that followed helped boost his popularity through the 1990s. Economic expansion, along with budget cuts, tax increases, and declining unemployment, produced a budget surplus in 1998, the first since 1969. Despite a substantial tax cut in 1997 that reduced levies on estates and capital gains and provided tax credits for families with children and for higher education, the surplus grew. The seemingly inexorable growth of government debt had turned around.

Clinton failed, however, to provide universal health insurance and curb skyrocketing medical costs. Under the direction of First Lady Hillary Rodham Clinton and with very little congressional consultation, the administration proposed an ambitious, complicated plan that the health care industry charged would increase taxes and government interference in medical decisions. Congress enacted piecemeal reform enabling workers who changed jobs to retain health insurance and underwriting health care for five million uninsured children, but affordable health care for all remained elusive.

Pledging to change the face of government to one that "looked like America," Clinton built on the gradual progress women and minorities had made since the 1960s. For example, African Americans and women had become mayors in major cities from New York to San Francisco. Virginia had elected the first black governor since Reconstruction, and Florida the first Latino. In the executive branch, Clinton appointed the most diverse group of department heads ever assembled, including six women, three African Americans, and two Latinos. Secretary of Commerce Norman Y. Mineta became the first Asian American to hold a cabinet post. Janet Reno became the first female attorney general and Madeleine K. Albright the first female secretary of state. Clinton's judicial appointments had a similar cast, and in 1993 he named the second woman to the Supreme Court, Ruth Bader Ginsburg, whose arguments before she became an appeals court judge had won key women's rights rulings from the Supreme Court.

The Clinton Administration Moves Right

Although parts of Clinton's agenda fell within the liberal tradition, his presidency overall moved the Democratic Party to the right. The $4.4 trillion deficit he inherited precluded significant federal spending, and the 1994 elections swept away the Democratic majorities in Congress. Led by Representative Newt Gingrich of Georgia, Republicans claimed the 1994 election as a mandate for their "contract with America," a conservative platform to end "government that is too big, too intrusive, and too easy with the public's money" and to elect "a Congress that respects the values and shares the faith of the American family." Opposition from Democrats and moderate Republicans blocked passage of most of the pledges, but Gingrich succeeded in moving the debate to the right.

The most extreme antigovernment sentiment developed far from Washington in the form of grassroots armed militias. They celebrated white Christian supremacy and reflected conservatives' hostility to such diverse things as taxes and the United Nations. Claiming the need to defend themselves from government tyranny, they stockpiled weapons. The militia movement grew with passage of gun control legislation and after government agents stormed the headquarters of an armed religious cult in Waco, Texas, in April 1993, killing more than 80. On the second anniversary of that event, a bomb leveled a federal building in Oklahoma City, taking 169 lives in the worst terrorist attack in the nation's history up to that point.

Clinton bowed to conservative views on gay and lesbian rights, backing away from a campaign promise to lift the ban on gays in the military. When military leaders and key legislators objected, he reverted to a **"don't ask, don't tell" policy** in 1993, forbidding officials from asking military personnel about their sexuality but allowing the dismissal of soldiers who said they were gay or engaged in homosexual behavior. Eventually, more than ten thousand homosexuals were discharged. In 1996, Clinton signed the Defense of Marriage Act, prohibiting the federal government from recognizing state-licensed marriages between same-sex couples.

Nonetheless, gays and lesbians continued to make strides as attitudes about homosexuality became more tolerant. By 2006, more than half of the five hundred largest companies provided health benefits to same-sex domestic partners and included sexual orientation in their nondiscrimination policies. More than twenty-five states banned discrimination in public employment, and many of those laws extended to private employment, housing, and education. By 2009, gay marriage was legal in Massachusetts, Connecticut, Vermont, Iowa, Maine, and New Hampshire, and several states recognized civil unions and domestic partnerships, extending to same-sex couples rights available to married couples in legal matters such as inheritance, taxation, and medical decisions.

Clinton's efforts to cast himself as a centrist were apparent in his handling of the New Deal program Aid to Families with Dependent Children (AFDC), which most people called welfare. Public sentiment about poverty had shifted since the 1960s. Instead of blaming poverty on the lack of adequate jobs or other external circumstances, more people blamed the poor themselves and believed that welfare programs trapped the poor in cycles of dependency. Many questioned why they should subsidize poor mothers now that so many women had joined the labor force. Nearly everyone considered work better than welfare, but supporters of AFDC doubted that the economy could provide sufficient jobs at decent wages.

By vetoing two welfare reform bills, Clinton forced a less punitive measure, which he signed as the 1996 election approached. The **Personal Responsibility and Work Opportunity Reconciliation Act** abolished AFDC and with it the nation's fifty-year pledge to provide a minimum level of subsistence for all children. The law provided grants to the states to assist the poor, but it limited welfare payments to two years, regardless of whether the recipient could find a job, and it set a lifetime limit of aid at five years. Reflecting growing controversy over immigration, it also barred legal immigrants from obtaining food stamps and other benefits and allowed states to stop Medicaid for legal immigrants.

The End of Welfare When Congress ended Aid to Families with Dependent Children (AFDC), the welfare system established during the New Deal, and replaced it with Temporary Assistance for Needy Families (TANF), LuAnne St. Clair wondered how she and her five children would fare when her welfare payments ended. Like other welfare recipients, American Indian mothers had to overcome the problems of acquiring job training and child care so they could find employment. But Indian women also faced the lack of sufficient jobs on reservations where they had strong family, cultural, and religious ties. In 1997, a year after the passage of TANF, St. Clair worried that she would have to leave the White Earth Reservation in Mahnomen, Minnesota, to find work. AP Images/Dawn Villella.

In its first decade, the law produced neither the horrors predicted by its critics nor the successes promised by its advocates. As intended, it did force single mothers to seek employment, cutting welfare rolls from 12.5 million to 4.5 million between 1996 and 2006. Yet not all former welfare recipients became self-supporting. Forty percent of former welfare mothers were not working regularly after being cut from the rolls, and those who did find jobs earned on average only about $12,000 a year. More than one-third of children living in female-headed families still lived in poverty.

Clinton's signature on the new law denied Republicans a partisan issue in the 1996 presidential campaign. The president ran as a moderate who would save the country from extremist Republicans, while the Republican Party also moved to the center, nominating Kansan Robert Dole, a World War II hero and former Senate majority leader. Clinton won 49 percent of the votes; 41 percent went to Dole and 9 percent to third-party candidate Ross Perot. Although Clinton won reelection with room to spare, voters sent a Republican majority back to Congress.

Impeaching the President Clinton's magnetic and articulate style, his ability to capture the middle ground of the electorate, and the nation's economic resurgence enabled the self-proclaimed "comeback kid" to survive scandals and an impeachment trial in 1998. Early in his presidency, charges related to firings of White House staff, political use of FBI records, and "Whitewater"—the nickname for real estate dealings that the Clintons had conducted in Arkansas—led to an official investigation by an independent prosecutor. The president also faced a sexual harassment lawsuit filed in 1994 by a state employee. A federal court threw out that case in 1998, but another sexual scandal more seriously threatened Clinton's presidency.

In January 1998, Kenneth Starr, independent prosecutor for Whitewater, began to investigate the charge that Clinton had had sexual relations with a twenty-one-year-old White House intern and then lied about it to a federal grand jury. At first, Clinton vehemently denied the charge, but subsequently he bowed to the mounting evidence against him. Starr prepared a case for the House of Representatives, which in December 1998 voted to impeach the president on two counts: perjury and obstruction of justice. Clinton became the second president (after Andrew Johnson, in 1868) to be impeached by the House and tried by the Senate.

The Senate trial took place in early 1999. Most Americans condemned the president's behavior but approved of the job he was doing and opposed removal from office. Some saw Starr as a fanatic invading individuals' privacy. One man said, "Let him get a divorce from his wife. Don't take him out of office and disrupt the country." Those favoring removal insisted that the president must set a high moral standard for the nation and that lying to a grand jury, even over a private matter, was a serious offense. A number of senators did not believe that Clinton's actions constituted the high crimes and misdemeanors required by the Constitution for conviction. With a two-thirds majority needed for that result, the Senate voted 45 to 55 on the perjury count and 50 to 50 on the obstruction of justice count. A majority, including some Republicans, seemed to agree with a Clinton supporter that the president's behavior, though "indefensible, outrageous, unforgivable, shameless," did not warrant his removal from office.

The investigation that triggered events leading up to impeachment ended in 2000 when the independent prosecutor reported insufficient evidence of illegalities related to the Whitewater land deals. Although more than 60 percent of Americans gave Clinton high marks on his job performance throughout the scandal, it distracted him from domestic and international problems and precluded the possibility of significant policy advances in his last years in office.

The Booming Economy of the 1990s Clinton's ability to weather the impeachment crisis owed much to the prosperous economy, which in 1991 began its longest period of expansion in U.S. history. During the 1990s, the gross domestic product grew by more than one-third, thirteen million new jobs were created, inflation remained in check, unemployment reached 4 percent—its lowest point in twenty-five years—and the stock market soared.

The president took credit for the thriving economy, and his policies did contribute to the boom. He made deficit reduction a priority, and in exchange the Federal Reserve Board and bond market traders lowered interest rates, encouraging economic expansion by making money easier to borrow. Businesses also prospered because they had squeezed down their costs through restructuring and laying off workers. Economic problems in Europe and Asia helped American firms become more competitive in the international market. And the computer revolution and the application of information technology boosted productivity.

People at all income levels benefited from the economic boom, but the gaps between the rich and the poor and between the wealthy and the middle class, which had been growing since the 1970s, failed to narrow. This persistence of inequality was linked in part to the growing use of information technology, which increased demand for highly skilled workers, while the movement of manufacturing jobs abroad diminished opportunities and wages for the less skilled. In addition, deregulation and the continuing decline of unions hurt lower-skilled workers, tax cuts had favored the better off, and the national minimum wage failed to keep up with inflation.

Although more minorities than ever attained middle-class status, in general people of color remained lowest on the economic ladder, reflecting Colin Powell's observation that "race still casts a shadow over our society." For instance, in 2005 the median income for white households surpassed $50,000, but it stood at only $31,000 and $36,000 for African American and Latino households, respectively. Asian American median family income exceeded that of whites, primarily because some Asian American groups, such as Japanese Americans, had more education and more wage earners. In 2005, poverty afflicted about 25 percent of blacks, 22 percent of Latinos, and 11.1 percent of Asian Americans, in contrast to 8.3 percent of whites.

Q: **What policies of the Clinton administration reflect the president's efforts to move his party to the right?**

The United States in a Globalizing World

America's economic success in the 1990s was linked to its dominance in the world economy. From that position, President Clinton tried to shape the tremendous transformations occurring in a process called globalization—the growing integration and interdependence of national citizens and economies. Building on the initiatives of his predecessors, Clinton lowered a number of trade barriers, despite stiff opposition from critics who emphasized the economic deprivation and environmental devastation that often resulted. Debates likewise arose over the large numbers of immigrants entering the United States.

Clinton agreed with Bush that the United States must retain its economic and military dominance over all other nations. The president took military action in Somalia, Haiti, the Middle East, and eastern Europe, and he pushed hard to ease the conflict between Israel and the Palestinians. Yet no new global strategy emerged to replace the containment of communism as the decisive factor in the exercise of American power abroad.

Defining America's Place in a New World Order In 1991, President George H. W. Bush declared a "new world order" emerging from the ashes of the Cold War. As the sole superpower, the United States was determined to let no nation challenge its military superiority or global leadership. (See "Global Comparison.") Yet policymakers struggled to define guiding principles for deciding when and how to use the nation's military and diplomatic power in a post–Cold War world. Combating Saddam Hussein's naked aggression seemed the obvious course of action in 1991, but dealing with other areas of instability proved more difficult.

Africa, where civil wars and extreme human suffering rarely evoked a strong American response, was a case in point. In 1992, guided largely by humanitarian concern, President Bush had attached U.S. forces to a UN operation in the small northern African country of Somalia, where famine and civil war raged. In 1993, President Clinton allowed that humanitarian mission to turn into "nation building"—an effort to establish a stable government—and eighteen U.S. soldiers were killed. After Americans saw film of Somalis dragging a soldier's corpse through the streets, the outcry at home suggested that most citizens were unwilling to sacrifice lives when no vital interest seemed threatened. Indeed, both the United States and the United Nations stood by in 1994 when more than half a million people were massacred in a brutal civil war in the central African nation of Rwanda.

Countries with the Highest Military Expenditures, 2005

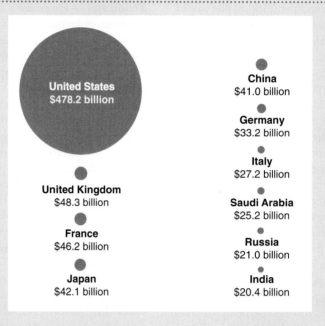

United States
$478.2 billion

China
$41.0 billion

Germany
$33.2 billion

Italy
$27.2 billion

Saudi Arabia
$25.2 billion

Russia
$21.0 billion

India
$20.4 billion

United Kingdom
$48.3 billion

France
$46.2 billion

Japan
$42.1 billion

During the Cold War, the military budgets of the United States and the Soviet Union were relatively even. For example, in 1983 U.S. military expenditures stood at $217 billion, compared to $213 billion for the USSR. Even before the Iraq War, which began in 2003, the U.S. military budget constituted 47 percent of total world military expenditures. That proportion rose to 48 percent in 2005, with the United States spending nearly ten times as much as its nearest competitor. The U.S. defense budget reflects the determination of Democratic and Republican administrations alike to maintain dominance in the world, even while the capacities of its traditional enemies have been greatly diminished.

As always, the United States was more inclined to use force nearer its borders, but in the case of the Caribbean country of Haiti, it gained international support for intervention. After a military coup overthrew Jean-Bertrand Aristide, the democratically elected president of Haiti, thousands of Haitians tried to escape political violence and poverty, many on flimsy boats heading for Florida. In 1994, Clinton got the United Nations to impose economic sanctions on Haiti and to authorize intervention by U.S. troops. Hours before U.S. forces were to invade Haiti, the military leaders promised to step down. U.S. forces peacefully landed and began disarming Haitian soldiers, and Aristide was restored to power. Initially a huge success, U.S. policy continued to be tested as Haiti faced grave economic challenges and political instability.

In Eastern Europe, the collapse of communism ignited a severe crisis. During the Cold War, the Communist government of Yugoslavia, a federation of six republics, had held ethnic tensions in check, and many Muslims, Croats, and Serbs had grown accustomed to living and working together. After the Communists were swept out in 1989, ruthless leaders exploited ethnic differences to bolster their power, and Yugoslavia splintered into separate states and fell into civil war.

The Serbs' aggression under President Slobodan Milosevic against Bosnian Muslims in particular horrified much of the world, but European and U.S. leaders hesitated to use military force. As reports of rape, torture, and mass killings in Bosnia increased, American leaders worried about the image of the world's strongest nation unwilling to stop the violence. Finally, in 1995, Clinton ordered U.S. fliers to join NATO forces in intensive bombing of Serbian military concentrations. That effort and successful offensives by the Croatian and Bosnian armies forced Milosevic to the bargaining table. After representatives from Serbia, Croatia, and Bosnia hammered out a peace treaty, Clinton then agreed to send twenty thousand American troops to Bosnia as part of a NATO peacekeeping mission.

In 1998, new fighting broke out in the southern Serbian province of Kosovo, where ethnic Albanians, who constituted 90 percent of the population, demanded independence. The Serbian army brutally retaliated, driving out one-third of Kosovo's 1.8 million Albanian Muslims. In 1999, NATO launched a U.S.-led bombing attack on Serbian military and government targets that, after three months, forced Milosevic to agree to a peace settlement. Serbians voted Milosevic out of office in October 2000, and he died in 2006 while on trial for genocide by a UN war crimes tribunal.

Elsewhere, Clinton remained willing to deploy U.S. power when he could send missiles rather than soldiers, and he was prepared to act without international support or UN sanction. In August 1998, bombs exploded at the U.S. embassies in Kenya and Tanzania, killing 12 Americans and more than 250 Africans. Clinton retaliated with missile attacks on terrorist training camps in Afghanistan and facilities in Sudan controlled by Osama bin Laden, a Saudi-born millionaire who financed the Islamic-extremist terrorist network linked to the embassy attacks. Clinton also launched air strikes against Iraq in 1993 when a plot to assassinate former president Bush was uncovered, in 1996 after Saddam Hussein attacked the Kurds in northern Iraq, and repeatedly between 1998 and 2000 after Hussein expelled UN weapons inspectors. Whereas Bush had acted in the Gulf War with the support of an international force that included

Breakup of Yugoslavia

Arab states, Clinton acted unilaterally and in the face of Arab opposition.

To ameliorate the Israeli-Palestinian conflict, a major source of Arab hostility toward the West, Clinton used diplomatic rather than military power. In 1993, due largely to the efforts of the Norwegian government, Yasir Arafat, head of the Palestine Liberation Organization (PLO), and Yitzhak Rabin, Israeli prime minister, recognized the existence of each other's states for the first time and agreed to Israeli withdrawal from the Gaza Strip and Jericho, allowing for Palestinian self-government there. In July 1994, Clinton presided over another turning point as Rabin and King Hussein of Jordan signed a declaration of peace. Yet difficult issues remained to be settled: control of Jerusalem; the fate of Palestinian refugees; and the more than 200,000 Israeli settlers living in the West Bank, the land seized by Israel in 1967, where 3 million Palestinians were determined to establish their own state. Clinton's last effort to broker negotiations between the PLO and Israel failed in 2000, and continuing violence between Israelis and Palestinians strengthened anti-American sentiment among Arabs, who saw the United States as Israel's ally.

Israel and PLO sign accords, 1993
Israel and Jordan sign peace treaty, 1994
Progress of Israeli-Palestinian negotiations halts and violence escalates, 2000
Israel withdraws from Gaza, 2005
Israel at war with Hezbollah in Lebanon, 2006
Israel invades Gaza, 2008

Events in Israel since 1989

Debates over Globalization The Clinton administration moved energetically on the economic side to speed up the growth of a "global marketplace." The process of globalization had begun in the fifteenth century, when Europeans began to trade with and populate other parts of the world. Between the U.S. Civil War and World War I, products, capital, and labor crossed national boundaries in ever-larger numbers. In that era, globalization was based on imperialism; Western nations took direct control of foreign territories, extracted their natural resources, and restricted manufacturing. Late-twentieth-century globalization, in contrast, advanced among sovereign nations and involved the industrialization of less developed areas, such as Korea and China. Other distinguishing marks of the more recent globalization were its scope and intensity: New communications technologies such as the Internet and cell phones connected nations, corporations, and individuals at much greater speed and much less cost than ever before.

Building on efforts by Presidents Reagan and Bush, Clinton sought to speed up globalization, seeking new measures to ease restrictions on international commerce. In November 1993, he won congressional approval of the **North American Free Trade Agreement (NAFTA)**, which eliminated all tariffs and trade barriers among the United States, Canada, and Mexico. Organized labor and others fearing loss of jobs and industries to Mexico lobbied vigorously against NAFTA, and a majority of Democrats opposed it, but Republican support ensured approval. In 1994, the Senate ratified the General Agreement on Tariffs and Trade (GATT), establishing the World Trade Organization (WTO) to enforce substantial tariff reductions and elimination of import quotas among some 135 member nations. And in 2005, Clinton's successor, George W. Bush, got Congress to lower more trade barriers with the passage of the Central American–Dominican Republic Free Trade Agreement (CAFTA-DR).

The free trade issue was intensely contested. Much of corporate America welcomed the elimination of trade barriers. "Ideally, you'd have every plant you own on a barge," remarked Jack Welch, CEO of General Electric. Critics linked globalization to the weakening of unions, the erosion of the social safety net provided for workers since the 1930s, and the growing gap between rich and poor. Demanding "fair trade" rather than simply free trade, they wanted trade treaties to require decent wage and labor standards. Environmentalists wanted countries seeking increased commerce with the United States to eliminate or reduce pollution and prevent the destruction of endangered species.

In November 1999, tens of thousands of activists dramatized the globalization debate when they gathered in Seattle, Washington, to protest a meeting of the WTO. Protesters charged the WTO with

THE PROMISE OF TECHNOLOGY

The Internet The Internet began as a product of government funding inspired by the Cold War. In response to the Soviet launch of *Sputnik*, President Eisenhower in 1958 created the Advanced Research Projects Agency (ARPA) to push research on technology. In 1969, the U.S. Department of Defense established ARPANET, a system that routed digitized messages between computers in order to provide security for military secrets and to enable communications during an enemy attack. In 1980, fewer than two hundred networks were connected, mostly at universities and research centers. By the year 2000, a majority of Americans and millions around the world logged on to what had come to be called the Internet at home or at work to send and receive e-mail, shop, chat, download music, read the news, conduct research, and more. Even the poorest countries had some access to the Internet. Here, Buddhist monks stand outside an Internet café in the Cambodian capital of Phnom Penh in December 2000. Phillip Lopez/AFP/Getty Images.

promoting a global economy that destroyed the environment, devastated poorer developing nations, and undercut living standards and wages for workers. At the Seattle demonstrations and elsewhere, U.S. labor unions emphasized the flight of factory jobs to developing nations as corporate executives sought cheaper labor to lower production costs. Tico Almeida, fresh out of college, was thrilled to hear "workers and unions from rich and poor countries alike stand together and say, 'We want rules for workers' rights to be integrated into the global economy.'"

Globalization controversies often centered on relationships between the United States, which dominated the world's industrial core, and the developing nations on the periphery, whose cheap labor and lax environmental standards caught the eye of investors. United Students against Sweatshops, for example, attacked the international conglomerate Nike, which paid Chinese workers $1.50 to produce a pair of shoes selling for more than $100 in the United States. Yet leaders of developing nations actively sought foreign investment, insisting that wages deemed pitiful by Americans offered people in poor nations a much better living than they could otherwise obtain. At the same time, developing countries often pointed to American hypocrisy in advocating free trade in industry while heavily subsidizing its own agricultural sector. "When countries like America, Britain and France subsidize their farmers," complained a grower in Uganda, "we get hurt."

Whereas globalization's cheerleaders argued that everyone would benefit in the long run, critics focused on the short-term victims. "International trade and global financial markets are very good at generating wealth," conceded American businessman George Soros, "but they cannot take care of other social needs, such as the preservation of peace, alleviation of poverty, protection of the environment, labor conditions, or human rights." The critics enjoyed a few successes. In 2000, President Clinton signed an executive order requiring an environmental impact review before the signing of any trade agreement. Beyond the United States, officials from the World Bank and the International Monetary Fund, along with representatives from wealthy economies, promised in 2000 to provide poor nations more debt relief and a greater voice in decisions about loans and grants. According to World Bank president James D. Wolfensohn, "Our challenge is to make globalization an instrument of opportunity and inclusion—not fear."

The Internationalization of the United States

Globalization was typically associated with the expansion of American enterprise and culture to other countries, yet the United States experienced the dynamic forces of globalization within its own borders. Already in the 1980s, Japanese, European, and Middle Eastern investors had purchased American stocks and bonds, real estate, and corporations such as Firestone and 20th Century Fox. Local communities welcomed foreign capital, and states competed to recruit foreign automobile plants. American non-union workers began to produce Hondas in Marysville, Ohio, and BMWs in Spartanburg, South Carolina. By 2002, the paychecks of nearly 4 million American workers came from foreign-owned companies.

Globalization was transforming not just the economy but American society as well, as the United States experienced a tremendous surge of immigration. By 2006, the nation housed 35.7 million immigrants who constituted 12.4 percent of the population. The 20 million who arrived between 1980 and 2005 surpassed the previous peak immigration of the first two decades of the twentieth century and exhibited a striking difference in country of origin. Eighty-five percent of the earlier immigrants had come from Europe; by the 1980s, almost half of the new arrivals were Asians, and nearly 40 percent came from Latin America and the Caribbean. Consequently, immigration changed the racial and ethnic composition of the nation. By 2004, Asian Americans numbered 13 million, while 41 million Latinos constituted—at 14 percent—the largest minority group in the nation.

The promise of economic opportunity, as always, lured immigrants to America, and the Immigration and Nationality Act of 1965 enabled them to come. Although the law set an annual ceiling of 270,000 immigrants, it allowed close relatives of U.S. citizens to enter above the ceiling, thus creating migration chains. In addition, the Cold War dispersal of U.S. military and other personnel around the world enabled foreigners to learn about the nation and form relationships with citizens. Moreover, during the Cold War, U.S. immigration policy was generous to refugees from communism, welcoming more than 800,000 Cubans after Castro's revolution in 1959 and more than 600,000 Vietnamese, Laotians, and Cambodians after the Vietnam War.

The racial composition of the new immigration heightened the century-old wariness of native-born Americans toward newcomers. Pressure for more restrictive policies stemmed from beliefs that immigrants took jobs from the native-born, suppressed wages by accepting low-paying employment, or eroded the dominant culture and language. Americans expressed particular hostility toward immigrants who were in the country illegally—an estimated 12 million in 2008—even though the economy depended on their cheap labor. The Immigration Reform and Control Act of 1986, which penalized employers who hired undocumented aliens but also granted amnesty to some 2 million illegal immigrants who had been in the country before 1982, did little to stem the tide.

The new immigration was once again making America an international, interracial society. The largest numbers of immigrants flocked to California, New York, Texas, Florida, New Jersey, and Illinois, but new immigrants dispersed throughout the country much more than did those of the early twentieth century. Taquerias, sushi bars, and Vietnamese restaurants appeared in southeastern and midwestern towns; cable TV companies added Spanish-language stations; and the international sport of soccer soared in popularity. Mixed marriages also displayed the growing fusion of cultures, recognized in 2000 on Census Bureau forms where Americans could check more than one racial category. Only half-joking, the famous golfer Tiger Woods called himself a "Cablinasian" to reflect his mixed heritage of Caucasian, black, American Indian, and Asian.

Like their predecessors, the majority of post-1965 immigrants were unskilled and poor. They took the lowest-paying jobs, including farm and yard work, child and elder care, and cleaning services—work that employers insisted native-born Americans would not do. Yet a significant number of immigrants were highly skilled workers, sought after by burgeoning high-tech industries. For example, in 1999 about one-third of the scientists and engineers employed in California's Silicon Valley had been born abroad.

Q: Who criticized free trade agreements and why?

President George W. Bush: Conservatism at Home and Radical Initiatives Abroad

The election of **George W. Bush** in 2000 marked the second time that a son of a former president gained the White House. But the younger Bush pushed an agenda that was closer to Ronald Reagan's than that of George H. W. Bush. He signed key legislation to improve public school education and to subsidize prescription drugs for elderly citizens. But he also persuaded Congress to pass enormous tax cuts that favored the wealthy, reduced environmental protections, and tipped the balance on the Supreme Court with two conservative appointments. The tax cuts, along with spending on new international and domestic crises, turned the substantial budget surplus that Bush had inherited into the largest deficit in the nation's history.

As Islamist terrorism replaced communism as the primary threat to U.S. security, the Bush administration launched a war in Afghanistan in 2001 and expanded the federal government's powers to investigate and detain individuals. In distinct contrast to his father's multilateral and cautious approach to foreign policy, George W. Bush adopted a policy of unilateralism and preemption by going to war against Iraq in 2003. He won reelection in 2004, but even at huge costs, stability in Iraq and Afghanistan remained elusive, and Bush confronted serious foreign and domestic crises in his second term. Democrats capitalized on widespread dissatisfaction with his administration to gain the presidency and control of Congress in 2008.

The Disputed Election of 2000 Clinton's presidency ended with a flourishing economy, and public opinion polls indicated that a majority of Americans agreed with the Democrats on most issues. Yet his vice president, Albert Gore, failed to succeed him in 2000. To many voters, Gore seemed stiff and pompous and too willing to change his positions for political advantage. He was further burdened with the taint of Clinton administration scandals.

George W. Bush won the Republican nomination after a series of richly funded, hard-fought primaries. The oldest son of former president George H. W. Bush, he had earned degrees from Yale and Harvard, worked in the oil industry, and served as governor of Texas since 1994. Inexperienced in national and international affairs, Bush chose for his running mate a seasoned official, Richard B. Cheney, who had served in the Nixon, Ford, and first Bush administrations.

Many observers predicted that the amazingly strong economy would give Gore the edge, and he did surpass Bush by more than half a million votes. Once the polls closed, however, it became clear that Florida's 25 electoral college votes would decide the presidency. Bush's tiny margin in Florida prompted an automatic recount of the votes, which eventually gave Bush an edge of 537 votes.

Meanwhile, the Democrats asked for hand-counting of Florida ballots in several heavily Democratic counties where machine errors and confusing ballots may have left thousands of Gore votes unrecorded. The Republicans, in turn, went to court to try to stop the hand-counts. The outcome of the 2000 election hung in the balance for weeks as cases went all the way to the Supreme Court. Finally, a bitterly divided Supreme Court ruled five to four against further recounts, and Gore conceded the presidency to Bush on December 13, 2000. For the first time since 1888, a president who failed to win the popular vote took office (Map 31.3). Despite the lack of a popular mandate, the Bush administration set out to make dramatic policy changes.

The Domestic Policies of a "Compassionate Conservative" Bush's appointments, like Clinton's, brought significant diversity to the executive branch. He chose African Americans Colin Powell as secretary of state and Condoleezza Rice first as national security adviser and subsequently as secretary of state when Powell resigned in January 2005. Five of Bush's top-level appointees were women, including Secretary of Labor Elaine L. Chao, the first Asian American woman to serve in the cabinet.

Bush had promised to govern as a "compassionate conservative." A devout born-again Christian, he immediately established the White House Office of Faith-Based and Community Initiatives to encourage religious and community groups to participate in government programs aimed at prison inmates, drug addicts, the unemployed, and others. The religious right praised the initiatives, but others charged that they violated the constitutional separation of church and state, and federal courts ruled

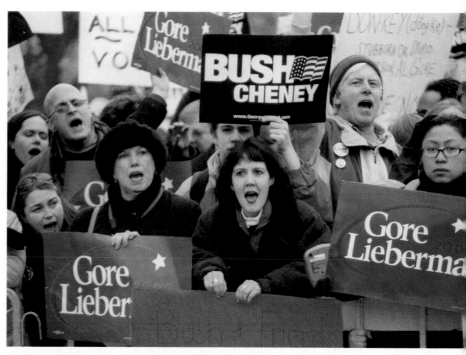

The Disputed Election While attorneys representing presidential candidates George W. Bush and Al Gore pursued lawsuits over the counting of ballots that would determine who won Florida's twenty-five electoral college votes, partisan supporters took to the streets. Here, backers of both sides rally outside the Supreme Court in Washington, D.C., on Monday, December 11, 2000, the day before the Court issued its five-to-four ruling that ended the hand-recounts of ballots and consequently secured the presidency for Bush. Critics charged that the five justices who voted to stop the recounts had applied partisanship rather than objectivity to the case, pointing out that if those justices had followed their custom of favoring state over federal authority, they would have allowed Florida to continue the recounts. AP Images.

in more than a dozen cases that faith ministries were using government funds to indoctrinate the people they served.

Bush's fiscal policies were more compassionate toward the rich than toward average Americans. In 2001, he signed a bill reducing taxes over the next ten years by $1.35 trillion. A 2003 tax law slashed another $320 billion. The laws heavily favored the rich by reducing income taxes, phasing out estate taxes, and cutting tax rates on capital gains and dividends. They also provided benefits for married couples and families with children and offered tax deductions for college expenses.

The administration insisted that the tax cuts would promote economic growth and jolt the economy out of the recession that had begun in 2000. The economy did recover, but opponents stressed inequities in the tax cuts and pointed to a mushrooming federal deficit — the highest in U.S. history — that surpassed $400 billion in 2004. Republicans had traditionally railed against budget deficits, but now many saw them as a way to limit the federal government. The deficit shot up to more than $400 billion again in 2008 and the next year

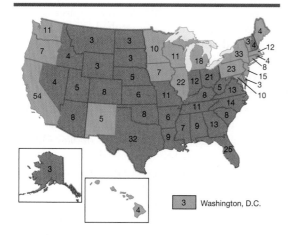

Candidate	Electoral Vote	Popular Vote	Percent of Popular Vote
George W. Bush (Republican)	271	50,456,062	47.8
Al Gore (Democrat)	267	50,996,862	48.4
Ralph Nader (Green Party)	0	2,858,843	2.7
Patrick J. Buchanan (Reform Party)	0	438,760	0.4

3 — Washington, D.C.

MAP 31.3 The Election of 2000

surpassed $1 trillion as the government struggled to combat a recession. The national debt rose to $9.6 trillion, making the United States increasingly dependent on China and other foreign investors who held more than half of the debt.

Bush used regulatory powers that did not require congressional approval to weaken environmental protection as part of his larger goals of reducing government regulation, promoting economic growth, and increasing energy production. The administration opened millions of wilderness acres to mining, oil, and timber industries and relaxed environmental requirements under the Clean Air and Clean Water Acts. To worldwide dismay, the administration withdrew from the **Kyoto Protocol** on global warming, signed in 1997 by 178 nations to reduce greenhouse gas emissions.

While environmentalists pushed for measures to limit American energy consumption, the administration called for more rapid development of energy resources. During his second term, as gasoline prices reached all-time highs in 2005, Bush signed the Energy Policy Act, a compromise bill providing $14 billion in subsidies to producers of oil, coal, nuclear power, and alternative sources of energy. But when gas prices shot up even higher in 2008, Congress blocked the president's efforts to lift restrictions on offshore drilling for oil, and it continued to thwart his calls to allow drilling for oil in the Arctic National Wildlife Refuge.

Conservatives hailed Bush's appointment of two new Supreme Court justices. In 2005, John Roberts, who had served in the Reagan and George H. W. Bush administrations, was named chief justice. Bush then replaced the moderate Sandra Day O'Connor with Samuel A. Alito, a staunch conservative who won confirmation by a narrow margin. While the Court stood up to the administration in rulings on the rights of accused terrorists, it evidenced the rightward tilt on cases concerning abortion, gun control, sex discrimination in employment, and regulation of business.

In contrast to the partisan conflict over judicial appointments and tax and environmental policy, Bush won bipartisan support for the **No Child Left Behind (NCLB) Act** of 2002, marking the greatest change in federal education policy since the 1960s and substantially extending the role of the federal government in public education. Promising to end, in Bush's words, "the story of children being just shuffled through the system," the law required every school to meet annual testing standards, penalized failing schools, and allowed parents to transfer their children out of such schools. It authorized an increase in federal aid aimed primarily at the poorest districts, but not enough for Senator Paul Wellstone of Minnesota,

one of the few critics of the education bill, who asked, "How can you reach the goal of leaving no child behind on a tin cup budget?" In addition to struggling to finance the new standards, school officials began to criticize the one-size-fits-all approach and pointed to family and community impoverishment as sources of student deficiencies.

The Bush administration's second major effort to co-opt Democratic Party issues constituted what the president hailed as "the greatest advance in health care coverage for America's seniors" since the start of Medicare in 1965. In 2003, Bush signed a bill authorizing prescription drug benefits for the elderly and at the same time expanding the role of private insurers in the Medicare system. Most Democrats opposed the legislation, charging that it left big gaps in coverage, subsidized private insurers with federal funds to compete with Medicare, banned imports of low-priced drugs, and prohibited the government from negotiating with drug companies to reduce prices. Legislators of both parties worried about the cost of the new drug benefit. Although the law's requirement that beneficiaries choose from dozens of private insurance plans made the program confusing, more than 80 percent of the elderly who signed up for the benefit were at least "somewhat satisfied" with the program. Medical costs overall continued to soar, and the number of uninsured Americans surpassed 40 million in 2008.

One domestic undertaking of the Bush administration found little approval anywhere: its handling of **Hurricane Katrina**, which in August 2005 devastated the coasts of Alabama, Louisiana, and Mississippi and ultimately resulted in some fifteen hundred deaths. The catastrophe that ensued when New Orleans levees broke, flooding 80 percent of the city, shook a deeply rooted assumption held by Americans, even conservatives who were devoted to limited government: that government owed its citizens protection from natural disasters. Federal, state, and local officials failed the citizens of New Orleans in two ways: They had not built the levees to withstand such a deluge, and they failed to rescue citizens when the levees broke and flooded their homes.

New Orleans residents who were too old, too poor, or too sick to flee the flooding spent anguished days waiting on rooftops for help; wading in filthy, toxic water; and enduring the heat, disorder, and lack of basic necessities at the convention center and Superdome, where they had been told to go for safety and protection. "How can we save the world if we can't save our own people?" wondered one Louisianan. Thousands of volunteers rescued the stranded, helped evacuees in distant cities, and traveled to the Gulf coast to assist with reconstruction. Millions more opened their pocketbooks to aid the victims. Yet the immense private generosity and the superb response of a few groups, such as the U.S. Coast Guard and the Louisiana Department of Wildlife and Fisheries, could not make up for the feeling that the nation had failed some of its citizens when they needed it most. Since so many of Katrina's hardest-hit victims were poor and black, the disaster also highlighted the severe injustices and deprivations remaining in American society.

The Globalization of Terrorism The response to Hurricane Katrina contrasted sharply with the Bush administration's decisive reaction to the horror that had unfolded four years earlier on the morning of **September 11, 2001**. In the most deadly attack ever launched on American soil, nineteen terrorists hijacked four planes and flew three of them into the twin towers of New York City's World Trade Center and the Pentagon in Washington, D.C.; the fourth crashed in a field in Pennsylvania. The attacks took nearly 2,800 lives, including U.S. citizens and people from ninety countries. The nation, indeed the world, was stunned.

The hijackers were members of Osama bin Laden's **Al Qaeda** international terrorist network, some of whom had been living in the United States for several years. Organized from bin Laden's sanctuaries in Afghanistan, where the radical Muslim Taliban government had taken control, the attacks reflected several elements of globalization. Technological advances and increased mobility facilitated bin Laden's worldwide coordination of Al Qaeda. Moreover, Islamic extremists were enraged by the spread of Western goods, culture, and values into the Muslim world, as well as by the 1991 Persian Gulf War against Iraq and the stationing of American troops in Saudi Arabia, bin Laden's homeland. Bin Laden sought to rid the Middle East of Western influence and install puritanical Muslim control. Whether poor or middle class, living in Middle Eastern homelands governed by undemocratic and corrupt governments or in Western cities where they felt alienated and despised, the 9/11 terrorists and others who came after them saw the West, especially the United States, as the evil source of their humiliation and the supporter of Israel's oppression of Palestinian Muslims. In the wake of the September 11 attacks, President Bush's public approval rating skyrocketed as he sought a global alliance against terrorism and won at least verbal support from most governments.

On October 11, the United States and Britain began bombing Afghanistan, and American special forces aided the Northern Alliance, the Taliban government's main opposition. By December, the Taliban government was destroyed, but bin Laden had not been captured, and numerous Al Qaeda forces had escaped or remained in hiding throughout the world. Afghans elected a new national government, but although the United States still had 27,000 troops in Afghanistan seven years later, economic stability and physical security remained out of reach.

At home, the balance between liberty and security tilted. Throughout the country, anti-immigrant sentiment revived, and anyone appearing to be Middle Eastern or practicing Islam was likely to arouse suspicion. Authorities arrested more than a thousand Arabs and Muslims, and a Justice Department study later reported that many people with no connection to terrorism spent months in jail, denied their rights. "I think America overreacted . . . by singling out Arab-named men like myself," said Shanaz Mohammed, who was jailed for eight months for an immigration violation.

In October 2001, Congress passed the **USA Patriot Act** by huge majorities. The law gave the government new powers to monitor suspected terrorists and their associates, including the ability to pry personal information about individuals from libraries, universities, and businesses, while allowing more exchange of information between criminal investigators and those investigating foreign threats. It soon provoked calls for revision from both conservatives and liberals. Kathleen MacKenzie, a councilwoman in Ann Arbor, Michigan, explained why the council opposed the Patriot Act: "[A]s awful as we feel about September 11 and as concerned as we were about national safety, we felt that giving up [rights] was too high a price to pay." A security official countered, "If you don't violate someone's human rights some of the time, you probably aren't doing your job."

Insisting that presidential powers were virtually limitless in times of national crisis, Bush stretched his powers as commander in chief until he met resistance from the courts and Congress. In 2001, the administration established special military commissions to try prisoners captured in Afghanistan and taken to the U.S. military base at Guantánamo, Cuba. But in 2006, responding to a suit filed by one of the approximately five hundred detainees who had languished there for years, the

> "I think America overreacted . . . by singling out Arab-named men like myself," said Shanaz Mohammed, who was jailed for eight months for an immigration violation in the wake of September 11.

Afghanistan

Supreme Court ruled five to three that Congress had not authorized such tribunals and that they violated international law. That year, congressional leaders became openly critical of the administration for wiretapping phone calls made and received by U.S. residents without obtaining the warrants required by law.

The government also sought to protect Americans from future terrorist attacks through the greatest reorganization of the executive branch since 1948. In November 2002, Congress authorized the new **Department of Homeland Security** (DHS), combining 170,000 federal employees from twenty-two agencies that had responsibilities for various aspects of domestic security. Chief among the department's duties were intelligence analysis; immigration and border security; chemical, biological, and nuclear countermeasures; and emergency preparedness and response. During the new department's first six years, no terrorist attacks were launched in the United States, but doubts grew about its effectiveness when its subagency, the Federal Emergency Management Agency (FEMA), failed in its response to Hurricane Katrina.

Unilateralism, Preemption, and the Iraq War

The Bush administration sought collective action against the Taliban, but on most other international issues, it adopted a go-it-alone approach. In addition to withdrawing from the Kyoto Protocol on global warming and violating international rules about the treatment of military prisoners, it scrapped the 1972 Antiballistic Missile Treaty in order to develop the space-based Strategic Defense Initiative (SDI) first proposed by Ronald Reagan. Bush also withdrew the nation from the UN's International Criminal Court, and he rejected an agreement to enforce bans on the development and possession of biological weapons—an agreement signed by all of America's European allies.

Nowhere was the new policy of unilateralism more striking than in a new war against Iraq, a war endorsed by Vice President Dick Cheney and Secretary of Defense Donald H. Rumsfeld, but not by Secretary of State Colin Powell. In his State of the Union message in January 2002, Bush identified Iraq, Iran, and North Korea as an "axis of evil." His words alarmed political leaders in Europe and Asia, who insisted that those three nations posed entirely

Iraq

different challenges and who preferred to emphasize diplomacy rather than confrontation.

Nonetheless, addressing West Point graduates in June, President Bush proclaimed a new policy for American security based not on containment but on preemption: "Traditional concepts of deterrence will not work against a terrorist enemy whose avowed tactics are wanton destruction and the targeting of innocents; whose so-called soldiers seek martyrdom in death and whose most potent protection is statelessness." Because nuclear, chemical, and biological weapons enabled "even weak states and small groups [to] attain a catastrophic power to strike great nations," the United States had to "be ready for preemptive action." The president's claim that the United States had the right to start a war was at odds with international law and with many Americans' understanding of their nation's ideals. It distressed most of America's great-power allies.

The Bush administration moved deliberately to apply the doctrine of preemption to Iraq, whose dictator, Saddam Hussein, appeared to be in violation of UN resolutions from the 1991 Gulf War requiring Iraq to destroy and stop further development of nuclear, chemical, and biological weapons. In November 2002, the United States persuaded the UN Security Council to pass a resolution requiring Iraq to disarm or face "serious consequences." When Iraq failed to comply fully with new UN inspections, the Bush administration decided on war. Making (subsequently refuted) claims that Hussein had links to Al Qaeda and harbored terrorists and that Iraq possessed weapons of mass destruction, the president insisted that the threat was immediate and great enough to justify preemptive action. Despite opposition from the Arab world and most major nations—including France, Germany, China, and Russia—which preferred to give the UN inspectors more time, the United States and Britain invaded Iraq on March 19, 2003, supported by some thirty nations (see Map 31.1). Coalition forces won an easy and decisive victory, and Bush declared the end of the **Iraq War** on May 1. Saddam Hussein remained at large until December 2003.

Chaos followed the quick victory over Hussein. Damage from U.S. bombing and widespread looting resulting from the failure of U.S. troops to secure order and provide basic necessities left Iraqis wondering how much they had gained. "With Saddam there was tyranny, but at least you had a salary to put food on your family's table," said a young father from Hussein's hometown of Tikrit. A Baghdad hospital worker complained, "They can take our oil, but at least they should let us have electricity and water." Five years after the invasion, Iraqis had less electricity than they had had before the war, and a majority lacked access to clean water. Continuing violence had caused 2 million to flee their country and displaced 1.9 million within Iraq.

The administration had not planned adequately for the occupation and sent far fewer forces to Iraq than it had deployed in 1991 in response to Iraq's invasion of Kuwait. The 140,000 American forces in Iraq came under attack almost daily from remnants of the former Hussein regime, religious extremists, and hundreds of foreign terrorists now entering the chaotic country. Seeking to divide Iraqis and undermine the occupation, terrorists launched deadly assaults on such targets as the UN mission in Baghdad and Red Cross headquarters, as well as on major mosques and Iraqi citizens, resulting in the death of tens of thousands.

The war became an issue in the presidential campaign of 2004, which registered the highest voter turnout since 1968. Massachusetts senator John Kerry, the Democratic nominee, criticized Bush's unilateralist foreign policy and the administration's conduct of the war. A slim majority of voters, however, indicated their belief that Bush would better protect American security from terrorist threats than Kerry. The president eked out a 286 to 252 victory in the electoral college, winning 50.7 percent of the popular vote to Kerry's 48.3 percent and carrying Republican majorities into Congress.

In June 2004, the United States transferred sovereignty to an interim Iraqi government, and in January 2005 about 58 percent of Iraqis eligible to vote risked their safety to elect a national assembly. The daunting challenges facing the national assembly were to write a constitution, satisfy Iraq's sharply divided political blocs, and decide to what extent Islamic religious law would shape the new government. Violence escalated against government officials, Iraqi civilians, and occupation forces. A nineteen-year-old Iraqi confined to his house by his parents, who feared he could be killed or lured into terrorist activities, said, "If I'm killed, it doesn't even matter because I'm dead right now." By 2006, when U.S. military deaths approached 3,000 and Iraqi civilian casualties reached tens of thousands, public opinion polls in the United States found that a majority of Americans believed that the Iraq War was a mistake.

The president's father, George H. W. Bush, had refused to invade Iraq at the end of the 1991 Gulf War. He explained that Colin Powell, Dick Cheney, and other advisers agreed that "unilaterally exceeding the United Nations' mandate would have destroyed the precedent of international response to aggression that we hoped to establish." The first Bush administration resisted making the nation "an occupying power in a bitterly hostile land," refusing to incur the "incalculable human and political costs" that such an invasion would produce.

By 2006, his son's very different approach was subject to criticism that crossed party lines and included leading military figures. Critics acknowledged that the U.S. military had felled a brutal dictator, but coalition forces were not sufficiently numerous or prepared for the turmoil that followed the invasion, nor did they find the weapons of mass destruction or links to Osama bin Laden that administration officials had insisted made the war necessary. Rather, in the chaos induced by the invasion of Iraq, more than a thousand terrorists entered Iraq—the place, according to one expert, "for fundamentalists to go . . . to stick it to the West."

The war and occupation exacted a steep price not only in dollars but also in American and Iraqi lives, U.S. relations with the other great powers, and the nation's reputation in the world, especially among Arab nations. Revelations of prisoner abuse in the Abu Ghraib prison in Iraq and in the Guantánamo detention camp housing captives from the Afghan war further tarnished the U.S. image. Anti-Americanism around the world rose to its highest point in history. The budget deficit swelled, and resources were diverted to Iraq from other national security challenges, including the stabilization of Afghanistan, the elimination of bin Laden and Al Qaeda, and the threats posed by North Korea's and Iran's pursuit of nuclear weapons.

Voters registered their dissatisfaction in the 2006 congressional elections, turning control of both houses over to the Democrats for the first time since 1994. President Bush replaced Secretary of Defense Donald Rumsfeld, and the administration displayed more willingness to work with other nations in dealing with Iraq, Iran, and North Korea. Yet Bush clung to the goal of bringing democracy to the Middle East, even as the situation in Iraq deteriorated. Despite opposition from Democrats in Congress, who wanted a timetable for withdrawal from Iraq, in 2007 the administration began a troop surge that increased U.S. forces there to 160,000. The surge, along with actions by Iraqi leaders, contributed to a dramatic reduction in terrorist violence, and the administration began planning for the eventual withdrawal of U.S. forces by the end of 2011.

Barack Obama and the Promise of Change

Despite the improving situation in Iraq, President Bush's approval ratings sank below 30 percent, posing severe difficulties for the Republican Party in the 2008 elections. The Republicans nominated John McCain, former Vietnam war hero and

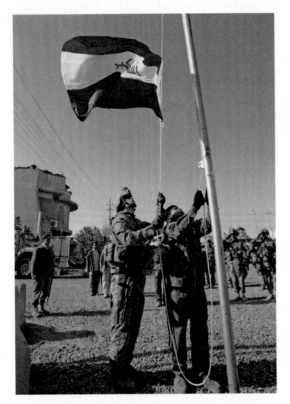

Transferring Authority to Iraqis In March 2007, as part of the troop surge in Iraq, U.S. forces set up three joint security stations in Ghazaliya, one of the most dangerous areas around Baghdad. By 2009, the counterinsurgency strategy had produced significant results. Attacks throughout Iraq fell sharply, while U.S. military deaths dropped from 904 in 2007 to 314 in 2008. The improved security fed Iraqis' determination to regain control of their country. Marking one of many steps in this process, in January 2009 U.S. forces transferred full control of Joint Security Station III in Ghazaliya to the Iraqi army. Here, U.S. Army Specialist Anthony Perez and an Iraqi soldier raise the Iraqi flag above the station. AP Images/Karim Kadim.

longtime senator from Arizona, who defeated more conservative contenders in the primaries and chose Alaska governor Sarah Palin as his running mate, the second woman to run for vice president on a major party ticket. Even more historic changes occurred in the Democratic Party when **Barack Obama** edged out **Hillary Rodham Clinton**, the former first lady and then senator from New York, in closely contended battles that continued until the last primaries in June.

Born to a white mother and a Kenyan father and raised in Hawaii and Indonesia, Obama was the first African American to head the *Harvard Law Review*. He settled in Chicago, served in the Illinois Senate, and won election to the U.S. Senate in 2004. At the age of forty-seven, Obama won the Democratic nomination with a combination of

brilliant campaign strategy based on grassroots and Internet organizing, a charismatic personality, and the ability to speak to deep-seated longings for a new kind of politics and racial reconciliation. He won 53 percent of the popular vote and defeated McCain 365 to 173 in the electoral college, while Democrats increased their majorities in the House and Senate (Map 31.4).

Obama promised to work across party lines on a series of reforms in health care, education, and the environment. But by his inauguration, more immediate problems commanded his attention. Fueled by a breakdown in financial institutions that had accumulated trillions of dollars of bad debt, a recession hit the economy in 2008. The financial crisis was so severe that Congress passed the Bush administration's $700 billion Troubled Assets Relief Program to inject credit into the economy and shore up banks and other businesses. Home mortgage foreclosures skyrocketed, major companies went bankrupt, and unemployment surpassed 9.4 percent in summer 2009, the highest rate in more than twenty-five years. While Iraq had become more stable, Afghanistan and Pakistan remained dangerous trouble spots, new fighting broke out in Gaza between Israel and the Palestinians, and the economic crisis stretched around the globe. The first African American president faced the most daunting challenges at home and abroad since the time of Franklin Roosevelt.

Q: Why did the United States invade Iraq in March 2003?

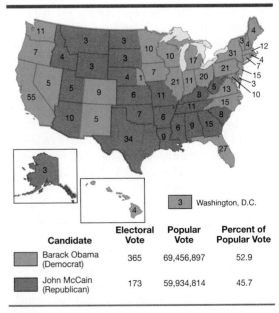

Candidate	Electoral Vote	Popular Vote	Percent of Popular Vote
Barack Obama (Democrat)	365	69,456,897	52.9
John McCain (Republican)	173	59,934,814	45.7

MAP 31.4 The Election of 2008

Conclusion: Defining the Government's Role at Home and Abroad

On March 21, 2003, some 225 years after the birth of the United States, Colin Powell referred to the unfinished nature of the American promise when he declared that the question of America's role in the world "isn't answered yet." In fact, the end of the Cold War, the rise of international terrorism, and the George W. Bush administration's doctrines of preemption and unilateralism sparked new debates over the long-standing question of how the United States should act beyond its borders.

Nor had Americans set to rest questions about the role of government at home. In a population so greatly derived from people fleeing oppressive governments, Americans had debated for more than two centuries what responsibilities the government could or should shoulder and what was best left to private enterprise, families, churches, and other voluntary institutions. Far more than other democracies, the United States had taken the path of private rather than public obligation, individual rather than collective solutions. In the twentieth century, Americans had significantly enlarged the federal government's powers and responsibilities, but the last three decades of the twentieth century had seen a decline of trust in government's ability to improve people's lives, even as a poverty rate of 20 percent among children and a growing gap between rich and poor survived the economic boom of the 1990s.

The shifting of control of the government back and forth between Republicans and Democrats from 1989 to 2008 revealed a dynamic debate over the role of government in domestic affairs. The protections enacted for people with disabilities during the first Bush administration and Bill Clinton's incremental reforms in some social areas built on a deep-rooted tradition that sought to realize the American promise of justice and human well-being. Those who mobilized against the ravages of globalization worked internationally for what populists, progressives, New Deal reformers, and many activists of the 1960s had sought for the domestic population: protection of individual rights, curbs on laissez faire capitalism, assistance for victims of rapid economic change, and fiscal policies that placed greater responsibility on those best able to pay for the collective good. Even the second Bush administration, which sought a more limited role for the federal government, supported the No Child Left Behind Act and the prescription drug program for the elderly, and it departed from traditional conservative policy and won congressional approval for a gigantic program to bail out

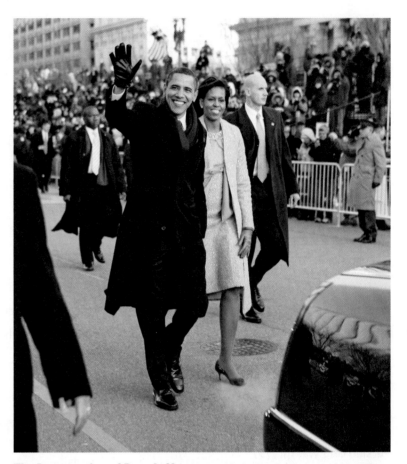

The Inauguration of Barack Obama President Barack Obama and his wife, Michelle, walk down Pennsylvania Avenue after his inauguration at the Capitol on January 20, 2009. In his inaugural address, Obama spoke of "this winter of our hardship," referring to economic crisis, wars in Iraq and Afghanistan, and other challenges facing the nation. While the most people ever to attend an inauguration absorbed his sober message, the feelings of sheer joy and hope that suffused the crowds were not diminished. AP Images/Doug Mills/Pool.

failing businesses when a severe financial crisis hit the economy in 2008.

The United States became ever more deeply embedded in the global economy as products, information, and people crossed borders with amazing speed and frequency. Although the end of the Cold War brought about unanticipated cooperation between the United States and its former enemies, globalization also contributed to international instability and the threat of deadly terrorism to a nation unaccustomed to foreign attacks within its own borders. In response to those dangers, the second Bush administration departed from the multilateral approach to foreign policy that had been built up by Republican and Democratic administrations alike since World War II. Toward the end of his second term, however, Bush worked to improve international relationships, and the unprecedented celebrations at home and abroad when Barack Obama won the presidency signaled the promise of a new era in American relations with the world.

Reviewing the Chapter

★ REVIEW QUESTIONS Q:

Use key terms and dates to support your answer

1. Why did George H. W. Bush lose the presidency in 1992? (pp. 775–82)

2. What policies of the Clinton administration reflect the president's efforts to move his party to the right? (pp. 782–85)

3. Who criticized free trade agreements and why? (pp. 785–90)

4. Why did the United States invade Iraq in March 2003? (pp. 790–96)

★ MAKING CONNECTIONS

Draw on key terms, timeline, and review questions

1. How did George H. W. Bush continue the policies of his predecessor, Ronald Reagan? How did he depart from them?

2. President Bill Clinton called himself a "New Democrat." How did his policies and goals differ from those of Democrats in the past?

3. In the late twentieth century, economic globalization transformed the United States. Explain what globalization is, and describe how it affected the U.S. economy and population in the 1990s.

4. The terrorist attacks of September 11, 2001, were unprecedented. What gave rise to the attacks? How did the nation respond?

FOR PRACTICE QUIZZES AND OTHER STUDY TOOLS, see the Online Study Guide at **bedfordstmartins.com/roarkcompact**.

★ SUGGESTED READINGS

John F. Harris, *The Survivor: Bill Clinton in the White House* (2005). A balanced account by a White House reporter.

George Packer, *The Assassins' Gate: America in Iraq* (2005). A journalist's narrative of the decision to go to war and its consequences on the ground.

David M. Reimers, *Other Immigrants: The Global Origins of the American People* (2005). A comprehensive account of the new immigration.

Joseph E. Stiglitz, *Globalization and Its Discontents* (2002). An explanation of the globalization debate by a Nobel Prize–winning economist.

Richard Wolffe, *Renegade: The Making of a President* (2009). A reporter's narrative of Obama's presidential campaign that offers insights into his background and character.

Lawrence Wright, *The Looming Tower: Al-Qaeda and the Road to 9/11* (2006). A riveting account of the roots of Islamic militancy and the organizing of the 9/11 attacks.

FOR MORE BOOKS ABOUT TOPICS IN THIS CHAPTER, see the Online Bibliography at **bedfordstmartins.com/roarkcompact**.

FOR ADDITIONAL FIRSTHAND ACCOUNTS OF THIS PERIOD, see Chapter 31 in Michael Johnson, ed., *Reading the American Past,* Fourth Edition.

FOR WEB SITES, IMAGES, AND DOCUMENTS RELATED TO TOPICS AND PLACES IN THIS CHAPTER, visit Make History at **bedfordstmartins.com/roarkcompact**.

★ TIMELINE

1988	• Republican George H. W. Bush elected president.
1989	• Communism collapses in Eastern Europe; Berlin Wall falls. • United States invades Panama.
1990	• Americans with Disabilities Act.
1991	• Persian Gulf War.
1992	• Democrat William Jefferson "Bill" Clinton elected president.
1993	• Israel and PLO sign peace accords. • North American Free Trade Agreement (NAFTA). • Clinton announces policy for gays in the military. • Family and Medical Leave Act.
1994	• United States sends troops to Haiti. • General Agreement on Tariffs and Trade (GATT) establishes World Trade Organization (WTO).
1995	• Bombing of federal building in Oklahoma City.
1996	• Personal Responsibility and Work Opportunity Reconciliation Act. • President Clinton reelected.
1997	• Tax cut enacted.
1998	• United States bombs Iraq and terrorist sites in Afghanistan and Sudan. • President Clinton impeached.
1999	• Senate trial fails to approve articles of impeachment. • United States, with NATO, bombs Serbia.
2000	• Republican George W. Bush elected president.
2001	• **September 11.** Terrorists attack World Trade Center and Pentagon. • United States attacks Afghanistan, driving out Taliban government. • USA Patriot Act. • $1.35 trillion tax cut.
2002	• No Child Left Behind Act. • Department of Homeland Security established.
2003	• United States attacks Iraq, driving out Saddam Hussein. • Prescription drug coverage added to Medicare.
2004	• George W. Bush reelected president.
2005	• Hurricane Katrina. • Central American–Dominican Republic Free Trade Agreement (CAFTA-DR).
2007	• Bush begins troop surge in Iraq.
2008	• Worst financial crisis since the Great Depression. • Democrat Barack Obama elected president.

Documents

For additional documents, see the DocLinks feature at Make History at bedfordstmartins.com/roarkcompact.

The Declaration of Independence

In Congress, July 4, 1776,

THE UNANIMOUS DECLARATION OF THE THIRTEEN UNITED STATES OF AMERICA

When in the course of human events, it becomes necessary for one people to dissolve the political bands which have connected them with another, and to assume, among the powers of the earth, the separate and equal station to which the laws of nature and of nature's God entitle them, a decent respect to the opinions of mankind requires that they should declare the causes which impel them to the separation.

We hold these truths to be self-evident, that all men are created equal; that they are endowed by their Creator with certain unalienable rights; that among these, are life, liberty, and the pursuit of happiness. That, to secure these rights, governments are instituted among men, deriving their just powers from the consent of the governed; that, whenever any form of government becomes destructive of these ends, it is the right of the people to alter or to abolish it, and to institute a new government, laying its foundation on such principles, and organizing its powers in such form, as to them shall seem most likely to effect their safety and happiness. Prudence, indeed, will dictate that governments long established, should not be changed for light and transient causes; and, accordingly, all experience hath shown, that mankind are more disposed to suffer, while evils are sufferable, than to right themselves by abolishing the forms to which they are accustomed. But, when a long train of abuses and usurpations, pursuing invariably the same object, evinces a design to reduce them under absolute despotism, it is their right, it is their duty, to throw off such government and to provide new guards for their future security. Such has been the patient sufferance of these colonies, and such is now the necessity which constrains them to alter their former systems of government. The history of the present King of Great Britain is a history of repeated injuries and usurpations, all having, in direct object, the establishment of an absolute tyranny over these States. To prove this, let facts be submitted to a candid world:

He has refused his assent to laws the most wholesome and necessary for the public good.

He has forbidden his governors to pass laws of immediate and pressing importance, unless suspended in their operation till his assent should be obtained; and, when so suspended, he has utterly neglected to attend to them.

He has refused to pass other laws for the accommodation of large districts of people, unless those people would relinquish the right of representation in the legislature; a right inestimable to them, and formidable to tyrants only.

He has called together legislative bodies at places unusual, uncomfortable, and distant from the depository of their public records, for the sole purpose of fatiguing them into compliance with his measures.

He has dissolved representative houses repeatedly for opposing, with manly firmness, his invasions on the rights of the people.

He has refused, for a long time after such dissolutions, to cause others to be elected; whereby the legislative powers, incapable of annihilation, have returned to the people at large for their exercise; the state remaining in the mean-time exposed to all the danger of invasion from without, and convulsions within.

He has endeavoured to prevent the population of these States; for that purpose, obstructing the laws for naturalization of foreigners, refusing to pass others to encourage their migration hither, and raising the conditions of new appropriations of lands.

He has obstructed the administration of justice, by refusing his assent to laws for establishing judiciary powers.

He has made judges dependent on his will alone, for the tenure of their offices, and the amount and payment of their salaries.

He has erected a multitude of new offices, and sent hither swarms of officers to harass our people, and eat out their substance.

He has kept among us, in times of peace, standing armies, without the consent of our legislature.

He has affected to render the military independent of, and superior to, the civil power.

He has combined, with others, to subject us to a jurisdiction foreign to our Constitution, and unacknowledged by our laws; giving his assent to their acts of pretended legislation:

For quartering large bodies of armed troops among us:

For protecting them by a mock trial, from punishment, for any murders which they should commit on the inhabitants of these States:

For cutting off our trade with all parts of the world:

For imposing taxes on us without our consent:

For depriving us, in many cases, of the benefit of trial by jury:

For transporting us beyond seas to be tried for pretended offences:

For abolishing the free system of English laws in a neighboring province, establishing therein an arbitrary government, and enlarging its boundaries, so as to render it at once an example and fit instrument for introducing the same absolute rule into these colonies:

For taking away our charters, abolishing our most valuable laws, and altering, fundamentally, the powers of our governments:

For suspending our own legislatures, and declaring themselves invested with power to legislate for us in all cases whatsoever.

He has abdicated government here, by declaring us out of his protection, and waging war against us.

He has plundered our seas, ravaged our coasts, burnt our towns, and destroyed the lives of our people.

He is, at this time, transporting large armies of foreign mercenaries to complete the works of death, desolation, and tyranny, already begun, with circumstances of cruelty and perfidy scarcely paralleled in the most barbarous ages, and totally unworthy the head of a civilized nation.

He has constrained our fellow citizens, taken captive on the high seas, to bear arms against their country, to become the executioners of their friends, and brethren, or to fall themselves by their hands.

He has excited domestic insurrections amongst us, and has endeavored to bring on the inhabitants of our frontiers, the merciless Indian savages, whose known rule of warfare is an undistinguished destruction of all ages, sexes, and conditions.

In every stage of these oppressions, we have petitioned for redress; in the most humble terms; our repeated petitions have been answered only by repeated injury. A prince, whose character is thus marked by every act which may define a tyrant, is unfit to be the ruler of a free people.

Nor have we been wanting in attention to our British brethren. We have warned them, from time to time, of attempts made by their legislature to extend an unwarrantable jurisdiction over us. We have reminded them of the circumstances of our emigration and settlement here. We have appealed to their native justice and magnanimity, and we have conjured them, by the ties of our common kindred, to disavow these usurpations, which would inevitably interrupt our connections and correspondence. They, too, have been deaf to the voice of justice and consanguinity. We must, therefore, acquiesce in the necessity which denounces our separation, and hold them as we hold the rest of mankind, enemies in war, in peace, friends.

We, therefore, the representatives of the United States of America, in general Congress assembled, appealing to the Supreme Judge of the world for the rectitude of our intentions, do, in the name, and by authority of the good people of these colonies, solemnly publish and declare, that these united colonies are, and of right ought to be, free and independent states: that they are absolved from all allegiance to the British Crown, and that all political connection between them and the state of Great Britain is, and ought to be, totally dissolved; and that, as free and independent states, they have full power to levy war, conclude peace, contract alliances, establish commerce, and to do all other acts and things which independent states may of right do. And, for the support of this declaration, with a firm reliance on the protection of Divine Providence, we mutually pledge to each other our lives, our fortunes, and our sacred honor.

The foregoing Declaration was, by order of Congress, engrossed, and signed by the following members:

JOHN HANCOCK

New Hampshire
Josiah Bartlett
William Whipple
Matthew Thornton

Massachusetts Bay
Samuel Adams
John Adams
Robert Treat Paine
Elbridge Gerry

Rhode Island
Stephen Hopkins
William Ellery

Connecticut
Roger Sherman
Samuel Huntington
William Williams
Oliver Wolcott

New York
William Floyd
Phillip Livingston
Francis Lewis
Lewis Morris

New Jersey
Richard Stockton
John Witherspoon
Francis Hopkinson
John Hart
Abraham Clark

Pennsylvania
Robert Morris
Benjamin Rush
Benjamin Franklin
John Morton
George Clymer
James Smith

George Taylor
James Wilson
George Ross

Delaware
Caesar Rodney
George Read
Thomas M'Kean

Maryland
Samuel Chase
William Paca
Thomas Stone
Charles Carroll, of
    Carrollton

North Carolina
William Hooper
Joseph Hewes
John Penn

South Carolina
Edward Rutledge
Thomas Heyward, Jr.
Thomas Lynch, Jr.
Arthur Middleton

Virginia
George Wythe
Richard Henry Lee
Thomas Jefferson
Benjamin Harrison
Thomas Nelson, Jr.
Francis Lightfoot Lee
Carter Braxton

Georgia
Button Gwinnett
Lyman Hall
George Walton

Resolved, That copies of the Declaration be sent to the several assemblies, conventions, and committees, or councils of safety, and to the several commanding officers of the continental troops; that it be proclaimed in each of the United States, at the head of the army.

The Constitution of the United States

Agreed to by Philadelphia Convention, September 17, 1787. Implemented March 4, 1789.

Preamble

We the people of the United States, in order to form a more perfect union, establish justice, insure domestic tranquility, provide for the common defense, promote the general welfare, and secure the blessings of liberty to ourselves and our posterity, do ordain and establish this Constitution for the United States of America.

Article I

Section 1 All legislative powers herein granted shall be vested in a Congress of the United States, which shall consist of a Senate and a House of Representatives.

Section 2 The House of Representatives shall be composed of members chosen every second year by the people of the several States, and the electors in each State shall have the qualifications requisite for electors of the most numerous branch of the State Legislature.

No person shall be a Representative who shall not have attained to the age of twenty-five years, and been seven years a citizen of the United States, and who shall not, when elected, be an inhabitant of that State in which he shall be chosen.

Representatives and direct taxes shall be apportioned among the several States which may be included within this Union, according to their respective numbers, *which shall be determined by adding to the whole number of free persons, including those bound to service for a term of years and excluding Indians not taxed, three-fifths of all other persons.** The actual enumeration shall be made within three years after the first meeting of the Congress of the United States, and within every subsequent term of ten years, in such manner as they shall by law direct. The number of Representatives shall not exceed one for every thirty thousand, but each State shall have at least one Representative; *and until such enumeration shall be made, the State of New Hampshire shall be entitled to choose three, Massachusetts eight, Rhode Island and Providence Plantations one, Connecticut five, New York six, New Jersey four, Pennsylvania eight, Delaware one, Maryland six, Virginia ten, North Carolina five, South Carolina five, and Georgia three.*

When vacancies happen in the representation from any State, the Executive authority thereof shall issue writs of election to fill such vacancies.

The House of Representatives shall choose their Speaker and other officers; and shall have the sole power of impeachment.

Section 3 The Senate of the United States shall be composed of two Senators from each State, *chosen by the legislature thereof,* for six years; and each Senator shall have one vote.

Immediately after they shall be assembled in consequence of the first election, they shall be divided as equally as may be into three classes. The seats of the Senators of the first class shall be vacated at the expiration of the second year, of the second class at the expiration of the fourth year, and of the third class at the expiration of the sixth year, so that one-third may be chosen every second year; and if vacancies happen by resignation or otherwise, during the recess of the legislature of any State, the Executive thereof may make temporary appointments until the next meeting of the legislature, which shall then fill such vacancies.

No person shall be a Senator who shall not have attained to the age of thirty years, and been nine years a citizen of the United States, and who shall not, when elected, be an inhabitant of that State for which he shall be chosen.

The Vice-President of the United States shall be President of the Senate, but shall have no vote, unless they be equally divided.

The Senate shall choose their other officers, and also a President *pro tempore,* in the absence of the Vice-President, or when he shall exercise the office of President of the United States.

The Senate shall have the sole power to try all impeachments. When sitting for that purpose, they shall be on oath or affirmation. When the President of the United States is tried, the Chief Justice shall preside: and no person shall be convicted without the concurrence of two-thirds of the members present.

Judgment in cases of impeachment shall not extend further than to removal from the office, and disqualification to hold and enjoy any office of honor, trust or profit under the United States: but the party convicted shall nevertheless be liable and subject to indictment, trial, judgment and punishment, according to law.

Section 4 The times, places and manner of holding elections for Senators and Representatives shall be prescribed in each State by the legislature thereof; but the Congress may at any time by law make or alter such regulations, except as to the places of choosing Senators.

The Congress shall assemble at least once in every year, and such meeting *shall be on the first Monday in December, unless they shall by law appoint a different day.*

Section 5 Each house shall be the judge of the elections, returns and qualifications of its own members, and a majority of each shall constitute a quorum to do business; but a smaller number may adjourn from day to day, and may be authorized to compel the attendance of absent members, in such manner, and under such penalties, as each house may provide.

Passages no longer in effect are in italic type.

Each house may determine the rules of its proceedings, punish its members for disorderly behavior, and with the concurrence of two-thirds, expel a member.

Each house shall keep a journal of its proceedings, and from time to time publish the same, excepting such parts as may in their judgment require secrecy; and the yeas and nays of the members of either house on any question shall, at the desire of one-fifth of those present, be entered on the journal.

Neither house, during the session of Congress, shall, without the consent of the other, adjourn for more than three days, nor to any other place than that in which the two houses shall be sitting.

Section 6 The Senators and Representatives shall receive a compensation for their services, to be ascertained by law and paid out of the treasury of the United States. They shall in all cases except treason, felony and breach of the peace, be privileged from arrest during their attendance at the session of their respective houses, and in going to and returning from the same; and for any speech or debate in either house, they shall not be questioned in any other place.

No Senator or Representative shall, during the time for which he was elected, be appointed to any civil office under the authority of the United States, which shall have been created, or the emoluments whereof shall have been increased, during such time; and no person holding any office under the United States shall be a member of either house during his continuance in office.

Section 7 All bills for raising revenue shall originate in the House of Representatives; but the Senate may propose or concur with amendments as on other bills.

Every bill which shall have passed the House of Representatives and the Senate, shall, before it become a law, be presented to the President of the United States; if he approve he shall sign it, but if not he shall return it with objections to that house in which it shall have originated, who shall enter the objections at large on their journal, and proceed to reconsider it. If after such reconsideration two-thirds of that house shall agree to pass the bill, it shall be sent, together with the objections, to the other house, by which it shall likewise be reconsidered, and, if approved by two-thirds of that house, it shall become a law. But in all such cases the votes of both houses shall be determined by yeas and nays, and the names of the persons voting for and against the bill shall be entered on the journal of each house respectively. If any bill shall not be returned by the President within ten days (Sundays excepted) after it shall have been presented to him, the same shall be a law, in like manner as if he had signed it, unless the Congress by their adjournment prevent its return, in which case it shall not be a law.

Every order, resolution, or vote to which the concurrence of the Senate and House of Representatives may be necessary (except on a question of adjournment) shall be presented to the President of the United States; and before the same shall take effect, shall be approved by him, or being disapproved by him, shall be repassed by two-thirds of the Senate and House of Representatives, according to the rules and limitations prescribed in the case of a bill.

Section 8 The Congress shall have power

To lay and collect taxes, duties, imposts, and excises, to pay the debts and provide for the common defense and general welfare of the United States; but all duties, imposts and excises shall be uniform throughout the United States;

To borrow money on the credit of the United States;

To regulate commerce with foreign nations, and among the several States, and with the Indian tribes;

To establish an uniform rule of naturalization, and uniform laws on the subject of bankruptcies throughout the United States;

To coin money, regulate the value thereof, and of foreign coin, and fix the standard of weights and measures;

To provide for the punishment of counterfeiting the securities and current coin of the United States;

To establish post offices and post roads;

To promote the progress of science and useful arts by securing for limited times to authors and inventors the exclusive right to their respective writings and discoveries;

To constitute tribunals inferior to the Supreme Court;

To define and punish piracies and felonies committed on the high seas and offences against the law of nations;

To declare war, grant letters of marque and reprisal, and make rules concerning captures on land and water;

To raise and support armies, but no appropriation of money to that use shall be for a longer term than two years;

To provide and maintain a navy;

To make rules for the government and regulation of the land and naval forces;

To provide for calling forth the militia to execute the laws of the Union, suppress insurrections and repel invasions;

To provide for organizing, arming, and disciplining the militia, and for governing such part of them as may be employed in the service of the United States, reserving to the States respectively the appointment of the officers, and the authority of training the militia according to the discipline prescribed by Congress;

To exercise exclusive legislation in all cases whatsoever, over such district (not exceeding ten miles square) as may, by cession of particular States, and the acceptance of Congress, become the seat of the government of the United States, and to exercise like authority over all places purchased by the consent of the legislature of the State, in which the same shall be, for erection of forts, magazines, arsenals, dock-yards, and other needful buildings; — and

To make all laws which shall be necessary and proper for carrying into execution the foregoing powers, and all other powers vested by this Constitution in the government of the United States, or in any department or officer thereof.

Section 9 *The migration or importation of such persons as any of the States now existing shall think proper to admit shall not be prohibited by the Congress prior to the year one thousand eight hundred and eight; but a tax or duty may be imposed on such importation, not exceeding ten dollars for each person.*

The privilege of the writ of habeas corpus shall not be suspended, unless when in cases of rebellion or invasion the public safety may require it.

No bill of attainder or ex post facto law shall be passed.

No capitation, or other direct, tax shall be laid, unless in proportion to the census or enumeration herein before directed to be taken.

No tax or duty shall be laid on articles exported from any State.

No preference shall be given by any regulation of commerce or revenue to the ports of one State over those of another; nor shall vessels bound to, or from, one State be obliged to enter, clear, or pay duties in another.

No money shall be drawn from the treasury, but in consequence of appropriations made by law; and a regular statement and account of the receipts and expenditures of all public money shall be published from time to time.

No title of nobility shall be granted by the United States: and no person holding any office of profit or trust under them, shall, without the consent of the Congress, accept of any present, emolument, office, or title, of any kind whatever, from any king, prince, or foreign state.

Section 10 No State shall enter into any treaty, alliance, or confederation; grant letters of marque and reprisal; coin money; emit bills of credit; make anything but gold and silver coin a tender in payment of debts; pass any bill of attainder, ex post facto law, or law impairing the obligation of contracts, or grant any title of nobility.

No State shall, without the consent of Congress, lay any imposts or duties on imports or exports, except what may be absolutely necessary for executing its inspection laws: and the net produce of all duties and imposts, laid by any State on imports or exports, shall be for the use of the treasury of the United States; and all such laws shall be subject to the revision and control of the Congress.

No State shall, without the consent of Congress, lay any duty of tonnage, keep troops, or ships of war in time of peace, enter into any agreement or compact with another State, or with a foreign power, or engage in war, unless actually invaded, or in such imminent danger as will not admit of delay.

Article II

Section 1 The executive power shall be vested in a President of the United States of America. He shall hold his office during the term of four years, and, together with the Vice-President, chosen for the same term, be elected as follows:

Each State shall appoint, in such manner as the legislature thereof may direct, a number of electors, equal to the whole number of Senators and Representatives to which the State may be entitled in the Congress; but no Senator or Representative, or person holding an office of trust or profit under the United States, shall be appointed an elector.

The electors shall meet in their respective States, and vote by ballot for two persons, of whom one at least shall not be an inhabitant of the same State with themselves. And they shall make a list of all the persons voted for, and of the number of votes for each; which list they shall sign and certify, and transmit sealed to the seat of government of the United States, directed to the President of the Senate. The President of the Senate shall, in the presence of the Senate and House of Representatives, open all the certificates, and the votes shall then be counted. The person having the greatest number of votes shall be the President, if such number be a majority of the whole number of electors appointed; and if there be more than one who have such majority, and have an equal number of votes, then the House of Representatives shall immediately choose by ballot one of them for President; and if no person have a majority, then from the five highest on the list said house shall in like manner choose the President. But in choosing the President the votes shall be taken by States, the representation from each State having one vote; a quorum for this purpose shall consist of a member or members from two-thirds of the States, and a majority of all the States shall be necessary to a choice. In every case, after the choice of the President, the person having the greatest number of votes of the electors shall be the Vice-President. But if there should remain two or more who have equal votes, the Senate shall choose from them by ballot the Vice-President.

The Congress may determine the time of choosing the electors, and the day on which they shall give their votes; which day shall be the same throughout the United States.

No person except a natural-born citizen, *or a citizen of the United States at the time of the adoption of this Constitution*, shall be eligible to the office of President; neither shall any person be eligible to that office who shall not have attained to the age of thirty-five years, and been fourteen years a resident within the United States.

In cases of the removal of the President from office or of his death, resignation, or inability to discharge the powers and duties of the said office, the same shall devolve on the Vice-President, and the Congress may by law provide for the case of removal, death, resignation, or inability, both of the President and Vice-President, declaring what officer shall then act as President, and such officer shall act accordingly, until the disability be removed, or a President shall be elected.

The President shall, at stated times, receive for his services a compensation, which shall neither be increased nor diminished during the period for which he shall have been elected, and he shall not receive within that period any other emolument from the United States, or any of them.

Before he enter on the execution of his office, he shall take the following oath or affirmation:—"I do solemnly swear (or affirm) that I will faithfully execute the office of the President of the United States, and will to the best of my ability preserve, protect and defend the Constitution of the United States."

Section 2 The President shall be commander in chief of the army and navy of the United States, and of the militia of the several States, when called into the actual service of the United States; he may require the opinion, in writing, of the principal officer in each of the executive departments, upon any subject relating to the duties of their respective offices, and he shall have power to grant reprieves and pardons for offenses against the United States, except in cases of impeachment.

He shall have power, by and with the advice and consent of the Senate, to make treaties, provided two-thirds of the Senators present concur; and he shall nominate, and by and with the advice and consent of the Senate, shall appoint ambassadors, other public ministers and consuls, judges of the Supreme Court, and all other officers of the United States, whose appointments are not herein otherwise provided for, and which shall be established by law: but Congress may by law vest the appointment of such inferior officers, as they think proper, in the President alone, in the courts of law, or in the heads of departments.

The President shall have power to fill up all vacancies that may happen during the recess of the Senate, by granting commissions which shall expire at the end of their next session.

Section 3 He shall from time to time give to the Congress information of the state of the Union, and recommend to their consideration such measures as he shall judge necessary and expedient; he may, on extraordinary occasions, convene both houses, or either of them, and in case of disagreement between them, with respect to the time of adjournment, he may adjourn them to such time as he shall think proper; he shall receive ambassadors and other public ministers; he shall take care that the laws be faithfully executed, and shall commission all the officers of the United States.

Section 4 The President, Vice-President and all civil officers of the United States shall be removed from office on impeachment for, and on conviction of, treason, bribery, or other high crimes and misdemeanors.

Article III

Section 1 The judicial power of the United States shall be vested in one Supreme Court, and in such inferior courts as the Congress may from time to time ordain and establish. The judges, both of the Supreme and inferior courts, shall hold their offices during good behavior, and shall, at stated times, receive for their services a compensation which shall not be diminished during their continuance in office.

Section 2 The judicial power shall extend to all cases, in law and equity, arising under this Constitution, the laws of the United States, and treaties made, or which shall be made, under their authority; — to all cases affecting ambassadors, other public ministers and consuls; — to all cases of admiralty and maritime jurisdiction; — to controversies to which the United States shall be a party; — to controversies between two or more States; — *between a State and citizens of another State;* — between citizens of different States; — between citizens of the same State claiming lands under grants of different States, and between a State, or the citizens thereof, and foreign states, citizens or subjects.

In all cases affecting ambassadors, other public ministers and consuls, and those in which a State shall be party, the Supreme Court shall have original jurisdiction. In all the other cases before mentioned, the Supreme Court shall have appellate jurisdiction, both as to law and fact, with such exceptions, and under such regulations, as the Congress shall make.

The trial of all crimes, except in cases of impeachment, shall be by jury; and such trial shall be held in the State where said crimes shall have been committed; but when not committed within any State, the trial shall be at such place or places as the Congress may by Law have directed.

Section 3 Treason against the United States shall consist only in levying war against them, or in adhering to their enemies, giving them aid and comfort. No person shall be convicted of treason unless on the testimony of two witnesses to the same overt act, or on confession in open court.

The Congress shall have power to declare the punishment of treason, but no attainder of treason shall work corruption of blood, or forfeiture except during the life of the person attainted.

Article IV

Section 1 Full faith and credit shall be given in each State to the public acts, records, and judicial proceedings of every other State. And the Congress may by general laws prescribe the manner in which such acts, records, and proceedings shall be proved, and the effect thereof.

Section 2 The citizens of each State shall be entitled to all privileges and immunities of citizens in the several States.

A person charged in any State with treason, felony, or other crime, who shall flee from justice, and be found in another State, shall on demand of the executive authority of the State from which he fled, be delivered up, to be removed to the State having jurisdiction of the crime.

No Person held to service or labor in one State, under the laws thereof, escaping into another, shall, in consequence of any law or regulation therein, be discharged from such service or labor, but shall be delivered up on claim of the party to whom such service or labor may be due.

Section 3 New States may be admitted by the Congress into this Union; but no new State shall be formed or erected within the jurisdiction of any other State; nor any State be formed by the junction of two or more States, or parts of States, without the consent of the legislatures of the States concerned as well as of the Congress.

The Congress shall have power to dispose of and make all needful rules and regulations respecting the territory or other property belonging to the United States; and nothing in this Constitution shall be so construed as to prejudice any claims of the United States, or of any particular State.

Section 4 The United States shall guarantee to every State in this Union a republican form of government, and shall protect each of them against invasion; and on application of the legislature, or of the executive (when the legislature cannot be convened), against domestic violence.

Article V

The Congress, whenever two-thirds of both houses shall deem it necessary, shall propose amendments to this Constitution, or, on the application of the legislatures of two-thirds of the several States, shall call a convention for proposing amendments, which, in either case, shall be valid to all intents and purposes, as part of this Constitution, when ratified by the legislatures of three-fourths of the several States, or by conventions in three-fourths thereof, as the one or the other mode of ratification may be proposed by the Congress; provided *that no amendments which may be made prior to the year one thousand eight hundred and eight shall in any manner affect the first and fourth clauses in the ninth section of the first article;* and that no State, without its consent, shall be deprived of its equal suffrage in the Senate.

Article VI

All debts contracted and engagements entered into, before the adoption of this Constitution, shall be as valid against the United States under this Constitution, as under the Confederation.

This Constitution, and the laws of the United States which shall be made in pursuance thereof; and all treaties made, or which shall be made, under the authority of the United States, shall be the supreme law of the land; and the judges in every State shall be bound thereby, anything in the Constitution or laws of any State to the contrary notwithstanding.

The Senators and Representatives before mentioned, and the members of the several State legislatures, and all executive and judicial officers, both of the United States and of the several States, shall be bound by oath or affirmation to support this Constitution; but no religious test shall ever be required as a qualification to any office or public trust under the United States.

Article VII

The ratification of the conventions of nine States shall be sufficient for the establishment of this Constitution between the States so ratifying the same.

Done in convention by the unanimous consent of the States present, the seventeenth day of September in the year of our Lord one thousand seven hundred and eighty-seven and of the Independence of the United States of America the twelfth. In witness whereof we have hereunto subscribed our names.

GEORGE WASHINGTON
PRESIDENT AND DEPUTY FROM VIRGINIA

New Hampshire
John Langdon
Nicholas Gilman

Massachusetts
Nathaniel Gorham
Rufus King

Connecticut
William Samuel Johnson
Roger Sherman

New York
Alexander Hamilton

New Jersey
William Livingston
David Brearley
William Paterson
Jonathan Dayton

Pennsylvania
Benjamin Franklin
Thomas Mifflin
Robert Morris
George Clymer
Thomas FitzSimons
Jared Ingersoll
James Wilson
Gouverneur Morris

Delaware
George Read
Gunning Bedford, Jr.
John Dickinson
Richard Bassett
Jacob Broom

Maryland
James McHenry
Daniel of St. Thomas Jenifer
Daniel Carroll

Virginia
John Blair
James Madison, Jr.

North Carolina
William Blount
Richard Dobbs
   Spaight
Hugh Williamson

South Carolina
John Rutledge
Charles Cotesworth
   Pinckney
Charles Pinckney
Pierce Butler

Georgia
William Few
Abraham Baldwin

Amendments to the Constitution (including the six unratified amendments)

(Although the first ten amendments to the Constitution are commonly known as the Bill of Rights, only Amendments 1–8 actually provide guarantees of individual rights. Amendments 9 and 10 deal with the structure of power within the constitutional system. The Bill of Rights was promised to appease Antifederalists who refused to ratify the Constitution without guarantees of individual liberties and limitations to federal power. After studying more than two hundred amendments recommended by the ratifying conventions of the states, Federalist James Madison presented a list of seventeen to Congress, which used Madison's list as the foundation for the twelve amendments that were sent to the states for ratification. Ten of the twelve were adopted in 1791. The first on the list of twelve, known as the Reapportionment Amendment, was never adopted [see the next column]. The second proposed amendment was adopted in 1992 as Amendment XXVII [see page A-12].   — Ed.)

Amendment I

Congress shall make no law respecting an establishment of religion, or prohibiting the free exercise thereof; or abridging the freedom of speech, or of the press; or the right of the people peaceably to assemble, and to petition the government for a redress of grievances.

Amendment II

A well-regulated militia being necessary to the security of a free State, the right of the people to keep and bear arms shall not be infringed.

Amendment III

No soldier shall, in time of peace, be quartered in any house without the consent of the owner, nor in time of war, but in a manner to be prescribed by law.

Amendment IV

The right of the people to be secure in their persons, houses, papers, and effects, against unreasonable searches and seizures, shall not be violated, and no warrants shall issue but upon probable cause, supported by oath or affirmation, and particularly describing the place to be searched, and the persons or things to be seized.

Amendment V

No person shall be held to answer for a capital, or otherwise infamous crime, unless on a presentment or indictment of a grand jury, except in cases arising in the land or naval forces, or in the militia, when in actual service in time of war or public danger; nor shall any person be subject for the same offence to be twice put in jeopardy of life or limb; nor shall be compelled in any criminal case to be a witness against himself, nor be deprived of life, liberty, or property, without due process of law; nor shall private property be taken for public use without just compensation.

Amendment VI

In all criminal prosecutions, the accused shall enjoy the right to a speedy and public trial, by an impartial jury of the State and district wherein the crime shall have been committed, which district shall have been previously ascertained by law, and to be informed of the nature and cause of the accusation; to be confronted with the witnesses against him; to have compulsory process for obtaining witnesses in his favor, and to have the assistance of counsel for his defence.

Amendment VII

In suits at common law, where the value in controversy shall exceed twenty dollars, the right of trial by jury shall be preserved, and no fact tried by a jury shall be otherwise reexamined in any court of the United States, than according to the rules of the common law.

Amendment VIII

Excessive bail shall not be required, nor excessive fines imposed, nor cruel and unusual punishments inflicted.

Amendment IX

The enumeration in the Constitution, of certain rights, shall not be construed to deny or disparage others retained by the people.

Amendment X

The powers not delegated to the United States by the Constitution, nor prohibited by it to the States, are reserved to the States respectively, or to the people.

Unratified Amendment

Reapportionment Amendment (proposed by Congress September 25, 1789, along with the Bill of Rights)

After the first enumeration required by the first article of the Constitution, there shall be one Representative for every thirty thousand, until the number shall amount to one hundred, after which the proportion shall be so regulated by Congress, that there shall be not less than one hundred Representatives, nor less than one Representative for every forty thousand persons, until the number of Representatives shall amount to two hundred; after which the proportion shall be so regulated by Congress, that there shall not be less than two hundred Representatives, nor more than one Representative for every fifty thousand persons.

Amendment XI

[Adopted 1798]

The judicial power of the United States shall not be construed to extend to any suit in law or equity, commenced or prosecuted against one of the United States by citizens of another State, or by citizens or subjects of any foreign state.

Amendment XII

[Adopted 1804]

The electors shall meet in their respective States, and vote by ballot for President and Vice-President, one of whom, at least, shall not be an inhabitant of the same State with themselves; they shall name in their ballots the person voted for as President, and in distinct ballots the person voted for as Vice-President, and they shall make distinct lists of all persons voted for as President, and of all persons voted for as Vice-President, and of the number of votes for each, which lists they shall sign and certify, and transmit sealed to the seat of government of the United States, directed to the President of the Senate;—the President of the Senate shall, in the presence of the Senate and House of Representatives, open all the certificates and the votes shall then be counted;—the person having the greatest number of votes for President shall be the President, if such number be a majority of the whole number of electors appointed; and if no person have such majority, then from the persons having the highest numbers not exceeding three on the list of those voted for as President, the House of Representatives shall choose immediately, by ballot, the President. But in choosing the President, the votes shall be taken by States, the representation from each State having one vote; a quorum for this purpose shall consist of a member or members from two-thirds of the States, and a majority of all the States shall be necessary to a choice. And if the House of Representatives shall not choose a President whenever the right of choice shall devolve upon them, before *the fourth day of March* next following, then the Vice-President shall act as President, as in the case of the death or other constitutional disability of the President.

The person having the greatest number of votes as Vice-President shall be the Vice-President, if such number be a majority of the whole number of electors appointed; and if no person have a majority, then from the two highest numbers on the list the Senate shall choose the Vice-President; a quorum for the purpose shall consist of two-thirds of the whole number of Senators, and a majority of the whole number shall be necessary to a choice. But no person constitutionally ineligible to the office of President shall be eligible to that of Vice-President of the United States.

Unratified Amendment

Titles of Nobility Amendment (proposed by Congress May 1, 1810)

If any citizen of the United States shall accept, claim, receive or retain any title of nobility or honor or shall, without the consent of Congress, accept and retain any present, pension, office or emolument of any kind whatever, from any emperor, king, prince or foreign power, such person shall cease to be a citizen of the United States, and shall be incapable of holding any office of trust or profit under them or either of them.

The Civil War and Reconstruction Amendments (Thirteenth, Fourteenth, and Fifteenth Amendments)

(In the four months between the election of Abraham Lincoln and his inauguration, more than 200 proposed constitutional amendments were presented to Congress as part of a desperate attempt to hold the rapidly dissolving Union together. Most of these were efforts to appease the southern states by protecting the right to own slaves or by disfranchising African Americans through constitutional amendment. None were able to win the votes required from Congress to send them to the states. The relatively innocuous Corwin Amendment seemed to be the only hope for preserving the Union by amending the Constitution.

The northern victors in the Civil War tried to restructure the Constitution just as the war had restructured the nation. Yet they were often divided in their goals. Some wanted to end slavery; others hoped for social and economic equality regardless of race; others hoped that extending the power of the ballot box to former slaves would help create a new political order. The debates over the Thirteenth, Fourteenth, and Fifteenth Amendments were bitter. Few of those who fought for these changes were satisfied with the amendments themselves; fewer still were satisfied with their interpretation. Although the amendments put an end to the legal status of slavery, it took nearly a hundred years after the amendments' passage before most of the descendants of former slaves could begin to experience the economic, social, and political equality the amendments had been intended to provide.   —Ed.)

Unratified Amendment

Corwin Amendment (proposed by Congress March 2, 1861)

No amendment shall be made to the Constitution which will authorize or give to Congress the power to abolish or interfere, within any State, with the domestic institutions thereof, including that of persons held to labor or service by the laws of said State.

Amendment XIII

[Adopted 1865]

Section 1 Neither slavery nor involuntary servitude, except as a punishment for crime whereof the party shall have been duly convicted, shall exist within the United States, or any place subject to their jurisdiction.

Section 2 Congress shall have power to enforce this article by appropriate legislation.

Amendment XIV

[Adopted 1868]

Section 1 All persons born or naturalized in the United States, and subject to the jurisdiction thereof, are citizens of the United States and of the State wherein they reside. No State shall make or enforce any law which shall abridge the privileges or immunities of citizens of the United States; nor shall any State deprive any person of life, liberty, or property, without due process of law; nor deny to any person within its jurisdiction the equal protection of the laws.

Section 2 Representatives shall be appointed among the several States according to their respective numbers, counting the whole number of persons in each State, excluding Indians not taxed. But when the right to vote at any election for the choice of Electors for President and Vice-President of the United States, Representatives in Congress, the executive and judicial officers of a State, or the members of the legislature thereof, is denied to any of the male inhabitants of such State, being twenty-one years of age and citizens of the United States, or in any way abridged, except for participation in rebellion, or other crime, the basis of representation therein shall be reduced in the proportion which the number of such male citizens shall bear to the whole number of male citizens twenty-one years of age in such State.

Section 3 No person shall be a Senator or Representative in Congress, or Elector of President and Vice-President, or hold any office, civil or military, under the United States, or under any State, who, having previously taken an oath, as a member of Congress, or as an officer of the United States, or as a member of any State legislature, or as an executive or judicial officer of any State, to support the Constitution of the United States, shall have engaged in insurrection or rebellion against the same, or given aid or comfort to the enemies thereof. Congress may, by a vote of two-thirds of each house, remove such disability.

Section 4 The validity of the public debt of the United States, authorized by law, including debts incurred for payment of pensions and bounties for services in suppressing insurrection or rebellion, shall not be questioned. But neither the United States nor any State shall assume or pay any debt or obligation incurred in aid of insurrection or rebellion against the United States, or any claim for the loss or emancipation of any slave; but all such debts, obligations, and claims shall be held illegal and void.

Section 5 The Congress shall have power to enforce, by appropriate legislation, the provisions of this article.

Amendment XV

[Adopted 1870]

Section 1 The right of citizens of the United States to vote shall not be denied or abridged by the United States or by any State on account of race, color, or previous condition of servitude.

Section 2 The Congress shall have power to enforce this article by appropriate legislation.

The Progressive Amendments (Sixteenth–Nineteenth Amendments)

(No amendments were added to the Constitution between the Civil War and the Progressive Era. America was changing, however, in fundamental ways. The rapid industrialization of the United States after the Civil War led to many social and economic problems. Hundreds of amendments were proposed, but none received enough support in Congress to be sent to the states. Some scholars believe that regional differences and rivalries were so strong during this period that it was almost impossible to gain a consensus on a constitutional amendment. During the Progressive Era, however, the Constitution was amended four times in seven years.   — Ed.)

Amendment XVI

[Adopted 1913]

The Congress shall have power to lay and collect taxes on incomes, from whatever source derived, without apportionment among the several States, and without regard to any census or enumeration.

Amendment XVII

[Adopted 1913]

Section 1 The Senate of the United States shall be composed of two Senators from each State, elected by the people thereof, for six years; and each Senator shall have one vote. The electors in each State shall have the qualifications requisite for electors of [voters for] the most numerous branch of the State legislatures.

Section 2 When vacancies happen in the representation of any State in the Senate, the executive authority of such State shall issue writs of election to fill such vacancies: Provided, that the Legislature of any State may empower the executive thereof to make temporary appointments until the people fill the vacancies by election as the Legislature may direct.

Section 3 This amendment shall not be so construed as to affect the election or term of any Senator chosen before it becomes valid as part of the Constitution.

Amendment XVIII

[Adopted 1919; repealed 1933 by Amendment XXI]

Section 1 After one year from the ratification of this article the manufacture, sale, or transportation of intoxicating liquors within, the importation thereof into, or the exportation thereof from the United States and all territory subject to the jurisdiction thereof, for beverage purposes, is hereby prohibited.

Section 2 The Congress and the several States shall have concurrent power to enforce this article by appropriate legislation.

Section 3 This article shall be inoperative unless it shall have been ratified as an amendment to the Constitution by the legislatures of the several States, as provided by the Constitution, within seven years from the date of the submission thereof to the States by the Congress.

Amendment XIX

[Adopted 1920]

Section 1 The right of citizens of the United States to vote shall not be denied or abridged by the United States or by any State on account of sex.

Section 2 Congress shall have the power to enforce this article by appropriate legislation.

Unratified Amendment

Child Labor Amendment (proposed by Congress June 2, 1924)

Section 1 The Congress shall have power to limit, regulate, and prohibit the labor of persons under eighteen years of age.

Section 2 The power of the several States is unimpaired by this article except that the operation of State laws shall be suspended to the extent necessary to give effect to legislation enacted by Congress.

Amendment XX

[Adopted 1933]

Section 1 The terms of the President and Vice-President shall end at noon on the 20th day of January, and the terms of Senators and Representatives at noon on the 3rd day of January, of the years in which such terms would have ended if this article had not been ratified; and the terms of their successors shall then begin.

Section 2 The Congress shall assemble at least once in every year, and such meeting shall begin at noon on the 3rd day of January, unless they shall by law appoint a different day.

Section 3 If, at the time fixed for the beginning of the term of the President, the President-elect shall have died, the Vice-President-elect shall become President. If a President shall not have been chosen before the time fixed for the beginning of his term, or if the President-elect shall have failed to qualify, then the Vice-President-elect shall act as President until a President shall have qualified; and the Congress may by law provide for the case wherein neither a President-elect nor a Vice-President-elect shall have qualified, declaring who shall then act as President, or the manner in which one who is to act shall be selected, and such person shall act accordingly until a President or Vice-President shall have qualified.

Section 4 The Congress may by law provide for the case of the death of any of the persons from whom the House of Representatives may choose a President whenever the right of choice shall have devolved upon them, and for the case of the death of any of the persons from whom the Senate may choose a Vice-President whenever the right of choice shall have devolved upon them.

Section 5 Sections 1 and 2 shall take effect on the 15th day of October following the ratification of this article.

Section 6 This article shall be inoperative unless it shall have been ratified as an amendment to the Constitution by the Legislatures of three-fourths of the several States within seven years from the date of its submission.

Amendment XXI

[Adopted 1933]

Section 1 The eighteenth article of amendment to the Constitution of the United States is hereby repealed.

Section 2 The transportation or importation into any State, Territory, or Possession of the United States for delivery or use therein of intoxicating liquors, in violation of the laws thereof, is hereby prohibited.

Section 3 This article shall be inoperative unless it shall have been ratified as an amendment to the Constitution by conventions in the several States, as provided in the Constitution, within seven years from the date of the submission thereof to the States by the Congress.

Amendment XXII

[Adopted 1951]

Section 1 No person shall be elected to the office of the President more than twice, and no person who has held the office of President, or acted as President, for more than two years of a term to which some other person was elected President shall be elected to the office of President more than once. But this article shall not apply to any person holding the office of President when this Article was proposed by the Congress, and shall not prevent any person who may be holding the office of President, or acting as President, during the term within which this Article becomes operative from holding the office of President or acting as President during the remainder of such term.

Section 2 This article shall be inoperative unless it shall have been ratified as an amendment to the Constitution by the legislatures of three-fourths of the several States within seven years from the date of its submission to the States by the Congress.

Amendment XXIII

[Adopted 1961]

Section 1 The District constituting the seat of Government of the United States shall appoint in such manner as the Congress may direct: A number of electors of President and Vice-President equal to the whole number of Senators and Representatives in Congress to which the District would be entitled if it were a State, but in no event more than the least populous State; they shall be in addition to those appointed by the States, but they shall be considered for the purposes of the election of President and Vice-President, to be electors appointed by a State; and they shall meet in the District and perform such duties as provided by the twelfth article of amendment.

Section 2 The Congress shall have the power to enforce this article by appropriate legislation.

Amendment XXIV

[Adopted 1964]

Section 1 The right of citizens of the United States to vote in any primary or other election for President or Vice-President, for electors for President or Vice-President, or for Senator or Representative in Congress, shall not be denied or abridged by the United States or any State by reason of failure to pay any poll tax or other tax.

Section 2 The Congress shall have the power to enforce this article by appropriate legislation.

Amendment XXV

[Adopted 1967]

Section 1 In case of the removal of the President from office or of his death or resignation, the Vice-President shall become President.

Section 2 Whenever there is a vacancy in the office of the Vice-President, the President shall nominate a Vice-President who shall take office upon confirmation by a majority vote of both Houses of Congress.

Section 3 Whenever the President transmits to the President pro tempore of the Senate and the Speaker of the House of Representatives his written declaration that he is unable to discharge the powers and duties of his office, and until he transmits to them a written declaration to the contrary, such powers and duties shall be discharged by the Vice-President as Acting President.

Section 4 Whenever the Vice-President and a majority of either the principal officers of the executive departments or of such other body as Congress may by law provide, transmit to the President pro tempore of the Senate and the Speaker of the House of Representatives their written declaration that the President is unable to discharge the powers and duties of his office, the Vice-President shall immediately assume the powers and duties of the office as Acting President.

Thereafter, when the President transmits to the President pro tempore of the Senate and the Speaker of the House of Representatives his written declaration that no inability exists, he shall resume the powers and duties of his office unless the Vice-President and a majority of either the principal officers of the executive department[s] or of such other body as Congress may by law provide, transmit within four days to the President pro tempore of the Senate and the Speaker of the House of Representatives their written declaration that the President is unable to discharge the powers and duties of his office. Thereupon Congress shall decide the issue, assembling within forty-eight hours for that purpose if not in session. If the Congress, within twenty-one days after receipt of the latter written declaration, or, if Congress is not in session, within twenty-one days after Congress is required to assemble, determines by two-thirds vote of both Houses that the President is unable to discharge the powers and duties of his office, the Vice-President shall continue to discharge the same as Acting President; otherwise, the President shall resume the powers and duties of his office.

Amendment XXVI

[Adopted 1971]

Section 1 The right of citizens of the United States, who are eighteen years of age or older, to vote shall not be denied or abridged by the United States or by any State on account of age.

Section 2 The Congress shall have power to enforce this article by appropriate legislation.

Unratified Amendment

Equal Rights Amendment (proposed by Congress March 22, 1972; seven-year deadline for ratification extended to June 30, 1982)

Section 1 Equality of rights under the law shall not be denied or abridged by the United States or by any State on account of sex.

Section 2 The Congress shall have the power to enforce, by appropriate legislation, the provisions of this article.

Section 3 This amendment shall take effect two years after the date of ratification.

Unratified Amendment

D.C. Statehood Amendment (proposed by Congress August 22, 1978)

Section 1 For purposes of representation in the Congress, election of the President and Vice-President, and article V of this Constitution, the District constituting the seat of government of the United States shall be treated as though it were a State.

Section 2 The exercise of the rights and powers conferred under this article shall be by the people of the District constituting the seat of government, and as shall be provided by Congress.

Section 3 The twenty-third article of amendment to the Constitution of the United States is hereby repealed.

Section 4 This article shall be inoperative, unless it shall have been ratified as an amendment to the Constitution by the legislatures of three-fourths of the several states within seven years from the date of its submission.

Amendment XXVII

[Adopted 1992]

No law, varying the compensation for the services of the Senators and Representatives, shall take effect, until an election of Representatives shall have intervened.

Facts and Figures: Government, Economy, and Demographics

PRESIDENTIAL ELECTIONS

Year	Candidates	Parties	Popular Vote	Percentage of Popular Vote	Electoral Vote	Percentage of Voter Participation
1789	**GEORGE WASHINGTON (Va.)***				69	
	John Adams				34	
	Others				35	
1792	**GEORGE WASHINGTON (Va.)**				132	
	John Adams				77	
	George Clinton				50	
	Others				5	
1796	**JOHN ADAMS (Mass.)**	Federalist			71	
	Thomas Jefferson	Democratic-Republican			68	
	Thomas Pinckney	Federalist			59	
	Aaron Burr	Dem.-Rep.			30	
	Others				48	
1800	**THOMAS JEFFERSON (Va.)**	Dem.-Rep.			73	
	Aaron Burr	Dem.-Rep.			73	
	John Adams	Federalist			65	
	C. C. Pinckney	Federalist			64	
	John Jay	Federalist			1	
1804	**THOMAS JEFFERSON (Va.)**	Dem.-Rep.			162	
	C. C. Pinckney	Federalist			14	
1808	**JAMES MADISON (Va.)**	Dem.-Rep.			122	
	C. C. Pinckney	Federalist			47	
	George Clinton	Dem.-Rep.			6	
1812	**JAMES MADISON (Va.)**	Dem.-Rep.			128	
	De Witt Clinton	Federalist			89	
1816	**JAMES MONROE (Va.)**	Dem.-Rep.			183	
	Rufus King	Federalist			34	
1820	**JAMES MONROE (Va.)**	Dem.-Rep.			231	
	John Quincy Adams	Dem.-Rep.			1	
1824	**JOHN Q. ADAMS (Mass.)**	Dem.-Rep.	108,740	30.5	84	26.9
	Andrew Jackson	Dem.-Rep.	153,544	43.1	99	
	William H. Crawford	Dem.-Rep.	46,618	13.1	41	
	Henry Clay	Dem.-Rep.	47,136	13.2	37	
1828	**ANDREW JACKSON (Tenn.)**	Democratic	647,286	56.0	178	57.6
	John Quincy Adams	National Republican	508,064	44.0	83	

*State of residence when elected president.

Year	Candidates	Parties	Popular Vote	Percentage of Popular Vote	Electoral Vote	Percentage of Voter Participation
1832	**ANDREW JACKSON (Tenn.)**	Democratic	687,502	55.0	219	55.4
	Henry Clay	National Republican	530,189	42.4	49	
	John Floyd	Independent			11	
	William Wirt	Anti-Mason	33,108	2.6	7	
1836	**MARTIN VAN BUREN (N.Y.)**	Democratic	765,483	50.9	170	57.8
	W. H. Harrison	Whig			73	
	Hugh L. White	Whig	739,795	49.1	26	
	Daniel Webster	Whig			14	
	W. P. Mangum	Independent			11	
1840	**WILLIAM H. HARRISON (Ohio)**	Whig	1,274,624	53.1	234	78.0
	Martin Van Buren	Democratic	1,127,781	46.9	60	
	J. G. Birney	Liberty	7,069		—	
1844	**JAMES K. POLK (Tenn.)**	Democratic	1,338,464	49.6	170	78.9
	Henry Clay	Whig	1,300,097	48.1	105	
	J. G. Birney	Liberty	62,300	2.3	—	
1848	**ZACHARY TAYLOR (La.)**	Whig	1,360,099	47.4	163	72.7
	Lewis Cass	Democratic	1,220,544	42.5	127	
	Martin Van Buren	Free-Soil	291,263	10.1	—	
1852	**FRANKLIN PIERCE (N.H.)**	Democratic	1,601,117	50.9	254	69.6
	Winfield Scott	Whig	1,385,453	44.1	42	
	John P. Hale	Free-Soil	155,825	5.0	—	
1856	**JAMES BUCHANAN (Pa.)**	Democratic	1,832,995	45.3	174	78.9
	John C. Frémont	Republican	1,339,932	33.1	114	
	Millard Fillmore	American	871,731	21.6	8	
1860	**ABRAHAM LINCOLN (Ill.)**	Republican	1,866,452	39.8	180	81.2
	Stephen A. Douglas	Democratic	1,375,157	29.4	12	
	John C. Breckinridge	Democratic	847,953	18.1	72	
	John Bell	Union	590,631	12.6	39	
1864	**ABRAHAM LINCOLN (Ill.)**	Republican	2,213,665	55.1	212	73.8
	George B. McClellan	Democratic	1,805,237	44.9	21	
1868	**ULYSSES S. GRANT (Ill.)**	Republican	3,012,833	52.7	214	78.1
	Horatio Seymour	Democratic	2,703,249	47.3	80	
1872	**ULYSSES S. GRANT (Ill.)**	Republican	3,597,132	55.6	286	71.3
	Horace Greeley	Democratic; Liberal Republican	2,834,125	43.9	66	
1876	**RUTHERFORD B. HAYES (Ohio)**	Republican	4,036,298	48.0	185	81.8
	Samuel J. Tilden	Democratic	4,288,590	51.0	184	
1880	**JAMES A. GARFIELD (Ohio)**	Republican	4,454,416	48.5	214	79.4
	Winfield S. Hancock	Democratic	4,444,952	48.1	155	
1884	**GROVER CLEVELAND (N.Y.)**	Democratic	4,874,986	48.5	219	77.5
	James G. Blaine	Republican	4,851,981	48.3	182	
1888	**BENJAMIN HARRISON (Ind.)**	Republican	5,439,853	47.9	233	79.3
	Grover Cleveland	Democratic	5,540,309	48.6	168	
1892	**GROVER CLEVELAND (N.Y.)**	Democratic	5,555,426	46.1	277	74.7
	Benjamin Harrison	Republican	5,182,690	43.0	145	
	James B. Weaver	People's	1,029,846	8.5	22	
1896	**WILLIAM McKINLEY (Ohio)**	Republican	7,104,779	51.1	271	79.3
	William J. Bryan	Democratic-People's	6,502,925	47.7	176	

Year	Candidates	Parties	Popular Vote	Percentage of Popular Vote	Electoral Vote	Percentage of Voter Participation
1900	**WILLIAM McKINLEY (Ohio)**	Republican	7,207,923	51.7	292	73.2
	William J. Bryan	Dem.-Populist	6,358,133	45.5	155	
1904	**THEODORE ROOSEVELT (N.Y.)**	Republican	7,623,486	57.9	336	65.2
	Alton B. Parker	Democratic	5,077,911	37.6	140	
	Eugene V. Debs	Socialist	402,283	3.0	—	
1908	**WILLIAM H. TAFT (Ohio)**	Republican	7,678,908	51.6	321	65.4
	William J. Bryan	Democratic	6,409,104	43.1	162	
	Eugene V. Debs	Socialist	420,793	2.8	—	
1912	**WOODROW WILSON (N.J.)**	Democratic	6,293,454	41.9	435	58.8
	Theodore Roosevelt	Progressive	4,119,538	27.4	88	
	William H. Taft	Republican	3,484,980	23.2	8	
	Eugene V. Debs	Socialist	900,672	6.1	—	
1916	**WOODROW WILSON (N.J.)**	Democratic	9,129,606	49.4	277	61.6
	Charles E. Hughes	Republican	8,538,221	46.2	254	
	A. L. Benson	Socialist	585,113	3.2	—	
1920	**WARREN G. HARDING (Ohio)**	Republican	16,143,407	60.5	404	49.2
	James M. Cox	Democratic	9,130,328	34.2	127	
	Eugene V. Debs	Socialist	919,799	3.4	—	
1924	**CALVIN COOLIDGE (Mass.)**	Republican	15,725,016	54.0	382	48.9
	John W. Davis	Democratic	8,386,503	28.8	136	
	Robert M. La Follette	Progressive	4,822,856	16.6	13	
1928	**HERBERT HOOVER (Calif.)**	Republican	21,391,381	57.4	444	56.9
	Alfred E. Smith	Democratic	15,016,443	40.3	87	
	Norman Thomas	Socialist	881,951	2.3	—	
	William Z. Foster	Communist	102,991	0.3	—	
1932	**FRANKLIN D. ROOSEVELT (N.Y.)**	Democratic	22,821,857	57.4	472	56.9
	Herbert Hoover	Republican	15,761,841	39.7	59	
	Norman Thomas	Socialist	881,951	2.2	—	
1936	**FRANKLIN D. ROOSEVELT (N.Y.)**	Democratic	27,751,597	60.8	523	61.0
	Alfred M. Landon	Republican	16,679,583	36.5	8	
	William Lemke	Union	882,479	1.9	—	
1940	**FRANKLIN D. ROOSEVELT (N.Y.)**	Democratic	27,244,160	54.8	449	62.5
	Wendell Willkie	Republican	22,305,198	44.8	82	
1944	**FRANKLIN D. ROOSEVELT (N.Y.)**	Democratic	25,602,504	53.5	432	55.9
	Thomas E. Dewey	Republican	22,006,285	46.0	99	
1948	**HARRY S. TRUMAN (Mo.)**	Democratic	24,105,695	49.5	303	53.0
	Thomas E. Dewey	Republican	21,969,170	45.1	189	
	J. Strom Thurmond	States'-Rights Democratic	1,169,021	2.4	38	
	Henry A. Wallace	Progressive	1,156,103	2.4	—	
1952	**DWIGHT D. EISENHOWER (N.Y.)**	Republican	33,936,252	55.1	442	63.3
	Adlai Stevenson	Democratic	27,314,992	44.4	89	
1956	**DWIGHT D. EISENHOWER (N.Y.)**	Republican	35,575,420	57.6	457	60.6
	Adlai Stevenson	Democratic	26,033,066	42.1	73	
	Other	—	—		1	
1960	**JOHN F. KENNEDY (Mass.)**	Democratic	34,227,096	49.9	303	62.8
	Richard M. Nixon	Republican	34,108,546	49.6	219	
	Other	—	—		15	
1964	**LYNDON B. JOHNSON (Texas)**	Democratic	43,126,506	61.1	486	61.7
	Barry M. Goldwater	Republican	27,176,799	38.5	52	

Year	Candidates	Parties	Popular Vote	Percentage of Popular Vote	Electoral Vote	Percentage of Voter Participation
1968	**RICHARD M. NIXON (N.Y.)**	Republican	31,770,237	43.4	301	60.9
	Hubert H. Humphrey	Democratic	31,270,533	42.7	191	
	George Wallace	American Indep.	9,906,141	13.5	46	
1972	**RICHARD M. NIXON (N.Y.)**	Republican	47,169,911	60.7	520	55.2
	George S. McGovern	Democratic	29,170,383	37.5	17	
	Other	—	—	—	1	
1976	**JIMMY CARTER (Ga.)**	Democratic	40,830,763	50.0	297	53.5
	Gerald R. Ford	Republican	39,147,793	48.0	240	
	Other	—	1,575,459	2.1	—	
1980	**RONALD REAGAN (Calif.)**	Republican	43,901,812	51.0	489	54.0
	Jimmy Carter	Democratic	35,483,820	41.0	49	
	John B. Anderson	Independent	5,719,722	7.0	—	
	Ed Clark	Libertarian	921,188	1.1	—	
1984	**RONALD REAGAN (Calif.)**	Republican	54,455,075	59.0	525	53.1
	Walter Mondale	Democratic	37,577,185	41.0	13	
1988	**GEORGE H. W. BUSH (Texas)**	Republican	47,946,422	54.0	426	50.2
	Michael S. Dukakis	Democratic	41,016,429	46.0	112	
1992	**WILLIAM J. CLINTON (Ark.)**	Democratic	44,908,254	43.0	370	55.9
	George H. W. Bush	Republican	39,102,282	38.0	168	
	H. Ross Perot	Independent	19,721,433	19.0	—	
1996	**WILLIAM J. CLINTON (Ark.)**	Democratic	47,401,185	49.2	379	49.0
	Robert Dole	Republican	39,197,469	40.7	159	
	H. Ross Perot	Independent	8,085,294	8.4	—	
2000	**GEORGE W. BUSH (Texas)**	Republican	50,456,062	47.8	271	51.2
	Al Gore	Democratic	50,996,862	48.4	267	
	Ralph Nader	Green Party	2,858,843	2.7	—	
	Patrick J. Buchanan	—	438,760	0.4	—	
2004	**GEORGE W. BUSH (Texas)**	Republican	61,872,711	50.7	286	60.3
	John F. Kerry	Democratic	58,894,584	48.3	252	
	Other	—	1,582,185	1.3	—	
2008	**BARACK OBAMA (Ill.)**	Democratic	69,456,897	52.9	365	56.8
	John McCain	Republican	59,934,814	45.7	173	

PRESIDENTS, VICE PRESIDENTS, AND SECRETARIES OF STATE

The Washington Administration (1789–1797)

Vice President	John Adams	1789–1797
Secretary of State	Thomas Jefferson	1789–1793
	Edmund Randolph	1794–1795
	Timothy Pickering	1795–1797

The John Adams Administration (1797–1801)

Vice President	Thomas Jefferson	1797–1801
Secretary of State	Timothy Pickering	1797–1800
	John Marshall	1800–1801

The Jefferson Administration (1801–1809)

Vice President	Aaron Burr	1801–1805
	George Clinton	1805–1809
Secretary of State	James Madison	1801–1809

The Madison Administration (1809–1817)

Vice President	George Clinton	1809–1813
	Elbridge Gerry	1813–1817
Secretary of State	Robert Smith	1809–1811
	James Monroe	1811–1817

The Monroe Administration (1817–1825)

Vice President	Daniel Tompkins	1817–1825
Secretary of State	John Quincy Adams	1817–1825

The John Quincy Adams Administration (1825–1829)

Vice President	John C. Calhoun	1825–1829
Secretary of State	Henry Clay	1825–1829

The Jackson Administration (1829–1837)

Vice President	John C. Calhoun	1829–1833
	Martin Van Buren	1833–1837
Secretary of State	Martin Van Buren	1829–1831
	Edward Livingston	1831–1833
	Louis McLane	1833–1834
	John Forsyth	1834–1837

The Van Buren Administration (1837–1841)

Vice President	Richard M. Johnson	1837–1841
Secretary of State	John Forsyth	1837–1841

The William Harrison Administration (1841)

Vice President	John Tyler	1841
Secretary of State	Daniel Webster	1841

The Tyler Administration (1841–1845)

Vice President	None	
Secretary of State	Daniel Webster	1841–1843
	Hugh S. Legaré	1843
	Abel P. Upshur	1843–1844
	John C. Calhoun	1844–1845

The Polk Administration (1845–1849)

Vice President	George M. Dallas	1845–1849
Secretary of State	James Buchanan	1845–1849

The Taylor Administration (1849–1850)

Vice President	Millard Fillmore	1849–1850
Secretary of State	John M. Clayton	1849–1850

The Fillmore Administration (1850–1853)

Vice President	None	
Secretary of State	Daniel Webster	1850–1852
	Edward Everett	1852–1853

The Pierce Administration (1853–1857)

Vice President	William R. King	1853–1857
Secretary of State	William L. Marcy	1853–1857

The Buchanan Administration (1857–1861)

Vice President	John C. Breckinridge	1857–1861
Secretary of State	Lewis Cass	1857–1860
	Jeremiah S. Black	1860–1861

The Lincoln Administration (1861–1865)

Vice President	Hannibal Hamlin	1861–1865
	Andrew Johnson	1865
Secretary of State	William H. Seward	1861–1865

The Andrew Johnson Administration (1865–1869)

Vice President	None	
Secretary of State	William H. Seward	1865–1869

The Grant Administration (1869–1877)

Vice President	Schuyler Colfax	1869–1873
	Henry Wilson	1873–1877
Secretary of State	Elihu B. Washburne	1869
	Hamilton Fish	1869–1877

The Hayes Administration (1877–1881)

Vice President	William A. Wheeler	1877–1881
Secretary of State	William M. Evarts	1877–1881

The Garfield Administration (1881)

Vice President	Chester A. Arthur	1881
Secretary of State	James G. Blaine	1881

The Arthur Administration (1881–1885)

Vice President	None	
Secretary of State	F. T. Frelinghuysen	1881–1885

The Cleveland Administration (1885–1889)

Vice President	Thomas A. Hendricks	1885–1889
Secretary of State	Thomas F. Bayard	1885–1889

The Benjamin Harrison Administration (1889–1893)

Vice President	Levi P. Morton	1889–1893
Secretary of State	James G. Blaine	1889–1892
	John W. Foster	1892–1893

The Cleveland Administration (1893–1897)

Vice President	Adlai E. Stevenson	1893–1897
Secretary of State	Walter Q. Gresham	1893–1895
	Richard Olney	1895–1897

The McKinley Administration (1897–1901)

Vice President	Garret A. Hobart	1897–1901
	Theodore Roosevelt	1901
Secretary of State	John Sherman	1897–1898
	William R. Day	1898
	John Hay	1898–1901

The Theodore Roosevelt Administration (1901–1909)

Vice President	Charles Fairbanks	1905–1909
Secretary of State	John Hay	1901–1905
	Elihu Root	1905–1909
	Robert Bacon	1909

The Taft Administration (1909–1913)

Vice President	James S. Sherman	1909–1913
Secretary of State	Philander C. Knox	1909–1913

The Wilson Administration (1913–1921)

Vice President	Thomas R. Marshall	1913–1921
Secretary of State	William J. Bryan	1913–1915
	Robert Lansing	1915–1920
	Bainbridge Colby	1920–1921

The Harding Administration (1921–1923)

Vice President	Calvin Coolidge	1921–1923
Secretary of State	Charles E. Hughes	1921–1923

The Coolidge Administration (1923–1929)

Vice President	Charles G. Dawes	1925–1929
Secretary of State	Charles E. Hughes	1923–1925
	Frank B. Kellogg	1925–1929

The Hoover Administration (1929–1933)

Vice President	Charles Curtis	1929–1933
Secretary of State	Henry L. Stimson	1929–1933

The Franklin D. Roosevelt Administration (1933–1945)

Vice President	John Nance Garner	1933–1941
	Henry A. Wallace	1941–1945
	Harry S. Truman	1945
Secretary of State	Cordell Hull	1933–1944
	Edward R. Stettinius Jr.	1944–1945

The Truman Administration (1945–1953)

Vice President	Alben W. Barkley	1949–1953
Secretary of State	Edward R. Stettinius Jr.	1945
	James F. Byrnes	1945–1947
	George C. Marshall	1947–1949
	Dean G. Acheson	1949–1953

The Eisenhower Administration (1953–1961)

Vice President	Richard M. Nixon	1953–1961
Secretary of State	John Foster Dulles	1953–1959
	Christian A. Herter	1959–1961

The Kennedy Administration (1961–1963)

Vice President	Lyndon B. Johnson	1961–1963
Secretary of State	Dean Rusk	1961–1963

The Lyndon Johnson Administration (1963–1969)

Vice President	Hubert H. Humphrey	1965–1969
Secretary of State	Dean Rusk	1963–1969

The Nixon Administration (1969–1974)

Vice President	Spiro T. Agnew	1969–1973
	Gerald R. Ford	1973–1974
Secretary of State	William P. Rogers	1969–1973
	Henry A. Kissinger	1973–1974

The Ford Administration (1974–1977)

Vice President	Nelson A. Rockefeller	1974–1977
Secretary of State	Henry A. Kissinger	1974–1977

The Carter Administration (1977–1981)

Vice President	Walter F. Mondale	1977–1981
Secretary of State	Cyrus R. Vance	1977–1980
	Edmund Muskie	1980–1981

The Reagan Administration (1981–1989)

Vice President	George H. W. Bush	1981–1989
Secretary of State	Alexander M. Haig	1981–1982
	George P. Shultz	1982–1989

The George H. W. Bush Administration (1989–1993)

Vice President	J. Danforth Quayle	1989–1993
Secretary of State	James A. Baker III	1989–1992
	Lawrence S. Eagleburger	1992–1993

The Clinton Administration (1993–2001)

Vice President	Albert Gore	1993–2001
Secretary of State	Warren M. Christopher	1993–1997
	Madeleine K. Albright	1997–2001

The George W. Bush Administration (2001–2009)

Vice President	Richard Cheney	2001–2009
Secretary of State	Colin Powell	2001–2005
	Condoleezza Rice	2005–2009

The Obama Administration (2009–)

Vice President	Joseph R. Biden	2009–
Secretary of State	Hillary Rodham Clinton	2009–

SUPREME COURT JUSTICES

Name	Service	Appointed By	Name	Service	Appointed By
John Jay*	1789–1795	Washington	Samuel Blatchford	1882–1893	Arthur
James Wilson	1789–1798	Washington	Lucius Q. C. Lamar	1888–1893	Cleveland
John Blair	1789–1796	Washington	**Melville W. Fuller**	1888–1910	Cleveland
John Rutledge	1790–1791	Washington	David J. Brewer	1889–1910	B. Harrison
William Cushing	1790–1810	Washington	Henry B. Brown	1890–1906	B. Harrison
James Iredell	1790–1799	Washington	George Shiras	1892–1903	B. Harrison
Thomas Johnson	1791–1793	Washington	Howell E. Jackson	1893–1895	B. Harrison
William Paterson	1793–1806	Washington	Edward D. White	1894–1910	Cleveland
John Rutledge†	1795	Washington	Rufus W. Peckham	1896–1909	Cleveland
Samuel Chase	1796–1811	Washington	Joseph McKenna	1898–1925	McKinley
Oliver Ellsworth	1796–1799	Washington	Oliver W. Holmes	1902–1932	T. Roosevelt
Bushrod Washington	1798–1829	J. Adams	William R. Day	1903–1922	T. Roosevelt
Alfred Moore	1799–1804	J. Adams	William H. Moody	1906–1910	T. Roosevelt
John Marshall	1801–1835	J. Adams	Horace H. Lurton	1910–1914	Taft
William Johnson	1804–1834	Jefferson	Charles E. Hughes	1910–1916	Taft
Henry B. Livingston	1806–1823	Jefferson	Willis Van Devanter	1910–1937	Taft
Thomas Todd	1807–1826	Jefferson	**Edward D. White**	1910–1921	Taft
Gabriel Duval	1811–1836	Madison	Joseph R. Lamar	1911–1916	Taft
Joseph Story	1811–1845	Madison	Mahlon Pitney	1912–1922	Taft
Smith Thompson	1823–1843	Monroe	James C. McReynolds	1914–1941	Wilson
Robert Trimble	1826–1828	J. Q. Adams	Louis D. Brandeis	1916–1939	Wilson
John McLean	1829–1861	Jackson	John H. Clarke	1916–1922	Wilson
Henry Baldwin	1830–1844	Jackson	**William H. Taft**	1921–1930	Harding
James M. Wayne	1835–1867	Jackson	George Sutherland	1922–1938	Harding
Roger B. Taney	1836–1864	Jackson	Pierce Butler	1923–1939	Harding
Philip P. Barbour	1836–1841	Jackson	Edward T. Sanford	1923–1930	Harding
John Catron	1837–1865	Van Buren	Harlan F. Stone	1925–1941	Coolidge
John McKinley	1837–1852	Van Buren	**Charles E. Hughes**	1930–1941	Hoover
Peter V. Daniel	1841–1860	Van Buren	Owen J. Roberts	1930–1945	Hoover
Samuel Nelson	1845–1872	Tyler	Benjamin N. Cardozo	1932–1938	Hoover
Levi Woodbury	1845–1851	Polk	Hugo L. Black	1937–1971	F. Roosevelt
Robert C. Grier	1846–1870	Polk	Stanley F. Reed	1938–1957	F. Roosevelt
Benjamin R. Curtis	1851–1857	Fillmore	Felix Frankfurter	1939–1962	F. Roosevelt
John A. Campbell	1853–1861	Pierce	William O. Douglas	1939–1975	F. Roosevelt
Nathan Clifford	1858–1881	Buchanan	Frank Murphy	1940–1949	F. Roosevelt
Noah H. Swayne	1862–1881	Lincoln	**Harlan F. Stone**	1941–1946	F. Roosevelt
Samuel F. Miller	1862–1890	Lincoln	James F. Byrnes	1941–1942	F. Roosevelt
David Davis	1862–1877	Lincoln	Robert H. Jackson	1941–1954	F. Roosevelt
Stephen J. Field	1863–1897	Lincoln	Wiley B. Rutledge	1943–1949	F. Roosevelt
Salmon P. Chase	1864–1873	Lincoln	Harold H. Burton	1945–1958	Truman
William Strong	1870–1880	Grant	**Frederick M. Vinson**	1946–1953	Truman
Joseph P. Bradley	1870–1892	Grant	Tom C. Clark	1949–1967	Truman
Ward Hunt	1873–1882	Grant	Sherman Minton	1949–1956	Truman
Morrison R. Waite	1874–1888	Grant	**Earl Warren**	1953–1969	Eisenhower
John M. Harlan	1877–1911	Hayes	John Marshall Harlan	1955–1971	Eisenhower
William B. Woods	1880–1887	Hayes	William J. Brennan Jr.	1956–1990	Eisenhower
Stanley Matthews	1881–1889	Garfield	Charles E. Whittaker	1957–1962	Eisenhower
Horace Gray	1882–1902	Arthur	Potter Stewart	1958–1981	Eisenhower

*Chief Justices appear in bold type.
†Acting Chief Justice; Senate refused to confirm appointment.

Name	Service	Appointed By
Byron R. White	1962–1993	Kennedy
Arthur J. Goldberg	1962–1965	Kennedy
Abe Fortas	1965–1969	L. Johnson
Thurgood Marshall	1967–1991	L. Johnson
Warren E. Burger	1969–1986	Nixon
Harry A. Blackmun	1970–1994	Nixon
Lewis F. Powell Jr.	1972–1988	Nixon
William H. Rehnquist	1972–1986	Nixon
John Paul Stevens	1975–	Ford
Sandra Day O'Connor	1981–2006	Reagan
William H. Rehnquist	1986–2005	Reagan

Name	Service	Appointed By
Antonin Scalia	1986–	Reagan
Anthony M. Kennedy	1988–	Reagan
David H. Souter	1990–2009	G. H. W. Bush
Clarence Thomas	1991–	G. H. W. Bush
Ruth Bader Ginsburg	1993–	Clinton
Stephen Breyer	1994–	Clinton
John G. Roberts Jr.	2005–	G. W. Bush
Samuel A. Alito Jr.	2006–	G. W. Bush
Sonia Sotomayor	2009–	B. Obama

FEDERAL SPENDING AND THE ECONOMY, 1790–2007

Year	Gross National Product (in billions)	Exports	Imports	Federal Budget (in billions)	Federal Surplus/Deficit (in billions)	Federal Debt (in billions)
1790	NA	20	23	0.004	0.00015	0.076
1800	NA	71	91	0.011	0.0006	0.083
1810	NA	67	85	0.008	0.0012	0.053
1820	NA	70	74	0.018	−0.0004	0.091
1830	NA	74	71	0.015	0.100	0.049
1840	NA	132	107	0.024	−0.005	0.004
1850	NA	152	178	0.040	0.004	0.064
1860	NA	400	362	0.063	−0.01	0.065
1870	7.4	451	462	0.310	0.10	2.4
1880	11.2	853	761	0.268	0.07	2.1
1890	13.1	910	823	0.318	0.09	1.2
1900	18.7	1,499	930	0.521	0.05	1.2
1910	35.3	1,919	1,646	0.694	−0.02	1.1
1920	91.5	8,664	5,784	6.357	0.3	24.3
1930	90.4	4,013	3,500	3.320	0.7	16.3
1940	99.7	4,030	7,433	9.6	−2.7	43.0
1950	284.8	10,816	9,125	43.1	−2.2	257.4
1960	503.7	19,600	15,046	92.2	0.3	286.3
1970	977.1	42,700	40,189	195.6	−2.8	371.0
1980	2,631.7	220,600	244,871	590.9	−73.8	907.7
1990	5,832.2	393,600	495,300	1,253.2	−221.2	3,266.1
2000	9,848.0	1,070,054	1,445,438	1,788.8	236.4	5,701.9
2005	12,520.8	1,283,753	1,995,320	2,153.9	−318.3	7,905.3
2007	13,937.0	1,645,726	2,345,983	2,568.2	−162.0	8,950.7

SOURCE: *Historical Statistics of the U.S., Colonial Times to 1970* (1975) and www.census.gov.

POPULATION GROWTH, 1630–2000

Year	Population	Percent Increase	Year	Population	Percent Increase
1630	4,600	—	1820	9,638,453	33.1
1640	26,600	473.3	1830	12,866,020	33.5
1650	50,400	89.1	1840	17,069,453	32.7
1660	75,100	49.0	1850	23,191,876	35.9
1670	111,900	49.1	1860	31,443,321	35.6
1680	151,500	35.4	1870	39,818,449	26.6
1690	210,400	38.9	1880	50,155,783	26.0
1700	250,900	19.3	1890	62,947,714	25.5
1710	331,700	32.2	1900	75,994,575	20.7
1720	466,200	40.5	1910	91,972,266	21.0
1730	629,400	35.0	1920	105,710,620	14.9
1740	905,600	43.9	1930	122,775,046	16.1
1750	1,170,800	30.0	1940	131,669,275	7.2
1760	1,593,600	36.1	1950	150,697,361	14.5
1770	2,148,100	34.8	1960	179,323,175	19.0
1780	2,780,400	29.4	1970	203,302,031	13.4
1790	3,929,214	41.3	1980	226,542,199	11.4
1800	5,308,483	35.1	1990	248,718,302	9.8
1810	7,239,881	36.4	2000	281,422,509	13.1

SOURCE: *Historical Statistics of the U.S., Colonial Times to 1970* (1975) and www.census.gov.

Birthrate, 1820–2000

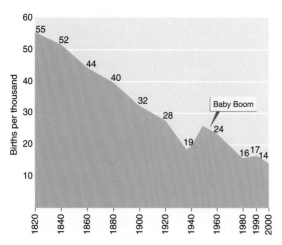

SOURCE: Data from *Historical Statistics of the U.S., Colonial Times to 1970* (1975) and www.census.gov.

Life Expectancy, 1900–2000

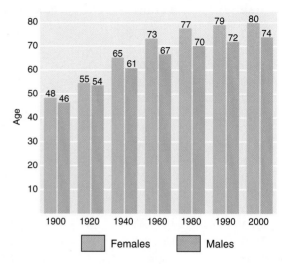

SOURCE: Data from *Historical Statistics of the U.S., Colonial Times to 1970* (1975) and www.census.gov.

Major Trends in Immigration, 1820–2000

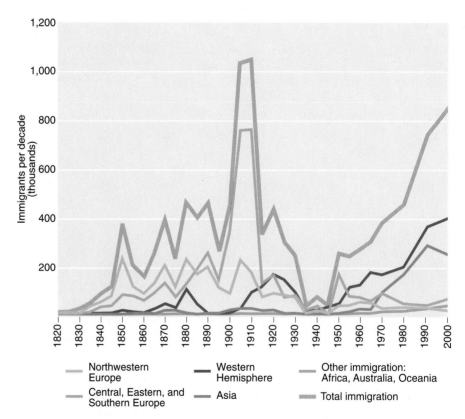

SOURCE: Data from *Historical Statistics of the U.S., Colonial Times to 1970* (1975) and www.census.gov.

Research Resources in U.S. History

For help refining your research skills, finding what you need on the Web, and using the Web effectively, see "Online Research and Reference Aids" at bedfordstmartins.com/roarkcompact.

While doing research in history, you will use the library to track down primary and secondary sources and to answer questions that arise as you learn more about your topic. This appendix suggests helpful indexes, references, periodicals, and sources of primary documents. It also offers an overview of electronic resources available through the Internet. The materials listed here are not carried at all libraries, but they will give you an idea of the range of sources available. Remember, too, that librarians are an extremely helpful resource. They can direct you to useful materials throughout your research process.

Bibliographies and Indexes

American Historical Association Guide to Historical Literature. 3rd ed. New York: Oxford University Press, 1995. Offers 27,000 citations to important historical literature arranged in forty-eight sections covering theory, international history, and regional history. An indispensable guide recently updated to include current trends in historical research.

American History and Life. Santa Barbara: ABC-Clio, 1964–. Covers publications of all sorts on U.S. and Canadian history and culture in a chronological and regional format, with abstracts and alphabetical indexes. Available in computerized format. The most complete ongoing bibliography for American history.

Primary Resources

There are many routes to finding contemporary material for historical research. You may search your library catalog using the name of a prominent historical figure as an author; you may also find anthologies covering particular themes or periods in history. Consider also the following special materials for your research.

THE PRESS

American Periodical Series, 1741–1900. Ann Arbor: University Microfilms, 1946–1979. Includes periodicals from the colonial period to 1900. Available in microfilm and as an online database.

Herstory Microfilm Collection. Berkeley: Women's History Research Center, 1973. A microfilm collection of alternative feminist periodicals published between 1960

and 1980. Provides an interesting documentary history of the women's movement.

New York Times Index. New York: New York Times, 1913–. Many libraries have this newspaper on microfilm going back to its beginning in 1851. An index is available to locate specific dates and pages of news stories. See also *ProQuest Historical Newspapers.*

ProQuest Historical Newspapers. Available at many libraries, a database of full-text articles from dozens of newspapers, including the *New York Times* for 1851–2001, the *Washington Post* for 1877–1988, and the *Los Angeles Times* for 1881–1984.

Readers' Guide to Periodical Literature. New York: Wilson, 1900–. This index to popular magazines started in 1900; an earlier index, *Poole's Index to Periodical Literature,* covers 1802–1906.

DIARIES, PAMPHLETS, BOOKS

The American Culture Series, 1493–1875. Ann Arbor: University Microfilms, 1941–1974. A microfilm set, with a useful index, featuring books and pamphlets published between 1493 and 1875.

American Women's Diaries. New Canaan: Readex, 1984–. A collection of reproductions of women's diaries. There are different series for different regions of the country.

The March of America Facsimile Series. Ann Arbor: University Microfilms, 1966. A collection of more than ninety facsimiles of travel accounts to the New World published in English or English translation from the fifteenth through the nineteenth centuries.

Women in America from Colonial Times to the Twentieth Century. New York: Arno, 1974. A collection of reprints of dozens of books written by women describing women's lives and experiences in their own words.

GOVERNMENT DOCUMENTS

Congressional Record. Washington, D.C.: Government Printing Office, 1874–. Covers daily debates and proceedings of Congress. Earlier series were called *Debates and Proceedings in the Congress of the United States* and *The Congressional Globe.*

Foreign Relations of the United States. Washington, D.C.: Department of State, 1861–. A collection of documents from 1861, including diplomatic papers, correspondence, and memoranda, that provides a documentary record of U.S. foreign policy.

Public Papers of the Presidents. Washington, D.C.: Office of the Federal Register, 1957–. Includes major documents issued by the executive branch from the Hoover administration to the present.

Serial Set. Washington, D.C.: Government Printing Office, 1789–1969. A huge collection of congressional documents, available in many libraries on microfiche, with a useful index.

LOCAL HISTORY COLLECTIONS

State and county historical societies often house a wealth of historical documents; consider their resources when planning your research. You may find yourself working with material that no one else has analyzed before.

Internet Resources

The following online sources are good places to find historical information. You can also search the Web using any of a number of search engines. Bear in mind that there is no board of editors screening Internet sites for accuracy or usefulness. Be critical of all sources, particularly those found on the Internet. When this book went to press, the sites listed below were active and maintained.

The American Civil War Homepage. **sunsite.utk.edu/civil-war**. A comprehensive resource bank on the American Civil War. Maintained by George Hoemann of the University of Tennessee, the site contains letters, documents, photographs, information about battles, links to other sites, and regiment rosters.

American Memory: Historical Collections for the National Digital Library. **memory.loc.gov/ammem/index.html**. A Web site that features digitized primary source materials from the Library of Congress, among them African American pamphlets, Civil War photographs, documents from the Constitutional Convention of 1774–1790, materials on woman suffrage, and oral histories.

Historical Text Archive. **historicaltextarchive.com**. One of the oldest and largest Internet archives of historical documents, articles, photographs, and more. Includes sections on Native American, African American, and U.S. history, in which can be found texts of the Declaration of Independence, the Constitution of Iroquois Nations, World War II surrender documents, and a great deal more.

Index of Native American Resources on the Internet. **hanksville.org/NAresources**. A vast index of Native American resources organized by category, including oral history, written history, geographical areas, timelines, and photographs.

A central place to search for information on Native American history.

Internet Resources for Students of Afro-American History and Culture. **libraries.rutgers.edu/rul/rr_gateway/research_guides/history/afrores.shtml**. A good place to begin research on topics in African American history. The site is indexed and linked to a wide variety of sources, including primary documents, text collections, and archival sources on African American history.

Make History. **bedfordstmartins.com/makehistory**. Comprising the content of five online libraries—Map Central, the Bedford Image Library, DocLinks, HistoryLinks, and PlaceLinks—Make History provides access to relevant digital content including maps, documents, and Web links. Searchable by keyword, topic, date, or specific chapter of *The American Promise.*

NativeWeb. **nativeweb.org**. One of the best organized and most accessible sites on Native American issues, *NativeWeb* combines an events calendar and message board with history, statistics, a list of news sources, archives, new and related sites that are updated each week, and documents.

Perry-Castañeda Library Map Collection. **lib.utexas.edu/maps/**. The University of Texas at Austin library has put over seven hundred U.S. maps on the Web along with hundreds of other historical and contemporary maps from around the world.

Smithsonian Institution. **si.edu**. Organized by subject, such as military history or Hispanic/Latino American resources, this site offers selected links to sites hosted by Smithsonian museums and organizations. Content includes images, book suggestions, maps, and links.

Supreme Court Collection. **law.cornell.edu/supct/**. This database can be used to search for information on various Supreme Court cases. Although the site primarily covers cases that occurred after 1990, there is information on some earlier historic cases. The justices' opinions, as originally written, are included.

United States Holocaust Memorial Museum. **ushmm.org**. This site contains information about the Holocaust Museum in Washington, D.C., and the Holocaust in general, plus links to related sites.

Women and Social Movements in the United States, 1600–2000. **womhist.alexanderstreet.com**. Available at many libraries, this database brings together hundreds of documents, links, and bibliographies documenting women's activism in public life.

WWW-VL History Index. **vlib.iue.it/history**. A vast list of more than 1,700 links to sites of interest to historians, arranged by general topic and by continent and country. The United States history page includes links to online research tools as well as links arranged by topic and historical period.

A Note to Students: This list of terms is provided to help you build your historical vocabulary. Many of these terms refer to broad, enduring concepts that you may encounter not only in further studies of history but also when following current events. For definitions and discussions of words not included here, consult a dictionary and the book's index, which will point you to topics covered at greater length in the book.

affirmative action Policies established in the 1960s and 1970s by governments, businesses, universities, and other institutions to overcome the effects of past discrimination against specific groups such as racial and ethnic minorities and women. Measures to ensure equal opportunity include setting goals for admission, hiring, and promotion; considering minority status when allocating resources; and actively encouraging victims of past discrimination to apply for jobs and other resources.

agribusiness Farming on a large scale, using the production, processing, and distribution methods of modern business. Farming became a big business, not just a way to feed a family and make a living, in the late nineteenth century as farms got larger and more mechanized. In the 1940s and 1950s, specialized commercial farms replaced many family-run operations and grew to an enormous scale.

alliance system The military and diplomatic system formulated in an effort to create a balance of power in pre–World War I Europe. Nations were bound together by rigid and comprehensive treaties that promised mutual aid in the case of attack by specific nations. The system swung into action after the Austrian archduke Franz Ferdinand was assassinated in Sarajevo on June 28, 1914, dragging most of Europe into war.

anarchist A person who rebels against established order and authority. An anarchist believes that government of any kind is unnecessary and undesirable and should be replaced with voluntary cooperation and free association. Anarchists became increasingly visible in the United States in the late nineteenth and early twentieth centuries. They advocated revolution, and their numbers grew through appeals to discontented laborers. Anarchists frequently employed violence in an attempt to achieve their goals. In 1901, anarchist Leon Czolgosz assassinated President William McKinley.

antebellum A term that means "before a war" and commonly refers to the period prior to the Civil War.

antinomian A person who does not obey societal or religious laws. In colonial Massachusetts, Puritan authorities accused Anne Hutchinson of antinomianism because she believed that Christians could achieve salvation by faith alone. They further asserted, incorrectly, that Hutchinson also held the belief that it was not necessary to follow God's laws as set forth in the Bible.

archaeology A social science devoted to learning about people who lived in the past by studying physical artifacts created by humans. Most but not all archaeological study focuses on the history of people who lived before the use of the written word.

Archaic A term applied to various hunting and gathering cultures that descended from Paleo-Indians. The term also refers to the period of time when these cultures dominated ancient America, roughly 8000 BP to between 2000 and 1000 BP.

artifacts Material remains studied and used by archaeologists and historians to support their interpretations of human history. Examples of artifacts include bones, pots, baskets, jewelry, furniture, tools, clothing, and buildings.

artisan A term commonly used prior to 1900 to describe a skilled craftsperson, such as a cabinetmaker.

Bill of Rights The term commonly used to identify the first ten amendments to the U.S. Constitution (the last of which was ratified in 1791). The Bill of Rights guarantees individual liberties and defines limitations to federal power. Many states made the promise of the prompt addition of a bill of rights a precondition for their ratification of the Constitution.

black nationalism A term linked to several African American movements emphasizing racial pride, separation from whites and white institutions, and black autonomy. Black nationalism gained in popularity with the rise of Marcus Garvey and the Universal Negro Improvement Association (1917–1927) and later with the Black Panther Party, Malcolm X, and other participants in the black power movements of the 1960s.

bloody shirt A refrain used by Republicans in the late nineteenth century to remind the voting public that the Democratic Party, dominated by the South, was largely responsible for the Civil War and that the Republican Party had preserved the Union. Republicans urged their constituents to "vote the way you shot."

bracero program A policy begun during World War II to help with wartime agriculture in which Mexican laborers (*braceros*) were permitted to enter the United States and work for a limited period of time but not to gain citizenship or permanent residence. The program officially ended in 1964.

brinksmanship A Cold War practice of appearing willing and able to resort to nuclear war in order to make an enemy back down. Secretary of State John Foster Dulles was the foremost proponent of this policy.

Calvinism The religious doctrine of which the primary tenet is that salvation is predestined by God. Founded by John Calvin of Geneva during the Protestant Reformation, Calvinism required its adherents to live according to a strict religious and moral code. The Puritans who settled in colonial New England were devout Calvinists. *See also* predestination.

checks and balances A system in which the executive, legislative, and judicial branches of the government curb one other's power. Checks and balances were written into the U.S. Constitution during the Constitutional Convention of 1787.

civil disobedience The public and peaceful violation of certain laws or government orders by individuals or groups who act out of a profound conviction that the laws or directives are unjust or immoral and who are prepared to accept the consequences of their actions. Civil disobedience was practiced most famously in U.S. history in the black freedom struggle of the 1960s.

civil service The administrative service of a government. This term often applies to reforms following the passage of the Pendleton Act in 1883, which set qualifications for U.S. government jobs and sought to remove such jobs from political influence. *See also* spoils system.

closed shop An establishment in which every employee is required to join a union to be employed.

Cold War The hostile and tense relationship that existed between the Soviet Union on the one hand and the United States and other Western nations on the other from 1947 to 1989. This war was said to be "cold" because the hostility stopped short of armed (hot) conflict, which was warded off by the strategy of nuclear deterrence. *See also* deterrence.

collective bargaining Negotiation by a group of workers (usually through a union) with their employer concerning rates of pay and working conditions.

collective security An association of independent nations that agree to accept and implement decisions made by the group, including going to war in defense of one or more members. The United States resolutely avoided such alliances until after World War II, when it created the North Atlantic Treaty Organization (NATO) in response to the threat posed by the Soviet Union. *See also* North Atlantic Treaty Organization.

colonization The process by which a country or society gains control over another, primarily through settlement.

Columbian exchange The transatlantic exchange of goods, peoples, and ideas that began when Columbus arrived in the Caribbean in 1492, ending the age-old separation of the hemispheres.

communism (Communist Party) A system of government and political organization, based on Marxist-Leninist ideals, in which a single authoritarian party controls the economy through state ownership of production, as a step toward reaching the final stage of Marxist theory in which the state dissolves and economic goods are distributed evenly for the common good. Communists around the globe encouraged the spread of communism in other nations in the hope of fomenting worldwide revolution. At its peak in the 1930s, the Communist Party of the United States worked closely with labor unions and insisted that only the overthrow of the capitalist system by its workers could save the victims of the Great Depression. After World War II, the Communist Soviet Union was held to be a direct threat to American democracy, prompting the Cold War. *See also* Cold War.

conscription Compulsory military service. Americans were first subject to conscription during the Civil War. The Selective Service Act of 1940 marked its first peacetime use. *See also* draft.

conservatism A political and moral outlook dating back to Alexander Hamilton's belief in a strong central government resting on a solid banking foundation. Currently associated with the Republican Party, conservatism today places a high premium on military preparedness, free market economics, low taxes, and strong sexual morality.

consumer culture (consumerism) A society that places high value on, and devotes substantial resources to, the purchase and display of material goods. Elements of American consumerism were evident in the nineteenth century but really took hold in the twentieth century, with installment buying and advertising in the 1920s and with the postwar prosperity of the 1950s.

containment The U.S. foreign policy developed after World War II to hold in check the power and influence of the Soviet Union and other groups or nations espousing communism. The strategy was first fully articulated by diplomat George F. Kennan in 1946–1947.

covenant An agreement or pact; in American history, a religious agreement. The Pilgrims used this term in the Mayflower Compact to refer to the agreement they made with one another to establish a law-abiding community in which all members would work together for the common good. Later, New England Puritans used the term to refer to the agreement they made with God and one other to live according to God's will as revealed through Scripture. *See also* Halfway Covenant.

cult of domesticity The nineteenth-century belief that a woman's place was in the home, where she should create a haven for her husband, who was working in the outside world. This ideal was made possible by the separation of the workplace and the home and was used to sentimentalize the home and women's role in it. *See also* separate spheres.

culture A term that connotes what is commonly called "way of life." It refers not only to how a group of people supply themselves with food and shelter but also to their family relationships, social groupings, and religious ideas and to other features of their lives.

de-industrialization A long period of decline in the industrial sector. The term often refers specifically to the decline of manufacturing and the growth of the service sector of the economy in post–World War II America. This shift and the resulting loss of manufacturing were caused by more efficient and automated production techniques at home, increased competition from foreign-made goods, and the use of cheap labor abroad by U.S. manufacturers.

democracy A system of government in which the people have the power to rule, either directly or indirectly, through their elected representatives. Believing that direct democracy was dangerous, the framers of the Constitution created a government that gave direct voice to the people only in the House of Representatives. They placed a check on that voice in the Senate by offering unlimited six-year terms to senators, who were elected by the state legislatures to protect them from the whims of democratic majorities. The framers further curbed the perceived dangers of democracy by giving each of the three branches of government (legislative, executive, and judicial) the ability to check the power of the other two. *See also* checks and balances.

détente French for "loosening." The term refers to the easing of tensions between the United States and the Soviet Union during the Nixon administration.

deterrence The linchpin of U.S. military strategy during the Cold War. The strategy of deterrence dictated that the United States would maintain a nuclear arsenal so substantial that the Soviet Union would refrain from attacking the United States and its allies out of fear that the United States would retaliate in devastating proportions. The Soviets pursued a similar strategy.

disfranchisement The denial of suffrage to a group or individual through legal or other means. Beginning in 1890, southern progressives preached the disfranchisement of black voters as a "reform" of the electoral system. The most common means of eliminating black voters were poll taxes and literary tests.

domino theory The assumption underlying U.S. foreign policy from the early Cold War until the end of the Vietnam War that if one country fell to communism, neighboring countries also would fall under Communist control.

doves Peace advocates, particularly during the Vietnam War.

draft (draftee) A system for selecting individuals for compulsory military service. A draftee is an individual selected through this process. *See also* conscription.

emancipation The act of freeing a person from slavery or bondage. The emancipation of American slaves, a goal shared by slaves and abolitionists alike, occurred with the passage of the Thirteenth Amendment in 1865.

English Reformation *See* Reformation.

Enlightenment An eighteenth-century philosophical movement that emphasized the use of reason to reevaluate previously accepted doctrines and traditions.

evangelicalism The trend in Protestant Christianity stressing salvation through conversion, repentance of sin, and adherence to Scripture, and the importance of preaching over ritual. During the Second Great Awakening in the 1830s, evangelicals worshipped at camp meetings and religious revivals led by exuberant preachers. *See also* Second Great Awakening.

fascism An authoritarian system of government characterized by dictatorial rule, disdain for international stability, and a conviction that warfare is the only means by which a nation can attain greatness. Nazi Germany and Mussolini's Italy are the prime examples of fascism.

federal budget deficit The situation resulting when the government spends more money than it takes in.

feminism The belief that men and women have the inherent right to equal social, political, and economic opportunities. The suffrage movement and second-wave feminism of the 1960s and 1970s were the most visible and successful manifestations of feminism, but feminist ideas were expressed in a variety of statements and movements as early as the late eighteenth century and continue to be expressed in the twenty-first.

finance capitalism Refers to investment sponsored by banks and bankers and the profits garnered from the sale of financial assets such as stocks and bonds. The decades at the end of the twentieth century are known as a period of finance capitalism because banks and financiers increasingly took on the role of stabilizing markets and reorganizing industries.

flexible response Military strategy employed by the Kennedy and Johnson administrations designed to match a wide range of military threats by complementing nuclear weapons with the buildup of conventional and special forces and using them all in a gradual and calibrated way as needed. Flexible response was a departure from the strategy of massive retaliation used by the Eisenhower administration.

franchise The right to vote. The franchise was gradually widened in the United States to include groups such as women and African Americans, who had no vote when the Constitution was ratified. *See also* suffrage.

free labor Work conducted free from constraint and in accordance with the laborer's personal inclinations and will. Prior to the Civil War, free labor was an ideal championed by Republicans (who were primarily northerners) to articulate individuals' right to work how and where they wished and to accumulate property in their own names. The ideal of free labor lay at the heart of the North's argument that slavery should not be extended into the western territories.

free silver The late-nineteenth-century call by silver barons and poor American farmers for the widespread coinage of silver and for silver to be used as a base upon which to expand the paper money supply. The coinage of silver created a more inflationary monetary system that benefited debtors. *See also* gold standard.

free soil The idea advanced in the 1840s that Congress should prohibit slavery within the western territories. "Free soil, free speech, free labor, and free men" became the rallying cry of the short-lived Free-Soil Party.

frontier A borderland area. In U.S. history, the borderland between the areas primarily inhabited by Europeans or their descendants and the areas solely inhabited by Native Americans.

fundamentalism Strict adherence to core, often religious, beliefs. The term has varying meanings for different religious groups. Protestant fundamentalists adhere to a literal interpretation of the Bible and thus deny the possibility of evolution. Muslim fundamentalists believe that traditional Islamic law should govern nations and that Western influences should be banned.

gag rule A procedural rule invoked to prohibit discussion or debate on a particular subject in a legislative body. From 1836 to 1844, a series of gag rules prevented the House of Representatives from discussing the large number of anti-slavery petitions from abolitionist groups that flooded that chamber.

gender gap An electoral phenomenon that became apparent in the 1980s when men and women began to display different preferences in voting. Women tended to favor liberal candidates, and men tended to support conservatives. The key voter groups contributing to the gender gap were single women and women who worked outside the home.

globalization The spread of political, cultural, and economic influences and connections among countries, businesses, and individuals around the world through trade, immigration, communication, and other means. In the late twentieth century, globalization was intensified by new communications technology that connected individuals, corporations, and nations with greater speed at low prices. This led to an increase in political and economic interdependence and mutual influence among nations.

gold standard A monetary system in which any circulating currency was exchangeable for a specific amount of gold. Advocates for the gold standard believed that gold alone should be used for coinage and that the total value of paper banknotes should never exceed the government's supply of gold. The triumph of gold standard supporter William McKinley in the 1896 presidential election was a big victory for supporters of this policy. *See also* free silver.

gospel of wealth The idea that wealth garnered from earthly success should be used for good works. Andrew Carnegie promoted this view in an 1889 essay in which he maintained that the wealthy should serve as stewards and act in the best interests of society as a whole.

government bonds Promissory notes issued by a government in order to borrow money from members of the public. Such bonds are redeemable at a set future date. Bondholders earn interest on their investments.

Great Awakening The widespread movement of religious revitalization in the 1730s and 1740s that emphasized vital religious faith and personal choice. It was characterized by large open-air meetings at which emotional sermons were given by itinerant preachers.

Great Society President Lyndon Johnson's domestic program, which included civil rights legislation, antipoverty programs, government subsidy of medical care, federal aid to education, consumer protection, and aid to the arts and humanities.

guerrilla warfare Fighting carried out by an irregular military force usually organized into small, highly mobile groups. Guerrilla combat was common in the Vietnam War and during the American Revolution. Guerrilla warfare is often effective against opponents who have greater material resources.

Halfway Covenant A Puritan compromise that allowed the unconverted children of the "visible saints" to become "halfway" members of the church and to baptize their own children, even though they were not full members of the church because they had not experienced full conversion. Massachusetts ministers accepted this compromise in 1662, but the compromise remained controversial throughout the seventeenth century.

hard currency (hard money) Money coined directly from, or backed in full by, precious metals (particularly gold).

hawks Advocates of aggressive military action or all-out war, particularly during the Vietnam War. *See also* War Hawks.

holding company A system of business organization in which competing companies are combined under one central administration in order to curb competition and ensure profit. Pioneered in the late 1880s by John D. Rockefeller, holding companies, such as Standard Oil, exercised monopoly control even as the government threatened to outlaw trusts as a violation of free trade. *See also* monopoly; trust.

horizontal integration A system in which a single person or corporation creates several subsidiary businesses to sell a product in different markets. John D. Rockefeller pioneered the use of horizontal integration in the 1880s to control the refining process, giving him a virtual monopoly on the oil-refining business. *See also* vertical integration; monopoly.

impeachment The process by which formal charges of wrongdoing are brought against a president, a governor, or a federal judge.

imperialism The system by which great powers gain control of overseas territories. The United States became an imperialist power by gaining control of Puerto Rico, Guam, the Philippines, and Cuba as a result of the Spanish-American War.

indentured servitude A system that committed poor immigrants to four to seven years of labor in exchange for passage to the colonies and food and shelter after they arrived. An indenture is a type of contract.

iron curtain A metaphor coined by Winston Churchill in his commencement address at Westminster College in Fulton, Missouri, in 1946 to refer to the political, ideological, and military barriers that separated Soviet-controlled Eastern Europe from the rest of Europe and the West following World War II.

isolationism A foreign policy perspective characterized by a desire to have the United States withdraw from the conflicts of the world and enjoy the protection of two vast oceans.

Jim Crow The system of racial segregation that developed in the post–Civil War South and extended well into the twentieth century; it replaced slavery as the chief instrument of white supremacy. Jim Crow laws segregated African Americans in public facilities such as trains and streetcars and denied them basic civil rights, including the right to vote. Jim Crow developed at the time that the doctrine of "separate but equal" became institutionalized.

Keynesian economics A theory developed by economist John Maynard Keynes that guided U.S. economic policy from the New Deal to the 1970s. According to Keynesians, the federal government has a duty to stimulate and manage the economy by spending money on public works projects and by making general tax cuts in order to put more money into the hands of ordinary people, thus creating demand.

laissez-faire The doctrine, based on economic theory, that government should not interfere in business or the economy. Laissez-faire ideas guided American government policy in the late nineteenth century and conservative politics in the twentieth century. Business interests that supported laissez-faire in the late nineteenth century accepted government interference when it took the form of tariffs or subsidies that worked to their benefit. A broader use of the term refers to the simple philosophy of abstaining from interference.

land grant A gift of land from a government, usually intended to encourage settlement or development. The British government issued several land grants to encourage development in the American colonies. In the mid-nineteenth century, the U.S. government issued land grants to encourage railroad development and, through the passage of the Land-Grant College Act (also known as the Morrill Act) in 1862, set aside public land to support universities.

liberalism The political doctrine that government rests on the consent of the governed and is duty-bound to protect the freedom and property of the individual. In the twentieth century, liberalism became associated with the idea that government should regulate the economy and ensure the material well-being and individual rights of all people.

liberty The condition of being free or enjoying freedom from control. The term also refers to the possession of certain social, political, or economic rights, such as the right to own and control property. Eighteenth-century American colonists invoked the principle to argue for strict limitations on government's ability to tax its subjects.

manifest destiny A term coined by journalist John O'Sullivan in 1845 to express the popular nineteenth-century belief that the United States was destined to expand westward to the Pacific Ocean and had an irrefutable right and God-given responsibility to do so. This idea provided an ideological shield for westward expansion and masked the economic and political motivations of many of those who championed it.

McCarthyism The practice of searching out suspected Communists and others outside mainstream American society, discrediting them, and hounding them from government and other employment. The term derives from Senator Joseph McCarthy, who gained notoriety for leading such repressive activities from 1950 to 1954.

mercantilism A set of policies that regulated colonial commerce and manufacturing for the enrichment of the mother country. Mercantilist policies ensured that the American colonies in the mid-seventeenth century produced agricultural goods and raw materials to be shipped to Britain, where they would increase wealth in the mother country through reexportation or manufacture into finished goods that would then be sold to the colonies and elsewhere.

Middle Passage The crossing of the Atlantic (as a slave destined for auction) in the hold of a slave ship in the eighteenth and nineteenth centuries. Conditions were unimaginably bad, and many slaves died during these voyages.

military-industrial complex A term first used by President Dwight D. Eisenhower to refer to the aggregate power and influence of the armed forces in conjunction with the aerospace, munitions, and other industries that produced supplies for the military in the post–World War II era.

miscegenation The sexual mixing of races. In slave states, despite the social stigma and legal restrictions on interracial sex, masters' almost unlimited power over their female slaves meant that liaisons inevitably occurred. Many states maintained laws against miscegenation into the 1950s.

monopoly Exclusive control and domination by a single business entity over an entire industry through ownership, command of supply, or other means. Gilded Age businesses monopolized their industries quite profitably, often organizing holding companies and trusts to do so. *See also* holding company; trust.

Monroe Doctrine President James Monroe's 1823 declaration that the Western Hemisphere was closed to further colonization or interference by European powers. In exchange, Monroe pledged that the United States would not become involved in European struggles. Although Monroe could not back his policy with action, it was an important formulation of national goals.

nationalism A strong feeling of devotion and loyalty toward one nation over others. Nationalism encourages the promotion of the nation's common culture, language, and customs.

nativism Bias against immigrants and in favor of native-born inhabitants. American nativists especially favor persons who come from white, Anglo-Saxon, Protestant lines over those from other racial, ethnic, and religious heritages. Nativists may include former immigrants who view new immigrants as incapable of assimilation. Many nativists, such as members of the Know-Nothing Party in the nineteenth century and the Ku Klux Klan through the contemporary period, voice anti-immigrant, anti-Catholic, and anti-Semitic sentiments.

New Deal The group of social and economic programs that President Franklin Roosevelt developed to provide relief for the needy, speed economic recovery, and reform economic and government institutions. The New Deal was a massive effort to bring the United States out of the Great Depression and ensure its future prosperity.

New Right Politically active religious conservatives who became particularly vocal in the 1980s. The New Right criticized feminism, opposed abortion and homosexuality, and promoted "family values" and military preparedness.

New South A vision of the South promoted after the Civil War by Henry Grady, editor of the *Atlanta Constitution*, that urged the South to abandon its dependence on agriculture and use its cheap labor and natural resources to compete with northern industry. Many southerners migrated from farms to cities in the late nineteenth century, and northerners and foreigners invested a significant amount of capital in railroads, cotton and textiles, mining, lumber, iron, steel, and tobacco in the region.

North Atlantic Treaty Organization (NATO) A post–World War II alliance that joined the United States, Canada, and Western European nations into a military coalition designed to counter the Soviet Union's efforts to expand. Each NATO member pledged to go to war if any member was attacked. Since the end of the Cold War, NATO has been expanding to include the formerly Communist countries of Eastern Europe.

nullification The idea that states can disregard federal laws when those laws represent an overstepping of congressional powers. The controversial idea was first proposed by opponents of the Alien and Sedition Acts of 1798 and later by South Carolina politicians in 1828 as a response to the Tariff of Abominations.

oligopoly A competitive system in which several large corporations dominate an industry by dividing the market so each business has a share of it. More prevalent than outright monopolies during the late 1800s, the oligopolies of the Gilded Age successfully muted competition and benefited the participating corporations.

paternalism The idea that slavery was a set of reciprocal obligations between masters and slaves, with slaves providing labor and obedience and masters providing basic care and direction. The concept of paternalism denied that the slave system was brutal and exploitative. Although paternalism did provide some protection against the worst brutality, it did not guarantee decent living conditions, reasonable work, or freedom from physical punishment.

planters Owners of large farms (or, more specifically, plantations) that were worked by twenty or more slaves. By 1860, planters had accrued a great deal of local, statewide, and national political power in the South despite the fact that they represented a minority of the white electorate. Planters' dominance of southern politics demonstrated both the power of tradition and stability among southern voters and the planters' success at convincing white voters that the slave system benefited all whites, even those without slaves.

plutocracy A society ruled by the richest members. The excesses of the Gilded Age and the fact that just 1 percent of the population owned more than half the real and personal property in the country led many to suggest that the United States was a plutocracy.

pogrom An organized and often officially encouraged massacre of an ethnic minority; usually used in reference to attacks on Jews.

popular sovereignty The idea that government is subject to the will of the people. Before the Civil War, this was the idea that the residents of a territory should determine, through their legislatures, whether to allow slavery.

Populism A political movement that led to the creation of the People's Party, primarily comprising southern and western farmers who railed against big business and advocated business and economic reforms, including government ownership of the railroads. The movement peaked in the late nineteenth century. The Populist ticket won more than 1 million votes in the presidential election of 1892 and 1.5 million in the congressional elections of 1894. The term *populism* has come to mean any political movement that advocates on behalf of the common person, particularly for government intervention against big business.

pragmatism A philosophical movement whose American proponents, William James and John Dewey, stated that there were no eternal truths and that the real worth of any idea lay in its consequences. Dewey tested his theories in the classroom, pioneering the role of process over content in American education and encouraging students to learn by doing. American pragmatists championed social experimentation, providing an important impetus for progressive reform in the early part of the twentieth century.

predestination The idea that individual salvation or damnation is determined by God at, or just prior to, a person's birth. The concept of predestination invalidated the idea that salvation could be obtained through either faith or good works. *See also* Calvinism.

progressivism (progressive movement) A wide-ranging twentieth-century reform movement that advocated government activism to mitigate the problems created by urban industrialism. Progressivism reached its peak in 1912 with the creation of the Progressive Party, which ran Theodore Roosevelt for president. The term *progressivism* has

come to mean any general effort advocating for social welfare programs.

Protestantism A powerful Christian reform movement that began in the sixteenth century with Martin Luther's critiques of the Roman Catholic Church. Over the centuries, Protestantism has taken many different forms, branching into numerous denominations with differing systems of worship.

Protestant Reformation *See* Reformation.

Puritanism The ideas and religious principles held by dissenters from the Church of England, including the belief that the church needed to be purified by eliminating elements of Catholicism from its practices.

Reformation The reform movement that began in 1517 with Martin Luther's critiques of the Roman Catholic Church, which led to the formation of Protestant Christian groups. The English Reformation began with Henry VIII's break with the Roman Catholic Church, which established the Protestant Church of England. Henry VIII's decision was politically motivated; he had no particular quarrel with Catholic theology and remained an orthodox Catholic in most matters of religious practice.

reform Darwinism A social theory, based on Charles Darwin's theory of evolution, that emphasized activism, arguing that humans could speed up evolution by altering the environment. A challenge to social Darwinism, reform Darwinism condemned laissez-faire and demanded that the government take a more active approach to solving social problems. It became the ideological basis for progressive reform in the late nineteenth and early twentieth centuries. *See also* laissez-faire; social Darwinism.

republicanism The belief that the unworkable model of European-style monarchy should be replaced with a form of government in which supreme power resides in the hands of citizens with the right to vote and is exercised by a representative government answerable to this electorate. In Revolutionary-era America, republicanism became a social philosophy that embodied a sense of community and called on individuals to act for the public good.

scientific management A system of organizing work, developed by Frederick Winslow Taylor in the late nineteenth century, to increase efficiency and productivity by breaking tasks into their component parts and training workers to perform specific parts. Labor resisted this effort because it de-skilled workers and led to the speedup of production lines. Taylor's ideas were most popular at the height of the Progressive Era.

Second Great Awakening A popular religious revival that preached that salvation was available to anybody who chose to take it. The revival peaked in the 1830s, and its focus on social perfection inspired many of the reform movements of the Jacksonian era. *See also* evangelicalism.

separate spheres A concept of gender relations, which developed in the Jacksonian era and continued well into the twentieth century, holding that women's proper place was in the home (the private sphere) and men's was in commerce and politics (the public sphere). The doctrine of separate spheres eroded slowly over the nineteenth and twentieth centuries as women became more and more involved in public activities. *See also* cult of domesticity.

social Darwinism   A social theory, based on Charles Darwin's theory of evolution, that all progress in human society was the result of competition and natural selection. Gilded Age proponents such as William Graham Sumner and Herbert Spencer claimed that reform was useless because the rich and poor were precisely where nature intended them to be and intervention would retard the progress of humanity. *See also* reform Darwinism.

social gospel movement   A religious movement in the late nineteenth and early twentieth centuries founded on the idea that Christians have a responsibility to reform society as well as individuals. Social gospel adherents encouraged people to put Christ's teachings to work in their daily lives by actively promoting social justice.

socialism   A governing system in which the state owns and operates the largest and most important parts of the economy.

social purity movement   A movement to end prostitution and eradicate venereal disease, often accompanied by the censorship of materials deemed "obscene."

spoils system   An arrangement in which party leaders reward party loyalists with government jobs. This slang term for *patronage* comes from the saying "To the victor go the spoils." Widespread government corruption during the Gilded Age spurred reformers to curb the spoils system through the passage of the Pendleton Act in 1883, which created the Civil Service Commission to award government jobs on the basis of merit. *See also* civil service.

state sovereignty   A state's autonomy or freedom from external control. The federal system adopted at the Constitutional Convention in 1787 struck a balance between state sovereignty and national control by creating a strong central government while leaving the states intact as political entities. The states remained in possession of many important powers on which the federal government cannot intrude.

states' rights   A strict interpretation of the Constitution that holds that federal power over the states is limited and that the states hold ultimate sovereignty. First expressed in 1798 through the passage of the Virginia and Kentucky Resolutions, which were based on the assumption that the states have the right to judge the constitutionality of federal laws, the states' rights philosophy became a cornerstone of the South's resistance to federal control of slavery.

strict constructionism   An approach to constitutional law that attempts to adhere to the original intent of the writers of the Constitution. Strict construction often produces Supreme Court decisions that defer to the legislative branch and to the states and restrict the power of the federal government. Opponents of strict construction argue that the Constitution is an organic document that must be interpreted to meet conditions unimagined when it was written.

suffrage   The right to vote. The term *suffrage* is most often associated with the efforts of American women to secure voting rights. *See also* franchise.

Sun Belt   The southern and southwestern regions of the United States, which grew tremendously in industry, population, and influence after World War II.

supply-side economics   An economic theory based on the premise that tax cuts for the wealthy and for corporations encourage investment and production (supply), which in turn stimulate consumption. Embraced by the Reagan administration and other conservative Republicans, this theory reversed Keynesian economic policy, which assumes that the way to stimulate the economy is to create demand through federal spending on public works and general tax cuts that put more money into the hands of ordinary people. *See also* Keynesian economics.

temperance movement   The reform movement to end drunkenness by urging people to abstain from the consumption of alcohol. Begun in the 1820s, this movement achieved its greatest political victory with the passage of a constitutional amendment in 1919 that prohibited the manufacture, sale, and transportation of alcohol. That amendment was repealed in 1933.

third world   Originally a Cold War term linked to decolonization, *third world* was first used in the late 1950s to describe newly independent countries in Africa and Asia that were not aligned with either Communist nations (the second world) or non-Communist nations (the first world). Later, the term was applied to all poor, nonindustrialized countries in Latin America as well as in Africa and Asia. Many international experts see *third world* as a problematic category when applied to such a large and disparate group of nations, and they criticize the discriminatory hierarchy suggested by the term.

trickle-down economics   The theory that financial benefits and incentives given to big businesses in the top tier of the economy will flow down to smaller businesses and individuals and thus benefit the entire nation. President Herbert Hoover unsuccessfully used the trickle-down strategy in his attempt to pull the nation out of the Great Depression, stimulating the economy through government investment in large economic enterprises and public works such as construction of the Hoover Dam. In the late twentieth century, conservatives used this economic theory to justify large tax cuts and other financial benefits for corporations and the wealthy.

Truman Doctrine   President Harry S. Truman's assertion that American security depended on stopping any Communist government from taking over any non-Communist government—even nondemocratic and repressive dictatorships—anywhere in the world. Beginning in 1947 with American aid to help Greece and Turkey stave off Communist pressures, this approach became a cornerstone of American foreign policy during the Cold War.

trust   A corporate system in which corporations give shares of their stock to trustees, who coordinate the industry to ensure profits to the participating corporations and curb competition. Pioneered by Standard Oil, such business practices were deemed unfair, were moderated by the Sherman Antitrust Act (1890), and were finally abolished by the combined efforts of Presidents Theodore Roosevelt and William Howard Taft and the sponsors of the 1914 Clayton Antitrust Act. The term *trust* is also loosely applied to all large business combinations. *See also* holding company.

vertical integration   A system in which a single person or corporation controls all processes of an industry from start to finished product. Andrew Carnegie first used vertical integration in the 1870s, controlling every aspect of steel production from the mining of iron ore to the manufacturing of the final product, thereby maximizing profits by eliminating the use of outside suppliers or services. *See also* horizontal integration.

virtual representation   The notion, propounded by the British Parliament in the eighteenth century, that the House of Commons represented all British subjects—wherever they lived and regardless of whether they had directly voted for their representatives. Prime Minister George Grenville used this idea to argue that the Stamp Act and other parliamentary taxes on British colonists did not constitute taxation without representation. The American colonists rejected the argument, insisting that political representatives derived authority only from explicit citizens' consent (indicated by elections), and that members of a distant government body were incapable of adequately representing their interests.

War Hawks   Young Republicans elected to the U.S. Congress in the fall of 1810 who were eager for war with Britain in order to legitimize attacks on Indians, end impressment, and avenge foreign insults. *See also* hawks.

welfare capitalism   The idea that a capitalistic industrial society can operate benevolently to improve the lives of workers. The notion of welfare capitalism became popular in the 1920s as industries extended the benefits of scientific management to improve safety and sanitation in the workplace as well as to institute paid vacations and pension plans. *See also* scientific management.

welfare state   A nation or state in which the government assumes responsibility for some or all of the individual and social welfare of its citizens. Welfare states commonly provide education, health care, food programs for the poor, unemployment compensation, and other social benefits. The United States dramatically expanded its role as a welfare state with the provisions of the New Deal in the 1930s.

Yankee imperialism   A cry raised in Latin American countries against the United States when it intervened militarily in the region without invitation or consent from those countries.

yeoman   A farmer who owned a small plot of land that was sufficient to support a family and was tilled by family members and perhaps a few servants.

Spot Artifact Credits

p. 389 (Bible): Anacostia Museum, Smithsonian Institution, Washington, D.C.; p. 398 (ticket): Collection of Janice L. and David J. Frent; p. 402 (plow): Courtesy Deere & Company; p. 403 (election artifact): Collection of Janice L. and David J. Frent; p. 419 (decorative shirt): Image courtesy of National Park Service, Nez Percé National Historical Park. Catalogue #BIHO1256; p. 420 (moccasins): Photo Addison Doty, Santa Fe, N.M.; p. 422 (silver bar): The Oakland Museum; p. 427 (bucket): Kansas State Historical Society; p. 440 (lamp): Picture Research Consultants & Archives; p. 441 (telephone): Smithsonian Institution, Washington, D.C.; p. 448 (cigarettes): Courtesy of Duke Homestead and Tobacco Museum; p. 470 (sewing machine): National Museum of American History, Smithsonian Institution, Washington, D.C.; p. 471 (typewriter): National Museum of American History, Smithsonian Institution, Washington, D.C.; p. 477 (baseball, card, and glove): Smithsonian Institution, Washington, D.C.; p. 478 (faucet): Picture Research Consultants & Archives; p. 493 (dagger): Library & Archives Division, Historical Society of Western Pennsylvania; p. 494 (paycheck): Chicago Historical Society, Archives and Manuscrip. Department; p. 499 (button): Collection of Janice L. and David J. Frent; p. 504 (magazine cover): Granger Collection; p. 519 (token): The Western Reserve Historical Society, Cleveland, Ohio; p. 534 (IWW poster): Library of Congress; p. 535 (flag): National Museum of American History, Smithsonian Institution; p. 547 (machine gun): National Museum of American History, Smithsonian Institution, Behring Center; p. 551 ("Save Wheat" poster): Herbert Hoover Presidential Library; p. 553 (suffrage bird): Collection of Janice L. and David J. Frent; p. 560 (IWW poster): Picture Research Consultants & Archives; p. 574 (refrigerator): From the Collection of The Henry Ford; p. 577 (Hughes book): Picture Research Consultants & Archives; p. 579 (button): Private Collection;

p. 582 (*This Side of Paradise*): Matthew J. & Arlyn Bruccoli Collection of F. Scott Fitzgerald, University of South Carolina; p. 589 (movie poster): Collection of Hershenson-Allen Archives; p. 597 (wheelchair): FDR Library/photo by Hudson Valley Photo Studio; p. 598 (1932 buttons): Collection of Janice L. and David J. Frent; p. 605 (*Grapes of Wrath*): Granger Collection; p. 609 (WPA poster): Picture Research Consultants & Archives; p. 628 (panzer): U.S. Army Ordnance Museum Foundation, Inc.; p. 629 (Good Neighbor button): Collection of Colonel Stuart S. Corning, Jr./Picture Research Consultants, Inc.; p. 639 (Double V button): Private Collection; p. 647 (atomic bomb): National Archives; p. 654 (Truman and Churchill button): Collection of Janice L. and David J. Frent; p. 663 (baseball card): The Michael Barson Collection/Past Perfect; p. 663 (banner): Dr. Hector P. Garcia Papers, Special Collections & Archives, Texas A&M University, Corpus Christi, Bell Library; p. 669 (Korean DMZ sign): Diana Walker/Time Life Pictures/Getty Images; p. 675 (sign): NEW Traffic Safety; p. 687 (*The Feminine Mystique*): W. W. Norton & Company, Inc. N.Y.C., © 1963; p. 690 (album cover): Chess Records; p. 691 (NAACP button): Collection of Janice L. and David J. Frent; p. 701 (food stamps): Getty Images; p. 705 (pennant): Private Collection; p. 709 (Indian resistance button): Collection of Janice L. and David J. Frent; p. 711 (ticket): Picture Research Consultants & Archives; p. 714 (magazine): Young Americans for Freedom; p. 726 (beret): West Point Museum, United States Military Academy, West Point, N.Y.; p. 734 (Vietnam button): Picture Research Consultants & Archives; p. 734 (antiwar button): Collection of Janice L. and David J. Frent; p. 749 (magazine): Young Americans for Freedom; p. 761 (bumper sticker): Courtesy, Christian Coalition; p. 775 (poster): National Museum of American History, Smithsonian Institution, Behring Center; p. 782 (logo): Americorps; p. 789 (documents): Nolo.